The Peninsular War

CHARLES ESDAILE

The Peninsular War

A NEW HISTORY

THE PENINSULAR WAR
Copyright © Charles Esdaile, 2003.
All rights reserved. No part of this book may be used or reproduced
in any manner whatsoever without written permission except in the
case of brief quotations embodied in critical articles or reviews.

First published 2003 by PALGRAVE MACMILLAN™
175 Fifth Avenue, New York, N.Y. 10010 and
Houndmills, Basingstoke, Hampshire, England RG21 6XS.
Companies and representatives throughout the world.

PALGRAVE MACMILLAN is the global academic imprint of the
Palgrave Macmillan division of St. Martin's Press, LLC and of
Palgrave Macmillan Ltd. Macmillan® is a registered trademark in the
United States, United Kingdom and other countries. Palgrave is a reg-
istered trademark in the European Union and other countries.

ISBN 1-4039-6231-6

Library of Congress Cataloguing-in-Publication Data available from
the Library of Congress.

First published in 2002 by Allen Lane, an imprint of Penguin Books.

First PALGRAVE MACMILLAN edition: June 2003.

10 9 8 7 6 5 4 3 2 1

Printed in the United States of America.

For Martin Blinkhorn, who first put me on the road, and Pilar Bravo Lledó, without whom I would still be on it.

Contents

CONTENTS

Preface

At first sight a new history of the Peninsular War – the great struggle that convulsed the Iberian Peninsula between 1808 and 1814 following its invasion by Napoleon Bonaparte – may appear superfluous. After all, in Britain, France, Portugal and Spain alike, a series of imposing histories of the war have been published that appear to leave little room for anything other than derivative pot-boilers. In fact a fresh work is sorely needed. Part of the problem is that this great weight of historiography now shows its age very badly. As 'old' history written very much in terms of battles, campaigns and great men, it is blind to the fresh currents of historical work that for at least the last fifty years have been revolutionising our understanding of the past. At the same time, it is disfigured by a combination of national myth, cultural prejudice and political partisanry. In Britain, for example, the Duke of Wellington so dominates the scene that many English-language histories of the Peninsular War turn out to be mere recitations of his victories. In France we find a deep desire to explain the conflict in terms of the Napoleonic legend. And in Spain and Portugal a succession of liberals, neo-absolutists, authoritarian nationalists and Marxists have all sought to hijack the war for their own purposes.

Viewed as a subject in its own right, then, the Peninsular War deserves fresh consideration. But the conflict cannot just be viewed in this fashion. A vital episode in the history of modern Spain and Portugal, it was also a part of the wider Napoleonic Wars. If this aspect of the question is considered, a fresh history of the struggle can be seen to be still more justified. With the publication of a succession of new works that have redefined our understanding of Napoleon and his wars, there is clearly room for a re-evaluation of the part played by the Peninsular War. Why, for example, did the emperor intervene in Spain and Portugal? Why was he defeated there? And, above all, to what extent did the Iberian struggle contribute to the formation of the great coalition that overthrew Napoleon in 1814? As for Spain and Portugal, meanwhile, a serious gap remains in their historiography. Whilst a massive growth of interest in local history has greatly enriched our under-standing of such subjects as conscription, *la guerrilla*, the nature of political authority and the impact of French reform, little of this material has been synthesised even for the benefit of Iberian audiences, let alone made available to readers lacking the benefits of Spanish and Portuguese. Still worse, perhaps, the few general works that exist on the subject are now increasingly dated, being dominated by a fascination with concepts whose validity is at the very least open to serious question. If the idea of 1789 as a bourgeois revolution has been comprehensively demolished, for example, is it really possible to go on making use of the same language when it comes to 1808?

Last but not least, a review of the historiography of the Peninsular War suggests that there is a strong need to pull military and political treatments of the subject together. If historians such as Oman were woefully ignorant of the political context of battle, so historians such as Artola have been just as ignorant of the military context of reform. War and politics go hand in hand. Britain's predominance, for example, cannot be understood without a discussion of the nature of the uprising of 1808, the response of the Iberian peoples to the war against Napoleon, and the social and economic background against which the struggle took place. Yet, by the same token, neither the triumph of the Spanish liberals, nor the restoration of Spanish absolutism, nor the place of the Peninsular War in the history of Iberia as a whole, can be understood without a grasp of the conflict's battles and campaigns, or, more broadly, the military experience which they afforded. Self-evident as all this is, the failure of generations of historians to blend the military with the civil may seem somewhat surprising. In fact, it was all but inevitable. Deeply hostile to, and, indeed, prejudiced against, military history, the academic community has on the whole surrendered its study to writers who lack the sources, languages, institutional support and intellec-tual formation necessary to see beyond the smoke and dust of battle. In recent years things have begun to change – a succession of academics have, for example, transformed our knowledge of 'people's war' in France – but with regard to Spain and Portugal the process has as yet hardly begun. Hence the need for a new general history. Whether this will be any more successful than its predecessors is, however, another matter.

A book that has been some twenty years in the making incurs far more debts of gratitude than any author can ever repay, not least to the various sources of research funding – in this case, the British Academy, the Leverhulme Trust, the University of Southampton and the University of Liverpool – that have made it possible. At the head of the list of people, perhaps, comes

Simon Winder and Ellah Allfrey at Penguin, without whom it would not have seen the light of day, and Martin Blinkhorn at the University of Lancaster, who first pointed me in the direction of the Peninsular War. Great encouragement, too, came from Christopher Allmand, whose years as my Head of Department at the University of Liverpool were marked by much patience and sympathy. The staff of all the libraries and archives at which I have worked have without exception been kindness and helpfulness themselves, but in this context I should particularly like to thank Christopher Woolgar, Karen Robson, Sue Donnelly and Mary Cockerill at the University of Southampton; Ian Jackson at the University of Liverpool; Nieves Sánchez Hidalgo, Estrella Valentín-Fernández Fernández, Inmaculada Martín Múñoz, Amalia Jiménez Morales, Ana Sanz Robles, Jesus Rodríguez Izquierdo, Maribel Baenas Pérez, Paqui Mateo Macias, and Yolanda Ruiz Estebán at the Biblioteca Nacional; and, above all, the gracious Pilar Bravo Lledó of the Archivo Histórico Nacional, whose matchless generosity at a moment of total technological failure not only far surpassed the call of duty, but stands as the very acme of the warmth that I have experienced at the hands of so many people in Spain. Others whom I should like to remember in this context include Leopoldo Stampa of the Ministerio de Asuntos Exteriores, Marta Requena, Concha Bocos, Rafael Agasagasti, William and Sonia Chislett, Emilio de Castro, Dolores Schilling, Jo Klepka, Enrique Mardones, Fernando Fanjul, Antonia Rodríguez, Jesus Maroto, José María Espinosa de los Monteros, Santiago Nistal and Maribel Piqueras. Also worthy of note here are my fellow researchers, Azucena Pédraz Marcos, Nuria Carmena Jiménez, Leonor Hernández Enviz, Grahame Harrison, Susan Lord, Mari-Cruz de Carlos (to whom I am indebted not just for much friendship and hospitality, but for her assistance with the illustrations) and Satoko Nakajima, whose company has provided me with insight and relaxation alike. And, in the publishing world, I owe many thanks to Lionel Leventhal of Greenhill Books, not just for his great personal generosity, but also for his sterling efforts to bring the memoir literature of the Napoleonic Age to the attention of a wider public.

Turning now to my fellow labourers in the Napoleonic vineyard, as so often before, I must first pay tribute to my dear friend and esteemed colleague, Rory Muir, who, despite years of exposure to my manuscripts, has once again lavished every possible care and attention upon the current work, whilst at the same time enlightening me on many aspects of the subject with which I am less familiar than I should be. Amongst those who have also at various times been kind enough to provide me with encouragement and good counsel have been Neville Thompson, Alan Forrest, Jeremy Black and

Michael Broers, whilst from Don Horward of Florida State University I have received, in addition, much hospitality in the course of numerous visits to the Consortium on Revolutionary Europe and the Strozier Library at Tallahassee. Two young historians in Spain who have proved of great assistance to me are Arsenio García Fuertes and Jorge Sánchez Fernández, but much kindness has also been shown me by Vittorio Scotti-Douglas, Paddy Griffith, John Tone, Alicia Laspra Rodríguez, Esteban Canales, Lluis Roura, Antonio Moliner Prada, Franciso Carantoña Alvarez, Antonio Carrasco Alvarez and Herminio Lafoz Rabaza. From them all I have learned a great deal, whilst it is a source of considerable regret to me that considerations of space have made it impossible to pay adequate tribute not only to their work, but also to that of the many other scholars whose writings have enriched this study. Needless to say, however, such errors as may have crept into its pages are the fault of no one but the author (at all events they most certainly are not the fault of the copy-editor, Sue Dickinson, who has been the very model of efficiency, patience and dedication).

Good to me though all my friends in the Napoleonic field have been, it is to my family that my debts are greatest. To my mother and my father, though he is now dead, I still owe more than I can say (including, not least, the copy of Oman presented me as a graduation gift!). But, above all, my beloved wife, Alison, remains the great woman behind this not very great man, and Andrew, Helen, Maria-Isabel, and Bernadette, whose arrival enlivened the last chapters of this work, are the dearest, best and most loving of children. To you all, *un abrazo*.

Liverpool, 23 March 2001.

NOTE ON THE TEXT

All translations of Spanish and French sources quoted in the text are the author's own.

List of Illustrations

List of Maps

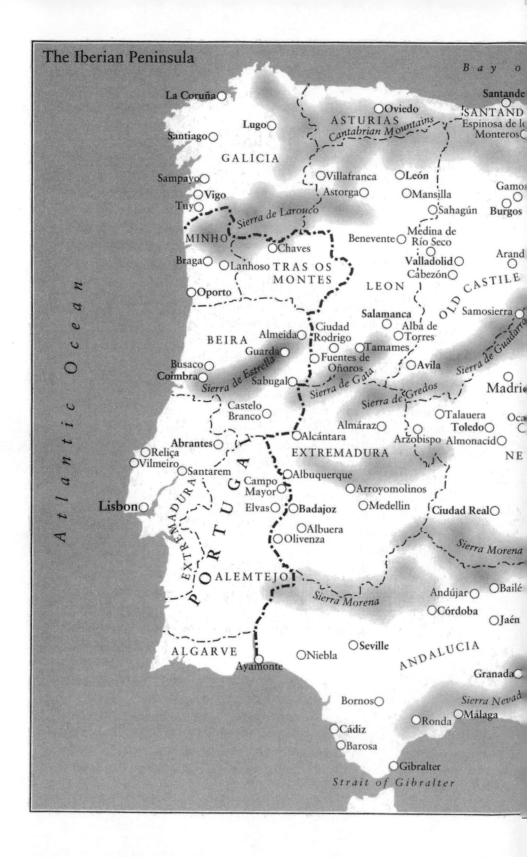

The Iberian Peninsula

Bay o

Atlantic Ocean

La Coruña

Santande
SANTAND
Espinosa de l
Monteros

Lugo

Oviedo

ASTURIAS
Cantabrian Mountains

Santiago

GALICIA

Sampayo
Villafranca
León
Gamo

Vigo
Astorga
Mansilla

Tuy
Sahagún
Burgos

Sierra de Larouço

Benevente
Medina de
Río Seco

MINHO
Chaves
Arand

Braga
Lanhoso
TRAS OS
MONTES
Valladolid
Cabezón
LEON
OLD CASTILE

Oporto
Salamanca
Samosierra

BEIRA
Almeida
Ciudad
Rodrigo
Alba de
Torres
Sierra de Guadarr

Guarda
Tamames

Busaco
Fuentes de
Oñoros
Avila

Coimbra
Sabugal
Sierra de Estrella
Sierra de Gata
Madri

Castelo
Branco
Sierra de Gredos

Almáraz
Talauera
Oca

Abrantes
Alcántara
Arzobispo
Toledo

Reliça
EXTREMADURA
Almonacid
NE

Vilmeiro
Albuquerque

Santarem
Campo
Mayor
Arroyomolinos

Lisbon
EXTREMADURA
PORTUGAL
Elvas
Badajoz
Medellin
Ciudad Real

Albuera
Olivenza

ALEMTEJO
Sierra Morena

ALGARVE
Sierra Morena
Andújar
Bailé

Córdoba
Jaén

Seville
ANDALUCIA

Ayamonte
Niebla
Granada

Sierra Neva

Bornos
Ronda
Málaga

Cádiz
Barosa

Gibralter
Strait of Gibralter

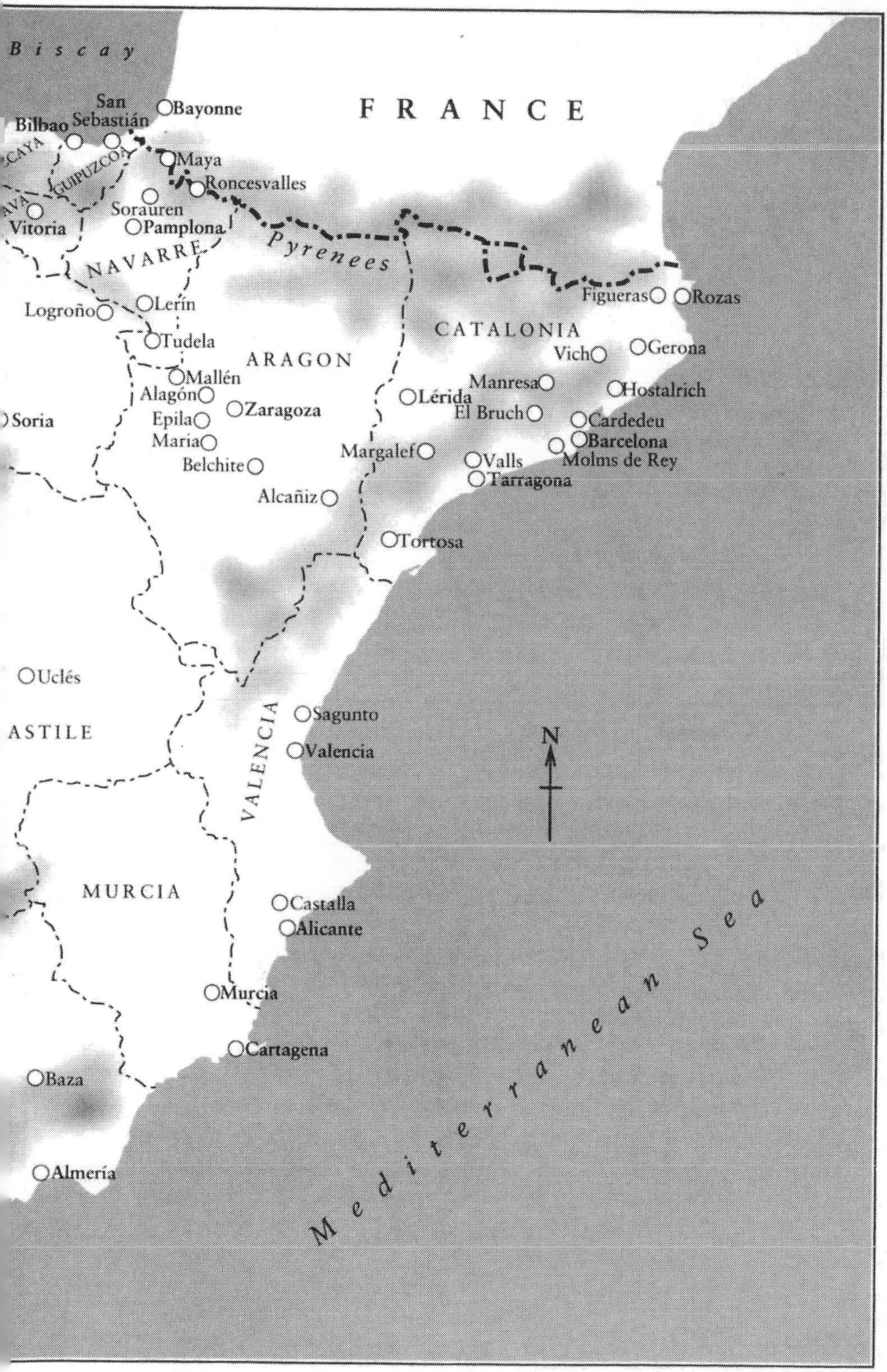

B i s c a y

F R A N C E

San
Bilbao Sebastián ○Bayonne
○Maya
VIZCAYA Roncesvalles
GUIPUZCOA
ALAVA Sorauren
Vitoria Pamplona
NAVARRE *P y r e n e e s*

Figueras○ ○Rozas
CATALONIA
Logroño○ ○Lerín
Vich○ ○Gerona
○Tudela
ARAGON Manresa○ ○Hostalrich
Mallén ○Lérida
Alagón○ El Bruch○ Cardedeu
Soria Epila○ ○Zaragoza Barcelona
Maria○ Margalef○ Molms de Rey
Belchite○ Valls○
Alcañiz○ ○Tarragona

○Tortosa

○Uclés

VALENCIA
CASTILE ○Sagunto N
○Valencia

MURCIA
○Castalla *M e d i t e r r a n e a n   S e a*
○Alicante

○Murcia

○Cartagena
○Baza

○Almería

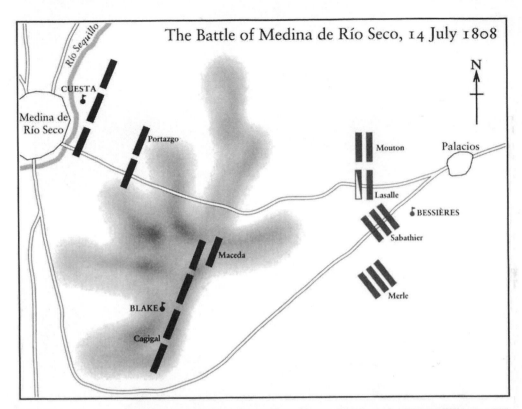

The Battle of Medina de Río Seco, 14 July 1808

Río Seguillo

N

CUESTA

Medina de Río Seco

Portazgo

Mouton

Palacios

Lasalle

BESSIÈRES

Sabathier

Maceda

Merle

BLAKE

Cagigal

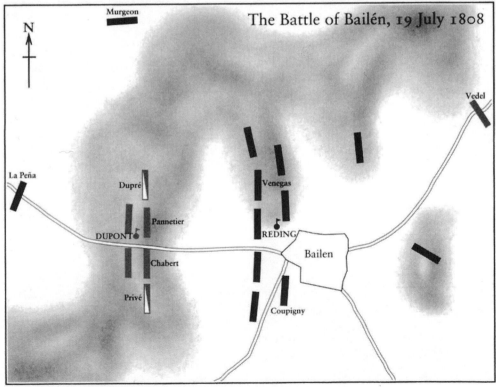

The Battle of Bailén, 19 July 1808

Murgeon

N

Vedel

La Peña

Dupré

Venegas

DUPONT

Pannetier

REDING

Bailen

Chabert

Privé

Coupigny

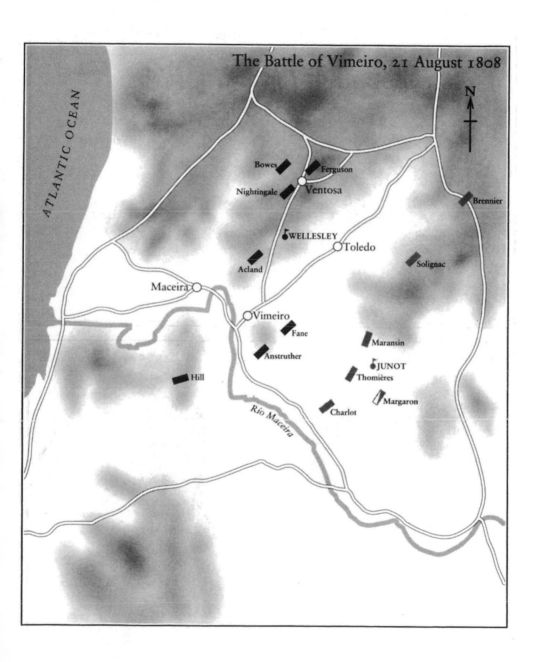

The Battle of Vimeiro, 21 August 1808

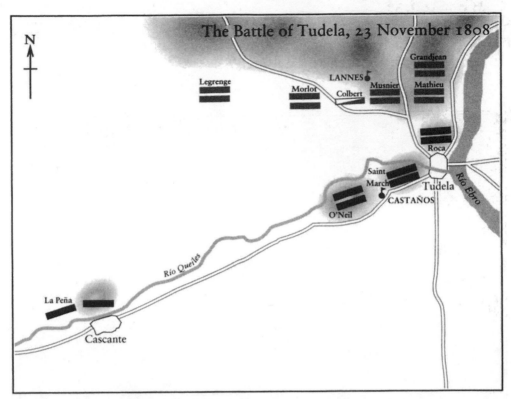

The Battle of Tudela, 23 November 1808

Legrenge

Morlot

Colbert

LANNES

Musnier

Grandjean

Mathieu

Roca

Saint March

Tudela

Río Ebro

CASTAÑOS

O'Neil

Río Queiles

La Peña

Cascante

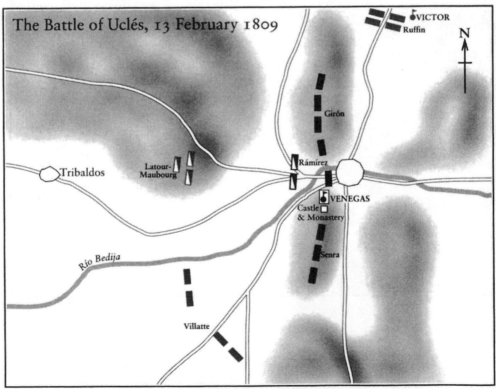

The Battle of Uclés, 13 February 1809

VICTOR

Ruffin

N

Girón

Latour-Maubourg

Rámírez

Tribaldos

VENEGAS

Castle & Monastery

Senra

Río Bedija

Villatte

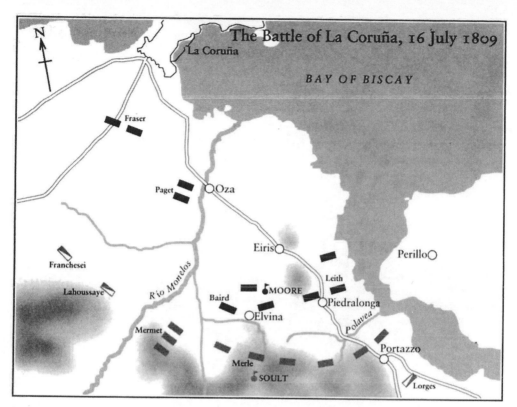

The Battle of La Coruña, 16 July 1809

La Coruña

BAY OF BISCAY

Fraser

Paget

Oza

Eiris

Perillo

Franchesei

Lahoussaye

Río Monelos

Leith

Baird

MOORE

Elvina

Piedralonga

Mermet

Polavea

Portazzo

Merle

SOULT

Lorges

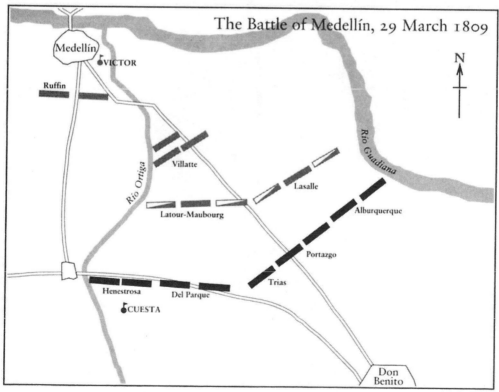

The Battle of Medellín, 29 March 1809

Medellín

VICTOR

N

Ruffin

Río Ortiga

Villatte

Río Guadiana

Lasalle

Latour-Maubourg

Alburquerque

Portazgo

Trias

Henestrosa

Del Parque

CUESTA

Don
Benito

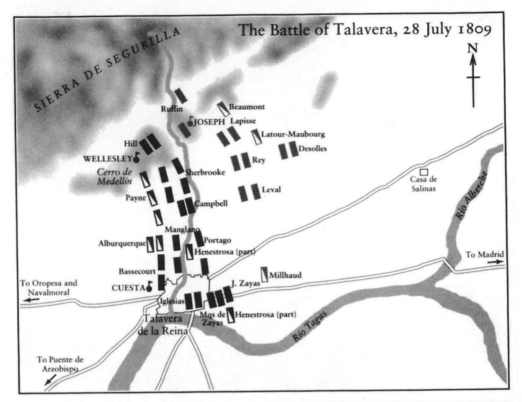

The Battle of Talavera, 28 July 1809

N

SIERRA DE SEGURILLA

Ruffin
JOSEPH
Beaumont
Lapisse
Hill
Latour-Maubourg
WELLESLEY
Desolles
Cerro de Medellín
Rey
Sherbrooke
Payne
Casa de Salinas
Campbell
Leval
Río Alberche
Manglano
Alburquerque
Portago
Henestrosa (part)
To Madrid
Bassecourt
Millhaud
CUESTA
J. Zayas
To Oropesa and Navalmoral
Iglesias
Mqs de Zayas
Henestrosa (part)
Talavera de la Reina
Río Tagus
To Puente de Arzobispo

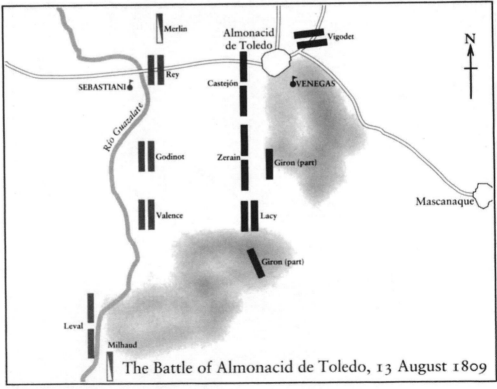

N

Merlin
Almonacid de Toledo
Vigodet
Rey
SEBASTIANI
Castejón
VENEGAS
Río Guazalate
Godinot
Zerain
Giron (part)
Valence
Mascanaque
Lacy
Giron (part)
Leval
Milhaud

The Battle of Almonacid de Toledo, 13 August 1809

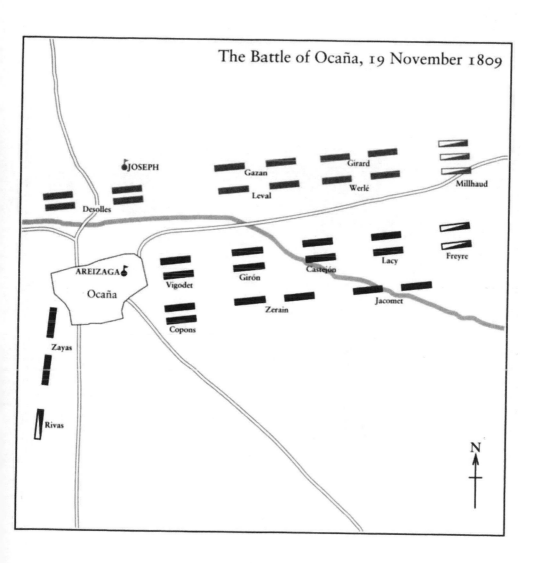

The Battle of Ocaña, 19 November 1809

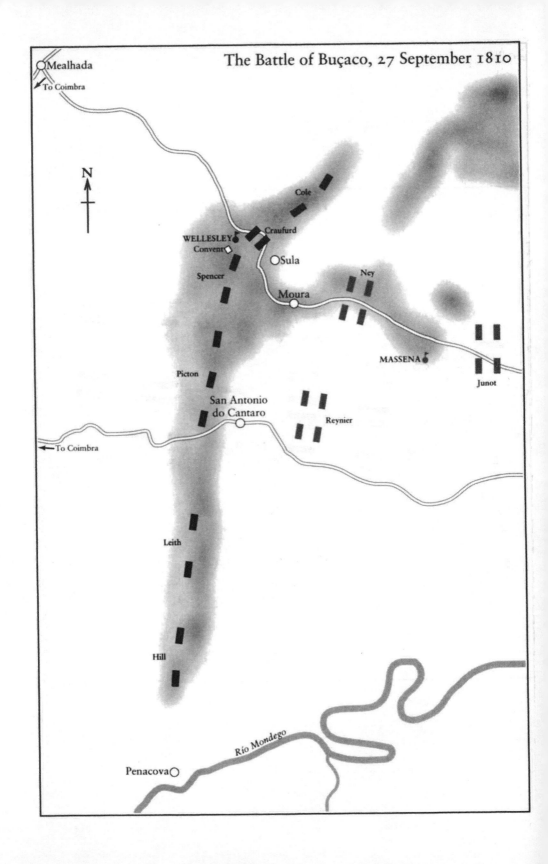

The Battle of Buçaco, 27 September 1810

N

Mealhada
To Coimbra

Cole

Craufurd

WELLESLEY
Convent

Sula

Spencer

Ney

Moura

MASSENA

Junot

Picton

San Antonio
do Cantaro

Reynier

To Coimbra

Leith

Hill

Río Mondego

Penacova

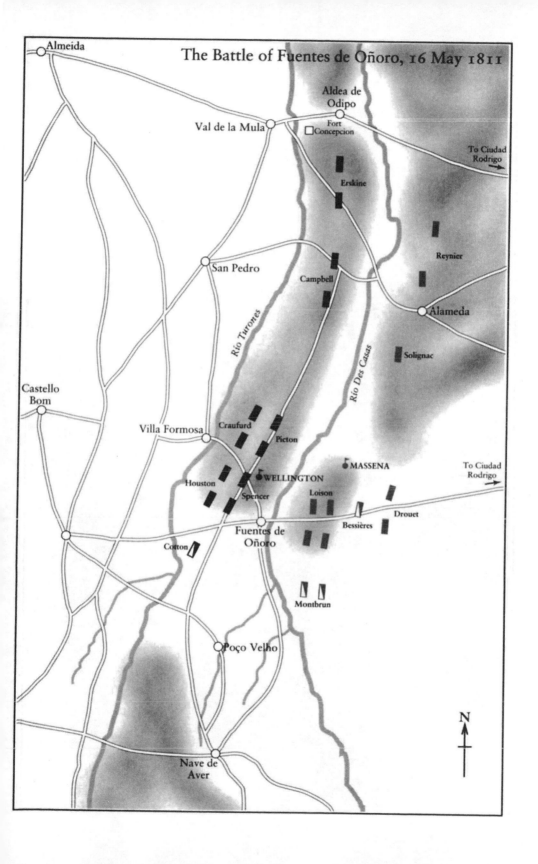

The Battle of Fuentes de Oñoro, 16 May 1811

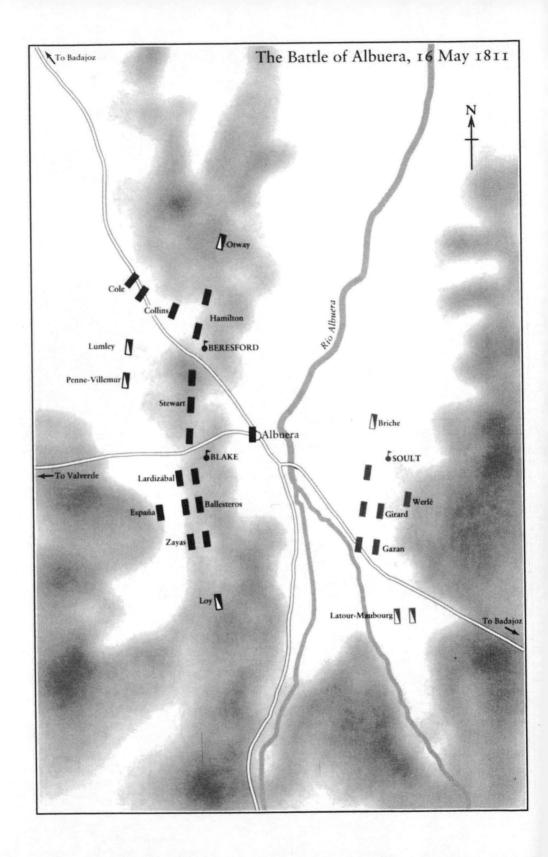

The Battle of Albuera, 16 May 1811

N

To Badajoz

Rio Albuera

Otway

Cole
Collins
Hamilton
BERESFORD
Lumley
Penne-Villemur
Stewart
Briche
Albuera
SOULT
BLAKE
To Valverde
Lardizábal
Werlé
España
Ballesteros
Girard
Zayas
Gazan
Loy
Latour-Maubourg
To Badajoz

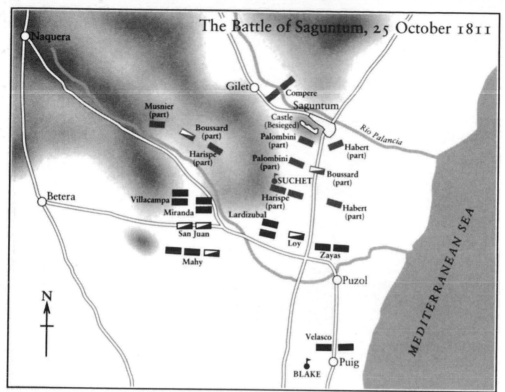

The Battle of Saguntum, 25 October 1811

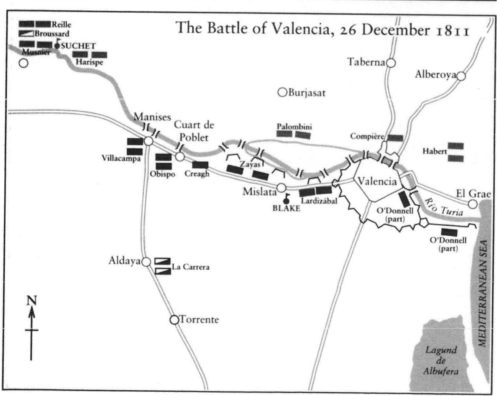

The Battle of Valencia, 26 December 1811

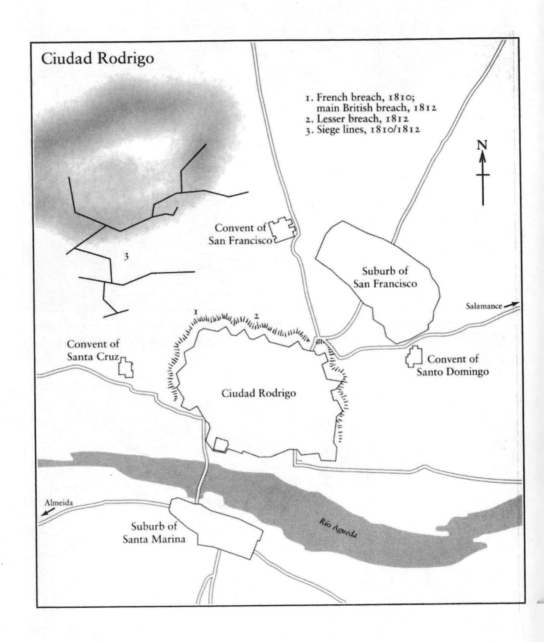

Ciudad Rodrigo

1. French breach, 1810;
   main British breach, 1812
2. Lesser breach, 1812
3. Siege lines, 1810/1812

N

3

Convent of
San Francisco

Suburb of
San Francisco

Salamance →

Convent of
Santa Cruz

1   2

Convent of
Santo Domingo

Ciudad Rodrigo

Río Agueda

Almeida ←

Suburb of
Santa Marina

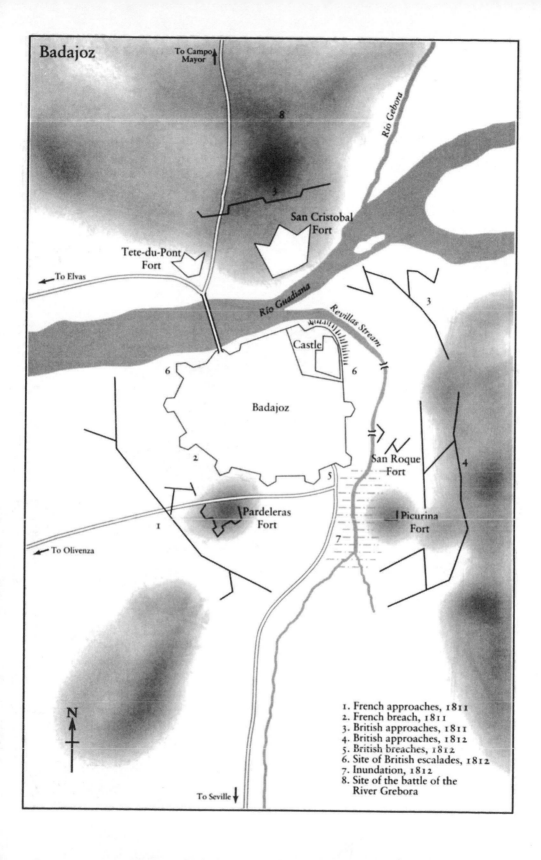

Badajoz

To Campo
Mayor

8

Río Gebora

3

San Cristobal
Fort

Tete-du-Pont
Fort

To Elvas

Río Guadiana

Revillas Stream

3

Castle

6

6

Badajoz

2

San Roque
Fort

4

5

Picurina
Fort

1

Pardeleras
Fort

To Olivenza

7

N

To Seville

1. French approaches, 1811
2. French breach, 1811
3. British approaches, 1811
4. British approaches, 1812
5. British breaches, 1812
6. Site of British escalades, 1812
7. Inundation, 1812
8. Site of the battle of the
   River Grebora

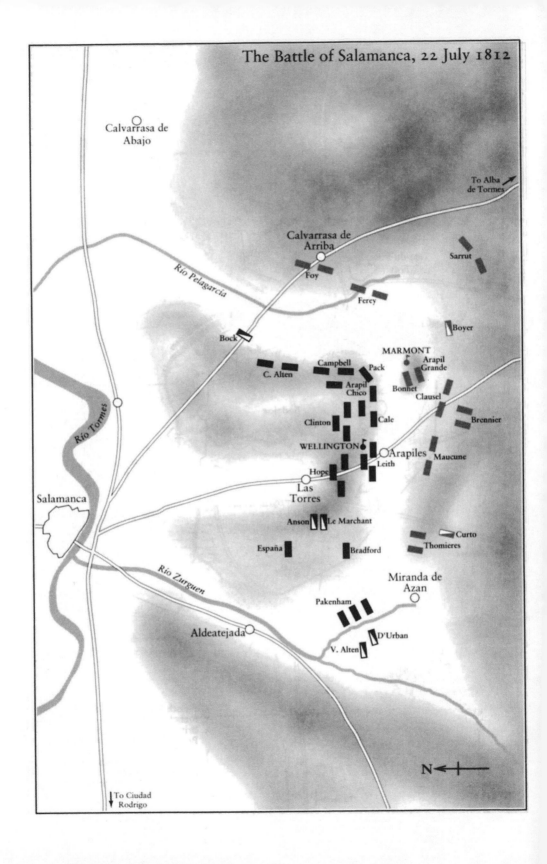

The Battle of Salamanca, 22 July 1812

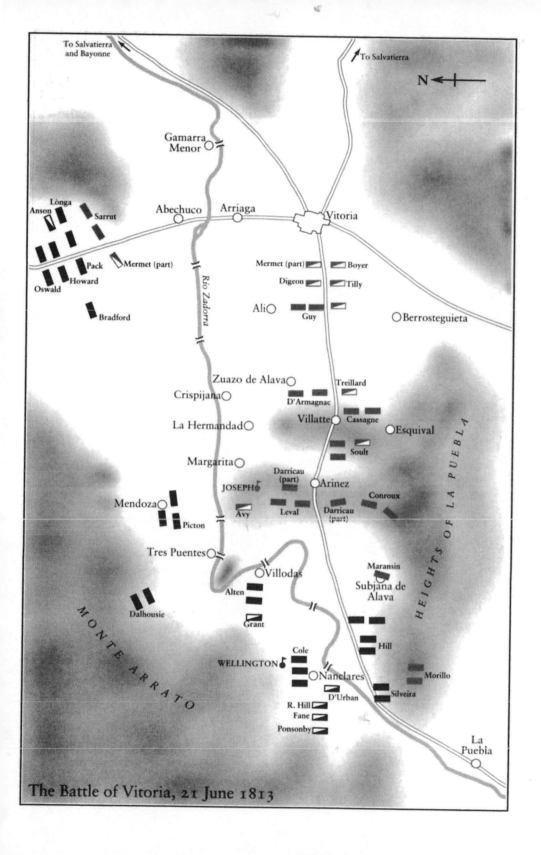

The Battle of Vitoria, 21 June 1813

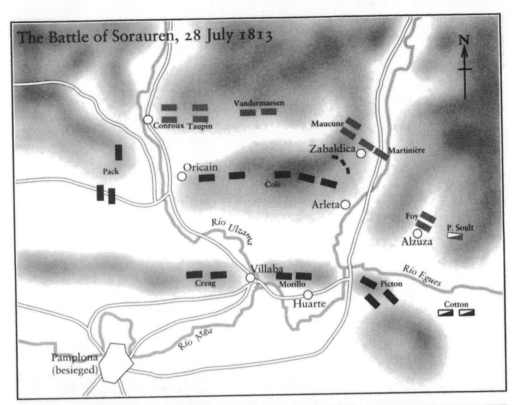

The Battle of Sorauren, 28 July 1813

Vandermaesen

Conroux Taupin

Maucune

Zabaldica Martinière

Pack

Oricain

Cole

Arleta

Foy
P. Soult
Alzuza

Río Ulzama

Río Egues

Creag

Villaba
Morillo
Picton

Huarte
Cotton

Río Arga

Pamplona
(besieged)

N

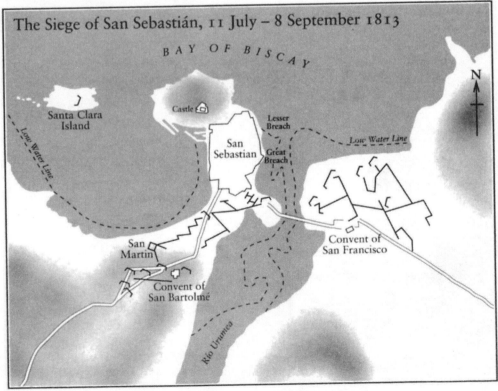

The Siege of San Sebastián, 11 July – 8 September 1813

BAY OF BISCAY

N

Santa Clara
Island

Castle

Low Water Line

San
Sebastian
Lesser
Breach

Great
Breach

Convent of
San Francisco

San
Martin

Convent of
San Bartolmé

Río Urumea

I

Lisbon

THE ORIGINS OF THE
PENINSULAR WAR

Weary, ragged and dishevelled, the French troops crested the rise. Gleaming in the distance, they could see the broad waters of the River Tagus, with, beside them, the towers of Lisbon. To reach this spot near the town of Sacavem, they had endured weeks of forced marching in torrential rain across some of the roughest country in the Iberian Peninsula. Indeed, thousands of their comrades had fallen by the wayside, all that was left being a handful of picked grenadiers. Still worse, it was all for nothing. Another European capital was on the point of falling to Napoleon, true, but the chief prize was vanishing before the invaders' very eyes, the Tagus being filled with the sails of a large convoy of shipping heading for the open sea. Going with them were the Portuguese royal family, the Portuguese navy, the contents of the treasury, and thousands of the country's leading citizens. Napoleon, in short, had been foiled.

But why had the emperor intervened in Iberia? Admirers of the emperor have on the whole sought to explain his actions in the context of either political idealism (the desire to extend the benefits of the French Revolution), family loyalty (the need to find thrones for Napoleon's numerous brothers and sisters) or strategic necessity (the strategic demands of a war that was none of his own making). For their opponents, meanwhile, the answer lies rather in dreams of conquest, hatred of the Bourbons, dissatisfaction with Spain as an ally, and the character of the emperor himself. Whichever view is taken, there is general agreement that in the summer of 1807 he was at the zenith of his power. Master of Holland, Switzerland, northern Italy and a much expanded France, in the autumn of 1805 he had been confronted by Britain, Russia, Austria, Sweden and Naples. In a matter of months, however, crushing victories at Ulm and Austerlitz (Slavkov) had produced the surrender of Austria; the cession of Venetia to the French-controlled Kingdom of Italy, of the Tyrol and Vorarlberg to Bavaria, and of the Dalmatian littoral to France; the occupation of Naples; the evacuation of all British and Russian forces from the central European theatre; and the conversion of Prussia into a *de facto* French ally. Russia and Britain, indeed, had themselves considered peace, only for their overtures to founder on Napoleon's ambition, the emperor's conduct in fact becoming so immoderate that within a year Prussia had been forced to go to war to defend her interests. Heavily defeated at Jena and Auerstädt on 14 October 1806, the Prussian armies had then for the most part surrendered without a fight. Having in the meantime occupied Berlin and inaugurated the Continental Blockade – his great master-plan for forcing the British out of the war by economic means – the emperor went on to invade Poland and East Prussia. Repulsed in a bloody draw at Eylau (Bagrationovsk) in early February 1807, on 14 June he secured his revenge, shattering the main Russian army at Friedland (Pravdinsk) and forcing Alexander I to sue for peace.

Negotiated during the famous meeting between Napoleon and Alexander at Tilsit (Sovetsk), the treaties that followed brought with them both a major reorganisation of Eastern Europe and a great increase in Napoleon's power. Already master of Germany, whose constituent states he had reorganised and united in the Confederation of the Rhine, the emperor turned his attention to Poland, whilst at the same time settling scores with Prussia. Thus, the latter was stripped of all her Polish territories, the bulk of these lands being formed into a new vassal state known as the Grand Duchy of Warsaw. As for her western lands, these became the basis of the Grand Duchy of Berg and the Kingdom of Westphalia, of which the former was given to Joachim Murat, who was married to Napoleon's younger sister, Caroline, and the latter to his younger brother, Jerome. In the later Treaty of Berlin, meanwhile, the Prussians were also compelled to pay a heavy indemnity and restrict their army to 42,000 men.

With Prussia humbled and Germans and Poles alike firmly incorporated in the Napoleonic system, there yet remained Russia. Unusually for him, Napoleon had in fact treated her with great magnanimity at Tilsit, not only employing his considerable personal charm to captivate the somewhat naive Alexander I, but sparing him the indignity of an indemnity and tossing him a slice of Prussian Poland. Beneath the surface, however, Russia was simply being snared as an instrument of the emperor's purposes. Thus, easily persuaded to join the Continental Blockade – in Russia as elsewhere, resentment of Britain was rife – Alexander also agreed to put pressure on Sweden, Denmark and Austria to do the same, to go to war against Britain, recognise the Napoleonic settlement in the rest of Europe, allow the French to resume control of the much-disputed Ionian Islands, and generally give the emperor *carte blanche*.

Napoleon, then, was in a commanding position. Russia was friendly,

Prussia shattered, and Austria temporarily neutralised. Thrones or other suitable positions had been found for most of the emperor's brothers and sisters as well as a variety of other figures connected with the régime – Joseph was King of Naples, Louis, King of Holland; Jerome, King of Westphalia; Murat and Caroline, Duke and Duchess of Berg; Elise, Duchess of Parma; Eugene de Beauharnais, Viceroy of Italy; and Marshal Berthier, Prince of Neufchâtel – so that familial duty could be said to have been well satisfied. By the same means, meanwhile, Napoleon had established a network of 'family courts' that could legitimise the Bonaparte dynasty, attract the loyalty of the aristocracy, and promote French culture. Ruling at his whim as they did, Napoleon's satellite rulers could also be expected to remain loyal to his rule, as could those princes who had survived the emperor's earlier reorganisation of Germany.

Setting aside Spain – notionally a close ally, but one that in practice had increasingly to be kept under observation – the one disappointing feature of the situation was the continuing failure to defeat Britain. However, supreme at sea though she was, the latter's position was far from unassailable. Indeed, her strategic difficulties were enormous. In the first place, her only allies were Sweden and Sicily (whither the King and Queen of Naples had fled following the occupation of their mainland domains in 1806), neither of whom possessed the capacity to defend itself unaided, let alone conduct the large-scale military campaigns that Britain needed from coalition partners. On the contrary, both needed defending, when troops were exactly what the British were short of. Whilst the number of men they had under arms had soared, far too many of them were serving in forces that could not be required to serve abroad. Still worse, neither Britain nor her colonies could be entirely stripped of regular troops. Though the British strove to employ local auxiliaries and foreign manpower, the result was that they did not have sufficient men to do very much themselves. Nor was raising a respectable field army the only problem: setting aside the dangers of storm and shipwreck, transporting even the most modest expeditionary force required large numbers of specialised ships, whilst simply getting the forces involved on and off ship was a most complex undertaking.

These difficulties were doubly unfortunate for they forced Britain back on methods of war – above all, blockade and colonial aggrandisement – that could not but antagonise potential partners on the Continent whilst at the same time confirming suspicions that the British were determined to avoid the sort of commitment they required of their allies. Nor were the methods of warfare on which they relied particularly cost-effective: colonial offensives were notoriously wasteful in terms of lives, whilst blockading

Europe's coasts inflicted immense wear and tear on the Royal Navy. Some amelioration in the demands on Britain's resources was at hand – by the end of July 1807 expeditionary forces that she had sent to South America and Egypt had capitulated in exchange for their evacuation – but even so the sinews of war were clearly at a premium.

The political foundations of the British war effort were no more solid. In office since March 1807, the Portland administration may have been more committed to the struggle than its predecessor, the so-called Talents, but it was also very vulnerable. Amongst Whigs like Richard Sheridan, Earl Grey and Lord Holland, it was felt that Napoleon personified the cause of progress. In the course of the 1790s, a number of Whigs – most famously Edmund Burke, but also the current Prime Minister, Lord Portland – had become supporters of the war, but this gain had been offset by the defection of a number of disillusioned Tories to the peace party. Meanwhile, if the failure of the talks of 1806 had temporarily silenced the peace party, the Portland administration was also hampered by other factors. The Foreign Secretary, George Canning, was a man of questionable judgement whose determination to defeat the French blinded him to political realities, and made him impatient with more circumspect colleagues. To make matters worse, Portland himself was aged and unwell, whilst the Cabinet also had to run the risk of losing the support of the throne. In ordinary circumstances, the latter would not have been an issue, King George III loathing Napoleon and sharing his ministers' antipathy to the Catholic emancipation that was the foremost domestic issue of the day, but the king was prone to bouts of porphyria that periodically left him completely incapacitated and threatened to replace him with the pro-Whig Prince of Wales.

However, Britain's stability cannot just be measured in terms of Westminster. Just as important was the Continental Blockade. Over the course of time and by dint of changing circumstances, Britain was able to circumvent the effects of the Blockade by developing new markets and building up undercover links with the Continent, but in 1807 it was by no means clear that matters would work out so well, and all the more so as that year had seen the United States move in the direction of a total embargo on all trade with Britain. Hit by both a squeeze on exports and a general increase in the price of raw materials, indeed, many industries were in the grip of a severe slump. Matters being worsened still further by the actions of French commerce raiders and a poor harvest, the handloom weavers of Lancashire mounted an impressive campaign to petition Parliament for a minimum wage, whilst many northern merchants and manufacturers began to organise petitions for peace. Hand in hand with these demands, meanwhile, went others for political change: in the general elections of 1807, for example, Westminster, then the most representative seat in the country, returned the popular demagogues, Sir Francis Burdett and Lord Cochrane, on a platform of electoral reform.

For victory to come, then, Napoleon probably had only to wait. Waiting, however, was not in his nature, and he was in any case obsessed by the constant need to secure fresh triumphs and thereby, as he put it, ensure that he continued to be feared. In consequence, no sooner were the discussions at Tilsit over than he was looking around for a new target. The obvious choice was Portugal. Pretexts for an attack were plentiful: she was not part of the Continental Blockade, had been defaulting on the indemnity she had been paying France since the 'War of the Oranges' of 1801, and had frequently allowed British warships to revictual from her shores. There was much to gain: Portugal possessed wealthy colonies and a substantial fleet. And finally she ought to present few problems: her army was minimal and her ruler, the Prince-Regent, João, notoriously dull-witted.

The result was not long in coming. On 19 July 1807 the emperor sent orders to his Foreign Minister, Talleyrand, to the effect that Portugal was to be instructed to close its ports to Britain's shipping, arrest all British subjects, confiscate all British merchandise, and declare war. Within a few days, meanwhile, word had also gone out to concentrate a large force at Bayonne preparatory to a march on Lisbon. Such a march, of course, could only be made across Spain, but this presented few difficulties. For years the Spanish royal favourite, Manuel de Godoy, had been trying to get Napoleon to intervene in Portugal, and he was delighted with the news. Unsettled by rumours that Fernando IV of Naples was to be persuaded to surrender Sicily to Joseph Bonaparte in exchange for the Balearic Islands, he may also have seen co-operation as a means of propitiating Napoleon. Occupation forces were therefore soon being mobilised in Galicia, León and Extremadura, the Spanish ambassador in Lisbon also being ordered at all times to take his cue from his French counterpart.

Threatened by France and Spain alike, Portugal now found herself in a situation that was perilous in the extreme. Often wrongly stigmatised as a decayed despotism in which obscurantism vied with inefficiency, under the leadership of the Marques de Pombal, the chief minister of José I (1750–1777), she had in fact become the very model of enlightened absolutism. Key reforms included the complete reorganisation of the government of empire and metropolis alike, a great reduction in the power of the Church and the nobility, the establishment of a modern army, and the creation of a modern system of education. The arts and sciences had been encouraged, and everything possible done to stimulate economic development, whether it was through the abolition of religious discrimination, the implementation of measures designed to prevent any erosion of the slave labour-force that worked the estates of Brazil, the introduction of new crops in the empire, the extension of Portugal's role in the slave trade, or the stimulation of Portuguese exports. Pombal had long since vanished from the scene – indeed, he had ended his life in disgrace – but his influence had survived and allowed textiles and the wine trade to thrive. Nor had the Revolutionary and Napoleonic Wars been much of a setback. There had been war with France from 1793 to 1797 and a brief Spanish invasion in 1801 (see below), but hostilities had been nominal and trade buoyant, whilst the definitive peace treaty had cost her no more than the cession of a small part of the Alentejo and the payment of indemnities to Madrid and Paris.

Napoleon's sudden ultimatum spelled disaster, however. As the eighteenth century had progressed the Brazilian gold, sugar and tobacco that had hitherto been the bedrock of Portugal's well-being had begun either to run out or to fall in value. Some relief was obtained by the discovery of diamonds and an increase in the cultivation of cotton, but even so the emphasis had increasingly begun to shift to the metropolis' own products and manufactures. As Britain took a large part of the wine that was Portugal's chief export, joining the Continental Blockade was unthinkable, and yet fighting France and Spain was not much of an option either: whilst some attempt had been made to reorganise the army since the peace of 1801, no more than twenty thousand men were under arms out of a theoretical total of some forty-eight thousand.

In the circumstances, then, the only hope was either to conciliate Napoleon whilst at the same time avoiding a total breach with London, or to enlist British support while staving off Napoleon. Needless to say, the chief minister – António de Araújo de Azevedo – attempted both courses of action. Thus, whilst Napoleon was told that Portugal was prepared to declare war on Britain and close her ports to her ships, Araújo jibbed at agreeing to arrest her subjects or seize her goods. As for the British, they were secretly informed that hostilities would be confined to form alone, the Portuguese simultaneously requesting their assistance.

Napoleon as yet being unready to go to war – the troops concerned had to be scraped together from a variety of depots all over France, whilst their Spanish counterparts faced enormous logistical difficulties – Lisbon was therefore told that it need only detain British subjects on a provisional basis and sequester rather than confiscate their goods, the original deadline of 2 September also being extended for a further month. Yet this meant nothing:

thanks to Britain's recent bombardment of Copenhagen and seizure of the Danish fleet, the emperor was more inclined to severity than ever.

In Portugal, the government's resolve was stiffening. Although news had now been received that no aid would be forthcoming from the British, reports from Paris suggested that Napoleon's entourage could be bribed into dissuading him from taking action. As a mark of good faith, the batteries that protected Lisbon from the sea were therefore placed in a state of defence and six thousand troops thrown into the coastal fortress of Peniche, but Napoleon was once again told that the government would not go beyond its original agreements, and large amounts of gold and jewels were placed at the disposal of certain confidential agents in Paris. Whether a more positive answer would have made any difference is unclear, but Napoleon now had all the pretext that he needed whilst his intervention force – the so-called First Corps of Observation of the Gironde – was ready for action. No sooner had he received the Portuguese answer, then, than he ordered its commander, General Junot, to cross the frontier.

Whilst all this had been going on, Madrid had been making little trouble (aside from anything else, on 29 August French troops had suddenly invaded the so-called Kingdom of Etruria*). Nevertheless, deeply mistrustful of Godoy, the emperor decided to bind the Spaniards to his plans even more closely. In consequence, 25 September saw the emperor make contact with Godoy's personal representative in Paris – one Eugenio Izquierdo – and agree the Treaty of Fontainebleau. In brief, Portugal was split into three with the north handed over to the King and Queen of Etruria, the centre kept under military occupation until the end of the war and then disposed of according to circumstance, and the south given to Godoy, Napoleon in the meantime agreeing both to guarantee the existing domains of the Spanish Bourbons and to allow Carlos IV to style himself 'Emperor of the Two Americas'.† Also settled was the question of how Portugal would actually be occupied, the basic plan being that 28,000 French and 13,000 Spanish troops would march on Lisbon from León, whilst another 16,000 Spaniards moved across the frontier from Galicia and Extremadura. Meanwhile, a

---

* Originally the Duchy of Tuscany, Etruria had been ceded to the Bourbons in 1801 in the person of Carlos IV's eldest daughter and her Italian consort. However, with Etruria having become a centre of smuggling and espionage, Napoleon had resolved on its annexation. Spain's only hope of compensation lying in Portugal, co-operation with the emperor therefore became all the more important.

† In terms of Portugal's modern provinces, the northern zone roughly corresponded to Minho, Douro Litoral and Alto Douro; the central to Beira Litoral, Beira Alta, Beira Baixa, Lisboa, Ribatejo, and Alto Alentejo; and the southern to Baixo Alentejo and Algarve.

further 40,000 French soldiers would be assembled at Bayonne to ward off British raids, although it was agreed that these troops would not enter Spain without the prior agreement of Madrid.

By the time that Fontainebleau was formally ratified on 29 October 1807, French troops were already deep inside Spain. Last-minute efforts at negotiation by the Portuguese had been quashed by threats that, unless they surrendered forthwith, the house of Bragança would be deposed, and on 18 October the first French forces started crossing the Spanish frontier. At their head marched the notoriously fiery and ambitious General Jean Andoche Junot, a close associate of Napoleon who had first met him at the siege of Toulon in 1793 and had since distinguished himself in Italy, Egypt and Palestine, as well as serving as French ambassador to Lisbon. Nicknamed 'The Tempest', Junot had his sights set on glory – he had never had an independent field command, had missed the dramatic campaigns of 1805–1807, and been denied the marshal's baton that had fallen to so many of his colleagues – whilst, apart from a few battalions composed of Swiss mercenaries or the scrapings of the old Hanoverian and Piedmontese armies, the 25,000 men that he commanded were all veteran units of the French line.

Despite persistent heavy rains that tired Junot's troops and slowed their advance, Fontainebleau therefore looked set to become a reality. Yet already a series of events in Spain were rendering it a dead letter. At the centre of this crisis stood the hated royal favourite, Manuel de Godoy, but to understand the tension that surrounded him we must first pay some attention to the context in which he had the misfortune to operate. The details of the situation will be addressed in due course, all that needs to be said for the moment being that the period from 1788 to 1807 had witnessed a transformation in the history of Spain. In 1788 – the year when the great enlightened absolutist, Carlos III, had been replaced on the throne by his son, Carlos IV, she had been a world power. Consisting of the Philippines, Cuba, Puerto Rico, Trinidad, Santo Domingo, the whole of southern and central America (with the exception of Brazil and the Guyanas), and large parts of the present-day United States, including Texas, Arizona, New Mexico, California and Florida, her colonial empire brought her income that in the period 1786–1790 averaged 540,000,000 reales. Fabulously rich in terms of their resources – silver, for example, was mined in vast quantities in Peru and Mexico – these territories for the past thirty years had been exploited ever more ruthlessly: in the period 1756–1760 revenue had only averaged 304,000,000 reales. Being in large part the product of private commerce and investment, only a fraction of this money – perhaps

100,000,000 reales per year – ever reached the treasury, but even so Spain still possessed that other hallmark of world power: a fleet that in 1788 numbered 76 men-of-war and 51 frigates, and included the 136-gun *Santísima Trinidad*, which was then the largest ship in the world. Permanent alliance with France in the form of the so-called Family Compact bought Spain security in Europe and support against Britain. And finally in the person of Carlos III, who had come to the throne in 1759, Spain had possessed a monarch of immense vigour and personal dynamism, who was determined to extract the utmost from his dominions both at home and abroad, and not afraid to take on the vested interests of the Church, the nobility and the commercial élite.

All, alas, was not what it seemed, the façade of power and dynamism masking many structural problems. Trade links with the empire were extraordinarily weak, whilst the colonies now cost so much to govern and defend that they were verging on becoming a drain on the treasury. The navy had endless problems finding the manpower it needed to sail its ships, whilst, with the burden of imperial defence increasingly transferred to colonial militias, the army was a mere skeleton. Indeed, recent military operations – the siege of Gibraltar of 1780–82 and a series of descents on the Moors – had not been encouraging. At present this was not too much of an issue, for the Spanish armed forces had just about managed to meet the demands placed on them, but the auguries for the future were not good: with frustration steadily increasing among the *criollos* of America, for example, what would occur if a revolt broke out there? What, too, would ensue were the Family Compact with France to be revoked? Still worse, colonial revenue was irreplaceable: as we shall see, Spain was not devoid of economic development, but growth was patchy, whilst domestic taxation was impeded by the immunities enjoyed by the Church and the nobility. With much of the country desperately poor, too, there was no way that the domestic market could absorb the products of Spanish industry, just as there was no way that Spanish industry could produce enough to keep the colonists from turning to the merchants and manufacturers of other countries.

If Spain cannot be said to have been in decline, her great-power status was at least precarious. Still worse, between 1788 and 1808 there occurred a series of events that shattered it beyond repair, plunging the élites into confusion and uncertainty and large sections of the populace into untold misery. Structuralists will contend that the loss of the colonies was inevitable, but, whilst that may well be the case, the fact remains that the catalyst was provided by the wars of 1793–5, 1796–1802 and 1804–8. At the same time, it may further be argued that without these same wars the circumstances would have been very different: Spain might still have lost her empire, albeit probably at a somewhat later date, but she would not have experienced the trauma and turmoil that actually became her lot. And, as it was, Godoy and Carlos IV found themselves coping both with a disintegrating situation for which they ultimately paid the price and a foreign predator who was blind to the limits of Spanish power: not the least of Napoleon's delusions in the aftermath of Tilsit was that Spain was a veritable 'sleeping giant' that had only to be given an efficient administration for her collapsing fortunes to be transformed. No longer, however, would the government in Madrid preside over a world power in its own right: just as the wealth of the Spanish empire would henceforward pour into the French treasury, so the Spanish navy and colonial militias would become agents of French imperialism.

So much for the context. Who, though, was Manuel de Godoy? An obscure scion of the provincial nobility, Godoy had first come to Madrid in 1787 as a private soldier in the royal bodyguard, and had quickly attracted the attention of María Luisa, the wife of the future Carlos IV, on account of his 'manly bearing'. No sooner had Carlos III died, then, than Godoy succeeded in gaining the favours of the royal couple to such an extent that by 1792 he held the rank of captain general (field marshal), was a grandee of the first class, and had been appointed chief minister. Astonishing as this last promotion may appear, however, it was not the result of mere caprice. With his court the focus of a bitter struggle between the rival factions known as the 'wigs' and the 'cravats', Carlos felt that the safest course was to award power to a man whose loyalty was owed to him alone. Yet power did not equate to security. Whether or not he was genuinely the queen's lover (and it is probable that he never was), the belief that he owed his position only to his sexual prowess could hardly be avoided. At the same time, too, his advancement angered the grandees who dominated the court, and all the more so because his advent as chief minister had aborted what they had seen as an opportunity to reverse the Bourbons' creeping erosion of their status.* Lacking a power base of his own, Godoy could only rely on continued royal favour and his own patronage. Neither could be depended

---

* In brief, in March 1792 the head of the 'wigs', the Conde de Floridablanca, had been replaced as chief minister by the head of the 'cravats', the Conde de Aranda. Because the 'wigs' were associated with officials of relatively humble origins who had been advanced by the Crown pushing through enlightened reform and the 'cravats' with the old-established titled aristocracy, Aranda's accession to power seemed to herald a retreat from the policies of Carlos III. By the same token, of course, his replacement by Godoy – seemingly, a typical 'wig' – was a disaster for the 'cravats'.

on – the former could be withdrawn at any time, whilst the latter was likely to win him as many enemies as it did friends – but year in, year out, Godoy made sure that he wrote to the king and queen several times a day so as to keep them appraised of his every decision. As for his palace, it was constantly thronged with 'almost all those distinguished by their birth, their position, their wealth, or their reputation . . . young gallants who had . . . gone there to show themselves off and seek conquests in matters of love, and persons of dubious reputation who wanted to mingle with their betters and . . . secure some advantage or other'.[1]

Thoroughly demonised as he later was, it is worth paying some attention to Godoy's qualities and character. Whilst no one would pretend that the favourite was either a paragon of virtue or a genius, he was by no means lacking in talent. On the contrary, his letters show a man of considerable grasp, whilst he was not foolish enough to think that he could dispense with the advice of men such as the artillery expert, Tomás de Morla. Independent observers also frequently recognised that he had his good points. If Lady Holland was deeply critical, remarking that his 'only ambition . . . is to amass immense wealth', and further that 'habitual and constitutional indolence impede the execution of any great enterprise', her husband was more charitable, recognising that, 'never in his heart a friend of the Church', he showed a genuine desire 'to reform abuses . . . to improve the condition of the people of Spain, and, above all, to reward, encourage and promote every kind of useful talent'.[2] Similarly, in 1807 Blanco White wrote that his patronage was 'not always . . . the reward of flattery or . . . servility', that 'he showed great respect for talents and for literature', and that 'he was not void of . . . vague wishes of doing good'.[3] And, 'instant statesman' though he was, he was no country bumpkin:

His manner . . . was graceful and attractive. Though he had neither education nor reading . . . his whole deportment announced . . . that mixture of dignity, politeness, propriety and ease, which the habits of good company are supposed exclusively to confer. He seemed born for a high station. Without any effort he would have passed wherever he was for the first man in society.[4]

Godoy's circumstances were not made any easier by the fact that in March 1793, Spain was dragged into war with revolutionary France. Though less damaging in its impact than its successors, the struggle was still disquieting enough. The Spanish troops went hungry, whilst the invasion of Roussillon that was their chief contribution to the fighting was marred by much hesitation and indecision and eventually became bogged down before the walls of Perpignan. The following year, indeed, the Spaniards were driven out. A counter-invasion of Catalonia was confined to its northern fringes, but by now the army was exhausted – it had, after all, never expected to have to fight a war with France. As for popular enthusiasm for the war, it had long since ebbed (if, indeed, it had ever existed). In consequence, the early summer of 1795 saw the French overrun the Basque provinces and reach the Ebro, hostilities then being brought to an end by a treaty signed at Basel on 22 July.

For a brief moment Godoy was genuinely popular, whilst a grateful Carlos IV rewarded him with the title of Prince of the Peace, France's terms having proved remarkably generous. However, Britain was now certain to threaten the Spanish empire, whilst in April 1796 the then General Bonaparte invaded Italy and proceeded to sweep all before him, thereby threatening the important marriage interests that the Bourbons had established there. In short, a fresh alliance with France was essential in the form of the Treaty of San Ildefonso of 18 August 1796 and with it, less than two months later, came war with Britain.

If Godoy had actually been the idler of legend, it is possible that his position might have been much easier. However, the favourite was rather impelled by the conflict to turn to reform. In doing so, however, he immediately jeopardised the chief bastion of his rule. Already aged forty in 1788, Carlos IV was a man of limited intelligence whose chief passions were hunting, collecting clocks and watches and playing practical jokes on his courtiers. Though not inclined to surrender the very real advantages that the enlightened absolutism personified by Carlos III had brought to the Spanish monarchy, he was also deeply fearful of revolution. All too well aware that the fall of Louis XVI had begun with a 'revolt of the aristocracy', he was therefore bound to be antagonistic towards Godoy's reforms, whilst at the same time being highly susceptible to the insinuations of the very groups whom Bourbon policy had always sought to muzzle. Last but not least, reform would also hit the monarchy itself. As the Danish ambassador wrote in January 1799:

Whilst the people groan in misery . . . the queen squanders money on her favourites. At present this position is occupied by a certain . . . Mallo,* a former *garde du corps* of neither talent nor reputation.[5]

---

* At this point Godoy was out of office, having been dismissed in September 1798 as a result both of differences over military policy and of pressure from France, which rightly suspected his intentions. Yet his influence survived. Thus, the new ministry, which was centred on the reformers, Francisco de Saavedra, Mariano Luis de Urquijo and Gaspar Melchor de Jovellanos, was very much his creature and had been appointed at his suggestion.

Godoy, then, was riding for a fall. That said, his instincts *were* perfectly sound. At the heart of his policy was an insistence that he would 'never trust the French'.[6] As he later wrote, 'In so far as France is concerned, the only thing that can be counted on is that the French will never be friends of anything other than their own interests.'[7] In consequence, his first target was the army, which he was determined should be given an adequate system of recruitment, a modern system of tactics and a better-trained officer corps, and pruned of such costly encumbrances as the royal guard. From 1796 onwards, he therefore became engaged in a spasmodic campaign to secure these goals, only to find that his every effort was blocked by the protests of powerful vested interests within the military establishment, vetoed by the throne, or derailed by popular opposition. When the great crisis came, little had been achieved other than to tinker with a few details and pack the high command with his favourites. Also, with financial worries deepening, soldiers and even officers went hungry and unpaid: 'The state of the troops blockading Gibraltar was such that on many days each company had to detach a number of soldiers to gather wild herbs and roots for their meals,' wrote one observer, whilst the Danish ambassador complained, 'The officers of the army and navy are not paid, and I have frequently had captains knocking on my door to ask me for a hand-out.'[8] Far from building up a party in the army, then, Godoy earned the hatred of some officers, especially in the royal guard (whose strength he did at least succeed in halving), the contempt of many others, and the loyalty of virtually none.

Nor was the army the only institution to be alienated by the régime. Under great financial pressure, eager to win some credit with caroline bureaucrats, determined to create a clientele amongst the hierarchy, and much influenced by the thinking of such liberal economic theorists as Gaspar Melchor de Jovellanos, the state also turned its attention to the Church. In consequence, the latter found that the regalist pressure of the past century was greatly intensified, with much use being made of the state's control of ecclesiastical appointments. More dramatically, a start was also made on the expropriation of the Church's wealth: by 1808 it had been stripped of something over fifteen per cent of its property (which was very considerable, some twenty per cent of arable land being in the hands of the clergy). To suggest that the process turned the whole ecclesiastical establishment against Godoy would be an exaggeration, for there were plenty of clerics – the so-called Jansenists – who favoured reform. For all that, however, much of the clergy did come to hate Godoy, reformists being angry at his failure to give them full support, traditionalists unable to diassociate him from this *desamortización*, and all shades of opinion united in their condemnation of his lifestyle, which was, beyond doubt, extremely scandalous. As if it was not bad enough that, despite having taken the hand of Carlos IV's niece, he lived openly with his mistress, Pepita Tudó, there were constant rumours that he sold favours for sex. 'His Excellency', wrote the young officer, Pedro Agustín Girón, 'was pretty much inclined to the fair sex. To please him and lend oneself to his desires was the surest way to favour, whilst it was always women who most had his ear. In consequence, there were many men so base that they brought their wives and daughters to the audience of that . . . voluptuous vizier.'⁹ As one diplomat wrote:

The number of women to be found in the Ministry of State was truly scandalous . . . Husbands . . . were never the ones who came to solicit favours, whilst even of the celibate . . . those who did so were few enough, their interests . . . rather being represented by wives, mothers or prostitutes. In this way the anteroom of the minister-favourite became a great seraglio.¹⁰

To return to revenue, it was not just the Church that was targeted. With the cost of the war with England mounting and the government bonds issued to finance the struggle perpetually depreciating, the need for fresh money was pressing. Yet the economic situation was extremely poor, and it therefore seemed unwise to pass the burden on to the mass of the population: indeed, there had already been fierce anti-taxation disorders in Galicia in 1791. If the era of Godoy was one of opportunity for men of property, it was also one of increased pressure. Thus, from 1798 onwards *pudientes* were subjected to a series of forced loans, whilst new taxes were imposed on servants, horses, mules and carriages, on all rental income, and on the establishment of new *mayorazgos*.

Driven by the desire to prepare Spain for a renewed conflict with France which he believed to be inevitable, Godoy was therefore pushing the frontiers of reform far beyond those attained by the governments of Carlos III. Meanwhile, the economic, cultural and educational issues that had been central to the caroline enlightenment also continued to be pressed. Price regulation was lifted from all manufactures; a new weekly newspaper was sent to all parish priests in an attempt to spread knowledge of modern agricultural methods and popularise the works of such foreign writers as Young and Bentham; a variety of technical colleges were started; and Jovellanos assisted with the publication of his seminal *Informe de Ley Agraria*, a treatise that proposed wholesale *desamortización*. Faced by these reforms, the French diplomat, Bourgoing, waxed lyrical:

The present moment seems to be the most favourable of any that has for a long time occurred. A minister in the flower of his age, to whose will everything is subservient, and who appears seriously intent on the welfare of his country; a monarch to whom the purity of his manners and a robust constitution promise length of years; abundance of excellent plans [and] of men of genius to conceive new ones ... a nation in which the government is so organised ... that the discontented may with ease ... be kept in awe ... How many circumstances here conspire to facilitate the execution of projects of national improvement![11]

This judgement, however, was a shade over-optimistic. It was not just that *ilustrados* such as Jovellanos who should have been natural allies of Godoy were alienated by his licentiousness and venality. Within the government the favourite faced a 'Trojan horse' in that a worried king and queen insisted on the inclusion in the reformist ministry of 1798 of the traditionalist Marqués de Caballero as Minister of Grace and Justice. A man of whom it was said that he was neither gracious nor just nor *caballero* (i.e. gentlemanly), Caballero spent the next few years harassing the cause of reform, and in fact succeeded in persuading Carlos to dismiss many of its leading supporters (Jovellanos was even imprisoned) and to clamp down on the Jansenists, many of whom were sent into internal exile. Outside the government, meanwhile, élite resentment of Godoy found a focus in the Prince of Asturias, or heir to the throne, Prince Fernando. Emotionally stunted and neglected by his parents, Fernando came to hate Godoy, believing that he had stolen the affection of *los reyes*. Such adolescent jealousy – in 1800 Fernando was sixteen – might have counted for nothing, had he not become surrounded by a number of figures with a grudge against Godoy, most notably the cleric, Juan de Escoíquiz, the Duque del Infantado, and the Conde de Montijo.* To make matters worse, in 1801 the favourite had been fully restored to favour. Thanks to French pressure, in 1801 Spain had been forced to go to war against Portugal in order to put pressure on Britain. Fearing, perhaps, that another general might perform the role of Lafayette in France, Carlos appointed Godoy to take command of the Spanish army. The resultant 'War of the Oranges't proved victorious, but so many problems were experienced that Godoy was then given the specially created post

---

* Of these figures, Escoíquiz was a Jansenist who had been made Fernando's tutor, only to be dismissed after voicing imprudent criticisms of Godoy's government and foreign policy; Infantado a grandee who had seen a valuable estate taken from him and given to Godoy after he had been accused of exercising unlawful *señorial* rights in its respect; and Montijo the son of a countess persecuted by Caballero on account of her Jansenism.
† So-called because Godoy sent María Luisa a basket of oranges picked, under fire, from the glacis of the fortress of Elvas.

of generalissimo with the brief of resuming the military reforms curtailed in 1798 (a position which he combined with the role of *eminence grise*: though not a minister, he remained very much at the centre of affairs).

To return to Godoy's enemies at court, the real heart of the growing conspiracy was not Fernando at all, but rather the magnates headed by Infantado and Montijo. For such men, one fact stood out above all else. Throughout the eighteenth century the old aristocracy had been increasingly under threat, whether it was from the growth of the bureaucracy, the creation of a new 'nobility of service', or the erosion of the link that had hitherto firmly linked the concept of nobility with that of martial prowess. 'From that bitter period', lamented an anonymous commentator, 'dates the humiliation of the nobility of Spain', whilst, as the Duke of Wellington later remarked:

The grandees! I give you my word . . . they are no more . . . than the valets . . . are in my house. Are you aware that they cannot leave Madrid without the king's permission, and that such permissions are granted seldom, and only for a couple of months? And, still more: they are so abased as to consider leaving the court . . . the greatest misfortune.[12]

In 1794, indeed, Montijo had been sent into internal exile for protesting at the aristocracy's prostration. The ignorant and cowardly Fernando being the perfect puppet, Infantado and Montijo therefore decided to make use of him to put things to rights, to which end they convinced Fernando that the favourite intended to oust him from the succession, matters being much helped in this respect by the prince's marriage in October 1802 to María Antonia of Naples, the princess detesting *los reyes*, Godoy, and the French alliance in approximately equal measure. Alas for Spain, however, Fernando was not well served by his advisers. A vain and superficial character possessed of boundless ambition, Escoíquiz was a blind admirer of Napoleon seemingly devoid of foresight (indeed, the emperor later described him as 'the true author of all the ills of Spain'[13]). 'Till called upon to take an active part in affairs . . . thought to possess great capacity for them', Infantado was described as '*un sot*, and the greatest I think I ever met with' and 'a giddy pate, much given to wantonness', whilst García de León y Pizarro remarked that 'his head was so weak that he always moved in the opposite direction to that of sense and reason'.[14] As for Montijo, he was described as 'a bold man full of knowledge, but one possessed of so frivolous and unquiet a character that he could only play a role in the most agitated epoch', and even as 'one of the worst and most turbulent men to have flourished in our day'.[15]

Whilst factious courtiers and a rebellious crown prince might provide sufficient explanation for a palace revolution, they cannot account for events of the magnitude of those which now followed. To understand the cataclysm that Spain was about to experience, we must move beyond the court to the burgeoning social crisis precipitated by the war with Britain. Until 1795 Spain had escaped relatively unscathed from the Revolutionary Wars. From 1796 conflict with Britain brought a dramatic change, however. Despite her powerful navy, Spain was unable to prevent the blockade of her ports, whilst the length of her sea lanes rendered her particularly vulnerable to commerce raiding. Some trade still got through, whilst the British even licensed the export of a few products, but even so the impact was disastrous, whilst the flow of bullion from the empire was also interrupted: hence the financial difficulties that helped precipitate the assault on the Church.

Had Spain been economically stagnant, this development need not have mattered. However, the reign of Carlos III had seen her exports increase dramatically. At the same time, in some areas agriculture had switched to cash crops, whilst industry had experienced a certain modest growth. In Catalonia, for example, the peasantry had increasingly turned to the production of wine and brandy, whilst an important cotton industry had grown up around Barcelona that by the late 1780s employed as many as 100,000 workers. In Guadalajara the wool factory – the largest and most ambitious of a whole series of industrial establishments set up by successive Bourbon monarchs as models for future development – by 1791 had 24,000 employees. In Valencia, boosted by the ready availability of the raw material, a silk industry existed that at its greatest extent had more than four thousand looms. In Granada there was another silk industry that employed some two thousand looms in 1798, a woollen industry with over seventy different manufacturers, and much cultivation of the hemp and flax demanded by the shipyards of Cartagena. In Seville, the famous tobacco factory employed over 1,500 people, whilst barrel-making and other crafts related to the colonial trade gave employment to many artisans in and around Cádiz. Around Santander the liberalisation of commerce and establishment of several foundries and shipyards led to an economic boom based on flour, iron, leather, forestry, charcoal-making, and basket-work. And finally, as well as developing as a major centre for the export of Castilian wool and grain, Bilbao was the centre of an important iron industry that in 1790 sent four thousand tons of iron goods to the empire alone.

Of course, neither industry nor agriculture produced wholly for the empire or even for the export market in general: only fifty per cent of Spanish exports went to the empire, whilst the proportion of Spanish agricultural and industrial production that went abroad was gradually falling. Yet the war's effects should not be minimised. By 1805, for example, cotton was employing only some 30,000 people in Catalonia. Elsewhere things were even worse. Raw materials often came by sea, as did much of the imported grain on which whole areas of the country were more or less dependent. In addition, the navy and merchant marine formed a market for a whole host of ancillary industries, whilst giving work to thousands of muleteers, woodcutters, stevedores and the like. With the British patrolling the seas more or less unmolested, the war's impact was therefore catastrophic, and all the more so as there was no room for manoeuvre: many industries were hopelessly archaic, the domestic market in recession, and a protectionist France positively hostile to Spanish exports.

In fairness to Godoy, it must be said that Spain's alliance with France was not the only cause of her difficulties. On the contrary, she was also assailed by an extraordinary crop of natural disasters that included unseasonal weather, floods, droughts, earthquakes and even plagues of grasshoppers. With considerable proportions of the harvest repeatedly lost and the population experiencing steady growth (between 1752 and 1797 it increased by approximately ten per cent), the result was, first, several subsistence crises, and, second, a great acceleration of the inflation that had been afflicting Spain since the 1780s. And, as if all this was not enough, large parts of Spain were swept by terrible epidemics of malaria and yellow fever.

All these disasters were inflicted on a country that was already in the grip of serious tension. As might be expected, agricultural issues were well to the fore. In the Cantabrian mountains, for example, the problem was essentially one of access to the forests that cloaked the hillsides. Vital to the region's peasantry as a source of food and pasturage, this had for some time been under increasing threat. On the one hand, the industries that had sprung up along the coast were consuming ever greater quantities of timber (by the 1790s wood was having to be brought in from as far away as Burgos). On the other, especially in the Basque country, the richer elements of the peasantry – indeed, the term is really a misnomer in this context – were steadily advancing their position at the expense of their poorer fellows. Thus, large amounts of land that had been used as common pasturage were cleared and brought under the plough, whilst many smallholders were forced to sell out. With many municipalities forced to embark on the sale of the common lands, by the first years of the nineteenth century a powerful group of middling and even large proprietors had therefore emerged who were quick to monopolise the last vestiges of Basque peasant democracy (in all the Basque provinces the assemblies associated with their traditional *fueros* had survived).

In other parts of the country the problem was rather more financial. Throughout Spain the *campesinos* were obliged to pay the traditional dues of tithes and first fruits to the Church. In addition to these ecclesiastical levies, there were also the dues owed under the feudal system. Although the feudal lord – the *señor* – might be the monarch, an absentee grandee, a member of the petty provincial nobility, a monastery or convent, a bishopric, one of the four medieval military orders, or even a municipal corporation, a very great number of Spain's villages, towns and even cities were subjected to such obligations. The details varied from place to place, but in general the *señor* was owed as much as a quarter of all produce as rent for the land and a variety of other dues and fees, enjoyed a series of monopolies on such activities as milling and baking, controlled local government, and ran his own courts, thereby being enabled to exploit the commons for his own profit and tax the most basic agricultural activities. Nor were the *señores* the only *pudientes*, most of Spain being dominated by a powerful *rentier* class composed of lawyers, officials, merchants and others who rented the *señores'* land, and then either sublet it at a great profit to peasant smallholders or alternatively farmed it with armies of landless labourers. For such men, meanwhile, common sidelines were usury and speculation. And on top of all this there was heavy taxation, the people being subjected to a bewildering variety of taxes, levies and monopolies.

To make matters worse, the Spanish countryside was already desperately poor. Only in a very few areas such as parts of Navarre and Catalonia was life tolerable. Otherwise the picture was uniformly grim. In Galicia, for example, the land was subdivided into tiny plots that were too small to support a family. In Old Castile and La Mancha, farms were better-sized but burdened by poor soil, low rainfall and rack-renting. And in Extremadura and Andalucía the classic form of farming was the great estate given over to vines, cereals or olives farmed by landless labourers who had access to employment for only part of the year. As a result, war and natural disaster meant complete destitution, the catastrophe being intensified by the damage done by *desamortización* to Church charity (in this respect it is also worth noting that a decree of 15 September 1803 gave those who bought Church land *carte blanche* to raise rents as they wished). Hospitals, poorhouses and orphanages were crammed to overflowing; many peasants lost their smallholdings; desperate labourers and their families fled to the cities in search of work only to find that there was no choice but for them to swell the ever-growing crowds of beggars, thieves and prostitutes; dockers, muleteers, artisans and out-workers lost their employment by the thousand; and the countryside was terrorised by gangs of bandits and desperate *jornaleros* out to find work by any means available. Meanwhile, of course, the *pudientes* were able to extend their estates at bargain prices (in that they were able to buy Church land with depreciated state bonds), escape the worst effects of taxation, shrug off or evade the pressures of the state, drive up rents and engage in wholesale grain speculation.

Thus far we have spoken of the crisis of the *antiguo régimen* very much in social and economic terms. Important though these were, it also had a political and ideological dimension. Let us take, for example, the question of the army, which was thoroughly detested. In the first place, and most obviously, it was the first line of defence against such activities as riot, smuggling and banditry. In the second, it was an economic burden: every time a regiment moved, it was entitled to requisition all the carts and mules that it needed, whilst the populace also had to pay the cost of any soldiers billeted in their homes. In the third, officers and men alike were notorious for the bullying manner which they adopted towards civilian society, further offence being caused by the presence of large numbers of foreign mercenaries and deserters. And, in the fourth, it was a constant reminder of the threat of compulsory military service, the brunt of which was borne almost exclusively by the poor.*

If the army was a constant source of irritation, even more was this the case with the régime's cultural policy. Crudely speaking, under Carlos III and Carlos IV alike this aimed at civilising the masses. To combat Spanish backwardness what was needed was the encouragement of education and cleanliness, the spread of enlightenment, the elimination of vice, and the inculcation of a new work ethic. Hence the régime's support of the Societies of Friends of the People, interest in popular education, aversion to bullfighting, construction of new cemeteries away from populated areas, and determination to purify Spanish Catholicism of many of the popular traditions with which it was adulterated. So far, so good, perhaps, but there was also a darker side to the story. Some of its aspects were simply ridiculous, as witness the attempt to replace both *la zarzuela* and the classical drama of the Golden Age with a new 'enlightened' theatre, and, still more so, the insistence that the populace should shed their traditional dress (the all-enveloping cloak typical of lower-class men was regarded as an ideal cover for bandit daggers). Others, however, were downright sinister, for also

---

* Known as the *sorteo*, the formal system of conscription was so unpopular that, after a short-lived experiment in the 1770s, the régime had resolved never to use it except in time of war (a situation that Godoy was desperate to change). However, the populace remained subject to the constant threat of *levas* – the forced impressment of vagrants and the destitute.

encompassed by the policy were the criticism of charity, the denunciation of all forms of holiday and popular entertainment, the desire to eradicate all manifestations of folk-culture (even traditional songs and carols were frowned upon), and the criminalisation of poverty. Underlying the whole was a terror of the common people – *el populacho* – that is almost palpable: ignorant, savage, brutal, irrational and vicious, they had to be subjected to a diet of constant labour and denied any outlet for their emotions.

All this was dangerously provocative. For a population such as that of eighteenth-century Spain, the various communal rituals and celebrations that were so hated by the *ilustrados* were the very stuff of life. Welcome interruptions in an otherwise unending round of drudgery and boredom, they were also vital manifestations of identity. For Carlos III and the various ecclesiastical reformers whom he patronised, such traditional ceremonies as the burial of the sardine in Murcia may have been examples of the darkest ignorance and superstition, but for the towns involved they were the life-blood of the community, and the source of much local pride. Take them away, indeed, and the people would be deprived of the supernatural help that was its only protection against misfortune, a fear that could only be intensified given the growing tendency of traditionalist preachers to argue that Spain's ills stemmed from divine punishment of Godoy. Allied to all this was the question of xenophobia, and, particularly, francophobia. In many parts of Spain, economic rivalry, the presence of a substantial French community, folk memories of the War of the Spanish Succession, and, most recently, the anti-revolutionary propaganda associated with the war of 1793–1795 had led to considerable anti-French feeling. Yet, with the *petimetre* – the fashionable young fop who affected French dress and French manners, and peppered his speech with gallicisms in order to curry favour and demonstrate his own superiority – already becoming something of a stock figure, and the Enlightenment being portrayed by traditionalist clerics as a satanic plot, in popular eyes for what did Bourbon cultural policy stand if not frenchification and the destruction of Spain's very identity? Just as early manifestations of Bourbon reformism had helped provoke serious disturbances in 1766, so Godoy was playing with fire in continuing to impose it in the Spain of the 1790s; indeed, of all his actions there was probably none more unpopular than his prohibition of bullfighting in 1805.

Hardly surprisingly, by 1800 Spain was in a state of ferment. Peasant risings occurred in Galicia and Asturias in 1790–1791, Galicia in 1798, Valencia in 1801, and Bilbao in 1804, there were bread riots in Segovia, Madrid and many *pueblos* in La Mancha, whilst numerous communities attempted to mount a legal challenge against their *señores*. As for the demands of the Church, many peasants pretended that they had produced less than was actually the case, or circumvented the tithes altogether by introducing new crops which were not specifically subject to them. Finally, there was also much resistance to the régime's political and social reforms. In the Basque provinces, for example, the notables were outraged by Godoy's attempts to whittle away the *fueros* still further in accordance with the centralising policies of Carlos III, and they engaged in a fierce campaign of obstruction and propaganda. More humbly, all over Spain, townsfolk and peasants who had been forced to see their loved ones buried in new-fangled municipal cemeteries stole their bodies back at night and tried to restore them to the protection of the old resting-places; more particularly, in Madrid the growing *afrancesamiento* of the court was met by the swaggering *majos* – shopkeepers, artisans, taverners and labourers who, together with their women, dressed in exaggeratedly traditional style and took pleasure in picking fights with *petimetres*.

To return to national politics, it was the existence of this complex web of resentment, resistance, hunger and despair that enabled the anti-Godoyist faction in the court to reach out to the people, and all the more so as the fashion which had emerged amongst the nobility of mingling with the Madrid crowd in disguise gave the conspirators an ideal means of spreading scurrilous rumours. Thus it was that when María Antonia of Naples met an early death, stories spread that she had been poisoned; still worse, it was put about that Godoy was plotting to seize the throne, the conspirators also distributing a series of insulting cartoons making much of Godoy's supposed relationship with the queen; Fernando, meanwhile, was portrayed as an injured innocent who would rescue Spain from all her ills.

Effective though this propaganda was, there is no reason to suppose that at this stage Spain was heading for anything more serious than the riots of 1766 (when mob violence had toppled an equally unpopular chief minister). What changed the situation was Spain's ever more precarious international position. In this respect it cannot be denied that Godoy's aims had gone disastrously astray. Far from being enabled to rebuild her strength, Spain rather had been seriously weakened. On the one hand, with the government deprived of much of the revenues of the American empire, there was little that Godoy could have done to strengthen the Spanish army even had his plans encountered less opposition. On the other, even such strength as Spain had was dissipated with the Spanish fleet suffering a number of serious defeats, and Portugal being invaded in 1801. Following the French lead, peace was signed with Britain in March 1802 – the price was the loss of Trinidad – but in little more than a year Britain and France were at war again. Conscious of the dangers of a fresh conflict, Godoy made frantic efforts to stay neutral, but in the event the best he could do was to persuade Napoleon to allow Spain to redeem the pledges made in the Treaty of San Ildefonso by a subsidy of six million francs per month. Onerous as this arrangement was (the government had to raise the necessary money by means of an extortionate loan on the Paris market), it did not even achieve its aims: arguing that in reality Spain remained allied to France, Britain went back to war with her in October 1804. The result was a return to economic disruption and, above all, the catastrophic defeat at Trafalgar on 21 October 1805, in which the bulk of Spain's remaining seapower was destroyed.

Trafalgar was not the killing blow of legend. Spain had really ceased to be a naval power before a single cannon had been fired. Ships she had in abundance, but already there were not the means to fit them out, and neither the training and experience to sail them nor the resources to build more (major naval construction had effectively ceased in 1797). Nor should the trauma of the battle be exaggerated. Counting the many men who drowned as their shattered ships foundered in the terrible storm that set in after the battle, Franco-Spanish casualties may have numbered as many as 14,000 men, of whom at least 5,000 were Spaniards. Amongst the coastal communities that provided Spain's sailors, this was certainly a blow, but at the popular level the impact was negligible. Except for those who had lost family in the battle, even the educated classes were not much moved by it: Spain, after all, still had plenty of warships, and there was no reason to think that the defeat had any particular significance. If poets such as Quintana penned many odes to the combat, their theme was dead heroes rather than a dead empire. The navy, it was generally agreed, had fought with honour, whilst the government reinforced this impression by showering the survivors with promotions and adding extra increments to the pensions paid to the widows of those who had been killed.

Yet defeat still rankled, for the fleet was perceived as having put to sea at the behest of a France that was not prepared to defend Spain's interests. On the contrary, indeed, Napoleon snubbed Madrid at every turn. With the very *raison d'être* of the alliance scattering the seabed off Trafalgar, the empire now under direct threat (Britain was not only patronising such revolutionaries as Francisco Miranda, but had occupied Montevideo and Buenos Aires), and his own popularity at a new low, Godoy began to cast around for some form of escape. Encouraged by friendly overtures from Russia, in the autumn of 1806 Godoy was presented with what seemed the perfect opportunity in the form of war between France and Prussia. Contemporary wisdom holding that the Prussian army was the best in

Europe, he immediately issued a proclamation calling Spain to arms. Great was the consternation in Madrid, therefore, when Napoleon smashed the Prussians at Jena and Auerstädt. Desperate to escape the emperor's wrath, Godoy maintained that his actions had been directed not against the French but the British – cannily phrased, his proclamation had not specified whom Spain was supposed to fight – congratulated Napoleon on his victories, and agreed both to join the Continental Blockade and dispatch a division of 14,000 men for service with the *grande armée* (commanded by the Marqués de la Romana, this ended up in Denmark as part of the assistance sent her when she attacked Sweden in company with Russia in February 1808).

With the signing of the Treaty of Fontainebleau, it appeared that salvation was at hand, but in fact the appearance of the French armies coincided with a dramatic deterioration in the situation. In addition to doing all that they could to blacken the favourite's reputation and ensure that the machinery of power could be immediately taken over by them should Carlos IV die, the *fernandino* conspirators had early in 1807 decided to guarantee the succession of their figurehead by marrying Fernando into the Bonaparte family (the fact that the only possible candidates were very junior did not deter them). Secret negotiations were opened with the French ambassador, in the process of which Fernando was persuaded to write a letter openly begging Napoleon's protection. However, tipped off that a plot was afoot, in a dramatic confrontation at the royal palace of El Escorial on 27 October, Carlos and María Luisa confined the prince to his quarters and ordered an investigation into his affairs. Fernando's papers apparently revealed little more than that he hated Godoy, wanted him imprisoned, and had been in some sort of contact with Napoleon. None the less, the king and queen decided that the prince had been plotting their overthrow. Bullied into admitting that this had indeed been his aim, Fernando was eventually pardoned, but those he named as his collaborators – Escoíquiz, Infantado, Montijo and various others – were arrested and, despite the collapse of an attempt at a show trial, sent into internal exile.

For Godoy, all this was a catastrophe, the general (and wholly incorrect) view being that the whole affair had been an audacious attempt to eliminate Fernando, and the banishment of Escoíquiz *et al.* a monstrous abuse of justice. Even more disastrously, meanwhile, the affair convinced Napoleon of either the need for, or the possibility of, intervention. Which is the case, it is impossible to say. The emperor knew that Godoy could not be trusted and was dissatisfied with Spain's performance as an ally, but had hitherto expressed no intention of taking any hand in her affairs. Yet the idea that she might be transformed into another family monarchy can hardly have been alien to his mind: there had been talk of such a move since at least 1804, whilst, anxious for a throne, the dashing Murat was actively promoting the idea. Whatever the truth of the matter, things now started to happen. Charged by Carlos IV with complicity in Fernando's plotting, the emperor announced that the prince was under his protection and forbade any mention of France in connection with Fernando and his accomplices, and on 13 November ordered the 25,000 men he had been holding in reserve at Bayonne – the Second Corps of Observation of the Gironde – to cross the frontier into northern Spain. Meanwhile, fresh troops – the Corps of Observation of the Ocean Coasts and Division of Observation of the Western Pyrenees – were concentrated at Bourdeaux and Saint-Jean-Pied-du-Port under Marshals Moncey and Bessières, and magazines established at Bayonne and Perpignan, strenuous attempts also being made to acquire as much intelligence as possible about Spain's armed forces, fortresses, roads and political situation.

The confrontation in El Escorial, then, led directly to French intervention, but whether Napoleon as yet intended to overthrow the Bourbons is another matter. As Marshal Bessières told one of his aides-de-camp, 'So long as Napoleon remains in power, no European throne can be filled by a Bourbon.'[16] Nor had the Spanish state done much to rehabilitate itself in his eyes. As usual, mobilisation had gone very slowly, whilst news was soon reaching the emperor that Junot's forces, which by now were massing on the Portuguese frontier, were going hungry.* Yet despite all this there is still no evidence that he was planning a change of dynasty prior to the end of 1807. In January 1808, indeed, Napoleon was still thinking of a marriage alliance: meeting his estranged brother, Lucien, in Mantua, he persuaded him to send his daughter, Charlotte – the only Bonaparte girl available – to Paris as a bride for Fernando.

If Napoleon was undecided, he was certainly keeping his options open, whilst his preparations were stimulated still further by the news that 7,000 British troops had arrived at Gibraltar from Sicily. Commanded by General Pierre Dupont, the 25,000-strong Second Corps of Observation of the Gironde was therefore moved from Vitoria to Valladolid, where it was ideally placed to march on Madrid, the Corps of Observation of the Ocean Coasts and Division of Observation of the Western Pyrenees sent to replace

---

* The fact that this was Napoleon's own fault was ignored: the original plan had been to advance into Portugal from León, but a mistaken belief that it would be quicker to march via Abrantes had led Napoleon to shift Junot to the barren Tagus valley. Given no forewarning of this move, the Spaniards were unable to prepare for it, and so the troops went hungry.

it in Navarre and the Basque provinces, and yet another new formation – the Division of Observation of the Eastern Pyrenees – mobilised at Perpignan. Not counting the forces of Junot, over 50,000 French troops were now in Spain, and still others massing on the frontiers. Small wonder, then, that Godoy was starting to feel distinctly alarmed.

Before looking at the events that followed, however, we must first return to Portugal, where João and Araújo had now agreed to implement all Napoleon's demands immediately, and were asking only for a guarantee of the Bragança dynasty. Their efforts, however, were to no avail. Concerned that the British might send an army to Lisbon, Napoleon ordered Junot to hasten his march (hence the shift to the Tagus valley). Exhausted by the difficult march they had to make to reach the Tagus, on crossing the frontier on 19 November, his troops found themselves facing a mere track that led through a barely populated desert of mountain and scrub. What followed was beyond doubt a terrible ordeal, as witness the account of General Foy:

The army suffered incessantly from the bad weather. In Portugal the autumnal rains are a positive deluge . . . Twenty times a day the columns of infantry were broken in fording the swollen . . . rivers. The soldiers straggled along at random, and, ceasing to be restrained by the ties of discipline and the presence of their leaders, they had no longer the appearance of an army, but rather of a medley of individuals exasperated by distress.[17]

Driven on mercilessly at a rate of over twenty miles a day, more than half the troops had fallen sick or turned to marauding by the time Junot regained a better road at Abrantes, whilst he also had to abandon most of his guns. So desperate was the situation, indeed, that the French commander had to form the élite companies of his first two divisions into provisional battalions, and it was with these men, no more than 1,500-strong, that he finally marched into Lisbon on 30 November.

For the Spaniards, meanwhile, things had not gone much better. According to Thiébault, 'General Caraffa's Spanish division lost 1,700 or 1,800 men from hunger or fatigue, drowning in torrents or falling down precipices.'[18] This, surely, is an exaggeration, but even so it is clear that the confusion was considerable. As Girón remembered of the first day's march:

It seemed impossible that that short and easy march could have been directed by soldiers. Units got lost, the soldiers dispersed, and in a word the disorder and confusion reached such a point that I can affirm that I have never seen its equal in the wake of the most complete defeats.[19]

Once again it was a poor advertisement for the Bourbon state, and one that Napoleon was unlikely to forget. All the more was this the case as Spain was currently acquiring greater prominence in his strategic plans. Thus, the operations that he was planning in the Mediterranean – the conquest of Sicily, the relief of the beleaguered garrison of Corfu, and the invasion of Egypt – made Spanish naval support very valuable, and yet the Spanish navy was in a pitiable condition. Reduced to perhaps fifteen serviceable men-of-war, even these were mostly in need of many repairs, whilst crew, spares and supplies were all extremely scanty. Only with the greatest difficulty, indeed, were six ships from Cartagena got to sea with the aim of joining the French squadron at Toulon. With all this, of course, Napoleon was much displeased, and all the more so as nothing would dissuade him from the belief that, thanks to her empire in America, Spain was awash with money. If this potential was not realised, the reason was simple: the Spaniards were corrupt; the Spaniards were inefficient; the Spaniards were incompetent; all that was needed therefore was the strong hand of France.

Already, though, the strong hand of France had failed in Portugal. João may have attempted to propitiate Paris, but he had also been careful to keep open his links with the British, who had promised to help the royal family escape to Brazil. Preparations for flight were therefore soon under way, and on 29 November a convoy of eight men-of-war, four frigates and twenty-four merchantmen put to sea and headed for the Atlantic, where it was met by the British naval squadron that had been sent to blockade the Tagus some weeks since. With them went not just the whole of the royal family, but the entire contents of the treasury and the national archives, many works of art, and large numbers of the nobility, the bureaucracy, and the wealthier inhabitants of Lisbon, attended by perhaps half the coin in circulation in the country. Also safely aboard ship, meanwhile, was the British merchant community and much of its trading stock.

Back in Lisbon the entry of the invaders was hardly a triumphal one, the few men that accompanied the frustrated Junot resembling nothing more than the remnants of a beaten army: so exhausted were they that many of them could not carry their own muskets. Some units had been reduced to one tenth of their original strength, whilst it was not for three weeks that the French commander could count upon the services of even 10,000 men. 'The state we were in . . . is hardly credible', wrote Thiébault. 'Our clothing had lost all shape and colour; I had not had a change of linen since Abrantes. My feet were coming through my boots.'[20] With the aid of the Spaniards, however, the country was gradually subjected to military occupation, garrisons being placed in such towns as Oporto, Setúbal, Faro, Almeida and

Elvas. Meanwhile, a determined effort was made to overawe the populace; the property of all those who had fled to Brazil was confiscated, along with much Church plate and all the estates of the royal family; an indemnity of 100,000,000 francs imposed; and the army formed into a new Portuguese Legion and sent off to garrison duties in Germany (it was eventually destroyed in Russia in 1812). As for the regency that had been left behind by João, it was abolished and replaced by a new 'council of government', the Bragança dynasty being finally proclaimed to have been overthrown on 1 January 1808.

As was usual with France's conquests, however, pillage and exploitation were cloaked in the guise of benevolence and reform. Thus, Junot had entered Lisbon proclaiming that its inhabitants had nothing to fear from him, and in fact made repeated efforts to ensure that his troops behaved in a reasonable fashion (forbidding them, for example, to frequent taverns after seven o'clock in the evening). There soon appeared, too, a translated version of an address which Napoleon had recently made to the clergy of Milan in which he maintained himself to be a loyal friend of the Catholic Church. The British, it was claimed, had imprisoned João, whilst Junot's every action was dressed up as an act of grace and favour (much was made, for example, of the abolition of the army), and numerous promises made of improvements in education and public works. Meanwhile, a start was also made on the sort of political, social and economic change that characterised the rest of the Napoleonic empire: a *corregedor-mór* was appointed to head the administration in each province in the style of the French *prefect*; discussions were initiated on a constitution; many convents and monasteries were suppressed; and beggars and street vendors were persecuted in the name of public order.

Rewarded for his efforts by Napoleon with the title of Duke of Abrantes, Junot could count on a number of collaborators. Not the least amongst these, of course, were many representatives of the resident French community. Most of them being engaged in commerce, they naturally welcomed the eclipse of their British rivals and provided the French commander with a large number of officials, including every single one not just of the new *corregedores* but also of the ministers whom Junot appointed to head the various arms of the administration. That said, however, there was no lack of Portuguese assistance. Bedazzled by dreams of sharing in the glory of the *grande armée*, for example, large numbers of army officers volunteered for service with the new Portuguese Legion, whilst, in line with developments in other states, the nobility, the bureaucracy, the intelligentsia and the commercial classes all provided the French with many adherents. With the Church urging submission to the new régime, Junot therefore had no difficulty in filling the ranks of the administration or, indeed, in assembling a delegation that in April 1808 travelled to France to ask Napoleon to give the French commander the throne.

If the educated classes gave the French much assistance, matters were by no means as rosy as Junot was inclined to pretend. On the contrary, from the earliest days of French occupation there was a considerable degree of violence and unrest. Whether this was overtly political is unclear: whilst the appearance of growing numbers of anti-French posters and handbills was unambiguous in its message of loyalty to the Braganças, the same cannot be said with any certainty of the fights that quickly began to break out between the French soldiery and members of the populace. Nor should much be made of the fact that the roads were becoming more and more dangerous: with the economy in chaos, the magistracy denuded of personnel and the populace experiencing a severe increase in taxation, an upsurge in lawlessness was inevitable. As Foy points out, indeed, entering Lisbon the French encountered 'swarms of robbers and vagabonds' who had 'flocked from their hiding holes' and engaged in 'scenes of disorder like those of which [the capital] was the theatre after the earthquake of 1755'.[21] As for the fact that nearly one third of the Portuguese Legion had deserted by the time that it crossed the frontier into Spain, heavy rates of desertion were nothing new. Yet the violence with which the French responded – according to Foy, an inhabitant of Mafra was executed merely for 'uttering invectives against the French army'[22] – inevitably encouraged xenophobic tendencies. At the same time, the collaborators included many men who had benefited from Pomballine reforms that had concentrated wine production in fewer hands but ruined many peasants in the process. Nor were the circumstances of Junot's arrival much help because the Portuguese had seen not 'heroes of a superior species, colossusses, demigods', but mere men, and not just that but men with 'hardly enough strength to keep the step . . . [and] nothing but rusted firelocks and cartridges imbued with water'.[23]

Though the French staged elaborate celebrations and festivities, the crowds that they attracted were hardly proof that Junot's rule was popular. Only events in Spain sufficed to transform unrest into revolt, however. Here Napoleon remained set on regeneration, but uncertain as to how to proceed. At this point he was still free to depose Carlos IV and replace him with Fernando, whom he knew to be not only extremely compliant, but also much loved by the people. Why, then, did he fail to embark upon so obvious a course? The answer is simple: Spain appeared to be in a state of utter disintegration; her army was ill-prepared for war; and he was constantly being told by the various agents he had sent across the Pyrenees that there was a general disposition to accept any solution that he cared to impose. The Spanish Bourbons could not be trusted, whilst there was no reason to believe that a régime headed by Fernando VII would be any more efficient than one headed by Carlos IV. Lucien, it transpired, was unwilling to permit the match between Charlotte and Fernando. And, finally, with ever larger numbers of troops in Spain, there simply seemed no reason why he should not solve the problem in a radical fashion that would at one and the same time reinforce his prestige, ensure that Spain was transformed and create another throne for his family. Who, after all, could frustrate such a course? The Spanish army was decrepit, and popular revolt in his experience at best a minor threat to be accepted and crushed as a matter of course. Warned by Fouché that Spain might not be an easy target, he therefore exploded:

What are you talking about? Every reflecting person in Spain despises the government; the Prince of the Peace . . . is a scoundrel who will himself open the gates of Spain for me. As to the rabble . . . a few cannon shots will quickly disperse them.[24]

To the very end Napoleon kept his options open – 'Murat assured me in 1814,' wrote Lord Holland, 'that he had no instructions . . . Not a syllable had been communicated to him of the object of his expedition'[25] – but the end of the Bourbon dynasty was now looming. Hence the letter that he sent to Alexander I of Russia on 2 February 1808 suggesting a march of 50,000 French and Russian troops on Constantinople from their respective bases in present-day Croatia and Romania with a view to partitioning the Ottoman empire, the aim being to buy off possible Russian objections to the blow to the balance of power presented by the removal of the Bourbons.

At all events developments now gathered pace. Backed up by heavy reinforcements, between 9 and 12 February the Divisions of the Eastern and Western Pyrenees crossed the border into Navarre and Catalonia, occupied Pamplona and Barcelona, and seized control of the citadels that dominated the two cities. By now thoroughly alarmed, the Spanish government had for some time been pressing for an explanation of France's conduct, whilst at the same time requesting the implementation of the promised partition of Portugal and requesting a Bonaparte bride for Fernando. To all these communications the emperor had replied with a mixture of disdain and obfuscation, whilst at the same time continuing to proclaim his friendly intentions. Faced by increasing evidence of French duplicity, Godoy responded by ordering the Spanish troops in Portugal to return to Spain, (most got away apart from those in Lisbon of whom the majority were disarmed and interned). The 24th of February, meanwhile, brought another shock. In a long memorandum Napoleon accused Spain of disunion and bad faith and announced that he no longer considered himself bound by Fontainebleau. Spain was now promised the whole of Portugal, true, but in exchange she would have to surrender all the territory that she possessed between the River Ebro and the Pyrenees and sign a permanent and unlimited alliance with France.

The point of this *démarche* is rather unclear, but the most likely explanation seems to be that Napoleon hoped at one and the same time to justify his conduct hitherto and provoke the Spaniards into a resistance that would give him the pretext he needed to overthrow the monarchy. If this is the case, then he was certainly successful, Carlos IV agreeing with Godoy and his other advisers that he should initiate preparations for flight to America by way of Seville. The court already having moved to the palace of Aranjuez on the River Tagus south of Madrid, it was well placed for such a move, but, to gain time, the favourite also ordered the royal guard to move there from its barracks in Madrid, whilst at the same time directing a variety of Spanish troops to hold the line of the Tagus. Garrisons stationed in the French zone of occupation were ordered to make no resistance and a conciliatory response was made to Napoleon's demands, but, even so, nothing could disguise the fact that war was imminent. As a miserable Godoy lamented, 'I am in such a state . . . that I should like to put on . . . a sack and go and hide in a corner.'[26]

The French, meanwhile, were on the move again. On 20 February, Joachim Murat had been appointed to the command of the 60,000 French troops who were now in Spain, whilst on 2 March he was ordered to establish his headquarters in Vitoria, where he soon received the support of a 6,000-strong detachment of the Imperial Guard. On 6 March the French occupied the fortress of San Sebastián, Murat the next day receiving instructions to launch the forces of Dupont and Moncey southwards towards Madrid, whose occupation, the emperor's lieutenant was told, was to be followed by the dispatch of Godoy and the Spanish royal family to a meeting with Napoleon at either Burgos or Bayonne. Though half-hearted efforts were still made to convince the Spaniards that all was well – the march on Madrid, for example, was explained by talk of securing Cádiz against the British besieging Gibraltar, or even sending troops to north Africa – the gloves were clearly off. As Napoleon wrote to Murat, 'I hope with all my heart that that there will be no war, and am only taking so many precautions because it is my habit to leave nothing to chance. But if there is a war, your position will be a very good one.'[27]

The trap, then, was about to shut, but events were now disrupted by fresh developments. For Fernando and his supporters – the so-called *fernandinos* – the war that now threatened was unthinkable. First of all, they remained convinced that the emperor intended to place Fernando on the throne or, at least, get rid of Godoy, and, second, they believed – quite rightly – that war would lead to defeat and the overthrow of the entire dynasty. Terrified of what might occur, Fernando therefore summoned Montijo, and ordered him to organise a rising that could present the emperor with a *fait accompli* in the form not only of a new régime, but of a new monarch only too eager to throw himself on Napoleon's mercy and do his will in every particular. Fernando, in short, would have been king, but he would have gone down in history not as *el deseado* but as *el afrancesado*.

In stirring up revolt, there was little difficulty. Across the Peninsula there was a widespread conviction that the French were out to do no more than rescue Fernando from the clutches of Godoy. 'Our troops', wrote Lejeune, 'had been welcomed in Spain . . . and the loyal populace, who . . . received us as if we were their brothers, impatiently awaited the day when the emperor . . . would remove the hated minister.'[28] Acting from ignorance as much as intent, the French had done nothing to dampen such hopes:

The French . . . knew not what was the work which they were destined to perform, but, hearing nothing from their hosts but curses upon the authors of the misfortunes of the country, they associated themselves with the public indignation, and . . . repeated that the army was come into Spain only to execute justice upon a villain.[29]

Nor at this point had Napoleon assumed the demon-like qualities that he was soon to acquire in the eyes of most Spaniards. Amongst the educated classes, indeed, he was widely admired – the emperor himself later remarked that the régime was 'never afraid of him' and 'looked on him as a defender of royalism'[30] – whilst, influenced by vague ideas that the emperor had saved the Church from the revolutionaries, the *populacho* were content to follow the lead of their betters. As Foy wrote, 'It was obvious that the reign of Napoleon had entirely effaced the antipathy of Catholic Spain to [the] new France.'[31] Yet beneath the surface trouble was brewing. 'The soldiers', wrote the young English seminarian, Robert Brindle, 'were quartered in private houses and brought distress and misery into every family. Their right to anything which they chose to covet few had the hardihood to call in question. If complaint were made, it must be preferred to a French officer, and insult or an additional grievance were the result.'[32]

At this stage virtually the only troops actually at Aranjuez were the royal guard, whose aristocratic officer corps had never forgiven Godoy either his lowly origins or the fact that he had cut its size by half. Meanwhile, the population of Aranjuez were wholly dependent on the court for their prosperity, and were currently much swelled by the hordes of courtiers and retainers who travelled with the royal family on their seasonal migrations from one royal palace to the next. At the same time, many of the villages around Madrid happened to be fiefs of the leading *fernandinos* and could thus be galvanised into action by economic means. Yet such economic means were probably barely needed. As the populace retained a touching faith in the protection supposedly afforded them by the monarch, the news that the king intended to abandon them caused as much fear as the idea that Godoy might evade his doom caused fury. Disguised as one 'Uncle Joe', Montijo had within a very few days succeeded in massing a large crowd around the palace at Aranjuez, and whipping the guards' hatred of Godoy to fever pitch. Initially it seems that the plan was for the revolt to be sparked off by the departure of the royal family, but, thanks to Carlos' vacillation, such an event stubbornly failed to materialise. However, in the end no catalyst was needed. As the Secretary of State, Pedro Cevallos, informed the Secretary of the Council of Castile: 'About one o'clock in the morning [of 18 March] there occurred a clash between some hussars and Guardias de Corps, and this was followed by the assembly of many soldiers and civilians who had taken fright at rumours that the king and queen and royal family were leaving.'[33] The hussars referred to were members of Godoy's recently formed personal bodyguard – 'a troop of brilliantly uniformed soldiers who were regarded by their fellows with envy and hated by the people'[34] – the violence with which they were assaulted setting the scene for three days of mayhem. Nor was the trouble confined to Aranjuez. In Madrid, for example:

Hardly had night fallen than a furious crowd invaded the house of Don Diego, the younger brother of the favourite. Having smashed in the doors and discovered that the building was empty, they began to throw all its rich furniture out of the windows . . . until they had made an enormous pile of tables, beds, wardrobes and pianos, to which they set fire . . . When the *plebe* had finished enjoying this . . . costly bonfire, they . . . headed for the house of the Príncipe de Branciforte, Godoy's brother-in-law. However, a notice had been put on the door . . . announcing that the property of the favourite and his close relatives had been confiscated . . . This was enough to calm down the rioters, and they spent the rest of the night processing through the streets . . . and drinking at the cost of the taverners . . . [The next day] the whole garrison . . . were called out of their barracks by bands of women bearing pitchers of wine in their hands, and . . . the soldiers, mixing with the people, bore in their firelocks the palm branches which, as a precaution against lightning, are commonly hung at the windows.[35]

In Toledo a bust of Godoy was hung from a gibbet; in San Lucar de Barrameda a botanical garden he had established was wrecked, and, last but not least, in Zaragoza, radicalised by recent regulations that had extended the academic year by three months, the students of the university forced their lecturers to barricade themselves into the building's cloister and seized the portrait of the favourite that hung in the main lecture hall. Placed on a makeshift hurdle, it was then dragged through the streets to the broad street known as the Coso that served as a *plaza mayor*. There, wrote one of the leaders, 'We made a bonfire whose flames leapt higher than the roofs, whereupon, having been well kicked and spat upon, His Excellency . . . was thrown upon the fire.'[36]

Back in Aranjuez, the king and queen were terrified. With the bulk of the guard in a state of rebellion and the favourite himself hiding in the attic of his palace, whence he had fled as the mob poured through the main door, Carlos IV quickly agreed to have Godoy arrested, but, under Montijo's orchestration, the disturbances continued unabated. Told by one regimental commander that only Fernando would enjoy the loyalty of the troops, Carlos and María Luisa caved in, and on the morning of 19 March abdicated the Crown into the hands of their son. Driven from his hiding-place by thirst, meanwhile, Godoy narrowly escaped a lynching, and was placed under close arrest.

For all its popular aspect, there is no doubt as to what the so-called *motín de Aranjuez* represented. Inspired by elements from outside its ranks though it may have been, a section of the army – in this case the royal guard – had sought to impose its views upon the body politic by 'pronouncing' against the régime. Challenged by this call to arms, Godoy and his royal patrons found that they had few defenders. The officer corps as a whole was disgruntled by the failure of the favourite's reforms to make any difference in its situation, and his orders to resist the French were already being widely disobeyed; much of the upper nobility and the Church was hostile; reformist circles had long since lost all faith in Godoy's political credentials; and the common people were in a state of open revolt. As for Fernando, he was seen as a saviour, the reception that he received when he rode into Madrid on 24 March being captured by Alcalá Galiano:

In truth, in all the different scenes of popular enthusiasm that I have witnessed, nothing . . . has ever equalled those which I now describe. The cheers were loud, repeated and delivered with . . . eyes full of tears of pleasure, kerchiefs were waved . . . from balconies with hands trembling with pleasure . . . and not for a moment did the passion . . . or the thunderous noise of the joyful crowd diminish.[37]

Popular though the new king was, his security was far from assured. Murat had occupied the city only the day before, and, despite increasingly abject attempts to win France's favour, refused to recognise Fernando; still worse, indeed, Carlos IV was persuaded to protest against his abdication and appeal to Napoleon for assistance. With the two rivals openly craving his mediation, the emperor was placed in an ideal position to recast the situation as he wanted, Carlos, María Luisa and Fernando alike being summoned to meet him for a conference at Bayonne (as a sop to the former king and queen, Godoy was rescued from captivity and whisked to safety in France). With all the protagonists in the drama united in his presence, Napoleon exploded the waiting bombshell: the rival kings were both to renounce the throne and hand it to the emperor. To this demand Carlos made no resistance, and on 5 May, after some days of unedifying squabbles, such feeble defiance as Fernando was willing to offer was also overcome, the throne now being formally signed over to Napoleon in exchange for generous pensions for the royal family and guarantees of territorial and religious integrity for Spain herself.

With the whole of the Peninsula now apparently subjugated, Napoleon appeared to have achieved his every objective. Even as the Bourbons departed to a decorous exile – Carlos, María Luisa and Godoy to Italy, and Fernando, his brother, Carlos, and uncle, Antonio, to Talleyrand's chateau at Valençay – however, the Peninsula was astir. Why, though, had the emperor acted as he had? For answer we can do no better than turn to Napoleon himself:

The old king and queen . . . had become the object of the hatred and scorn of their subjects. The Prince of Asturias was conspiring against them . . . and had become . . . the hope of the nation. At the same time [Spain] was ready for great changes . . . whilst I myself was very popular there. With matters in this state . . . I resolved to make use of this unique opportunity to rid myself of a branch of the Bourbons, continue the family system of Louis XIV in my own dynasty, and chain Spain to the destinies of France.[38]

The preoccupation with *raison d'état* is repeated in other sources. As he told Roederer, for example:

Spain . . . must be French. It is for France that I have conquered Spain; it is with her blood, her arms, her gold. I am French in all my affections . . . I do not do anything except for . . . love of France. I dethroned the Bourbons for no other reason than it was in the interest of France to assure my dynasty. I had nothing else in view except French strength and glory . . . I have the rights of conquest: call whoever governs Spain king . . . viceroy or governor general, Spain must be French.[39]

Setting this aside, however, opportunism was the key. Napoleon had been motivated neither by an altruistic desire to spread the benefits of freedom and enlightenment, nor by a gigantic strategic combination, nor by an overwhelming clan loyalty that made the creation of family courts the centrepiece of French foreign policy. Strategic, ideological and historical factors were present in his thinking, certainly, but in the last resort what mattered was, first, the emperor's character, and, second, the force of circumstance. Forever eager to demonstrate his prowess, impose his stamp upon affairs, and demonstrate his contempt for diplomacy, the emperor was confronted with a situation in which nothing seemed to stand between him and a stroke that was more audacious than anything that he had yet attempted. Never had he been more wrong.

2

Madrid

THE IBERIAN INSURRECTIONS, MAY–JUNE 1808

The men knelt together in the mild, spring night. One, a friar, bent forward in prayer. Before them loomed the shadowy figures of the firing squad, their greatcoats faintly luminous in the moonlight. A shouted order and a dozen muskets were levelled at the prisoners. At that moment there came a sudden movement. Straightening up, a man at the front of the group flung his arms wide, looked his killers full in the face, and opened his mouth one last time. Too late: the volley crashed out, and the huddled victims were flung back by the impact of the musket balls. What, the officer in command wondered, had the fellow been about to shout: an accusation, a plea for mercy, a scream of defiance? He would never know, and did not especially care either: all round the royal palace looming dark against the pre-dawn sky behind him, all along the narrow streets that led to the heart of the city, were strewn the dead of the day's fighting, and there were other executions to attend to yet. It was 3 May 1808.

Immortalised by Goya, this snapshot of the executions that took place at the Montaña del Príncipe Pío on the outskirts of Madrid in the wake of the dramatic rising of the Dos de Mayo had tremendous significance. The very ambiguity of its central figure is an arresting metaphor of the response of the Spanish people to the Napoleonic invasion, which, as we shall see, was much more complex than has generally been depicted. Nevertheless, the killings of 2 and 3 May were to reverberate around Spain in dramatic fashion, and in the process to usher in war and revolution alike.

The rising of the Dos de Mayo, of course, was hardly unexpected. Ever since the *motín de Aranjuez* Spain had been in ferment: attacks on *godoyistas* were frequent, whilst the failure of the French explicitly to recognise Fernando caused much discontent and in particular gave rise to the suspicion that they intended to bring back the favourite. In consequence, it was not very long before discontent raised its head. In Vitoria, for example, an angry crowd made a desperate attempt to prevent the king's departure for the French frontier, whilst the publication of Carlos IV's protest against his abdication caused a serious riot in Madrid. Meanwhile, a captain named Mottet was murdered in the *madrileño* village of Carabanchel Alto on 12 April by the priest on whom he was billeted, whilst Burgos saw a veritable precursor of the Dos de Mayo:

I was just going to make a sketch . . . of the beautiful bas-relief on the gate of the bridge, when I heard the cry, 'Death to the French!' and several musket shots. I ran as fast as I could to the guard in the Plaza Mayor, where our troops were under arms and ready for battle . . . We lost a few men from cross shots, but the shots fired by the . . . crowd, which charged us at a run, exhausted their ammunition . . . whilst our repeated orderly discharges . . . soon swept the place clear of our assailants.[1]

A conflagration was inevitable, and all the more so in Madrid with its excitable and xenophobic gangs of *majos* and *majas*. The city's mood was caught by the later dissident, José María Blanco y Crespo (better known by his *nom d'exil* of Joseph Blanco White):

The wildest schemes for the destruction of the French division at Madrid were canvassed almost in public and with very little reserve . . . Short pikes headed with a sharp cutting crescent were to be distributed to the spectators who used to range themselves behind the cavalry. At one signal the horses were to be houghed with these instruments and the infantry attacked with poignards. To remonstrate against such absurd and visionary plans . . . was not only useless but dangerous.[2]

By the beginning of May rumours were spreading through the streets that the Junta de Gobierno – the council of regency left behind by Fernando – was being pressurised into sending the last members of the royal family to Bayonne. Serious disturbances took place at Aranjuez on 1 May, and the appearance of two carriages before the royal palace the next day was therefore enough to draw a large crowd. Whipped to a frenzy by the sight of Carlos IV's youngest son, Francisco de Paula, it fell upon an aide-de-camp of Marshal Murat named Auguste Lagrange who had ridden up to assess the situation. Well aware of what was going on – his headquarters was only a few hundred yards away – Murat now took action. Mobilising the nearest available troops – a detachment of the Imperial Guard which he had been given as a personal escort – he ordered them to clear the scene. A few moments later a thunderous discharge rang out, and ten Spaniards lay dead or wounded on the cobbles, the survivors of the crowd hastily dispersing in search of shelter.

Within minutes of the sound of gunfire, the streets were full of confused and angry citizens. Catching up whatever weapons they could lay their hands on, they quickly fell on those Frenchmen unfortunate enough to be caught in the city (of which there were very few, almost all Murat's 10,000 troops being encamped in the surrounding open country). Something of the atmosphere that reigned in the city is conveyed by Antonio Alcalá Galiano:

I was getting dressed when my mother came in looking frightened. All she said to me were the . . . words, 'It has begun'.* There was no need to say what it was she was talking about . . . In a moment, having got dressed anyhow, I was in the street . . . Scattered shots began to be heard in the distance . . . On all sides bands of people were beginning to come together, although they were armed in such a ridiculous fashion that they had to be crazy to think that they could do away with French soldiers. I joined one that was led by a young lad who was some sort of artisan . . . and we headed for the Calle de Fuencarral. But some of them were insisting that we should go to the barracks and join the troops, and others that we should fall upon the French straight away . . . In sum, it was a case of regulars versus guerrillas.[3]

Quickly becoming disgusted with the disorderly nature of his companions, the nineteen-year-old Alcalá Galiano returned to his house. It was as well for him that he did. Outside the palace, the insurgents proved no match for Murat's guardsmen and were quickly put to flight. The rebellion, indeed, was doomed, for columns of French troops were soon pouring into the city from all sides. For a description of the scenes that took place, we have no better source than Blanco White:

The main column came up the Calle Mayor, whose four- and five-storey houses afforded the inhabitants the best possible means of venting their fury on the French soldiers without exposing themselves to their arms. Those who had muskets fired from the windows, and the rest threw down tiles, bricks and heavy pieces of furniture.[4]

Advancing along the main streets, the invaders steadily drove the crowds back towards the central square known as the Puerta del Sol. Attacked from several directions at once by both infantry and cavalry, those defenders who had not already melted away were then overwhelmed. All that was left thereafter was a small group of soldiers and civilians who had seized control of the army's main artillery depot under the command of two junior officers named Daoíz and Velarde, but, after putting up a gallant fight, these diehards, too, were wiped out. By two o'clock in the afternoon, all was quiet. Some 200 Spaniards lay dead, perhaps the same number had been wounded, and 300 more, most of them prisoners taken in the fighting, were

* 'Ha empezado.'

executed during the night. As for the occupiers, their losses had been 31 dead and 114 wounded.

Thus ended the famous revolt of the Dos de Mayo. As far as such tumults went, it had not been particularly impressive, but for all that it was to have profound effects. In the first place, the fighting was replete with images of popular heroism and French brutality: many of the insurgents had fought with little more than their bare hands; the dead included a number of women, including, most famously, a young girl named Manuela Malasaña who was shot dead at the artillery depot; and it was rumoured that even possessing a pair of scissors had been enough to procure a death sentence. As Foy admits, 'Among those who were condemned were men who had not fought, and whose only crime was that of having had about them large knives, or other sharp instruments. They were executed without the assistance of a priest . . . a circumstance which still more exasperated a religious people.'[5] In the second, the story got about that the affair had been a premeditated attempt to massacre the entire population of Madrid. And in the third, the revolt discredited much of the political apparatus of Bourbon Spain at a stroke.

So important is this development that it must be discussed at some length. When Fernando departed for Bayonne he had left behind a structure of government headed by the Junta de Gobierno. Originally presided over by Fernando's uncle, the Infante Don Antonio, it was composed of the ministers who had been appointed by the new king to head the five ministries – Foreign Affairs, War, Finance, Navy, and Grace and Justice – which since the reign of Carlos III had constituted the heart of the Spanish administration. Uncomfortably coexistent with the departments over which these five officials presided were the organs through which Spain had been governed prior to their formation, including most notably the Councils of Castile, the Indies, War, the Admiralty, the Treasury, the Military Orders, and the Inquisition. Lower down the scale this duplication was perpetuated in that Spain was divided into both thirty-two provinces, each headed by a Treasury official known as an Intendent, and fourteen military regions, each headed by a Viceroy, Captain General or Commandant General.* Most important towns were controlled by powerful magistrates known as *corregidores*, whilst mention ought also to be made of the various regional courts of justice and councils of administration, the most important of these being

---

* The military regions were Galicia, Asturias, Navarre, Old Castile, Aragón, Catalonia, Extremadura, New Castile, Valencia and Murcia, Seville, Granada, the Campo del Gibraltar, the Balearic Islands and the Canary Islands.

the Chancellories of Granada and Valladolid and the Audiences of Galicia, Seville, Aragón, Catalonia, Asturias and Extremadura. In the short time that Fernando had been upon the throne before he left for Bayonne, there had been little chance to make any significant changes in the thousands of officials and army officers who staffed this system. New heads had been found for all the ministries; the Duque de Infantado appointed president of the Council of Castile; an old enemy of Godoy, the tough and experienced Gregorio García de la Cuesta, had been made Captain General of Old Castile; and a few officials driven from their posts by popular fury. Otherwise, however, the system was entirely unchanged.

In the current climate the fact that the administration was still permeated by *godoyismo* could not but render it extremely suspect. Adding fuel to the flames were at several other problems. Foremost of these was the manner in which the provincial administration was effectively headed by the army. Thus, the Captains General presided over the Chancellories and Audiences and played a prominent role in their discussions; responsible for its supply, the Intendents were closely linked with the army, wore uniform and were paid the same honours as senior officers; and many *corregidores* were officers who were at the same time the military governors – in effect, Captains General in miniature – of the towns to which they were appointed. With senior generals traditionally occupying many positions of state and the officer corps possessed of a large number of fiscal and legal privileges known as the *fuero militar*, Spain genuinely appeared a military monarchy. Well, then, might Jacob write, 'The power which the governor of Cádiz possessed . . . was so considerable that it more resembled the authority of an individual sovereign than the delegate of a king of Spain', or Swinburne that the Marqués de la Mina 'governed Catalonia . . . more like an independent sovereign than like a subject invested with a delegated authority'.[6]

If this was the case, it was no accident: having come to the throne by force, the Bourbons were intimately linked with the army, whilst, like all eighteenth-century absolutists, they had found it exceedingly useful in their constant struggle to undermine the independence of the privileged orders. However, in a number of ways the results were counterproductive. The Bourbon army had indeed played a significant role in subordinating the nobility and eroding provincial privilege (for the extension of conscription to areas such as Navarre and Catalonia had been an important tool of centralisation), but the privileges heaped upon the officer corps ensured that it generated considerable friction. Officers were able largely to escape the ordinary civil and ecclesiastical courts, impose military justice on most of those caught up in disputes with them, and generally take first place in a society obsessed with status: aside from taking precedence at all civic and religious functions, they possessed the right to wear uniforms and swords and were generally credited with having the pick of the *cortejo* system.* As Townsend wrote, 'The principal *cortejos* in the great cities are the canons of the cathedrals, but where the military reside they take their choice and leave the refuse for the Church.'[7] Given that the eighteenth century was a time of increasing prosperity in which the American trade had brought great wealth to many families, many civilian notables had come to regard them with jealousy and desire a share in their good fortune, and all the more so as many officers affected a most arrogant demeanour. Symbolic of this jealousy was the emergence of gentlemen's fashions of a type that aped officers' uniforms, 'without which', wrote Blanco White, 'a well-born Spaniard is almost ashamed to show himself'.[8] Also visible was a growing belief that a standing army was an economic burden, a danger to public morality – soldiers were regarded as drunken, diseased and brutal louts who corrupted all those with whom they came into contact – and an endless source of provocation to the *populacho*. And, with official hostility to all forms of provincial particularism growing, in Asturias, Navarre and the three Basque *señorios*,† the army's role in crushing Catalan self-government in the early eighteenth century could not be forgotten.

Much of the sting might have been taken out of the situation had civilian notables enjoyed a reasonable degree of access to the officer corps, and, in particular, its senior ranks. This, however, was not the case. Unless the would-be entrant was prepared to serve a long and difficult apprenticeship in the rank and file in the hope of one day making the rank of sergeant and thereby gaining access to the hypothetical possibility of promotion from the ranks, the only means of becoming an officer was to seek a position as a cadet. Prospective cadets had to demonstrate that they were of noble origin, but in itself this was no great problem, as most of those involved were *hijosdalgo* (approximately five per cent of the population could claim to be nobles at the end of the eighteenth century, including many of the families who made up the heart of what was to become the Spanish bourgeoisie). Rather, the issue was what happened after the ranks of the officer corps had been entered. Except in the artillery, where promotion was traditionally by

---

* Space, alas, does not allow for a discussion of this fascinating custom, which can best be described as a form of institutionalised adultery in which married women selected eligible males (churchmen included) to be their escorts-cum-companions-cum-lovers, and openly appeared with them in society.

† The Basque *señorios* were Vizcaya, Guipúzcoa and Alava. Together with Asturias and Navarre, in 1808 they still possessed medieval assemblies dominated by the local *pudientes*.

seniority, what counted was favour, and, in particular, favour at court. Whilst it would be wrong to imagine that all officers above a certain rank were members of the titled nobility, the result was none the less a situation of considerable disequality in which young men from favoured families could be generals by their mid-twenties whilst others soldiered on as perpetual subalterns. Meanwhile, promotion was slowed down still further by the facts, first, that there were too many officers; second, that many officers were awarded brevet ranks, or *grados*, that effectively gave them first call on such vacancies as became available; and, third, that officers were not just competing with colleagues in their own units, it being very common for officers on their way up to be transferred from one unit to another.

If all this was irritating to civilian notables eager to reinforce the position of their families by acquiring access to the military estate – an issue which the problems and opportunities engendered by the French Wars made still more pressing – it was even more so to the many officers who found themselves trapped in the lower ranks of the line regiments.* Forbidden to marry until they reached the rank of captain and left to vegetate in miserable provincial towns, they were forced to watch whilst their more fortunate fellows gravitated to comfortable postings in Madrid, or secured prolonged leaves of absence. To add insult to injury subaltern officers were both ill paid and hard hit by the soaring inflation that Spain had been experiencing even before 1792. 'Prices have reached such a level', it was complained, 'that for some time the officer has not been able to subsist on the pay which is accorded him'.[9]

The army, then, was deeply divided, but this was not the end to the problems that beset the body politic. Setting aside the somewhat similar difficulties that beset officialdom in general, the years prior to 1808 had witnessed the emergence of an aristocratic and ecclesiastical faction dedicated to reversing the reforms introduced over the years by the Bourbon monarchy. For this group Aranjuez had represented a great triumph and they were naturally concerned to perpetuate their influence whilst at the same time eradicating all those who could be regarded either as allies of reform or partisans of Godoy. At the opposite end of the spectrum there existed a very different current of opinion. A loose clique of noblemen, academics, churchmen, officials and entrepreneurs, these men looked not backwards but forwards, favouring an intensification of reform and, in

---

* The officer corps of the royal guard – a preserve of the titled nobility or those with connections at court – was far better off: not only was promotion faster, but in the Guardias de Corps troopers were rated as ensigns, captains as brigadiers, and colonels as field marshals.

particular, greater *desamortización*. As yet far from being consciously revolutionary, they were nevertheless both eager to play a part in affairs and ready to steer them in a direction that fitted with their views.

If a variety of interest groups existed that in one way or another resented or were seeking to challenge the political order, the picture is further complicated by the fact that the arbitrary character of the Spanish administration in general, and of the régime of Godoy in particular, ensured that the country was filled with individuals who had some real or imagined grievance against the authorities. Whether they were merchants who had gone bankrupt or been imprisoned for fraud, churchmen denied a benefice, or young men disappointed in their search for office, all of them had every reason to leap at any chance of revenge that offered itself.

It was precisely that chance that now emerged. To return to the authorities, the brief interim that divided the arrival of the French in Madrid from the departure of Fernando for Bayonne had, of course, been characterised by a concerted attempt to win over Napoleon. Every effort had been made to maintain order and reassure the populace, and it was only when it finally became apparent that things were going wrong that the Junta de Gobierno became more obstructive. By then, however, the fact that Fernando was firmly in the power of the French made it difficult for the Junta to do more than adopt delaying tactics and deliver ineffectual protests: indeed, the first message that the new king sent it from Bayonne specifically ordered it to do nothing that might endanger his safety. Utterly bewildered, the Junta requested clearer instructions and in the meantime decreed the formation of a committee of generals and bureaucrats that could take its place were it to be arrested, but its hesitant progress towards a breach with the French had not gone very far before Madrid erupted in revolt.

The Dos de Mayo therefore rendered the position of the authorities quite impossible. Having hitherto done their best to maintain order – at Aranjuez the raiders had even been faced down with the aid of Spanish troops – they appeared to have been a party not just to manoeuvres against the Bourbon monarchy, but also to what was being widely represented as premeditated massacre. With the Junta even now making strenuous efforts to ensure that the populace kept quiet, the way had been opened for a massive settling of accounts. To understand what followed, it is important to realise that Spain was not completely occupied. On the contrary, although some 90,000 French troops were currently in the country, these were for the most part concentrated along an axis that stretched from Toledo through Madrid, Aranda de Duero, Burgos, Victoria, Pamplona and San Sebastián to the French frontier at Irun. Thus, the area around Madrid and Toledo was held by the Second Corps of Observation of the Gironde and the Corps of Observation of the Ocean Coast under Dupont and Moncey; the capital itself by the detachment of the Imperial Guard attached to Murat; and Burgos, Alava, northern Navarre and Guipúzcoa by the Corps of Observation of the Western Pyrenees under Marshal Bessières. Otherwise, apart from Barcelona and Figueras, which was garrisoned by the newly promoted Corps of Observation of the Eastern Pyrenees under General Duhesme, Spain was entirely free of occupation, and, what is more, possessed of substantial armed forces. Some of the Spanish forces were still in Portugal, true, whilst others were stationed in areas controlled by the French or absent in Denmark under the command of La Romana, but, even so, at least 100,000 men were ready for action.

But numbers were not everything. The army of 1808 suffered from numerous defects. Recruited from a mixture of foreign deserters and mercenaries, volunteers, and criminals, vagrants and unemployed labourers who had been pressed as *levas*, all of whom served for eight years, the army was composed of two regiments of guard infantry, two regiments of guard cavalry, thirty-nine regiments of line infantry, six regiments of Swiss infantry, twelve regiments of light infantry, forty-three regiments of provincial militia, twelve regiments of heavy cavalry, eight regiments of dragoons, four regiments of light cavalry, four regiments of artillery and a single regiment of sappers and miners. To explain Spain's repeated defeats in the war that followed, much scorn has traditionally been heaped upon the officer corps. However, rather more important were certain defects in the army's organisation.

First and foremost there was the question of its cavalry. Always a major strike force in Napoleonic warfare, in Spain cavalry acquired still greater importance because of the rolling plains which covered so much of the country. In the years prior to 1808, however, a variety of problems – amongst others, the parsimony resulting from years of building up the navy at the expense of the army, and the shortage of decent horses discussed at greater length next – had led to the cavalry being allowed to constitute a rather smaller proportion of the army than was the case elsewhere, whilst the 26 regiments that it did have were not only, like the rest of the army, short of men, but possessed only about half the 18,000 horses that they needed. As if this was not bad enough, centuries of mule-breeding had both ruined the quality and reduced the numbers of the mounts available. No matter whether it was classified as light or heavy cavalry, as dragoons or chasseurs, or as line or élite, Spain's cavalry was unlikely to be able to make much of an impact on the battlefield.

Stronger than the cavalry though they were, the artillery and infantry also had their difficulties. Thus, although it was well trained and equipped with the French Gribeauval system of howitzers and field pieces – reckoned the best in the world – the artillery, too, was plagued by the question of animals. Except in the case of the horse artillery – which was little better off than the cavalry – the teams needed to move the guns were only recruited on mobilisation, whilst the lack of horses ensured that they tended to be composed of mules and oxen, both of which were slow and hard to manage. There being no corps of artillery drivers, the teams had also to be conducted by civilians who were all too prone to absconding with their beasts as soon as danger threatened. As for the infantry, it was organised on an obsolescent model that separated light from line and thereby ensured that there were rarely adequate numbers of troops trained to fight in skirmish order at the right place at the right time.* All this admitted, however, the army of 1808 was no worse than many other forces of the period, most of its difficulties revolving around the military and political situation that emerged when war finally broke out. How, though, did war come about? At this point we must return to the aftermath of the Dos de Mayo. Shocked and bewildered by what had happened, scores of refugees were soon fleeing the capital for the provinces, and it was therefore not long before the story of the rising had spread throughout the country. Still more dramatically, meanwhile, a chance meeting between two senior officials in the town of Móstoles twelve miles to the south of Madrid led to the issue of a general call to arms that was quickly transmitted throughout Extremadura and western Andalucía.

Within a matter of days, therefore, most of mainland Spain knew of the Dos de Mayo. Had what followed genuinely been the spontaneous movement beloved of the traditional account, the country should have sprung to arms straight away, but nothing of the sort occurred. There were a number of disturbances, true, the places affected including Ciudad Rodrigo, Córdoba and Oviedo, but the populace was still interested in little more than rooting out the supposed partisans of Godoy and providing against a surprise attack. At all events, attempts actually to raise a revolt against the French proved abortive: in Extremadura the acting Captain General, the Conde del Torre del Fresno, and the commander of the Spanish division withdrawn by Godoy from the Alentejo, the Marqués del Socorro, called the populace to arms only to be resolutely ignored; an attempt on the part of Asturias' medieval

---

* In line with distinctions that had emerged in the latter half of the eighteenth century, all footsoldiers were defined as either 'line' or 'light' infantrymen, of which the former in theory fought in traditional shoulder-to-shoulder 'close-order' formations, and the latter in spread-out 'open-order' ones. In Napoleon's forces, however, all infantry battalions possessed special companies trained to fight as skirmishers.

estates to do the same broke down in disorder; and plans on the part of the Captain General of the Campo del Gibralter, Francisco Javier Castaños, to declare war at the head of his 9,000 troops were abandoned after a much disillusioned Socorro, who had taken refuge in Cádiz rather than resume his duties as Captain General of Seville, warned him to keep quiet.

Socorro, Torre del Fresno and Castaños aside, the authorities remained supine. Shaken though they were by Bayonne and the Dos de Mayo, they were not prepared to champion a war against the French, reasoning that the only results would be, first, a bloodbath, and, second, an intolerable threat to the social order. Though some little time was required to act upon it – hence the delay that ensued before the pot finally boiled over – for the numerous 'out' groups that littered Spanish society and politics, this was a godsend. In brief, all over Spain a variety of forces came together to organise a rising, though few of the conspiratorial cells that emerged were operating in anything other than a vacuum. In every place, indeed, the plan was to 'pronounce' against the French and hope that the rest of the country would accept the leadership of the conspirators. Only in Valencia, Oviedo, Seville, Zaragoza and Tenerife, however, is it possible to reconstruct the genesis of the revolt.

Taking Valencia first of all, there emerged a conspiratorial group consisting of Vicente, Manuel and Mariano Bertrán de Lis, all of whom were leading members of a powerful merchant family with important interests in the grain trade, several subaltern officers, a doctor and a cleric. In Oviedo, meanwhile, the lead was taken by a group that included the president of the provincial estates, two canons of the cathedral, a number of middle-ranking officials, and several local notables who were to become leading liberals (the most important were Agustín Argüelles and the Conde de Toreno). In Seville the chief figures were a failed merchant named Nicolás Tap y Núñez who had just been released from prison and blamed Godoy for his incarceration, a grandee named the Conde de Tilly, and two officials of the cathedral chapter. In Zaragoza we have José Palafox, a prominent local noble with a commission in the king's personal bodyguard and strong links with the party of aristocratic reaction, several local nobles, the respected merchant, Lorenzo Calvo de Rozas, and the officers who commanded the Zaragoza element of the *resguardo* (a polyglot assembly of local security forces). And in Tenerife the leader was the Captain General's deputy, Carlos O'Donnell, an ambitous malcontent who had acquired a deep hatred for his superior, saw revolt as the best means of escaping accusations of *godoyismo*, and had no difficulty in winning over a number of officers of the garrison and local notables bent on high office.

Wherever we look, then, we see the same thing. Believing that an opportunity was at hand to advance their sectional aims, avenge their wrongs, or secure greater prominence, malcontents and dissidents of all sorts came together to plot insurrection. To achieve this goal they subverted the populace. In Seville, 10,000 reales was spent on suborning the garrison and securing the services of a gang of thugs who could act as cheerleaders for Tap and Tilly. In Valencia, there was a paid strike force of 500 peasants recruited from the notoriously turbulent *huerta* that surrounded the city. In Oviedo a similar force was recruited from volunteers paid four reales per day. In Zaragoza the conspirators made contact with Mariano Cerezo and Jorge Ibort, both of whom were *labradores* of considerable influence with the populace (why this should have been the case is not clear, but it is possible that they had links with banditry or smuggling). And in Tenerife the requisite intermediaries were discovered in a disgraced Augustinian friar and a well-known bandit, whilst here, too, money was freely disbursed to hire the requisite crowd.

From the beginning, then, the rising's objective was not just to resist the French but also to secure material changes in the body politic. With the authorities preaching submission and the populace in a state of ferment, all that was lacking was a suitable catalyst, and, thanks to Napoleon, this was not slow to put in an appearance. Although the emperor had succeeded in overthrowing the Bourbon dynasty, he had not yet announced his plans for the throne. In this respect matters had been slow to develop, but the final collapse of his attempts to marry Fernando to the daughter of his estranged brother, Lucien (whose opposition he made a serious attempt to overcome), and the *motín de Aranjuez* together convinced Napoleon that drastic action was essential, the result being that on 27 March he wrote to his younger brother, Louis, offering him the Crown. Knowing full well that this was designed to strip him of his Dutch power base, the independent-minded Louis' response was a stinging negative, however. Thus Napoleon turned instead to his youngest sibling, Jerome, but the latter had only recently been installed as King of the new German state of Westphalia and also refused to budge. Lucien being an impossibility, there remained only his oldest brother, Joseph, and on 10 May the latter was ordered to report for duty post-haste.

Ostensibly head of the Bonaparte clan and since 1806 King of Naples, Joseph was an easy-going figure who was both much in awe of his imperial brother and vain enough to relish the idea of being King of Spain, and on 23 May he therefore set off from his capital. Confident of securing his agreement, meanwhile, Napoleon could finally announce Spain's fate.

Implicit in the abdication of Carlos IV and Fernando VII was the recognition that he had the right to dispose of the throne as he wished. In consequence, Murat was ordered to get the Junta de Gobierno to ask the emperor to appoint Joseph to the throne, and nominate 150 prominent figures who could participate in a conference on Spain's future at Bayonne. And ten days later the emperor himself issued a grandiloquent proclamation promising to remedy the country's ills, establish a constitution, and give it a ruler as wise and benevolent as himself.

As yet the name of Joseph Bonaparte had not been publicly mentioned but by the end of May the whole of Spain was in revolt. In this respect what really mattered was the removal of Fernando VII. Held up as he had been as a paragon of virtue, tenderness and generosity who wished only to see his people happy and prosperous, for thousands upon thousands of the *populacho, el rey deseado* represented their only hope of salvation. In his person there were bound up visions of peace, justice and freedom that were as millennial as they were at odds with Fernando's real nature and the views of those promoting his cause. Notwithstanding the Dos de Mayo, until the very last moment popular reactions were contained by ignorance, uncertainty, bewilderment, and the hope that all might yet come right, but on 20 May the official gazette formally announced that Fernando had abdicated. This was the end: all hope of relief had been swept away and, what is more, swept away as a result of what appeared to be treason on the part of the *godoyistas* who still filled the army, navy and civil administration. With wild rumours circulating that the young men of Spain were to be conscripted *en masse* by the French, the conspiratorial cells that had sprung up in the wake of the Dos de Mayo were overnight provided with the genuine crowds which they needed to make their revolution.

Whilst the news of Fernando's abdication provoked risings all over Spain, the details of what happened varied dramatically from place to place. Amidst the welter of different stories there were three basic models. In the first, and probably the most common, the arrival of the gazette of 20 May, news of insurrection in other parts of Spain, or revolutionary emissaries from neighbouring cities, provoked massive popular demonstrations – the fruit of panic, collective hysteria and inchoate social protest – that in turn brought about the formation of new organs of political authority, the role of the conspirators in these instances being essentially reactive (where they were present at all: in a number of cases no evidence of conspiracy has been found). In the second, a rather smaller group, conspiratorial cells took the initiative themselves, precipitating a crisis, and imposing their own political solutions. And, in the third, the legitimate authorities themselves raised the flag of revolt and co-opted other elements of the old order to help them lead it. Within these three basic patterns there is still much room for differentiation, however. One obvious question is the extent to which the authorities of Bourbon Spain succeeded in taking control of the revolution. More immediately pertinent, though, is the extent to which the *populacho* were able to satisfy the veritable lust for blood typified by events at the town of Almaraz where the *alcalde mayor* was told by the crowd, 'We want to kill someone, Sir. They have killed one person in Trujillo, one or two more in Badajoz, and someone else in Mérida, and we do not want to be left behind. Sir, we want to kill a traitor.'[10]

Examples of the first pattern that can be picked out from what may be described as the first wave of risings – those that took place without any knowledge of revolt elsewhere – include Cartagena and Valencia (23 May), Zaragoza and Murcia (24 May) and León (27 May). Thus, in Cartagena red cockades – the traditional badge of the Bourbon monarchy – were handed out to the people, and the garrison brought out in support of the rising, whereupon the Captain General (in this instance a naval officer, Cartagena being the capital of one of Spain's three naval departments) and the military governor were arrested, and a provincial junta established under a prominent admiral. In Zaragoza, meanwhile, where José Palafox had been hiding out at a property belonging to his family outside the city, the conspirators' agents were easily able to steer the crowds into calling for him to lead them, whereupon a delegation was sent to bring him back to the city, the Captain General imprisoned, and the young guards officer installed as *de facto* dictator. That the whole affair was got up from the start is confirmed by the tone of Palafox's memoirs. Written in the third person, these describe how he was meditating on what best to do, when he suddenly heard 'a multitude of armed civilians' coming towards his hiding-place. For a moment he believed all was lost, but 'what was his surprise when, surrounding the house, the crowd found out that Palafox was there, and began to fire their fowling pieces in the air at the joy of the discovery'. Very soon, all was well:

Bathed in tears at the terrible fate of their king, the men declared their firm resolution to avenge that atrocious perfidy and . . . sacrifice everything they had rather than recognise the usurper. Unable to speak for the emotion, joy and love that he felt, Palafox could not withstand these honourable patriots' demands for him to place himself at their head and lead them in their noble attempt to . . . free the fatherland.[11]

In Valencia, by contrast, the conspirators faced somewhat greater difficulties. As one of their leaders wrote:

Without any clear idea of what to do, the people roamed in great masses through every district of the city, crying, 'Death to the traitors! Death to Napoleon! Long live Fernando VII, our religion and our fatherland!' They moved like the waves of the sea, without object or concert; everything was confusion and disorder; they had no leader to guide them; every person had a different rumour to relate, and nobody could come to an agreement as to what to do, although everybody was filled with the same sentiments and working for the same goal.[12]

Apparently taken by surprise, they were only able to take control of the crowds with some difficulty, and even then only at the cost of admitting to their ranks a number of brazen adventurers. Alarmed at the threatening demeanour of the *populacho*, they also had little option but to accept the assimilation of the old order with the new, the provincial junta that was eventually formed consisting not just of the conspirators, but also of the Captain General, the Intendent, a number of senior officials of the military and financial administration, and the entire city council. Finally, in Murcia and León, where there were no conspiracies, crowds filled the main squares baying for the blood of traitors, denouncing *desamortización* – a particular theme in León – and demanding the proclamation of Fernando VII. The demonstrators were no less radical than their counterparts elsewhere, but with no one to direct them, the crowds were aimless and confused, with the result that all the authorities had to do to regain control was to proclaim their loyalty to Fernando VII and form provincial juntas that were in reality nothing more than an agglomeration of the existing organs of political and social power. As to the spirit which motivated them, it was hardly the stuff of legend. Thus:

The same spirit of insurrection and fury has been observed amongst the inhabitants of this town [of Monforte de Lemos] as that which has already had such sad effects in other cities. More than once movements have begun against . . . men who have been the target of false, vague or imaginary accusations, whose intention has been the justification of disorderly excesses . . . Moved by these considerations . . . the members of the *ayuntamiento* met with other sensible citizens . . . to think about the best means of preventing the terrible ills to which all this could give rise. Convinced that in the current circumstances . . . the ordinary means of justice cannot either quieten the general fermentation or contain disorder, they decided to . . . form a junta composed of . . . the persons of greatest confidence in the town, and to invest it with all the . . . powers that it could possibly be given.[13]

This pattern of spontaneous disturbances being seized upon with a greater or lesser degree of success by disaffected elements, or bamboozled and contained by the old order, was by far the most prevalent and was repeated in Granada, Santander, Valladolid, Ciudad Rodrigo, Cádiz, La Coruña and Badajoz. Only rarely, by contrast, did the crowd have to be prodded into action by the agents of conspiracy. Thus, the only definite examples are Oviedo (25 May) and Seville (26 May), both of which rose in revolt in the course of the first wave of uprisings. Of events in the former city we have a particularly clear account from Ramón Alvarez Valdés, who witnessed them as a university student. Thus:

In the evening of [20 May] there met Ponte, Busto, Ballesteros, Merconchini, Lastra, Toral, Argüelles, Cifuentes, Argüelles Cabezada, and the Vizconde de Matarrosa, who had just arrived from the capital. Burning with patriotism and indignation . . . they all agreed that they should . . . enter the lists with no greater delay than the time necessary to recruit the greatest number of inhabitants that could be mustered . . . the plan being that these should be paid four reales per day . . . Pooling what money they had . . . they divided it into equal parts, and gave it to Ponte, Argüelles, Cifuentes and Merconchini, who then went off in different directions . . . Meanwhile, Busto* . . . had already arranged matters at the arms factory, where he had made contact with the manager, Silva, two foremen and a number of armourers. The plan was to take over the factory, arm the recruits and divide them into three columns, which would then head by different routes for the Plaza Mayor.[14]

Three days went by without an increasingly nervous Busto having any idea as to how his confederates were getting on. Much to his relief, however, in the late afternoon of 24 May, Ponte appeared with the news that he alone had 2,000 peasants waiting in readiness outside the city, and that his three fellows were not far away. After that events moved swiftly:

Busto and Ponte having agreed as to what should be done, the latter left to unite his forces with the other columns of peasants . . . and then led them very silently through the outskirts of the city in the direction of the arms factory. Silva having been forewarned by Busto . . . they got in without difficulty and had very soon been armed. They were then immediately divided into three groups, of which the first was headed by Don Gregorio Piquero, the second by Merconchini and the third by Don Ramón de Llano Ponte. The first . . . was to seize the Casa-Regencia,† whilst the others invaded the Plaza Mayor from different directions and massed in front of the building in support. At eleven o'clock Piquero . . . placed himself at the head of his

---

* The leader of the conspiracy, José García del Busto, who currently occupied the post of Procurador General in the Asturian estates. The arms factory referred to was one of Spain's eight musket works.
† The residence of the Comandante General, one Juan Crisostomo de la Llave.

column, and placing some of the most enthusiastic at their head . . . took La Llave's guards . . . by surprise.[15]

There was no resistance. A terrified La Llave surrendered, and on the stroke of midnight the cathedral bells rang out to proclaim the rebellion. Rushing into the streets, the inhabitants, who had hitherto taken no part in events, then joined the throng, but nothing can disguise the fact that what had occurred had been nothing more nor less than a *coup d'état*.

As for the provincial juntas that resulted from such events, it is hardly a surprise to find that they contained many malcontents and dissidents (examples include the Conde de Tilly in Seville and the liberals, Toreno and Flórez Estrada, in Oviedo). Not so, of course, the juntas that resulted from the third model, of which examples include those of Ronda, Segovia, Córdoba, Jaén, Lérida, Santa Cruz de Tenerife, Palma de Mallorca and Castaños' headquarters at San Roque, for here, unchallenged by either riot or subversion, the *antiguo régimen* remained wholly intact. Writing of events in his own garrison, for example, the then lieutenant-colonel, Pedro Agustín Girón, could not be clearer as to their nature:

The excitement that was sweeping . . . Andalucía having begun to be felt in Ronda, on 1 June the town council received a dispatch from the supreme junta that had been created in Seville. In an instant a junta had been created from the *regidores*, the other authorities of the town, and a number of prominent citizens.[16]

As a result of this rather confused and amorphous wave of revolt, by the beginning of June 1808 large parts of Spain were in a state of open rebellion. Rebellion, however, did not mean revolution. Most towns of any size now had emergency administrations – two exceptions were Cádiz, where the town council still held sway, and Zaragoza, which was in the sole charge of José Palafox – but the resultant juntas hardly constituted the bourgeois revolution of Marxist legend. In Murcia, for instance, the junta consisted of the bishop, an archdeacon, two priors, seven members of the old *ayuntamiento*, two of the city's magistrates, five prominent members of the local aristocracy, including Carlos III's chief minister, the Conde de Floridablanca, and five serving or retired army or navy officers, all of them of high rank. In Ciudad Rodrigo, meanwhile, we see nine serving officers, including the pre-war deputy governor and the commanders of all the units that had made up the garrison; five retired officers, of whom two were brigadiers and one an erstwhile *regidor perpetuo*; a local nobleman possessed of a position at court; the Intendent; two officials of the old *consejos*; and the bishop and seventeen other members of the local clergy. Some of the juntas, true, included men in the vanguard of Spanish liberalism, but in very few cases were such figures in the ascendant. As for those instances where outsiders had succeeded in entering the corridors of power, they were in many cases interested in little other than the fruits of office, and very often enjoyed their triumph for no more than a matter of days (both Tap and Rico, for example, shortly found themselves under arrest on trumped-up charges). With the populace altogether absent – the occasional 'tribunes of the people' that one finds were clearly trusties of the local notables – the most that can be said was that there had been a shift in the balance of power, with the army, in particular, having lost much of its ascendancy.

This is not, of course, to say that the situation in Patriot Spain was one of total harmony. In many juntas men who were identifiably liberal in their beliefs sat side-by-side with representatives of both Bourbon reformism and the political and social opposition which this had provoked, whilst the rising had not put an end to longstanding personal jealousies and family rivalries. If conflict was likely within the ranks of most of the juntas, beyond them the situation was even worse. Such cities as Zaragoza, Seville and Valencia did not necessarily command the loyalty of all the towns in their sphere of influence (to take one example, the little Aragonese town of Molina was in theory an independent *señorio* and therefore rejected the rule of Zaragoza; oddly enough, it does not appear to have joined the rising at all until 18 June). In such cases, it was at least logical that the major cities should prevail, but what was to be done in Galicia, which was divided into seven separate provinces and possessed at least two possibilities for a capital, or for that matter in New Castile and Catalonia where Madrid and Barcelona were in the hands of the French? Also likely to cause problems was the position of the army, as in Old Castile where a combination of habit, fear of the mob and Cuesta's sheer force of character had persuaded the local juntas to accept his rule. And, last but not least, there also remained the question of the formation of a new central government, much though the Junta of Seville might have liked to consider the question closed in the wake of its assumption of the title of 'Supreme Junta of Spain and the Indies'.

If the new patterns of authority were extremely muddled, certain things are very clear. First and foremost, whether the élites had captained revolt or merely sought to appropriate its leadership, and whether, too, they wished to continue, intensify or reverse the process of political, social and economic reform that had gripped Spain since 1759, they were at one in recognising that the populace were in a dangerous mood. In many parts of the country, indeed, the revolt had been accompanied by considerable violence, whilst there had been hundreds of murders. The majority of these, true, had been of French civilians – most of them merchants and their families – who had found themselves trapped in rebel territory.* Yet many of the dead rather were Spaniards and, what is more, representatives of property, power and authority. Tarred by the brush of treason, the Bourbon authorities were easy targets for *fernandino* agitators, mutinous soldiers, or simply angry crowds out to exact revenge on the *antiguo régimen*. Amongst the dead were several generals (Torre del Fresno in Badajoz, Socorro in Cádiz, Filanghieri in Galicia, Borja in Cartagena, Cevallos in Valladolid); the governors of Tortosa, Castellón de la Plana, Ciudad Rodrigo and Villafranca de Panadés; the postmaster of Ciudad Rodrigo; the *corregidores* of Vélez Málaga, Jaén and Madrigal; the *procurador mayor* of Seville; the town clerk of Tortosa; and a range of private individuals, from Godoy's brother-in-law, Pedro Trujillo, through men who had been in one way or another connected with his policies, to prominent local notables such one Bernabé Portillo, a landowner who had been experimenting with the introduction of cotton-growing in the Málaga area. Also murdered in one or two cases were the wives and even children of the men concerned. Even joining the rebellion was no protection: Filanghieri and Cevallos both died after they had done so, whilst in Santa Cruz de Tenerife, despite the fact that the Captain General – the Marqués de Casa Cagigal – had declared for Fernando VII, O'Donnell overthrew him anyway.

Typical of the scenes that accompanied the killings were those witnessed in Ciudad Rodrigo:

It was three o'clock in the afternoon when an extraordinary commotion was suddenly noted in the streets. Large numbers of people having soon gathered together, this soon became an outright tumult. Throwing aside the bounds of subordination and decorum, the crowds began to shout, 'Death to the governor and the other traitors!' Prepared for this eventuality, the junta asked the bishop . . . to send emissaries to persuade the rioters to desist from their atrocious project . . . but the confusion, the shouting and the sheer density of the crowd prevented their . . . counsel from being heard . . . All was in vain, and . . . by a little past four the governor, one of his adjutants, a French merchant and the postmaster were no more.[17]

Still more graphic is the account of Robert Brindle, trapped in his seminary at Valladolid:

---

* In by far the worst single atrocity of its type, 330 men, women and children were massacred in Valencia by a gang of assassins headed by a friar named Baltasar Calvo who had been refused a place on the provincial junta and seems to have hoped to terrify the new authorities into changing their mind.

The multitude . . . paraded the streets . . . with fowling pieces, pruning hooks and such other weapons as they could procure. The Captain General of the province during this time was General Cuesta. Though a true patriot and a skilful officer, yet it was impossible for him to restrain the populace from the most grievous outrages. Don Francisco Cevallos, governor of Segovia, having been obliged to evacuate that fortress, sought refuge in Valladolid. It since appears that the place was in the worst possible state of defence . . . But no sooner had he entered Valladolid than the cry of traitor was raised and in a moment the poor man was literally torn to pieces. The Captain General was a spectator of this horrid spectacle, but so far from being able to restrain the violence of the mob [that] the cry was even raised against himself, and a gallows erected for his execution.[18]

But the trouble was not just confined to the murder of supposed traitors. On the contrary, the *populacho* also engaged in overt social protest, matters being further inflamed by the continuation of the same old faces in the new organs of local government. Tenant farmers protested against high rents; agricultural labourers tried to occupy the land or demanded higher wages; and there was a widespread refusal to pay the tithe. Examples of such unrest are widespread, but perhaps the most dramatic comes from Castellón de la Plana. Thus:

On 19 June [1808] . . . a gang of malcontents assembled . . . in the town, and ran through the streets, disturbing the public peace and shouting 'Long live the King, the Fatherland and the Faith! Death to the traitors!' Having murdered the governor, Coronel Don Pedro Lobo, and a landowner named Felix de Jiménez, they followed these execrable excesses with an attempt on the life of the commissary, Don José Ramón de Santi . . . In addition, the insurgents broke into the Capuchin nunnery, and freed all the prisoners in the public gaols by force.[19]

Very often the catalyst for such riots related to the war. In Pontevedra, for example, the story was that the populace was about to be sold to the French and sent off in handcuffs, in Santiago that enemy troops were disembarking on the coast, in Ribadeo that a French spy was in the town, and in Ronda that preparations were afoot for a French-style terror. In the words of Girón:

My wife stayed in Ronda for the first part of the campaign, and did not escape a fright at the hands of popular injustice . . . One day my house was assaulted by a crowd of vagabonds, who, in spite of her pleas, turned out everything on the pretext that I had . . . a guillotine hidden there, the fruit of this patriotic visit being the theft of all my knives, swords and fowling pieces.[20]

Such vigilantism is not to be taken at face value, however. Even if some of the rioters acted in good faith, the general impression is one of agrarian revolt. As the Conde de Noroña lamented of Galicia, 'Beneath the surface there burns a spirit of insurrection.'[21]

From the very beginning, then, the new authorities were faced by a major problem of public order. Impelled though they were by military necessity, their efforts to raise new armies were also intended to contain the mob. At all events, mobilisation began immediately. All round Spain proclamations were issued calling for volunteers and ordering the conscription of large numbers of men between the ages of sixteen and forty, whilst these were coupled with a comprehensive attempt to unite the populace behind the struggle. Multifarious in its forms – there were newspapers, poems, odes, ballads, cartoons, pamphlets, plays, posters, proclamations, patriotic addresses, lives of Napoleon, denunciations of Godoy and even spoof French gazettes – and fuelled by the new authorities, powerful elements of the Church, and hundreds of private individuals driven by idealism or ambition, the main aspects of this propaganda offensive were simple enough. For most of the reign of Carlos IV, it was argued, Spain had been dominated by a venal and incompetent favourite – 'a man full of ambition, greed and ineptitude, openly given over to every vice in the most bare-faced manner' whose rule was characterised by 'a badly directed war against France, an onerous peace settlement, the . . . discredit of the treasury, and a series of shameful misfortunes'.[22] Having brought her to the brink of ruin and conspired to seize the throne, Godoy had finally betrayed the country to France in a vain attempt to save his skin and prevent the accession to the throne of the best of all possible kings. Meanwhile, in France there had arisen the person of Napoleon Bonaparte, a cruel and cynical adventurer who had usurped the throne, plunged his country into endless wars of conquest, employed deceit and treachery as an integral part of policy, enslaved half of Europe, and sought to establish himself as a veritable God upon the earth. 'In the history of great political revolutions', wrote Melchor Andario, 'there is no equal of Bonaparte: he is the greatest monster ever to have been vomited forth by the anger of heaven to inundate the world with crimes and calamities. In any review of his actions, one stumbles at one moment on the customs of Caligula, at another on the cruelties of Nero.'[23] Still more explicit was the language of the *Juicio Imparcial, Cristiano y Político sobre el Pérfido Cáracter del Emperador de los Franceses*:

He is, like Attila, the scourge of God . . . the most terrible gift that . . . an angry deity could visit upon the earth . . . He is a monster who wishes to stretch out his sharp claws from east to west and from north to south and rob everything, destroy everything, annihilate everything.[24]

Determined to eradicate the liberties of a people whose independent spirit offended his megalomania as much as its wealth stimulated his greed, the emperor had seized upon the opening offered him by Godoy's stupidity, and was now seeking to enslave the Spaniards as well – it was repeatedly claimed that one of Napoleon's principal objects was to conscript Spain's manpower for service in his unhappy legions – whilst at the same time furnishing one more throne for his insatiable family. Spain, then, was faced by the greatest threat she had ever experienced to her liberty, her religion – much was made of the fact that Napoleon had (supposedly!) freed the Jews, legalised divorce and publicly flirted with Islam during his stay in Egypt – and her prosperity, whilst she had also been cruelly cheated of the new golden age that would supposedly have been brought by Fernando VII.

If Spain's predicament was great, however, she need fear nothing. Thus, having detailed at length the iniquities of Napoleon and Godoy, not to mention the qualities of *el rey deseado*, the propagandists went on to ridicule the idea that Napoleon was a military genius and pour scorn upon his armies. Miserable slaves, the latter could not stand before a nation united in enthusiasm for a just and holy cause. And that the nation was united, of course, there was no doubt: everywhere volunteers were coming forward in their thousands and the new authorities were swamped with donations of every sort. Spain had powerful armed forces and excellent fortresses, whilst she could also call upon the support of Great Britain – it was not long, as we shall see, before the insurgents had elicited the assistance of London – and an empire that was the source of boundless supplies of bullion. Spanish heroism might also inspire the rest of Europe to throw off its chains in its turn. Indeed, it might even be hoped that the French would be so horrified by Napoleon's madness in invading Spain that they would get rid of the tyrant themselves.

As we shall discover, in the long run these exhortations fell on deaf ears. Yet for various reasons there was initially a rush of volunteers. So grim was Spain's economic situation that the offer of pay was quite enough to obtain considerable numbers of recruits. All the more was this the case as the uprising had fallen plumb in the middle of one of the slackest periods of the agricultural year – the long gap between planting and harvest. Landed proprietors, merchants and master craftsmen could not only cut a patriotic figure by conjuring up large numbers of recruits, but also had many means of forcing the groups who were economically dependent upon them to take up arms. And finally there was little concept of what was to come: fear of the French, for example, was easy to indulge when all that seemed to be required of a soldier was a few days' guard duty on the walls of his home town (few volunteers, let it be said, joined the regular army, most of the men who were forthcoming enlisting in new units that were not only much better paid, but seen primarily as local militias).

The mobilisation of the populace, meanwhile, implied the formation of a new army. In large parts of Spain – Extremadura, Aragón and Old Castile – first-line troops were few and far between, the insurgents being backed by little more than the *resguardo*, various garrison units,* and a number of officers and men who had fled districts occupied by the French. Elsewhere things were better – Andalucía, Valencia and Galicia all had substantial garrisons, for example, but even so the desire for patronage still ensured the creation of many new regiments. Full of raw recruits, however, such units had also for the most part to be officered by men who had no military experience whatsoever, and the results were singularly unimpressive. For a good example of the spectacle provided by such troops we can do no better than turn to Girón's description of the forces raised in Córdoba:

Half a league from the city we saw a great crowd of horsemen coming towards us along the road, and after a short while we saw that it was General Echávarri followed by a numerous mass of poorly mounted and worse armed men that he called his cavalry. There were more than 1200 of them, most of them on horses, and the rest on mules. They had saddles of every style – and some of them none at all – and arms of various centuries ranging from the dagger to the rapier. Such was the confusion in which they rode that, as they went by, they left a saddled horse abandoned in the road.[25]

If the new army was defective in its organisation, there were also problems with its composition. Whereas infantrymen could be improvised relatively quickly, this was simply not possible with either cavalrymen or gunners. Not only was much more time needed for their training, but cavalry and artillery required resources that many of the new authorities simply did not have. If cannon were sometimes available, hiring draught animals was very expensive, whilst there was a desperate shortage of horses. A few new squadrons of horsemen did appear – the most famous were the handful of *garrochistas* who fought at Bailén as the Lancers of Jérez and Utrera – but the vast majority of the new troops had perforce to be infantry. In most

---

* In addition to her front-line troops, Spain possessed numerous companies of urban militia, invalids and garrison artillery.

cases it proved possible to hand out muskets and bayonets, but uniforms were in short supply whilst it was impossible to provide more than a tiny proportion of the tents, blankets and other equipment required for service in the field.

Poorly organised and ill-equipped, the new levies were extremely undisciplined and much given to riot and mutiny: indeed, even attempts to school them in the rudiments of drill were frequently met with violent resistance. Nor were they prepared to serve outside their home districts, if indeed they were prepared to serve at all (and many were not: within days many juntas were being forced to address the question of desertion). Mercifully enough, however, 40,000 regular troops were available in Andalucía, 9,000 in the Levante, and 20,000 in Galicia, whilst the Canaries, the Balearic Islands and the African enclave of Ceuta all possessed substantial garrisons that could be transported to the Peninsula at need. Smaller forces were available in some other areas, too, whilst many soldiers were arriving from the areas held by the enemy: in Barcelona, especially, the French let such Spanish soldiers who wished to do so melt away in the direction of the Patriot zone, whilst there were several cases of entire regiments simply abandoning their posts and marching for the nearest Spanish army. Also involved were the Spanish forces in Portugal. Originally 25,000 strong, the division sent to the Alentejo had already been withdrawn by Godoy, which left 9,000 men in and around Lisbon under Caraffa and another 6,000 in Oporto under Belesta. Apart from a daring few who made a break for it and eventually reached Badajoz, Caraffa's men were disarmed and imprisoned, but there was nobody to stop Belesta from doing exactly as he liked, and, no sooner had the news of the rising arrived, than he marched to join the Galician forces at Lugo.

From levies and regulars alike, meanwhile, a rudimentary military structure was beginning to emerge in the form of field armies based on Asturias, Galicia, Old Castile, Extremadura, Andalucía, the Levante, and, albeit somewhat belatedly, Catalonia. Political arrangements were also gradually acquiring a more rational form: in Galicia, for example, the independent juntas that had been formed in each of the main towns quickly established a regional government in La Coruña whilst the Juntas of León and Asturias were invited to send deputies to a supra-regional *cortes del norte*. At the same time, in many cities consideration was given to the establishment of a national government. Above all, however, the juntas of, first, Asturias and then La Coruña had made contact with London, their emissaries being received with acclamation and, as we shall see, promised a variety of aid.

All this, of course, was just as well for trouble was brewing. Lulled not only by the soothing messages which he continued to receive from Marshal Murat, but also his contempt for the Spaniards, the emperor did not regard the rising with any particular alarm. 'All these little events,' he told Talleyrand on 9 June, 'are being calmed by the direction that is being taken by the principal inhabitants ... of the kingdom, whilst ... the king's arrival will everywhere dissipate trouble, put an end to doubt and re-establish tranquillity'.[26] That said, however, he had lost none of his vigour. As he wrote to Marshal Bessières:

Once you have made yourself master of Santander by brute force, you should impose a contribution of 2,000,000 [francs], sequester the property of the bishop, disarm the town and the countryside, and make some severe examples. And with Santander and Zaragoza taken, you should march on León and Asturias ... Retrograde movements ... must never be adopted in people's wars.[27]

Napoleon's ardour was strengthened by the belief that the new régimes that he was implanting from one side of Europe to the other were implanted all the better for a judicious 'whiff of grapeshot'. As early as 16 April, indeed, he had noted in a memorandum on northern Spain, 'Marshal Bessières ... should fall on any ... village that rises in revolt or mistreats any soldier or courier ... In a campaign one terrible example ... is sufficient.'[28] But in Spain in particular added zest was lent to the enterprise by the emperor's conviction, whether real or affected, that revolt was the work of the Church; there is, for example, a certain glee in the words that he addressed to a delegation of clerics shortly after he came to Spain in November 1808. Thus: '*Messieurs les moines*, if you choose to meddle in our military affairs, I promise you that I shall cut off your ears.'[29]

Within a matter of days of the outbreak of revolt, then, in Old Castile, New Castile, Aragón and Catalonia alike, French columns were striking out for the nearest insurgent forces. In the event it was the Spaniards who fired the first shots, however. On 5 June two squadrons of French dragoons under a Captain Bouzat were attacked by insurgents at the northern entrance to the pass of Despeñaperros in the Sierra Morena and forced to retreat to the nearby town of Almuradiel, leaving behind a number of dead. Spain was at war.

3

Bailén

THE SUMMER CAMPAIGN OF 1808

Apart from the groans of the wounded, the battlefield had all but fallen silent in the sun of the midsummer afternoon. Along the high road that stretched towards the Spanish positions lay scattered the bodies of the last French reserves – a battalion of sailors* who had made a final heroic effort to break through – whilst what was left of the rest of the army huddled in the scanty shade provided by the olive groves and ilex trees that covered the slopes of the ridge they had breasted early that morning. Utterly exhausted and tortured by heat and thirst, the troops could fight no more. Wounded in the hip while leading forward the last charge, the French commander suddenly heard the crackle of musketry from the direction of the bridge over which his troops had marched on the way to the battlefield, and knew that the game was up. Calling a trusted aide-de-camp, he therefore dispatched him in the direction of the Spanish lines with instructions to negotiate a truce.

Four days later nearly 18,000 prisoners were marching into captivity in what became known as the capitulation of Bailén. Spain was overjoyed, Britain exultant, France dismayed, and Napoleon outraged. It was the greatest defeat the Napoleonic empire had ever suffered, and, what is more, one inflicted by an opponent for whom the emperor had affected nothing but scorn. What, then, had gone wrong?

To answer this question, we must first examine the role played by the emperor himself. At the heart of the problem was his persistent refusal to accept the possibility that he might face serious opposition in Spain. Popular risings were expected, certainly – indeed, they were almost to be welcomed – but it had throughout remained Napoleon's conviction that the Spanish army would either remain neutral or actively put itself at his orders. To this

---

* Frequently described as marines, this unit – the Marins de la Garde – was in fact composed of boatmen, having been raised to ferry Napoleon and his staff across the Channel in the invasion of Britain that was planned in the period 1803–1805.

end, Murat had been instructed to do everything that he could to win over its allegiance: 'Take command of the Spanish troops: take some good sergeants and make them sub-lieutenants; have them fraternise with the French forces . . . I suppose that the French ordinances and rates of pay are more generous than their Spanish counterparts: announce that from 1 June the Spanish soldiers will be treated in the same manner as the French ones.'[1] And as late as 3 June he was writing to Marshal Bessières as if the Spanish were his to command at will: 'A battalion of either the Spanish or the Walloon Guards ought to be coming under your command; if it does, you can tell Captain General Cuesta that he may take it under his orders, and send it wherever its presence is necessary for the peace of the countryside.'[2]

As a result of these delusions, the first Army of Spain was remarkably weak in numerical terms – at only 90,000 men, indeed, it was heavily outnumbered by the 114,000 regular troops available to the insurgents, let alone anything else that they might raise – whilst it was also largely composed of second-line forces of a distinctly unimpressive character. Thus, presented with a mass of fresh conscripts by the combination of Tilsit and his decision to call up the conscript 'classes' of 1808 and 1809 in advance, Napoleon had decided to use them to form either internal security units intended to hunt down deserters – the so-called 'legions of reserve' – or 'provisional' regiments of infantry and cavalry that of necessity lacked not only *esprit de corps* but also the hard kernel of veterans that had allowed the French armies in Germany and Poland to assimilate large numbers of conscripts without difficulty. To hand as they were – the *grande armée* was still cantoned in Prussia – it was mostly these troops that were sent to Spain, though many of them were hardly better trained than the levies they were to end up fighting. Indeed, many even of the regular units contained large numbers of raw recruits, the French infantry being in the process of a major reorganisation which saw the number of field battalions in each regiment rise from two to four. Augmenting these forces, meanwhile, were a number of foreign units. Of these, some were drawn from the regular armies of the satellite states and were therefore relatively reliable, but over half the men concerned were mercenaries, prisoners of war who had taken up arms under Napoleon rather than face a long spell of imprisonment, deserters on the run from their original employers, or impressed members of the defunct armed forces of such states as Portugal. Such men being notoriously unreliable, their presence hardly suggests that war was regarded as a serious possibility. Much the same is true, if not more so, indeed, with regard to the two battalions of Paris' municipal guard that also appeared in the French array, the most likely explanation for whose presence is that Napoleon wanted his capital to bathe in the reflected glory of what he assumed would be a mere promenade.

A particularly grim picture of the Army of Spain emerges from the writings of General Foy:

The troops ... had neither the consistency nor the vigour which are requisite for high enterprises; the *matériel* from which they were formed was the refuse of the great armies which remained undiminished in the presence of Europe. The officers were of two kinds, the one torn from the depots where they were waiting to be disbanded or put on half pay ... the others very young, just from school, whose inexperience stood in need of being guided by good examples. There were few non-commissioned officers, and few subjects from which they could be made. The cavalry consisted of nothing but young soldiers and young horses. The infantry was not composed of homogeneous elements; one battalion had only four or six companies, while another ... had eight or ten. After the legions of reserve and ... supplementary regiments had been created, then came 'marching regiments', in which were crowded together the forgotten ... detachments, the returned deserters and the men from the hospitals. No corporate spirit ... vivified these aggregations, formed today to be dissolved tomorrow ... Unacquainted with each other, unknown to their officers, whose names, even, they knew not, taken little care of, badly subsisted and irregularly paid, [the soldiers'] existence was fluctuating and precarious, like that of the ephemeral corps of which they formed a part.[3]

As for the training of most of the men, this was of precisely the standard that might have been expected:

On the fifteenth of March, we held exercises on a plain outside the town [of Valladolid], and General Malher was killed by a ramrod that a soldier had foolishly left in the barrel of his musket. An immediate inspection was carried out to discover the ... culprit: eighteen ramrods were missing from the section of the line the shot had been fired from.[4]

Just as suggestive are the generals that had been sent to Spain. Thus, of the four corps commanders, Dupont, Duhesme and Bessières had no experience of commanding anything larger than a division, whilst Moncey had a reputation for caution. Only the second two were marshals, and both of these owed their promotion to politics rather than martial prowess (the former was a crony of Napoleon's and the latter a Republican, who only appears to have received his marshal's baton in consequence of the need to conciliate the supporters of the disgraced General Moreau). All the real stars of the French high command were absent, whilst Murat had, or so he said, fallen sick, and was going home, thereby leaving the French with no other commander-in-chief than the distant figure of Napoleon himself (there was, true, Murat's deputy, Savary, but he was allowed little independence, and was in any case more a courtier than a front-line soldier).

If all this was unencouraging, the French did at least enjoy a strong position. Whilst the Spaniards were dispersed àround the country in half-a-dozen separate masses, the French were grouped around Madrid, Burgos and Barcelona. Realising his advantage, Napoleon therefore decided to attack the insurgents before they had got their forces ready for action. Thus, on the march to secure Seville and Cádiz since as early as 23 May, Dupont was directed to conquer Andalucía with the first of his three infantry divisions, his single cavalry division, the ill-fated *marins* and a new brigade composed of two regiments of Swiss infantry that had been caught in Madrid. Back in the capital, Moncey was ordered to march on Valencia with one infantry division and one cavalry brigade. Further north, meanwhile, Bessières was to strike at both Zaragoza and Santander simultaneously from his base at Burgos, whilst in Catalonia the isolated Duhesme, who had only 13,000 men, was expected not only to hold down Barcelona and keep open his communications with France, but to send forces to subject Lérida and Tarragona and then go on to join in the attack on Zaragoza and Valencia.*

That such a plan was wildly over-confident is with hindsight obvious, but at first all seemed to go well enough. Given the disposition of the Spanish forces, the first insurgents that were encountered were necessarily for the most part improvised levies rather than regular troops and these proved no match even for the distinctly unimpressive Army of Spain. Thus, on 6 June troops of Bessières' corps stormed insurgent Logroño and Torquemada, whose only defenders were a few armed civilians, whilst on 7 June it was the turn of Segovia, strengthened though the inhabitants were by the cannons and cadets of the artillery academy situated in the castle. Also on 7 June Dupont defeated a small force of regulars supported by a mass of levies outside Córdoba, which was then sacked without mercy, whilst on 8 June troops bound for Zaragoza took the town of Tudela in the face of an attempt to defend it on the part of the inhabitants and a number of levies sent up from Zaragoza under the command of Palafox's brother, the Marqués de

---

* A word on French organisation may be useful here. The smallest units were the infantry battalion and cavalry squadron, of which the first had around 600 men and the second around 100. Four battalions or four squadrons made up a regiment; two or three regiments a brigade; two or three brigades, together with a battery of foot or horse artillery, a division; and three or four divisions, together with some extra artillery, a corps. Each corps of the first 'Army of Spain' had a cavalry division, but in the autumn of 1808 this was reduced to a single brigade, and the bulk of the cavalry massed in a reserve of six divisions.

Lazan. On 12 June Cuesta was defeated at Cabezón when he attempted to defend the approaches to Valladolid, and on 13 and 14 June Palafox was defeated at Mallén and then again at Alagón, where he was lightly wounded. Finally, slightly delayed by the fact that some of the forces involved were recalled so as to assist in the defeat of Cuesta, on 21 June two more French columns stormed the passes of the Cantabrian mountains that led to Santander.

In all these actions events assumed a common pattern. Excited and uncontrollable, the raw levies that formed the bulk of the Spanish forces proved incapable of manoeuvring in the face of the enemy, whilst many of them barely knew how to use their weapons, having sometimes only been issued with muskets the day before they went into action. Happy enough to fire away at the French so long as they remained at a safe distance, the latter had usually no more than to make an offensive move for them to flee in panic, throwing away their arms, accusing their commanders of treason and leaving the few regulars involved to fend for themselves as best they could. Having run away, meanwhile, the levies invariably exposed themselves to the French cavalry, which were unleashed amongst them with terrible effect, sabring them unmercifully and taking hundreds of them prisoner. French casualties, meanwhile, in no case numbered more than a few dozen. Typical enough was the experience of Girón at Alcolea:

After having for some time subjected us to a fairly heavy bombardment . . . the enemy attacked the bridgehead. The small detachment that had been posted to hold the entrenchment having run out of ammunition, they had to fall back . . . Though caught at a disadvantage, the battalions of grenadiers and the half-battalion of the [regiment of] Campomayor . . . detained the enemy for some time, but, as was to be expected from their number and quality alike, they had soon forced the bridge, and . . . we had to retreat . . . At the bridge there appeared . . . neither General Echavarrí, nor any of the other figures who had made such a noise in Córdoba, whilst the battalions of armed civilians who were with us fled at the first cannon shots.[5]

So far so good, then. Severe punishment had been administered to the insurgents, whilst major towns that had fallen to the French included not just Córdoba and Segovia but also Valladolid and Santander. Yet all was not what it seemed. As early as 6 June, indeed, the French experienced an embarrassing check in Catalonia. Thus, the force of troops mustered by Duhesme to march on Lérida and Zaragoza amounted to a mere 3,200 men, all of them Italian troops drawn from Naples and the Kingdom of Italy. Immediately available to the Spaniards were no more than a desperately understrength regiment of line infantry and a handful of strays from Barcelona. Unlike most other parts of Spain, however, Catalonia had other forces on which it could rely. Thus, in common with Galicia and the Basque provinces, it could count upon the services of an irregular home guard known in this particular instance as the *somatén*. Organised on a parish basis and controlled by the civil authorities, this could be called out in the event of invasion and had gained much experience of fighting the French in the course of the invasion of 1794–95. No sooner had the Lérida column set out from Barcelona than a swarm of irregulars began to gather in its path. Commanded by a General Schwartz, the Italians at first made good time along the Barcelona–Lérida highroad, but on 6 June they were attacked at the defile of El Bruch. Convinced that he was under attack by regular troops – the *somaténes* were hidden amongst trees and rocks and accompanied by two young drummerboys who were later fused into the single figure of the legendary *tambor de Bruch* – Schwartz decided to retreat, only for his command to become so demoralised that it eventually lost all cohesion and dissolved in a *sauve qui peut*. Much alarmed, Duhesme then sent word to the troops he had sent southwards to fall back on the capital, and by 11 June his entire force was back in Barcelona.

The travails of the Corps of Observation of the Eastern Pyrenees were not yet over. Duhesme having now resolved to concentrate on securing his communications with the French frontier, which were protected only by a single battalion that had been left to hold the fortress of Figueras, he therefore headed for Gerona, whilst taking advantage of the opportunity to cow the *somaténes* by sacking many towns and villages along the way. The city, however, was well fortified and possessed of a proper garrison of infantrymen and gunners. Attacked on 20 June, it therefore repulsed two assaults, and forced the invaders to fall back on Barcelona. The capital was found to have been blockaded by the *somaténes* of the coastal districts, but these were soon driven away. More than that, though, Duhesme could not do. Recognising this, Napoleon sent a fresh division to the frontier under General Reille, but this was able to do no more than keep the highroad open as far as Figueras, the situation for the time being therefore sliding into stalemate.

Nor was Catalonia the only region where the French were baulked. In Aragón the commander of the 6,000-strong French force bearing down on Zaragoza, Charles Lefebvre-Desnouettes, had decided to rush the city. At first sight this looked easy enough, for setting aside the miserable perfomance of the Aragonese levies in the Ebro valley, it was protected by no more than its old medieval wall and possessed little in the way of artillery. Indeed, even

Palafox did not think it could be held, abandoning the city to its own devices on the pretext of the need to organise a relief force outside the city. What nobody counted on, however, was the populace. Unwilling to join the regular army and in practice not much interested in the war, the latter would nevertheless often put up a fierce fight when it came to the defence of their own homes, for not only were life and hearth at stake, but also powerful notions of community and local pride. Meanwhile, the inhabitants of Zaragoza had been particularly radicalised by the events of the *motín de Aranjuez*, had a certain tradition of anti-French feeling and possessed immense faith in the city's Virgén del Pilar. Thanks to much braggadocio on the part of Palafox, whose mediocre talents as a general were somewhat counteracted by a genius for propaganda, they were also sure of victory. Stiffened by the usual straggle of regulars, several thousands of the inhabitants therefore lined the walls and prepared to give a good account of themselves.

When the French appeared before the city on 15 June, they were therefore walking into a hornets' nest. Covered by a few field guns, columns charged the various gates and in several places got inside the walls, but there were many casualties in the process and they were unable to subjugate the defenders, who, ensconced behind walls, on rooftops, or in fortress-like convents, were fighting in conditions that were near perfect. After several hours the attackers were therefore forced to retreat in disorder. They did not go far, setting up camp in the plain to the west of the city, appealing for help to Bessières, and in the night of 23–24 June heavily defeating a rather foolhardy effort on the part of Palafox to drive them away at Epila. However, it was hardly an auspicious start, and one, moreover, that was soon to be repeated a third time.

Beaten off at Zaragoza and Gerona, the French still had troops marching on Valencia. However, they were lucky to reach it at all: not only were Moncey's troops almost entirely composed of raw conscripts, but the Levante was possessed of a reasonable garrison. In short, there was a good chance that the French might have been defeated *en route*, but nevertheless Moncey managed to outwit the Spanish commander, a nonentity named the Conde de Cervellón, and reach Valencia by a route that was guarded only by the lightest of forces. Easily brushing these aside, on 26 June Moncey appeared before the city and drove in a substantial force of regulars and levies that was sent out in an attempt to fend him off at San Onofre. However, the Spaniards escaped more or less unscathed, protected by the irrigation ditches, cactus hedges and fruit trees with which the whole area was covered. Moreover, when Moncey tried a storm the next day he found that the defences – a wall even weaker than that of Zaragoza – had been much strengthened, that part of the approaches had been flooded and that the defenders – a mixture of levies and civilian volunteers – were enthusiastic and determined. Once again, everything possible was done, but by nightfall Moncey had lost over a thousand of his eight thousand men, in consequence of which he was left with no option but to retreat.

This series of reverses did much to soften the impact of Napoleon's initial success: already, indeed, Patriot Spain's fecund propagandists were starting to claim that the heroic Spanish people had routed the veterans of Austerlitz and Jena. At this particular point, nothing could have been more embarrassing for the emperor. As we have seen, having once decided to overthrow the Bourbons, Napoleon had taken steps both to legitimise his actions and co-opt Spain's élites by summoning a conference of forty-seven prominent figures appointed by the Junta de Gobierno, twenty parish priests appointed by the Spanish bishops, and eighty-three elected representatives of the town councils, universities, chambers of commerce and local estates at Bayonne. However, no rules were ever established as to how the elections were actually to be carried out, whilst the uprising in any case rendered them out of the question. Indeed, fewer than 100 deputies ever assembled at Bayonne, a considerable number of those who were invited to attend either sending excuses, absconding *en route*, or simply refusing to go. Amongst those who did attend, however, were: the Archbishop of Burgos; the Inquisitor General; leading grandees such as the Príncipe del Castelfranco, the Duque de Fernán Núñez, the Duque del Infantado, the Duque del Parque and the Conde de Orgaz; the ministers Miguel José de Azanza and Gonzalo O'Farrill; several representatives of the Council of Castile; and a variety of other statesmen, officials and men of letters including the erstwhile ministers, Mariano Luis de Urquijo and Francisco Cabarrús.

Initially, it seems to have been intended that this body would formally petition Napoleon for the boon of Joseph Bonaparte as King of Spain, but so long did it take to get even the most skeletal body of deputies assembled at Bayonne that the emperor eventually decided not to wait, Joseph being announced as 'King of Spain and of the Indies' on 6 June. That being the case, the chief task of the assembly proved rather to be the discussion of the new constitution which Napoleon had publicly promised that Spain would enjoy. In the middle of May a draft had been sent to the Junta de Gobierno and the Council of Castile, but these bodies had jibbed at the massive changes in state and society which Napoleon's ideas presaged. Recognising that he could not proceed in the face of the concerted opposition of the élites, the emperor therefore drew back with good grace, elaborating a new document which went some way towards the criticisms that had been made of the original. Gone, then, were such ideas as universal conscription, freedom of conscience and freedom of property, the new constitution rather representing a compromise between the rival models of Napoleonic France and Bourbon Spain. Moreover, when the congress finally opened on 15 June the deputies were permitted to debate it at some length and even to put forward a number of amendments.

Finally promulgated on 7 July, the Constitution of Bayonne showed a Napoleon prepared to compromise with the *antiguo régimen* in order to smooth the way for his brother. At first sight there was little difference from the model of reform that had already been established elsewhere, as, for example, in the new German state of Westphalia. Provision, then, was made for a cabinet, modern ministries, a council of state and a bicameral *cortes* of very limited power, chosen in part by royal appointment, and in part by indirect election. Also seen were the abolition of torture, the separation of the revenues of Crown and State, the removal of all internal customs barriers and the establishment of freedom from arbitrary arrest, equality before the law – which implied, of course, an end to all privileges of birth and status – and freedom of movement, employment and occupation. But elsewhere concessions were on offer. Both the institution of the *mayorazgo* and the *fueros* of the Basque provinces were specifically recognised, albeit with the proviso of subsequent reform. The practice of all faiths other than Catholicism was banned. And the new *cortes* was given a flavour of tradition by the division of the lower chamber into three estates (clergy, nobility and people).

Backed by such a mixture of old and new, it was hoped that Joseph might secure the loyalty of both erstwhile caroline bureaucrats and the new generation of liberals, whilst at the same time doing as little as possible to alienate the traditionalist opposition. Before the experiment could be tried, however, the new king, who had arrived in Bayonne the day after its proclamation and had since then been charming everyone with the warmth of his personality, had first to be got to his capital. In this respect, however, considerable problems had arisen. Thus, despite the victory of Cabezón, the French had been too thinly stretched to hang on to Valladolid for very long, and had withdrawn further east so as to concentrate on covering the direct route from Madrid to Burgos and the French frontier. Establishing a new capital at León, Cuesta had quickly set about building a new army on the basis of the forces that had been defeated at Cabezón, such new recruits as could be got in from the local countryside, and a single regiment of levies that was grudgingly sent him by the Junta of Asturias. Having thus provided himself with some 9,000 men, the general began to put pressure on the Junta of Galicia to order its substantial regular army to help him strike a blow against the French. Eager to boost its reputation, the Junta proved willing enough to oblige. The new commander of the Galician forces was Joaquín Blake, the grandson of a Scottish Jacobite who had taken service with Spain. A cautious and relatively junior officer – at the time of the uprising he had been a mere brigadier – Blake would have much preferred not to risk his army in combat for some while yet and, having almost no cavalry, was all too well aware of the dangers of operating in the plains of Castile. However, by the end of the first week of July the Army of Galicia was on the march.

What followed was an omen for the future. To have any hope of success, the Spaniards needed to strike fast with all their forces, but the unwilling Blake in fact moved very slowly, whilst leaving two of his four infantry divisions behind him to cover his retreat (in fairness, he had also been directed to ensure that Galicia was left properly protected). By 13 July the two armies – for Blake had also insisted on keeping his army separate from that of Cuesta – had therefore only advanced as far as the town of Medina de Río Seco. Still worse, with scarcely 600 cavalry between them, the Spanish commanders had little or no idea of the movements of the enemy, whom they assumed to be concentrating in the area of Valladolid.

Disastrously for them, however, they could not have been more wrong. Having left only a small force to protect their communications with Madrid, the French had been somewhat alarmed by the Spanish offensive. However, whilst Marshal Bessières got together such men as he could, a detachment of the Imperial Guard was sent north from Madrid and a reserve division, and, what is more, one almost entirely composed of veteran troops, was sent to him from the French frontier. Even once these troops had reached him, the marshal was still possessed of a total of only 13,700 men, but the French commander had few fears about taking on the much larger numbers of Spaniards that could be fielded by Cuesta and Blake, whilst he was also well aware that his master was expecting him to end the threat to the Madrid highway (Joseph had by now not only entered Spain, but travelled as far as Burgos). Thanks to an enterprising officer named Rigny, he was also well informed, and on 13 July he therefore set out for Medina de Río Seco.*

---

* Rigny's adventures deserve to be retold. Caught by the rising in Santander, where he had been sent to arrest a British officer reported to be in the area, he had escaped arrest by passing himself off as the very man he had been to catch, and had then travelled back to Burgos, gathering much information and being wined and dined by the Patriot authorities in the process. As can be imagined, great was the consternation when he was finally spotted: 'The presence of Rigny in the marshal's suite produced a comical effect on the unfortunate Spaniards, the latter recognising in him the supposed British officer with whom they had discussed their hostile projects so freely.'[6]

At that town, meanwhile, Blake and Cuesta had drawn up their forces in defensive positions facing in the direction of Valladolid. Unfortunately for them, however, Bessières was coming not from there but from the north-east, the French commander having elected Palencia as his point of concentration. Still worse, they did not discover their mistake until the enemy were almost on them. With Bessières heading for their left flank and rear, a change in position was essential, but the fact that all was still in darkness ensured that the move miscarried, and the two armies ended up spread over several miles of rolling countryside in three separate fragments that were not even in sight of one another. When battle was joined on 14 July the issue was therefore not in doubt for a moment. Taken in flank, the Vanguard and First Division of the Army of Galicia were scattered by a dramatic cavalry charge, whilst the same force's Fourth Division was crushed attempting to get back into touch with its fellows. For a graphic description of the scene, we can do no better than turn to the account of a Spanish staff officer named Juan Moscoso:

The French columns slowly advanced in good order covered by an imposing screen of cavalry. Eventually they separated, one of them climbing the slopes of the heights on our left flank and the other moving towards our centre and right wing . . . Many officers and men distinguished themselves, but in a moment the whole line fell into disorder . . . A body of enemy cavalry rode up onto the . . . plateau, and the conscripts panicked and swept away the veterans in the confusion. What a spectacle! What desperation! Almost entirely abandoned by their companies, the officers ran sword in hand across the field trying to get their frightened men together, and we saw several shot dead by soldiers who were wildly firing their muskets in the air . . . Within a short time, in short, everything had fallen into confusion, and, in spite of the valour . . . of various . . . officers, there was nothing that could be done . . . to make the men return to their ranks.[7]

For a French view of the cavalry charge, we may turn to Emile de Saint-Hilaire, who was riding in the French second line:

We came up too late: the affair was almost over apart from over on the left where a regiment of Spanish infantry formed in square was still in good order . . . I thought that the shock would be terrible, but, no sooner had we charged than all the *barbes noires* . . . took to their heels without a shot, making dramatic signs of the cross and commending themselves to the protection of the Blessed Virgin. Sabres raised and splitting heads right and left, we followed them to the edge of the plain, only to be brought up short by a five-foot wall masking a deep ravine that offered them a sure refuge. Only one thing restored the Spaniards a little in our eyes. Seeing that he was about to be cut down, a young drummer-boy . . . stopped and waved his shako in the air, crying 'Long live the emperor!', in an attempt to save his life. At the sound of his shouts, an officer of his regiment who had already set his horse at the wall . . . crossed back again . . . and ran him through, indignantly . . . shouting, 'Death to all traitors!', only to fall dead, cut to pieces.[8]

With his allies from the Army of Galicia thoroughly beaten, Cuesta was left with nothing to do but retire from the field. Blake, too, escaped, but the Spaniards had lost at least one thousand dead or wounded, twelve hundred prisoners and thirteen guns.

French losses had been minimal – perhaps 400 men – whilst it was still relatively early in the day. However, fortunately for the Spaniards, who might otherwise have been virtually destroyed, no pursuit was attempted, the victors instead sacking Medina de Río Seco in an orgy of murder, rape and pillage (many of its nuns, for example, were driven to the largest church in the place and there violated by dozens of soldiers). At the same time, it was a day of blazing heat and, with the never very impressive River Sequillo almost dried up, the French were short of water: according to Foy, indeed, the soldiers complained, 'The Spaniards have taken the river away with them.'[9] Each blaming the other for the defeat, meanwhile, the Spanish generals separated at Benavente, with Blake heading back to Galicia and Cuesta aiming in the first instance for León. Followed to that city by Bessières, he then sent his infantry to the safety of Asturias, whilst he himself rode, with the few regular cavalry who had been serving with him ever since the start of hostilities, for still unoccupied Salamanca.

Victory, then, was incomplete. Yet Napoleon was delighted. 'It is a very great victory,' he wrote to Joseph. 'The most important event in the Spanish war, it has given a decided colour to affairs.'[10] With the Spanish threat scattered, Joseph entered Madrid on 20 July. However, his reception did not bode well for the future. To quote a French medical officer stationed in the city:

The garrison was placed under arms, and all the French went out to meet him. The Spanish people did not do the same: nobody was to be seen in the streets, and all the doors and windows were shut. A few curious citizens stuck their noses out to see the royal party go by, but they immediately slipped back inside for fear of being seen by indiscreet compatriots. The houses had been ordered to be hung with draperies, but the only people to comply with the regulations did so by hanging out dirty rags.[11]

To lend veracity to the occasion, indeed, a crowd had to be manufactured, the same observer noting that 'a number of porters and water carriers, veritable *lazzaroni*, who had been bribed and plied with drink, ran along beside King Joseph's triumphal carriage, crying like madmen, "God save the King!" '.[12] But all was in vain. To quote Joseph's close friend and adviser, Comte Miot de Melito, indeed, 'The silence and disdainful expressions of the inhabitants of Madrid ... was so striking that it would have been impossible to invest the occasion with greater solemnity.'[13] Nor was this all: the new Spanish army that Joseph had begun to form on the basis of the prisoners from Medina de Río Seco had for the most part deserted before they even reached the capital, whilst Joseph's party had also been abandoned by many of the dignitaries who had rallied to him at Bayonne.

It is here worth pointing out that, despite tales of scowling faces and muttered threats, not to mention occasional acts of defiance, the attitude of the populace of Madrid was clearly really one of indifference rather than outright resistance. Nevertheless, *el rey intruso* was deeply alarmed. Even at Bayonne he had been worried, but his fears had been crushed. As Miot writes of his arrival:

The emperor rode out to meet his brother some distance from Bayonne, and welcomed him with many marks of interest and affection. It was necessary to close his eyes to the dangers of the role which he was going to have to play, and only to allow him to see its brilliant side. On his arrival at Bayonne, Joseph found himself surrounded by all the seductions and grandeurs of royalty. He received the homages forced from the grandees of Spain, the deputies of the junta and the principal figures who had followed the old court ... At the same time, a veil was thrown over everything that was happening in Spain: there was no certain news to be had, and those few rumours that slipped through all the obstacles that had been erected to keep them out were stubbornly denied.[14]

All Joseph's concerns now returned with a vengeance, but, as was to happen on many occasions in the future, he had neither the strength nor the courage to refuse his new role. Installed in his capital, he therefore began to go through the motions of kingship. A new government composed of nine ministers appointed at Bayonne was formally installed, together with the Council of State demanded by the Constitution of Bayonne; a gazette was established; an amnesty issued for all insurgents who would surrender their weapons and take the oath of allegiance to the new monarch; a variety of audiences and ceremonies were held in the palace; and on 25 July Joseph was formally acclaimed King of Spain. All the time, meanwhile, every effort was made to instil a mood of celebration – public buildings were illuminated and the population treated to free bullfights and firework displays (which seem to have been well attended). Not surprisingly, conciliation was also very much the order of the day: the agnostic Joseph attended High Mass every day, whilst doing his best to ensure that the French forces did not mistreat the populace, the king having been genuinely shocked by the news of the sack of Medina de Río Seco.

As Joseph himself recognised, however, Spain would have to be conquered before it would accept him. Yet despite continued optimism on the part of Napoleon – to all his brother's gloomy letters, the emperor replied that all would be well – things were not going according to plan. Even as *el rey intruso* was entering Madrid, indeed, the arms of his imperial brother were experiencing total humiliation in Andalucía. But, before we look at events in the south, we must first return to Aragón. On 15 June, as we have seen, Zaragoza had succeeded in beating off an attempt to storm the city. Much disconcerted, the attackers had retired a short distance to await reinforcements, whilst the Marqués de Lazan, who had taken over from Palafox when the latter left the city, made frantic attempts to strengthen the walls and prepare for the fresh assault that he knew to be inevitable. Sure enough, a steady supply of fresh troops and heavy artillery was soon reaching the French, and on 28 June operations against the city were resumed under a new commander named Verdier. Thus, with the defenders distracted by a catastrophic explosion in their main powder magazine, the invaders drove the Spaniards off the heights that dominated the city from the south. With this preliminary move out of the way, on the morning of 2 July 3,000 troops attacked the walls, only to find that the defenders, who had by now been reinforced by a regiment of line infantry from Catalonia and much encouraged by the sudden reappearance of José Palafox, stood firm and put up a desperate resistance. Despite a few moments of crisis, moreover, the invaders were once again repelled with heavy losses, their defeat being accompanied by the emergence of one of the greatest popular icons of the Spanish struggle in the person of Agustina of Aragón – more precisely, Agustina Zaragoza Domenech – a Catalan girl who single-handedly saved a key position from falling into the hands of the enemy by seizing a linstock from a dying gunner (reputedly her lover) and firing a cannon into the very faces of the advancing French.

Much discouraged, Verdier now resigned himself to engaging in conventional siege operations. Thus, an elaborate system of trenches was dug before the walls and gradually extended closer and closer to provide cover for an assault force whilst the attackers also established a force on the north bank of the Ebro that was able considerably to restrict the reinforcements and supplies that had hitherto been able to reach the city by that route.* Despite a series of sorties, they were also able to seize a number of the outposts the latter had continued to maintain outside the walls in such monasteries as that of the Capuchins. Inside the city, meanwhile, Palafox and his subordinates did their best to maintain the morale of the population. Religious ceremonies abounded – on 25 July the feast of Saint James, for example, was celebrated with particular fervour – whilst printing presses continued to churn out a mixture of bombast and defiance. Nothing, however, could disguise the fact that a new attack was certain, and on the night of 31 July the bombardment of the city began. With sixty guns in place, whole sections of the city's flimsy defences were swept away, and in the afternoon of 4 August the French attacked again. This time there was no mistake: protected until the last minute by their trenches, the assault columns were able to scramble through the various breaches and establish themselves in the ruins of such buildings as the Church of Santa Engracia.

At this point the French might again have expected the city to surrender, but the defenders remained as defiant as ever. In the face of furious opposition, the attackers were therefore forced to fight their way yard by yard towards the heart of the city. Had they been able to keep going, they might well have triumphed – by the late afternoon many of the defenders were flagging, whilst news that the French had reached the broad central thoroughfare known as the Coso started a major panic and caused Palafox once again to abandon the city. However, the assault troops were much depleted, badly disordered, and increasingly tired and thirsty, a handful of Spaniards in consequence being able to initiate a counter-attack that flung back the enemy vanguard. With other defenders slipping through the city's narrow streets to attack their flanks and rear, the French could go no further, the end of the day therefore seeing them confined to a narrow finger of territory stretching from the walls to a point not far from the Coso.

What might have happened next is difficult to say: Verdier's forces were in no fit state to do much more, certainly, but the Spaniards were too disorganised to do more than keep up a steady fusillade and make spasmodic rushes at one French position or another. Across the Ebro, meanwhile, Palafox had reappeared with a convoy of reinforcements and ammunition, but it seems unlikely that his improvised troops would ever have had the

---

* A sizeable city by Spanish standards, Zaragoza stood on the south bank of the River Ebro which at this spot runs in a roughly west-to-east direction. It was connected to the northern bank by a single bridge at the end of which there stood two monasteries and a cluster of houses. Initially, however, this sector had been left unmolested, the French having enough troops to attack only the city's southern front.

capacity to evict the French. In short – an important point to make in view of the hyperbole that to this day surrounds the defence of Zaragoza – fresh troops might yet have won the day for Verdier. For reasons that will become clear, however, no such help was to arrive.

We now come to the campaign of Bailén. For a variety of reasons, Dupont had not advanced beyond Córdoba. On 10 June Cádiz lost much of its immediate importance when the remnants of the French fleet defeated at Trafalgar were forced to surrender after a brief cannonade. Meanwhile, the French commander had got wind of the concentration of the Spanish garrison, whilst he was also cut off from Madrid. No sooner had the insurrection broken out than the population of New Castile and eastern Andalucía had flung themselves upon every Frenchman that they could find. Couriers, invalids, convoys, forage parties and even a general and his wife were attacked and murdered, sometimes in circumstances of the most revolting cruelty. Particularly dreadful was the scene at Manzanares, where an entire hospital was massacred:

I went down into . . . the gardens, whereupon my eyes were assaulted by a most shocking spectacle. Some fifty corpses . . . allowed us to assess the barbarity of these cowardly assassins. Some had been beaten to death, others had had their heads smashed in by axes, and still others had been . . . plunged into cauldrons of boiling oil. The limbs of these unfortunates had been so shrivelled up . . . that a man of the height of five and one half feet appeared to possess that of no more than three.[15]

As for the reinforcements that were hastily dispatched from Madrid – Dupont's second division – they found their route repeatedly contested by bands of armed peasants, most notably at Valdepeñas, where the populace is reputed to have barricaded the streets and defended themselves with boiling oil, fowling pieces, farm implements, knives and even cooking utensils.

Much alarmed, Dupont was disturbed enough first to curtail his march at Córdoba, and then on 16 June to fall back as far as Andújar. Getting into touch here with the division that had been sent down from Madrid (commanded by General Vedel, it was posted to hold the town of Bailén), he then settled down to wait on events whilst sending out a punitive expedition to sack Jaén as the nearest insurgent capital. Why Dupont delayed at Andújar is something of a puzzle, for he had clearly abandoned all hope of subjugating Andalucía and would have been better advised to fall back on New Castile. However, a tough and experienced veteran who had won much renown in the Austerlitz campaign, the French commander was hoping for a marshal's baton, and therefore unwilling to make so public an admission of failure; at the same time, too, like many of Napoleon's generals, he simply was not used to the burdens of independent command, whilst at the same time being terrified of his master's wrath. Yet, protected though he was by the River Guadalquivir, which ran from east to west to the south of his men's positions, his 17,000 troops were not only distinctly unimpressive but also threatened by an army of at least 33,000 Spaniards of whom a large majority were regulars. Undeterred by the recent French visit, moreover, irregular bands commanded by agents of the Junta of Jaén were pressing in upon his communications. Still worse, his men were falling sick in large numbers, and spread out between Andújar and Bailén, about the only good news being that a third division was now being sent from Madrid. Commanded by Jacques Gobert, this arrived at Bailén on 7 July and was given the task of watching the highroad from there to La Carolina, the result being that Dupont now had some 20,000 troops south of the Sierra Morena (it is symptomatic of the rather improvised nature of the French response to the uprising that this third division came not from Dupont's own corps, of which one division still remained in Madrid, but rather from that of Moncey).

Retribution was not long in coming. Under the command of General Castaños, the four-division-strong Spanish Army of Andalucía had soon moved up to a position a few miles to the south of Andújar and elaborated a plan of attack. In brief, whilst part of the Spanish army pinned Dupont down at Andújar, two divisions would cross the river south of Bailén and descend on his rear, whilst another force composed largely of new levies worked its way around the French forces from the west before attacking from the north. Finally, a further two thousand levies would move around Dupont's eastern flank and attempt to block his retreat through the Sierra Morena. By all the normal rules, this was madness. As Castaños had little idea that Dupont had received reinforcements, the Spaniards were running the risk of being defeated in detail, for Dupont could easily have united his forces and struck at the various Spanish detachments in turn. Even if he remained as passive as the plan required, neither of the two main Spanish forces was really strong enough to defeat either Dupont on the one hand or Vedel and Gobert on the other.

But for once fortune favoured the Spaniards. Operations began on 14 July when the division of General Reding appeared on the southern bank of the Guadalquivir at the ferry of Mengíbar and attacked the French outpost that had been stationed there. Not much came of this other than the fact that Vedel hastily rushed most of his men to support the detachment posted to watch the river, but on 15 July Castaños feinted against Andújar.

Shaken by the Spanish demonstration, Dupont therefore sent orders for Vedel to send him some assistance. In doing so, he made it quite clear that his subordinate need only send a brigade and, further, that he should continue to watch the river, but, misled by a rather feeble show on the part of Reding, Vedel left only two battalions at the river and marched for Andújar with almost his entire division.

Thus began a chain of misadventures. At dawn on 16 July Reding confounded Vedel's expectations by once again moving up at Mengíbar. Sending for help, Vedel's detachment received the support of only a few battalions of Gobert's division, with the result that 4,000 French troops were left to face more than 9,000 Spaniards. Taking up a defensive position behind a tributary of the Guadalquivir called the Gaudiel, they put up a brave fight, but eventually Gobert was killed and his men routed. Believing, perhaps, that to go on would be to court defeat, Reding then fell back across the river, the fact being that by the time Dupont heard of Gobert's defeat, all was much as it had been when Vedel had marched to join him at Andújar.

Dupont was not to know this, but he did now have a large part of his forces united under his direct command. In consequence, two possibilities were open to him in that he could either have attacked Castaños or marched on Reding. Either course of action offered an excellent chance of success – Dupont outnumbered Castaños by two to one and Reding by three to two – but, not knowing how many troops were facing him, the French general was unwilling to push south across the Guadalquivir, whilst he was equally unwilling to give up his chief Andalusian base. Rather than keeping his army together, he therefore added a few cavalry to Vedel's division and ordered him to defeat Reding whilst he himself continued to hold Andújar.

There followed another bizarre mistake. On 17 July Vedel marched as ordered on Bailén, only to find that there were no Spanish troops in the vicinity. Misled by reports of Spanish forces far to the east – in fact these were the troops not of Reding but of the column that had been sent to block the passes of the Sierra Morena – Vedel jumped to the conclusion that the victors of the Gaudiel had marched along the highroad towards the mountains, and therefore pushed on in their supposed wake. Passing the night at Guarromán, the following day he reached La Carolina and was there relieved to pick up the forces defeated on 16 July, the latter having retreated thither rather than falling back on Andújar.

All this represented a serious want of judgement on the part of Vedel and all the more so as he had more than enough cavalry to discover the true situation. As it was, this now slid still further towards disaster. Having spent the previous day resting his men behind the Guadalquivir, Reding had now been joined by a second division under Coupigny and on 18 July he recrossed the river, his intention being to take Bailén from the French troops that he assumed were holding it. Arriving before the town, like Vedel before them, they found it empty, however, and in consequence made camp preparatory to marching to attack Dupont.

Back at Andújar Dupont had finally come to the conclusion that something had gone seriously wrong. Castaños' attack had still not materialised whilst it was clear that large numbers of Spanish troops were loose in his rear (though not at Bailén: everything that Dupont knew suggested that the interlopers were not only much further east, but separated from his forces by Vedel). News having arrived that Vedel had marched on the passes, late in the evening of 17 July he therefore finally resolved to evacuate Andújar in favour of Bailén. Getting the army moving was no easy matter, however – aside from anything else, the sack of Córdoba had left it encumbered with an immense quantity of plunder of all sorts – and it was therefore not for another twenty-four hours that Dupont's forces finally set off. Even then, progress was very slow, the size of the French baggage train ensuring that it was not far short of dawn before Dupont's vanguard had arrived in the vicinity of Bailén. Still worse, Dupont was completely unprepared for battle: indeed, believing that the only danger came from Castaños, he had placed his best troops at the rear of the column and given the van to one of his miserable 'Legions of Reserve'.

Tramping through the darkness, the French advance guard crossed a tributary of the Guadalquivir known as the Rumblar, and began to make its way through a band of low hills that runs from north to south a mile to the west of Bailén, only for the peace of the olive groves and holm-oak that covered the area to be shattered by a fusillade of shots. Although they firmly believed that Dupont was still at Andújar, Reding and Coupigny had posted a few pickets in the hills, and the men concerned had opened fire. Taken by surprise, the Spanish pickets were quickly driven in, but the firing nevertheless alerted the Spaniards to the fact that they were under attack, and their forces therefore rushed to take up a fighting position. At the southern end of what became the Spanish line a few troops got on to the hill known as the Haza Walona, whilst the right was posted on a projecting spur called the Cerro Valentín, but otherwise they were stationed on level ground just to the west of Bailén.*

---

* Anglophone readers may note that this account of the Spanish position differs considerably from that given in Oman, who argues that the Spaniards were posted on the hills. There is, however, no evidence that this was the case.

Whilst the Spaniards were taking up their positions, the equally astonished French were themselves struggling to deploy. Whilst his leading infantry moved into columns of attack on the hills above the Spaniards, Dupont ordered up his chief cavalry units, one of the brigades involved immediately proceeding to attack the Spanish centre in an attempt to win time. Driven off with some loss, the horsemen then fell back, whilst the two batteries of four-pounder guns, which was the only artillery that the French had thus far managed to bring up, opened up on the enemy. Too few and lacking in power to be very effective, however, the French guns were overmatched by their Spanish opponents', which were mostly of a much heavier calibre. Throughout the battle, indeed, the Spanish guns were to make a great impression: 'So well was our artillery served', wrote one participant in the battle, 'that it almost did not waste a shot.'[16] When the leading French infantry – the Fourth Legion of Reserve and a battalion of Napoleon's Swiss troops – finally advanced to the attack at around seven in the morning, they therefore faced an impossible task. Arrayed in four battalion columns with a cavalry brigade on either flank, they were shot to pieces and forced to retreat. Heavily outnumbered and desperate to break through – Reding had some 17,000 men to his own 11,000 – Dupont brought up fresh troops and tried again, only to experience renewed failure. The French cavalry drove the Spanish left off the Haza Walona and repelled a force that advanced on the other wing, but their infantry were first shattered by artillery fire and then put to flight by a successful cavalry charge.

Seeing the French recoil in disorder, Reding ordered forward more troops on his right, and within a few minutes these had outflanked the French left. Much alarmed, Dupont ordered up a fresh infantry brigade and some of his increasingly exhausted cavalry, and after a sharp fight the interlopers were driven off. On the other hand, a second attack on the part of the infantry that had gone forward at the beginning of the day was easily repelled, their retreat having to be protected by yet another cavalry charge. In despair, Dupont then ordered up his last reserves – the battalion of Seamen of the Guard and the four battalions of 'Spanish' Swiss that had been added to his command when he left Madrid – and, with the aid of a few other troops who were still in reasonable order, mounted one last assault against the enemy centre. Once again, however, the Spanish artillery tore great gaps in the French ranks, whilst Dupont himself was wounded in the hip. The cavalry and seamen seem none the less to have reached the Spanish front line, but they were too few in numbers to make any impression and had eventually to fall back. As for the Swiss, they for the most part immediately went over to their former comrades.

With his entire command exhausted and used up, Dupont had been thoroughly beaten (though it has to be said that he was the author of his own downfall: for all the Spaniards' numerical advantage, he might have cut his way through, had he only brought up all his forces for a single attack). At the same time, not only was there no news of Vedel, to whose doings we must shortly return, but the Spaniards were closing in on his rear. Thus, although Castaños had been extremely slow to discover the departure of the French from Andújar and slower still to respond, one of the two divisions that he had kept with him was at last approaching the Rumblar, whilst the flanking column that had been sent out to circle round the French from the north had suddenly appeared in the vicinity of Dupont's ill-protected baggage train. Left with no alternative, the French commander sent to Reding to ask for an armistice, this being something that the latter was only too glad to grant (not only were his own troops exhausted, but he was no more aware of Vedel's whereabouts than Dupont, and, still worse, could not be certain that he was not about to fall on his own rear). What Reding did not have, however, was the authority to negotiate the terms of a capitulation, the result being that a mixed deputation had to be sent off in search of Castaños.

It was now the middle of a blazing summer afternoon – 'The heat', remembered Girón, 'got worse every moment; there were points when I thought I was going to suffocate'[17] – time enough, it might have been thought, for Vedel to have marched the sixteen miles from La Carolina. Had he done so promptly, the result of the action would have been very different, for Vedel had under his command not only his own division, but also that of the dead Gobert, the whole making a total of some 9,000 men. At first, all went well enough: having realised the previous day that he had made a serious error, Vedel had immediately decided to return to Bailén, and at five o'clock in the morning of 19 July he had set out with his troops from La Carolina. The march, however, was not pushed with any rapidity – it took some five hours for the column to cover the first eight miles – and at Guarromán Vedel halted to allow his men to rest and cook a meal. Not until two o'clock in the afternoon did he get moving again, and that despite the fact that the noise of the fighting could be clearly heard in the distance. By this time, of course, the cannonade had died away, thereby dissipating what little sense of urgency Vedel displayed still further, and it was therefore another three hours before he finally came in sight of the small force Reding had posted to watch his rear.

Why Vedel acted in this fashion has never been fully explained. However, whether he was motivated by scorn for the Spaniards, a desire not to overtire his troops, or even dislike of Dupont, the damage was done. Ignoring Spanish protests that an armistice had been agreed, Vedel launched a vigorous attack on the few troops facing him, and succeeded in taking 1,000 prisoners. Indeed, not until a direct order reached him from Dupont ordering him to desist would he do so, his division eventually bivouacking some way back along the highroad.

Thus ended a day of confusion and slaughter. Some 2,000 of Dupont's troops lay dead or wounded on the battlefield, whilst perhaps 800 more had changed sides. As for the survivors, they were bereft of food and water, utterly demoralised, and totally lacking in cohesion, as well as being menaced by large numbers of fresh troops. Despite the arrival of Vedel, there was therefore little option but for Dupont to make the best terms he could. There followed several days of complex negotiations, but on 23 July 17,635 men laid down their arms. Handing over his sword to Castaños, Dupont is supposed to have said, 'You may well, General, be proud of this day; it is remarkable because I have never lost a pitched battle until now – I who have been in more than twenty.' Quick as a flash, however, came the reply, 'It is the more remarkable because I was never in one before in my life.'[18] A little later, meanwhile, their ranks were joined by battalions that had been dropped off to protect the road to Madrid at Santa Cruz de Mudela and Manzanares. In theory, officers and men alike were to be repatriated to France by sea, whilst the former were allowed to retain their personal baggage (a clause which gave rise to claims that Dupont had surrendered with no other object than to safeguard his plunder).

Few of the men taken at Bailén were ever to return to France: abused and mistreated from the start, they were denied repatriation, confined on hulks in Cádiz harbour, and eventually dispatched to the barren Balearic Island of Cabrera, where half of them starved to death. However, Dupont, Vedel and a small number of senior officers were allowed to sail for home. Needless to say, their reception was unpleasant in the extreme. Unable to conceive of how a French army could come to grief at Spanish hands, unwilling to admit the shortcomings in his own handling of the situation, furious with his subordinates' generalship, and convinced that the surrender had been motiv-ated by nothing more than a desire to retain the spoils of war, the emperor responded with a tirade of spectacular proportions. 'In all the history of the world,' he raged, 'there has never been anything so stupid, so inept or so cowardly ... From the very dispatch of General Dupont, one can see perfectly that everything has been the result of the most inconceivable incompetence.'[19] In consequence, Dupont, Vedel and various other officers were arrested (originally, they were to have been court-martialled, but in fact the only one to suffer this fate was Dupont, and even then not until *raisons d'état* made it seem necessary early in 1812). All Napoleon's fury, however, could not undo the damage. Stunned by what had occurred, on 1 August Joseph, who had no more than 23,000 troops with him in Madrid and was labouring under the impression that thousands of vengeful Spaniards were about to fall on him, evacuated the capital and fell back on Old Castile, whilst ordering Verdier to abandon the siege of Zaragoza and Bessières to retire from León, the entire French army ultimately taking shelter behind the Ebro.

As if all this was not bad enough, by this time Duhesme had also suffered fresh misfortunes. In so far as events in his area are concerned, we left a fresh division assembling on the frontier under Reille, whilst Duhesme himself licked his wounds in Barcelona. It being quite obvious that nothing further could be attempted until Gerona had been captured, on 10 July he therefore set off for that town once again with the bulk of his forces, having first sent a message to Reille to the effect that he should attempt to meet him there. By 24 July 13,000 French troops had therefore assembled before the town (though not without much trouble with the *somaténes*), and siege operations were soon under way. The latter, however, were not at all well-conducted, as well as being hampered by the nature of the terrain and other difficulties, whilst the garrison had been reinforced in the nick of time by a regiment dispatched from the Balearic Islands. Progress was therefore extremely slow, whilst the absence of the bulk of Duhesme's forces from Barcelona ensured that the Spaniards were able to embark the substantial garrison of the Balearic Islands and send it to Tarragona, which now became the capital of the Catalan insurrection (landing on the Catalan coast with his men, the erstwhile Captain General of the Balearic Islands, Juan Miguel de Vives, at the same time took over the command of all operations in the province). Aided by the local *somaténes*, these forces now closed in on the 3,500 men Duhesme had left in Barcelona, which was closely blockaded, whilst a handful of regulars under a brigadier called the Conde de Caldagués were sent to help the populace of the district that surrounded Gerona to harass Reille and Duhesme.

Very much a man of action, Caldagués was joined by many *somaténes*, whilst he had soon persuaded the defenders of Gerona to try a dramatic move. Thus, on 16 August almost all the regular troops in the garrison suddenly attacked the works on the hills that dominated the town from the east, whilst Caldagués appeared in their rear. Completely taken by surprise, the French were routed and forced to abandon their positions. Their casualties had been relatively few, but, even if they now managed to drive off

Caldagués, their numbers were simply not sufficient to allow them both to besiege Gerona and to prevent further attempts at relief. Rather than risk disaster, their commanders preferred to withdraw and that same night Duhesme was therefore on the march for Barcelona and Reille for Figueras. The latter got away easily enough, but the former's route lay first through rough hill country and then along the coast, the result being that he was harassed not just by the *somaténes* but also by a British frigate that was in the area. As a result retreat turned into rout, Duhesme only getting away by abandoning all his guns and baggage and taking to mule tracks across the hills. Safety was eventually attained, certainly – Vives made no attempt to stop him getting into the city – but all that he could now hope to do was to hold out until help should arrive.

Thus ended the first campaign of the war. Setting aside the situation in Portugal, to which we shall turn in the next chapter, Joseph, Bessières, Moncey and Verdier were huddled together around the towns of Miranda de Ebro and Logroño; Duhesme was blockaded in Barcelona; and Reille isolated at Figueras, about the only good news being that a belated insurrection in Vizcaya had been mercilessly crushed by the dispatch of a punitive expedition. Not only had thousands of French soldiers been killed or taken prisoner, but El Bruch, Gerona, Zaragoza, Valencia and, above all, Bailén all constituted the stuff of legend, Patriot Spain's ever growing legion of propagandists leaping to take advantage of them and glory in the heroism of the Spanish people. Needless to say, in the process much scorn was heaped on Napoleon, who was popularly represented as having been reduced to a state of abject terror. As for the unfortunate Joseph, his liking for women had been quickly noted, whilst the retreat to the Ebro saw rumours that he and his staff had emptied the wine cellars of a mansion which they briefly occupied at Calahorra, and it was therefore soon being put about that he was a drunkard – a habit particularly offensive in Spanish eyes – and a womaniser. Hence his nicknames of Tío Copas (Uncle Cups), the Rey de Copas (the King of Cups), Pepe Botella (Joe Bottle) and, more obscurely, Pepino (an obvious play on Pepe, *pepino* – 'cucumber' – also has a certain phallic connotation).

If Napoleon was furious, then, it was hardly surprising. Based though his Spanish policy had been on a series of errors and miscalculations, the empire had been seriously compromised. Thus, in Germany nationalists were comparing Palafox with Arminius (the Teutonic leader who had wiped out a Roman army in AD 9); in Prussia proponents of a fresh war were claiming that there was no reason why their countrymen should not match the example of the Spaniards; and in Austria a war party was dreaming of stirring up a Spanish-style uprising in the recently lost Tyrol. Complain though Joseph might that the war was unwinnable and that the Spaniards would never accept his rule, retribution was therefore soon in train.

There was little chance of the Spaniards being able to resist the hammer blow that was about to descend upon them. Despite all the bombast about the heroic Spanish people defeating the veterans of the *grande armée*, the French forces had for the most part consisted of a mass of ill-organised raw recruits, and popular resistance was limited in its impact. Armed civilians had fought with great courage in the defence of beleaguered Spanish cities, but, except where the ground they occupied was so strong as to be nearly inaccessible, in the field they had proved a complete liability. Problems occurred even when they fought as guerrillas. In Catalonia, for example, the *somaténes* might have proved adept at harassing the French, but they were also unreliable and notoriously unwilling to serve outside their home districts, as well as being, as we shall see, much inclined to pillage. As for Spain's victories, they have all to be placed in their proper perspective: Zaragoza, Valencia and Gerona would all have fallen had the French possessed more troops; Bailén had been lost by the French rather than won by the Spaniards; and El Bruch was a mere skirmish. Particularly instructive in this respect are Wellington's views on Bailén:

I believe no-one was more surprised at the result of Bailén than Castaños himself . . . I knew Dupont afterwards . . . a very able man, but he took fright and did not understand the Spaniards. Later in the war the French would have marched over the Spaniards instead of capitulating to them. Their general would have said, 'Retirez-vous, coquins!'.[20]

Last but not least, it is all too clear that with one or two exceptions, the brunt of the fighting had actually been done by the regular army. If Spain was to survive, she therefore had but one hope, and that was to acquire not only substantial foreign aid but also much larger and more effective armed forces than those which she currently had at her disposal. Victory at Bailén having muffled that message, the future was bleak in the extreme.

4

Vimeiro

THE LIBERATION OF PORTUGAL, AUGUST 1808

It was 15 June 1808. The House of Commons was crowded and in an excited mood. For the past week London had been feverishly discussing the extraordinary news from Spain that the northern province of Asturias had risen in revolt against the Corsican ogre, and it was known that the great topic of the day was at last to be discussed at Westminster. The celebrated Whig playwright, Richard Brinsley Sheridan, planned a great speech for the occasion, but proceedings were delayed by other business, and by the time that he rose to speak he had unfortunately got so drunk as to be incapable of coherent speech. Nevertheless, knowing that he was essentially lauding Spain's heroism to the skies and proposing that Britain should fly to her assistance, the Foreign Secretary, George Canning, knew full well how to respond. Promising 'every practicable aid', he proclaimed that the government would 'proceed upon the principle that any nation of Europe that starts up with a determination to oppose . . . the common enemy . . . becomes instantly our essential ally'.[1]

This exchange marks the beginning of Britain's involvement in the Peninsular War, and, by the same token, a considerable shift in her fortunes in the struggle against Napoleon. From it would stem her engagement in a prolonged campaign on the Continent of Europe and the end of the situation in which she could be accused, in Sheridan's words, of doing no more than 'filching sugar islands'. If only through happenstance, Britain could now play the part of a great military power as well as a great naval one, and evade charges that she was acting purely in her own selfish interests and fighting to the death of the last Austrian. Both at home and abroad, meanwhile, the British government was presented with major advantages. Their revolt's complex origins being barely understood, it seemed that the Spanish people had rejected Napoleon and all his works. As the emperor had continued to use the rhetoric of the French Revolution, domestic radicals and foreign 'Jacobins' alike had been inclined to rally to his cause, but now Britain found herself in the camp of freedom. Opposition from such sources was never wholly silenced, true, but Britain, and with her all Napoleon's opponents, had suddenly acquired a new moral legitimacy.

If the enormous nature of these advantages was not yet fully understood, the Portland administration's enthusiasm was entirely comprehensible. Britain was experiencing considerable political and economic difficulties, whilst the occupation of Portugal had shut off an important outlet for her trade. Meanwhile, the attack that she had launched against Spanish America had on 5 July 1807 come to an inglorious end with the capitulation of the entire British army at Buenos Aires, whilst her chief remaining ally, Sweden, had just been attacked by Russia. The year 1807 had seen success in Denmark, but in general the picture was not one of a sort calculated to please either Canning or the Secretary for War and the Colonies, Lord Castlereagh, both of whom were anxious to strike a real blow at the French, and increasingly concerned at the criticism to which they were being subjected in press and Parliament. Some effort had been made to help Sweden – in April 10,000 troops had been sent to Goteborg under Sir John Moore – but the main focus of attention now became Iberia and its dominions. A 5,000-strong division under Sir Brent Spencer had been collected at Gibraltar with orders to attack Lisbon, Ceuta or Mahón. Meanwhile, some 13,000 men were at Cork ready for a descent on the territory known today as Venezuela in the hope that this might precipitate a general revolt.

Spain, then, was already a major focus for the Portland administration, and all the more so as by late May news had been received from the governor of Gibraltar, Sir Hew Dalrymple, who had been in touch with Castaños, that revolt was possible in southern Spain. In the event, however, it was from Asturias that the call first came, for no sooner had she rebelled than two emissaries – the Vizconde de Matarrosa (soon to be the Conde de Toreno) and an academic named Andrés Angel de la Vega – took ship for England. The result was a storm of excitement. *The Times* and other leading newspapers pressed for immediate help for Asturias, whilst assorted men of letters went into perfect raptures at Spain's heroism. Meanwhile, the Asturian deputies were treated to many banquets and accorded the hospitality of some of the greatest households in the kingdom, the excitement being whipped up still further by the publication of numerous pamphlets and caricatures. For something of the spirit of the moment one has only to turn to private letters of the period. For example:

What a magnificent series of events is passing before us in Spain . . . I cannot describe to you the interest I feel in the Spanish cause. It exceeds anything except perhaps that which I felt in the first moments of the French Revolution. May the Spaniards obtain perfect liberty, and raise the Goddess for the admiration of mankind from that abyss in which the French have left her.[2]

Doubts did exist in some sectors, true: George III, for example, was dubious and one or two ministers downright hostile. Yet inaction was unlikely: men of the most contradictory political beliefs were wildly excited by the Asturian rising, whilst it was simply too good an opportunity to miss. As early as 2 July, then, Gijón saw the arrival of 34 guns, 12,000 swords and large quantities of ammunition, whilst about £100,000 in Spanish coin was dispatched from England (rather less useful were the arms captured from the Spanish armada sent back in token of reconciliation from the Tower of London!).* Meanwhile, a three-man military mission was sent to Oviedo to assess what else was needed. Nor was this the limit to the Portland administration's enthusiasm. The Asturian delegation, which was soon joined by others from Galicia and Seville, had not asked for troops, but the dispatch of a British army was soon under consideration. So far as this was concerned, there were fewer constraints than normal. Recent reforms in the army's recruitment – primarily, the authorisation of embodied members of the militia to volunteer for service in the line – offered the hope of a steady supply of fresh men; the need to provide against French invasion had been much reduced; and forces were available for immediate action in the shape of Spencer's troops, the division that had been assembled at Cork, and a couple of brigades that had been about to raid the invasion port of Boulogne. Just as vital, the necessary transports were also available, whilst the last few years had also seen a process of reform that promised to improve the army's hitherto somewhat dubious combat reputation. Although the troops mostly continued to be recruited from the 'scum of the earth' – the urban and rural poor and enemy deserters and prisoners of war – in many regiments flogging was being replaced by a more humane system of discipline, whilst a system of infantry tactics was being evolved that was eventually to be the best in Europe.

An army of reasonable quality could easily be got together, then, but what was Britain fighting for? Discussion of Britain's war aims in the French Wars has often centred on claims that are extremely partisan. On the one hand it is claimed that she was striving to free Europe from tyranny, and on

* References to the financial aid sent to Spain are complicated by the wide variety of Spanish coins and the different terms used to describe them. In brief, the basic unit of account was the silver real of which there were about 100 to the pound; 20 reales made one peso or dollar, the sum dispatched to Asturias in fact constituting 500,000 dollars.

·the other that she was struggling to roll back the advance of the French Revolution, and at the same time eliminate the economic challenge of a France on the brink of her own industrial revolution. The truth, of course, is far more complex. No more altruistic than any of the other powers, Britain certainly had no intention of liberating the whole of the Continent from French control. As for the *ancien régime*, she had long since abandoned any pretence that she was fighting for a Bourbon restoration. With French competition in industry and commerce, a worry that was chronic rather than acute, the fact was that, if he would only accept certain conditions, Napoleon had little to fear from Britain. What those conditions were had been decided at the time of the Treaty of Amiens in 1802. Even on the Rhine, France might have her natural frontiers, and that despite the fact that she would thereby retain hold of Belgium and part of Holland. Returned, too, would be most, if not all, of her colonies, whilst in principle, if Spain or any other country wished to establish an alliance with Paris, then there was nothing to stop them from doing so. And, above all, Napoleon could continue to rule France. What was intolerable, however, was the idea that he could simply trample the principles of legitimism and international law under foot. The agreement signed at Amiens had been thrown over, and since then state after state had been annexed to France or transformed into a Bonaparte-ruled satellite. By fighting France, then, Britain was seeking to curb Napoleon's power, and in Iberia she had in concrete terms no other aim than to restore the Bourbons and the Braganças to their respective thrones. This, of course, was not the whole story. From the start it was recognised that friendship with Spain and Portugal, and, in particular, access to their American empires, carried with it the possibility of immense commercial benefit. But in the end Napoleonic intervention in Iberia symbolised everything that Britain was fighting against: even had there been no insurrection in the Peninsula, retreat across the Pyrenees would still have figured heavily in British terms for a peace settlement.

Where, though, should the British army be sent? Troops were not welcome in Spain, but by the end of June fresh possibilities had come to light in Portugal. Although Portugal had been occupied without resistance, the presence of Napoleon's forces had, as we have seen, given rise to considerable unrest. By the summer of 1808 this had been greatly inflamed by hardship, for economic activity was largely at a standstill, whilst large numbers of servants had been thrown out of work by the flight of so many members of the propertied classes. In consequence, the Spanish revolt could not but destabilise the French position. First to move were the mountainous districts of Tras-os-Montes and Entre Douro e Minho left ungarrisoned by the departure of the Spanish forces from Oporto on 6 June. Oporto itself did not move – although a junta was formed under the governor, Luis de Oliveira, it did no more than seek to maintain order whilst sending secretly to Junot for assistance – but on 6 June Chaves was taken over by the people, to be followed in close succession by Braga, Vila Pouca, Bragança and Melgaço. Whether this movement amounted to anything more than a glorified *jacquerie* is unclear. In towns such as Bragança and Vila Nova de Foz Coa men of property were attacked as traitors, Jews, heretics or even witches, whilst in Arcos de Val de Vez the town hall was sacked, the archives burned, the price of basic foodstuffs fixed, the export of bread prohibited, the collection of debts suspended, and conscription, the tithes, the Church's fees for baptisms, weddings and funerals, and the feudal dues all ended. However, as the movement spread across the country – on 16 June it reached the Algarve, on 18 June Oporto, and on 24 June the Alentejo and Beira – the local notables were quick to seize control, their task much assisted by there being no trouble at all in some areas. In Oporto, for example:

The populace only wanted someone to appear that would invite them to rise in defiance of the present government. Such were found, and a cry of 'Viva o Principe!' spread like wildfire. Hundreds assembled in great confusion and fury. The torrent directed their steps towards the depots. Lock and key were no embarrassment . . . and all that thought proper supplied themselves with arms . . . The town, as may be supposed, continued in a state of the greatest fermentation . . . but at any rate such ardour is good. What is really extraordinary is that no accident has happened during these days of tumult and confusion. It was most natural to fear that some evil-disposed person might have taken advantage of such times, and satisfied private resentment with murder.[3]

Whatever the revolt's nature, it quickly gathered pace. Collaborators and Frenchmen were quickly rounded up, French detachments attacked (for example, at Faro and Mezao Frio), contact established with the British, and fresh armed forces emerged on the basis of veterans of the old army, civilian volunteers, the insurgent zone's units of provincial militia,* and the *ordenança*, which was an irregular home guard very much akin to the Catalan *somatén*. Indeed, there was even a new national government, the junta that had been formed in Oporto under the leadership of Archbishop Antonio de Sao José de Castro quickly securing the allegiance of the rest of the country.

The revolt, then, was not going to be overawed. As for Junot, he was in

---

* Consisting of forty-eight regiments, the militia was, as in Spain, a force of part-time conscripts mobilised in time of war.

trouble. Only in Lisbon and a few other such towns – Abrantes, Almeida, Elvas, Alcoutim and Vila Real do Santo Antonio – were the French present in reasonable force, whilst many even of these garrisons were clearly in danger of being starved into surrender. At any time, British troops might land somewhere on the coast; Lisbon was restless and excited; Junot was encumbered with several thousand Spanish prisoners; all communications with Spain had been cut; and no help was forthcoming from the powerful Russian fleet that happened to be moored in the Tagus.* What was to be done? Some consideration was given to the idea of marching for Spain, but Junot was unwilling to give up his dominions and fearful of what Napoleon would do if he retreated without a fight. The obvious alternative was to concentrate around Lisbon, but reaching the commanders of the various outlying detachments proved extremely difficult as many couriers were ambushed and murdered. However, by mid-July most of the detachments concerned had reached the capital, the only troops left behind being the garrisons of Elvas and Almeida. As the French had fallen back, they had also exacted a heavy toll of the insurgents: to the accompaniment of wholesale slaughter – General Loison, indeed, boasted that he had killed 4,000 of the insurgents in a few days – Beja and Guarda had been sacked, and many villages burned to the ground.

Terror solved nothing, however. Lisbon, for example, had already experi-enced a major panic in the course of the great Corpus Christi festivities: 'While the procession was walking, a great tumult arose . . . Legs and arms were broken. Poor ladies . . . with their clothes torn half off their backs were screaming for help; others fainting.'4 Whether this was the fruit of a plot to assassinate Junot, as the French alleged, is unclear, but far from abating, the excitement only grew. To quote Junot's wife, Laure:

Some months before, the Portuguese monks and priests had faked a number of miracles to influence the spirit of the people, and it was also put about that King Sebastian, who had died three centuries earlier in Africa, would return. Spread about by the clergy, these stupidities excited popular passions: the populace now gathered on Lisbon's highest points so as the better to see the arrival of the messiah-king, and crowds surrounded the statue of Joseph I, which had, it was said, turned about twice on its base. The result of this baseness was the murder of several Frenchmen.5

---

* Withdrawn from its Aegean base the previous autumn under the terms of the Treaty of Tilsit, this force had been on its way home via the Atlantic, but had put in to Lisbon for fear of British attack. Unfortunately for Junot, however, its commander, Dmitri Senyavin, was hostile to Alexander's alliance with France, and therefore refused to land the troops and cannon that the French general begged him for.

All this was not without its funny side – 'It was at that time that a miraculous chicken laid an equally miraculous egg . . . embossed with the words, "Death to the French!" '[6] – but, in Portugal as in Spain, the war was beginning to exhibit a savagery which was to mark it out from conflict in most of the rest of Europe at this time. Why this should have been the case is easy to understand. At the simplest level the invaders were frightened by the people, the rugged countryside, and their own crushing sense of isolation. They therefore sought security in the reign of terror that was in any case a standard tool of French occupation policy. Meanwhile, the French were convinced that they were representatives of the highest expression of European culture and civilisation: just as France had throughout the eighteenth century been at the forefront of art, literature, architecture and political philosophy, the Revolution had demonstrated the superior courage and intelligence of her inhabitants. Though they saw themselves as liberators, the French armies therefore affected an arrogance which only served to compound the vices – drunkenness, vandalism, licentiousness and plunder – characteristic of every army of the period, whilst in the Peninsula matters were made still worse by the fact that the inhabitants were regarded as little more than savages. This was in part a function of the primitive conditions typical of Spain and Portugal; in part, a function of their terrible poverty; and in part a function of the importance of the Catholic Church, the French armies being a confirmed refuge of the anti-clericalism that had marked the Revolution. Whether it was in their superstition, their love of bullfighting, or their willingness to engage in the most bloodthirsty atrocities, the inhabitants seemed truly beyond the pale. Given that they could also be argued to be in breach of the laws of war – civilians who engaged in armed combat forfeited all right to quarter – and were frequently in revolt against the entire social order, they could hardly expect the most gentle of treatment, and yet every act of repression merely inflamed their anger and encouraged the perpetration of further acts of barbarity.

Though horror crowded upon horror, the situation in Portugal remained a stalemate: whilst he dispatched sorties against the insurgents – both Leiria and Evora were sacked and their defenders massacred – Junot did not possess the strength to crush the rebellion; by the same token, meanwhile, lacking arms, ammunition and trained troops, the insurgents could not hope to evict the French from their central redoubt (indeed, they could hardly fight them at all: most of their pitchfork-wielding levies were unwilling to serve beyond the confines of their own districts). What tipped the balance was British intervention.

Portugal had not at first figured as an objective of the Portland administration. If only because of the huge interest in Asturias, Spain was
undoubtedly the government's preferred destination for its forces. Yet none
of the Spaniards were at this point asking for British troops, for Britain's
record of seizing Spanish territory made a British landing an extremely
sensitive issue. With the Junta of Oporto – now renamed the Junta do
Supremo Governo – clamouring for help, and the prospect of both neutralis-
ing Senyavin's Russian fleet and securing Lisbon's harbour dangling before
their eyes, it was not long before London had decided that the Cork division
was to sail for the Tagus, though its commander was also given leave to
embark on operations in Spain should opportunity offer.

The extraordinary discretion allowed to the British commander by his
government is testimony to the faith that was placed in him, it being here,
of course, that we first encounter the figure of the future Duke of Wellington,
Sir Arthur Wellesley. Born in Dublin on 1 May 1769 as the third son of a
family deeply embedded in the Anglo-Irish aristocracy, Wellesley was educated at Eton and in France, and in March 1787 he had entered the British
army as an ensign. Armed with money, patronage and dedication, the young
officer found advancement no difficulty: by September 1793 he was both a
lieutenant-colonel and a member of the Irish parliament. Sent to fight the
French in the campaigns in Flanders and Holland in 1793–95, he was so
disgusted by the mismanagement he witnessed that he briefly considered a
career in civil office, but failure to obtain the necessary preferment soon
made him abandon the idea in favour of service with his regiment in
India. A year after his arrival in the sub-continent, where his brother, Lord
Mornington (soon Marquess Wellesley), had just become Governor-General
of all Britain's extensive territories, war broke out with the Indian state of
Mysore, and by January 1799 Wellesley was in the field as, in effect, a corps
commander.

In considerable debt, Wellesley had been eager for war. At all events
India made his fortune. After playing a prominent role in the capture of
Seringapatam, he was made Governor of Mysore and spent two years
putting down a variety of opponents of British rule, before being given
command of the army eventually sent against the Mahratha Confederacy.
Now a major-general, the autumn of 1803 saw him win major victories at
Assaye and Argaon, and in the spring of 1805 he returned to England in
triumph, whereupon he was elected to the Commons. Command of a
brigade in the army sent to besiege Copenhagen in 1807 followed, as did
appointment as the Portland administration's Chief Secretary for Ireland,

and by 1808 Wellington had gained the friendship and respect of both Canning and Castlereagh, whilst he had also been made a lieutenant-general. A natural choice for the expedition to Venezuela, no attempt was made to remove him from the command when the decision was taken to switch it to the Peninsula. No sooner had Wellesley sailed from Cork on 12 July, however, than news arrived from Portugal that the French garrison there was much larger than had originally been reported. More troops would therefore be needed and so the Cabinet resolved to reinforce its initial contingent with the troops of Spencer and Moore (it had become clear that the Spaniards had no intention whatsoever of allowing the former to garrison Cádiz in the manner which the government had originally intended; as for the latter, relations with the Swedes having broken down, he was sailing for England in disgust). Given that a few other troops were also available in England, the whole force would amount to some 40,000 men, but this meant that Wellesley would have to relinquish command: still very junior, he was unacceptable to the Duke of York – the commander-in-chief – as head of an army of the size that the government was now envisaging. Probably for political reasons, the command was therefore offered to Lord Chatham, a senior general who had the post of Master General of the Ordnance in the Portland administration. Chatham proving unable to go out to Portugal immediately, Sir Hew Dalrymple was appointed interim commander, the latter then being given the much liked, amenable, highly experienced but not very bright Sir Harry Burrard as his deputy.

For all this, the government has been much criticised, but in fact it had a major problem on its hands in that the Duke of York wanted the command. Ever since the operations in Flanders in 1793–95, the duke had enjoyed the confidence of neither Parliament nor public, and yet he could be passed over only in favour of an extremely senior general. Hence the choice of Chatham, who was also almost certainly being seriously considered as a replacement for the elderly and ineffectual Duke of Portland. Why, however, the need for Dalrymple and Burrard? Admirers of Sir John Moore have suggested that their sole purpose was to block their hero from gaining the command. In some ways the idea is not so implausible, for Moore was not the paragon of legend, but rather a very difficult character, scornful of politicians, impatient of the civil power, and convinced that he had been cheated of his rightful glory. Opinionated, vain and highly strung, he was also much given to intrigue and complaint and had strong connections with the Whigs, whilst he seems to have been especially disliked by Canning. Yet in the end none of this affected the government's thinking. Aside from there being no reason to think ill of Chatham, Dalrymple and Burrard, Dalrymple in particular had greater first-hand knowledge of the Peninsula than anyone else in the British army, good contacts with Castaños, and so far had managed things extremely well, whilst Burrard, too, brought some useful qualities with him, even if it was only a talent for smoothing ruffled feathers.

What, though, of Wellesley? Only discovering his supersession some days prior to his troops' arrival in Portugal, he was much aggrieved, but affected an icy dignity, promising that he would not precipitate action with the enemy in the hope of winning glory for himself. However, this was precisely what he was being encouraged to do. Unable to keep him in command, Castlereagh hinted that he should press on with operations in the little time left to him before Dalrymple or Burrard could reach Portugal, whilst the former was told in no uncertain terms that he should give Wellesley the most prominent role in operations that he could. In some ways this support is surprising, for Wellesley was in practice little more likeable than Moore. Though he might shun ostentation and bombast, a mixture of shyness, intellectual arrogance and aristocratic hauteur had produced a demeanour that was at best curt and distant, and at worst intolerant of human frailty and capable of great injustice. Even less attractive, meanwhile, was his habit of seeking scapegoats for his frustrations in a manner that took little account of reality, whilst he was devoted to the noose, the lash and the punishment parade, contemptuous of notions of democracy and political progress, obsessed with the concept of order, and inclined to regard the mob – and, by extension, his soldiers – with a mixture of fear, contempt and loathing. Yet all his faults could not also conceal the key fact that he was a military genius. As was apparent from his achievements in India, his icy manner reflected a cool detachment that allowed him constantly to outthink the enemy, to get the best out of any ground, and to maximise the strong points of his own forces. Also helpful was a forte for logistics and an eye for detail. Liked he may not have been, but respect and confidence he inspired in abundance.

Having sailed from Cork on 12 July, Wellesley outpaced the rest of his convoy and made for La Coruña to confer with the insurgent authorities. From them he gathered that his troops would be neither needed nor welcome in northern Spain – the Junta was full of news of imaginary Spanish victories and insistent that the situation was well in hand. Receiving firm news of the revolt in northern Portugal, he in consequence decided to try his hand there instead. The Junta of Oporto proving all too eager for British assistance – it was short of men and arms alike – by 1 August Wellesley's division was disembarking in Mondego Bay, halfway between Oporto and Lisbon, being joined there a few days later by the forces of Sir Brent Spencer. By this time, Wellesley had received the orders subordinating him to Dalrymple and Burrard, but until their arrival he remained in command. Faithful to his promises that he would not act precipitately, he spent over a week readying his forces for the campaign – in particular, it was necessary to gather in large numbers of draught animals, pack mules and baggage wagons – but on 9 August he marched southwards with over fourteen thousand men organised in six brigades. With him, however, there were only three of the five batteries of artillery available, the other two having been left behind for want of horses, together with a third of the only cavalry regiment that had been attached to his command.

Overcoming such logistical difficulties was to prove one of the greatest problems that Wellesley was to face in Spain and Portugal. Another such problem was his relations with the local authorities. Whilst the Junta of Oporto and its military commander, Bernardino Freire, did provide his forces with considerable numbers of mules and carts, they also made extravagant demands for arms and supplies and allegedly seized food intended for the British. For the time being, however, such problems were overshadowed by the question of fighting the French. With 26,000 men rather than the 18,000 estimated by the British, Junot had enough troops to take the offensive. Thus, whilst a small division was sent out under General Delaborde to slow down the British advance, the French commander organised a powerful striking force. Many troops were left to garrison Lisbon, but even so 13,000 men had soon been gathered together to attack the British, who were steadily advancing southwards parallel with the coast. Already, however, the first shots of the British campaign in the Peninsula had been fired: an advance guard of riflemen had clashed with a French outpost at Obidos on 15 August, whilst Delaborde made a stand near the village of Roliça two days later. Intent on fighting a delaying action, the French general was manoeuvred out of his first position without difficulty, but one of the columns sent against his second position attacked prematurely, the British losing nearly five hundred casualties before driving Delaborde from the field. It had been a sharp fight:

We rapidly approached the field of battle, and found a difficulty at first getting within range. The hills on which the enemy were posted were high, and too perpendicular to attempt a direct ascent. Our staff officers, however, discovered certain chasms or openings, made . . . by the rain, up which we were led . . . the enemy playing upon us all the time . . . Our Colonel . . . said, 'Charge'; we did so, but I could go no further, having received a wound in my leg . . . Captain Culley . . . was wounded in both legs. Serjeant Hill . . . was . . . wounded in the head.[7]

Roliça, though, was a mere overture, albeit one that gave cause for reflection. In the words of a soldier who arrived in the Peninsula some time later:

The personal enmity to Napoleon, and the violent party prejudices in England, were so great, that the most absurd stories of the want of order and valour of his troops gained immediate credence there, and many of the English army believed that they had but to show themselves, and the French would fly. The bravery with which their attack was met . . . was a matter of great surprise.[8]

Much more serious was the battle that took place at the coastal village of Vimeiro on 21 August. Wellesley had come down to the sea to pick up two brigades of reinforcements, and it was here that Junot chose to attack him in the hope that his army could be trapped and destroyed. In this, he was to be disappointed. By the time that the French attacked, the reinforcements had already disembarked, and Wellesley had posted his troops on several hills that encompassed Vimeiro and were in part protected by a deep ravine. It was a good position. In the words of one participant:

The village of Vimeiro stands in a valley . . . at the eastern end of a high mountainous range which extends westwards to the sea. In front of the village is a hill of inferior altitude, terminating in a plateau of considerable extent . . . On the left is another strong ridge of heights, stretching to the eastward, and terminating on the right in a deep ravine.[9]

By 1808, meanwhile, a British army on the defensive was no laughing matter, a series of measures having been taken that were designed to take the edge off French assaults. How the latter were delivered varied considerably, but a common feature was their employment of a very heavy screen of skirmishers – infantrymen who fought spread out in open order, made such use as they could of cover, and took their time with regard to loading and firing. Such men could inflict heavy losses on a defending force and spread confusion by picking off key officers, but were very difficult to deal with by traditional close-order troops. Realising this, the British had greatly increased the number of skirmishers which they could deploy themselves. Thus, by 1808 in the guards and line infantry each battalion possessed a light company that was specifically trained for skirmish operations, and every 'centre' company a number of sharpshooters. Several battalions were also armed with rifles rather than muskets and two regiments of light infantry supposedly could fight in their entirety in open order.* As yet the system was not developed systematically or to its fullest extent, but already the basic idea had sunk in: French attacks were to be confronted with a strong force of skirmishers that could keep their light troops away from the defending line and slow down the progress of the attack, thereby exposing the attackers to the ravages of long-range artillery fire for a longer period (not that the British were strong in this respect: for logistical reasons, until late in the war their cannon were fewer in numbers and much lighter than those of the French).

Nor was this an end to the matter. However strong, gallant and well-trained, no skirmish screen could possibly hope to hold out for ever. Sooner or later, then, the French would come within musket range of the defenders who would invariably be arrayed in a two-deep line (despite misconceptions to the contrary, the British also sometimes used columnar formations, just as the French sometimes used line, but in the British army it was very rare for any other formation than the line to be used on the defensive). According to the traditional account, what then happened was that the attackers would be struck down by a hail of musketry, the British infantry firing volley after volley until the French were brought to a halt and forced to flee, but it is now thought that the preferred technique was rather to fire a single volley, cheer and then charge forward with the bayonet. Yet in the last resort the result was the same: the British infantry had evolved a series of procedures that, when coupled with Wellesley's habitual use of the reverse slope of hills to hide his troops till the last minute, made them an exceedingly dangerous enemy.

Outnumbered as he was, Junot's only hope was probably to stake everything on a single massive assault, but he instead chose to split his forces, sending some of his troops to circle round the British position from the east whilst himself assaulting Wellesley's left flank, which rested on the village of Vimeiro. To reach the latter, the French had first to conquer the isolated hill in front of the village. However, covered with vineyards and pine trees and held by some of Moore's best troops, including all his riflemen and light infantrymen, this proved a difficult objective. In the words of one rifle officer:

---

* Most British infantry regiments had one or two battalions, each of which had ten companies (one grenadier, eight centre and one light in guards and line units). As in all other armies, most men were armed with muzzle-loading, flintlock, smoothbore muskets which were deadly *en masse* but notoriously inaccurate as individual weapons. Rifles, by contrast, were slower to fire, but, thanks to special loading techniques and grooved barrels, much more accurate and possessed of a much longer range.

The night before the battle I belonged to a picket of about 200 riflemen . . . We were posted in a large pine wood . . . About eight o'clock in the morning . . . a cloud of light troops, supported by a heavy column of infantry, entered the wood, and, assailing the pickets with great impetuosity, obliged us to fall back for support on the Ninety-Seventh Regiment. As soon as we had got clear of the front of the Ninety-Seventh . . . that regiment poured in such a well-directed fire that it staggered the resolution of the hostile column, which declined to close . . . with them. About the same time the second battalion of the Fifty-Second, advancing through the wood, took the French in flank, and drove them before them in confusion. On the pickets being driven in, I joined my own brigade, which was on the left of the Ninety-Seventh. Here the business was beginning to assume a serious aspect. Some heavy masses of infantry, preceded by a swarm of light troops, were advancing with great resolution . . . In spite of the deadly fire which several hundred riflemen kept up on them, they continued to press forward . . . until the old Fiftieth Regiment received them with a destructive volley, following it instantly with a most brilliant . . . charge with the bayonet, which broke . . . in utter dismay and confusion this column.[10]

Two attacks were beaten off with ease in this fashion, and the French suffered heavy casualties: 'I saw regular lanes torn through their ranks as they advanced . . . and we pelted away upon them like a shower of leaden hail.'[11] At the same time, a desperate attempt to outflank the hill was put to flight by a number of units that had been in reserve, the discomfiture of the French being completed by a sudden charge by Wellesley's handful of dragoons (although, in a fault typical of British cavalry throughout the war, the latter proceeded to get out of control and ride into the very midst of the French position where they were in turn crushed by Junot's cavalry reserve).

Whilst the defenders of Vimeiro and its hill had thus been standing firm, Wellesley had been marching most of the rest of his troops across their rear to counter Junot's turning movement. Ascending the heights in the British commander's left rear at two different points, the troops concerned – a mere two brigades – therefore ran into overwhelming numbers of redcoats and were routed after a sharp fight whose most notable element was again the British use of 'shock' tactics rather than firepower. Short of mounted troops, the British were unable to derive all the profit from their successes that they might have done, but even so more than two thousand Frenchmen had been killed, wounded or taken prisoner, whilst Junot had also lost over half his cannon.

Secured at the moderate cost of only 720 casualties, Vimeiro had been a fine achievement, which had been strongly suggestive both of Wellesley's skills as a general and the potential of the British infantry. To Wellesley's fury, however, a much greater triumph was thrown away. The French were in total disarray and Junot, whose behaviour in the action had been so odd as to give rise to charges that he was either drunk or suffering from a touch of the sun, in a state of moral collapse. Had a general advance been ordered the result must have been total disaster. But Wellesley's period of grace had run out, for the reinforcements had been accompanied by Sir Harry Burrard. Not landing until after the action had begun, the latter made no attempt to interfere in the repulse of Junot, but an advance was a different matter, and, despite Wellesley's pleas, he refused to sanction the slightest forward movement, believing, first, that Wellesley was a distinctly rash commander who had only risen to prominence because of his political connections, and, second, that the French were receiving reinforcements.

Thanks to Burrard, Junot was allowed to get off in good order. Yet the French situation remained extremely serious: the army was badly shaken; the British were known to be expecting further reinforcements; the insurgent forces were closing in; and the Lisbon crowd was restive and excited. Although the British still failed to move, on 22 August Junot therefore resolved to try for a capitulation on terms that would see the French returned home by sea. Whether Junot was actually expecting to be able to brazen things out is not apparent, but the fact is that his ploy was astonishingly successful. The day after the battle, Dalrymple had also appeared. Mistrustful of Wellesley and angry at the terms of his appointment, he was also discouraged by the army's transport problems, inclined to downplay the effects of Vimeiro, and convinced that the French could hold their own. Thus it was that Dalrymple vetoed the march on Lisbon proposed by Wellesley – a march which incidentally stood a good chance of trapping Junot's beaten army – and greeted the arrival of the French emissaries with some relief (according to Madame Junot, the general sent to open negotiations even heard him whisper to Burrard, 'We are not in a very good situation; let us hear him').[12] Thus it was, too, that, after a lengthy series of discussions, the main points of the French proposals were all accepted. Junot and his men were to be embarked for a French port in British ships and allowed to depart without having to lay down their arms even in form, whilst they were permitted to take with them their cannon, baggage and personal possessions. Their civilian supporters and collaborators – both French and Portuguese – were guaranteed life, liberty and property and permitted to take ship with Junot if they so wished. Included in the capitulation were not just Junot's field army and the garrison of Lisbon, but also the forces holding Almeida and Elvas. All that the French had to promise in return was to leave the fortifications they occupied intact, to leave behind any cannons they had seized from the Portuguese army, and to free all their prisoners.

Known as the Convention of Sintra, these terms caused considerable controversy. Already smarting at the fact that the French had been granted an armistice without any reference to their own representatives, the Portuguese were infuriated by the generosity of the terms Junot had been granted, matters being made still worse by the French interpreting 'personal property' as including a wide variety of loot, and in general adopting the most arrogant of attitudes. For example:

I proceeded to Lisbon . . . where I saw the French army . . . An extraordinary sight it was, for they had their standards displayed in the square of Belem with as much *sangfroid* as if they had been the victorious army, and had dictated the agreements.[13]

Setting aside these issues, even the military aspects of the convention were questionable. No attempt was made to stipulate that Junot's troops should not be employed again in Spain or Portugal, for example, or to insist that they should at least be deprived of their much needed horses and draught animals.

Sintra, in short, was a serious embarrassment: despite frantic attempts to force the French to disgorge their plunder, the Portuguese were furious, Porter, for example, writing of how they 'stood staring at each other as if uncertain of whether a mine or one of their old earthquakes had sprung under their feet', and Warre that 'the mob would have . . . destroyed the homes of everybody connected with the French, and even now, if a French deserter or spy . . . is found, the cry of "He Frances" is enough, unless some English are near, to have him murdered'.[14] Nor was the army much better pleased: according to Morley, the convention 'crushed every hope and withered every laurel'.[15] Yet there was little doubt that it was in principle defensible. In the wake of Dalrymple and Burrard's blunders, indeed, sensible observers recognised that it was genuinely attractive. As Leach wrote:

The aspect . . . of affairs was totally changed . . . when the flag of truce came in. The enemy then had possession of all the defensible positions between us and Lisbon, independent of the citadel and different forts near the capital. This would have enabled General Junot to protract the contest for a length of time, whilst the game of the British clearly was to root out their opponents with as little delay as possible . . . not only on account of the lateness of the season, but because the presence of our army would be desirable in Spain.[16]

Such, however, was not the way in which the agreement was seen in England. In the wake of Bailén, what was expected was great victories, whilst the first news that had reached the country gave the unfortunate impression that Junot had surrendered altogether. The result was a storm of protest. From the king downwards, almost every sector of public opinion was appalled at the opportunity that appeared to have been thrown away, and on 21 September Dalrymple was recalled to London to account for his conduct (Burrard, by contrast, was allowed for the time being to remain in Portugal as caretaker commander, though he too went home once Moore had arrived to replace him). A few days earlier, meanwhile, an equally disgusted Wellesley had himself sailed for home on the pretext afforded by the death of his deputy in the post of Chief Secretary for Ireland.

In view of the furore it might have been thought that this would have been the end of Wellesley's career. In a bitter denunciation of the convention, for example, the poet, William Wordsworth, wrote that he was 'utterly unworthy of the station in which he had been placed'; that 'he magnified himself and his achievements'; and that 'here was a man, who, having not any fellow feeling with the people he had been commissioned to aid, could not know where their strength lay, and therefore could not turn it to account'.[17] To make matters worse, Dalrymple had done his best to imply that the convention was in large part Wellesley's responsibility, whilst the Wellesley clan's many enemies were determined to exploit the situation for all it was worth. Disappointed though they were, however, Castlereagh and, rather less willingly, Canning upheld his cause, whilst he was also warmly received by George III. As for the court of enquiry that was convened by the government, the report that it issued on 22 December could be read as exonerating him altogether. In consequence, Wellesley survived the crisis in good enough order to have hopes of another army. Not so Dalrymple and Burrard, both of whom were damned with such faint praise as to make it clear that they could never be offered a command again, the former in addition being severely reprimanded by the government.

Despite the controversy, the Sintra affair posed no threat to continued British involvement in the Peninsula. In so far as the situation there was concerned, by 18 September the bulk of the French forces in Portugal had taken ship for France, the only exception being the garrisons of Almeida and Elvas, which, blockaded by Portuguese forces on the one hand and Spanish ones on the other, had to be rescued by detachments of British troops. Also dealt with was the Russian squadron, which surrendered on terms that saw its men sent back to Russia, and its ships impounded in Britain. Meanwhile, Lisbon had been occupied amidst scenes of general rejoicing:

At length, when . . . the national flag of Portugal once again waved on the citadel . . . there was such a combination of *vivas*, sky-rockets, ringing of bells, singing, dancing, screeching, crying, laughing . . . embracing in the streets . . . as must render every attempt at description hopeless.[18]

In control was a new regency created from three members of the original council left behind by João, two representatives of a list of possible substitutes drawn up by the prince, and two representatives of the Portuguese resistance movement, including the Bishop of Oporto. As for the British army, it had now been swelled by the troops of Sir John Moore, who had also replaced Dalrymple (who had left for London on 3 October).

With Portugal settled, the British could once again turn their attentions to Spain. Contact with the new Spanish government had established that a British army would now be welcome, but autumn had brought a change to British attitudes to the Peninsula. On the one hand Sintra had shattered the political consensus of June 1808, for Whigs and radicals were naturally inclined to make use of it as a means of overthrowing the Portland administration. On the other the government had become increasingly irritated with the Spaniards. Not least of the reasons was the ever more importunate demands of the Spanish missions to London. To these petitions the British had responded with considerable generosity – the Asturians alone received £350,000 in specie, 9,000 shirts, 10,000 pairs of shoes, 6,000 packs, 26 cannon, 20,000 muskets, 14,000 pikes, 12,000 swords, 1,600 pistols, 1,080 barrels of powder, 2,752,155 musket cartridges, 18,600 artillery charges, and 2,500 camp kettles, whilst the total of the money sent to the various juntas amounted to £1,100,000 – but the various liaison officers and military missions which they had dispatched to the Peninsula or otherwise succeeded in attaching to the Spanish armies had begun to send back news of a most alarming sort. If the various juntas that headed the Spanish revolt could not be faulted in their commitment to the struggle, it was all too apparent that they tended to regard it in a most parochial fashion, their sole concern being the protection of their own provinces. Thus, such levies as they managed to raise were often kept at home, while in many cases attempts were also made to lay hands upon such forces of the regular army as happened to be found within their borders. As for the aid supplied by the British, it, too, was being hoarded for the use of the provinces in which it had been disembarked. To make matters worse, the juntas were experiencing considerable difficulties in organising any sort of war effort and imposing their authority.

Had the Spaniards been more honest in their accounts of what was going on the situation might have been more acceptable, but it was becoming apparent that they were either living in a fool's paradise or guilty of deliberate deceit. Bailén, true, had been a great victory, but it had not, as we shall see, been followed up: the various Spanish authorities were bitterly at odds with one another, a new central government was only just beginning to take shape, and there was no commander-in-chief of any sort. In consequence, the dispatches of Britain's liaison officers made dramatic reading. To quote Phillip Roche, for example, the provincial juntas were 'not only quarrelling with each other about idle privileges and pre-eminences, but . . . occupying a large portion of their time in very futile discussions', whilst for William Parker Carroll, the juntas were 'solely activated by narrow-minded, short-sighted policy, never extending their views beyond the precincts of their respective districts'.[19] Equally, from Seville William Cox complained, 'The recent successes of their army, the ostentatious reception of the conqueror, and the pompous celebration of their victories are circumstances which . . . have tended much to strengthen the idea conceived of by this junta of their supposed superiority.'[20] Still worse:

This junta have shown too evident signs of a wish to aggrandize themselves and a disinclination to afford those aids to other provinces which they have had it in their power to grant not to afford just grounds of suspicion that their boasted loyalty and patriotism have at times been mixed with unworthy considerations of self-interest and personal advantage. They are every day making promotions in the army without much attention to merit, and giving away employments . . . which they really have no right to dispose of.[21]

Though relying on the Spaniards would clearly be most unwise, the question still arose of what should be done with the British expeditionary force. Galicia, Asturias and the Basque provinces having from the very beginning of the war been an object of the government's attentions, it was only natural that they should now resurface as a possible theatre of operations, and all the more so as the Asturians were requesting the dispatch of a large force of cavalry. This, for many reasons, was neither possible nor desirable, whilst only slightly less unrealistic was Castlereagh's pet scheme for a rapid descent on Bilbao in an attempt to cut off the French retreat from Madrid. So rapid was the French flight to the Ebro, however, that the Secretary of State's scheme was out of date almost as soon as it was committed to paper, and it was eventually agreed that the army should be concentrated on the borders of Galicia and León preparatory to assisting in the expulsion of the French from Spain. Exactly what assisting in the expulsion of the French meant was left to the discretion of its commander, however, and in this respect it was unfortunate that the man who now occupied that post was Sir John Moore.

One of the heroes of the traditional British version of the Peninsular War, Moore has invariably received favourable treatment at the hands of its chroniclers. As we have already seen, however, there was another side to the story. Moore was a difficult character on extremely poor terms with the government, which he blamed for the misfortunes and indignities that he had experienced in the course of his abortive mission to Sweden.* Further angered by a variety of other circumstances – he felt, for instance, that he had been treated very casually on his return from Sweden and resented not being given the Spanish command straight away – he was also openly scornful of Castlereagh's military plans, deeming them 'plausible verbose nonsense' and 'a sort of gibberish'.[22] The ministry liking him no more than he liked the ministry, it is therefore somewhat surprising that he got the command at all, but there was nothing else to be done, Chatham still not being ready to take the field.

Although Moore's differences with the government were to have an unfortunate influence in the subsequent campaign, the Portland administration was doing everything that it could to ensure success. Not the least of its concerns was to unite Patriot Spain under a single political and military authority. As early as 20 August 1808 Castlereagh was urging Dalrymple to take such steps as he could to secure the appointment of a commander-in-chief, whilst the failure of the Spaniards to make such an appointment led not only to formal protests but suggestions that the Spanish generals should be persuaded to operate in accordance with a common plan drawn up for them by the British. As for the question of political authority, the parochialism of the provincial juntas was countered by threats of the withdrawal of support and the very same day that Dalrymple was ordered to press for a Spanish commander-in-chief, the juntas' representatives in London were informed that no further aid would be forthcoming until their masters had formed a new central government.

How far British pressure was instrumental in the formation of the body – the Junta Suprema Central – that eventually supplied this want is unclear, but in one respect at least the British did succeed in making a substantial contribution to the Spanish cause. As will be recalled, in 1807 a sizeable Spanish force had been sent to assist the *grande armée*. After taking part in the siege of the Swedish fortress of Stralsund, this body had been cantoned

---

* Events in Sweden make for a complex story, but, in brief, they culminated in Moore being forced to flee Stockholm in disguise.

in Denmark, which was now at war with both Britain and Sweden. Scattered through the Danish archipelago, far from home and interspersed with considerable numbers of Dutch, French and Danish troops, there had appeared little risk that the 14,000 men involved would cause much trouble, but to make doubly certain the greatest efforts were made to encourage loyalty to the emperor and prevent them hearing of events in Spain. Thus, it was not until 24 June that their commander, the Marqués de la Romana, was finally informed of the accession of Joseph Bonaparte. What then happened is a matter of some conjecture, but La Romana was eventually persuaded to seek the help of the British squadron that was blockading the Belgian coast, and after much careful planning it was arranged that all the troops in the division should revolt and make for a safe refuge from which they could be evacuated. Things did not go entirely according to plan – several units were disarmed or forced to surrender – but between 7 and 11 August 9,000 troops were concentrated on the island of Langeland. Some delay then ensued, but the Spaniards were safe enough and on 21 August they embarked on British ships and put to sea, finally disembarking at Santander on 11 October.

Thus ended the British role in what may broadly be defined as the heroic period of the Peninsular War. Immense quantities of material and financial aid had been supplied to the Spanish and Portuguese insurgents; Portugal had been liberated at minimal cost; the army had given substantial proof of its tactical efficiency; a reasonable plan had been reached with regard to the support that should be given to the Spanish armies in the fresh fighting that seemed likely to ensue before the close of the year; and the bulk of La Romana's division was rescued from Denmark. At the same time Britain had been able to act with speed and efficacy, whilst it had succeeded in securing considerable influence in Portugal and Spain alike: had not both countries apparently acceded to British demands that they should establish new central governments, for example? In short, the British government could feel well pleased: Sintra might have been both a disappointment and an embarrassment, but its favourite and most trusted general had emerged from the furore if not unscathed then at least not so damaged as to prevent him from being employed in the future, whilst there seemed little doubt that the ripples that it had caused in Britain and Portugal alike would soon be smoothed away.

In practice, however, the situation was by no means so rosy. The dispatch of so many troops to Portugal had ensured that there would be a considerable delay before operations could commence in Spain. There were also serious problems with the Spaniards: inherent in the sudden Spanish interest in

British troops, for example, lay the desire not just to receive assistance but also to obtain command over them. Equally a desire was beginning to emerge amongst the British to further their influence in Spain or even to impose their own political solutions. With the British army in the hands of an officer who was not only highly ambitious but deeply frustrated, at odds with the ministry, notoriously suspicious of the government's representatives abroad, and possessed of a prickly disposition, trouble was certain, and all the more so given the thunderbolt that was in preparation across the River Ebro.

5

Somosierra

The line of mountains loomed dark in the mist, their summits shrouded in cloud. Ahead of the French army the highroad disappeared into a deep cleft in the hills, the precipitous slopes of which were covered with scrub and boulders. From the defile there came the sound of heavy fighting, whilst it was apparent that the advance had been stalled. Spurring forward into the defile at the head of his staff, the emperor surveyed the scene through his telescope. Turning to one of his aides-de-camp, he ordered that the way should be cleared by the squadron of Polish light horse that was serving as his personal bodyguard. Utterly astonished, several of the officers around the emperor protested that the task was impossible, but Napoleon was adamant: the Poles would charge. Joined by the aide-de-camp who had carried the fatal message, in a few moments they were clattering towards the Spanish positions. Assailed by the fire of sixteen cannon, the cavalrymen within a matter of seconds lost half their strength, and had to fall back. Rallied by General Montbrun, however, they returned to the charge and this time were successful. The men serving the guns died to a man, the rest of the Spaniards fled, and the French were left to resume their march. With neither troops nor defensible positions left between the emperor and Madrid, the war seemed almost over.

The action fought at the pass of Somosierra on 30 November 1808 marked the culmination of a dramatic campaign that had seen the French army more than avenge Bailén. The Spanish armies had been swept aside, whilst the emperor had reached the very gates of Madrid. At the heart of this situation, it has often been argued, was the influence of Bailén. All over Patriot Spain men of letters, priests and office-seekers were continuing to rush into print to legitimise the rising against Napoleon, advance their own solutions to Spain's problems, awaken popular enthusiasm for the struggle, and obtain official favour. Whilst newspapers and broadsides carrying highly coloured accounts of the fighting appeared on all sides, they were supplemented by hundreds of proclamations, poems and pamphlets. In all this literature the message was the same: Spanish heroism had triumphed over the 'conquerors of the world'. Napoleon was claimed to be in an agony of terror and remorse; victories invented where none had taken place; Spanish defeats played down or even denied altogether; and foolish rumours of all sorts given the greatest credence. In all this, a considerable part was played by the anti-militarism that had become a commonplace feature of Spain's intellectual milieu. As a good example here one might cite the immense attention lavished on the famous *garrochistas* who had fought at Bailén. A mere handful of men, these lance-wielding cattle herders had played only a minor role in the fighting, and yet were the heroes of the hour.

For a good account of the excited atmosphere that prevailed at this time, we have only to turn to Robert Brindle of the English College:

Every place resounded with acclamation of victory and there was scarcely one Spaniard who did not already imagine their troops at the gates of Paris, and Bonaparte tottering on his throne. Such, indeed, was the enthusiasm that if any feared another eruption from the French, it would have been looked upon as treason to express such fears. This state of affairs continued for two or three months during which time not one unpleasant tiding was permitted to reach our ears ... We reposed great confidence in the Spanish army and ... as we heard for some time no song but the song of victory, we were unwilling to change our tune.[1]

The results were most unfortunate. Never enthusiastic about going to war, the Spaniards in effect were told that they did not have to, whilst the authorities were persuaded that they could let sleeping dogs lie rather than press conscription too hard. Meanwhile, a climate had been created that could not but encourage a determination to exploit the rising for selfish ends. Thus, many local notables proved quite barefaced in their corruption and maladministration. Although other instances may be found – for example, the formation of new regiments for no better reason than to provide commissions for relatives, clients and adherents of all sorts – nowhere was this more the case than with regard to conscription. Reports of the protection of *pudientes*, relatives, friends, allies and dependants and of the acceptance of bribes are therefore numerous – in Granada the cost of exemption was between 300 and 400 reales – whilst rackets of all types abounded. In the words of one petition, for example, 'In this town [Vivero] ... the men of power and influence have managed to escape from a charge which should be general. Some have gained exemption on the grounds that they are nobles [and] others on grounds that they are officials'.[2] Equally, 'Half of those who are called up are allowed to go free, some thanks to money, others thanks to blackmail, and still others thanks to a thousand different tricks and frauds.'[3] And finally, 'In many provinces the quota has still not been achieved ... nor will it be achieved, because the chief inhabitants, who should have offered their sons straight away, have had them exempted as nobles ... In the province of Cuenca all the towns are full of young men, but, what with bribes and blackmail ... those who do not want to go stay at home.'[4]

With money, indeed, it was even possible to play at being a soldier without ever having to experience the rigours of life in the field. Particularly important here were the numerous corps of 'distinguished volunteers' that sprang up all over Patriot Spain. Thus, in exchange for paying the cost of their uniform and equipment, men could enlist in units whose only duties were to mount guard on city walls, inject civic life with a certain degree of military pomp, add a degree of lustre to the new authorities, and maintain the prerogatives of the propertied classes. Hardly surprisingly, these units soon acquired an evil reputation. The Voluntarios Distinguidos de Cádiz – a force later lauded to the skies by liberals eager to find a model for a new army – was described as 'battalions of cupids' composed of 'a multitude of infamous men of evil habits who ... possess neither merit, nor subordination, nor inclination to the true object for which their arms were created'.[5] As for the Junta Central's personal guard – the grandiloquently named Voluntarios de Honor de la Universidad de Toledo – it was written:

If it is wished in part to put things right ... these soldiers who call themselves the Estudiantes de Toledo ... should be expelled from the city. Your Majesty has no idea of the ... ruin that they are causing ... There is not a married woman who because of them has not fallen out with her husband, not a widow who has not emptied her house to take up with them, not a maiden who has not abandoned father and honour at their instigation ... They have neither king nor religion, and recognise no difference between day and night, both of which they spend in the tavern.[6]

Sparing of their sons, the wealthy were equally parsimonious when it came to the subject of their riches. Often giving little themselves, they rather sought to coerce donations from their dependants and social inferiors whilst at the same time ensuring that the cost of the war was by one means or another passed on to the populace. Indeed, the juntas were widely accused of corruption: the Junta of Granada was reputed to have stolen at least 5 million reales, whilst of the Junta of Córdoba it was written that every evening it was 'wasting on dinners what the poor give for the army'.[7] Much of the money made by the juntas came from bribes – the secretary of the Junta of Galicia, for example, was accused of having obtained up to

1,600,000 reales in this fashion – but there are also reports of the juntas engaging in an *ad hoc* programme of *desamortización* that saw the sale of both common lands and the properties of the Church.

All this could not have been more unfortunate. If the populace had taken to the streets in May 1808, it was at best with a view to protecting themselves (there was a strong belief that the Dos de Mayo had been the result of a premeditated attempt to massacre the citizens of Madrid). Beyond that, what mattered was avenging themselves on their social superiors and, in particular, all those groups who had enriched themselves under Godoy: very soon, warned one writer, 'the sovereign power will have been taken over by the poor, and these will exterminate the rich and the French alike'.[8] Whilst the accession of Fernando VII had been greeted with great excitement, and his overthrow genuine dismay, this did not mean that the people were devoted to the new monarch *per se*. On the contrary, as one perceptive British officer noted of the Spanish peasantry, 'had they been permitted to live in peace, it would have been a matter of the greatest indifference to them whether their king was Joseph, Ferdinand or the ghost of Don Quijote'.[9] With Fernando having been presented as a kind of 'Prince Charming' who would put all things right and usher in a golden age of peace and prosperity, the people's real loyalty was rather to a Spain in which they would no longer be subject to the demands of Church, State and *señor*. Willing enough though they were to riot against *godoyismo*, they had no desire to fight the French, and all the more so as military service had always been particularly hated. Try though Patriot propaganda might to emphasise the brutality of the *grande armée* or Napoleon's greed for foreign manpower, there was, meanwhile, no disguising the fact that *los de siempre* were still in control, nor, for that matter, the anger of the populace. Thus:

The Junta . . . of Ciudad Real . . . is not the work of . . . the people . . . Its members are Godoys, traitors, egoists and thieves who clubbed together so that the people would . . . not get at their money. From Infantes, Manzanares and Madridejos come documents that show . . . the injustices . . . that they have been perpetrating . . . The province is scandalized, for everybody knows that they are malignant rogues.[10]

With the French absent from most of Spain and Patriot propaganda insistent that victory was a foregone conclusion, the consequences were easy to predict. Volunteers came forward, certainly, but in smaller numbers than have generally been represented, whilst enlistment was clearly influenced by the payment of substantial bounties, pressure on the part of masters or landlords, and the fact that early summer was a time when many day labourers could find no work. As early as 31 May 1808 the Junta of Seville was complaining that many recruits were in practice unwilling to serve, and, further, that even the regular army was experiencing serious desertion. Meanwhile, no sooner were the new regiments, formed in the wake of the uprising, confronted with the prospect of being marched off to fight the French than the troops began to desert in droves. Draft evasion was also common: 'Married men being then exempt from the contributions required to fill up the ranks', noted the British officer, John Patterson, 'all the youthful fellows in the neighbourhood espoused themselves in order to avoid the Junta's levies.'[11]

Patriot Spain therefore began to experience precisely the same problems visible in Revolutionary and Napoleonic France. Large numbers of men fled their homes for mountains, cities, neighbouring provinces or even other countries. 'In this city', complained the Junta of Santiago, 'the young men who have been conscripted into the army can often be heard complaining of the large number of their fellows who have fled to . . . Portugal in order to avoid being enlisted.'[12]* Everywhere such men mingled with groups who were already living on the margins of society. Joined by many refugees from the Spanish armies, such men had little option but to turn to banditry. 'From experience', wrote one anonymous Galician memorialist, 'it has become clear . . . that the thieving deserters who infest the highways have become so numerous that it is impossible to go from one house to the next.'[13] Nor was Galicia the only area affected. From the vicinity of Cádiz one government agent reported that the whole area was swarming with 'bad Spaniards, who, having either deserted or fled from being enlisted, have necessarily become thieves and wrongdoers, robbing passers-by . . . sacking farms, and [oppressing] the [inhabitants] with more inhumanity than the . . . French'.[14]

A problem that was to dog the Allies throughout the war, the collapse of order in the Patriot zone, was exacerbated by economic paralysis. As fighting spread across the country, so established trade routes and centres of industry were disrupted. For example, the flour mills around Santander which fed the colonial market could no longer rely upon a steady supply of grain from the wheatlands of Old Castile. To make matters worse the commercial community often came under direct attack. Even Spanish merchants often found themselves under attack as suspected *afrancesados*, whilst, as we have seen, the substantial number of French entrepreneurs who had settled in Spain everywhere found themselves in great danger. The Valencian massacre remains exceptional in its horror, but it was not alone: for example, serious

---

* The men concerned did not escape scot-free, however: lacking any means of support, many eventually appear to have enlisted in the volunteer units then being raised in Oporto by the British adventurer, Sir Robert Wilson (see below).

disturbances also took place in La Coruña. Many businesses, then, were physically eliminated, whilst the war also led to a crisis in credit as great banking families, such as the Dutari brothers of Madrid, saw their profits collapse. Nor did the war even bring much in the way of fresh opportunity: if the British lifted their blockade, for example, they made no attempt to check the flow of contraband to South America and used their newfound friendship with Spain to make fresh inroads in the domestic market. Worth thirteen million reales per year in 1808, the value of goods smuggled in via Gibraltar alone had by 1812 reached sixty-five million. Centred in an area controlled by the French, meanwhile, the Catalan cotton industry could neither get its goods to America, nor obtain adequate supplies of raw materials, nor even, protected as she was by the Continental System, sell its products in France. As for the Patriots, deprived of both Catalan cotton and, to a lesser extent, brandy, they could not hope to maintain even the pre-war supply of goods to America, transatlantic exports soon falling by some seventy-five per cent.

Misery was guaranteed, but not all draft evaders fled their homes, for to do so carried with it many dangers and disadvantages. To take just one example, in November 1808 the Junta of Mondoñedo reported that it had arrested 'various men who we know with reasonable certainty to have concealed their sons'.[15] In most localities, then, there existed many elements that had a direct interest in resisting the new authorities, whilst such levies as could be raised were also much given to violent protest. Nor did it help, first, that *motines* could always be camouflaged by a veneer of patriotic enthusiasm; second, that local notables who had failed to secure what they regarded as an adequate degree of power and influence were not above making use of the mob; and, third, that the numerous place-seekers and adventurers who had fastened on the rising as a means of making their way in life had nothing to lose in whipping up a tumult. Not surprisingly, riot was a constant danger. In Galicia *sorteos* were frequently disrupted by angry mobs; in Valencia several regiments of levies had to be disbanded after attempts to reduce their excessive pay – initially more than double that of the regular army – led to mutiny; in Oviedo the newly raised Regimiento de Castropol took a leading part in rioting that broke out on 19 June; and in Madrid the liberation of the city following the battle of Bailén was marred by brawling, pillage and murder. Thus, the commander of the forces who had entered the city, General Llamas, narrowly escaped death at the hands of his own men; the city was stripped bare of the stores left behind by the French; and the pre-war Intendent, Luis Vigury, put to death by a mob that dragged his body through the streets.

All too aware of just how vulnerable they were, the *pudientes'* initial response was a mixture of carrot and stick. Figures with particular influence amongst the populace were eulogised, awarded pensions or found figure-head positions, and the populace themselves flattered and fêted. From time to time, too, money was thrown to the crowd, free bullfights organised, or the poor feasted at the public expense. But the chief thrust of the response was repressive. The propaganda of the new authorities, for example, con-tained a series of more or less coded messages that spelled out the attitude that was expected of the *populacho*, whilst desperate attempts were made to retain the services of even small parties of regular troops. Quick to appear, too, were a variety of rudimentary security commissions, police forces and anti-bandit patrols, not to mention a flood of ordinances that sought to regulate and control the populace's every move. Firearms were prohibited; householders were enjoined to make certain that their dependants did not disturb the peace; people were forbidden to gather in the streets; taverners were ordered not to let customers linger over their drinks or engage in gaming or drunkenness; many forms of public entertainment were curtailed; travel was banned unless sanctioned by permit; tight restrictions were imposed on the letting of rooms; and vagabonds, beggars, peddlars and prostitutes were threatened with imprisonment, forced labour or impress-ment. As if this was not enough there were calls for a general régime of prayer and penitence – special religious processions, ceremonies and other services abounded – whilst the *populacho* were specifically instructed to respect the social hierarchy and adopt a suitably deferential attitude towards their superiors.

For the populace, of course, all this was a grave disappointment. Still worse, the new regulations threatened to curtail many important sources of income. As the juntas were also beginning to make use of the situation to further the interests of the *pudientes* in matters social and economic – in Asturias, for example, a system of rent controls that dated from the days of Carlos III was abolished – all that efforts to coerce the *populacho* achieved was a vicious circle of alienation, riot and repression. As it soon became all too obvious to the juntas that they simply did not have the means to maintain order in the face of wholesale revolt, the result was a reluctance to provoke the populace more than could be avoided. If the *quinta* offered certain advantages, it just as clearly carried with it the threat of trouble, whilst educated opinion had always associated it with labour shortages, drunken-ness, sexual licence and venereal disease. Hardly surprisingly, then, in many parts of Spain attempts were made to restrict the number of conscripts sent to the army, or to ensure that the brunt of the burden fell on unpopular groups. Around the coast many towns tried to escape by claiming that their men were permanently registered for service with the navy and therefore exempt from duty on land, whilst in Andalucía a common target was Galician migrant labourers who could be rounded up as vagrants. Claims, too, were made that no men could be found, or that all those available were needed to defend their homes or help round up bandits and deserters.

Militarily, then, Spain presented a depressing picture in the wake of the French retreat to the Ebro. British observers were shocked. To quote the commissary, Schaumann, for example:

The more one sees of the Spaniards, the more discouraged one gets. Everything that has been so blatantly trumpeted in the papers about their enthusiasm, their great armies and the stampede to join them is simply lies. It often looks as if Spain were not even willing to defend herself. In all the hamlets, villages and towns, the inhabitants . . . lounge about in their hundreds, completely apathetic, indifferent and gloomy, and sunk in their idleness. Is this the daring, patriotic and impetuous race about which the press have raved so bombastically?[16]

Populous though they were, León and the two Castiles raised no more than a few thousand levies, whilst the Junta of Seville was reduced to offering free pardons to bandits, smugglers and deserters who would enlist. Meanwhile, in Catalonia attempts to form a new volunteer army on the basis of the *somaténes* met with no success whatsoever, the latter in the meantime becoming notorious for pillaging friend and foe alike. By November, true, perhaps as many as 100,000 fresh troops had been scraped together, but even so the figure is hardly an impressive one by comparison, say, with the effort made by France in 1793–94.

Had every soldier available to the Spaniards been sent in rapid pursuit of the French, something might yet have been achieved, but the shortage of soldiers and breakdown of what was at best a haphazard system of recruitment were not the only problems faced with regard to mobilisation. The question of equipment and supply was desperate. Despite the copious assistance that had been received from the British, many troops were lacking in weapons, clothing and footwear, whilst others were soon enduring severe hunger. Far worse, however, was the juntas' ambition and rivalry. Not only were many of the new authorities extremely parochial in their attitude to the war, but some were bent on petty geo-strategic ends of their own. A prime example here was the Junta of Seville. Having arrogated to itself the title of 'Supreme Junta of Spain and the Indies' at the beginning of the uprising and secured the somewhat naive allegiance of Castaños, this body had embarked on an unrivalled campaign of aggrandisement. Denied the national leadership to which it aspired, it was determined at least to subjugate Andalucía and was only narrowly prevented from dispatching troops against the Junta of Granada when the latter sought to assert its independence. Not content with this, the Junta of Seville engaged in dreams of annexing southern Portugal and tried to keep Castaños' army in Andalucía rather than letting it follow up the retreat of the French. Less ambitious in their scope but just as unfortunate were the activities of the commander of the forces of the Junta of Badajoz, General José Galluzo, who for a full month refused to recognise the Convention of Sintra and lift the blockade he had imposed on French-held Elvas.

Elsewhere things were not much better. If the Junta of Valencia quickly dispatched divisions to Madrid and Zaragoza under Llamas and Saint March, the Juntas of Jaén and Granada tried to recall the troops that they had sent to Castaños' army, whilst the Juntas of Galicia and Asturias were very reluctant to allow their troops to advance beyond their frontiers at all. Last but not least, Cuesta was determined to preserve the independence of the few thousand levies that he had been able to assemble in the vicinity of Salamanca in the guise of the Army of Castile, and was therefore most disinclined to let them move forward for fear that their lack of numbers meant they would inevitably be subordinated to another general.

The consequence of such behaviour was not hard to foresee. After Bailén, Joseph Bonaparte had been terrified that the Spaniards would fall upon him from all sides, but nothing of the sort occurred. Madrid was evacuated by the French on 1 August, but it was nearly a fortnight before any Patriot troops reached the city, and even then these consisted only of the division sent up from Valencia. Castaños did not appear until 23 August, whilst he, too, was accompanied by only one division, the other three that made up his command having been kept back by the Junta of Seville. Bound up with all this, of course, is the issue of the concentration of authority. A central government was yet to emerge, and until it did there was no hope of appointing a commander-in-chief. Amongst the generals, there was some talk of at least agreeing on a candidate for such a role, but such were the divisions in their ranks that even this remained a pipe dream. Thus, Cuesta and Blake had been enemies ever since Medina de Río Seco; Palafox saw Castaños as an obstacle to his plans to complete the revolution that had been begun at Aranjuez; Castaños was mistrustful of both Cuesta and Palafox; and the young and foolish Duque de Infantado was despised by all and sundry, not least because he had briefly rallied to the cause of Joseph Bonaparte. All that a conference held on 5 September could agree was therefore a vague plan of campaign that called for Blake to push into Vizcaya and Palafox into Navarre, the aim being to surround the French, who were commonly supposed to be starving, disease-ridden and demoralised.

Gradually, the obstacles in the way of a general advance were overcome, and by late September the Army of Galicia, an Asturian division under Acevedo, the Army of Castile, two divisions of the Army of Andalucía, and Saint March and Llamas' Valencians had all reached the Ebro, whilst successful forays had been carried out against Bilbao and Sangüesa. However, the remaining two divisions of the Army of Andalucía had been so much delayed that they were only now reaching Madrid, whilst the Army of Extremadura had not even left its home province. Campaigning, it seemed, had taken second place to politicking, and, in particular, the formation of a new central government. The need for some such body had been recognised from the very beginning, but it was not until the liberation of Madrid that the issue assumed a practical character, and all the more so as the Council of Castile – a body which had since May played a leading role in collaborating with the invaders – was attempting to put itself forward as the rightful government.

What, though, was to be done? For commentators of many shades of opinion the obvious solution was the appointment of a regency, but there was no agreement as to who should exercise such a function, nor, still less, as to who should decide on the identity of the regent or regents. Put forward by such figures as José Palafox, meanwhile, it was hard not to associate such plans with personal ambition and the pursuit of the sectional aims of Church and aristocracy, whilst the civilian notables at the heart of the provincial juntas had little desire to see, as seemed likely, power placed in the hands of some general. Just as problematic, was the formation of a *cortes* that could elect a government, for there was neither a national assembly of any sort nor any idea of how one might be assembled or how much time would be needed to implement such a scheme. *Faute de mieux*, there thus seemed little option but for the various provincial authorities to establish a central council – a central junta, in fact – that could function as an interim government.

No sooner had this suggestion been generally accepted, however, than fresh problems arose. Whilst it was quickly agreed that the new body should meet in some neutral location – after some deliberation the choice fell on Aranjuez – and that each of the juntas or other authorities concerned should be allotted two representatives, many questions were unclear. What, for example, was the relationship that should exist between the Junta Central and the provincial bodies from which it stemmed? What was the role of the Junta Central in the long term? For that matter, what bodies should be represented in its ranks? There being little common ground on any of these issues, almost any solution was bound to provoke controversy. Meanwhile, any new Junta was certain to face the bitter hostility of significant elements in the Patriot camp. For the Palafoxist faction – the spearhead of all those who wished to turn back the clock of Bourbon reform – its very formation was a defeat that was both personal and political, whilst many representatives of the old Bourbon administration were equally unhappy at the way in which the Council of Castile had been sidelined.

Most prominent amongst these disaffected elements was the tough and uncompromising General Cuesta who was now not only at loggerheads with Blake, but also with the civilian authorities that had emerged in his dominions, the Junta of León having taken advantage of the fact that it had had to flee to the frontiers of Galicia following Medina de Río Seco to throw off his authority. Aided and abetted by Infantado, he had tried to persuade Castaños of the need for a group of generals to seize power, but the victor of Bailén was too sensible (or possibly too cautious) to consider so foolhardy a notion. Nevertheless, Cuesta was still capable of making trouble. Thus, early in September the Junta of León selected two representatives to attend the Junta Central on its behalf in the person of its erstwhile president, Antonio Valdés – an admiral and sometime Minister of Marine – and the Vizconde de Quintanilla. To reach Madrid from their refuge of Ponferrada, however, they had to cross territory controlled by Cuesta, the latter promptly having them imprisoned in the castle of Segovia, whilst at the same time ordering the appointment of two replacements by the Chancellory of Valladolid, which he regarded as the only legitimate source of political authority in his Captain Generalcy. In doing so, however, he merely demonstrated the limits of military power. Castaños would not back him – on the contrary, he accused him of risking 'a military anarchy, which, after shedding torrents of blood, will make us fall into the hands of our enemies'[17] – and the general therefore had no option but to surrender his prisoners, relinquish his command and travel to Aranjuez to account for his conduct.

Victory saddling the Junta with many enemies, this triumph was double-edged, but Patriot Spain did at least acquire a new administration. Composed of representatives of Aragón, Asturias, the Canaries, Old Castile, Catalonia, Córdoba, Extremadura, Galicia, Granada, Jaén, León, Madrid, the Balearic Islands, Murcia, Navarre, Seville, Toledo and Valencia, the Junta Suprema Central Gubernativa del Reino was solemnly installed in the royal palace of Aranjuez on 25 September. Having assembled, the delegates quickly appointed a council of ministers, divided themselves up into five sub-committees on the basis of one for each of the old ministries, and established both a secretariat and a separate Junta General de Guerra, it being the task of this last body to advise the Junta on military matters and co-ordinate the movements of the armies. There was, however, little inclination to appoint a commander-in-chief, a role that not only recalled Godoy's position as *generalísimo*, but hinted at both Caesarism and the reassertion of the army's primacy in the governance of Spain. More fundamentally still, perhaps, to the horror of many of its progenitors, a mixture of logic and personal ambition drove the Junta to lay claim to the sovereign power and specifically reject the idea that they were mere deputies at the service of the provincial juntas.

Aranjuez may therefore be said to have witnessed a second revolution. In what sense may this revolution be interpreted, however? According to many Spanish historians, the Junta Central was a leading instrument of a classic bourgeois revolution in which an old feudal order was overthrown by a new middle class. This is an exaggeration: there was nothing revolutionary about the thirty-five grandees, army officers, town councillors, churchmen and bureaucrats who at one time or another sat upon it, whilst the long manifesto that it published on 10 November was at best ambiguous, on the one hand promising reform but on the other speaking of the restoration of Spain's ancient constitution. Nevertheless, despite certain measures which suggest a more traditionalist agenda – it suspended the sale of clerical property, rescinded the 1767 expulsion of the Jesuits, and appointed a new Inquisitor General – it could hardly *not* push on with reform. Not only were most of its leading figures – its first president, the Conde de Floridablanca; its secretary, Martín de Garay; and the Asturian writer and economist, Gaspar Melchor de Jovellanos – all associated with the enlightened absolutism of Carlos III and Carlos IV, but it could not escape from what seemed the wholly negative record of Godoy, the ease with which Napoleon had subverted the Bourbon state, the growing threat to the social order, and the demands of the war effort.

Whether anything dramatic would have come from all this is another matter. The few known radicals associated with the Junta Central – most notably, the leading playwright and journalist, Manuel José Quintana – certainly envisaged a liberal revolution in the style of that which was to be pushed through in the *cortes* of Cádiz after 1810. Moreover, gathering round Garay – a man of considerable capacity who appears to have been quickly won over to their ideas – they formed a pressure group known as the *junta chica* and did their best to advance their plans. However, their views were not supported even by Jovellanos, who was a strong exponent of scientific education, economic liberalism and *desamortización*, and had from 1800 to 1808 been imprisoned by the Inquisition for his pains. Nor were they much respected even by men of enlightened views. Lord Holland, for example, wrote that the *junta chica* 'was composed of young men of more ardour and imagination than experience or prudence, who had imbibed their notions of freedom from the encyclopedists of France, rather than . . . the immediate wants of their own country'.[18] Sooner or later, too, the ambiguity that characterised the manifesto of 10 November would have had to be abandoned, thereby unleashing the wrath of carolines and traditionalists alike. Given that 1809 witnessed decrees that unified all the old councils into a single body and, in principle at least, put an end to the levies on industrial and commercial profits known as the *alcabalas*, *cientos* and *milliones*, it is nevertheless fair to say that the Junta Central did not neglect reform. What is even clearer, meanwhile, is that it did not neglect the war. On the contrary, indeed, the Junta ordered a *quinta* sufficient to raise an army of 550,000 men, confirmed the principle of universal conscription already introduced by many of the provincial juntas, tried to obtain large numbers of horses from Morocco, decreed the formation of what amounted to a national guard – the so-called *milicias honradas* – imposed a variety of emergency 'war contributions' and forced loans, encouraged the production of arms and equipment, and ordered the provincial juntas to open public subscriptions for the clothing of the army.

British observers were scathing on the subject of the new government. For example:

The central junta have certainly not done and are not doing their duty. They have sacrificed the public interest to their own private views of ambition and advantage. The people think so and unless a more energetic government is immediately formed the people will interfere.[19]

To quote the same observer again:

The government do nothing. They are insensible to the danger and neglect the precautions required . . . They are more occupied with trifles and nonsense about their own rank and state than with great national measures.[20]

What was lacking was neither goodwill nor energy. Far more problematic was the question of how the Junta's orders were to be enforced. In this respect, its chief agents were the provincial juntas, and yet these bodies had suddenly discovered that they had created a serious threat to their authority and independence (aside from anything else, no sooner had the new government been formed than the British had switched all aid from them to the Junta Central). At the same time, the Junta was also being sabotaged by enemies within its own ranks – above all, the supporters of José Palafox – and the continued opposition of the Council of Castile, which was effectively claiming that the new government was illegitimate. If 'the people' thought anything, it was because of a whispering campaign. Barely a week after the Junta came into being, indeed, the British diplomat, Charles Vaughan, was writing:

The central junta are sometimes ... spoken of with contempt, and I know not whether to attribute it to the bad characters of some of its members, or to a jealousy of the growing influence of the people. It is something represented as ridiculous the people exercising the power of the crown, and the slowness of their proceedings is complained of.[21]

Even had co-operation been more forthcoming, however, on a local level there still remained the problem of popular unrest or, to put it another way, the desire of the propertied classes not to push the populace too far. If the Junta Central failed in its most pressing duty in the autumn of 1808, then, it must also be asked whether any other administration could have managed better.

From the point of view of the Junta Central the way out was obvious. Obtain a dramatic military victory and it might secure the respect of its subordinates whilst at the same time reassuring the British and making certain of their continued support. However, given the numerous defects of its troops such a prospect was unlikely. Gone, at least for the most part, were the disorderly crowds of armed civilians of the first weeks of the war, but gone too, in effect, was the old Bourbon army, whose regiments had lost many veterans to desertion on the one hand, and been swamped by raw recruits on the other. Typical, perhaps, was the Valencian division of General Llamas (the troops who had run amok in Madrid in August), which Alcalá Galiano describes as having 'loose breeches, cloaks, long, tangled and greasy locks hanging ... down their backs, and round hats with patriotic cockades, slogans, or badges of the Virgin and the saints', and 'in general ... mixing the ridiculous with the ferocious'.[22] On all sides, indeed, there prevailed inexperience, shortages of food, clothing and equipment, and a desperate want of cavalry and artillery. Of the Galician forces it was written, 'It is impossible to describe the wretched appearance of this army, in want of everything and a mixture of peasants in their different costumes', and of the Army of Castile that it was 'a complete mass of miserable peasantry, without clothing, without organisation, and with few officers worthy of the name'.[23]

With time and good fortune, perhaps, many of these defects could have been remedied but matters were compounded by the quality of the officer corps, which is generally agreed to have been very poor. Only too typical, it seems, was one Antonio Terán. A captain of the León infantry regiment, he was accused of being 'a coward unworthy of his epaulettes' and reported to be living in Vigo with 'a prostituted adulteress' whose husband was in America.[24] From Valencia, meanwhile, come reports of courts martial of 'Don Mariano Usel, Colonel of the Regimiento de la Fé ... for the poor organisation of the unit, embezzlement of funds and other acts ... [and] against some officers of the Regimiento de Turia ... for their excesses, lack of subordination, mistreatment of local justices, and murder of several Frenchmen in Murviedro'.[25] It would be tempting to attribute the blame for this situation entirely to the influx of new officers who had entered the army in 1808, for many of the insurgent authorities had certainly showered commissions upon friends and dependants without any regard for their suitability. When the Supreme Council of War was charged with the task of examining Spain's defeats the following year, for example, it concluded that this rash of appointments had had the most serious effects and proposed that every commission issued since 1808 should be annulled. Yet this is too simplistic an explanation of the problem. Many of the men appointed to command the new regiments were actually drawn from the mass of retired and supernumerary officers that had existed before 1808, whilst it was not just outside the army that there was a problem. To quote Francisco Javier de Cabanés, a regular officer who was perhaps the best military analyst that Spain produced in the Peninsular War, 'In those moments of effervescence [i.e. the uprising], alongside a number of officers ... who deserved to be plucked from the ranks of the subalterns, there were promoted many whose ability was unworthy of the ... positions conferred upon them.'[26]

Reports of misconduct amongst the officer corps are in any case so common that it is impossible to believe that the problem was confined to any one group within its ranks. Aside from the question of incompetence, absenteeism was common. Rather than enduring the miseries of active service, many officers seized any pretext to travel to such cities as Cádiz, Seville and La Coruña, in which sanctuaries, like Terán, they lived in the best style that they could afford, the whole issue being compounded by the cavalier fashion in which many generals appointed serving officers to be their aides-de-camp. On the battlefield, many officers displayed the most abject cowardice, the problem becoming so serious that the Junta Central was eventually driven to order all infantry officers below a certain rank to be deprived of their horses. Lack of leadership was compounded by indiscipline. Excessive numbers of soldier-servants were employed, for example, with the result that many troops were removed from the fighting line. Fanciful non-regulation uniforms were very much *de rigueur* – 'Had 100,000 men been collected from the different European armies, the officers could not have exhibited a greater variety of dress . . . Everyone seems to wear . . . his own fancy, and deems it sufficient if it be military'[27] – and gambling and whoring were widespread. Thus:

The soldier who abandons himself like a brute to the bribed flattery of prostitutes, to excess of wine . . . or to the lamentable distraction of gambling can never shelter in his breast the . . . heroic sentiments of a . . . patriot. Although our armies suffer to a greater or lesser extent from all these moral infirmities, the most general . . . is gambling. A large part of our officers being immersed in it, they ignore their obligations . . . occupy the hours that they should spend in study in its pursuit, offer a pernicious example to the soldiery, debase themselves in the lowest fashion, and . . . look on everything other than winning and losing with the most stupid indifference.[28]

Essential to all and sundry were large quantities of baggage, and, in the case of senior officers, servants, barbers, cooks and valets, whilst corruption was widespread whether it involved falsifying troop returns or commandeering much-needed transport.

There were, of course, exceptions to the rule, but, with officers of this sort, improvement was unlikely. Desertion, for example, was encouraged, and all the more so because the men were all too frequently dressed in costumes that resembled civilian clothing, whilst straggling was also a constant problem. Steadiness on the battlefield, too, was not much to be found. Though occasionally capable of the utmost heroism, most Spanish troops were prone to attacks of panic that could lead to entire regiments – indeed, in one case an entire army – fleeing the field at the first shots. Why this was the case is not hard to understand:

Crowds flocked to bear arms, but while untaught to bear them were . . . hazarded all at once in the field, creating confusion from the want of military knowledge of their leaders as well as their unsteadiness . . . Though in some instances I have observed that the . . . new militia . . . have acted against the enemy with peculiar resolution and resistance, it has always been in . . . strong passes, or woods, or where knowledge of the country has peculiarly favoured them. Almost in every instance where reliance has been placed upon the favourable results of a general action . . . a failure has been the consequence.[29]

Even when the Spaniards stood their ground (and they often did so, particularly when placed in strong defensive positions), the state of their drill was generally so poor that they were incapable of performing anything other than the simplest manoeuvres. Thus, units might defend themselves or advance against the enemy with determination, but even then they generally lost their formation, whilst, asked to change their front or form square, they were likely to fall into inextricable disorder. Once put to flight, there was almost no hope of rallying them: 'The men all fight desperately . . . but, as is to be expected in such raw levies, once routed their confusion is great.'[30]

Such were the other problems experienced by the army that these deficiencies proved fatal. Thus, even in infantry combats, the Spaniards were likely to be outmatched. The marked lack of skirmishers of the early days of the war was gradually remedied, but want of training and confidence ensured that the French *tirailleurs* were invariably able to drive back their Spanish counterparts and inflict heavy losses on the immobile battle lines behind them. Accentuating the weakness of the infantry was a shortage of artillery. Logistical factors always ensured that too few guns were brought to the battlefield, whilst those that were seem rarely to have been concentrated for maximum effect. Worst of all, however, was the issue of the cavalry. Too small a proportion even of the old army, this could not, for obvious reasons, be expanded in the same manner as the infantry, whilst even those units that managed to take the field were invariably both understrength and hampered by the poor quality of their horses. In a straight clash with their French counterparts, then, the Spanish cavalry were invariably overborne with the result that they increasingly tended to just turn and run. In fleeing, however, they were certain to expose the infantry, who over and over again found themselves being ridden down by a torrent of horse that suddenly appeared in flank or rear. As General Francisco Copons complained, 'The arm of which the enemy make greatest use is their cavalry, and it is necessary to meet it with equal force. Thanks to the state in which we find ourselves, this is not possible, but it is essential for us to do what we can.'[31]

The tactical inferiority of the Spanish armies was exacerbated by the poor quality of their commanders. Few generals, perhaps, could have wrested very much from forces of the sort that Patriot Spain put into the field, whilst it is also the case that better troops might have permitted the emergence of talent that in the event lay hidden. At the same time, a few generals displayed great physical courage, won renown for the skilful defence of some fortress or proved themselves to be competent subordinates or divisional commanders. Yet the picture still remains fairly bleak. Not helped by headquarters that were frequently filled with well-connected young noblemen who had little idea how to fulfil their responsibilities, too often Spanish generals misread the enemy's intentions, failed to send out adequate patrols, took up vulnerable positions, adopted impractical dispositions, failed to react to hostile moves, or allowed their forces to be defeated in detail. So monotonous, indeed, was one scenario that it aroused comment on the part of the enemy:

They prejudged the event of the battle by their own ardent desire to . . . destroy their enemies; ignorant of the art of manoeuvring . . . they placed themselves in long shallow lines in plains where the superiority of our tactics and our cavalry must necessarily give us the advantage. This order of battle, bad even for well manoeuvred troops, deprived the Spaniards of the power of . . . concentrating themselves to resist our masses.[32]

In 1808 or any subsequent year, then, any Spanish army that took the field was likely to be defeated, but the situation was worsened still further by the fact that defeat was unlikely to be anything but very heavy. In mountainous areas, things might not be too bad, but much of Spain was composed of rolling tableland devoid of woods, villages and enclosures. 'My road from Astorga', wrote one British officer travelling across Old Castile, 'lay through a vast open space extending from five to twenty or more miles on every side without a single accident of ground which would enable a body of infantry to check a pursuing enemy or cover its own retreat'.[33] In such terrain an army with cavalry superiority could wreak terrible havoc on a defeated foe, the latter being likely to lose not only thousands of casualties but also all its guns and baggage. In Spain, in particular, hundreds of soldiers could be relied upon to take advantage of a defeat to attempt to return home or fall in with some guerrilla band or bandit gang.

Military operations, in short, were likely to be a costly business that would try Patriot resources to the limit. This was made even worse by a strategic situation that was extremely unfavourable to the Spanish cause. The first meeting of the Junta Central's Junta General de Guerra (a body composed of Castaños, the Conde de Montijo, the Marqués de Castelar – a senior officer of the royal guard – and an admiral named Ciscar) had confirmed the plan of campaign that had been worked out at the conference of 5 September, and for good measure agreed a major reorganisation of the Patriot forces. The troops of Galicia, Asturias and, when they arrived, La Romana were to form the Army of the Left; those of Castaños, Llamas, Cuesta and Galluzo the Army of the Centre; those of Palafox and Saint March and a further Valencian division under O'Neill the Army of Reserve; and the forces of Catalonia, reinforced by one division dispatched from Zaragoza and another sent up from Granada, the Army of the Right. Most significantly in view of the presence of Montijo, who was not only a ringleader in the *motín de Aranjuez* but also a connection of the Palafox family, it was agreed that all conscripts should be sent to the front via the Army of Reserve.* Yet the planned attack was the fruit not of military realities, but of the bombastic outpourings of the popular press, the pernicious influence of Bailén and the precarious position of the Junta Central. Indeed, it was little more than madness. The Armies of the Left and Reserve were separated by a yawning gulf that was supposed to be filled up by the still absent British and the Army of Extremadura, whilst the extension of the Spanish flanks into Vizcaya and Navarre had pulled the 80,000 troops who had reached the front into a great crescent that allowed the 65,000 men whom the Spaniards were trying to surround to operate on interior lines. Already, indeed, a sudden French offensive had routed the erstwhile Army of Castile at Logroño and cut off part of one of Castaños' Andalucian divisions at Lerín. With most of the Spanish troops, at best, of mediocre quality and suffering miserably for want of food and winter clothing, a grim description of their situation is provided by Juan Manuel Sarasa, a young private in the Zamora infantry regiment who had escaped from Denmark with the forces of La Romana:

We were encamped in the Berrón district for fifteen days. For the first three we received no rations of any sort until the evening of the third when some cattle arrived. So great was our hunger that we did not bother to butcher them properly, but simply hacked off such chunks as we could. The meat we set to roast, but, absolutely overcome, we snatched it from the fires before it was barely warm. As for bread we received none at all. I bought a loaf for 100 reales . . . and to eat it I had to hide from my comrades.[34]

Well might the British liaison officer, Whittingham, write:

I fear the result of this action. The French are concentrated, and we are considerably scattered. Their troops are all equal; ours, some bad and some good. They have the advantage of unity of command; we are directed by three generals, all independent of each other.[35]

This already bad situation was now to get much worse. At the end of the first week of November the Allied centre was still only held by two divisions of the Army of Extremadura. Still worse, delay was compounded by intrigue.

---

* The benefit of this measure to the Palafoxists is clear. With all new recruits channelled through Palafox's own army, it would be possible for the Aragonese commander to deny fresh men to his rivals whilst at the same time building up his own power base.

Ever since Bailén, Castaños' prominence had been a source of both anger and embarrassment to the faction centred on José Palafox, for Castaños was both a nominee of enlightened absolutism and a fierce opponent of military rule. Removing him from his command had therefore quickly become a major objective, and the Palafoxists were well placed to do this. Setting aside the presence of Montijo, the Aragonese commander had also secured a seat in the Junta Central for his younger brother, Francisco. The result of this was that Jackson was soon writing, 'Castaños is at present very unpopular in Madrid, and such is the state of the public mind . . . that I would not answer for his life should he prove unsuccessful.'[36] Not long had passed, indeed, before a special commission had been dispatched to the Army of the Centre composed of Francisco Palafox, Montijo and the Marqués de Coupigny, an officer who had commanded one of the divisions that had blocked Dupont's way at Bailén and had ever since been bitterly jealous of his erstwhile commander.

The results of this mission were predictable enough, but before discussing them we must first examine the French. Bailén had, as we have seen, embarrassed and enraged Napoleon. Far from ordering the evacuation of the Peninsula as the Spaniards hoped, he resolved to go to Spain himself; made repeated attempts to halt Joseph's retreat; directed some 130,000 men of the *grande armée*, including the Imperial Guard, four army corps and four divisions of heavy cavalry, to head for Spain; sent for further reinforcements from Naples, the Kingdom of Italy and the Confederation of the Rhine; ordered fresh levies in France; offered Britain peace in exchange for the recognition of Joseph Bonaparte; and secured his rear by sanctioning Russian annexation of Finland, Moldavia and Wallachia, and threatening Austria and Prussia with complete destruction if they stood in his way. Come what may, then, Spain was to be secured. Indeed, it had become the very touchstone of Napoleon's foreign policy. For it, the emperor was prepared to jeopardise domestic peace (so great were the numbers of conscripts he now needed that there was no option but to call up 80,000 fresh men from the already plundered 'classes' of 1806–1809, as well as to take 60,000 from that of 1810); for it, the British were to be offered a peace that would have left them in possession of virtually all France's colonies in the wider world; and for it, again, Russia was to be permitted greatly to strengthen her position in the east. Yet in truth Napoleon had little option. Guided above all by questions of personal prestige, he could not back down for fear that the spell that he had woven on Continental Europe would otherwise be broken, thereby encouraging Austria, Russia and Prussia to seek vengeance and the *Rheinbund* states to seek shelter elsewhere. In judging his actions at this point, however, we should avoid hindsight. We know that the Spanish war was to cause Napoleon untold difficulties, certainly, but nothing had occurred to alter the emperor's contempt for Spanish capabilities, whilst the forces that the British could send to Spain were so small by his standards that there seemed little doubt they could simply be swamped. In short, what was envisaged was a lightning campaign that would see the French sweep across the face of the entire Peninsula, leaving the emperor free to return to the task of defeating the British and overawing Europe.

Energetic though the emperor's response was, October was much advanced before the first of the forces he had detached from the *grande armée* had crossed the Spanish frontier. Once they had done so, however, success seemed assured. In the first place, the French forces were no longer the improvised miscellany of the first Army of Spain. Many units of this force remained, but their soldiers were now experienced campaigners, whilst the old 'provisional regiments' and 'legions of reserve' had all been reorganised into ordinary regiments of the line. As for the troops from Germany, these had been forced to absorb large numbers of fresh recruits, but were dominated by strong cadres of veterans. With the new arrivals, too, could be expected the structures and techniques that had made the *grande armée* so successful elsewhere. The bulk of the French forces would be concentrated in Navarre and the Basque provinces under the command of Napoleon himself. Organised in seven army corps, a cavalry corps and a general reserve, of which the most important component was the Imperial Guard, the army was also much better led than before, the generals sent to Spain including Ney, Victor, Lefebvre, Mortier, Soult and Lannes. Unlike in the summer, there was also a master-plan that envisaged a massive offensive against the Spanish centre followed by a drive on Madrid and turning movements against each of the isolated Spanish wings. Coming up behind, meanwhile, were still more troops, including the corps that had been repatriated with Junot from Portugal.

Assured of strategic superiority, the new Army of Spain was also certain to be impressive on the battlefield. Often composed of scratch formations that had received little training, the first French troops in Spain had only rarely been able to fight in the style that had brought so many victories elsewhere. Now, Napoleon's forces would be able to show all their tactical virtuosity. Particularly noteworthy in this respect was their striking power. Massed in corps and army-level reserves, heavy twelve-pounder guns would first be used to batter the target. Once the defenders had been suitably softened up, the infantry would then be sent in to open a breach in their line. In traditional British accounts, great emphasis has been placed on the idea that dense columns of French troops preceded by a few skirmishers simply hurled themselves on the enemy in an attempt to break through by impetus alone. However, there were clearly a wide range of variations on the theme. For example, attacks could be delivered either in line alone or in a mixture of line and column, whilst another method was to form a dense screen of skirmishers and gradually wear the enemy down. Even when reliance was placed on shock tactics, different methods could be employed. One such, certainly, was to mass entire brigades, divisions or even corps into gigantic masses that were so close-packed that their only hope of victory was to keep moving. More often, however, the individual battalions would be deployed in such a fashion that if checked they could shake out into line, just as their parent brigades and divisions would be arranged in ways that allowed freedom of manoeuvre and, in particular, the use of reserves. Flexibility was the key, whilst, if things were properly managed, the infantry could rely on close support from both artillery and cavalry. Once a break-through had been achieved, victory could always be consolidated by the army's cavalry reserve – separate formations of dragoons and cuirassiers whose task it was to charge through the hole that had been smashed in the enemy line, sweep away any remaining opposition and turn defeat into rout.

The ability to concentrate overwhelming resources against a single sector of the enemy line and deliver blows of massive power and effect was likely to be particularly effective against an opponent as unwieldy and ill-trained as the Spaniards, and had played an important role in earlier campaigns. However, it was not the only factor that had brought victory after victory to Napoleon. Just as vital was the great flexibility brought to the French army by its organisation into a system of brigades, divisions and corps. By 1808, true, this was no longer the advantage that it had been even a few years before – its benefits had gradually been appreciated by other armies and its rudiments were in use by both the British and the Spaniards – but the system was still better developed amongst Napoleon's forces than it was anywhere else, whilst its virtues both on and off the battlefield remained undoubted.

The efficacy of France's military system was not just limited to the manner in which it could employ its soldiers, however. Just as impressive was Napoleon's ability to socialise the men who fell into his clutches. Thus, in neither France nor the rest of the Napoleonic empire was conscription any more popular or equitable than it was in Spain. Yet once the young men concerned had actually been inducted into the army, they found that they had become part of a machine that was adept in persuading them to accept their lot. In part, of course, this was the result of necessity – hundreds of miles from home, conscripts would generally think twice before running away – but the army also promoted both a sense of isolation from civilian society and strong bonds of comradeship and *esprit de corps*. A particularly important factor here was the manner in which competition between different units had been carefully nurtured by Napoleon whilst emulation was also important in the motivation of the individual soldier. If the idea that every drummerboy had a marshal's baton in his knapsack was a myth, the individual soldier could still aspire to humbler forms of promotion and advancement. A transfer to one of the élite companies of a man's own battalion, a posting to the Imperial Guard, the award of the Legion of Honour – a decoration that, almost uniquely, was open to all ranks of the army – or a career as a junior officer were all real possibilities, whilst even the mere fact of long service earned the right to colourful stripes on the soldier's sleeve. For all their official prohibition, meanwhile, looting and other more serious forms of misbehaviour were also widely tolerated, whilst the soldiers were not beaten or flogged as they were in other armies. Add to this Napoleon's ability to remember individual soldiers and his extraordinary personal charisma, and it will be appreciated that morale was remarkably high.

A military machine of truly awesome stature was therefore about to strike the divided, outnumbered and ill-fed Spaniards. Yet it was not without its defects. What drove its individuals was not love of country, but in the last resort personal ambition. And, if the lowest of its soldiers could hope for loot, higher status and more pay, the higher one advances up the hierarchy, the greater one finds the stimuli to have been. The marshals who led the French armies in Spain were soldiers of considerable talent, but as individuals they were deeply flawed. Like their imperial master, they were ultimately little more than adventurers who had no hesitation in jettisoning anything or anyone who had become an encumbrance to them. Republicans in the early 1790s, they now served the man who had killed the Republic, just as in 1814 they were to offer their services to the Bourbons, in March 1815 to line up behind the so-called 'liberal empire', and in July 1815 to become royalists again. To save themselves, in fact, they would happily lay down the life of a friend: when Ney was executed by the Bourbons in 1815, no fewer than five other marshals signed his death warrant. Of mixed origin – some were nobles who would probably have made general even under the *ancien régime*, and others commoners whom it would have doomed to obscurity – all of them had made their fortune by hitching their star to that of Napoleon. Titles, estates and pensions had been lavished upon them, and still they were greedy for more: with Murat now King of Naples, indeed, they had become insatiable. And, as Napoleon intended, ambition bred rivalry, and greed jealousy, the marshalate being renowned for its feuds and hatreds. Whenever the emperor was in personal command of the *grande armée*, as, of course, he now was, the problem was kept under control, for the desire of the marshals to please their master was generally stronger than their desire to do down their rivals. But take the emperor away, and matters would be very different. Thus far in the history of the Napoleonic Wars, this had not happened, but Spain and Portugal were soon to see the emperor leave his commanders to it and return to Paris. Discussion of the chaos that resulted is not appropriate at this point, but if they behaved as independent satraps, found all sorts of reasons not to co-operate with one another, laid hands on men and money meant for others, looted their dominions unmercifully, and ignored the authority of the unfortunate Joseph, it was only to be expected.

Indeed, even with the emperor present, things could go wrong, and in this case spare the Spaniards from complete catastrophe. According to Napoleon's grand design, the forces facing the troops which had pushed into the Basque provinces on the one hand and Navarre on the other should have been left well alone until the French had broken through at Burgos and sent troops to surround them. On the French right flank, however, the army of General Blake, which had taken up a strong position at the village of Amorebieta a few miles to the south-east of Bilbao, was confronted by the corps of Marshal Lefebvre. Eager for glory, the latter could not resist the temptation to act on his own account, and on 29 October he therefore attacked. Fought in dense fog and drizzle, the battle that followed was not much of a victory for the French – 'The First Regiment of Catalonia . . . received the attack with the greatest coolness and kept up a very regular fire by platoons, maintaining their position against an enemy nearly five times their number . . . The most veteran troops could not possibly have displayed more soldierlike firmness or more *sangfroid* in action'[37] – but it was quite enough to discomfort Blake who proceeded to evacuate Bilbao and retire south-westwards towards the headwaters of the Ebro. Several days of confused manoeuvring followed as Lefebvre and his neighbour, Victor, sought to trap Blake, but on the whole the Spaniards had the better of the exchange, whilst the Army of the Left ended up in a much less exposed position than had initially been the case.

At the very outset, then, Napoleon's plan was spoiled. Irritated though he was by Lefebvre's impetuosity, however, the emperor had no intention of staying his hand. On 6 November, indeed, he had arrived at Vitoria, active operations beginning four days later with an attack on the Spanish positions outside Burgos. Occupied as these were by only two divisions of the erstwhile Army of Extremadura, the result was a foregone conclusion. Arrayed in an open plain to the east of the city at Gamonal, the Spaniards were broken almost immediately by a massive cavalry charge and fled in panic, leaving the invaders to sack Burgos at their leisure. Also lost were at least 3,000 casualties and all the Spaniards' guns and baggage, French losses, by contrast, amounting to no more than 100 men. And with Burgos taken Napoleon was at liberty to pursue his master-plan: by 11 November substantial French forces were heading northwards for Reinosa on the one hand and southwards for Aranda on the other.

With disaster threatening, the Spaniards proved luckier than they deserved. To the north the Army of the Left had, on 10 November, taken up a strong defensive position at Espinosa de los Monteros where it was joined by the infantry of the division of the Marqués de la Romana (the cavalry had been sent off to acquire new horses). Well-placed though his troops were, however, Blake was in no state to fight: many men had fled, fallen sick or been cut off; he had no cavalry; all but six of the army's guns had been sent to the rear; the weather was appalling; and the soldiers were suffering from a want of food, tents, blankets and greatcoats. To his immediate front was the corps of Marshal Victor, whilst that of Marshal Lefebvre was swinging south to get round his right flank. Prudence dictated immediate retreat, but, perhaps fearing retribution if he failed to put up a fight, Blake instead stood firm and, as a result, on 10 November was attacked by Victor. Numbers on the field were about equal – 21,000 Frenchmen to 23,000 Spaniards – and it was therefore a matter of some credit to Blake that every attack launched by Victor's troops was beaten back in a day of furious fighting. As one of the defenders remembered:

We had hardly taken up our positions when the enemy attacked us with great impetus, but their arrogance came to grief in the face of the valour and serenity of our division. Letting our opponents approach to within ten paces, with every volley we brought down an entire column. The enemy repeated their attacks with fresh troops, but each time ... they were beaten back, leaving mountains of corpses in front of our lines.[38]

In the circumstances, it might have been better to have retired in the night, for the attackers had gone into action in a somewhat piecemeal fashion and had also concentrated on the section of line held by the veteran division that had been rescued from Denmark, which was conceivably the best force in the entire Spanish army. However, fearing that a retreat in the face of the enemy could not but lead to disaster, Blake hung on in the hope of inflicting a reverse serious enough to allow him to get away unmolested. This was not to be: when the invaders attacked again the following day, they did so in a much more circumspect and co-ordinated fashion, choosing as their target the weak Asturian division of Acevedo and making much use of firepower rather than headlong assaults in column. For a while fighting was intense. 'As soon as [the Spaniards] saw us', wrote one participant, 'they . . . sent out . . . a very large number of skirmishers to harass our right from behind the shelter of a stone wall which flanked it. Seven small artillery pieces of a sort carried by mule-back, together with a battery stationed in front of their line, then opened up on us with canister and wounded a number of men.'[39] But skirmishing was very much a French speciality, and with their commander and many other officers shot down by snipers, the Asturians were soon in flight. Attacked in both front and flank, the rest of the army soon gave way in its turn. Amongst the last to fall back were the men of La Romana:

With the river barring our route just behind us and the enemy in possession of the only bridge . . . there was no option but to wade across . . . Once on the other side we had to climb a very steep slope . . . exposed to the terrible fire which the enemy directed at us from the other bank. In this short time I was hit by seven bullets, but fortunately not one of them cost me a scratch. When I saw the state in which they had left my clothes, I raised my gaze to heaven and gave thanks to the Almighty.[40]

By nightfall the Spaniards were streaming westwards towards Reinosa, only to find their way blocked by Marshal Soult, who, leading the corps hitherto led by Bessières northwards from Burgos to cut off Blake's retreat, had just captured his artillery and baggage as it was retiring westwards along the southern fringes of the Cantabrian mountains. With Victor and Lefebvre also bearing down on the tattered remnants of Blake's army, which casualties and desertion had now reduced to only some 12,000 men, there was only one thing to do. Thus, abandoning everything, Blake fled northwards to the sea and then doubled back south-westwards towards the city of León. Conducted in incessant rain and snow through some of the highest mountains in Spain, however, this retreat broke the Army of the Left as a fighting force: barely half its 40,000 men reached León, whilst even those who did were penniless, starving, disease-ridden and lacking arms and ammunition. As La Romana, who had been ordered to take over, wrote on 9 December:

I have now assembled 20,000 men . . . but I can make no movement against the enemy because I do not have any cavalry nor a greater supply of musket cartridges than forty rounds per man. I lack many arms which the troops lost in their disorderly retreat and many units have no camp kettles in which to prepare their meals. There is not a real in the army's coffers, and the troops have not been paid for the last month ... The draught and pack mules have not been paid for, and their owners work with the greatest ill will.[41]

Besides Blake, Napoleon's other main target was the large concentration of Spanish troops hanging about the southern and eastern fringes of Navarre. News of the French breakthrough at Burgos should have had the Army of the Centre and such part of the Army of Reserve as was not needed for the defence of Zaragoza falling back in the direction of Madrid, but nothing of the sort transpired. On the contrary, over a week was wasted in bitter disputes between Castaños and Palafox, whilst the waters were further muddied by the intervention of the commission dispatched to the former's headquarters by the Junta Central. With the French bearing down on them from the direction of both Vitoria and Aranda, from where Napoleon had ordered Marshal Ney to march eastwards to take them in the rear, the two Spanish commanders eventually agreed to concentrate their forces along a line stretching southwards from the Ebro at Tudela to the northern flanks of the Sierra de Moncayo at Tarrazona. However, even under the best of conditions this line would have been too long to be held by the 45,000 men who eventually came up, whilst the defenders also failed to keep a proper watch. When the French attacked on the morning of 23 November, in fact, many of the Spaniards, above all those of the Army of Reserve, were still taking up their positions, whilst others failed to respond at all. Concentrating the vast majority of their forces against the Spanish right, the French broke through with little or no difficulty. All that saved the Spaniards from complete disaster, indeed, was the fact that Ney failed to make an appearance until 26 November, the distance that he had to cover simply being too great for him to have had any chance of fulfilling the emperor's intentions. Though roughly handled – a Prussian nobleman fighting for the French describes their line of retreat as being 'littered with corpses'[42] – the two divisions of the Army of Reserve that had been present on the field were therefore able to reach Zaragoza without too much difficulty, being joined in their retreat by most of the Valencian division originally commanded by Llamas. As for the Army of the Centre's Andalusian divisions, they eventually regrouped at Calatayud, from where, much harried by pursuing French troops and the ravages of hunger, disease and winter weather, they retired southwards in the direction of New Castile.

In moving southwards in this fashion, Castaños had had faint hopes of saving Madrid, but there was little chance of him getting there before the French, whilst even if he had arrived in time his 20,000 half-starved and exhausted fugitives would have made little difference. Napoleon, however, was taking no chances: even before Tudela had been fought, 45,000 men were bearing down on the capital. Garrisoned only by 12,000 veterans of Bailén, whose battalions had still not marched for the front, and devoid of fortifications, Madrid was an easy target. As noted at the beginning of this chapter an attempt was made to halt the invaders at the Somosierra pass, but even this was bungled, several thousand of the defenders ending up trapped on the wrong side of the mountains and left with no option but to flee to Segovia where the 9,000 survivors of Gamonal had also found refuge. Having burst through the pass on 30 November, the French had Madrid at their mercy, the troops who had held the pass having been ordered by their commander, San Juan, to retire on El Escorial. With the emperor at the gates, the populace took to the streets and demanded that an attempt be made to defend the city. Terrified of the mob, the authorities gave way and established a junta of defence which handed out such arms as were available and ordered the construction of barricades and ditches. For a brief moment all was activity:

The capital presented a grandiose spectacle: on all sides both sexes ran . . . to pull up paving stones, dig up earth, carry stone . . . The docility and zeal shown by the populace . . . were amazing . . . The least word was enough to have them throwing metal cooking utensils and items of wool and cotton from the balconies to help make bullets and wadding. In order to hold up the French inside the city windows were stuffed with mattresses, whilst the streets were blocked with . . . furniture of every sort.[43]

Defiant though the *populacho* were, however, all this was so much froth. Many of the defence works were poorly planned and executed, whilst the whole enterprise was doomed by the failure adequately to secure the heights that dominated the city. As for the would-be defenders, meanwhile, few of them were properly armed, whilst they also showed the usual propensity to disorder, lynching one of the members of the junta on the pretext that a number of the musket cartridges they had been given had proved to be filled with sand.

If the Junta of Defence sent out desperate appeals for help, it was therefore hardly surprising. However, the survivors of Gamonal and Somosierra were in no condition to be of much assistance, and the troops of Castaños and Moore still too far away. Bloodshed might yet have been averted – anxious not to compromise Joseph more than absolutely necessary, Napoleon repeatedly offered the authorities reasonable terms – but such was the inhabitants' excitement that the latter did not dare to accept them. On 3 December, therefore, the emperor ordered a demonstration against the city. The result was only too predictable. Many of those who had received arms never appeared at the barricades, whilst most of those who did 'cried "Death or victory!", and fled'.[44] Only the fact that Napoleon did not press the attack beyond seizing the commanding heights of the present-day Retiro Park saved the city from being occupied at once, whilst surrender was not postponed for more than a few hours: with the mob cowed, the Junta of Defence capitulated the very next day, though not before most of the regular troops in the city had hastily marched for the Tagus. Many cobbles having been torn up to build defences, the inhabitants 'gained nothing but the trouble of repaving their principal streets'.[45]

As was to be expected, the fall of Madrid produced a general collapse in the Spanish position in central Spain. What little remained of the Army of the Centre – during the retreat from Tudela it had lost fully half its men – had on 2 December been at Guadalajara. Now commanded by Manuel La Peña – Castaños had received a dispatch ordering him to return to Aranjuez to take up his duties as president of the Junta Central's advisory committee of generals – its battered remnants had attempted to reach Madrid by means of a circuitous march that eventually brought them to a town a few miles south of the capital. Learning that the latter had fallen, it then fled eastwards and eventually reached Cuenca where command was assumed by Infantado. Its sufferings, meanwhile, had been terrible. To quote its new commander:

I saw a ruined army and troops who presented a most distressing experience. Some were entirely barefoot, others almost naked, and all disfigured ... by the most ravenous hunger (there were many who had had no bread for eight days ... and many had died along the roads and in the mountains). They appeared more like corpses than men ready to defend their fatherland.[46]

As for the forces at Segovia, these had clamoured for a march on the capital, only to revolt and flee for the Tagus. Eventually got together at Talavera, along with a few troops who had escaped from Madrid and Somosierra, they then lynched San Juan – his crime was apparently that he had been the commander of Godoy's personal bodyguard – and were only finally got into some sort of order by Galluzo, who had just been reinstated by the Junta Central. As for this last body, accompanied by crowds of desperate civilians – one estimate is that no fewer than 14,000 people fled Madrid – it had evacuated Aranjuez on 1 December, making first for Extremadura and finally for Seville, which it reached on 17 December. Along the way, however, the scene had been one of the utmost chaos:

Abandoned ammunition wagons, blown-up cannon, shots in the air and crowds of troops dressed in every colour set the scene for the full horror of a rout . . . A more extraordinary picture cannot be imagined. Groups of 100 or 200 or more soldiers of every arm were coming by commanded by a sergeant or a corporal, whilst their officers turned up in groups of half a dozen accompanied by their servants, their units having ceased to exist . . . The uproar and disorder were horrific and announced a terrible catastrophe.[47]

The great offensive in central Spain had not been the only disaster to assail the Spaniards. In Catalonia, too, the French had also been on the attack. As we have seen, by August 1808 the invaders had got into considerable difficulties in that province, half their troops being blockaded in Barcelona and the remainder pinned down in the vicinity of Figueras. In planning his counter-attack in Spain, however, Napoleon had not forgotten them. On the contrary, three new divisions were formed from various French and Italian units to assist them. In all, indeed, over 18,000 reinforcements appeared on the Catalan front, command of which was now given to the experienced and capable Marshal Gouvion Saint-Cyr. Conscious, perhaps, of the extreme difficulty of forming a new regular army in Catalonia, where conscription was for historical reasons particularly hated, the Junta Central had resolved on the dispatch of reinforcements of its own – one division was detached from Palafox for the purpose and another formed at Granada under Reding from a mixture of new levies and troops withdrawn from Castaños, whilst the British were asked to send thither the Spanish troops they had freed at Lisbon – but it was some time before any of these troops could arrive. Disaster, then, was soon threatening on the Catalan front as well. Now headed by the Captain General of the Balearic Islands, Juan Miguel de Vives, the Army of the Right remained inactive, Saint-Cyr therefore being left to take the offensive. Operations began early in November with an attack on Rosas, whose excellent harbour made it a convenient base for ships seeking to prevent the provisioning of Barcelona by sea. Besieged on 7 November, it held out determinedly, but by 5 December the walls had been breached and the defenders forced to surrender. Next on the list was the relief of Barcelona, and by 11 December a strong force of troops was therefore heading southwards. In marching on Barcelona Saint-Cyr was taking a risk, for the Spaniards possessed a great superiority in numbers and could easily have surrounded him. However, in the event too many troops were left to watch Barcelona. Faced by fewer than 10,000 men, the French gained a victory at Cardedeu on 16 December, and reached Duhesme the following day. At least 18,000 Spanish troops were still nearby, but, drawn up behind the River Llobregat around Molíns de Rey, at dawn on 21 December they were attacked, outflanked and put to flight with the loss of all their guns and baggage.

So ended the great French counter-offensive. Madrid, Burgos, Santander and Bilbao had been reoccupied; Barcelona relieved; Rosas taken; and important victories won at Gamonal, Espinosa, Tudela, Somosierra, Cardedeu and Molíns de Rey. The Armies of the Left and Right had been routed, the Army of the Centre split into three (the survivors of Gamonal, Somosierra and Madrid; Castaños' Andalucian divisions at Cuenca; and the Valencians that had taken refuge with Palafox), and the Army of Reserve confined in Zaragoza. Meanwhile, thousands of men were dead, wounded or missing; hundreds of guns and incalculable quantities of stores in the hands of the French; and the new government a fugitive. And, faced with disaster, the populace had shown little fight. In Valladolid, for example:

All was now bustle and confusion. The French were said to be at the gates of the city . . . Men, women and children [were] wandering up and down uttering the most pitiful cries and with terror and dismay painted on their countenances . . . The doors of the nunneries were thrown open by the bishop's order, and many venerable ladies who for the space of fifty years had never trodden unhallowed ground were now obliged to leave the grave which they had prepared for themselves.[48]

All of this was predictable. Once Napoleon had resolved on avenging Bailén, nothing could have staved off defeat. That said, such a disaster might yet have been avoided. Much has been made in this respect of the unfortunate role supposedly played by the Patriots' early successes in fostering a mood of over-confidence, but this is something that has been much exaggerated. Of far greater influence was, first, the disaffection of the populace; second, the oligarchy's fear of disorder; and, third, the machinations of such figures as Palafox. In short, what confronted Patriot Spain in the winter of 1808 was as much a political as it was a military problem, for continued resistance, let alone recovery, would in the end only be possible if faction could be defeated and order restored. With the Spanish armies in tatters, these objectives seemed unattainable. Indeed, no sooner had Madrid fallen than French troops had started to push south and west. For a brief while everything hung in the balance, but there was as yet one force that had not been touched by disaster. Almost unknown to the French as its presence was, the British army was finally ready for action, and, what is more, about to strike.

6

La Coruña

THE CAMPAIGN OF SIR JOHN MOORE,
DECEMBER 1808–JANUARY 1809

The people of Portsmouth looked on in horror at the spectacle that was emerging from the harbour. The British expeditionary force had returned home, but there was no grand parade through the streets, no pomp or colour, no tale of victory. What appeared seemed rather to be the mere wreckage of an army. Dressed in torn and faded uniforms, many of the soldiers were clearly wounded or sick, whilst all of them were filthy, haggard and exhausted. As for horses, there were none, the cavalry marching on foot with an air of particular dejection. As was already known, meanwhile, their commander was dead, cut down in a moment of victory that was looking more dubious by the minute, whilst dark stories were circulating of betrayal, incompetence and treachery. What had gone wrong?

What indeed? The answer is complex and many-faceted, but the situation seemed clear enough. The British army had been driven ignominiously from the Iberian Peninsula, suffering heavy casualties in the process; the Spanish forces were in ruins; the alliance with Patriot Spain had been put in jeopardy; Portugal had been rendered vulnerable to a fresh invasion which there seemed to be little chance of stopping; the Portland administration had been destabilised and left wide open to the attacks of an opposition that was increasingly restive; and, to cap it all, Napoleon was boasting of a great victory, accusing the British of betrayal and revelling in the imposition of a series of reforms that allowed him to make still further claim to the title of hero and liberator. All this was all the more shocking in view of what had gone before. The Convention of Sintra, certainly, had been an embarrassment, but nobody had ever doubted the calibre of the troops, whilst Sir John Moore's difficult temperament and differences with the ministry were not well enough known to detract from his reputation as a bold and enterprising officer of great promise. Such was the influence of Bailén and the constant stream of propaganda emanating from Patriot Spain that great hopes had continued to be entertained. In this respect, indeed, matters had been made still worse by Britain's successful rescue of La Romana's division from Denmark, for, composed of veteran troops who had not been caught up in the turmoil of events in Spain, it had given an impression of the Spanish army as a whole that was distinctly misleading.

Yet catastrophe had always been a strong possibility. With the populace hostile to conscription, the authorities too weak to enforce their writ, the world of politics rent by personal jealousy, ideological difference and provincial particularism, and the army beset by manifold difficulties, it was never likely that a counter-offensive could have been withstood. The most that Sir John Moore's army could ever have done would therefore have been to reduce the scale of disaster. Posted in the vicinity of Burgos – the position which the Spaniards, at least, intended that he should adopt – the British commander's 40,000 troops would at least have had a chance of checking the French on-rush and, in particular, preventing a Gamonal-style break-through, thereby affording Castaños and Blake a chance of escaping from their exposed positions in much better order. A retreat in the direction of Portugal would certainly have followed, but so many French troops would undoubtedly have marched in pursuit of Moore that the Spaniards might just have been able to hold the line of the Sierra de Guadarrama and thereby retain Madrid. In the long run, the city would still almost certainly have been lost, but substantial Spanish forces would probably have escaped beyond the River Tagus, whilst the panic and disintegration that marked the campaign of November and December 1808 might have been avoided. Of course, other scenarios were also possible – so badly were the British outnumbered that they might easily have been annihilated in some climactic battle somewhere in Old Castile – but, for all that, it is at least arguable that Moore's failure to appear on the Ebro was a matter of some regret.

The origins of the British army's presence in Spain have already been explored. As we have seen, in August 1808 it had been agreed that it should be concentrated on the frontiers of Galicia and León – a remote district safe from any possible French attack – and a plan of campaign elaborated with the Spaniards. Reasonable enough from London's point of view; however, Moore looked at this scheme in a very different light. Having had to extract the garrisons of Elvas and Almeida from blockade, British troops were now spread across wide expanses of central Portugal so that merely getting them to the area that had been designated for them would take a considerable time, and all the more so as the only practicable way of doing so was to route the entire force by La Coruña (as in fact his orders, which were only sent out on 25 September, specifically laid down). Acting entirely on his own initiative, he therefore decided to make his point of concentration not the isolated and poverty-stricken district of Ponferrada, but rather the city of Salamanca, reasoning that Sir David Baird would be able to shift his division southwards from La Coruña in no more time than it would take him to get his troops across the border from Portugal. All of this was perfectly understandable – a landing, Moore believed, would result in 'a corps lost' whereas 'a march, well conducted, will do this army much good'[1] – whilst the change did not overtly conflict with the spirit of the government's instructions, and ought in ordinary circumstances to have speeded up British intervention (although even then the British still could not have been ready for action at Salamanca before mid-November at the earliest). Yet it has to be said that Moore was also scornful of the government's capacity for strategic thought and eager for military glory. Still worse, he failed to win any extra time: not, indeed, until the first week of December was the army finally united. In part the delay was caused by factors beyond Moore's control – the structural shortcomings of the British army, the sloth displayed by Dalrymple before his departure, a desperate shortage of specie, mistakes on the part of officialdom at home, the difficulty of securing adequate transport, and the obstructive behaviour of the Junta of Galicia. There is also, however, the complex question of the roads which the army used for its march into Spain. In brief, whilst the bulk of the infantry marched on Salamanca north-eastwards from Lisbon across Beira, the artillery, the cavalry and some further footsoldiers were placed under the command of the capable Sir John Hope and ordered to make use of the main Lisbon– Madrid highway, which ran across the Alentejo, through Extremadura and up the Tagus valley. This arrangement does not deserve the scorn sometimes heaped upon it: it took account of the season of the year, the condition of the various roads and the station of the various units of the army inside Portugal. But for the British to get into action quickly, it relied on Hope finding a way across the rugged mountains that separated the Tagus valley from León: clearly, Moore could not go into action without his horse and guns. Despite the existence of at least two roads that led in the right direction, this Hope completely failed to do. The reasons have never been explained, but the result was that his corps ended up taking a tremendous detour. Marching up the length of the Tagus valley, it turned north just west of Madrid, picked up the main highway from the capital to the north-west, and then had to travel a considerable distance back towards the Portuguese frontier.

Whatever the truth of the matter, the British army ended up being for some time exposed to defeat in detail in the plains of the *meseta* should the French break through, as in fact they did, when they might have been safely ensconced in the mountains of Galicia. For this, perhaps, Moore can be forgiven. Not so, alas, his behaviour during the time he spent at Salamanca following his arrival there on 13 November. As if the news of Gamonal and Espinosa were not bad enough, it became ever more apparent that the new Spanish government had no means of enforcing its authority, that there was no one with whom Moore could elaborate a plan of campaign, that the chances of the British army being kept supplied with adequate stocks of food were tenuous in the extreme, that enthusiasm for the war amongst the populace was totally lacking, and that it would be a considerable time before he could be joined by Baird, whose troops were currently spread out far to the north over the best part of one hundred miles of road between Lugo and Astorga. To say that this was an awkward predicament was putting it mildly, and Moore would have been foolish indeed had he not been deeply alarmed. As he complained:

If I had had sooner a conception of the weakness of the Spanish armies, the defenceless state of the country, the apparent apathy of the people, and the selfish imbecility of the government, I should certainly have been in no hurry to enter Spain, or to have approached the scene of action until the army was united ... There seems to be neither an army, generals nor a government. I cannot calculate the power of a whole people determined and enthusiastic if persons are brought forward with ability to direct it, but at present nothing of this kind appears ... We are here on our own ... in complete ignorance of the plans and wishes of the Spanish government. Indeed, as far as I can learn, the Junta ... are incapable of forming any plan or coming to any fixed determination.[2]

In fairness to him, Moore did resolve to hang on until such time as he could be joined by Baird and Hope, but his decision to remain at Salamanca did not mean that he was a happy man. By the last days of November he was regularly receiving desperate appeals from both the British ambassador – a protégé of Canning's named John Hookham Frere who shared the ministers' general dislike of Moore and placed unbounded trust in Spanish enthusiasm – and the Junta Central itself to do something to help the Patriot cause. Yet everything Moore knew suggested that the optimistic bombast in which Frere and the Junta were wont to cloak their appeals had no basis in fact, whilst his capacity actually to do anything remained as limited as ever: as late as 28 November none of Baird's troops had passed Astorga, whilst Sir John Hope was still some seventy miles to the east. Fearing disaster, he in consequence tried to re-write history. 'They have been buoyed up in England', he claimed, 'by the false information transmitted by the officers sent to the various Spanish armies, who had neither sense nor honesty to tell the truth, so that Lord Castlereagh has very little idea of the situation in which we are here.'[3] The result, he continued, was that 'this army was sent infinitely too far forward', when in fact, as he wrote to Baird, it really ought to have gone to Andalucía: 'I know that you should have landed at Cádiz, and [that] I should have met you at Seville, where the army could have been united and equipped, but it was ordered otherwise, and it is our business to make every effort . . . to obey our orders . . . as far as lies in our power.'[4]

Breathtaking in its dishonesty, this farrago of untruth is worsened still further by the fact that Moore himself had always recognised that he was taking a risk in ignoring his instructions. As he had written whilst still in Portugal, 'If the French are kept . . . a good way behind the Ebro, then all will be well, but if they . . . assume the offensive and are able to force back the Spaniards before we can get together, our position will not be so pleasant.'[5] If he was in a 'terrible scrape', then, it was largely one of his own making. Yet Moore genuinely had much to complain about. It was not just, for example, that none of the inhabitants seemed willing to serve in the army. Still worse was the fact that they were in many cases openly hostile. In Ciudad Rodrigo, for example, 'something like a commotion' almost took place 'in consequence of our soldiers having requested a little salt from the people on whom they were billeted', and, still worse, 'An officer of the Seventy-Ninth unfortunately got involved in a dispute, and, while passing through one of their dark and narrow streets, was barbarously assassinated by an unknown hand.'[6] Similarly, at Alcántara, 'They received us . . . with an inhospitality they durst not have ventured had they not believed us to be friends.'[7] The general complaint is summed up by the commissary, Augustus Schaumann:

The people here have the cool effrontery to look upon the English troops as exotic animals who have come to engage in a private fight with the French, and now that they are here all that the fine Spanish gentlemen have to do is to look on with their hands in their pockets. They do not regard us in the least as allies who are prepared to shed their blood for Spain; they simply look upon us as heretics. In our billets it is as much as we can do to get a glass of water.[8]

The last straw came on 28 November when news arrived of Tudela. Arguing that he had not been sent to Spain to fight the entire French army on his own, Moore decided on retreat and readied his troops for departure whilst ordering Baird to march on La Coruña and Hope to head directly for Portugal.

Almost immediately, however, the situation changed, for Moore heard, first, that having been given the command of all the Spanish forces in north-western Spain, La Romana had succeeded in rallying the remains of the Army of the Left at León, and, second, that Madrid was making a serious attempt to defend itself. With the French showing no signs of moving west, Moore decided that retreat would lead to certain disgrace, and all the more so as he once again had an army of all arms at his disposal, Hope now being only fifteen miles away at Alba de Tormes. In consequence, on 5 December he countermanded his earlier instructions. As he wrote:

Madrid still holds out. This is the first instance of enthusiasm shown; there is a chance that the example may be followed . . . Upon this chance I have . . . taken measures to form our junction whilst the French are wholly occupied with Madrid. We are bound not to abandon the cause as long as there is hope . . .[9]

If this decision did not come soon enough to avert a violent confrontation between Moore and Frere (who behaved, it has to be said, with culpable stupidity), it did change the whole direction of the campaign. Thus, the British commander had resolved to strike eastwards into Old Castile in the hope that this would compel the emperor to turn aside from Madrid. In a very short time, of course, news arrived that the capital had fallen, but even so the same logic held good in that an attack on Old Castile would be certain to distract the French from marching on Portugal or Andalucía. Having left Salamanca on 11 December, meanwhile, Moore was reinforced in his determination by the arrival at his headquarters of a captured dispatch from Napoleon to Soult in which the latter was informed of the whereabouts of the rest of the French army and instructed to launch an offensive westwards from his current position on the River Carrión some forty miles east of León. One of Soult's three infantry divisions being at Santander and his cavalry brigade in the Tagus valley, there seemed every chance that he could be overwhelmed before he could receive any help, for the marshal was a long way from the nearest support, whilst it was clear that the French had no idea that the British were anywhere in sight. Originally the plan had been to occupy Valladolid, but Moore therefore ordered his men to keep marching north, thereby getting into direct touch with both Baird and La Romana. In the wake of their flight from Espinosa de los Monteros, contact with the Spaniards did not prove very encouraging, but the junction with Baird meant that by 20 December well over 25,000 British troops were concentrated at Mayorga. Though he had now both discovered the British threat and been reinforced by a full division of cavalry from Valladolid, Soult was still very vulnerable: on 21 December, indeed, one of his cavalry brigades was attacked and beaten at Sahagún de Campos by two regiments of British hussars.

Often criticised for 'galloping at everything', the British cavalry distinguished themselves at Sahagún. Covered with vines, the ground was unsuitable for cavalry, whilst the French had taken up a position behind a deep ditch. In the words of one participant:

As soon as the enemy's order of battle was formed, they cheered in a very gallant manner and immediately began firing. The Fifteenth then halted, wheeled into line, huzzaed and advanced. The interval betwixt us was perhaps 400 yards, but it was so quickly passed that they had only time to fire a few shots before we came upon them ... The shock was terrible: horses and men were overthrown, and a shriek of terror, intermixed with oaths, groans, and prayers for mercy, issued from the whole extent of their front. Our men, although surprised at the depth of the ranks, pressed forward until they had cut their way quite through the column. In many places the bodies of the fallen formed a complete mound of men and horses ... It was allowed by everyone who witnessed the advance of the Fifteenth that more correct movements, both in column and in line, were never performed at a review.[10]

With the rest of the army soon in occupation of Sahagún as well, it seemed that Soult was on the point of being dealt a crushing blow, but in the event Moore decided that his men should rest for forty-eight hours, so that it was not until nightfall on 23 December that the army marched out to attack the French, who were waiting for them at Carrión de los Condes. No sooner had the orders for the advance been dispatched, however, than dramatic news arrived from the south in the form of a report that masses of French troops were debouching from the Sierra de Guadarrama into the plains of Old Castile. In short, the game was up: Napoleon had finally discovered the presence of the British army and was heading north to wipe it out. The time having come to cut and run, fresh orders were sent out and to their complete consternation the British forces found themselves being stopped and turned around.

Though the astonished troops were not to know it, their goal was now the sea. However, before we examine the events that followed we must first look at the developments that succeeded the occupation of Madrid in the French camp. At the time of the fall of the capital and for some time afterwards, Napoleon and his forces had remained blissfully unaware of the fact that the British army was still a player in the campaign. Thus, no French troops having advanced west of a line stretching from Valladolid to Avila, only the vaguest impression had been obtained of the British presence in Spain, whilst it had been generally assumed that such forces as had been involved were now in full flight for Lisbon. Troops were therefore dispatched to such towns as Talavera, Toledo, Ocaña and Tarancón, but none in the direction of Salamanca. What this presaged, of course, was a move on Portugal and Andalucía, but in the meantime Napoleon had plenty of other matters on his mind. First and foremost amongst these was the political settlement of Spain, the emperor's opening gambit here being to announce that he was going either to assume the Spanish throne himself or to divide the country up into a number of military regions headed by French governors. However, all this was simply a ruse. What Napoleon really wanted, apart from a pretext for appearing magnanimous, was a show of recognition, and this he got: invited to swear loyalty to Joseph Bonaparte on the Blessed Sacrament in ceremonies held in churches throughout the capital on 13 December, the city's civil and ecclesiastical dignitaries and thousands of ordinary citizens complied with the imperial will, whereupon it was duly announced that *el rey intruso* was to be allowed to resume his throne.

Joseph's restitution, however, was for the time being a matter of form alone. In the Constitution of Bayonne Napoleon considered that he had been forced to make a number of humiliating concessions to traditionalist opinion in Spain, and he was now determined to ensure that his new vassal state would conform much more strictly with the rest of the empire. Napoleon knew, though, that, anxious to conciliate Spanish opinion and gain acceptance as monarch, Joseph would be unlikely to go along with the changes that he wanted to make. In consequence, to the king's intense chagrin, Joseph was confined to the suburban palace of El Pardo, whilst his imperial brother settled everything to his own satisfaction in what became known as the Decrees of Chamartín (the village in which Napoleon had his headquarters). At a stroke these abolished monopolies, internal tariff barriers, feudal dues and rights of private jurisdiction; dissolved two-thirds of all Spain's religious communities; opened the way for monks and nuns to return to civil life; abolished the Inquisition; and put on sale all property belonging to the religious institutions that had been suppressed. At the same time, despite the continued affectation of moderation, to reform was added proscription. The capitulation had guaranteed the life, freedom and property of all those who submitted to the emperor, but, on the pretext that it had been violated by the flight of such few regular troops as had been in the city when it was attacked, the French ruler declared it null and void and proceeded to make a large number of arrests, those affected including several members of the Junta of Defence, the president of the Council of Castile, various noblemen who had deserted Joseph after initially swearing loyalty to his cause, and the entire Council of the Inquisition. Given that many of those involved lost their property, that many further confiscations were planned, and that all the goods involved were immediately put on sale in their turn, the scale of the assault on the traditional social structure was therefore greatly increased.

Joseph, it need hardly be said, was most unhappy at much of this. Setting aside the fact that Napoleon's actions threatened in a variety of ways to alienate the populace, the Decrees of Chamartín had not even been issued in his name. Feeling that his position had been undermined, he threatened to abdicate. The trouble was, however, that Joseph was not the man to act on such a threat. On the one hand he was so overawed by his younger brother that breaking with him presented almost insuperable psychological difficulties, whilst on the other he was addicted to wealth and luxury and much in love with the idea of being a king. Excellent judge of human nature that he was, Napoleon was well aware of this, and in consequence called Joseph's bluff by offering him a variety of lesser positions in exchange for the Spanish throne. This producing the desired result, the emperor switched from stick to carrot, inviting his brother to accompany him on a brief visit to the capital and flattering him with promises of understanding and support.

For over two weeks after the fall of Madrid all seemed to go well. Yet Napoleon was living in a fool's paradise. Whilst the populace had proved not only hostile to conscription, but also – at least for the most part – unwilling to take up arms even in defence of their own homes, this did not mean that French occupation met with no resistance whatsoever. On the contrary, the winter of 1808 saw the real beginnings of *la guerrilla* – the irregular struggle that was to plague the French zone of occupation for the rest of the war. Far more complex than at first appears, this phenomenon is best discussed in some other context. Suffice to say that the territory that the invaders had just overrun quickly became the haunt of assorted bands of marauders. At this time for the most part little more than bandit gangs made up of a mixture of outlaws, deserters, draft evaders and destitute *campesinos*, these men quickly began to cause serious problems for the French, even if their actions were in most cases driven not by patriotism but necessity. Even before the fall of Madrid, there had been trouble: sent with a dispatch from Lannes to Napoleon in late November, Marbot found the bodies of several Frenchmen who had been murdered along the way, including a cavalry officer nailed upside down to a barn door with a fire lit beneath his head, and was twice attacked by parties of guerrillas.

If Moore's operations were being conducted with a sure grasp of the positions and intentions of the enemy, it was in large part due to the guerrillas' capture of large numbers of French couriers. Not until 15 December was Soult informed that Moore was on the move, whilst Napoleon did not hear of the matter for another four days. Once the news had come in, however, the emperor moved with great speed and decision. Although he had resolved on an offensive on Lisbon, to which end cavalry were already pushing westwards down the Tagus, the main body of his army still remained in the vicinity of Madrid. Instantly disposable were some 40,000 men including the Imperial Guard, King Joseph's royal guard (a small force of foreign deserters and prisoners of war), the corps of Marshal Ney and two stray infantry divisions belonging to the corps of Lefebvre and Victor. Further away in an arc stretching from Talavera to Guadalajara there were the remaining troops of Victor and Lefebvre – in each case two infantry divisions and a cavalry brigade – a brigade of light cavalry detached from the corps of Marshal Soult, three divisions of dragoons and the independent infantry division of General Desolles. These troops being more than sufficient to hold off the remnants of the Spanish armies, with the exception of Joseph's guard the whole of the central reserve was therefore immediately ordered to march in the direction of Valladolid in the hope that the British might be cut off from Portugal. Not only that, indeed, but messages were sent out to a division of dragoons that had been sent to hold Avila, another that had recently arrived at Burgos and the corps of General Junot, which was strung out between that city and the French frontier, either to join the chase or to reinforce the beleaguered Soult.

Despite the fact that 80,000 men were now bearing down upon him, Moore was in fact in little danger. For one thing the French onrush was slowed by appalling weather conditions. In the Sierra de Guadarrama, for example, the troops were struck by a terrible blizzard:

Next day a furious snowstorm, with a fierce wind, made the passage of the mountains almost impassable. Men and horses were hurled over precipices. The leading battalions actually began to retreat, but Napoleon was resolved to overtake the English at all costs. He . . . ordered that the members of each section should hold one another by the arm. The cavalry, dismounting, did the same. The staff was formed in similar fashion, the emperor between Lannes and Duroc . . . and so, in spite of wind, snow and ice, we proceeded, though it took us four hours to reach the top.[11]

Further north, meanwhile, although the snow turned to rain, 'the roads were all but impassable: we had met with no such mud anywhere else but in Poland and Champagne'.[12] All this caused the French terrible suffering. Coignet, for example, remembers fording a freezing river and emerging with his legs 'as red as lobsters', whilst Chlapowski wrote, 'Horses and men sank deep into the mud . . . I was told that some soldiers who could not keep up . . . took their own lives for fear of falling into the hands of the Spanish guerrillas whose bands were roaming the country.'[13]

Setting the weather aside, Moore was so far to the north that it was unlikely that a force coming from Madrid would ever have been able to cut him off. The emperor's only chance, indeed, was that his opponent would be caught unawares, but Moore was well aware of the danger and fled westwards as soon as he got news that Napoleon was on the march, whilst he had also long since requested that his transports should be sent round from Lisbon to La Coruña. Vigorous action on the part of Soult, it is true, might just have slowed Moore down enough to allow Napoleon's forces to get behind him, but the marshal elected to wait for the first of the reinforcements that were being sent up to him from Burgos and then was slowed down by pouring rain and a series of skilful rearguard actions on the part of the British cavalry.

By 27 December, then, the whole of Moore's army had got to relative safety on the western bank of the River Esla between Benavente and Valencia de Don Juan, and the following day there may be said to have commenced the long march that became known in the annals of the British army as the 'retreat to Corunna'. Thus, covered by a rearguard of cavalry and light infantry, which managed to capture General Lefebvre Desnouettes in a fierce skirmish outside Benavente, the main body of Moore's forces struck out north-west for Astorga. At that town they came up with the remnants of the Army of the Left, the latter force having been forced to evacuate the positions which it had been holding around León by the advance of Soult's troops from the Carrión after a sharp reverse at Mansilla de los Mulos. Even if it was no fault of the Spaniards, whose only other lines of retreat were blocked by either snow or the enemy, this encounter with his allies was not at all to Moore's taste, the latter having for logistical reasons asked La Romana to retire not westwards towards Astorga but northwards towards Oviedo. As he had feared, indeed, the result was chaos, the Army of the Left now being in a worse state than ever. Wrote one soldier, 'I can conceive of no description of it . . . It had more the appearance of a large body of peasants driven from their homes, famished and in want of everything, than a regular army. Sickness was making dreadful havoc amongst them.'[14] To quote Gordon, meanwhile, 'This Spanish force amounted to about 6,000 men in the most deplorable condition. They were all ill-clothed; many were without shoes and without arms; a pestilential fever raged amongst them; they had been without bread for several days and were quite destitute of money.'[15] Desperate for food they therefore fell on the town and the British baggage trains alike and the result was a general free-for-all that had soon spread to the redcoats as well.

All this came as a great shock to many British officers. 'What was our surprise,' wrote Cadell, 'to see such troops instead of the fine army we had so often heard was to join us.'[16] That said, however, at least the Allied armies were united and possessed of a secure line of retreat, whilst they also had access to substantial stocks of arms, ammunition, food, clothing and an excellent defensive position: the town itself was fortified and could have been held as an outwork, whilst the main forces held the passes through which ran the main road to La Coruña immediately to the north-west. Yet no stand was attempted, both armies rather, on 30 December, getting under way for Galicia. Why this should have been the case is a subject that has generated much controversy, whilst the whole episode plunged relations between the British and the Spaniards into crisis. Part of the problem was certainly logistical – the Astorga position could not be supplied indefinitely – but the heart of the issue was that, on personal and political grounds alike, Moore was determined to take no more risks with his army. Coupled to all this was the fact not only that La Romana's troops were clearly in no state to fight, but also that discipline in the British army, too, was breaking down. The trouble had begun when the army passed through Benevente a few days before. With bitterness at the Spaniards running high, troops billeted in the castle vandalised its magnificent interior unmercifully, whilst the soldiery and their women fell on the town's wine cellars and engaged in the first of what was to become a series of mass drinking bouts. Meanwhile, the confusion was increased still further by the decision to shed some of the army's stores, in the course of which the troops got hold of yet more alcohol.

In military terms, Moore's decision to retreat was therefore probably sensible enough, but in other respects it was a disaster. Having first failed to appear in time to meet Napoleon's counter-offensive and then allowed Madrid to fall without firing a shot, the British now seemed to be abandoning Spain altogether. At all events, La Romana was furious, for many of the supplies stored at Astorga had been intended for his army, whilst Moore had initially promised him that he would defend the town. However, there was worse to come. As the British fell back, so drunkenness, exhaustion – at one point Moore forced his men to march for thirty-six hours without a break – hunger and discontent led to widespread straggling. Left with no other means of survival, all those concerned had no option but to turn to pillage, but whilst some men continued to stumble along in the wake of the army and did no more than take what they needed, even they were not disposed to look especially kindly on the civilian population, whilst many others saw the situation as a glorious opportunity to indulge their worst vices. Though some battalions held together well enough, the path of the army was therefore marked by a trail of arson, theft, rape and murder.

Stories of the disorders witnessed during the retreat are legion. Typical of the horrors inflicted on the civilian populace is the sight seen by Gordon on 1 January 1809:

In the afternoon we passed through a large village which had been completely gutted by fire. The wretched inhabitants were sitting amidst the trifling articles of property they had been able to seize from the flames, contemplating the ruins of their homes in silent despair. The bodies of several Spaniards who had died of hunger and disease, or perished from the inclemency of the weather, were lying scattered around and added to the horrors of the scene. The village had been burned by some of our infantry.[17]

Porter confirms such scenes, writing, 'The poor cottagers were plundered, and multitudes of homeless, destitute people were continually hastening to the officers as they came up, imploring them for a redress which was out of their power to bestow.'[18] But worst of all, perhaps, was the fate of Bembibre. To quote Blakeney:

Bembibre exhibited all the appearance of a place lately stormed and pillaged. Every door and window was broken, every lock and fastening forced. Rivers of wine ran through the houses and into the streets, where lay fantastic groups of soldiers . . . women, children, runaway Spaniards and muleteers, all apparently inanimate . . . while the wine oozing from their lips and nostrils seemed the effect of gunshot wounds . . . The music was perfectly in character: savage roars announcing present hilarity were mingled with groans issuing from fevered lips disgorging the wine of yesterday; obscenity was public sport.[19]

Marching in near continuous rain and snow, even those troops who remained with the colours presented a sorry sight. The Spanish muleteers deserted, wagon after wagon was abandoned, and even the headquarters' supply of ready cash had to be thrown into a ravine. Meanwhile, the road became littered with dead men and horses and abandoned equipment of all sorts, the many blazing supply dumps only adding to the appearance of rout. As for the soldiers, typical enough was the experience of Stephen Morley:

We had neither an adequate supply of food or clothing, and our feet were dreadfully hurt from want of shoes; many were actually barefooted . . . The poor women were deeply to be pitied. One of them . . . with no covering but her tattered clothes . . . gave birth to a son . . . The road all the way was strewed with men unable to proceed . . . Discipline was forgotten, none commanded, none obeyed . . . Seeing smoke issue from a large building off the road, I crawled rather than walked to it. It was something like a barn, and full of our men who had made a fire. I found a spare corner, and putting my pouch under my head, fell into a sound sleep . . . When I awoke, I was told the army . . . had gone on.[20]

The French then coming up, like many such men, Morley was taken prisoner. The group that he was with put up a fierce fight, however, one of the few bright spots of the retreat being the manner in which bands of stragglers repeatedly clubbed together in desperate 'last stands'. Most famous of such incidents was one which took place near Betanzos in the last stages of the retreat in which a sergeant named William Newman rallied a group of about a hundred men and fought off a group of French cavalry.

The troops' fighting spirit was not broken, then. Yet the retreat remains a dark chapter in the history of the British army. Let us turn, for example, to the account of the Marqués de la Romana:

The English have seized . . . the mules and oxen that drew our army's artillery, munitions and baggage train; they have insulted and mistreated . . . our officers . . . They have stolen all the mules of the . . . inhabitants of Benevente and the *pueblos* of the Tierra de Campos, and have left a multitude of carts abandoned by the wayside, some of them broken down and others smashed up on purpose. They have without necessity killed and eaten the oxen that pulled these carts and have not paid their value. They have killed three magistrates and various other inhabitants. After allowing anyone who wanted to to drink their fill without paying a penny, they have poured away all the wine in the cellars. They have not paid for the carts and animals that they have used to move their women and their immense baggage trains. In some *pueblos* the commissaries have refused to give receipts for the supplies made available to them by the justices, whilst in others they have arbitrarily reduced the sums that were asked of them. In a word the French themselves could not have found agents better calculated to whip up hate of the British than the army commanded by General Sir John Moore.[21]

However, if the Spaniards gained a distinctly negative view of their allies, the reverse was also true. From the moment that the British troops had entered Spain, disillusionment had been growing at the unwillingness of the inhabitants to enlist in the regular army, not to mention the laxity and incompetence that were perceived to be the chief characteristics of the Spanish authorities. To these doubts, meanwhile, were added stories of treason and betrayal – there seemed, for example, to be no other explanation for the fall of Madrid – whilst the miserable condition of La Romana's forces was hardly calculated to inspire confidence in Spain's powers of resistance. To be fair, indeed, the behaviour of these troops was not much better than that of the British, as witness the experience of the parish priest of the village of San Andrés del Rabanedo in the wake of the battle of Mansilla de los Mulos:

The streets and houses ... were strewn with the dead and dying. What with the stench and filth of the former and the cries and groans of the latter, a more horrible spectacle had never been seen ... All this was accompanied by robbery, insult and outrage as men besieged by hunger or accustomed to a life of crime assailed road and home alike. Seeing me come out of a privy, a group of stragglers went in and searched the excrement, believing that I must have gone in to hide some money ... It was not possible to move an inch without exposing oneself to every sort of vexation.[22]

As the retreat proceeded, too, so stories began to spread of hostility and even murder, whilst there was also much anger at the general failure of the populace to offer anything in the way of resistance. In Schaumann's words:

The apathy with which the inhabitants of this mountain country ... have witnessed our misery is revolting. They were to be seen in large armed hordes far away from us in the mountains ... when ... they might have been very useful to us and covered our retreat. But not only did these puffed-up patriots ... give us no assistance, but they also took good care to remove all cattle and all foodstuffs out of our way ... and in addition murdered and plundered our own men who fell out left and right along the road.[23]

However, if the seeds of serious problems were being sown in Anglo-Spanish relations, at least the Allied armies survived. The Army of the Left succeeded in reaching the safety of the wild mountains that border the northern frontier of Portugal, whilst French attempts to drive in the British rearguard at Cacabellos and Constantino were repulsed with ease. As for the enemy, not only were many troops withdrawn from the pursuit of Moore's army, but the emperor himself decided to return to France, having come to the conclusion that his presence was no longer needed. So much did the outlook improve, indeed, that Moore even offered battle with his whole force in an extremely strong position outside Lugo, even if he did eventually decide to take the road again when the French declined to attack immediately. There was further chaos in the march from Lugo to La Coruña – the weather continued to be atrocious, whilst the men were even more mutinous and exhausted than before – but, aside from two brigades that had been detached from the main column in the early stages of the march to secure Vigo, by 12 January the army had reached the sea.

At La Coruña, however, fresh problems confronted Moore, for it was discovered that his ships had been held up. Although the delay was fairly short – they in fact appeared on 14 January – it was none the less sufficient for the French to approach within striking distance of the town. Amidst scenes of general destruction – La Coruña and its environs were crammed with stores and munitions of all sorts, most of which had to be burned or blown up – a start was made on getting the troops embarked. Whilst this was going on, 15,000 infantry and a few guns were sent out to occupy the line of heights that overlooked the town and its spacious harbour from the south and south-west. In this position on 16 January 1809 there was fought the battle of La Coruña. Despite serious problems of their own, the French, who were led by Marshal Soult, could bring up perhaps 16,000 men, including plenty of cavalry and artillery. Perceiving what he thought was a weak spot in the British line, the French commander threw the bulk of his troops against it in an attempt to split the defenders in two and trap their centre and left against the seashore. However, though subjected to heavy bombardment, the British threw back all the troops that reached the heights and captured the village of Elvina in a fierce counter-attack, and that despite the fact that Moore was fatally wounded by a cannonball whilst directing the movement of some reserves (he died that evening and was buried the following day on the southern ramparts of La Coruña). With the French cavalry prevented from charging by the stone walls, rocks and scrub that covered the whole area, the battle therefore petered out with the British still in possession of the field.

With this pretty small-scale affair – total casualties amounted to less than 2,000 men – the campaign was over. Despite some long-distance artillery fire, by the end of 17 January most of the British troops had been got safely aboard, and on the following day the whole armada sailed for home, La Coruña's understandably demoralised governor surrendering later the same day. At first sight, then, British intervention had ended in humiliation and disaster. At La Coruña, true, a reverse had been inflicted on the French. However, Sir John Moore was dead, over one fifth of his army were missing, and several thousand more sick or wounded, whilst the retreat had had all the appearances of a rout; if the army had saved all its guns, it had lost much of its baggage and been forced to destroy almost all the horses that had managed to reach La Coruña. Hundreds more men, meanwhile, were lost in winter storms in the Bay of Biscay and the Channel. Added to all this must be the loss or destruction of immense quantities of *matériel*, including, most spectacularly of all, 4,000 barrels of powder blown up in a great explosion on 13 January, as well as the occupation of the most heavily populated region in the whole of Spain, and in addition such important towns as Lugo and La Coruña.

Even worse than the physical losses suffered by the Allied cause was the immense damage that had been done to Anglo-Spanish relations. Misled by propagandistic journalists who had consistently claimed that Moore's army was much larger than it actually was and represented Sahagún as a great victory, Spanish opinion was genuinely shocked by the British departure, whilst fuel was added to the flames by the angry accounts of the Marqués de la Romana and other observers, the marquess openly accusing Moore of betrayal and bad faith. If much of this criticism was unfair, the behaviour of the army had also been singularly unhelpful. The presence of British troops in Spain was always likely to have led to a variety of cultural problems: the drunkenness habitual amongst many of the men was frowned upon, whilst Protestant hostility to popery ensured that officers and men alike were not always disposed to treat the Catholic Church with respect. However, the excesses of the retreat went far beyond friction and disrespect, the fact being that many of the British troops had behaved as badly as the enemy.

Needless to say, the issue cut both ways. British veterans of the campaign felt they had advanced into Spain in good faith only to find a country with neither enthusiasm for the struggle, nor competent leadership, nor adequate armies, and a country, moreover, in which, rather than being welcomed and assisted, they had from the start been lied to, deceived and treated as interlopers. Lip-service was in some instances paid to the idea that the common people were sound at heart, but contempt for the ruling élite was all but universal, matters not being helped by the decision of various public figures, such as the *de facto* head of the defence of Madrid and erstwhile governor of Cádiz, Tomás de Morla, to go over to the enemy. With treason seemingly rife, it followed that the British army had been betrayed and that Spain – which had at best appeared to be primitive, backward and superstitious – was not worth fighting for.

If all this was not enough, the campaign also led to turmoil in England. Inside the government, a furious Canning was nudged in a direction that was ultimately to threaten complete disaster. The war, he thought, was going very badly, whilst things now looked likely to get even worse. Still convinced that the Iberian Peninsula held immense strategic potential, he was deeply alarmed at the manner in which the experiences of the British army had produced widespread disillusionment with the Patriot cause amongst not just public opinion but even some of his colleagues. Even more infuriating, meanwhile, was the style in which the Opposition seized upon the campaign as a stick with which to beat the government – Whig after Whig demanded the publication of the official correspondence, pressed for the establishment of a parliamentary committee of enquiry, or simply lambasted almost every aspect of the government's Spanish policy. Eventually the storm blew itself out, but Canning was deeply disgruntled by the somewhat lacklustre defence put up by his fellow ministers, much distressed at the fashion in which criticism had focused on Frere, and left with the firm belief that something would have to be done. With a variety of other issues also conspiring to widen the rift – amongst them, a revival of pressure for political reform and Canning's impatient and mercurial character – by the spring of 1809 the Foreign Secretary was plotting a major Cabinet reshuffle.

In acting in this fashion, Canning sincerely believed that he could establish a stronger ministry which would be able to capitalise on the considerable underlying support for the administration in Parliament and fight a more effective war. Nor can he be accused of being moved by spite or personal ambition: though he did find Castlereagh cold, reserved and ineffectual, for example, Canning was not simply out to get rid of him, just as the various schemes that he eventually put forward in no case advanced his chances of becoming prime minister. Yet, that said, his behaviour was at best misguided and at worst irresponsible: a better prime minister could possibly be found than Portland, but only at the risk of major feud in the governing party, whilst the strategic situation was by no means as dire as Canning feared. A good case can be made for saying that far from betraying his trust, by striking at Napoleon's communications Moore had drawn a large part of the emperor's forces after him into northern Spain. In doing so, it is often argued that he had thwarted the capture of Lisbon and Cádiz and thereby cost Napoleon his only chance of a quick victory. This, perhaps, is going too far, but what is certainly true is that the battered Spanish armies had been afforded a valuable breathing space and the Junta Central given the chance to restore a modicum of order. From its nadir in December 1808, the Patriot cause therefore recovered, and this in turn ensured that the British would not abandon Spain altogether, as might otherwise easily have proved the case.

For the shattered remnants of the Army of the Centre things were still bad enough. In late December Galluzo's Extremadurans were driven from their base on the Tagus at the Puente de Almaraz by the corps of Marshal Lefebvre, and pursued halfway to Badajoz, the only reason why they escaped destruction being that the marshal misunderstood his orders and at the last minute fell back across the Tagus, marched through the towering Sierra de Gredos and occupied Avila. Even then its soldiers were scattered across the countryside, Lorenzo Calvo de Rozas writing that in the Tagus valley many 'dispersed soldiers' were 'molesting all the towns and villages'.[24] Meanwhile, matters of rather greater note were taking place in La Mancha where, left alone by the French, Infantado had been reorganising the Army of the Centre's Andalusian elements at Cuenca. By the middle of December, some 20,000 men had been got together and Infantado resolved to try a *coup de main*, sending half his forces westward under General Francisco Javier Venegas to attack the French cavalry screen that had been posted south of the Tagus. For various reasons, however, the plan miscarried, whereupon Infantado decided to bring up the rest of his troops and arranged a rendez-vous with Venegas at the town of Uclés. But the duke was a sluggish commander at best, whilst he faced many logistical problems. In consequence he was outmarched by the French, who had responded to the threat by sending as many men as they could to crush Venegas.

On 13 January 1809 there followed the battle of Uclés. Venegas' men had taken up defensive positions on the long west-facing ridge behind which the town is situated. Commanded by Marshal Victor, however, the French proved more than equal to the challenge, and quickly enveloped the southern end of the Spanish line, which broke and fled. No reserves having been stationed behind Venegas' position, there was no chance of repairing the damage, and the whole Spanish army was soon falling back. As yet the centre and right had maintained their order, and the defenders might therefore still have made an orderly retreat, but it was not to be: Marshal Victor had led a flanking column on a long detour around the northern flank of the position and with perfect timing now appeared in the Spanish rear. The result was disaster. To quote a French eyewitness, 'Several thousand Spaniards were obliged to throw down their arms. Terror seized their whole army, and the various corps which composed it precipitately fled on all sides.'[25] Several units maintained their order and tried to break out, but they, too, as Girón recounts, were soon in trouble:

Having got everything ready in a few moments, I ordered the attack to be beaten throughout the column, and we marched on the enemy . . . The latter advanced very close to us and . . . opened a very lively fire on our front and flank. In spite of my precise orders not to fire a shot, the battalion at the head of the column began to fire back. Realising that if it continued, we were lost, I immediately ran to the front . . . to get it to attack with the bayonet, but it was already falling back on account of its heavy losses and getting entangled with the battalion that was following it. In the course of my attempts to get it to stand . . . the horse that I was riding was hit by two musket shots . . . By now we were under terrible close-range fire from three directions, and the troops had got completely muddled up so that they formed a single mass. Not knowing how else to save themselves, various soldiers began to cry, 'Quarter! Quarter!', and to wave scarves and even shirts on their bayonets.[26]

In the end over 10,000 men were taken, less than one third of that number managing to escape the trap and rejoin Infantado. Amongst the survivors was Girón, who set spurs to his dying horse and galloped clear, just managing to outdistance a party of French cavalry in the process. Left with no more than 8,000 men, the duke then fled eastwards with the French in hot pursuit. Chased by the French as far as Cuenca, they lost much of their artillery and baggage in a skirmish at Tortola, but thereafter they were left alone, and, turning their faces to the south, made haste to gain the shelter of the Sierra Morena and, beyond it, Andalucía.

If the punishment visited on Galluzo and Infantado was severe, it was far from being the only damage inflicted on the Patriot cause. Far away to the north-east the Army of Reserve was still massed at Zaragoza, where it had been joined, it will be recalled, by two Valencian divisions that had originally been given to Castaños. With most of the French troops in the vicinity engaged in the pursuit of the Army of the Centre, Palafox and his men had for some weeks been left in peace. The French had not forgotten them, however, and, whilst the Aragonese forces were kept under observation by the corps of Marshal Moncey, Napoleon sent orders for the latter to be reinforced by the corps of Marshal Mortier, the intention being that the city should be placed under siege as soon as these reinforcements should have come up.

In all, once the units needed to cover the attackers' line of communications had been deducted, some forty thousand men would be available for the siege, these being supported by a train of sixty heavy guns and plentiful munitions and engineering equipment (particularly valuable in this respect were the makings of the pontoon bridge that would be needed if Zaragoza was to be besieged with any security or hope of success). Given the events of the previous siege, the caution that this displayed was entirely understandable, whilst it was rendered all the more necessary by the fact that the Aragonese capital was no longer an easy target. On the contrary, whilst continuing to animate the defenders with a barrage of extravagance, exaggeration and bombast, Palafox had massed 34,000 troops in the city, not counting the unknown number of armed civilians who might also participate in the fighting. Most of these men were new levies, but at least they had all received a modicum of training and been organised into proper regiments and could be expected to put up a much better fight behind fortications than they would in the open field. Cannon, arms and ammunition were plentiful, too, whilst the city's medieval defences had been hidden behind a line of earthworks and entrenchments which linked together the various convents and monasteries that lay just outside the walls, all of these having been transformed into makeshift forts. Also better protected were Monte Torrero and the trans-ebrine suburb of San Lázaro. Inside the city, streets had been barricaded, doors and windows blocked by barricades, walls loopholed, and houses linked by tunnels and passageways. And, last but not least, the population appeared genuinely determined to defend themselves. For example:

Such was the spirit of the inhabitants that upon the 27th and the 28th there was not a moment's cessation of work during day or night and every individual of every class was at work at the batteries . . . The ladies had enrolled themselves, and hundreds of women of the lower class, and formed companies in order to supply the different batteries with provisions, etc., during the siege.[27]

Given the general lack of interest in the war amongst the populace, it is difficult not to question this impression. Yet months of demagoguery, pride in Zaragoza's 'Virgin of the Pillar' as a focus of veneration and pilgrimage, religious faith, and the anti-revolutionary traditions instilled by the flight to Aragón of many French clergy in the 1790s had all had some effect. At the same time research on Britain and France has suggested that urban populations were generally more swayed by ideas of patriotism than were their rural counterparts even when they not under direct attack. We should not go too far in this respect: there were deserters even from Zaragoza, whilst Marbot attributes the collapse of resistance at the end of the siege to an act of generosity on the part of Marshal Lannes that convinced the defenders their lives would be spared. Nor can the constant French stories of the wholesale use of terror to force the troops to fight be wholly ignored. Yet the second siege of Zaragoza nevertheless turned into a horrific affair. The reinforcements needed for the siege taking some little time to arrive, operations did not begin until 21 December. After that, however, matters proceeded apace. As before, Monte Torrero was overrun on the first day of the fighting, whilst by the close of the year the city had been closely blockaded on both banks of the river, a pontoon bridge thrown across the Ebro, and considerable progress made on the attackers' trenches and gun emplacements. Thinly stretched by the arrival of orders directing the dispatch of a division to protect the direct road between Zaragoza and Madrid, not to mention the ravages of sickness, the attackers might have been seriously inconvenienced had Palafox used all his surplus troops to rush one particular sector of their front, but the plan seems never to have been considered, such sorties as did take place consisting of suicidal rushes by mere handfuls of men.

Though he did his best to hearten the defence, the fact was that Palafox was at best a mediocre commander. Meeting him for the first time, Girón

Pictured with his staff at Astorga on 2 January 1809, Napoleon spent barely two months in the Peninsula. Would the result of the war have been different had he commanded his forces in person?

(*above*) Carlos IV, María Luisa and members of the Spanish royal family. The young boy holding the queen's hand is Prince Francisco de Paula, whose appearance at a window of the royal palace sparked off the Dos de Mayo.

(*left*) Fernando VII. Briefly put on the throne in 1808, he was so eager to secure Napoleon's patronage that he has been described as the first *afrancesado*.

Lascivious and venal, Manuel de Godoy was nonetheless a shrewd statesman who struggled to equip Spain for the challenges of the Napoleonic era.

An angry crowd fills the courtyard of the royal palace at Aranjuez on 18 March 1808 as soldiers, peasants and retainers demand the head of Manuel de Godoy.

Fernando VII enters Madrid in triumph in the wake of the Motín de Aranjuez.

The first shots of the Peninsular War are fired outside the royal palace in Madrid on
2 May 1808 as the crowd tries to prevent the removal of the last members of the Spanish
royal family to France.

(*left*) Joseph Bonaparte. Handsome, sensitive and generous, the 'gentle Bonaparte' did not deserve his popular reputation as a drunkard, but lacked the strength to stand up to Napoleon.

(*right*) The Duque de Infantado, painted here some time after the war, was a ringleader in the plot that brought Fernando VII to the throne in 1808, but he proved of little worth as either general or statesman.

Napoleon receives news from his staff, whilst, in the background, the Imperial Guard's regiment of Polish light horse rides resolutely into the pass of Somosierra on 30 November 1808.

(*above*) José Palafox. Famed for his defence of Zaragoza, this young guards officer was in reality more a politician than a general.

(*left*) The Marqués de la Romana. Commander of the division marooned in Denmark in 1808, he was one of the few Spanish generals to win the approval of the British, but his political intrigues seriously jeopardised the Patriot cause.

professed himself astonished at his 'absolute nullity'.[28] Even more damning was the officer who commanded his artillery, Luis de Villaba, who condemned his 'conceit and nonsensical designs' and complained that 'all the maxims and doctrines of war that could have led us to . . . victory were ignored and trampled underfoot'.[29] Indeed, he had already made a serious error. In cramming so many men into Zaragoza, he had been responding to his desire for self-aggrandisement rather than any grasp of strategic reality. As Aragón had thereby been all but stripped of troops, the result was that there was little chance of operating against the besiegers' flanks and rear or, still more, organising a relief force. In opposition to this, of course, it can be argued that to leave troops outside the city was simply to expose them to a re-run of the disaster at Epila the previous summer, but this ignores the other result of Palafox's actions. Thus, Zaragoza was forced to accommodate far more men than were needed for its defence, whilst its already substantial population had been swollen by large numbers of refugees. With the city's buildings insufficient to shelter such an influx, the consequence was growing pressure on the city's magazines, severe overcrowding and, inevitably, disease. As Marbot writes, 'The peasants . . . had entered the town with their wives, their children, and even their herds and . . . lived mixed up with their beasts in the most disgusting state of filth.'[30] Very soon, indeed, the city was in the grip of a typhus epidemic so serious that within ten days it had rendered a third of the garrison *hors de combat*.

To the misery of disease was soon added that of bombardment, for by 10 January the French had completed all their siege batteries and armed them with cannon and munitions. Duly opening fire, they had soon wrought terrible damage on the Spanish front line, whilst at the same time succeeding in storming the vital monastery of San José, which had been converted into a detached work protecting the whole of the eastern and south-eastern faces of the city. Digging operations and bombardment continued for another fortnight, by which time all was ready for an assault on the walls themselves, and on 27 January Marshal Lannes, who had been sent by Napoleon to take command of the besiegers, duly ordered his men to storm the city.

With the walls breached in many places in the sector chosen by the attackers for the assault, the defenders could at this point have been expected to surrender. Palafox, however, rejected all Lannes' overtures, whilst his followers were still prepared to put up a fight. In consequence, the French attack was met by desperate resistance:

The main assault, made on 27 January, was one of the bloodiest days of the siege. Since dawn our batteries had concentrated their fire on widening the breaches. At nine o'clock those units designated for the assault moved forward . . . Of all the attacks on the right only one achieved even partial success – that on the breach by the Palafox battery. The . . . assault on the casa González, in which I took part, failed completely. We . . . just managed to get into the building, but were met by such a heavy fire . . . that we fell back rather quickly. Major Beyer . . . was seriously wounded, and the captain of my company . . . fell into enemy hands.[31]

Despite heavy casualties, the invaders eventually succeeded in establishing a lodgement inside the walls, but, as in the previous siege, even then the defenders would not give up. On the contrary, in a foretaste of battles far in the future, the French had to advance into the city house by house, blowing holes in partition walls and methodically slaughtering the defenders of each room. Amidst scenes of desperate courage, the Spaniards fought back, engaging in repeated counter-attacks and digging mines under many French positions, but, though increasingly exhausted, Lannes' men kept inching forward. Fighting even went on underground as mine was met by counter-mine, and rival parties of miners hacked at each other with picks and shovels. On 10 February matters rose to a fearsome climax with a French assault on the Spanish stronghold of the convent of San Francisco preceded by the explosion of a 3,000-pound mine:

At three o'clock in the afternoon . . . Breuille had the charge fired and the terrible explosion flung to a great height in the air a huge portion of the convent and the cloister. Hardly had the mass of falling debris reached the deep . . . crater which the explosion had opened, before the . . . men flung themselves into the convent and charged the retreating enemy with the bayonet . . . We had hoped that the Spanish would have been intimidated by the magnitude of this disaster . . . but our sudden attack only increased their fury. They contested every inch of ground . . . We had to pursue them to the very roofs . . . and those of us who were below saw many fling themselves from the top . . . rather than yield to their conquerors . . . Never in any war was there . . . a more terrible scene than that presented by the ruins . . . The . . . surrounding suburbs . . . were rendered horrible by the quantities of mutilated human remains with which they were strewn. Not a step could be taken without stumbling over torn limbs . . . hands or fragments of arms.[32]

Outside the city, meanwhile, considerable partisan activity notwithstanding, a variety of improvised relief forces were easily scattered or driven away. The end came on 18 February in the form of a fresh French attack that overran the whole of the left bank of the Ebro. With the defenders reduced to starvation rations, constantly exposed to a rain of mortar and howitzer shells, decimated by typhus, and less and less capable of holding back the

French, even Palafox, who was himself seriously ill, realised that all was lost, and, twenty-four days after the breaches had first been stormed, on 20 February the guns at last fell silent.

Thus ended the defence of Zaragoza. Badly led and deprived of all hope of relief, the city had never stood a chance. However, for all Palafox's blunders, the desperate resistance put up by the Army of Reserve and its civilian allies constituted a heroic epic that did much to counter the negative effects of the previous few months, whilst again making it much harder for the British to abandon the Patriot cause. Certainly, the evidence was impressive enough: much of the city lay in ruins, whilst only a third of the garrison remained on its feet, the 24,000 deaths that it had suffered having been augmented by those of 30,000 civilians. Defeat, then, had been heroic, but heroic defeats do not win wars. Sir John Moore had given the Junta Central the chance to rebuild its fortunes. Whether it could successfully do so was a different matter.

7

Oporto

CONQUEST FRUSTRATED, JANUARY–JUNE 1809

Panic gripped the steep streets leading down to the river. Carrying what they could, men, women and children rushed from their homes and made their way downhill. Mixed in with the frightened mass were equally terror-stricken soldiers, militiamen and beasts of burden, whilst columns of fugitive cavalry rode straight into the terrified crowd, trampling many unfortunates beneath their hooves. Desperate to escape – French soldiers were even now beginning to appear behind them – the whole mass rushed pell-mell onto the city's only bridge, only for those at the front suddenly to realise that they faced a yawning gulf. However, their screams proved fruitless. Fired on from the rear, those still on the quayside pushed onwards driving those ahead of them into the water. Screaming in terror, young and old were swept away, whilst behind them still more of the fugitives toppled from the bridge, were crushed to death in the press, or were accidentally cut down by Portuguese cannon firing from the further bank.

Witnessed at the fall of Oporto on 29 March 1809, these scenes marked the most dramatic moment in the implementation of the scheme of operations which Napoleon had drawn up for his generals on the eve of his return to Paris in January 1809. From their positions in Galicia and around Madrid, Soult and Victor were to conquer Portugal, whilst the French forces left in the occupied territories crushed the remaining bastions of resistance in those areas. Finally, with peace restored to the northern half of the Peninsula, Andalucía and the Levante would be invaded and the conflict brought to a close. In the emperor's mind, there was no reason why the war should not be over by the summer, and such was the disarray in the Patriot camp in both Spain and Portugal that it is hard to question his confidence altogether. Yet the abiding theme of the next few months is the story of how the French attempt to conquer the Peninsula was temporarily all but brought to a standstill. Despite plenty of victories, the summer of 1809 found the invaders little further forward than they had been six months earlier. At

first sight, such a situation seems somewhat surprising, the first weeks of
1809 finding the Spaniards in what appeared to be the last extremity, the
British toying with withdrawal, and the Portuguese in no fit state to face
invasion. Why, then, was nemesis postponed?

The traditional British answer to this question is a simple one. Sir John
Moore, it is claimed, drew so many of the invaders after him in the campaign
of December 1808–January 1809 that the French were forced to suspend
offensive operations on other fronts. Meanwhile guerrilla resistance erupted,
tying down many French troops and blunting such attacks as they actually
managed to make, whilst the British plied the Spaniards with aid, thereby
enabling them to rebuild their armies. This is a part of the truth, but only a
part of it. Just as important were the Spanish authorities, engaging as they
did in a constant struggle to rebuild the power and credibility of the state,
to render their field armies more effective and to encourage popular resistance. In striving for these goals they were not wholly successful – some of
what they did, indeed, in the end proved counter-productive – but, for all
that, their story cannot be ignored.

Forced to flee its original seat, held responsible for a series of catastrophic
defeats for which the only explanation, given the bombast characteristic of
Spanish propaganda, seemed to be wholesale treason, and deprived of its
president – Floridablanca was dying of bronchitis – the Junta Central was
certainly in desperate straits when it settled into its new capital of Seville at
the end of 1808. Still worse, the confusion was being exploited by a variety
of malcontents to pursue their own ends: the Junta of Seville, for example,
had resurrected its claim to be the supreme government, whilst Montijo had
made a daring bid to secure the Captain Generalcy of Andalucía. Hardly
had it reached safety than the Junta therefore issued a decree which dealt a
stinging blow to the pretensions of the provincial juntas. Dressed up in
flattering language though this document was, it none the less explicitly
subordinated them to the Junta Central, denied them legislative and military
authority, stripped them of many of the airs they had given themselves,
deprived them of much patronage, ordered them to submit regular reports
of their doings, and confined them to the administration of such matters as
conscription, requisitioning, taxation and propaganda. Just to make certain
that the provincial juntas were put in their place, meanwhile, twelve of the
Junta's members and a number of other special agents were sent out to act
as commissioners in the style of the *représentants en mission* of the French
Revolution. Indeed, in the north-west, completely cut off as it was from
Seville, even the authority of the army was revived in the cause of the

restoration of central control: as commander of the Army of the Left, La Romana was also given the role of viceroy of Old Castile, León, Asturias and Galicia.

Nor was the relationship between central and provincial juntas the only item on the government's agenda. Order had also to be restored to both the war effort and society as a whole. Correctly identifying the haphazard creation of new regiments as one of the chief problems which had hampered the army, for example, the Junta prohibited the formation of any more until all existing units had been brought up to strength. Concerned, too, about the burgeoning number of officers, it also ordered the investigation of the many commissions that had been granted by the new authorities and eventually ruled that many of them should be annulled. Finally, orders that it had issued the previous autumn ending the exemption of the nobility from compulsory military service were firmly reiterated, the provincial juntas also being prohibited from engaging in the practice that had grown up in some provinces of excusing anyone willing to hand over one or more horses and their saddles. Any recalcitrance was sharply slapped down. An example is Murcia where the local authorities had been using an outbreak of yellow fever as a pretext to keep its conscripts as a private army:

As the formation of any further new regiments is inconvenient at a time when the old ones are short of soldiers and full of officers drawing their pay . . . within the space of eight days the recruits must be sent off [from Murcia] in batches, and details provided both of the total number of recruits got together in accordance with the quota imposed on the Kingdom of Murcia, and of the number of recruits that have been sent off to the army hitherto.[1]

In all of this a major role was played by the Junta's advisory commission of generals, which, reconstituted in Seville, performed miracles in working through the hundreds of matters that were referred to it for consideration (even if some of its decisions were surprising, not the least of these being its rejection of proposals to establish a formal general staff).

Just as important, however, was the question of law and order. Thus, the countryside was swarming with draft evaders and bandits, whilst many cities had become home not just to men fleeing conscription, but also to numerous vagrants and refugees, few of whom had any means of support. Unrest, meanwhile, continued unabated. Lérida, for example, saw a dramatic rising in which an adventurer raised an angry mob, murdered several local dignitaries and seized the city's citadel. Attempting to evacuate Tarragona following the battle of Molíns de Rey, the Junta of Catalonia was almost lynched. In Jérez the town was taken over by hundreds of day labourers who wanted to put an end to conscription. In Murcia squabbles amongst the ruling élite interacted with popular anger and resentment to produce a rising in which the provincial junta was overthrown and the bishop assaulted. In Ribadeo an industrialist named the Marqués de Sargadelos, with a long history of disputes with the local inhabitants, was murdered by angry townsfolk. And in Don Bénito there had been a wholesale agrarian rising. Thus:

The town of Don Bénito . . . has been in the most deplorable condition ever since . . . a number of discontented porters, day labourers and artisans – men whose ignorance and immorality always inclines them to the worst – launched a furious attack . . . on the . . . town council at the very moment when the list of those eligible to be chosen for the defence of the fatherland was being drawn up, demanding land and crying that only the people with anything to lose should go to war. This outrage, which ended in the precipitate flight of the . . . council, which would otherwise have been murdered, has been followed by others which have caused respectable inhabitants the utmost consternation. Continually insulted . . . by these malignants, they have had to watch them . . . occupying the pastures rented out by their neighbours in the most disorderly fashion . . . These they have ploughed and harrowed, whilst in the meantime threatening anyone who opposed them with death.[2]

Stirred up though many of these events were by ambitious individuals or powerful local factions who had failed to secure what they regarded as their just deserts, they still demanded a clear response. In consequence, whilst commissions were issued to a variety of petitioners who claimed that they would be able to solve the bandit problem in their particular localities through the formation of security units of one form or another, further 'police' regulations were introduced. At the instigation of the Junta Central's commissioner, the Marqués de Villel, for example, in Cádiz it was ordered that all freemasons should be reported to the Inquisition; that all books and pamphlets of an irreligious or immoral nature should be confiscated forthwith; that trade and commerce should henceforward be characterised by equity and fair dealing; that vagrants, prostitutes and drunks should be imprisoned; that children should be kept off the streets and educated in a proper fashion; that theatres should not stage any piece that was improper, indecent or provocative; that all classes of society should abstain from luxury and excessive adornment; that all quarrels and rivalries should be eschewed or given up; and, finally, that the whole city should engage in constant prayer and penitence. Meanwhile, the Junta Central itself took action: on 3 January 1809, for example, draconian measures were issued against desertion; on 14 January an 'extraordinary tribunal of public security' was established in Seville; and on 19 February fresh orders laid down that all weapons in civilian hands should be surrendered immediately.

Closely linked with the question of law and order was that of popular resistance. In certain circumstances, of course, this was much to be welcomed – hence the instructions that were sent out enjoining every town and village in Spain to loophole its houses and barricade its streets in the hope of emulating the feats of Zaragoza, and the commissions issued to many individuals who volunteered to raise guerrilla bands or popular militias. Hence, too, the famous decree of the *corso terrestre* of 25 February 1809 that any money or other valuables seized from the French or their collaborators should become the property of those who had seized them. Nor was there any reason to doubt that irregular resistance was causing the French many problems. Ever since the start of the war, the Catalan *somaténes*, later supplemented by somewhat more permanent militias known as *miqueletes*, had been harassing every movement that the French made. In Aragón, Navarre and the Castiles, rather more *ad hoc* bands of irregulars were also starting to emerge. Most dramatic of all was the situation in Galicia. Throughout the summer and autumn of 1808 that large and heavily populated region had proved difficult to mobilise, there having been both a shortage of volunteers and considerable resistance to conscription. Like Catalonia, however, Galicia possessed a rudimentary home guard, known in this case as the *alarma*. With all adult males registered in this body, which also possessed its own officers and was already organised into parish companies, the arrival of the French was not long in eliciting a reaction. The British, true, had received little support and on occasion had even been attacked, but that did not mean to say that the requisitioning, looting and general ill-treatment which accompanied French occupation was ever likely to be tolerated. With the local clergy – a force of considerable influence given the Church's extensive properties in Galicia – also doing everything it could to whip up support for an insurrection, the province was soon up in arms. For a good account of the outbreak of the fighting in just one area, let us turn to the *Semanario Político, Histórico y Literario de la Coruña*:

On 25 January . . . General Fournier entered Mondoñedo with 700 cavalry. On the following day he sent 150 of them to the town of Ribadeo. No sooner had they arrived than they demanded bread, meat, wine, eggs, hay, barley and firewood from all the villages roundabout . . . These demands were backed up by all kinds of threats that were made only too credible by the robberies and other iniquities already committed in the places through which they had passed . . . All this led a number of honourable and distinguished patriots to persuade the peasantry that they should refuse to supply the rations which had been demanded of them . . . and within twenty-four hours the parishes of Cogela, Balboa, Sante, Villaosende, Cedofeita and Vidal had come together and elected as their chief, Don Melchor Díaz de la Rocha. On the twenty-ninth of the same month, 320 peasants armed with fowling pieces, pitchforks and pikes presented themselves in the early morning . . . 200 of them being sent to occupy the heights overlooking the bridge on the road from Mondoñedo to Rivadeo [at Nuestra Señora del Puente] and the others to watch Quintalonga . . . On the same day the 200 peasants blocking the road at Nuestra Señora del Puente attacked a group of Frenchmen travelling from Ribadeo to Mondoñedo. In this action five Frenchmen were killed . . . whereas our peasants suffered no losses at all, being sheltered from the enemy horsemen by walls and ditches. On the thirtieth the enemy . . . attacked Quintalonga, only to be thrown back by the 120 peasants who held that point . . . As a result of these happy successes, our countrymen took heart and their number increased considerably.[3]

Galicia being an extremely hilly area covered in woods and thickets, it was generally impossible to catch those responsible before they melted away, whilst prisoners were put to death in circumstances of the most revolting cruelty. With the French becoming more and more frustrated and infuriated, the reprisals which were their standard response to popular resistance were pursued with even more vigour than would normally have been the case, village after village being burned to the ground and their inhabitants slaughtered. Typical enough was the fate of the coastal town of Corcubión:

We rowed smartly up the bay, but had scarcely doubled the point . . . at the entrance of the harbour, when we observed . . . the French soldiers pouring into the wretched town from both sides of the valley. Many of the inhabitants rushed to the fishing boats on the beach, and, leaping into them indiscriminately, pushed into the stream. As we rowed up the harbour, we met hundreds of these poor people, half-dressed, screaming, and struggling hard to get beyond the reach of shot. Others fled along the sides of the hills towards the bay, hoping to be picked off the shore by boats or . . . to conceal themselves . . . amongst the rocks. Of these fugitives, great numbers were brought down . . . by the fire of the enemy . . . So completely hemmed in . . . were these wretched people that escape was almost impossible. The horror and confusion of this frightful spectacle were increased by the conflagration of the town, in the streets of which deeds of still greater atrocity were going on.[4]

Accompanied as they were by horrors of all sorts – at Fontaneira, for example, a woman caught in the streets had her breasts cut off – such tactics were catastrophic, on the one hand fuelling desires for revenge and on the other leaving many men with no other means of subsistence than pillage. Still worse, even submission was no protection. As one of Marshal Ney's aides-de-camp complained:

This is no longer a campaign that we are conducting; it is rather a devastation by ·bandits in uniform. And although [we officers] lament the situation, risking our lives to contain the soldiery, we are turned into murderers ... The towns and villages half-burned, the farm animals and mules killed or stolen, all the tools and instruments of the peasantry and artisans used as fuel because ... it is easier to throw them on the fire than cut down trees, all the churches sacked and profaned; this is all that is left of this kingdom.[5]

Dramatic though the Galician insurrection was, closer consideration shows that matters were by no means as simple as at first appeared. Nowhere was this more clear than in Catalonia. To the *somaténes*, themselves hungry and resentful, had rallied adventurers of dubious character and motive, deserters from the regular army, and a variety of bandits, smugglers and petty criminals. As such they did not present a pretty spectacle. To quote an officer sent to Catalonia with the division dispatched from Andalucía in the autumn of 1808:

Every day I hate these people more: they have no other God than money, and for it would sell their fatherland, their fathers, their saints and anything else that comes to hand ... The whole of the much vaunted Army of Catalonia is composed of bands of thieves who under the name of *somaténes* enter the towns and villages in almost the same manner as the French ... the only difference being that they are rather more skilful at robbing them.[6]

In addition to preying on friend as much as foe, the *somaténes* were also impossible to rely on. For example, the Junta Central's *représentant en mission* in the province complained that 'they are people on whom it is impossible to count for more than a few days' and Charles Doyle that 'they must be employed quickly or they will not be forthcoming'.[7] Most damning of all, however, was Joaquín Blake, who, as we shall see, was soon to acquire the Catalan command:

Let all the *somaténes* ... that Your Excellency can offer me come and welcome, but, given the fact that they will certainly increase our confusion, they should bring supplies with them so that they do not augment our misery as well. Only a little while ago Brigadier Casamayor saw 2,000 of these armed peasants disappear the moment that the assembly was sounded ... whilst a few nights back 3,000–4,000 fled from the command of Lieutenant-Colonel Juan Clarós. Let them come and give new proofs of their constancy by all means, but I will place no trust in . . . these people when it comes to attacking the enemy.[8]

The full complexity of the problems involved in irregular resistance was not to become apparent until much later, and will be discussed in another place. Nor shall we here discuss the various ways in which the *partidas* and other forms of irregular resistance quickly came to sap the Spanish war effort. Suffice to say that even at this early date there was clearly good reason for wanting to impose a greater degree of order. As a first step in this direction, on 28 December 1808 the Junta therefore issued a set of instructions for the organisation of guerrilla bands which laid down very clearly that the latter were not to allow themselves to be joined by men who had fled the regular army or were avoiding conscription, that they were not to become too big, that each band was to be commanded by a recognised leader who would automatically be given a commission as a regular officer, and that all the guerrillas should be subjected to the authority of the local military commander. Meanwhile, in Galicia army officers were put in charge of particular districts and encouraged to form the insurgents into regular units, whilst government commissioners were sent out to parts of Aragón and Old Castile with instructions both to stir up popular resistance and subordinate the bands to their authority.

The trouble with efforts to restore order and boost the authority of the government, however, was that they were likely to prove counter-productive. Both provincial juntas and insurgent chieftains, for example, were deeply resentful of the Junta Central's efforts to clip their military and political authority and frequently essayed resistance. Of particular note here is the situation that developed in Asturias, where the chronic parochialism of the junta combined with the reactionary proclivities of the Marqués de la Romana to produce a coup in which the marquess marched on Oviedo, overthrew its rulers and installed a new body of his own. The rights and wrongs of this coup can be debated, but there is considerable evidence that La Romana was motivated not by military considerations, but rather by hatred of revolution: the University of Oviedo having in recent years become a centre of progressive thought, the Junta of Asturias was dominated by such figures as the later liberal writer, Alvaro Flórez Estrada. But even if British claims that the Junta had failed to support the war effort are accepted, it is not clear that anything was achieved by the coup. In the words of the Conde de Toreno (himself a member of the first junta), 'Romana appointed another junta, but the arbitrary treatment of its predecessor had angered most of the inhabitants, and unseated . . . order and good government in the principality.'[9] Aware of its unpopularity, the new junta hardly met and for the rest of 1809 Asturias effectively had no government at all.

If the notables who controlled the juntas were unhappy, so were the populace, and all the more so as the various anti-bandit patrols that appeared tended to slip into crime themselves whilst providing the clients of the local *caciques* with a means of avoiding military service and generally behaving in the most arbitrary fashion. To quote one of the many anonymous notes sent to the Junta Central:

Those who have infected the *pueblos* with robbery and smuggling have been the very commissions that have been established for the persecution and extermination of bandits and wrongdoers. One man they imprison, whilst another they free. One man they threaten, whilst another they favour. There is no person of sense who is not horrified by such iniquity.[10]

In consequence of all this, there were further disturbances of which the worst were probably those that took place in Cádiz on 22 February 1809. A complex affair, these troubles in part stemmed from popular resentment of both Villel and attempts to encourage recruitment. Also important was hatred of customs officials – 'these jacks-in-office who with no other income than their salaries succeed in enriching themselves . . . enjoying every kind of luxury, and avoiding every sacrifice'[11] – and growing economic difficulties:

All the attention of the Junta is currently centred on the number of people living in Cádiz . . . It has grown a lot, whilst . . . depending as it does on foodstuffs brought in from outside, Cádiz is incapable of suddenly absorbing a large increase in population . . . Shortages are therefore imminent, and they cannot but fall most heavily on the poor . . . for whom the least increase in the price of necessities is a sentence of death.[12]

Yet the heart of the problem was constituted by the city's militia, the Voluntarios Distinguidos de Cádiz. Hearing that a battalion of foreign deserters and former prisoners of war was being moved to the city, this force concluded that it was about to be sent to the front. In little time at all, rumours were spreading that treason was afoot, and an angry crowd, in whose ranks were to be found many of the volunteers, took over the city, murdered the much-hated head of the customs guard, and besieged Villel in his lodgings.

Faced with these disturbances, the Junta Central responded with a number of judicious concessions: the Voluntarios were promised that they would never have to serve outside the city, conscription in the city was suspended, and the local police commission temporarily disbanded. At the same time, however, it was made clear that no further disorders would be tolerated. Cádiz's *alcalde mayor* issued a decree prohibiting all gatherings of more than five people, ordering the arrest of all minors found alone on the streets, and threatening women – a section of society believed to be particularly prone to unrest and disorder on account of their 'indiscreet persuasions and want of talent' – who failed to behave in a decorous fashion with solitary confinement. And on 3 March the Junta Central issued a decree ordering the most draconian punishment of all those involved in acts of public disorder.

By such means the crowd might be overawed, but there was still another problem that had to be faced. Many generals were vigorously opposed to the direction that the revolution had taken, either because they were deeply legitimist – Cuesta (who had in the confusion been appointed by the Junta of Extremadura to take charge of the new army it was raising on the basis of the fugitives from Gamonal and Somosierra) and La Romana – or because they were eager to pursue the goals of the aristocratic plot that had been shortcircuited by the overthrow of Fernando VII – Infantado, Francisco Palafox and Montijo. Also to be found was a degree of personal jealousy and ambition, with Cuesta, for example, still smarting from the loss of his Castilian command the previous autumn and Infantado bitterly resentful of having been relieved of command of the Army of the Centre after Uclés. The result was a variety of intrigues in which the various generals schemed both with one another and with other malcontents, including most notably the Junta of Seville, to orchestrate the downfall of the Junta Central. In the north-west, for example, La Romana effectively declared himself independent of the Junta's authority, whilst Montijo and Francisco Palafox even went so far as to instigate a short-lived rising in Granada in April 1809. This was crushed – 'The Junta [of Granada] . . . ordered the cavalry . . . to charge a small number of onlookers who had gathered in the Plaza Nueva, sent infantry . . . to occupy every street corner, and . . . raided the house of the Conde de Montijo'[13] – but even so the Junta could hardly feel complacent. The defects of its composition were obvious, and its new president, the Marqués de Astorga, open to ridicule. In the words of Lord Holland, 'The . . . Marquis of Astorga was the least man I ever saw in society, and smaller than many dwarfs exhibited for money. He . . . drove about with guards like a royal personage. They called him the *rey chico*.'[14] In consequence, 'Their popularity is now totally lost, and it is the universal wish that they may be removed, and an individual, or small council of regency, appointed to succeed them.'[15]

With matters in this state, it was essential for the Junta Central to secure the support of the British, of whom it continued to entertain the most exaggerated hopes (at this time it was, for example, being reported that the small British garrison that had remained in Lisbon under Sir John Cradock consisted of 70,000 men). In the wake of La Coruña, however, relations with London had been going from bad to worse. On 14 January 1809 Canning and the Spanish ambassador to London, Juan Ruiz de Apódaca, had signed a definitive treaty of peace, friendship and alliance that committed Britain to aiding Spain with all the means at her disposal and prohibited her from making a separate peace with France or recognising any other monarch than Fernando VII. But what aid to Spain meant in London was different from what it meant in Seville. What the Spaniards really wanted was men and money, but the Portland administration had little specie to spare, whilst the events surrounding Moore's retreat made the dispatch of another army distinctly problematic. All demands for financial aid were therefore refused, and the dispatch of troops made conditional on the admission of a British garrison to Cádiz as a gesture of good faith.

To no Spanish government would this have been acceptable. Just along the coast from Cádiz was the perpetual source of resentment constituted by Gibraltar, whilst the British had only given up Menorca, which they had held for much of the eighteenth century, in 1802. Nor was the retreat to La Coruña the best platform from which to launch such a demand. A spat might yet have been avoided, but the situation was complicated by events on the ground. Convinced that Cádiz was French for the taking, an over-zealous liaison officer named Sir George Smith took it upon himself to implore Cradock to send troops to occupy the city. As Cradock complied, when Frere presented the government's request in early February, a British force was actually present off Cádiz, the Junta Central therefore concluding that their allies were intent on a landing with or without their permission. In the circumstances only one answer was possible, but even so the incident strengthened British sentiment against the Spaniards still further. As one British soldier wrote:

Who could have thought that the . . . Spaniards . . . would refuse admittance to our army into Cádiz? Such, however, has been their return for our generous conduct, and it has fallen to our lot to suffer the mortification of the refusal.[16]

Setting these difficulties aside, there were in any case still other issues that stood in the way of increased British aid. Few British observers could be found, for example, who were not dissatisfied at the shape that had been given to the Spanish government, the arrangements that had been made for the command of the Spanish armies, or the training, organisation and general performance of the Spanish troops. Most thorny of all was the linked issue of British subsidies, free trade and Spanish America. Faced by ever-growing demands for aid, Canning had responded by stating that Britain's ability to respond would be contingent upon her gaining access to both American silver and the colonial trade, whilst at the same time suggesting the need for a reform in the relationship between metropolis and colonies. These demands were hardly altruistic – Britain stood to gain enormously – but the fact was that more specie and fresh markets were essential to Britain's war effort. Yet, again, no Spanish government could have submitted to such demands and certainly not the battered Junta Central, the latter knowing full well that any concessions of this sort would provide excellent ammunition for its enemies.

How, then, was the Junta Central to recover the British confidence that was so vital to its political, financial and military prospects? How, too, was it to face down its internal enemies, secure compliance with its decrees and restore order to Spanish society? In these circumstances, the only hope was a mixture of wheedling and remonstrance. On 12 March 1809 the Secretary General of the Junta Central, Martín de Garay, sent Canning a long memorandum in which he laid much emphasis on the heroism of the Spanish people and protested at the manner in which Britain had thus far failed to give all the support that it could to the Patriot cause, whilst at the same time hinting that greater aid would bring substantial concessions. Another way forward, meanwhile, lay in moves in the direction of political reform: the American colonies were declared to be an integral part of the Spanish state and granted the right of representation in the Junta Central, whilst on 22 May 1809 it was announced that a new *cortes* would assemble within a year and a general call issued for proposals for its organisation and agenda. Desperate efforts, too, continued to be made to encourage support for the war, with the Junta sponsoring a national competition for the composition of odes to heroic Zaragoza and holding lavish ceremonies to celebrate the first anniversary of the Dos de Mayo. But in the last resort the only effective answer was military victory, and, by extension, the adoption of an offensive strategy.*

If the Junta Central was once again ready for battle, it was the result of the combination of the breathing space won for it by Moore's campaign

---

* In fairness to the Junta it should be noted that the generals were just as eager for battle as the politicians, as witness a meeting of the Junta's advisory military commission on 4 March 1809 at which it was specifically resolved that the chief object of Spanish strategy should be the immediate liberation of Madrid.

and the defence of Zaragoza, and the arrival of copious outside aid: by May 1809 the British had provided the Spaniards with 155 artillery pieces, at least 200,000 muskets and over 90,000 complete uniforms, whilst patriotic contributions had started to come in from America that by December of the same year were worth 284,000,000 reales. What, though, of the French? Napoleon, as we have seen, had committed them to the conquest of Portugal and the suppression of resistance in Catalonia as the first steps in a campaign that by the end of the summer was supposed to have liquidated all opposition in the Peninsula. In elaborating this scheme, however, the emperor had been wildly over-optimistic. As powerful forces were needed to defend the territories occupied by the French, only a limited number of troops could be used for offensive operations. For the invasion of Portugal, the only troops available were the corps of Marshal Soult and Marshal Victor and a number of additional cavalry formations. What Napoleon was gambling on, of course, was a complete lack of resistance: of the Spaniards and Portuguese he was as contemptuous as ever, whilst he was completely unaware that the British still had troops in Lisbon. But there was a further flaw in his thinking. The population of most of the rest of Europe having remained quiet in the face of French conquest, there had been little need to protect lines of communication. In Spain, however, this was not so, whilst the invaders were still ringed by regular armies. For every step that the French advanced, then, men had to be dropped off to hold down the fresh gains and protect them from counter-attack. Yet, arguing that the Spanish armies were no threat and popular resistance a phenomenon that could be easily crushed, Napoleon actually withdrew a number of troops from the Peninsula.

Far from the first six months of 1809 seeing an end to the war, they rather marked a period of intense frustration for the French. From the very beginning, things went wrong. In the west, Soult was supposed to be in Lisbon by 10 February. Yet by the time that he had occupied La Coruña, El Ferrol and Vigo (all of which surrendered without a fight), handed over responsibility for Galicia to the corps of Marshal Ney, which had come up from Castile in his wake, regrouped his battered forces – his own corps and two extra cavalry divisions – and concentrated those of his men who were fit to fight on the Portuguese frontier at Tuy, it was already three days past that date. At the frontier, however, the way was blocked, for the road south across the River Miño was commanded by the fortress of Valença, whose governor refused point blank to surrender. After an abortive attempt at an amphibious crossing, the army had to look for another passage. This was eventually found at Orense fifty miles inland, but many men fell sick or were killed, whilst so many horses were lost that it proved necessary to send all the baggage and heavy guns back to Tuy under heavy guard. At Orense, meanwhile, still further time was lost in attempts to gather fresh supplies, hunt down La Romana's army, which was hiding in the hills east of the city, and put down the insurrection. Not until 9 March 1809, then, did Soult finally cross the frontier. With him were fewer than 22,000 men, a mere 20 guns, all of them light, and only the most limited supplies of food and ammunition, the French having had to limit themselves to what they could carry by mule train.

Weak though Soult was, the defenders were still weaker. The populace were unenthusiastic at the prospect of military service and much given to outbreaks of unrest (there were, for example, serious riots in Lisbon in early February); the local notables were frightened of popular vengeance; and the new authorities bitterly at odds with one another. Plans had been laid for a somewhat expanded army which would include a substantial force of light infantry, or *caçadores*; such men as could be found of the old army had been mobilised and augmented by some 25,000 conscripts; and Britain had been asked to supply a commander-in-chief who could take affairs in hand. However, although such an officer was quickly found in the person of William Beresford, a capable and experienced major-general who had served under Moore in 1808 and was known to be a friend of Wellesley, uniforms, arms, equipment, transport, baggage animals and cavalry mounts were all in short supply. As for training, this was badly deficient, whilst most of the officers of the old army had joined Junot's Portuguese Legion. Extremely conscious of the inexperience of their replacements, Beresford had immediately asked for British officers, but it would be many months before this solution could make much difference.

The result was a sorry picture. Many regiments of the regular army had still not been fully embodied, whilst the entire force was still scattered across the length and breadth of the country in its regimental recruitment districts. There were also forty-eight regiments of militia, but these in most cases lacked arms – many had had to be given pikes – whilst they were in any case even worse trained than the regular army. Finally, one must also mention the *ordenança* or home guard. Formed and armed in the style of the *somaténes* and *alarmas*, they were, like them, supposed to turn out in time of invasion. Organised into guerrilla bands, they might have been of some service, but stop an army they could not, whilst attempts to place them under arms on a permanent basis had led to much disorder. Lisbon was securely held by 16,000 British troops under Cradock and Almeida by the Loyal Lusitanian Legion – a tiny force of volunteers raised by the British adventurer, Sir Robert Wilson – but otherwise there was nothing. Well, then, might Harriet Slessor be despondent:

The country people declare that they will fight . . . They are willing to think . . . that they are capable of performing wonders. But let a formidable French army present itself . . . [and] confusion, dismay and distraction [will] be mingled in the probable annihilation of thousands.[17]

Soult's forces initially faced only the 12,000 men represented by the line regiments, militia and *ordenança* of the province of Tras-os-Montes. Commanded by Francisco da Silveira, these forces were soon in full retreat amidst scenes of riot and disorder, and within two days of crossing the frontier Soult had taken the border fortress of Chaves. Turning west, Soult then moved against a mass of about 25,000 *ordenança* commanded by General Bernardino Freire that had been mobilised to block the best route from Chaves to Oporto at Braga. Reaching these forces proved a costly affair – the French were harassed every step of the way – but on 20 March the French attacked. The combat was a short one. Positioned on some hills some miles east of Braga, the *ordenanças* had been joined by a handful of regulars and militia, and had constructed a number of redoubts armed with cannon. However, the defenders were in hopeless disarray – on 17 March, indeed, a thoroughly demoralised Freire had been murdered by a group of armed peasants after trying to flee his command – whilst the position was far too extensive for them. The result was inevitable: within a matter of minutes, the Portuguese were scattering in panic before Soult's cavalry.

Oporto, meanwhile, was in a state of utter confusion. Nominally governed by its bishop, who had come back from Lisbon to reclaim his old fief, it was in practice in the hands of the mob. Bands of *ordenanças* roamed the streets hunting down anyone whom they suspected of treason and murdering local notables associated with the pre-war régime, and there was also a terrible prison massacre. Although the northern approaches to the city had been blocked by earthworks, ditches and palisades, there was little chance of a successful defence. Attacked on the morning of 29 March, within two hours all 30,000 of the defenders were fleeing in terror. Hence the disaster we have already described. Built on a steep hillside running down to the River Duero, the city was a death-trap. Thousands of fugitives were cut down by the French and others were trampled or crushed to death. At the quaysides, meanwhile, boats were swamped and men, women and children thrown into the water. However, by far the worst scenes were witnessed at the only bridge across the river. Constructed from pontoons, it was gradually swamped by the weight of the crowd, leaving a gap in the middle into which hundreds, if not thousands, of soldiers and civilians were driven by the pressure of those behind. Temporarily attached to Marshal Soult's head-quarters, Joseph's aide-de-camp, Bigarré, was a horrified eyewitness:

Imagine 12,000–15,000 souls crowded together on the bank of a river crossed by a bridge of boats, whose centre has been pushed under the water. Imagine that mass . . . pressing forward to cross the bridge. Imagine those unfortunates being hurled into a gulf whose existence they only discovered at the last moment. Imagine them being exterminated by . . . Portuguese guns on the left bank of the Duero and the bayonets of the French at their heels.[18]

Elsewhere many defenders were massacred as they tried to give up, whilst there was also much pillage and rapine. Trapped in the bishop's palace, 200 militia fought to the death, but by nightfall it was all over: some 8,000 men, women and children lay dead for French losses of less than 500, whilst the booty included 200 guns, immense stocks of food and munitions, and 30 shiploads of wine.

Great victory as this was, the French could go no further. Worn down by constant skirmishes, exposed to the most terrible reprisals and prevented from foraging effectively, the troops were exhausted, demoralised and increasingly unruly. As for their commanders, they found that they were deprived of news and forced into courses of action – mass executions and the destruction of entire villages – that only stirred up resentment against them still further. As for Soult, he had conquered nothing. Oporto had been taken and petty garrisons left in Braga and one or two other places, but the Portuguese had closed in around him and completely cut him off. All too clearly, nothing further could be attempted until the forces supposed to be marching to Soult's aid had crossed the frontier. If the people in arms had not stopped the invasion of Portugal, they had at least checked its success.

What though of the forces that Napoleon had ordered to assist Soult? Consisting of the corps of Marshal Victor and some extra cavalry, to be of any help these troops would either have had to beat the Spanish Army of Extremadura and reduce the major fortresses of Badajoz and Elvas; brave the trackless wastes of the Tagus valley and capture Abrantes; or storm Ciudad Rodrigo and Almeida. It may therefore be doubted whether they would ever have got very far, but in the event they did not even reach the frontier. An attempt to probe the northern front was abandoned after Wilson succeeded in bluffing the forces facing him into believing that they were opposed by a large army, whilst Victor's next plan – a march on Badajoz – was checked by the sudden appearance of Cuesta's Army of Extremadura, which attacked the Marshal's troops at Medellín on 29 March in accordance with both the proclivities of Cuesta himself – he was a commander with a particularly tough and aggressive disposition – and the Junta Central's need for a powerful counter-offensive.

Traditionally, Cuesta has been savaged for his conduct of the battle that followed, but in fact his generalship was by no means foolish. The battlefield was an open plain, and the Spanish cavalry both outnumbered and out-classed. The French, meanwhile, had taken up a position between the River Guadiana and a tributary called the Ortiga that flowed into it from the south, Medellín being situated at the confluence of the two. Faced by this situation, Cuesta deployed his infantry in lines that were six men deep and therefore much more likely to be able to resist a cavalry charge.* As for the horse, it was split up in small forces on either flank and in the centre, the aim evidently being to support them at all times with infantry, and thereby thwart its superior French counterparts. The flanks of this array were protected by the Ortiga and the Guadiana, whilst its front was covered by a thick line of skirmishers and Cuesta's thirty guns, the latter being dragged along with the infantry for the purposes of close support.

To pretend that this arrangement had no faults would be futile. Thus, the Spanish line was at the outset stretched very thin by the need to rest the flanks on the two rivers, whilst the various units would have to be careful to maintain their alignment at all times for fear that the French cavalry might otherwise seize a gap and ride down the troops on either side. Yet the problem was not an insuperable one. Outnumbered four to three, Victor was not able to hold the Spaniards back, and, as the latter advanced, so the ever narrowing battlefield enabled them to thicken their array. For a time, then, it seemed that Cuesta might obtain a victory. 'The Spanish infantry,' wrote Sir George Jackson, 'behaved nobly. Though great numbers were without shoes and almost without clothing, they advanced with a coolness and resolution that would have done credit to veteran troops.'[19] 'The French artillery, heavier, more numerous and better served was severely felt', but, astonishingly, two regiments of dragoons which charged the Spaniards were

---

* There is some doubt here. Oman says that Cuesta's infantry was arrayed four deep, but this is certainly an error: in all armies but the British, the basic formation was a line three deep, whilst deeper formations were always multiples of this figure (in the pre-war Spanish army, for example, a column of companies had twelve ranks). However, such eyewitness accounts as we have do not help beyond implying that the infantry fought in line. But a line six deep does at least make sense. It could have been formed without difficulty (by forming each company at double depth), fitted the needs of the moment, and even tallies with Oman's four-deep claim if it is assumed that he was working from a source that referred to lines of double depth and forgot that in the Spanish service this would have produced two more ranks than it would have done in Wellington's army.

'repulsed with loss', whilst the Spanish skirmishers were 'so numerous and so bold that they frequently forced ours [i.e. their French counterparts] back to their ranks'.[20] But victory was not to be. Ordered to charge some French horse, the cavalry that had been attached to the Spanish right were taken by surprise by a sudden movement on the part of a squadron of enemy hussars. What followed was all too familiar.

Our hussars . . . then drowned the sound of the trumpet . . . by a . . . terrible shout of joy and fury. The Spanish lancers stopped; seized with terror, they turned their horses . . . and overthrew their own cavalry, which was behind them . . . Our hussars mingled with them indiscriminately [and] cut them down without resistance.[21]

On the other flank, too, disaster struck. As Cuesta wrote:

The left had arrived within half a pistol shot of the first enemy battery and was advancing with the bayonet to take it, when a strong force of enemy cavalry . . . charged to rescue it. Our infantry did not stop, but the Almansa and Infante line cavalry regiments, and . . . the Imperial Chasseurs of Toledo wavered . . . and, abandoning our array, fled at the gallop . . . I was behind . . . our left at the time, and seeing the flight of the three regiments, quickly rode over to contain the disorder . . . The corps of grenadiers, which was still advancing on the battery . . . was shouting, 'What is this? Come back! They are ours!' But it was all in vain. The cavalry could not be rallied, and so the enemy got into the rear of our infantry and achieved their disunion.[22]

With the division of dragoons of General Latour-Maubourg rolling up the infantry divisions of Henestrosa and Del Parque, Cuesta's forces had within a matter of moments been reduced to a crowd of fugitives – 'In an instant the army that was before us disappeared like clouds driven before the wind. The Spaniards threw down their arms and fled; the cannonade ceased and the whole of our army went off in pursuit of the enemy.'[23] Thanks to the open terrain, the result was disastrous: the fleeing Spaniards were cut down or taken prisoner in enormous numbers, whilst they also lost twenty guns and much of their baggage. By the end of the day, indeed, 10,000 men had become casualties, whilst many others had scattered deep into the countryside, many of them never to return. As for Cuesta himself, such is the opprobrium that has been heaped on him by British authors that a personal note is essential, for he clearly exposed himself to great danger. One of his aides-de-camp was cut down by a cannonball at his side, and he himself was wounded in the foot. Trying to rally some fugitives, he was in the end literally knocked down. Ridden over by friend and foe alike, he then found himself in the midst of the French, and was only saved from death by the courage of two of his nephews, who drove off his assailants and, with the aid of the British liaison officer, Benjamin D'Urban, 'pulled him out from under the horses' feet bruised and nearly senseless'.[24]

Fortunately for the Spaniards, the ability to exploit Medellín proved limited. Shaken by a harder fight than anything he had expected and much concerned at reports of the formation of local militias on the model of the *somaténes*, Victor decided to check his march until he had received news of Soult, of whose progress he remained entirely ignorant. More might have been achieved if Victor could have called upon further support from the Madrid area, but this was impossible, for the troops concerned were being kept fully occupied watching the much-tried Army of the Centre. Reconstituted in the Sierra Morena under the Conde de Cartaojal, this had just been beaten at Ciudad Real following an abortive attempt to surprise the forces guarding the southern approaches to Madrid, but it remained an army in being and in consequence could not just be ignored.

By the end of March, then, the most important part of Napoleon's plans for the conquest of the Peninsula had effectively stalled. But what of the pacification of the occupied territories? In the north the first priority was the subjugation of Galicia, but, despite Marshal Ney's best efforts, the revolt there proved impossible to put down. With only 17,000 men, he had had from the first to abandon any hope of garrisoning the entire province and instead chose only to hold such major towns as Villafranca, Lugo, Santiago, El Ferrol and La Coruña, whilst dividing the rest of his forces into mobile columns that kept open communications between the various bases and struck out in all directions hunting down the *alarmas*, burning villages, taking hostages and inflicting terrible atrocities upon the unfortunate populace. Yet the insurgents were rarely caught by the French columns and frequently inflicted numerous casualties on them, whilst every act of punishment or reprisal simply created fresh insurgents. Still worse, the French actually lost ground. Protected from blockade by the flying columns, the towns held by Ney's troops were safe enough, but, far to the south-west, the situation of Tuy and Vigo was very different. Held by invalids and other troops dropped off by Soult and completely out of touch with Ney, the two towns had quickly been surrounded in an attempt to starve them into submission. In the end Tuy's defenders were evacuated by troops sent up from Oporto by Soult, but on 27 March Vigo surrendered when the British landed some naval cannon and breached the main gate.

In view of the assumptions that tend to be made with regard to the nature of the so-called 'little war', it is important to note the identity of the forces that besieged Vigo. Whilst not troops of the old regular army, they were not just crowds of armed peasants either. On the contrary, at their heart was the División del Miño, which was a force consisting of five regiments of new levies organised by regular officers acting at the behest of La Romana and the Junta Central. Raised by conscription, dressed in uniform and trained to fight in the usual formations of the period, these men were soldiers if not, at the beginning, ones that were especially good. Nor could it be otherwise: lacking any means of subsistence, armed civilians could not be away from their homes for more than a few days. Yet even had this not been the case, there is still room to doubt the idea of a Galician people's war. The French could count on opposition wherever they actually appeared, but they had only to leave a district alone for it to remain quiet for weeks. Crowds of peasants might be induced by the hope of pay to put in a few hours of drill every week, but of fighting most of the time there was no thought. As Hall writes, for example:

On reaching the camp . . . we found the patriot army exercising by divisions . . . When we approached a general halt was ordered, and those who had muskets presented them as well they might, while those who had none went through the motions equally well with their pikes or staves formed out of scythes and reaping hooks . . . Under our auspices the peasantry continued to flock in from the adjacent country . . . although we could supply scarcely a twentieth part of these patriots with arms . . . And that small fraction not being supplied with officers, or disciplined, or organised in any way, it was really like children playing at soldiers.[25]

Even when actually called upon to fight, the *alarma* did not necessarily put up much of a fight:

When the enemy's toops reached the foot of the hill . . . the French infantry very coolly sat down on the grass to rest . . . Now was the moment . . . to make a rush down upon the wearied invaders, and . . . the patriots were ordered to advance to the attack, but . . . rather to trust to the effect of the rush downhill and to . . . the use of the bayonet than to the fire of their musketry. There was a great cheering of 'Viva! Viva!' upon these orders being given, and the Spaniards moved on to the charge in a style worthy of the days of their own Cid Campeador. But this lasted only until they came within a couple of gun-shots of the French troops, upon which . . . the patriots halted, and commenced a brisk fire directed towards the enemy . . . I am ashamed to say . . . it was now observable that more than half their number had gone off to the rear . . . while those who remained merely . . . fired off their pieces in the direction of the distant enemy . . . without working the smallest mischief on their foes . . . When the French came within musket-shot, they threw forward a few skirmishers, who commenced firing on the Spaniards. I need hardly add that the greater number of the now sadly reduced forces of the Patriots now took to their heels.[26]

Fortunately for the Spaniards, Galicia could rely not only on raw levies and disorderly home guards, but also on the battered Army of the Left. Got together by La Romana in the vicinity of the Portuguese frontier, this force was in a sorry state: at the beginning of February, indeed, 3,000 of its 10,000 men had no arms. But when Soult had appeared the marquess had skilfully kept out of harm's way (albeit at the cost of earning the punning nickname of Marqués de la Romerias – the Marquess of the Pilgrimages). Once free to attack the enemy, he had even gone over to the offensive, launching a surprise attack on the town of Villafranca del Vierzo – astonishingly enough, the only point held by the French between Lugo and Astorga. The garrison being quickly forced to surrender, the message was obvious: Ney was losing control.

Not until May did it prove possible for the French to do anything about the situation. Not having had any news of the province for months, Joseph ordered 7,000 troops to head across the frontier under General Kellermann. Meeting at Lugo, Ney and Kellermann decided to ensure first that the garrison of Asturias – the largest Spanish force in the region – could not intervene in favour of the insurgents. Abandoning all offensive operations in Galicia, Ney therefore concentrated one of his two divisions at Lugo, whilst Kellermann returned to León and sent a message to the governor of Santander, General Bonnet, asking him to co-operate as well. By the middle of May, then, three separate forces were moving into Asturias. Taken by surprise and deployed in scattered detachments along the frontier, the Spanish forces were overwhelmed and fled in all directions, Oviedo being entered on 20 May. There was no resistance:

From eleven o'clock in the morning of 18 May the bells of the cathedral and all the other churches of the city were rung to sound the alarm. The Marqués de Santa Cruz toured the streets, urging the inhabitants to take up arms, as did Canon Pedro de Nava . . . A few of the citizens did so, but seeing that no soldier put himself at their head, that nobody tried to organise them, that no other measures were being taken other than to ring the bells, make speeches and deliver sermons [and] that all was confusion and disorder . . . they lost heart . . . Consternation and fear were written in the faces of the city's inhabitants . . . Dazed and terrified, they fled to the towns and villages of the surrounding district . . . The roads and tracks were full of old and young of both sexes, of fathers of families, of young children. Everyone was trying to save what they could and carry off anything that might sustain them in their flight.[27]

Although Ney issued a proclamation promising the inhabitants that they would be well treated, submission spared the city nothing:

On the pretext that a few shots had been fired at the troops as they entered the city, they were ordered to sack it ... During the sack these latter-day vandals committed such excesses and cruelties that merely recounting them is enough to scare one out of one's wits. The cost of the damage done in almost all the buildings by the riotous soldiery in their attempts to uncover their pillage, of the fine furniture that was smashed, and of the personal effects, money and plate that were taken away, cannot begin to be calculated.[28]

On the surface the loss of Oviedo seemed a considerable humiliation for the Spaniards: caught in the midst of his purge of the Asturian authorities, for example, La Romana had to escape in a fishing boat, whilst the city had been the very symbol of the uprising. Yet in practice its only result was to leave the French overstretched in Galicia and Santander, both provinces now witnessing serious setbacks. In Galicia, Mahy struck north with the Army of the Left and blockaded Lugo, whilst the Division of the Miño marched on Santiago and occupied the city after defeating its garrison in a fierce battle. Meanwhile, Santander city was also taken, having been surprised by a division of the Asturian forces which had dodged the invaders and slipped through the mountains. Within a matter of days, then, Ney and Bonnet were racing back the way they had come, leaving Kellermann little option but to evacuate Asturias, which by the end of June was once again in Spanish hands.

Just as hard to subdue as Galicia and Asturias, meanwhile, was Catalonia, where the first priority was the conquest of the defiant fortress of Gerona, blocking, as this did, the main road between Barcelona and the border and affording the *somaténes* of the northern half of the province a secure base and place of refuge. In consequence, in January 1809 Napoleon had ordered the forces stationed in the area of the frontier under General Reille to move against it as soon as possible, even sending them a few German troops as reinforcements. The emperor had envisaged that the siege should begin no later than the middle of February, but Reille was not especially enthusiastic about his assignment, whilst it also took some time to amass the supplies, siege materials and heavy guns that would be needed, the French also continuing to be harassed by incessant irregular resistance. More might have been achieved had Saint-Cyr been able to march to Reille's assistance from the vicinity of Barcelona, but all chance of this was for some time rendered impossible by a further Spanish offensive. The French had been too weak to follow up their victory at Molíns de Rey, whilst Barcelona had very quickly once again been hemmed in by a cloud of *somaténes*. As a result, the Army of the Right, which was now commanded by Teodoro Reding, the Swiss officer who had blocked Dupont's escape at Bailén, had been able to recover its cohesion (to the plentiful food assured by the fact that it was positioned in one of the richest agricultural districts in the whole of Spain had been added a division of reinforcements that had been sent up from Andalucía). Reding, it seems, would have preferred simply to keep the army in being and wear down the French with raids and skirmishes, but the local populace were loud in their demands for action, and the Spanish general was soon being accused of cowardice and treason. By early February, then, the Army of the Right was on the move in an attempt to envelop the most advanced elements of Saint-Cyr's forces. Always risky, however, the plan went wrong, and a series of complex manoeuvres eventually led to Reding being cut off from his base at Tarragona by the French commander. Battle being joined north-west of Valls in the early morning of 25 February, the Spaniards tried to cut their way through. Initially only 6,000 strong, the French were steadily forced back – Doyle described Reding's men as 'perhaps the best troops in Spain'[29] – and by noon were in such disarray that the battle seemed lost. Had Reding pushed on, he would have scored a much-needed victory, but at this point he decided that his men needed a rest and fell back to some heights two miles to the west of the original battlefield. Saint-Cyr having soon been heavily reinforced, he therefore went over to the attack. Forming his two divisions into heavy brigade-sized columns that made changes of formation very difficult, his intention was essentially to put the Spaniards to flight by fear alone. In this he was completely successful: several volleys of musketry having had little effect on the advancing masses, the defenders turned and ran. Having already been wounded four times and seen two of his aides-de-camp cut down by his side in hand-to-hand combat, Reding was mortally hit. Very soon, it was all over – 3,000 Spaniards had been killed, wounded or captured, whilst they had also lost all their guns and baggage – and yet the offensive's effect had still been to win Gerona's defenders at least a month (not until the beginning of May, indeed, did the French close in on the city).

Nor was this the end of the trouble. In Aragón, too, the French were soon experiencing serious difficulties. Following the fall of Zaragoza, the two corps employed in the siege – those of Mortier and Junot* – had fanned out

---

* Some clarification is needed here. Junot had returned to Spain with the corps he had led to Portugal. This force, however, had since been amalgamated with Soult's corps, whereupon Junot had been given the corps of Marshal Moncey, who had been sacked on account of the slow pace of operations at Zaragoza.

eastwards and southwards, occupying town after town and advancing as far as the frontiers of Catalonia and Valencia. In the face of this advance the Spaniards were powerless – there was little, indeed, even in the way of popular resistance – but far away in Paris Napoleon was now increasingly concerned at the situation in Germany, where it was clear that Austria was planning to attack the emperor. To the consternation of King Joseph, Mortier's corps was therefore ordered to evacuate its positions and head for Bayonne. Entrusted with the whole of Aragón, Junot's corps could not cope, and all the more so as one of its infantry brigades had been sent off as escort for the long column of Spanish prisoners that had been packed off to the frontier following Palafox's surrender. Much encouraged, the irregular forces who had begun to appear in the more remote parts of the province took heart, and inflicted a number of reverses on the invaders. Meanwhile, the chances of suppressing the irregulars were nullified by the appearance of yet another Spanish field army in the shape of the 'Second Army of the Right', a new force put together under the politically dependable Blake on the basis of the one division of the old Army of Reserve that had not been caught up in the siege.

Frantic efforts in Valencia and Murcia having raised the size of Blake's forces to some 9,000 men, in mid-May they moved across the border and occupied Alcañiz. This was very bad news for the French, whose forces in Aragón were only 10,000-strong as well as being very low in morale. In their commander they were more fortunate, for the mercurial and increasingly eccentric Junot had just been replaced by General Suchet, an impressive leader who had hitherto led a division in the corps which he now inherited. Yet even he was hard pressed to deal with the crisis that followed. By cutting his garrisons to an absolute minimum, Suchet was able to put together 8,000 men, and with these troops he rushed to do battle with Blake at Alcañiz on 23 May. However, the Spaniards had occupied a very strong defensive position whose chief feature was a line of rocky hills, and Suchet therefore had to waste much time feeling out the enemy lines before committing himself to an attack. Not, then, till mid-afternoon did a heavy column of infantry emerge from the French positions and seek to storm the Spanish centre. Advancing uphill under heavy fire, the attackers were first brought to a halt, and then forced to retire in great disorder, whereupon a much discomforted Suchet ordered his men to fall back on Zaragoza, having lost perhaps 800 men. As for their morale it was lower than ever:

The non-success of this attack was tantamount to an absolute defeat in the eyes of the troops, which were already prone to fear and dejection . . . We had already distanced the Spaniards by nearly five leagues, when the First Division . . . was seized with a sudden panic. The terrified soldiers fancied that the enemy was close at their heels. The alarm rapidly spread under favour of the darkness; they fired upon each other and took to flight in the utmost confusion.[30]

Encouraged by this success – the first Patriot victory since Bailén – Blake waited a few days for reinforcements, and then struck westwards in an attempt to threaten Suchet's communications and force him to fight a second battle on unfavourable terms. No bad strategy – and one that clearly recognised the Spaniards' best chance of winning field actions was to make the French attack them in positions that nullified their many advantages on the battlefield – this soon produced the desired effect. On 14 June Suchet, who had spent the intervening period frantically trying to rally his troops, once more marched out of Zaragoza. Unfortunately for the Spaniards, however, Blake had detached many men to guard his own communications (in contrast to the over-confidence that marked many Spanish generals, Blake's besetting sin was doubt and hesitation). The battle that followed on 15 June at María was a bitter struggle. In the words of one of Suchet's officers:

The Spanish were showing considerable resolution and even gained ground . . . By noon our ammunition was running low and indeed had almost been exhausted. A burning sun bore down on our heads and we were dying from the heat and of thirst. I distinctly remember . . . one of my comrades . . . offering me his flask when it was hit by a ball and blown out of his hands.[31]

Yet thanks to Blake the fight was still lost. Assisted by a violent thunderstorm that blinded their opponents, the French were able to break the Spanish right and force the rest of the army to retreat.

Having lost the chance of liberating Zaragoza, Blake would have done best to fall back and rely on the partisans to force Suchet to give up the chase. However, fearful of popular or political retribution, he instead turned to fight a few miles south at Belchite. The result was disaster. Suchet had obtained many reinforcements, whilst the ground was by no means as strong as it had been at Alcañiz and María, but, even so, no one could have predicted what happened next. In the words of the British liaison officer, Charles Doyle:

The cannonading had not commenced five minutes when a grenade from the enemy fell amongst some of ours and blew them up. In one moment all was consternation and confusion, [and] the troops, panic-struck, gave way . . . The enemy's cavalry profited instantly by the alarm, and penetrating the broken line spread universal terror. The whole army dispersed and the retreat was most precipitate. General Blake with some other . . . officers was left literally alone upon the field![32]

A mortified Blake put this extraordinary affair down to a handful of 'rotten apples'. 'Fortune,' he wrote, 'could have been against us to the point that we were beaten, but I never would have expected that the troops under my command would have fled without fighting . . . I do not believe this to be the place to discuss the cause of these routs, which are unfortunately so common in our armies, but I must at least say that a few individuals who give a bad example can demoralise an army without its commander realising it.'[33] But the truth was much less kind to him, the fact being that his men had been demoralised by defeat, bad weather and a growing lack of confidence in Blake, who was by all accounts a colourless individual utterly devoid of charisma. And the fact remained that he had still lost his army. Though few men were killed or taken prisoner – the only troops who put up a fight were a single battalion that made a stand in the main square of the town – the 'Second Army of the Right' was no more, at least half its survivors taking the opportunity to disappear for good.

The elimination of Blake's army did not put an end to Suchet's travails, however, the French commander having had to pay a heavy cost for the victories of María and Belchite. Thus, in the absence of any enemy stronger than a few skeleton garrisons, irregular forces raised on the eastern frontiers of Aragón by the army officers, Felipe Perena and Ramón Gayán, had blockaded Zaragoza and Jaca and cut the main road to Madrid. Also active, meanwhile, were *partidas* raised in the south-west of the province by a variety of juntas that had sprung up in such isolated towns as Molina and Teruel. With major insurgent successes very much a possibility – Jaca, in particular, was held only by a small force of unwilling national guardsmen – Suchet was therefore for months thereafter forced to abandon field campaigns in favour of a series of punitive operations in the interior of his dominions. Much success was achieved, but even so the French forces found themselves under great pressure. In the words of Heinrich von Brandt:

It was a real see-saw battle between the partisans and ourselves: they were everywhere we were not, they disappeared upon our approach, escaped our clutches and re-appeared behind us. As most of the people of the region were on their side, they inevitably had all the advantages. We had to be vigilant at all hours of the day or night so as not to be taken by surprise and risk a loss of either life or honour.[34]

By the early summer of 1809, then, the French had little to show for months of hard fighting but the Tagus valley, a particularly barren and poverty-stricken strip of central Extremadura and a toehold in northern Portugal. Asked at one and the same time to hold down the territory that they held at the end of 1808, fend off the Spanish armies and conquer Portugal, they had simply been taxed beyond the limits of their resources. Only if massive reinforcements had been sent to them from France could they possibly have achieved their goal. But with war brewing with Austria, not a single man could be spared to go to King Joseph's assistance – indeed, it was only with the greatest difficulty that Napoleon was persuaded not to withdraw substantial troops from the Peninsula (Mortier's corps was, as we have seen, pulled out of its positions in Aragón for this purpose, but in the event the emperor relented and allowed it to move to Old Castile, where its presence was the key factor in enabling the French to march on Asturias). In consequence, the great offensive envisaged by Napoleon in January 1809 effectively ground to a halt. In Galicia, Aragón, Navarre and northern La Mancha, French columns periodically struck deep into the hills and laid waste towns and villages where insurgent juntas or guerrilla bands had established themselves, whilst in Catalonia siege operations were just beginning at Gerona, but the fact was that the initiative had passed to the Allies.

If the French were about to find not only that they could advance no further, but that they were badly over-extended, this did not mean that the triumphal march on Lisbon, Seville and Valencia envisaged by Napoleon was out of the question in the long term. On the contrary, for the Patriot cause retribution had as yet only been postponed. Not only would the defeat of Austria that could all too easily be foreseen allow the emperor to send substantial reinforcements to the Peninsula and even to return there himself, but the Junta Central's spoiling tactics carried with them a terrible price. Militarily speaking, for Spain the best strategy to adopt would have been one based on the defence of the substantial territories left in Patriot hands – southern and western Catalonia, the Levante, Andalucía, Extremadura, western León, southern Galicia, and Asturias. Protected by mountains and fortresses, the Spanish forces would have been a threat that would have been costly and time-consuming to eradicate, whilst their mere existence would have prevented the French from concentrating their full force against the guerrillas. Meanwhile, time would have been gained for the suppression of resistance to conscription, the accumulation of much larger armies, and the improvements of training and discipline. As we have seen, however, for political and diplomatic reasons, a defensive strategy was not an option. Yet by advancing the Spaniards lost far more than they gained. As the resultant battles were fought out in the open terrain of the *meseta*, their armies' glaring inadequacies were exposed more than ever, and, still worse, exposed in a situation in which the French enjoyed a central position whilst the Spaniards were operating on exterior lines. Meanwhile, desertion was encouraged, and losses incurred of a sort that the tatterdemalion Patriot cause simply could not sustain. Free Spain, in short, was bleeding to death.

8

Talavera

THE FALL OF THE JUNTA CENTRAL, JULY 1809–JANUARY 1810

The lines of British infantry lay in the blazing summer sun. Smoke from burning grass drifted into their eyes, but did little to shield them from the enemy. Indeed, in the distance eighty pieces of artillery sent cannonballs screaming towards them to obliterate a file of defenders or bounce harmlessly overhead. A handful of defending cannon fired back, but they were too few to make any difference, and all that the troops could do was to hug the ground in the hope that the storm would pass. It was with great relief that they suddenly realised that the enemy batteries had ceased firing, and that the dark masses of troops facing them were on the move. Across the intervening space, indeed, could be heard the rolling drumbeats of the pas de charge. Shots cracked out from the skirmishers that lined the British front, but the men involved were soon falling back, for they were far too few in numbers to make any impression on the array that was bearing down on them. The troops knew exactly what to do, however, a single volley fired at the last moment sweeping away whole ranks of men. Nor were the defenders finished: lowering their bayonets, they sprang forward with a great cheer and sent the surviving enemy scrambling for safety.

Based on the repulse of the divisions of Lapisse and Rey* at the battle of Talavera on 28 July 1809, this episode typifies an image of the Peninsular War that still remains dear to British hearts. In 1809, however, it epitomised neither British action in the war, nor the war itself. Setting aside La Coruña, in fact, Talavera was the only occasion in 1809 when British troops had to face a full-scale French assault in a set-piece battle, whilst victory was followed by a fresh retreat and new setbacks. What Talavera really epitomises, indeed, is failure, whether it was failure to develop effective methods of inter-allied co-operation, failure to reform the Spanish armies, failure to

---

* British accounts generally refer to the latter as Sebastiani's division. However, although originally commanded by that officer, by the time of Talavera it was led by General Rey, Sebastiani having been elevated to the command of the corps of which it was a part.

consolidate the authority of the Junta Central, or failure to revolutionise popular attitudes to the war. Despite a summer and autumn of bitter fighting, hopes of Allied recovery were therefore revealed to be illusory.

At the time that Talavera was fought, however, it must have seemed to many observers that the Allied cause was on the rise. Only in Catalonia were the French still on the attack, and even here they had run into difficulties, for their first goal – Gerona – was possessed of impressive defences, a large garrison of regular troops, and a governor of great professionalism, courage and resourcefulness in the person of the sixty-year-old Mariano Alvarez del Castro. Much to the ire of Napoleon, who responded by replacing Saint-Cyr with Marshal Augereau and Reille with Palafox's old opponent, General Verdier, for a variety of reasons operations did not even begin against the fortress until 24 May, and when they did progress was extremely slow. Not until the beginning of July, indeed, were the French in a position to launch an assault, but their chosen objective – the great citadel that crowned the heights overlooking the city – remained defiant, and two attempts to conquer it were therefore driven back with heavy losses.

Setback though this was, it was as nothing compared to events elsewhere, for these suggested that the French were not just stymied, but on the retreat. In June, as we have seen, the invaders had had to evacuate their short-lived conquests in Asturias, but by far the most dramatic developments had occurred in Portugal and Galicia. In the former the French invasion had stalled following the capture of Oporto, after which Soult had been effectively corralled in a small pocket of territory around the city (not that this dissuaded him from indulging in dreams of a Lusitanian monarchy). Nor had much time ensued before the British once again hove into view, the Portland administration having on 2 April decided to increase its forces in Portugal to 30,000 men and place them under the command of Sir Arthur Wellesley with orders to expel the French from the country.

This development was the fruit of a variety of factors including Canning's determination to maintain Britain's commitment to the Peninsula, the Junta Central's refusal to grant the British access to Cádiz, the determination of Wellesley's friends to see him restored to favour, and Wellesley's own submission of a long and prescient memorandum in which he argued: first, that the mere presence of a British army in Portugal would prevent the French from subduing the Spaniards; second, that Portugal could be placed in such a state of defence that the French would never be able to conquer her with a force of less than 100,000 men; and, third, that a remodelled Portuguese army could augment Britain's striking power sufficiently for her to think of liberating Spain. Beyond that, however, all that can be said for certain is that on 22 April 1809 Lisbon saw the arrival of a Sir Arthur Wellesley committed to an immediate attack on Soult, an intention in which he was encouraged by news that the forces of 'King Nicholas', as the marshal had become known, were riven with dissatisfaction (in brief, a plot – the so-called Argenton conspiracy – was afoot to overthrow Soult and bring his men over to the Allies).

By the beginning of May, then, 17,000 British and 11,000 Portuguese soldiers were poised to hit Oporto under Wellesley, whilst further east Beresford was marching northwards with a flanking column charged with the task of cutting Soult off from Spain. The result was a resounding victory. Forced to evacuate Oporto on 12 May after a surprise river crossing which saw a small party of British soldiers seize a large monastery on the town's eastern outskirts and beat off a series of desperate assaults, Soult ordered his men to head for León. Nor was this the end of his travails, for, reinforced by the Portuguese army that Silveira had managed to sustain east of Oporto, Beresford had succeeded in blocking his intended line of march. Threatened by a second Bailén, the marshal abandoned his guns and baggage and fled north along a precipitous mountain track that led in the direction of Galicia. Beset by enemies on all sides, soaked by pouring rain, and impeded by some of the roughest terrain in Portugal, he was on several occasions nearly trapped, but on 18 May he reached the frontier, having lost 4,000 men.

This bare account of the fighting should not be allowed to disguise the fact that the French occupation of northern Portugal had proved a grim affair. An English officer who had been billeted in Oporto in 1808, for example, returned to the house in which he had stayed to find it in a shocking condition:

To witness the destruction occasioned in this beautiful residence was truly pitiable . . . the fine balustrades [were] broken; the chandeliers and mirrors were shattered to pieces; all the portable furniture had been taken away and the remainder either wantonly burned or otherwise destroyed; the choice pictures were defaced, and the walls more resembled a French barrack than the abode of a Portuguese *fidalgo* from the obscene paintings that were daubed upon them. The beautiful garden was entirely ransacked; the charming walks and fragrant bowers torn up and demolished; the fountains broken to pieces.[1]

The same observer goes on to retail the story of a Portuguese gentleman having his brains blown out on the very eve of Soult's retreat by a French officer 'because he would not resign one of his daughters to gratify the abominable lust of this detestable assassin'.[2] Nor were things any better outside Oporto:

At midday . . . I passed a field where the French had bivouacked. All the furniture and even the crockery had been taken from the houses of a neighbouring village and brought into the field. The beds and the mattresses lay in rows in the mud. The drawers from the various articles of furniture had been used as mangers. Wardrobes had been transformed into bedsteads and roofs for the huts. The chairs, staircases and window frames had been used . . . as fuel for the kitchen fires . . . All the crosses and statues of the saints on the road had been thrown from their pedestals, and the almsboxes in front of them broken open and plundered, while all the altars and chapels had been ruined and polluted. In the churches even the graves had not been spared, and the sanctuaries had been rifled. Altar candlesticks, arms and legs of apostles and saints, torn vestments, chalices, prayer books and the like, mixed up with straw and filth, lay all about them.[3]

Small wonder, then, that the British came across French stragglers who had been nailed to barn doors, castrated and had their genitals stuffed in their mouths, nor that mobs of angry peasants clamoured to be allowed to murder the many prisoners who had fallen into the hands of the British. Nor was Galicia a safe haven, but its insurgents could do little more than harass the retreating columns, whilst both the Army of the Left and the Division of the Miño were far away attacking Santiago and Lugo. As the Anglo-Portuguese forces halted at the frontier, Soult's battered command was therefore able to make its way northwards to Lugo (from which the Spaniards had since withdrawn). What was to be done next, however? Soult was firmly in favour of marching on León, from where he could once again threaten Portugal, whilst at the same time re-equipping his men with the arms, clothes and shoes that they so badly needed. By contrast, Ney wanted the French to concentrate on Galicia which he reckoned could now be crushed once and for all, the two marshals between them being able to muster about 32,000 men. Eager to secure such succour as Ney could provide for his weary forces, Soult went along with the latter plan and made a show of marching against the Spaniards, but in his heart he never had any intention of assisting his fellow commander, and in fact proceeded immediately to evacuate Galicia on the pretext that his men were unfit for further operations. On 7 June, meanwhile, Ney ran into the Division of the Miño and was repulsed with heavy losses. Discovering Soult's treachery a few days later, the 'bravest of the brave' understandably threw in the sponge in his turn: in less than a month, indeed, Galicia was free.

Thus ended a campaign that had cost the empire both considerable embarrassment – for months the Patriot press had been full of tales of the insurgents' heroism – and the lives of thousands of troops. Exhibited in microcosm, meanwhile, were a number of lessons that Napoleon would have done well to bear in mind. However enthusiastic the insurgents – and there is clear evidence that at least some of the *alarmas* were more interested in pillage and private vendettas than fighting the French – they could probably in the end have been defeated, but this would have both taken a great deal of time and required either abandoning attempts to advance elsewhere or a massive injection of fresh troops into the Peninsula. As was shown even more clearly by Soult's invasion of Portugal, every square mile of captured territory had to be given a solid garrison. At the same time the presence of enemy armies – a vital element – created a need for still more troops. With the French set an impossible task, their willpower and morale alike were undermined. Meanwhile, growing anger and frustration encouraged atrocities of all sorts and intensified the rigours of occupation policies that were already very brutal. Victory, then, would take far more time, money and manpower than Napoleon had ever anticipated. Also clear was that still further delays were likely unless the emperor was prepared to adopt a rather different command structure from the one which he had bequeathed to his armies in January 1809. In theory, Joseph had been appointed the emperor's lieutenant in Spain, but his authority had been consistently undermined throughout Napoleon's stay in the country, whilst he was in any case a nonentity in military terms, the French commanders therefore being all too inclined to ignore him. With remote control from Paris no solution, the result was that the bitter rivalries which rent the marshalate often led to complete chaos. Even when the French commanders were disposed to co-operate with one another, however, they could rarely maintain contact. From this stemmed yet another problem in that the great envelopments and encirclements characteristic of Napoleon's campaigns were simply not possible in Spain. Even in the great counter-offensive of November–December 1808, the emperor's efforts in this respect had not worked perfectly, but with the subsequent growth in popular resistance such combinations became almost impossible.

The extent to which Napoleon became aware of these problems in the wake of the evacuation of northern Portugal and Galicia is unknown. What is true, however, is that he resolved, first, that enormous reinforcements should be sent to Spain at the earliest possible date (effectively the moment Austria was defeated), and, second, that the French armies should again concentrate on the destruction of the British, to which end Soult was given control not just of his own corps but also those of Ney and Mortier. Yet for the time being the forces *in situ* were on their own, and thus it was that in southern and western Spain, at least, the strategic initiative continued to lie with the Allies. In this respect, the latter's situation looked most promising. In Portugal, the British had received several thousand fresh troops, and were now massing for an attack on Victor, whilst their Portuguese allies kept watch on the frontier with León. With the Spaniards able to contribute the Army of Extremadura, which had been rebuilt to a size of some 36,000 men, and the 23,000-strong Army of the Centre, a great victory did not seem impossible.

Yet success was to prove elusive. In the first place, in the middle of June lack of food caused Victor to evacuate his exposed positions south of the Tagus and pull back towards Madrid. Undaunted, Wellesley and Cuesta elaborated a plan for a concentric advance on the capital itself. However, whilst any operation on exterior lines is absolutely dependent on co-operation, trust and co-ordination, in the summer of 1809 few qualities were more more lacking in central Spain. Cuesta and Wellesley, for example, were both prickly individuals who were all but certain to alienate one another. The Junta Central was terrified of Cuesta and strongly suspected the British of secretly being in league with one or more of the various groups that were plotting its downfall (in this respect it was unfortunate, first, that the prominent British liaison officer, Charles Doyle, was a noted intimate of Francisco Palafox, and, second, that La Romana enjoyed much British approval). Cuesta, meanwhile, believed that the British were scheming to have him replaced with the much more amenable Duque de Alburquerque. Francisco Javier Venegas, the commander of the Army of the Centre, was an enemy of Cuesta and a tool of the Junta Central. And, finally, Cuesta, Venegas and many other influential Spaniards could not but be alarmed by rumours that Wellesley was to be appointed Allied commander-in-chief.

Outside the senior ranks of the Allied armies, most of this probably had no impact. But rumours of power struggles at the top were little needed as a source of friction. For the Spaniards, bitter memories of rapine and pillage were now revived. Even before the British army left Portugal, it was clear that its behaviour was but little changed. Several soldiers who had committed outrages of one sort or another were reported to have been killed by the populace, whilst, as Wellington complained, 'The army behave terribly ill. They are a rabble who cannot bear success any more than Sir J. Moore's army could bear failure ... They plunder in all directions.'[4] Even more shocking than mere robbery was the callous brutality exhibited by many of the soldiery, as witness, for example, the behaviour of a soldier named John Clapham who, searching for firewood just after the army had entered Spain, entered a church and seized a coffin from the vault, leaving the body tipped out on the floor.

Such behaviour was probably inevitable. Set apart from the rest of society for years at a time and exposed to endless danger and privation, the soldiers were both brutalised and encouraged to revenge themselves upon the civilian world. 'I have seen', wrote Sherer, 'common men distributed through the empty palace of a nobleman . . . and I have observed in their countenances a jocular eagerness to smash and destroy . . . But this does not arise out of cruelty. No, in such a case a soldier feels himself lifted for a moment above his low and ordinary condition, while the banished owner of the proud mansion . . . appears humbled before him.'[5] Whatever the cause, the phenomenon was certainly troubling. To quote Thomas Browne, 'The [common soldiers] appeared to me to become daily more ferocious and less fit for return to the duties of citizens, and I sometimes apprehended that when they should be disbanded in England after the restoration of peace, the country would be overrun with pilferers and marauders of every description.'[6]

Yet the problem was not just confined to pillaging and vandalism. Also apparent was a superiority complex at least as striking as anything on display in the French army. From the very moment that they landed in Lisbon, the British felt that they were higher beings. The Portuguese capital, indeed, caused general horror, Bell calling it 'the most filthy town I had ever seen', and Bragge remarking that 'on setting your foot on land, you are almost overcome with the stench'.[7] The effect of such sights was not unnaturally to lead to the most unfavourable comparisons. To quote Porter:

The foul imagination of Dean Swift could not prefigure the scene that presented itself: a chaos of nastiness, poverty and wretchedness lay on every side. Rags or nakedness seemed the condition of every person who approached me . . . Not an inn is to be found in which you could pass the night without undergoing the tortures of a hell . . . I made an attempt to lodge in one, but had I been destined to pass my nocturnal hours in the most wretched hovel in England, or to have put up at this place, I should have preferred the former. It would be impossible to find in all Great Britain a habitation so ruinous, so ill-furnished, so filthy, and so infested with vermin, and yet this was the chief hotel in the city.[8]

Moving up country, or, for that matter, over the frontier into Spain, made little difference. Writing of the district between Almeida and Ciudad Rodrigo, for example, Simmons complained:

Our present quarters are truly miserable; on all sides stupendous mountains, the people wretched in the extreme, clothes hardly sufficient to cover themselves, and positively not a degree above savages . . . Of a morning they will turn out of their wretched cabins and are to be seen sitting in rows upon the ground . . . picking lice off themselves and out of each other's heads.[9]

'Positively not a degree above savages.' From this there stemmed a multitude of evils. With such attitudes compounded by ignorance of popular customs and dissastisfaction at the record of Spaniards and Portuguese alike in 1808, scorn was widespread. Thus, for Simmons, the Portuguese were 'not worthy of notice', whilst for Donaldson the Spaniards were 'a jealous minded, vindictive and and cowardly race, grossly ignorant and superstitious'.[10] Examples of the discourteous, rude and arbitrary treament of civilians are therefore legion. Travelling to Lisbon to recuperate after being wounded, Simmons, for example, thought nothing of forcibly impressing a Portuguese peasant to drive his cart, and then having his servant thrash the unfortunate man when the cart jolted his wounds; Kincaid of stealing food from starving Portuguese refugees; and Lawrence of robbing Spanish peasants who had come into the camp to sell wine. Less serious but more gratuitous is the story of an Irish soldier named Dennis, who, seeing a religious procession approaching with the Blessed Sacrament, wanted to avoid having to kneel in the dirt of a Lisbon street:

At last a lucky thought struck him. He snatched the hat out of the hand of a Portuguese who was kneeling before him, kneeled down on it and went though the ceremony with great gravity . . . The fellow who owned the hat durst not move until the procession had passed, and then, without giving him time to speak, Dennis clapped the hat on the owner's head and walked off.[11]

Generally speaking, the officer corps would not act in quite so outrageous a fashion, but even so it did little to remedy matters. Thus:

In some instances we experienced much hospitality from the people, but these occurrences were rare, for the Spaniards are naturally a lofty and distant people, and most unquestionably our officers did not endeavour by any act on their part to do away with this reserve . . . This is a fatal error . . . If the officers of the British army were to reflect upon the effect their conduct must have on the people of a different nation . . . they would at once come to the resolution of changing their tone . . . It is a singular fact, and I look upon it as a degrading one, that the French officers . . . made in the ratio of five to one more conquests than we did! How is this to be accounted for? The British officer has the advantage of appearance; his exterior is far before that of a Frenchman; his fortune, generally speaking, is ten times as great. But what of all this if the one accommodates himself to the manners . . . of those he is thrown amongst, while the other . . . sticks to his national habits, struts about, and not only despises, but lets it be seen that he despises, all he meets save those of his own nation?[12]

Arrogance, meanwhile, was both compounded and fuelled by anti-Catholicism. As Irishmen, many of the rank and file were Catholic, but the officers of the British army were staunchly Anglican, whilst a number of units were experiencing an upsurge in Methodism amongst the soldiers, and, in particular, the NCOs. If Spain and Portugal were backward, Catholicism was regarded as the culprit, whilst there was universal condemnation of many aspects of Catholic faith and practice. Statues, for example, were claimed to encourage idolatry and alms-giving laziness. Particular dislike was felt for the large numbers of clergy to be found everywhere, Patterson, for example, describing monks as 'living . . . in a state of lazy indolence . . . supported by the deluded multitude and supplied most plentifully with an abundance of good things'.[13] But greatest interest was aroused by the institution of the convent. Nothing could convince the officers of the army that the 'fair inmates' and 'lovely forsworns' had not been incarcerated against their will and there was general denunciation of what Swabey called 'the cruelty of immuring unfortunate youth in these diabolical cells'.[14] The result was a further crop of incidents. The Twenty-Third Light Dragoons got up a mock procession, complete with a fake bishop; Kincaid describes how monks were assaulted or pelted with snowballs; and there are numerous accounts of officers flocking round convents and attempting to strike up relationships with the nuns. Whether they were ever successful is unknown (although there are certainly stories to this effect), but on occasion stronger measures were taken:

Our doctor . . . got so merry he bolted off to a convent to release the nuns like a gallant knight! Many of the fair *señoritas* he knew there were pining for liberty, but the wily priests came to the rescue. There was a shindy, of course [for] a few officers of the baggage guard . . . collected their forces and joined the medico. They . . . had nearly forced an entrance when the second-in-command received a wound on the head and tumbled down the stairs. The doctor called off his troops to see after the wounded . . . and the holy priests made their escape, satisfied in preserving the dark-eyed maidens from the hands of such heretics.[15]

The Spaniards, then, were unlikely to find the British congenial companions. Needless to say, the latter were no better impressed. British memories of Spanish betrayal in the campaign of Sir John Moore were just as strong as Spanish ones of British misconduct. Famously, officers and men alike were shaken at the sight of Cuesta and his army. Still suffering from the effects of being wounded and trampled underfoot at Medellín, Cuesta was described as an 'infirm old man, so much so that he is obliged to be lifted into his saddle' and a 'deformed-looking lump of pride, ignorance and treachery'.[16] As for his troops, they aroused derision:

Falstaff's ragged regiment would have done honour to any force compared with the men before us. They were undisciplined, badly armed, and . . . almost naked. I can assure the reader that it was with the greatest difficulty we could avoid laughing right out of our faces, when officers out at elbows and knees stalked past carrying rusty old swords not worth lifting off the road. Hundreds of men with the most haughty countenances sported coats of many colours, while their inexpressibles bore unmistakable testimony to the difficulty experienced by the wearers in keeping the rags pinned about their legs.[17]

Add to all this the effect of pure happenstance – the fact, for example, that the Tagus valley was a poor region that had already been thoroughly plundered – and it will be seen that relations were bound to be bad. And so it transpired. In outline the Allied plan was that, whilst Venegas prevented the troops in La Mancha and Madrid – the corps originally commanded by Marshal Augereau and now led by General Sebastiani, and King Joseph's small reserve – from marching west, Wellesley and Cuesta would join forces in the Tagus valley and defeat Victor, whereupon Joseph and Sebastiani would have to retreat. Sebastiani and Joseph might, of course, ignore Venegas and join Victor, or Victor ignore Wellesley and join Joseph and Sebastiani, but neither possibility was especially worrying, for both would simply expose the capital to capture whilst posing few risks to the Allies. Whatever happened, in short, Madrid ought to fall, dealing a heavy blow to Napoleon in the process.

In almost no respect, however, did this plan succeed. Coming up against Victor east of the town of Talavera de la Reina in a strong position behind the River Alberche, Wellesley and Cuesta agreed to attack him on 23 July, only for the Spaniards to fail to move at the appointed time. Finding that Victor had in consequence been able to pull out safe and sound, Wellesley was furious. Why the Spanish general refused to move is not quite clear though the most probable explanation is that he suspected that he was being led into a trap. This suspicion was unfounded, but even so there were good military reasons for believing that a frontal attack of the sort planned was unwise. As even Wellesley recognised, 'The chances were not much in our favour.'[18] But that was not the issue, the central British complaint being that Cuesta had failed to inform them of his change of heart. As early as 17 June the British commander had complained that he was 'as obstinate as any gentleman at the head of an army need be', but now the situation had become impossible: 'I find,' wrote Wellesley, 'General Cuesta more and more impracticable every day. It is impossible to do business with him, and very uncertain that any operation will succeed in which he has any concern.'[19]

Fearful for the safety of his army, Wellesley therefore halted his advance. Also important was the question of logistics, however. Wellesley had only agreed to the offensive on condition that the Spaniards provided him with adequate supplies and transport. This was essential – at this point the British army lacked the permanent baggage train of later years and in consequence effectively had to live off the country – but, despite genuine goodwill on the part of the Spaniards, the Tagus valley was incapable of supplying the army's wants. A little food was forthcoming, but carts were not to be had, and the commissaries of some units were reduced to raiding the convoys that came up bringing food for the Spaniards. Even had Cuesta been less difficult, it is therefore clear that the British would not have advanced beyond the Alberche. As Wellesley told Castlereagh, 'I have not been able to follow the enemy as I would have wished on account of . . . my having found it impossible to procure even one mule or cart in Spain.'[20]

Unable to shift Wellesley, Cuesta decided to press on eastwards anyway, only on 25 July suddenly to run into not just Victor, but also Sebastiani and Joseph. What, then, had gone wrong? The answer lay with Venegas, who had not only advanced in the most dilatory fashion, but also turned aside to engage in useless demonstrations against Toledo (a town that is near-impregnable against troops coming from the south). What motivated this conduct is unclear, one possibility being that he had decided to sabotage Cuesta's operations out of sheer spite, another that he had been given secret instructions to hang back by the Junta Central, and still another that his hands were tied by an absurd scheme hatched by an adventurer named Domingo Soriano to secure the arrest of King Joseph and the surrender of a large part of the French army. Whatever the explanation, the result was that Joseph and Sebastiani felt able to join Victor. Some 46,000 men were therefore soon heading for the Allied armies. It was not just with these troops that Wellesley and Cuesta would be forced to contend, however. In León, Soult had been resting and re-equipping his battered corps, whilst Ney had just evacuated Galicia. Also available was the corps of Marshal Mortier, which was stationed further to the south-east in Old Castile. With Wellesley in the Tagus valley, the opportunity was too good to miss, and these troops too were soon on the march.

Given that the handful of troops that Wellesley and Cuesta had posted to watch their flank and rear were incapable of holding the mass that was about to descend upon them, it is probably just as well that Wellesley had decided to halt at the Alberche. However, he remained in some danger, for there was a very real possibility that Cuesta could have been overwhelmed by Joseph, Victor and Sebastiani when they moved west on 26 July. Fortunately for the Allies, however, a combination of good fortune and French bungling allowed Cuesta to escape the trap, with the result that by the morning of 27 July the Spaniards were back in touch with the British forces. The line of the Alberche being for a variety of reasons impossible to defend, the Allies then fell back a little further to a defensive position selected for them by Wellesley, covered by the British division of General Mackenzie. These troops, however, were neither as alert or as well-posted as they might have been, whilst the countryside around their headquarters – a substantial farm called the Casa de Salinas – was obscured by olive groves, pines and holm-oaks. Eager to see what was going on, Wellesley had ridden out to this building and mounted the tower that was its central feature, when suddenly a swarm of French infantry burst out of the scrub and attacked Mackenzie's troops. In this fight the British commander-in-chief came very close to being killed or captured – running for his life, he just got out of the main courtyard before the French burst in on the other side – whilst over 400 men became casualties, but he succeeded in rallying the division and bringing it safely back to the main Allied line.

To the accompaniment of a constant cannonade, both armies now began to deploy for battle. Moving up from the east through country covered by the same sort of scrub as had so hampered Mackenzie at the Casa de Salinas, the French occupied a position running from a low hill called the Cerro de Cascajal southwards across the plain that extended to the Tagus. Stationed at the edge of the woods and olive groves through which the French had come, their right and centre had an excellent field of fire and could move on the Allies over open ground, but their left was less well defined, the olives, pines, and holm-oaks covering the entire position and extending forward in a great belt that encompassed the town of Talavera and merged with the position occupied by the Allies.

If the terrain did not especially assist the French, it did not wholly favour the Allies either. For most of its length their position was marked by a small stream called the Portiña, but, except where it ran through a narrow ravine between the Cascajal and a somewhat steeper and higher eminence running more or less east–west, known as the Cerro de Medellín, that formed the Allied left, this was no obstacle whatsoever. Just before it plunged into the thickets that cloaked the southern end of the battlefield, it was overlooked by an isolated knoll known as the Pajar de Vergara, but otherwise the position was protected only by the Medellín. Some further help was derived from the groves and enclosures that filled the space between the Pajar and the Tagus, but, if they hampered cavalry charges and artillery bombardments, they at the same time exposed their defenders to the danger of being taken by surprise, masked their own cannon, and made it very difficult for them to manoeuvre. Meanwhile, most of the centre and left were extremely vulnerable to cannon fire: except on the rather narrow Medellín, there was no reverse slope of the sort that Wellesley so much favoured.

Held by the British from the Medellín to the Pajar and the Spaniards from the Pajar to the Tagus, the Allied position was really rather mediocre. Meanwhile, the Spanish army, as usual, contained too many raw troops – in a famous incident that took place as the rival forces were drawing up their lines, indeed, four battalions took to their heels at the sound of their own muskets after letting fly a massive volley at some French cavalry that had appeared far in the distance. Finally, the Allies were badly outgunned, Joseph, Victor and Sebastiani having between them brought eighty cannon to the battlefield and Wellesley and Cuesta only fifty-five. The French were somewhat outnumbered, true – Wellington and Cuesta could muster 53,000 troops to their 46,000 – but the rather slight advantage that this amounted to was completely nullified by the fact that, as the attackers, they could mass the bulk of their forces against the British or the Spaniards alone whilst containing the rest of the Allied array with a mere handful of cavalry.

Whilst either the British or the Spaniards could have been the target of the blow that followed, for a variety of reasons it fell upon the former. In this, at least, the Allies were fortunate. Far better trained than the Spaniards and much heartened by their victories in Portugal, the British could rely upon the tactical genius of Wellesley, whilst the weeks that had passed since the Oporto campaign had seen the formation of the army into permanent divisions and the attachment of at least a company of riflemen to every infantry brigade so as to give them a more effective skirmishing capacity. But Marshal Victor – the only one of the three French commanders on the field at this point – had never faced the British in battle. Determined to seize the lion's share of the glory, he did not even wait for the whole of the French forces to come up. Hardly had night fallen, then, than the division of General Ruffin moved forward against the Medellín. Apparently positioned in the wrong place, the defenders were taken by surprise and the scrub-covered and boulder-strewn slopes of the hill soon became the scene of a confused night action. Riding up to find out what was going on, the well-liked and jovial divisional commander, Sir Rowland Hill, was almost captured, and it was only after fierce fighting that the French were driven off.

Troublesome though it may have been, the night attack on the Medellín had therefore been a failure. However, though the defenders had now been alerted to the danger, Victor had not finished. At five o'clock in the morning the massed batteries of French artillery opened fire on Wellington's troops. Under cover of this terrible cannonade, Ruffin's troops again rolled forward across the Portiña. Arrayed in three regimental columns, they were soon moving up the steep slope on the further bank, assailed by no more than the fire of Hill's skirmishers (so dense was the cannon smoke that they were completely hidden from view). Waiting for them at the crest of the slope, however, were 4,000 British infantry. Thus, no sooner had Ruffin's men emerged from the smoke than they were assailed by a crashing volley that virtually wiped out their front ranks. After a brief exchange of fire, Hill's seven battalions charged their shaken enemies and in a matter of moments the whole of Ruffin's division was fleeing in disarray.

In the French camp this repulse caused consternation. Knowing that Soult was marching on Wellington's communications, Joseph, Sebastiani and the king's chief adviser, Marshal Jourdan, had been opposed to an assault, but their hands had been forced by Victor, an impetuous commander who had only become a marshal two years before and was possessed of something of an inferiority complex (an ex-ranker of no great intellect, he was the butt of many jokes). Desperate for victory, Victor therefore continued to advocate Wellesley's destruction. After much argument, this bravado carried the day – Joseph was frightened at the idea of what Napoleon might do if the British were allowed to escape and had just heard that Soult would take rather longer to reach the Tagus valley than had originally been hoped – and so preparations began for another assault. Chief amongst these was a heavy bombardment that caused serious losses. Schaumann, for example, describes how he saw a gunner 'flung aloft and [sail] through the air with arms and legs outspread like a frog' and Morley how a spent shot struck him on the hip at the same moment as another smashed through the open mouth of a man named Shaw who had been lying asleep beside him. Most graphic of all are the memories of Andrew Pearson:

Just as my company got into line, the captain told me to close the files to the right, and . . . at that moment a round shot passed through the bodies of the front and rear rank men, killing them both. I was struck with one of their muskets on the breast and stunned for a few minutes . . . A sergeant who assisted me up instantly reeled and fell, and was carried about six yards to the rear. I ran to him and inquired if he thought himself mortally hit, when he replied that the shot was in his pack. I at once examined it . . . and putting my hand into it brought out a twelve-pound shot.[21]

Whilst the French commanders were arguing with each other, the Portiña was witnessing scenes that were to become characteristic of the relationship between the British and the French armies in the Peninsular War. The only source of water on a battlefield assailed by the full heat of a Spanish summer, the lull in the fighting had made it a magnet for both sides. All along its course, then, enemies found themselves scooping water from the same stagnant pools, sharing food, wine and tobacco, and trying to talk to one another. Wrote one participant:

The water in the stream, which in the morning was clear and sweet, was now a pool of blood, heaped over with the dead and dying. There being no alternative, we were compelled to close our eyes and drink the gory stream. The French troops were equally ill off and . . . came down in thousands . . . to follow our example. In place of looking grimly at our enemies, we shook hands with them in the most friendly manner.[22]

It was an extraordinary scene, but also one that became increasingly commonplace as the war progressed. Revolted by Spanish and Portuguese cruelty, united by professionalism and hardship, and utterly alienated by the society in which they found themselves, it was but natural that the British and French should be drawn to one another. As time went on, an unwritten code therefore evolved that laid down all sorts of rules and conventions. Sentries were not to be shot at, unnecessary firing avoided, the wounded spared and succoured, prisoners treated with respect, and sources of food and water that lay in no man's land shared with the other side. Stories of officers exchanging letters for captured friends, asking for enemy newspapers or even dining with the other side are therefore commonplace, whilst ordinary soldiers could frequently be found scavenging for food and plunder side by side. The British officer who got so drunk in the French lines that he had to be carried home by four enemy soldiers and the French sentry who was found doing an Englishman's duty are probably apocryphal, but even so the phenomenon was widely remarked, not least by the Spaniards and Portuguese, amongst whom it caused considerable offence.

Unfortunately, the fraternisation could not last for ever. The French bombardment resumed, and by two o'clock in the afternoon all was ready. Whilst two of Victor's three infantry divisions – those of Ruffin and Villatte – threatened the Cerro de Medellín by moving along the long valley leading to the west that flanked its northern side, the two that Sebastiani had brought to the field – those of Leval and Rey – together with Victor's third division – that of Lapisse – surged forward against the Allied centre. The result was the bloody crisis of an already bloody day.

North of the Medellín, Wellesley was not much tested, for, anticipating the French move, he had sent most of his cavalry into the valley, where they were reinforced by a large contingent of Spanish troops sent over at his request by Cuesta. Advancing a little way, the French perceived that one of the two British cavalry brigades that had been sent to intercept them was riding towards them and they therefore halted and formed square. Undaunted, the cavalry – a mixture of British and German light dragoons – charged on, only to meet disaster. According to every British account, the horsemen suddenly encountered a hidden watercourse and were thrown into terrible confusion. This may be a piece of fabrication, but there is no question that the charge failed. Reaching the French squares in a blown and disordered state, the British cavalry had no chance of breaking them and for the most part wheeled aside, leaving a suicidal remnant to plunge on down the valley and be overcome by some French cavalry that had been waiting in reserve. Fortunately for the Allies, however, plenty of other troops had been sent to the valley, Ruffin and Villatte therefore deciding that discretion was the better part of valour.

Far more important was the situation in the centre, where the attack had been preceded by a further heavy bombardment. Arrayed side by side with Leval on the left, Rey in the centre and Lapisse on the right, the French moved forward in lines of battalion columns (the first – composed of Dutch and German troops – in a single line, and the second and third with a line of supports as well). Preceded by their skirmishers, the columns moved forward, but as they did so they were subjected to heavy artillery fire, the Pajar de Vergara having been reinforced by a number of Spanish guns. All along the front, meanwhile, the end result was the same. On the British right, the division of General Campbell, supported by a few Spanish battalions that were also caught up in the attack, met the French with a rapid succession of volleys, brought them to a halt and then forced them to retreat with a spirited bayonet charge which captured a battery of light artillery that was being brought up for the purposes of close support. Coming up against the crack division of General Sherbrooke, however, the divisions of Lapisse and Rey were subjected to rather different tactics. Allowed to approach to within fifty yards, they were assailed by a single volley and immediately charged by the redcoats. Cut down by the hundred, the French turned and ran, but at this point things again went wrong. In the words of Andrew Pearson:

It was too much for us to lie any longer, and, leaping up, we gave the well-known British cheer and charged. This was a movement for which they were not prepared, and we soon broke their front ranks, when they immediately fell back on the dense columns in the rear.[23]

Keyed up by long hours of lying motionless under artillery fire, Sherbrooke's troops rushed after the fugitives, only to run straight into their supports. Disordered, outnumbered and blown, they were immediately routed, with heavy casualties. Much encouraged, the French followed them up, but the only reserves that the British had left in the centre moved up and formed a fresh line, whilst from his vantage point on the Medellín Wellesley at the same time rushed a single battalion down the slope to join them. Allowing Sherbrooke's men to fall back through their ranks, these troops then confronted Lapisse and Rey and engaged them with a heavy fire that brought them to a halt. There followed a prolonged firefight in which both sides lost heavily, but, assailed by British cavalry as well as infantry, the French could eventually take no more and fell back.

It had been, in the phrase Wellington used of Waterloo, a near run thing. The centre was exhausted. 'A German sharpshooter', wrote Schaumann, '. . . looking quite black in the face from the sun, the dust, the gunpowder and perspiration . . . flung himself on the ground in an exhausted condition, assuring me he had fired off sixty charges. His tongue was cleaving to his palate with thirst; he was unable to fight any longer, and hardly ten of his company were still alive.'[24] Two brigade commanders were dead, and so many men had fallen that 'a line of Spanish cavalry was formed in the rear . . . to add to our apparent force'.[25] Marching toward the battlefield, the Light Division encountered crowds of British and Spanish fugitives who all claimed that the battle was lost, whilst the town of Talavera itself was in chaos:

The Spaniards . . . dashed in masses through the town, and, mixed up with vast quantities of baggage, blocked the streets . . . I watched this appalling tumult and confusion from my window. Even the inhabitants were packing and taking flight.[26]

Even now the battle was not over, for, as the remnants of Lapisse and Rey's divisions retired, Leval was moving forward again. However, raked by artillery fire from the Pajar, the advancing troops were again brought to a halt by the musketry of the defenders, whilst the attack was finished off altogether by Cuesta's troops who sallied out in some number and assailed the French left flank, the high point of this exploit being a spirited cavalry charge that not only inflicted many casualties but overran what remained of Leval's divisional artillery. For the French, this was the end. Very little of the infantry – the only troops who could make any impression on the Allied position – were still fresh; over seven thousand men had been killed or wounded; seventeen guns had been captured; and the entire army was badly demoralised. Desperate for victory to the last, Victor demanded that the battle be continued, but Joseph, Sebastiani and Jourdan over-ruled him, pointing out that the Allies were still intact and that there was even a danger that they might counter-attack. In consequence, although firing continued for some hours, by the middle of the night the entire French army was in retreat amidst shouts of 'A Bayonne! A Bayonne!'

Behind them they left some much-scarred opponents. Over five thousand British troops – one quarter of the force engaged – had been killed or wounded, as had several hundred Spaniards. 'Almost all my staff are either hit or have lost their horses,' wrote Wellesley, 'and how I have escaped I cannot tell. I was hit in the shoulder at the end of the action, but not hurt, and my coat shot through.'[27] To add to the horror, many of the injured had been burnt to death in grass-fires started by smouldering wadding. Food and water were deficient and the troops absolutely exhausted, whilst it was also necessary to devote considerable time to gathering up the surviving wounded. Yet on 29 July substantial reinforcements arrived in the shape of the first elements of what became the famous Light Division, and there seemed no reason to think that the next few days would not see the Army of the Centre force the French to retreat. Unknown to Wellesley and Cuesta, however, the situation was about to change dramatically. At this point news arrived that a large force of French troops had cleared the passes that separated the Tagus valley from Old Castile and León and occupied the important road junction of Plasencia some 100 miles to the west. Believing that far fewer troops were involved than was actually the case, the Allied commanders resolved that Wellesley should attack them with his army, whilst Cuesta continued to hold Talavera. Given that 50,000 men were concentrating at Plasencia, disaster threatened, but, not for the first time the Allies were rescued by their greater ability to keep watch on the enemy. Thus, a letter from Joseph to Soult from which it was possible to deduce the real situation was intercepted by a band of guerrillas and passed to Cuesta who immediately sent it on to Wellesley. Receiving this document in the nick of time, the latter halted his advance and hastily made for the crossing of the Tagus at Puente del Arzobispo. At Oropesa he was joined by Cuesta, who had just as hastily abandoned Talavera and rushed to catch him up. The Spanish general was eager to attack the French, but Wellesley insisted on retreating across the river. By dusk on 4 August, then, the British army was safely ensconced on the southern bank, where they were rather sulkily joined a day later by the Spaniards.

With the main Allied armies now south of the River Tagus, where they took up a position watching the Puente de Almaraz, the great hopes that the campaign had aroused were effectively at an end. In Madrid, especially, this caused great disappointment. As José Clemente Carnicero, a resident of the city who in 1814 incorporated his memories of French occupation into one of the first Spanish attempts at a general history of the Peninsular War, remembered:

A friend entered my room, and, seeing me in my accustomed state of calm, exclaimed, 'What? Do you really have such phlegm? Don't you know that the people are running through the streets full of joy . . . because King Joseph has surrendered his entire army? We are Spaniards again, and our troops are coming to take possession of . . . the palace this very afternoon.' 'I am delighted to hear it,' I replied, 'but we . . . had better watch out that it isn't a trick to get us to reveal our true feelings so that we can be pounced on later.' 'Watch out all you like,' he answered, 'but I'm telling you that it's the truth. Come and see for yourself.' We went round various streets . . . and in all of them we saw proof of what my friend had said. In some there were great crowds of people fraternising with unarmed Frenchmen . . . In others groups of men, women and children were running up and down congratulating each other at the happy news. And in still others troops of young girls from the poorer quarters were sallying out . . . to greet and make much of our men. It was being said that they had already entered the city, that General Castaños was already in the palace with a guard of halberdiers, that the British had come . . . In short, there was not a soul who did not appear to be convinced of the . . . reality of the news.[28]

False dawn though it was, at least the sight of the French wounded provided some consolation:

Although some of the more compassionate were filled with pity, for many citizens the sight of . . . entire wagon trains filled with wounded entering the city every minute . . . was a source of the utmost satisfaction. Some had lost limbs; some were nursing broken bones; some were being driven to utter the most lamentable screams; some were in their last agonies; and some were pleading for death . . . So excessive was the number of victims that even the general hospital's many . . . large and spacious rooms were not enough to take them, and it proved necessary to requisition . . . the women's hospital . . . and . . . the magnificent monastery of San Francisco . . . and even then the carts were kept waiting at the doors for many hours.[29]

The fighting, however, was far from over. On 8 August the strong rear-guard that had been left by Cuesta at Puente del Arzobispo was driven in in a surprise attack that inflicted heavy casualties on the Spaniards and cost them most of the guns captured on 28 July, Wellesley having handed them all over to Cuesta as being of greater use to the Spanish general than they were to him. Still worse, having spent the last two weeks doing nothing but demonstrate against Toledo and the southern approaches to Madrid, on

11 August the Army of the Centre was soundly beaten by Joseph and Sebastiani at Almonacid. The origins of this action are shrouded in mystery, for it is clear that Venegas could easily have got away to the Sierra Morena. Six days before the battle, however, three of his divisions were attacked in their positions at Aranjuez. This was not much of a fight – the French did no more than probe the crossings of the Tagus – but Venegas, who was not present on the field, was misled by his subordinates into thinking that they had won a major victory. Certainly, he was well pleased:

Not a soldier manoeuvred with anything but the greatest serenity and courage, and those men who carried the wounded to the rear hurried back to the ranks as soon as they had left their comrades at the field hospitals. The discipline and training of the encampment of Santa Elena have produced marvellous effects, and these troops of only four or five months can now march and counter-march without a single man getting in the wrong place.[30]

Rather than retreating, he therefore fell back no further than the town of Almonacid de Toledo, where he drew up his men around two prominent hills, the northernmost of which was crowned by a medieval castle. But the position was a very poor one: as Girón complained, 'Our disposition was bad, or, to be more precise, nonexistent: the troops were scattered about in accordance with the will of God, and not a single measure announced the existence of a plan, an idea or an inspiration.'[31] When the French attacked, they could therefore hardly fail to win. All the more was this the case as they were led with 'audacity and vigour'.[32] Sweeping around the Spanish left flank, which was entirely 'in the air', they quickly ascended the southernmost of the two hills. As commander of the Spanish division most threatened by the French advance, the observer best placed to tell the story is General Girón:

Having very quickly revealed their intention of making their main attack on our left wing, the enemy harassed it from the very first moment . . . One of our units was holding its own on the other side of the heights. Believing it my duty to support it, I marched to join it at the head of the first battalion of the regiment of Spanish Guards, but, before I could get there, it retreated in the greatest disorder, and I was forced to form line to contain the enemy. Realising that I could not hold back the force that was facing me in the plain, I retired to the heights which I had left. However, hardly had I reached them, when the troops who were fighting on my right . . . abandoned their positions in disorder. Left with no option but to try to rally them . . . I led them back to the summit of the hill, but, unfortunately, everything was in vain. Occupying the crest, the enemy opened fire on us. I ordered the Guards battalion and the Regiment of Ecija to fire back, but the disordered masses of the division which had broken collided with my units and disordered their formations. I therefore decided to retreat . . . With the heights that marked our left in their hands, the enemy had outflanked us, and they now descended to the plain to take us in the rear.[33]

Hemmed in by the two hills, the Spaniards were unable to manoeuvre, and very soon they were in full retreat. It had been a fierce struggle – the French acknowledged over 2,000 casualties – but, for all that, Joseph could feel well pleased.

With this unnecessary battle, there ended the campaign of Talavera. Fortunately for the Allies, the French were unable to exploit their success. As before, they simply lacked the strength to move on Portugal (as Soult in fact wished to do), Andalucía, Extremadura or the Levante without dangerously weakening their hold on their Castilian heartlands, which were already witnessing a considerable upsurge in guerrilla activity, whilst they were in any case badly in need of a rest. If this was the case, it was just as well, for Anglo-Spanish relations had sunk to an all-time low. Amongst officers and men of the British army, all sorts of stories were circulating of Spanish cruelty, hostility and indifference, matters not being helped by Cuesta's abandonment for want of transport of a large contingent of British wounded who had been left in his care. With food even more scarce after the battle than it had been beforehand, Mackinnon, for example, wrote:

In many places the magistrates showing evident marks of hostile inclination and nowhere inclined to serve us, the people of the country have everywhere treated the unfortunate men who have sacrificed themselves to save Spain with inhumanity and neglect . . . I was often obliged to use violent means to keep the men from starving.[34]

Still worse was the perception of George Simmons:

The French army was supplied by the villagers with a number of articles, whilst our army was nearly starving . . . Our Spanish friends infested every road for miles and robbed the peasantry who were bringing bread and vegetables to us for sale.[35]

The bitterness was intense. Despite the confusion witnessed by Schaumann, the Spaniards had fought well at Talavera, but this did not stop Wood from writing, 'There were about 30,000 of our allies . . . in line with us, but they were . . . neither attacked nor engaged during the conflict. My battalion being on the right of the line . . . I could plainly perceive their actions. They certainly fired, but I could not perceive what they fired at, nor did I afterwards see many of their troops dead on the field.'[36] Far from their efforts being recognised, indeed, the Spaniards were accused of cowardice, and of throwing away the fruits of British heroism. Many officers, indeed, expressed complete despair. 'No good, I am convinced, can ever be done for these people,' complained the engineer officer, Rice Jones. 'General Catlin Crauford has this day joined us with seven or eight new regiments, but for what purpose it is impossible to say. We begin to suspect that Ministers are mad enough to think of continuing to support the allies that we have found in this country.'[37]

But Rice Jones need not have worried. Of further co-operation, there was in the short term little chance. Wellesley was as furious as any of his men. First of all there was the question of food:

Since the 22nd of last month . . . the troops have not received ten days bread; on some days they have received nothing, and for many days together only meat . . . The cavalry . . . have not received, in the same time, three regular deliveries of forage . . . During a great part of this time . . . the Spanish armies received their regular rations daily . . . The consequence of these privations . . . has been the loss of many horses of the cavalry and artillery . . . The sickness of the army, from the same cause, has increased considerably . . . Indeed, there are few . . . officers or soldiers of the army who . . . are not more or less affected by dysentery.[38]

On top of this there was the issue of the Spanish army:

In the battle of Talavera . . . whole corps threw away their arms, and ran off in my presence, when they were neither attacked nor threatened with an attack, but frightened, I believe, by their own fire . . . When these dastardly soldiers run away, they plunder everything they meet, and in their flight from Talavera they plundered the baggage of the British army . . . I have found, upon enquiry and from experience, the instances of the misbehaviour of the Spanish troops to be so numerous, and those of their good behaviour so few, that I must conclude that they are troops by no means to be depended on.[39]

As to what should be done next, he had no doubt. Sheltering behind the fact that his orders laid down his first priority to be the defence of Portugal, Wellesley abandoned the Spaniards and set off for Badajoz, where he hoped to feed and rest his army in the fertile Guadiana valley.

In this decision, he was reinforced by London's reaction to Talavera. With Wellesley himself the Cabinet professed delight, and he was rewarded with the title of Viscount Wellington. But several factors suggested a need for caution. The Opposition would be certain to accuse the new peer of misjudgement, whilst rumours were already circulating that Talavera had been fought for no better reason than that of obtaining a title. A series of scandals had emerged with regard to the abuse of patronage in which the chief protagonists were none other than the Duke of York and Lord Castlereagh. And in private there was some dissatisfaction with Wellington, as we may now call him: perceived as over-confident, he had also given much offence by a series of intemperate letters in which he berated the government for, as he saw it, failing to send him enough money. In consequence, direct co-operation with the Spanish armies was made dependent on the establishment of a reliable system of supply, the admission of a British garrison to Cádiz, the appointment of Wellington as commander-in-chief of the Spanish armies, and the removal of General Cuesta. It being most unlikely, as the Cabinet recognised, that the Spaniards would agree to these conditions, it followed that Wellington would henceforth be confined to Portugal.

To return to the situation in the Peninsula, the lynchpin of the Anglo-Spanish alliance was now Wellington's elder brother, Richard, Marquess Wellesley, who had just replaced Frere as British ambassador. The reasons for this change are clear enough. A romantic who was deeply engaged with the Spanish cause, Frere had become a major focus of Opposition criticism, and could not be trusted to adopt the firm line that now seemed necessary. Wellesley, by contrast, was a senior figure of much experience of whom great things were expected, an old friend of Canning's, a keen supporter of the war in the Peninsula, and a natural partner for Wellington. But, for all his talents, his brief was an awkward one. Whilst conveying to the Junta Central the bad news that British armies should no longer be a factor in their planning, he was also expected to encourage military, political and administrative reform, whilst at the same time extracting a series of concessions with regard to such matters as the export of specie from the American colonies. Hardly had he arrived in Seville, meanwhile, than he found himself beset by his brother's retreat from the Tagus. Disappointed with Wellington even before the Talavera campaign – they felt, for example, that the British had not exerted themselves sufficiently in the pursuit of Soult after the victory at Oporto, and, further, that, instead of being kept back by Wellington to watch the frontier of Tras-os-Montes, the Portuguese army ought to have invaded León or Galicia – the Spaniards were outraged. Fortunately for the Allied cause, however, Wellesley realised that the British needed the Spaniards rather more than his political masters were prepared to admit. Whilst refraining from pressing the more extreme British demands, he therefore tried desperately to extract promises from the Junta of a sort that might halt the retreat to Portugal, whilst at the same time mounting a sterling defence of his brother's conduct.

For a little while matters hung in the balance, but in the end Wellington agreed for the time being to keep his army in the area of Badajoz. In this respect, then, Wellesley did much good, but in other ways he proved more maladroit. Like many British observers, he had a fixed notion of the Junta Central:

The Supreme Central Junta is neither an adequate representation of the crown, nor of the aristocracy, nor of the people, nor does it comprise any useful quality either of an executive council, or of a deliberative assembly, while it combines many defects which tend to disturb both deliberation and action . . . Omitting all question respecting the disposition of the Junta, it is evident that it does not possess any spirit of energy or activity [or] any degree of authority or strength, that it is unsupported by popular attachment or goodwill [and] that its strange and anomalous constitution unites the contradictory inconveniences of every known form of government without possessing the advantages of any . . . It is not an instrument of sufficient power to accomplish the purposes for which it was formed, nor can it ever acquire sufficient force or influence to bring into action the resources of the country and the spirit of the people with that degree of vigour and alacrity which might . . . repel a foreign invader.[40]

In consequence, Wellesley was soon urging a variety of reforms on the Junta. Some of these were merely platitudinous or irritating – the Junta hardly needed to be told, for example, that improvements were necessary in the state of the Spanish army – but others either threatened to destabilise the Alliance or played straight into the hands of the Junta's opponents. Thus, suggestions that there should be concessions to the American colonies could only imply changes in tariff policy that would favour Britain, whilst demands for a regency naturally encouraged the ambitions of Infantado, Francisco Palafox and La Romana. Indeed, in September Palafox and Infantado contacted Wellesley and sought his backing for a coup, Palafox having openly denounced the Junta Central and called for just such a body as Wellesley was demanding. Just as vocal were the old councils of the Bourbon state, which since July had been amalgamated in a single body. Realising that the British still needed them, the Junta therefore gave no more ground than they absolutely had to if they were to obtain the formal treaty of subsidy which they had been pressing for. With moves for a new *cortes* already under way, all that was done was to place executive power in the hands of a rotating committee of seven of its own members. For Wellesley, however, this was not enough, news of his dissent encouraging La Romana to publish an extremely provocative manifesto in which he threatened to resign from the Junta's ranks – he had earlier filled a vacancy for Valencia

– unless it reformed itself immediately (by which he meant that he should be declared sole regent).

Whatever good Wellesley may have done, he had therefore also destabilised the Junta Central. On 11 November, however, he left for home, having been recalled to become Foreign Secretary (in a spectacular denouement which had seen Canning and Castlereagh fight a duel, the former's schemes had produced both a new Cabinet headed by the much respected Spencer Perceval and his own departure for the political wilderness). In Spain, meanwhile, political disaffection, the need to regain British confidence, the impending fall – despite desperate resistance and some help from outside – of Gerona, and the danger that the Peninsula might soon be flooded with enemy troops released by the defeat of Austria were forcing the Junta to prepare a new offensive.

Despite Wellington refusing point blank to take part in the campaign, the late autumn therefore saw the Armies of the Left and Centre alike moving into central Spain. Heavily reinforced from Asturias on the one hand and Extremadura on the other, and given new commanders in the persons of the Duque del Parque and Juan Carlos Areizaga, the two armies were expected to converge on Madrid. Supporting them, meanwhile, was a much reduced Army of Extremadura under the Duque de Alburquerque (on 12 August Cuesta had been forced to relinquish his command on account of a stroke), the task of this force being to feint against the capital from the west. Operations began well enough. In mid-October Del Parque advanced from his base at Astorga with 40,000 men and took up a strong defensive position at Tamames. Arrayed on a ridge even stronger than the position Blake's men had occupied at Alcañiz, they could not have been better posted. Outnumbered two to one, the nearest French troops were therefore forced to retire with heavy casualties when they attacked on 18 October, and within a few days Del Parque was in Salamanca. In the first week of November, meanwhile, Alburquerque crossed the Tagus with his 10,000 men, whilst Areizaga advanced northwards from the Sierra Morena with another 55,000.

Again, though, things went wrong. Decisive action might have brought Areizaga a great victory, but in the event he dithered, allowing the French to force a battle on their terms at Ocaña on 19 November. Able to deploy over 50,000 men against fewer than 34,000 of the enemy, Areizaga still possessed the advantage of superior numbers, but his position was appalling, his forces being arrayed in two lines across an open plain with their right flank completely 'in the air'. Wearied by incessant marching and counter-marching, the troops were badly demoralised, whilst their quality was as bad as ever. Indeed, only the day before, the cavalry had been routed by a much smaller force of their French counterparts amidst the usual scenes of panic and disorder. As a result, 19 November was a foregone conclusion. For a little while, the Spanish infantry fought well enough, checking and even driving back the columns which the enemy – essentially the corps of Mortier and Sebastiani together with Joseph's personal reserve and some attached cavalry – sent against them. On the Spanish right, however, their 5,000 cavalry were routed almost in an instant by four brigades of French horse, which then proceeded to wheel right and hurl themselves on the infantry's flank and rear. Taken by surprise, the whole army then dissolved in chaos. Entire divisions laid down their arms, whilst the rest of the troops scattered in all directions. A few troops on the left maintained their order and conducted a gallant rearguard action, but even so Areizaga's casualties amounted to over 18,000 men, or fully one third of his army. Also lost were fifty of his sixty cannon and large quantities of arms, ammunition and supplies, whilst some ten thousand of the fugitives deserted rather than return to the colours (by comparison, French losses were a mere three hundred).

Nor was this the end of the woes that afflicted the Spanish cause. Far to the north November had seen Del Parque march eastwards in an attempt to isolate from Madrid those enemy troops who still remained in the region, the latter having fallen back behind the River Duero. Hearing at Medina del Campo of Areizaga's misfortunes, he hastily turned round and fled westwards, only to be caught at Alba de Tormes on 28 November by the vanguard of the troops sent to follow him. Composed entirely of cavalry, the French would not usually have been able to attack, but, encamped on either side of the River Tormes, the Spaniards had been taken unawares. Led by the notoriously ferocious François Kellermann the invaders therefore charged home with great violence. Though this was a gamble, it paid off: the three Spanish divisions on the wrong side of the river were routed with the loss of three thousand men and nine guns, whilst the disorderly retreat that followed saw the disappearance of immense numbers of deserters.

By the end of November, then, Patriot Spain was in a sorry state. In Catalonia, as we have seen, Gerona was on its last legs; Spain's two largest armies had been shattered; and the British army was preparing to leave the Guadiana (disgusted by what he regarded as the Junta's stupidity, Wellington was convinced that a French march on Lisbon could not be long delayed). To make matters worse, intelligence reports were received of large masses of fresh troops crossing the frontier from France. Thus, with Austria beaten, Napoleon had immediately ordered numerous reinforcements to take the road for Spain. Consisting of Junot's corps of the *grande armée*,* two divisions of the Young Guard, a division of German infantry, a new force of mounted police that had been raised for the specific purpose of fighting the guerrillas, a handful of stray regiments that had as yet failed to find a permanent home, and a mass of drafts and reinforcements for those units already in Spain, the whole amounted to some 138,000 men. And, as if all this was not enough, it was even rumoured that the emperor himself might again be coming to take charge of operations.

Distracted by his decision to take a new wife in the person of the Grand Duchess Marie-Louise of Austria, Napoleon did not appear, but, even so, time had run out for the Junta Central.

Deprived of the last vestiges of a British military presence, its own armies were being decimated by disease and desertion. By the New Year, indeed, Del Parque was down to a mere 9,000 men, whilst all that was left to defend Andalucía were perhaps 40,000 men in the form of the minuscule Army of Extremadura, which had managed to escape without mishap, and the remnants of the Army of the Centre. Even such men as were left could not be relied upon:

This whole district is full of stragglers and fugitives, whilst every day the number of those who desert the front line increases ... To paliate their scandalous behaviour, they claim that they are being left to die of hunger [and] that their own officers tell them to run away ... I do not believe any of this, but bands have been seen consisting of as many as ninety-three men ... whilst those militiamen who have confronted them have ... suffered a number of dead.[41]

With the exception of Badajoz, there were also no fortresses behind which the defenders could shelter. Last but not least, on 11 December Gerona, too, had fallen prey to starvation, by which time two-thirds of the garrison and half the inhabitants lay dead (also dead, however, were some fourteen thousand of their assailants, whilst the siege had not only neutralised the French forces in Catalonia for a full six months, but also allowed the Spaniards yet again to reduce Barcelona to a state of semi-starvation).

Heartened by the fact that the French initially showed no signs of advancing, the Junta frantically tried to mend its fences. Orders were issued for the

---

* A force which is not to be confused with either Junot's original corps, which had been split up in December 1808, or the troops now commanded by Suchet, this was a new unit that was mostly composed of fresh battalions raised from men conscripted in the spring of 1809 for service against Austria.

election of deputies to the new *cortes*, which it was announced would open on 1 March 1810. A levy of a further 100,000 men was announced and all remaining exemptions from military service abolished. Fresh edicts appeared against desertion. Church plate, table silver, personal jewellery, horses and draught animals were all made the subject of fresh requisitioning. An 'extraordinary contribution' that amounted to a graduated income tax was decreed. A start was made on the fortification of the passes that spanned the Sierra Morena. And, finally, Palafox and Montijo were imprisoned, and La Romana appointed to the Captain Generalcy of Valencia in an attempt to get him out of the way.

Mere energy was not enough, however. Whilst the goodwill of the Junta cannot be doubted, many of its measures were either poorly drafted or completely impracticable, whilst they in any case had little time to take effect. At the same time many local notables were disaffected, whilst there were few means of enforcing the government's decrees even if there had been more willingness to do so; so great was the problem of desertion and banditry that large areas of the countryside were completely out of control. Meanwhile, notables and *populacho* alike showed little enthusiasm for patriotic self-sacrifice: very little private wealth was ever handed in, whilst in Jaén an attempt to mobilise the home guard that had been formed in the wake of the uprising produced not a single man.

Lack of enthusiasm was not the end of the Junta's problems, however. On the contrary, the real cost of the offensive strategy that had been forced upon Patriot Spain now became apparent. Had the populace flocked to the colours by the thousand, they could neither have been armed nor equipped. Denuded by the need to equip army after army more or less from scratch, Spain's arsenals and magazines stood empty. And, as if matters were not bad enough already, the French chose this moment to advance on Seville. Traditionally, it has been argued that this decision neglected the obvious need to eliminate Wellington's army before doing anything else, whilst at the same time laying the French open to an eventual British counter-attack. But to argue in this fashion is short-sighted. To defeat Wellington, the French had first to end Spanish resistance, which in turn meant defeating every last Spanish field army and capturing every last Spanish fortress. As the immense reinforcements that were starting to flow across the Pyrenees promised to be more than sufficient to contain Wellington, a march on Seville was therefore logical, whilst it also satisfied a number of political imperatives. More money – a constant problem for Joseph, as we shall see – would be available for his government. Laughed at and snubbed by

Spaniard and Frenchman alike, Joseph would finally be taken seriously. And finally, eager to be loved, the king looked forward to winning Spanish opinion over by a show of beneficence and magnanimity.

Whatever else may be said of Joseph, he was not wrong to foresee victory. Scattered along the length of the Sierra Morena, the defenders had no chance of stopping the flood that burst upon them on 19 January 1810. In all, some 60,000 French troops – the corps of Victor, Mortier and Sebastiani together with a number of other formations – poured southwards to assault the Spanish positions. Overwhelmed at every point, Areizaga's men fled eastwards and southwards, leaving town after town to fall into the hands of the enemy. The result was revolution. Abandoning last-minute efforts to turn Seville into another Zaragoza, on 23 January the Junta Central decided to flee for the safety of Cádiz. Presented with a golden opportunity for revenge, its many enemies went to work with a will. Persuaded by a variety of agitators that it was guilty of treason – for weeks, in fact, pamphlets had been circulating accusing its members of being favourites of Godoy or agents of the French – the crowd took to the streets and released Palafox and Montijo, who then joined with the Junta of Seville in proclaiming themselves to be the government of Spain. Also in the plot was La Romana, who had never departed for Valencia, and was now rewarded with the command of the Army of the Left.

The new régime was shortlived, however. Only a small number of regular troops were available; the crowd hardly to be relied upon; and the city's defences mere earthworks. Not choosing to wait for the French, it therefore fled in its turn. Excited by numerous religious processions and acts of disorder, the crowd at first maintained an attitude of defiance, but no sooner had the French appeared before the walls on 31 January than resistance collapsed, a delegation of local officials eventually surrendering without a fight. With Jaén, Córdoba and Granada already gone the same way, the only show of resistance came at Málaga where the people overthrew the local authorities, only for the French to storm the town and execute the leaders of the insurrection.

A few places in the west and south aside, there now remained only Cádiz. By a near miracle, however, it was saved. Though a number of their colleagues had been attacked and arrested *en route*, the rump of the Junta Central had succeeded in reaching that city on 28 January, and the following day they handed over power to a five-man regency headed by General Castaños. At this stage the new capital was protected only by the puffed-up and self-congratulatory Voluntarios Distinguidos de Cádiz, but in the nick of time help arrived in the shape of the Army of Extremadura. Posted on the extreme left of the Spanish line, Alburquerque had foreseen the direction that events were likely to take, and had therefore come south with all speed. Having picked up a few stragglers *en route*, on 3 February he arrived at Cádiz, the result being that when the French summoned the city to surrender two days later they received a defiant answer.

With the initiation of what was to become the siege of Cádiz, there ended the war of the Junta Central. Battered and humiliated, that body was no more, but its record was by no means wholly discreditable, whilst in nominating its own replacement it had finally scotched efforts to establish a régime whose chief goal would have been the restoration of the position of the privileged orders: Spain was to have a regency, true, but its members were characterised less by aristocratic reaction than by caroline enlightenment, whilst its first president was the cautious and amenable Francisco Javier Castaños. For good or ill, with the convocation of the *cortes*, the way was also now open for reform. As for the military situation, Cádiz provided resistance with a powerful bastion that the French would find hard to overcome. Yet the overall picture was grim. So many men, so much territory and so much *matériel* had now been lost, that Spain's ability actually to wage war in any formal sense had been critically impaired. There was still some way to go, but even so the Patriot cause had taken the first steps on the road that would lead to eclipse, humiliation and the negation of the very reform programme that was now so eagerly expected.

9

Seville

THE BONAPARTE KINGDOM
OF SPAIN, 1808–1813

From all sides church bells rang out whilst rockets streaked through the sky and guns crashed out in salute. To the accompaniment of a buzz of excitement from the vast crowd that thronged the streets, many of the city's squares were ringing to the music of military bands whilst blue-uniformed troops looked on indulgently. The word suddenly running around that the king was coming, every pavement, every balcony, every door and every window was lined with expectant faces. And, even more suddenly, there he was. Gasps and exclamations of surprise filled the air: this was not the drunken, debauched and one-eyed figure of legend, but a handsome figure with a ready smile and a kindly expression. Pleased with what they saw, the crowd responded with delight, and soon cheers of 'Long live the King!' were mingling with pleas for work, bread and justice. As for the object of their adulation, he waved and nodded right and left and sat a little straighter in the saddle: never, wrote one of his supporters, had Joseph I, King of Spain, felt more certain of his throne.

Repeated, as they were, in city after city in Andalucía in February 1810, these scenes provide us with a useful opportunity to turn aside and examine the new state that lay at the heart of the Peninsular War. Napoleon's conquest of Spain had been resolved upon in the context of a policy that was already well established beyond the Pyrenees. From the 1790s onwards the French had been establishing satellite states ruled by friendly régimes and characterised by the establishment of political, social, judicial and military systems very closely modelled on the French pattern. Initially designed to harness local desires for progress or revolutionary change and encourage those desires elsewhere, by 1808 they had increasingly become mechanisms of exploitation and control whose purpose was essentially to defend the borders of *la grande France*, keep the imperial armies supplied with men and money, complement the spoils system that lay at the heart of the Napoleonic empire, and assimilate local élites in the structures of French supremacy – hence, for example, the numerous 'family courts' presided over by one or other of the emperor's numerous siblings. Exploitation, however, was coupled with reform. Powerful armies, flourishing treasuries and complicated systems of import and export control – the *sine qua non* of Napoleon's Continental Blockade – all required effective systems of administration, just as the élite participation on which the imperial régime depended had to be bought by such measures as the sale of ecclesiastical land or the establishment of the principle of the career open to talent. Hence, generations of imperial apologists were able to hide behind the notion that Napoleon's career was centred on an attempt to uphold the French Revolution against the cause of aristocratic and monarchical reaction.

Ludicrous though this idea may be, it is at least clear that by 1808 the French had a 'blueprint' for conquest that went far beyond mere military despotism. To argue, as some apologists have done, that Napoleon intervened in Spain out of a quixotic desire to fight against the superstition, obscurantism and backwardness of the 'black legend' may be nonsense, but the régime of Joseph Bonaparte was for all that founded on a genuine belief that Europe could be remade on the French model even if the basis of that drive was not ideological but rather political, financial and economic.

That said, reform was not a static concept, and *josefino* Spain could be said actually to have witnessed an intensification of the reform process. In earlier years this had been invested with at least a degree of autonomy in that the different states of the empire had been permitted to retain a variety of distinctive features. The Constitution of Bayonne, indeed, had conformed to this model. A relatively generous document in Napoleonic terms, it prohibited any religious faith other than Catholicism, recognised, for the time being at least, the privileges of the Basque provinces, and extended separate political representation to the nobility.

By the end of 1808, however, the drive for change was operating in a climate in which Napoleon was becoming dissatisfied with the satellite state as a tool of strategy. Too many of their rulers, his brothers and sisters included, were inclined to shy away from policies that would make them unpopular with their subjects, whilst the emperor was becoming convinced that the old order had to be broken rather than conciliated. Spain and Portugal, indeed, proved the point, for, from Napoleon downwards, the French insisted that the rising had been the work of the clergy. Berating a delegation of captured Spaniards at Vitoria in 1808, the emperor thundered, 'It is [the monks] who mislead and deceive you. I am as good a Catholic as they are, and I have no desire to threaten your religion.'[1] 'The clergy of the chief churches of Seville, Valencia, Valladolid and Zaragoza were trying to arouse the patriotic zeal of the people,' wrote Lejeune.[2] 'The Spanish priests', said Rocca, 'hated the French from patriotism and from interest, for they well knew that the intention was to abolish their privileges, and to deprive them of their riches and temporal power. Their opinion swayed that of the greatest part of the nation.'[3] Most graphic of all is the testimony of General Foy, however:

The Deity soon signified that the cause of the Spaniards was his own ... In the cavern of Covadonga in Asturias, so famous for having been the asylum of Pelayo and his brave followers, attentive and devout observers saw large drops of sweat trickle down the face of Our Lady of Battles. At Compostela a clinking of arms was heard ... on the tomb of Saint James, announcing that the ... glorious patron of Spain would again lead her armies to victory ... The miracles were a proof of the opinion of the clergy.[4]

In the Iberian Peninsula, then, the conciliation that had originally moulded French policy there was thrown aside, and a new model of reform pushed through that regarded difference not as a restriction but as a stimulus. Hence anti-clerical and anti-seigneurial policies were introduced that were noticeably sharper than had generally been the case hitherto. At the same time, the new style also informed procedure elsewhere, most notably in Rome, Tuscany and Berg, just as the constant snubs that were the lot of Joseph Bonaparte in 1808 and 1809 prefigured the manner in which Louis Bonaparte was ejected from Holland and Jerome Bonaparte stripped of half Westphalia.

The main outlines of the Bonaparte kingdom of Spain were, as we have already noted, laid out in the Constitution of Bayonne. Spain was to be a constitutional monarchy governed by such principles as equality before the law and equipped with a legislative apparatus that was broadly similar to that of France. These bases were never abandoned, for they were entirely consonant with the Napoleonic model. But most of the arrangements negotiated at Bayonne failed to materialise. With the exception of such organs of government as the council of state, for example, the constitution's political superstructure remained unbuilt, whilst its guarantees of personal liberty were simply ignored. Many of Napoleon's concessions therefore remained dead letters. If no legislative assembly was ever summoned, what price the nobility's recognition as a separate estate? For the true measure of the new state, indeed, we must rather turn to the Decrees of Chamartín, these essentially constituting an attempt to give reform a complexion that the emperor felt it was otherwise unlikely to attain. The fact was that he simply did not trust Joseph. 'Joseph,' he later said, 'has intelligence ... but he does not like work ... He knows nothing; he loves pleasure.'[5] According to his own account, indeed, he was openly contemptuous of him:

'What a curious notion you have of yourself,' I would say to him. 'Why, you are not even as good as the corporal of light infantry posted at your door. If you found yourself at the head of . . . a hundred men in front of the enemy . . . you would not know what to do. You would probably run away like a coward.'[6]

Realising that his survival depended on retaining the support of his imperial brother, Joseph was in broad outline prepared to go along with his policies. In any case, the Decrees of Chamartín were only objectionable to him to the extent that they had been forced upon him without consultation and introduced at what he considered to be a very bad time: seeing himself as a man of the Enlightenment, he was genuinely convinced that reform was the key to success. According to his propaganda machine, after all, what were his opponents fighting for but the preservation of feudal and ecclesiastical privilege? Ordered by Napoleon to compile a list of monasteries that were to be suppressed, he complied without demur, whilst his council of state promulgated a series of decrees which extended the changes still further. As can be imagined, these dealt primarily with the position of the Church and the various matters that had been left by the Constitution of Bayonne for further deliberation. As far as the former was concerned, there was a mixture of increased spoliation and tighter control. Having been ordered to dismiss all their novices, close their doors to any further applications, and confine themselves to their convents – a serious blow to the finances of the mendicant friars – on 18 August 1809 all the religious orders were dissolved, whilst the next few months witnessed the disappearance of a variety of ecclesiastical levies, of which the most important was the Voto de Santiago (a levy on grain paid to the Archbishopric of Santiago de Compostela in the lands of the Crown of Castile). For the time being the Church was allowed to retain the tithes (so long, that is, as it continued to make over to the state the many subventions it had traditionally surrendered from them), but it was stripped of its legal privileges (most notably, the right of all members of the clergy to be tried only by the ecclesiastical courts), deprived of most of its remaining patronage, and prohibited from ordaining any more priests until it had absorbed the large surplus of clergy that resulted from the dissolution of the orders.

As elsewhere, then, the Catholic Church suffered severely at the hands of the French empire, and all the more so when the picture is completed by such crimes as the cold-blooded murder of twelve priests and nuns at Uclés in February 1809, the pillage experienced by many churches and cathedrals, and the use of many religious buildings as storehouses, stables, barracks or improvised fortresses. Already thoroughly radicalised by years of propaganda that portrayed the French Revolution as the work of Satan, many Spanish churchmen were therefore inclined to claim that the French intended to destroy the Church altogether, making much of Napoleon's emancipation of the Jews, arrest of the Pope, and overtly cynical and indifferent attitude towards all religion. But this was unfair. The emperor may have been determined to impose the primacy of secular authority and utterly lacking in religious convictions, but he appreciated the value of the Church as a tool of social and political control and therefore had no intention of destroying it altogether. Included in the Decrees of Chamartín, therefore, were clauses intended to boost the financial position of the ignorant and impoverished parish clergy that fitted in closely with the desires of many reformist ecclesiastics. As for Joseph, no more pious than his brother, he was none the less careful to preserve a show of ostentatious observance, whilst at the same time doing his best to form a working relationship with the hierarchy and strengthen the Church at parish level. Those monks and friars who had been ordained as priests were encouraged to adopt a new parochial ministry, whilst in Seville, for example, ecclesiastical properties to the value of 300,000 reales were set aside for the upkeep of the city's parishes, a part of this sum being used to support 25 new curacies. In May 1809, meanwhile, Joseph had also specifically ordered that a proportion of the plate taken from religious houses that had been shut should be distributed amongst the parish churches, no fewer than ninety of which received help from this source in the area of Madrid alone.

Moving on to other matters, we come first to the question of Spain's territorial organisation and governance. Though dealt with only tangentially in the Constitution of Bayonne, there could be little doubt as to the implications of this document. Initially, Joseph contented himself with working within the apparatus that he had inherited from the *antiguo régimen* whilst at the same time placing responsibility for local government in many provinces in the hands of a variety of royal commissioners. However, after much preparation and debate, on 2 July 1809 Spain was divided into thirty-eight new provinces, each of which was headed by an Intendent appointed by King Joseph, whilst on 17 April 1810 these intendencies were converted into French-style prefectures and sub-prefectures. Named after their chief towns rather than, as in France, after their dominant geographical features, the new territorial divisions, which were all more or less equal in size, bore little relation to historic units of any sort.* To take Navarre as an example,

* The decision to retain the historic names of many old provinces in this fashion was none the less a significant concession. In France the *départements* boasted such names as Loire Inférieure, Manche and Bouches du Rhône.

part of it was joined with the Basque *señorio* of Guipúzcoa in a prefecture governed from Pamplona, and the rest conjoined with west-central Aragón in another based at Zaragoza. If Aragón thereby gained eastern Navarre, it lost its eastern fringes to Catalan Tarragona, however, whilst the remainder was split between Teruel and Huesca. Each prefecture, meanwhile, was to have its own district court and constitute an independent diocese, whilst the new units were grouped together in units of between two and four to form new military districts, the result being that there would in turn have to be a massive restructuring of the judicial, ecclesiastical and military ordering of the state. In practice, little progress was made in these areas, but in much of southern and central Spain by 1812 the prefectural system, at least, was becoming a reality.

Implicit in the Decree of 17 April 1810, there was, as can be observed, a direct threat to the foral provinces, which had hitherto been allowed to retain their traditional structures and generally treated in a lenient fashion. Thus, if Guipúzcoa was absorbed into a rump of Navarre, Vizcaya and Alava were joined in the prefecture of Vitoria. The issue of the *fueros* is one to which we shall return, but for the moment let us concentrate upon the general revolution in government of which the creation of the prefectures was a part. Beginning with the central authorities, on 18 August 1809 the bitter struggle that had for many years raged between new-fangled ministry on the one hand and traditional council on the other was resolved in favour of the former. Thus, the Councils of War, the Indies, the Treasury and the Military Orders were abolished and the Council of Castile was restricted to the functions of a supreme court of appeal, whilst the number of ministries was expanded from five to nine – Finance, Interior, Justice, Foreign Affairs, War, Police, Marine, Indies and Ecclesiastical Affairs. Equally, on 4 September 1809 all Spain's *ayuntamientos* were dismissed, the provincial authorities being ordered to proceed to the formation of new bodies chosen by election. Initially, the vote was restricted to property-owners noted for their enthusiasm for the French cause, but even so the old system of hereditary tenure had been completely overthrown and the number of councillors linked to the size of the population. With the Decree of 17 April 1810, meanwhile, the French model was introduced in full with councils at municipal, sub-prefectural and prefectural levels; mayors in every town; and very limited powers of election (as in France, only the smallest places could choose their councils themselves, larger ones having to submit a list of candidates for approval by higher authority). As for the administration of justice, the *alcaldes mayores*, or local magistrates, were deprived of the seats they had generally enjoyed in the municipalities, and, as laid down at

Bayonne, integrated in a uniform system of courts. Also worth noting here is the abolition of torture and the substitution of the noose by the supposedly more humane garrotte.

More specifically covered in the Constitution of Bayonne than the question of territorial organisation was that of legal and fiscal unification. Spain had been promised common civil, criminal and commercial codes, a unified judiciary and a uniform system of taxation. In so far as the legal codes were concerned, the original plan had been simply to impose the models that had been introduced in France since 1799, but on this point the emperor had given way, leaving the new régime to elaborate the documents that it needed by itself. To carry out the work required, in December 1809 a permanent sub-committee was established within the Council of State, and this eventually produced a document based on the Code Napoléon that accepted most of its principles whilst at the same time eliminating such contentious rights as that of divorce. Pressure of business prevented the new code's discussion, however, with the result that it was never introduced, *josefino* Spain therefore having to continue to rely on the Bourbon *Novísima Recopilación*. In the matter of taxation, meanwhile, matters were much the same. In the course of 1809 the Minister of Finance, Francisco Cabarrús, sketched out a new scheme that would have suppressed the multitude of existing levies, many of which applied only to part of the country, in favour of three new taxes levied on property, occupation and income, all of which would have applied to the whole of Spain. However, not until October 1810 did the first part of this scheme appear in the form of an annual impost of ten per cent of all rental income, whilst it was another year before there appeared the *patente industrial*, which was essentially an annual licence that had to be paid by all those involved in any sort of craft or business. Spain also being given a single tax and customs frontier – the Basque provinces and Navarre were effectively stripped of their immunity by a decree of 16 October 1809 – the principles of the Napoleonic empire were slowly entrenching themselves beyond the Pyrenees.

In addition to proposing new systems of law and taxation, the Constitution of Bayonne also promised a reorganisation of the exhorbitant national debt that had built up under Carlos IV. Amounting to almost 6,500,000,000 reales by 1808, this was guaranteed by the new régime, but that did not mean that the latter was prepared to take it on on the terms bequeathed to it by the Bourbons. As a leading financial expert, Cabarrús was particularly eager to do something about the problem, the result being the issue on 9 June 1809 of orders for all titles to the national debt to be surrendered in exchange for *cédulas de crédito*. These in turn could be used either to buy *bienes nacionales* – property seized from enemies of the régime and, above all, the Church – or to generate a dividend of four per cent per annum. On the same day, meanwhile, there also appeared a decree that both authorised the sale of the property seized by the government and laid down the rules for the manner in which this was to be carried out. Matters were complicated by the issue of fresh *cédulas* as rewards for those who had served the *josefino* régime, but, with much of the Bourbon debt effectively cancelled and plentiful amounts of property up for sale, on the surface it looked as if matters had genuinely been put on a new footing.

Reform of this sort was not the only activity in which the régime engaged. Joseph, for example, was eager to promote economic revival, and therefore introduced a number of measures that tied in closely with classic liberal theory. In addition to the internal customs barriers got rid of by the decree of 16 October 1809, various monopolies were abolished, whilst the régime also rid itself of the series of industrial enterprises, none of them very successful, that had been bequeathed to it by the *étatist* Bourbons. At the same time, a new stock exchange was set up in Madrid; Spain's primitive national bank, the Banco de San Carlos, was overhauled; the cultivation of such crops as potatoes, cotton and rice was encouraged; generous concessions were offered to all those willing to establish industrial concerns; a Conservatorio de Artes y Oficios was set up in Madrid as a repository of information relating to machines, tools and industrial processes; and the Reales Sociedades de Amigos del País – the learned societies established by Carlos III in order to promote innovation and the spread of modern science – given every encouragement.

Last but not least, recognition should also be given to Joseph's efforts to celebrate Spain's cultural heritage, and improve the environment in which her inhabitants lived. As interested as any of its counterparts elsewhere in the spread of education, on 6 September 1809 the régime ordered that state primary schools should be established in place of those run by teaching orders, whilst a further decree of 26 October laid down that each provincial capital should have a French-style *lycée*. More generous than his brother in the matter of female education, Joseph also set up a school for 150 girls in Madrid and decreed that similar institutions should be founded in the provinces, the administration of all these plans being placed in the hands of a new Committee of Public Instruction. Alongside this, meanwhile, there appeared an academy modelled on Napoleon's Institut de France in the shape of the National Institute for Arts and Sciences.

It is not, however, for his educational policy that Joseph Bonaparte is most remembered in the field of culture. It was Joseph who was responsible for the foundation (if not the idea) of the Museo del Prado and the first attempts at the official preservation and investigation of the remains of such sites as Roman Italica, whilst it was also Joseph who first laid out Madrid's botanical gardens and established Spain's first natural history museum. To him, too, Madrid owes a number of squares, not least the Plaza de Oriente in front of the royal palace, which were created in an attempt both to beautify the city and to provide work for the city's poor, just as it was in his reign that the inhabitants were for the first time given access to the palace gardens that were eventually to become the Retiro park. Implicit in these schemes, of course, was a concern for living standards that is, in the circumstances, laughable in its sincerity. Thus, the focus of a bloody war that caused untold miseries to the populace, Joseph genuinely wished them to enjoy open spaces, clean air and better health; hence the new parks and squares, and hence, too, the efforts that were expended on such matters as vaccination – ordered by Joseph Bonaparte in Madrid as early as July 1808 – street cleaning, waste disposal and funerals (like the Bourbons before him, Joseph was especially keen to put an end to the practice of church burials).

As may be observed, then, *josefino* Spain was characterised by a genuinely reformist impulse that was as marked as anything found in other parts of the Napoleonic empire. Indeed, further impetus was lent to the process by the fact that in many parts of Spain the administration was for much of the time not in the hands of King Joseph. For the latter there was often good reason at the very least to make haste slowly, or even to tone down certain measures of reform. On the ground, however, power was in the hands of Intendents, royal commissioners, and, ultimately, prefects who were often for various reasons less inclined to be circumspect than the king (a good example is Francisco de Amorós, an army officer and friend of Godoy who responded to the overthrow of the favourite with a one-man crusade against the *antiguo régimen*). At the same time, even in the early days so much influence was possessed by the local military commanders that Joseph's agents were able to exercise no power whatsoever, whilst consideration must also be given to the impact of territorial alienation. On 8 February 1810, growing irritation with his brother led Napoleon to order that the Basque provinces, Navarre, Aragón and Catalonia should be turned into military 'governments' whose authorities would be entirely independent of those appointed by King Joseph. Two months later, two more such units were created out of Burgos on the one hand and Valladolid, Toro, Palencia and, albeit temporarily, Avila on the other, whilst on 14 July Napoleon took the whole of Andalucía out of Joseph's hands and gave it to Soult, who was at the same time given the command of almost all the troops that had taken part in the offensive of January 1810. And, finally, mooted as early as October 1810 in an attempt to frighten Joseph into greater ferocity, in February 1812 Catalonia was to all intents and purposes annexed to the French empire (the decree concerned did not actually use the term 'annexation', but its provisions were such as to leave no doubt as to its implications). In all these cases, the result was the intensification of reform, the French commanders being not only convinced that the privileged orders were the motor of popular resistance, but, in the trans-ebrine regions at least, under orders from Napoleon to prepare the way for annexation.

Reform, then, cannot be analysed just from a consideration of the decrees that emanated from King Joseph's Council of State. In the Basque *señorios* and Navarre, the establishment of military 'governments' led to a full-scale assault on the *fueros*. A hard-liner with little respect for local sensibilities, the governor of the Basque provinces, General Thouvenot, immediately swept away the three *señorios'* traditional forms of self-government and gave each of them a small appointed council modelled on that of a French *département*. Still worse, their fiscal privileges were also abrogated, Thouvenot immediately imposing a series of unprecedented taxes that had within eighteen months raised 40,000,000 reales. In institutional terms, however, Navarre fared rather better – briefly abolished, her foral institutions were quickly re-established in an attempt to conciliate the local notables – but there, too, the *diputación* was appointed rather than elected, and executive power placed in the hands of a new police commission. In Catalonia the role of *eminence grise* to the occupation authorities fell into the hands of an *afrancesado* so pro-French in sympathy that he not only pressed for the introduction of the Code Napoléon in full, but advocated the introduction of conscription and complete annexation by France. Thanks to the support of the then commander of the French garrison, Marshal Augereau, a *ci-devant* Jacobin and common soldier much inclined to nurse delusions that the people had only to be freed from their chains to rally to the French cause, the result was a series of measures designed to refashion Catalonia on the French model. Last but not least, it should be noted that throughout the areas subjected to direct imperial control there appeared considerable numbers of French administrative personnel, giving the process of transformation still greater impetus.

French personnel or no French personnel, in Spain as elsewhere the implementation of reform rested on a substantial degree of collaboration on the part of the indigenous élites, for Napoleon never had sufficient trained administrators to supply more than a handful of the large numbers required. Matters should have been eased by the presence in the country of a sizeable

French community prior to 1808, but surprisingly little assistance was derived from this source (the most prominent example is Cabarrús, a Frenchman who had come to Spain to pursue a fortune in commerce in the 1770s), whilst Joseph was in any case very eager both to make his monarchy a genuinely Spanish institution and to win the support of the propertied classes. In theory the *josefino* state was characterised by the career open to talents, but in practice there was more continuity than change. The court was filled with leading grandees; the government and administration with Bourbon statesmen and officials; the officer corps with Bourbon army officers; and provincial and municipal government with representatives of the old local oligarchy. As witness the creation in October 1809 of the corps of *asistentes* – young men taken on as interns to learn the business of administration – even Napoleonic innovation made little difference, recruitment being restricted to those whose families could afford to pay a subvention of 24,000 reales a year.

If great care was taken not to threaten the position of the propertied classes, just as much effort was put into ensuring that service in the bureaucracy brought with it high rewards: Councillors of State, for example, were officially entitled to a salary of 100,000 reales a year, whilst even *asistentes* received 12,000. Nor were the prizes on offer solely financial: having abolished all Spain's existing orders of nobility, on 20 October 1809 Joseph created a new Spanish Royal Order, which was eventually awarded to over 600 churchmen, nobles, army officers and officials and carried with it a substantial pension, whilst there was even the possibility of a title (Minister of Foreign Affairs from 1811 to 1813, for example, Miguel José de Azanza became the Duque de Santa Fé).

Collaboration, then, offered financial gain and social advancement, whilst the French could also be relied upon to hang bandits, suppress rioters and back *señores* against agrarian disorder: sights such as the three gallows that Dorsenne kept permanently filled outside Burgos were in this sense as much a reassurance as they were a menace. Meanwhile, having obtained control, the invaders were in a position to use every means at their disposal to project a positive image of Napoleonic rule and manipulate society in their own interests. It is instructive, for example, that no sooner had the French arrived in Madrid in December 1808 than they held a grand review:

With a view to appealing to the eyes of the populace as he had previously appealed to their reason, and hoping to dispose them to accept with pride an alliance with so rich and powerful a nation as the French, the emperor ordered that . . . all the troops should appear in their most gorgeous uniforms at the review he intended to hold on the Prado. We all got ourselves up in gala array so as to be worthy of the grand occasion.[7]

Needless to say, these displays of pomp and ceremony were reinforced by a sustained offensive in the press. All over occupied Spain official gazettes appeared giving the régime's version of events and blackening the Patriot cause. Typical of one common theme was the *Gazeta de Sevilla* of 7 January 1812:

The guerrillas commit all the robberies imaginable: nobody is free of their plundering. Spanish, French, English, all alike are victims of their wickedness. Priests, magistrates, labourers, muleteers, nobody is spared . . . Such are the instruments which presently serve perfidious Albion . . . Not being able to conquer, by means of these men, the British oppress those whose independence they feign to protect.[8]

Typical of another is the proclamation on 25 March 1812 which described the *gaditano* régime as an 'infamous and illegitimate government . . . composed of the very scum of Spain, dependent on the caprice of an ignorant mob, dominated by British influence, and possessed of no more territory than the prison in which it resides . . . that has deceived the foolish Spaniards who submit to its tyranny by promising them an illusory liberty'.[9]

The effect of such broadsides is unknown, but it cannot be denied that for many life in the Patriot zone had been hazardous and distressing. Hence, perhaps, the extraordinary scenes witnessed in the course of Joseph's journey round Andalucía in 1810:

It is impossible to convey an adequate idea of the joy with which the population of Ecija, Jérez, Santa María, Ronda, Málaga, Granada and Jaén received the new king . . . In every town, the nobility, formed up as a guard of honour, came to congratulate him on his happy arrival, and swore to extend to him a devotion without limits. They even embraced his feet and his knees . . . Following their example, the people kissed his horse and prostrated themselves on the ground, crying, 'Long live King Joseph!', whilst I saw women of the lower classes . . . begging him to do them the honour of riding over their bodies . . . Men and women, young and old, everyone flocked to his lodgings to contemplate the features of the man they called their saviour. The great lords showered him with presents and wearied him with their protestations of attachment and love, and the populace begged for a look and a blessing. Amidst general acclamations, fireworks of a sort that had but rarely been seen in Spain were let off everywhere to add to the joy of the day. In the tableaux there appeared both insulting references to Joseph's predecessors and allegories in honour of the new king.[10]

Particularly amongst the lower classes, these transports of delight proved pretty ephemeral, but, even if the general disillusion was shared by the propertied classes, the latter also had to contend with the ever present fear of social exclusion. Merely by setting up a family court, for example, Joseph confronted grandees with the uncomfortable choice of either participating in the structures of his rule or abandoning the stage to *parvenu* rivals. Equally, at the level of the garrison town, the local oligarchy found that the French dominated social life. Bullfights, balls, receptions, reviews, firework displays, illuminations and even the theatre were all invested with political significance, just as the freemasonry that had begun to make some slight impact in Spain prior to 1808 was now injected with an imperial theme (thus, the many new lodges that were now formed often took such titles as 'La Estrella de Napoleón' or 'La Beneficiencia de Josefina').

To attend some reception hosted by a French officer or watch a bullfight thrown in honour of Napoleon's birthday was not the same, of course, as to accept a position of responsibility under *el rey intruso*. But the French also had other weapons. In Spanish society the right to wear uniform had for the past century been a coveted mark of status, hence the jealousy aroused by the officer corps, and hence too the popularity of the various corps of 'distinguished volunteers' and the like that had sprung up since 1808. In the wake of French occupation the only uniform to which the civilian could obtain access, however, was the dark blue coat, red facings and white breeches of Joseph's civic militia (see below). Also to be considered was the question of *desamortización*. With immense quantities of land being offered for sale at prices that were inclined to fall by the day, could any family abstain from taking part in the process? With many French officers being charming and polished individuals who cultivated an air of dash and gallantry – British memoirs are full of complaints at the greater success enjoyed by their enemies when it came to flirting with Spanish women – it was very difficult to avoid contact with the French altogether, and still harder to prevent contact from developing into co-operation and even recognition: oaths of allegiance to King Joseph, for example, were required not just of all office-holders of any sort, but also of all heads of families.

Punished as it was by sequestration of property, escape to the Patriot zone was not a practical possibility except for, say, officials with a secure position in government service, notables with property in the Patriot zone, or young men with a career to make and no family responsibilities. It was therefore inevitable that the French should have been able to obtain at least a measure of acquiescence amongst the propertied classes. Whilst often drawing the line at taking service with the French, and in some instances serving as spies or couriers, they accepted the presence of the occupying forces, and on occasion even struck up friendships with them. Typical of this coexistence is the case of Francisco de Goya, who remained in Madrid throughout the French occupation, painted Joseph's picture and documented the war in the masterpiece of studied ambiguity known as the *Desastres de la Guerra*. For many imperial officers, indeed, life could be reasonably comfortable. Let us, for example, take the case of the German, Heinrich von Brandt, who was an officer in one of Napoleon's Polish regiments. Stationed in Aragón after the fall of Zaragoza, he remarks that the French 'were not as universally hated as has since been alleged'.[11] The clergy, he agrees, were hostile, as were most of the peasantry, but the propertied classes and women in general were split:

In the middle classes older people were exclusively against us, but amongst those between twenty and thirty there were many *afrancesados* ... Although women, especially the mature ones, bitterly rebuked the French for their lack of religion and for their insatiable appetites ... during our wanderings we had the experience of meeting ardent francophiles, especially young brides with old husbands, or ... novices whose mother superiors had set them at liberty on the approach of the French.[12]

Whether or not this analysis is correct, Von Brandt had no difficulty striking up relationships with the people amongst whom he found himself. At Daroca, for example, he became friendly with a fugitive monk, whilst at Calatayud he met a seventeen-year-old postulant named Ines with whom he fell deeply in love. For a matter-of-fact account of how all barriers could be broken down, we need only turn to the memoirs of the cavalry officer and *beau sabreur*, Charles Parquin:

At Salamanca my duties as adjutant obtained for me excellent quarters in the house of a beautiful Spanish noblewoman ... whose husband, a colonel in the Spanish army, had died two years previously ... The first week she ... refused to see me and our only contact had been when I sent my card to her. Soon afterwards I sent a note to her and I employed bribery to learn from the maid who brought me chocolate every morning that her mistress watched from behind the curtains of her room when I mounted to leave the house ... This encouraging sign made me so bold as to ask if she would allow me to spend one hour each day in her company. This favour was granted me. Later on, as one can imagine, I did not stop there ... and, in short, I was happy, very happy indeed.[13]

With the lower classes, of course, relations were much less amicable. However, as time went on, the frenzied responses of the early days of the war died away. Particularly in towns where exposure to the French was constant, there rather developed a spirit of live and let live:

I do not know what may be the state of the public mind in the southern provinces of the Peninsula, but assuredly the feelings of all the provinces through which I have passed are decidedly inimical to the French and favourable to the common cause . . . At the same time, I am convinced that many of the middling classes of society lean towards the French and that in all the great towns the French have active friends and partisans. Even the patriotic feelings of the lower classes are of little use to their country. It is a passive feeling, which murmurs under the oppression and tyranny which it suffers, without exerting itself to remove or diminish what it complains of. The people pay their contributions and deliver up their mules, grain and provisions whenever they are demanded . . . by the enemy. Of course they complain of these exactions and are happy to see the English . . . But . . . it does the enemy no harm nor us any good.[14]

At particular times and in particular places, the *rapprochement* noted above could go even further, a good example being the spirit that prevailed in Madrid in the early months of 1809:

The day after [his return to the capital] and for many days afterwards, [Joseph] went out, showing himself in the streets and visiting the . . . hospitals. He got quite a good welcome, and there were signs of a general change in the spirit of the inhabitants . . . Aversion diminished, and hope and confidence appeared reborn, and it must be said that this change was the work of the king himself. His character served him marvellously in the circumstances in which he found himself: his affability . . . and, above all, the manner in which he in every instance chose Spaniards rather than Frenchmen pleased the nation. At the same time inertia, the evils of the war, the departure of the British . . . [and] the impossibility of resistance caused arms to be discarded and necks to be bent to a yoke that was found to be less burdensome than had been expected.[15]

Why, though, should resignation, acquiescence and personal friendship have in some instances gone as far as active collaboration? At the heart of the matter for many of those involved was clearly fear of disorder, the desire to ensure the survival of their own privileges and social status, and the belief that resistance was futile. Discussion of individual cases is not entirely helpful, but one might begin by noting a number of senior army officers who rallied to the French cause, including Fernando VII's own Minister of War, General Gonzalo O'Farrill, and the erstwhile governor of Cádiz, Tomás de Morla. Thus, both generals, of whom the former had joined Joseph at Bayonne and the latter following the surrender of Madrid, made it quite clear that they regarded war as an empty gesture that would produce only defeat and the collapse of the social order. Also worthy of note here is the support shown the *josefino* régime by substantial elements of the Church. Most clerical opinion was deeply hostile both to the emperor and to a France associated with the excesses of the Revolution. With matters made still worse by atrocity and anti-clericalism, many bishops fled their dioceses for the Patriot zone, just as many priests and friars preached holy war and on occasion took up arms against the French. Yet in Oviedo, Seville, Valencia and a variety of other cities, driven not just by fear of disorder but the belief that the coming of Joseph Bonaparte reflected the workings of divine providence, the hierarchy maintained the most cordial relations with the occupying forces and acted as agents of their propaganda. As Suchet acknowledged, for instance, the 'persuasive eloquence' of the Bishop of Zaragoza 'instilled a peaceful and conciliatory disposition into his flock'.[16] And finally it is no surprise to find either that the French conquest of Valencia saw the local grandees rally to the new masters of the city *en masse*, or that the organs of local government established by the French in the wake of their occupation of Asturias were largely composed of men who had been prominent in the province's old *ayuntamientos* and provincial assembly.

Also common were opportunism, calculation and an eye to the main chance. Particularly visible amongst the many prominent figures who rushed to join Joseph at Bayonne and then deserted him in the wake of Bailén (such as the Duque de Infantado and Fernando's Secretary of State, Pedro de Cevallos), such factors were also of great importance lower down the scale. Thus, the fact that the French for a long time seemed likely to win encouraged *pretendientes* and adventurers to take service under King Joseph (a good example here is the man who headed French intelligence in Barcelona under Duhesme and Saint-Cyr, Joaquín Casanova, an obscure individual who would have been hard put to it to find advancement but for the war). Equally, in the Church, in particular, there were plenty of clerics dissatisfied with their lot; hence, perhaps, the accounts that can be found of disrobed friars leading pro-French irregular bands, of parish priests and cathedral canons taking service with the French as local officials, and, for that matter, of nuns eager to elope with French officers.

Then, too, there was the issue of revenge and political exclusion. March 1808 had witnessed the downfall of many officers and officials associated with the régime of Godoy, and for such men there was little room in Patriot Spain. Filled with the desire for revenge, they therefore flocked to the French administration and armed forces. A prominent and particularly vigorous example is Amorós, but others include the erstwhile Intendent of Zaragoza,

Ignacio Garciny, who had been driven from the city by an angry mob at the time of the *motín de Aranjuez*, and went on to become *comisario regio* – in effect, governor – of Soria and La Rioja, and the head of the Bourbon artillery, General José Navarro Sangrán, who was appointed *comisario regio* in Old Castile.

Whilst the factors that we have looked at thus far cannot be said to have been absent from other cases as well, there were several groups of *afrancesados* who were united by ideas of a more positive sort. As we have seen, in the period leading up to 1808 a significant section of educated opinion had been won over to the cause of political and economic liberalism, and, in particular, to such key measures as the 'nationalisation' of the Spanish Church, the liberation of thought from the shackles of the Inquisition, the abolition of all restrictions on economic activity, the creation of a free market in land, and an end to the privileges of the nobility. Under the influence of Godoy, the period 1792–1808 was marked by the pursuit of many of these objectives, and yet such were Godoy's personal failings and the depths to which Spain's fortunes fell that the *ilustrados* became ever more disillusioned. Though many were encouraged by the rising of 1808 to believe that the way was now open for reform, others were horrified, realising, perhaps, that it was as much a protest against Spanish enlightenment as it was a protest against French aggression. In consequence, many *ilustrados* turned to the French in the conviction that Napoleon epitomised the cause of progress. Thanks to this belief, Joseph gained the support of a devoted band of *literati* which included the noted writers, Leandro Fernández de Moratín, José Marchena, Juan Meléndez Valdés and Alberto Lista, as well as a small number of dissident clergy whose thinking had been strongly infuenced by the Enlightenment, including the sometime official of the Inquisition, Juan Antonio Llorente, and the *sevillano* cathedral canon, José Isidoro Morales. Alongside these figures, meanwhile, could be found a second group of men consisting of ministers and bureaucrats associated with the caroline reforms who had survived to see the coming of the French. The product of a rigidly élitist movement that regarded the mass of the people as mere brutes, emphasised the principle of absolute monarchy, and sought as far as possible to civilise the conduct of war, they could not fail to be repelled by the events of 1808. Some of their representatives, true, swallowed their misgivings and rallied to the Patriots – one thinks here of Floridablanca and Jovellanos – but for others the only option was collaboration, and all the more so as the Napoleonic régime not only shared their contempt for the people, but seemed to represent a return to enlightened absolutism, whether it was in its religious toleration, its attack on the

Church, its expropriation of ecclesiastical property, its assault upon corporate privilege, its rationalisation of government, or its centralisation of power. In consequence, from the beginning of his reign Joseph could call on the services of not just Cabarrús, but also Mariano Luis de Urquijo, Miguel José de Azanza, and the Marqués de Caballero, all of whom had held ministerial posts in the reformist régimes of Carlos III and Carlos IV.

So far, we have for the most part only discussed collaboration amongst the upper ranks of society. Collaboration, however, was not just a phenomenon of the prominent. Thus, in addition to staffing a full administrative and judicial apparatus, the French were able to organise a small regular army, which at its greatest extent consisted of three guard, ten line and two light infantry regiments together with a variety of cavalry, artillery and engineer units, whilst at the same time mobilising substantial numbers of auxiliary regiments, civic guards and even anti-guerrilla guerrillas.* Largely undocumented as this phenomenon of rank-and-file *afrancesamiento* is, it is difficult to interpret. Marxian claims that it represents a positive identification on the part of the people with the Napoleonic revolution are impossible to substantiate, the reasons for collaboration probably being practical rather than ideological. Thus, in a situation where economic life was in chaos, prices soaring and hunger never far away, service with the French could constitute a vital source of income. At the same time it was also governed by a measure of self-interest, for the guerrillas not only brought down savage reprisals on the heads of many *pueblos* but were themselves much given to pillage. Local home guards of one sort or another therefore attracted a considerable amount of support – ten battalions of civic militia were formed in Madrid alone – but even so there were limits to the phenomenon of popular *afrancesamiento*. Thus, Joseph's Spanish regulars time and again melted away like snow, the king being able to rely only on the foreigners who made up his royal guard. As for the irregular forces employed to hunt down the guerrillas, whilst there are doubtless some interesting stories to uncover – who, for example, was the girl nicknamed La Colegiana who is supposed to have led a pro-French *partida* dressed as a man in 1813? – it is clear that many were in fact brigands who were simply using service with the French as a cover for their misdeeds.

However many Spaniards may have at one time or another taken up

---

* It is also worth pointing out that substantial numbers of Spanish prisoners of war escaped imprisonment in France by volunteering for service with the *grande armée* in the specially formed Régiment du Joseph-Napoléon.

arms as *juramentados*, collaboration at the popular level remained patently insubstantial. Nor, indeed, could this be otherwise: very few aspects of the French reform programme were of any immediate benefit to the populace, whilst most of them were actually harmful. Thus, the inclusion of the Basque provinces within the national customs frontier hit the local agricultural economy very hard; the attack on the Church deprived the populace of both poor relief and spiritual support; and the new cemeteries continued to give rise to fears of eternal damnation. To understand the negative impact of French reform in full, however, it is necessary to examine the interest that the French took in what was called the policing of society. We see here the idea of enlightenment as a civilising mission that would save the poor from themselves. By nature idle, improvident, dirty and given over entirely to vice, they would be made to work, taught useful trades, instilled with a sense of social responsibility, and deprived of the opportunity for debauchery. Yet, at best, poverty would be replaced by tyranny, for the implication was clearly that the populace would be placed under strict control, forced to conform to the norms of respectable society, injected with a sense of deference, denied any outlet for their frustrations, and stripped of their cultural autonomy. At the heart of the whole programme, in short, was fear of the mob. There was nothing inherently Napoleonic about all this – on the contrary, such ideas had been commonplace throughout eighteenth-century Europe – but, imbued as the French were with a sense of cultural superiority, the empire saw a particularly sustained attempt to put the theory into practice.

From the various police agencies established by the French – the most important was the Ministry of General Police whose formation was decreed by King Joseph on 6 February 1809 – there therefore flowed a flood of rules and regulations of every sort. Typical of these documents, perhaps, was the *Reglamento para la Entrada, Salida y Circulación de la Personas por Madrid* that appeared on 17 February 1809. This consisted of a list of minute rules concerning the movements of the populace in Madrid and, more especially, communication between the city and the outside world. Thus all outsiders who came into Madrid were expected to register with the police in exchange for a pass which allowed them to remain in the capital for a given time (permanent residents had already been registered when they had been required to swear allegiance to Joseph in December 1808). Meanwhile, visitors of any sort had to have their journey sanctioned by the authorities in the place from which they set out, just as nobody could leave the capital without a passport. Nor were things much better inside the city: free transit through the streets was allowed during the day, but even then pedestrians were enjoined to keep moving and prohibited from stopping to talk on street corners; at night, meanwhile, internal passes were required and all pedestrians required to carry torches.

It could be argued that, like the instructions that were later issued for all inhabitants to carry pass-books, these regulations are the fruit of nothing more than an attempt to prevent espionage, subversion and insurrection, but the question of support for the Patriot cause was generally left to specific decrees such as that issued by Soult in Seville on 7 May 1810 which threatened any *pueblo* that failed to resist the guerrillas, let alone collaborated with them, with the most draconian penalties. The real significance of the regulations is rather to be found in the numerous police orders whose bearing on the issue of security is little more than tangential. There were orders banning carters from driving too fast; orders restricting the movement of mule trains and wagons; orders concerning the tethering of horses; orders for sweeping the pavements and the removal of rubbish; orders for the conduct of market traders and peddlars; orders for the control of lodging houses; orders for the illumination of the streets at night; orders for the proper manner of carrying corpses to the cemetery; orders prohibiting dogs from being allowed to wander loose in the streets; orders for the confinement of all beggars in municipal hospitals or workhouses; and orders restricting the slaughter of animals to slaughterhouses or other designated places. There were orders regulating the organisation of carnival festivities, Holy Week processions and bullfights; orders prohibiting the wearing of cloaks, masks and disguises at fiestas; orders restricting the opening hours of taverns and gaming houses; orders enjoining the registration of prostitutes; orders prohibiting the consumption of alcohol in the streets; orders forbidding theatres to show anything that offended public decency; and orders banning the congregation of any more than the smallest groups of people in the streets. As one pamphlet put it, 'They will be telling us where to spit next.'[17] With their every action watched, the populace were deeply resentful, all the more so as the regulations were backed up by heavy fines and, as in similar cases in Patriot Spain, were the source of much inconvenience. As if it was not bad enough that the licences, permits and pass-books demanded by the invaders all cost money – to obtain the official *carta de seguridad*, for example, cost one real – the marginal activities that actually sustained much of the populace were criminalised, and this at a time when normal economic life was all but at a standstill. Also affected was virtually every type of cheap entertainment, even if it was only lounging in the sun. However much the French and their supporters might put it down to the fact that the *populacho* was too savage for the new habits to appeal, hostility and resistance were only to be expected.

All the more is this the case if we consider the rationale of French rule. Implicit both in the patterns of the Napoleonic empire in general, and in the motivation for French intervention in Spain in particular, was exploitation: indeed, for what reason had Napoleon placed his brother on the throne if it was not to ensure that Spain fulfilled the requirements of a reliable satellite state? As for the costs of invasion, these were, as everywhere else, to be borne by the territories occupied by the French armies. Last but not least, there was also the question of Napoleon's power base: loot, perhaps, was not the only factor that motivated the soldiery, but nor was it to be forgotten as a means of maintaining their morale; as for the marshals, generals and other grand dignitaries of the empire, more lands were always needed for the *donations* with which the emperor had been careful to ensure their loyalty.

The French, then, fell on the Peninsula like wolves. Outright brigandage was not approved of, on the grounds that it was bad for discipline and liable to prove counter-productive. To quote an edict of Marshal Berthier, 'The emperor is unhappy with the disorders that have been committed. Pillage annihilates everything down to the very army that engages in it.'[18] But such pious sermonising proved but little in the way of protection. As the French swept back across Spain in the winter of 1808, town after town witnessed the most appalling scenes. Burgos, for example, suffered very badly:

As we approached Burgos, we crossed the site of the affair of 10 November. It was still strewn with corpses, although the sad spectacle which it presented did not make as painful an impression on me as the state of that great city at the moment of our entrance. Absolutely deserted, almost all the houses had been pillaged and their furniture smashed to pieces and thrown in the mud; part of the city was . . . on fire; a frenzied soldiery was forcing every door and window, breaking down everything that stood in the way, and destroying more than they consumed; all the churches had been stripped; and the streets were encumbered with the dead and dying. In short, although it had not been defended, the city exhibited all the horrors of an assault.[19]

Also badly hit were Lerma, Aranda de Duero and Toledo. Wherever the French went, indeed, the story was much the same. To quote Rocca:

As soon as the main guard was posted, at a concerted signal the soldiers . . . precipitated themselves all together . . . through the city, and long after the arrival of the army shrieks were still heard, and the noise of doors broken open with hatchets and great stones.[20]

The result was a trail of destruction. Arriving at Burgos to take up the post of governor of Old Castile, Thiébault wrote that it 'looked like a desolate solitude – in parts a sink of filth' where 'famine, ruin, despair [and] pestilence prevailed, with death as the sole remedy'.[21] Elsewhere matters were even worse:

Continuing on our way we arrived . . . at Huerta [de Valdecarábanos] . . . without any other event than being challenged and interrogated by two parties of Frenchmen . . . But if these continual delays did not dampen our spirits, the horrible spectacle that we came across at . . . Aranjuez . . . filled us with pity. On the . . . Cuesta de Arineros three unfortunates were hanging from trees. Of the beautiful bullring nothing was left but the main walls, the same being true of many of the town's principal houses . . . The gardens, the promenades, in short everything that made the place so rich and beautiful . . . had been destroyed . . . At the end of the Puente Larga, another four men had been strung up with the difference that they had not only been hung, but nailed through their chests to the trees on which they had lost their lives . . . Husbands have seen their wives raped, fathers their daughters, sons their aged mothers, and there have even been cases in which the main square was used as the scene of their indescribable lascivities.[22]

To all this was added great financial pressure. As early as 18 August 1808, Joseph announced a levy of 8 per cent on the products of the year's harvest, whilst in late October a forced loan was imposed on those territories then occupied by the French that amounted in the case of Navarre alone to 7,300,000 reales. With the reconquest of Madrid in December 1808, the pressure increased still further, Napoleon making it quite clear to his brother that *josefino* Spain could expect to be plundered rather than subsidised. In Burgos, for example, the emperor had seized large stocks of wool and quinine with the intention of auctioning them in France, whilst he had seized the estates of the ten richest families to have been proscribed as *donations* and ordered Joseph to present him with fifty masterpieces for the Louvre. Aside from a loan of 25,000,000 francs that was agreed in July 1808 on the collateral of the Spanish crown jewels, less than 7,000,000 of which seem actually to have been paid, Napoleon was reluctant to give his brother financial aid, and instead insisted that he should fund his régime from what he could obtain in Spain. Nor would he relax France's tight tariff laws, effectively blocking the export of Spanish wool and thereby dealing a heavy blow to Joseph's treasury.

All this was a source of much grief to *el rey intruso*: at Burgos, indeed, such was his misery that he took to his bed for two days. A humane and generous man, he genuinely wanted his subjects to be happy, whilst, as he well knew, there was every reason not to overburden them. Ideally, then, he would have liked to rely solely on a combination of regular taxation and the exploitation of the wealth of the Church. But, not only did his officials have no access to large parts of the country, their ability to raise money was falling even where the French were in occupation: in Aragón, for example, tax revenue declined by a factor of more than one half in the course of 1809. As for the Church, success was limited. Much of its plate was confiscated, true, but on the whole *desamortización* proved a disappointment: whilst some money came in from the tithes paid to the religious foundations that had been suppressed and the auction of their plate and fittings, the land involved was largely paid for by the new *cédulas*, whose value was soon depreciating as rapidly as that of their Bourbon predecessors. With much the same true of the estates confiscated from supporters of the Patriot cause, Joseph was forced to move further and further away from the legality of which he dreamed. As early as December 1808 a forced loan was decreed of 20,000,000 francs, whilst in September 1809 this was followed by a second of 10,000,000.

To fiscal pressure was added the day-to-day burden of occupation. Distressing and unpleasant in itself, billeting was the source of much expense (the cost of housing a single officer, for example, was officially recognised as between eight and ten reales per day). On top of this, French commanders were from the beginning permitted to impose enormous war contributions wherever they went. To take the neighbouring cities of León and Palencia as an example, between December 1808 and October 1810 they were together mulcted of a total of some 2,500,000 reales. Added to this, of course, was wholesale requisitioning, whether it was of livestock, such as the 300 oxen demanded of Navarre in August 1808, food, such as the 300,000 rations required from Toledo in August 1812, or hospital supplies, such as the 2,600 sheets, 500 bolsters, 800 palliasses and 700 blankets demanded of Palencia in January 1809. Nor was any ceremony wasted in the imposition of such demands:

Whenever the French come here . . . they commit the greatest atrocities that Your Excellency can imagine. Three days ago they took 8,000–9,000 head of livestock . . . On the 23rd they took 714 *fanegas* of barley, and whilst some of them were loading up, the rest sacked fifty houses . . . Today they have taken 92 *fanegas* of barley and sacked three more houses . . . If I was to mention all the atrocities which they commit in the course of their comings and goings, Your Excellency would be astonished, for there is not a statue which they do not burn, nor a woman whom they do not molest. Indeed, at times they kill the women, as they do any man who does not give them what they demand.[23]

Fuelled by the greed of commanders such as Soult, who is believed to have stripped Andalucía of works of art worth 1,500,000 francs, such rapacity remained characteristic of French occupation until the very end – in May 1813, for example, the last days of French rule saw Salamanca faced by a demand for 300,000 reales – whilst Joseph's ability to do anything to remedy matters was reduced to an ever smaller compass. First had come the decrees of 8 February and 29 May 1810 which took the whole of northern Spain out of his control. And then, on 14 July 1810 not only was Andalucía given to Soult, but Joseph's vague supervisory powers over the French forces were taken away by grouping them into six independent armies (of the South, the Centre, Portugal, Aragón, the North and Catalonia), the king being formally reduced to the position of commander of the Army of the Centre.

Coming as it did in the midst of his triumphant tour of Andalucía, the first of these decrees came as a major shock for Joseph – 'I saw', wrote Miot, 'what a mortal blow it was for him'[24] – but at first he did nothing. To quote the same observer:

The hope of getting Napoleon to revoke his orders . . . made him postpone a decisive resolve. Instead, he carefully hid away the news that he had received, and we once again allowed ourselves to be lulled to sleep by the cheers of the crowds who in every town dogged our every pace.[25]

The political consequences of this situation were manifold. From the beginning Joseph had been convinced that his only hope in Spain was a policy of moderation. Unable to hold to this ideal in the matter of taxation, the king had at least consistently acted in a clement fashion, freeing prisoners of war, reprimanding officials who had acted in too arbitrary a fashion, and restoring property that had been seized unjustly to its rightful owners. But what happened now depended on the military authorities. The newly independent French commanders were not all mindless brutes – in eastern Spain Augereau and Suchet more or less adopted Joseph's policies as their own and in the latter case in particular scored some success – but the contempt which Napoleon heaped upon any talk of moderation destroyed all hope of magnanimity taking general root.

At the heart of the problem was the deepening split between Joseph and his younger brother. Soured on the one side by outrage over the behaviour of the French armies and the Decrees of Chamartín and on the other by dissatisfaction with the king's incompetent generalship and milksop ways, relations between the two had temporarily been patched up. As Miot notes, however, the truce proved shortlived:

Napoleon had only handed power to Joseph in form: the reality remained in his hands. Very quickly the king perceived this from the conduct of the French generals and officials that had remained in Spain, and the irritation which he felt was extreme. In his letters he complained bitterly of the independence which both groups affected in so far as he was concerned. The violence of the expressions which he used [and] the threats with which he accompanied his complaints . . . inflamed the resentment of the emperor, whilst the latter could not brook the fact that the king was affecting equality with him . . . Very soon the exchange of letters between them had ceased . . . Instead, the [emperor] sent his orders directly to the commanders of the French armies in Spain, and a host of measures that undermined Joseph's authority as king and commander-in-chief were carried out . . . without his participation and sometimes even his knowledge.[26]

With matters made worse, first, by the fact that Joseph's chief-of-staff, Marshal Jourdan, was widely perceived as a nonentity, and, second, by the king's determination to advance Spaniards rather than Frenchmen, the other agents of the emperor felt free to ignore Joseph even whilst they still remained nominally subject to his authority. Typical perhaps was the attitude of General Thiébault, who in the autumn of 1809 found himself hoist with his own petard when an attempt to drag his feet by allegations of ill-health was answered by a polite letter sympathising with his troubles and informing him that General Solignac would be arriving to take over forthwith. Thus:

Even in the case of a D'Armagnac,* this ill-concealed dismissal would have been scandalous; in my case, no name was bad enough for it. On the part of the king it was sheer impudence, for he was misusing a power which he had no right to claim. I had been appointed by the emperor, and could be removed only by him. But for the weakness of my condition, which did not allow me to master my temper, together with the tendency I always had to take advantage of every opportunity of seeing my wife once more, I should have appealed to the emperor, and Solignac would have left Burgos without having time to make a mess of the authority which he so scandalously misused.[27]

Far from being characterised by benevolence, French rule therefore continued to be marked by extreme brutality and the most arbitrary conduct. Hostage-taking, executions, massacres, burnings and sackings abounded, whilst there were many random killings, rapes and acts of plunder and humiliation. As for Joseph, he was left looking more and more ridiculous. At the very time that he was entering Seville in triumph and issuing an amnesty for all those who would join his cause, for example, Sebastiani was

* A reference to Thiébault's predecessor, Jean D'Armagnac, whom he accuses of brutality, corruption and incompetence.

sacking Málaga and extracting from it 12,000,000 reales. Still worse, even those areas which in theory remained under his authority were not safe, a raid on Avila by Marshal Ney in February 1810 stripping it of 6,000,000 reales, 12,000 *fanegas* of wheat and 500 head of cattle.

By the summer of 1810, then, Joseph had lost all control of the situation. With his income only one third of what he needed, his administration in chaos, his authority openly flouted, and Napoleon asking more and more of him – in January 1810, for example, it had suddenly been announced that the pay of the Peninsular armies was no longer to be found in Paris but in Spain and Portugal – the king felt that he had no option but to fight back. Desperate protests to Napoleon proving of little avail – the emperor swore that he had no money, insisted that Spain was awash with riches, and accused his brother of being too soft – Joseph became more and more angry and repeatedly threatened to abdicate. Napoleon, however, would only agree to his terms on condition that he persuaded the Patriots to surrender, and in the spring of 1811 the king therefore made a desperate bid to restore his fortunes by paying a surprise visit to France. Realising, perhaps, that he had gone too far, Napoleon responded with a display of charm and reassurance – justice, for example, was everywhere to be administered in the king's name; one quarter of all monies raised in the provinces was to be sent to Madrid; the generals were ordered to report to Joseph on a regular basis; and Joseph was to receive a subvention of 500,000 francs a month – and this proved sufficient to get the unhappy monarch to resume his burdens. However, it soon became apparent that nothing had changed: little money was received from Soult and the rest, whilst by the end of the year only 1,000,000 francs had arrived from France. With things soon as desperate as ever, Joseph was again forced to resort to extortion: on 23 July 1811 an extraordinary levy was imposed on grain, the city of Toledo alone being assessed at 1,500 *fanegas* of wheat and another 1,500 of barley. Once more Joseph considered abdication, but again Napoleon saved the situation, sending the king 380,000 francs, appointing him to the position of commander-in-chief of all the French forces in Spain, investing him with titular authority over the whole of Spain, and restoring Marshal Jourdan as his chief-of-staff (less flamboyant and opinionated than many of his fellows, Jourdan had become a trusted friend and confidant in the course of the time that he had spent in the same position in 1809, but in September of that year he had been forced to return home on account of ill-health).

Yet none of this made much difference. *El rey intruso* continued to be slighted and deprived of money at every turn. Meanwhile, dreams of convoking a *cortes* or embarking on a triumphal progress of the sort that had gone down so well in Andalucía in 1810 came to nothing for want of funds. All that could be done was to order the formation of the prefectural councils envisaged in the decree of 17 April 1810 (typically, these had never been established) in the hope that these might impose some restraint on the generals. But, getting harder and harder to staff the Bonapartist administration as it was, the measure had almost no effect. Further humiliated by being temporarily driven from his capital in August 1812 (though not before he had *faute de mieux* demanded that it produce the immense sum of 20,000,000 reales), Joseph had by the end of the year finally been reduced to a cypher. Thus, large numbers of functionaries, including some of his most trusted advisers, had decided that the game was up, whilst others, such as the aged Cabarrús, had now died. For a short period the court continued its daily round in a forlorn attempt at defiance – Joseph, indeed, displayed great courage and serenity – but the civil administration had been reduced to the purest improvisation, whilst all legislative activity had come to a halt. With Napoleon pressing for Madrid to be reduced to the status of an outlying garrison, the end could not be long delayed, and on 17 March 1813 Joseph left his capital for the last time. Until the last moment the king clung to the hope that there would be a miraculous change in the political. situation – hearing, for example, of the bitter disputes that rent the Allied camp as a result of Wellington's appointment to the command of the Spanish armies, he seemingly entertained dreams of wholesale defections – but no such reprieve offered itself. On the contrary, on 27 June 1813 *el rey intruso* found himself crossing the frontier amidst the wreckage of his beaten armies.

By then, however, all trace of the Bonaparte kingdom of Spain had been swept away. Why, though, had the enterprise proved so signal a failure? To this question an obvious and implicitly pro-Napoleonic answer is that, xenophobic, ignorant and priest-ridden, the Spanish people were persuaded to put up such opposition to French rule that the benefits of Napoleonic reform never became fully apparent to them. Just as obvious, but this time anti-French, is the argument that the *josefino* régime was never a reformist administration at all, but rather a military despotism pure and simple with no other goal than that of stripping Spain of its last real. But neither view is adequate. Just as Spanish resistance cannot be explained solely in terms of obscurantism, so King Joseph cannot be explained solely in terms of rapine. Thus, to deny that the *josefino* régime was reformist would be foolish: even if reform was in the long run seen by Napoleon as a necessary means of realising Spain's potential as a satellite state, the measures that flowed from Bayonne and Madrid were far-reaching in their implications and were in part intended to win Joseph general acceptance. In this, however, the French had miscalculated, for the sort of transformation that had been dreamed of in 1808 by the crowds that had taken over the streets of Madrid, Aranjuez and so many other places had hardly revolved around the creation of a French-style state able to impose greater and greater demands on the populace. The substitution of the modern garrotte for the traditional noose by King Joseph may therefore be regarded as a metaphor: modernity was replacing obsolescence; efficiency, decrepitude; and iron, rope. In short, the problem was not, as Jovellanos once put it, that French reform was foreign, but rather that it was reformist at all.

10

Pancorbo

THE EMERGENCE OF GUERRILLA WAR, 1808–1810

Tough and experienced, the French dragoons glanced around them. On all sides there was nothing to be seen but miles of rock and scrub backed by towering mountains. News having reached the commander of the post at the miserable village of Pancorbo that a band of guerrillas was about to stage an ambush somewhere between there and Miranda de Ebro, he had decided to send out a strong patrol. Nothing had happened as the men rode through the terrible gorge of Pancorbo – a long defile that enjoyed the reputation of being one of the most dangerous places in the whole of Spain – but, moving on, one of the soldiers suddenly caught the flash of sunlight on metal. Shouting the alarm, his commander soon had the dragoons galloping up the slope overlooking the road. Taken by surprise, a handful of figures rose out of the scrub and fled in confusion. Braver than the others, one or two stopped to fire the occasional shot, but most of them lost no time in mounting the horses they had left tethered in the rear. In the general confusion, two men flung themselves on the same horse whilst another grabbed a stirrup in the hope of being pulled to safety, only for the three of them to find their way blocked by a dragoon who flourished his blade and moved in for the kill, shouting triumphantly. From the scrub behind him, however, burst one of the leaders of the men who had attacked the French column. A Catholic priest, Father Jácobo, he emptied his pistols at the surprised dragoon who hastily spurred away. Still with the French in hot pursuit, the little party continued its dash for safety. Ahead of them loomed a large rock, and suddenly, from its summit there rang out a volley that tumbled several Frenchmen from their saddles and caused the others to swerve aside. Dismounting, the dragoons opened up with their carbines, but already the guerrillas were melting away. Their ambush had been sprung and a number of them killed, but they had lived to fight another day, and that, in a sense, was all that mattered.

Fought out near the village of Bugedo on the highroad from Madrid to the French frontier on 30 October 1809, this skirmish conjures up a vision of people's war that has come to epitomise the Iberian struggle against Napoleon. For most readers, indeed, two images will be conjured up by mention of the Peninsular War. On the one hand, there is the invincible 'thin red line' of Wellington's infantry, and on the other the cruel and sinister figure of the Spanish guerrilla: as is widely recognised, indeed, it was the struggle in Spain and Portugal that actually introduced the word to the English language.* Furthermore, it has long since become a historical commonplace to explain the defeat of the French through the juxtaposition of these two images. Thanks to the guerrillas, it is argued, the French armies were forced to remain spread out over the entire face of the Peninsula so that the numerically inferior Anglo-Portuguese forces could defeat them in detail. At the same time, the presence of Wellington's army in Portugal prevented the French from concentrating all their forces on the guerrillas, and thus saved the Spaniards from annihilation. Caught between British and Portuguese bayonets and popular hatred, the invaders found themselves enmeshed in a predicament – the famous 'Spanish mousetrap' – from which escape was all but impossible. For a variety of reasons, British, American, French, Spanish and Portuguese historians have all tended to emphasise this aspect of the war against the French at the expense of other forms of resistance and to treat the subject only in the most positive of terms. However, at the time opinions on the subject were bitterly divided, whilst there is also much evidence that the impact of the guerrillas was more ambiguous than has generally been argued. As this chapter will show, indeed, few aspects of the Peninsular War are more complex.

According to the traditional view, the subject is simplicity itself. The Spanish people were outraged at the overthrow of Fernando VII, and the French had only to appear amongst them for acts of spontaneous resistance to erupt. In the words of Marshal Suchet:

The . . . greater part of the population, sometimes without any distinction of age or sex, embarked on that active and obstinate species of contest which brought enemies upon us in all directions and exhausted us far more than regular engagements. Each district formed . . . its own *guerrilla* for the purpose of protecting its territory and co-operating in the common defence. Peasants, land owners, fathers of families, priests and monks unhesitatingly abandoned their dwellings . . . in order to swell the . . . bands forming against us.[1]

---

* The Spanish word 'guerrilla' actually means 'little war' rather than 'irregular fighter', and it is in fact customary to use the phrase *la guerrilla* as a generic term for the whole of the irregular struggle. The guerrillas themselves are more properly termed *guerrilleros*.

With matters made still worse by the arrogance and misbehaviour of the invading forces and the repression and atrocity in which they increasingly engaged – 'Had some of our amateurs of fine art . . . been picked out and shot', remarked Captain Elzéar Blaze, 'the war would not have become national . . . These dilapidations were the cause of the war to the death which the Spaniards waged against us'[2] – it was not long before the zones occupied by the imperial forces had been gripped by a savage irregular war. All the more was this the case as the Patriot authorities and many elements of the Church did everything that they could to incite the population to armed resistance. To quote Sébastian Blaze:

The monks skilfully employed the influence which they still enjoyed over Spanish credulity . . . to inflame the populace and excerbate the implacable hatred with which they already regarded us . . . In this fashion they encouraged a naturally cruel and barbarous people to commit the most revolting crimes with a clear conscience. They accused us of being Jews, heretics, sorcerers . . . As a result, just to be a Frenchman became a crime in the eyes of the country.[3]

Also helpful in explaining the rise of resistance, it could be argued, was the social, geographical and historical context of the Iberian Peninsula. For example, both Spain and Portugal were rugged countries which contained extensive stretches of inaccessible mountain and steppe. As Suchet noted:

The Spanish peninsula . . . is covered with lofty chains of mountains extending in all directions . . . supported by the internal plateau of the country . . . The result . . . is that the waters must . . . force their way to the sea . . . by . . . deep and rugged gullies . . . It is impossible to travel the distance of a few leagues without meeting one or many of these defiles . . . The ravines are generally dry, and yet impassable . . . In every . . . direction, communications are extremely difficult: the provinces are isolated from each other [and] the towns and villages separated by immense distances and built upon heights, or enclosed within walls, [and] surrounded by splendid forests of olive trees . . . Whole tracts of land are covered with broom and heath.[4]

In both Spain and Portugal, too, the populace were inured to hardship, suspicious of foreigners and well versed in ways of life – above all, banditry and smuggling – that were characterised by violence and involved constant skirmishes with the security forces. It was, indeed, the conviction of General Bigarré that the bedrock of the entire phenomenon was the 'customs guards and smugglers who covered the whole of the country under the Prince of the Peace', Captain Blaze, meanwhile, noting that, as the Spaniards were 'accustomed to extol the exploits of the robbers and smugglers', the chieftains 'have always been in readiness to become chiefs of the guerrillas'.[5]

Thanks to the *ordenança*, the *alarmas*, the *miqueletes* and the *somaténes* –
'forces that greatly tend to promote the national armament [and] might also
combine to render a sudden change from peace to war likely to prove even
acceptable to . . . the Spanish people'[6] – there was also a widespread tradition
of popular mobilisation against invasion, whilst the substantial mobilisation
of the war of 1793–95 had produced a considerable degree of military
experience (famous guerrilla leaders who had fought in this struggle included
Juan Martín Díez – El Empecinado – and Julián Sánchez García – El Charro)..

Repeated since Napoleonic times, these arguments have since been reinforced by other, more recent examples. Thus, resistance has frequently been
tied to poverty and growing social tension, the key factors here being, first,
the extent to which French occupation fuelled pauperisation and, second,
the collaboration of so many of the *pudientes*. Though detailed social
analysis was not a forte of the early nineteenth century, in support of this
view there is at least the common association of the guerrillas with robbery
and pillage. Thus, for Von Brandt, the strongest motive for their appearance
was 'the hope of plunder', whilst for the British observers, Sydenham and
Larpent, they were 'regular freebooters [who] subsisted on the pillage of the
country' and 'a sort of banditti'.[7] In the same way, it has also been claimed
that enlightened absolutism had made less progress in Spain and Portugal
than elsewhere with the result that the reforms of the new régime grated on
them far more than would otherwise have been the case. Tantamount to
suggesting that resistance was the product of backwardness – or, as the
French would have put it, of savagery, ignorance and want of civilisation –
this latter argument could be supplemented by arguing that Spain was
Catholic and therefore given over *ipso facto* to obscurantism, superstition
and counter-revolution. One here returns, of course, to common French
complaints: 'With regard to knowledge and the progress of social habits,
Spain was at least a century behind the other nations of the continent. The
. . . insular situation of the country and the severity of its religious institutions had prevented the Spaniards from taking part in the disputes and
controversies which had agitated and enlightened Europe.'[8]

Evidence for the argument that the guerrillas' essential characteristics
were their spontaneous origins, popular composition and ideological motivation is therefore not hard to find. As for their contribution to the struggle,
the invaders had begun to come under attack by bands of irregulars from
the earliest days of the war. In Andalucía, for example, the *alcalde mayor*
of Montoro, Juan de la Torre, led a band of peasants in a series of attacks
on Dupont's communications which, amongst other incidents, saw the
massacre of the seventy-strong guard that had been left to hold the Puente

de Alcolea following the occupation of Córdoba. De la Torre was quickly captured, but the whole district between Córdoba and the Sierra Morena was soon swarming with guerrilla bands led by such figures as Pedro de Valdecañas, José Cruz, Ramón Argote, Ignacio Gómez and Antonio Cuesta. Most famous of these early guerrillas, however, is Juan Martín Díez. Nicknamed 'El Empecinado', he is supposed from early April onwards to have led a group of twelve men in a series of attacks on French couriers in the neighbourhood of Aranda de Duero. In several cases, meanwhile, these actions were accompanied by a brutality that set the scene for the entire war, there being reports – possibly exaggerated – of men being stoned to death, boiled in oil, sawn in half, or buried up to their necks in the ground and left to die of thirst.

In those parts of Spain held by the French throughout, irregular resistance continued to simmer throughout the summer of 1808, as in Navarre where one Andrés Eguaguirre gathered together a force of 800 men in the vicinity of Estella and established a base at the mountain shrine of Santiago de Lóquiz. Navarre was always to be a focus of *la guerrilla*: by August 1809, indeed, it had become the haunt of the famous Martín Javier Mina y Larrea ('El Mozo'), whose exploits had soon acquired dimensions that were positively legendary. As the French zone of occupation expanded, however, so the phenomena of guerrilla resistance multiplied. Many of the initial bands in Old Castile had been eclipsed following the French retreat from Madrid – in some instances, as in that of El Empecinado, they were even persecuted by the Patriot authorities – but they now reappeared, whilst new groups emerged that were formed on the basis of fugitives from such defeats as that of Gamonal. As an example, we might cite the forces commanded by Juan Díaz Porlier that sprang to life in the area of Palencia early in 1809. These bands had soon been supplemented by others, of which the most prominent were those of Jerónimo Merino, Bartolomé Amor, Jerónimo Saornil, Tomás Príncipe ('Borbón') and Lucas Rafael. Also affected were the Basque provinces, León, Extremadura and La Mancha. Thus, Vizcaya became the beat of Francisco Longa and Antonio Jaureguí ('El Pastor'); León of cavalry raiders sent out from Ciudad Rodrigo, in whose ranks a peasant named Julián Sánchez García had soon obtained a commission; Extremadura of Toribio Bustamente; and La Mancha of Francisco Abad Moreno ('Chaleco'), Juan de Tapía, Juan Palarea ('El Médico') and, above all, El Empecinado, whose ever-growing band scored numerous successes in the region of Cuenca and Guadalajara. And, last but not least, mention should be made of Aragón. Initially cowed by the capture of Zaragoza, Aragonese resistance was revived by such leaders as Felipe Perena,

Ramón Gayán, Juan Baget, Miguel Sarasa ('Cholín') and Fidel Mallén, who achieved a number of successes, including forcing the surrender of 750 men who were cut off by a flash flood near Monzón, defeating two French columns in the vicinity of Jaca, and wiping out a patrol of 70 Frenchmen at Bernaus. After Belchite, meanwhile, the bands were reinforced by a strong *partida* formed on the basis of regular troops detached from Blake's army under Pedro Villacampa, the latter establishing a powerful base at the mountain sanctuary of Nuestra Señora del Tremedal and taking prisoner a company of the Fourteenth line at the Puerto del Frasno near Almunia on 29 August.

By the summer of 1809, then, the guerrillas were certainly making themselves felt. To quote Miot:

By that time the Junta had ... adopted the formidable system of guerrillas. Spread out in parties in every part of the territory ... that the French occupied, they did us more damage than the [Spanish] regular armies by intercepting all our communications and forcing us never to send out a courier without an escort or leave isolated soldiers on the roads ... Large parties of guerrillas ... often advanced to the gates of the capital. General Franceschi ... one of the most distinguished officers of the army, was taken prisoner by them, along with young Anthoine, a nephew of the king who was then an aide-de-camp of Marshal Soult. The hatred and fury of the Spaniards was carried to the last excess: they breathed vengeance and exercised it on any Frenchman who fell into their hands. This small-scale warfare quietly undermined us. We only possessed the ground actually occupied by our armies, and our power did not extend beyond it. The business of administration ceased, and there was neither order, nor justice, nor taxation.[9]

Such, too, was the impression of Heinrich von Brandt, who not only fought the guerrillas in Aragón but wrote what may be regarded as the first serious study of the Spanish guerrillas:

Local causes, added to hatred, revenge and other passions ... brought the mountaineers together ... From corps thus formed ... the boldest and most determined stepped forward as leaders ... As long as the guerrillas were thus constituted, they made no formidable appearance as a body, but were nevertheless extremely dangerous to the French. They formed the basis of an actual armament of the people, and were soon upon every road and path ... and eagerly seeking for plunder ... They rushed with the utmost rapidity upon their booty, or placed themselves in order of battle according to the nature of the undertaking ... As soon as the enterprise was completed everyone went his own way, and armed men were scattered in all directions ... Thus the communication on all roads was closed. Thousands of enemies were on the spot, though not a single one could be discovered; no courier could be dispatched without being taken; no supplies could set off without being attacked . . . At the same time, there existed no means of striking out at a combination of this kind. The French were . . . obliged to be constantly on their guard against an enemy, who, while continually flying, always reappeared, and who, without actually being seen, was everywhere. It was neither battles nor engagements which exhausted their forces, but the incessant molestations of an invisible enemy who, if pursued, became lost among the people, out of which he reappeared immediately afterwards with renewed strength. The lion in the fable, tormented to death by a gnat, gives us a true picture of the army at that period.[10]

Finally, much the same language is employed by the hussar officer, Rocca:

In these mountainous provinces of the north of the Peninsula, the French, although always conquerors where the . . . Spaniards showed themselves in battle, were not . . . the less assailed by clouds of armed mountaineers, who, never coming near to fight in close ranks, or body to body, retreated from position to position, from rock to rock, on heights, without ceasing to fire even in flying. It sometimes required entire battalions to carry an order of a battalion to another distant one. The soldiers, wounded, sick or fatigued, who remained behind the French columns, were immediately murdered. Every victory produced only a new conflict. Victories had become useless by the persevering and invincible character of the Spaniards, and the French armies were consuming themselves . . . in continual fatigues, nightly watchings and anxieties.[11]

When they moved south in 1810, the French merely took the problem with them. Whilst the towns of Andalucía on the whole rallied more or less willingly to King Joseph, the countryside remained hostile. Particularly determined centres of resistance were encountered in the mountains that fringed the coast – the Serranía de Ronda and the Alpujarras – where the chief figures were Andrés Ortiz de Zarate, José Serrano Valdenebro and Juan Fernández Cañas, a good example of their activities being the successful attack that they launched against the French garrison of Ronda on 9 March 1810. His regiment having been stationed in the district, Rocca was soon in the thick of the fighting:

On 1 May I was with a detachment of forty-five hussars commanded by a captain; we were going to seek, cut straw [look for fodder] . . . at some farms belonging to the village of Setenil . . . We said to each other, as we passed through a defile about half a league from the town [that] the enemy must have been very ill-advised not to have placed an ambuscade in that place . . . by which they might have done us a great deal of harm without running any risk themselves . . . When we had done foraging, we set out again by the same road . . . The captain, by whose side I was marching, repeated . . . that it was lucky that the enemy had not placed any ambuscade in the pass. He had scarcely spoken the words when four or five shots . . . killed the three last mules in the convoy and the trumpeter's horse, which was before us; our horses instantly stopped. The captain was to have marched on first, but the horse he rode . . . hesitated. Seeing this, I spurred my horse . . . and passed the defile alone. The *serranos* . . . discharged all their pieces as I passed. Two balls only reached me: the first passed through my left thigh; the other entered my body. The captain followed me . . . and arrived safe and sound at the other side of the pass, and of the whole detachment, there were only the last four men killed because the enemy suspended their fire for a few minutes while they loaded their guns a second time.[12]

However, fighting did not just take place in the Serranía de Ronda and the Alpujarras. In the area of Jaén, for example, numerous guerrilla bands operated in the Sierra de Segura and the Sierra de Cazorla of which the most notable appear to have been those led by Pedro de Alcalde, Juan Uribe and Bernardo Márquez. Finally, just to complete the story, later conquests – Asturias, for example, and Valencia – all produced *cabecillas* of their own, of which the most noted were Jaime Alfonso ('El Barbudo') and Agustín Nebot ('El Fraile') both of whom were to be active in southern parts of the Levante in 1812–13, whilst it should be noted, too, that resistance in areas with a long history of occupation did not just remain static. Thus, in Navarre, the capture of 'El Mozo' by the French was followed by the emergence of an even more effective commander in the person of his distant relative, Francisco Espoz Ilundaín, the latter being better known as Francisco Espoz y Mina, a *nom de guerre* that he took in an effort to associate himself with the triumphs of his predecessor. Equally 1810 saw the militias and scattered bands maintained by the Patriot junta that had managed to survive in the locality revivified by their amalgamation under the command of the retired army officer, José Joaquín Durán y Barazábal.

Wherever the French went, then, their presence provoked considerable irregular resistance. What, though, was the effect of *la guerrilla* on the war? First, and most obviously, it was beyond doubt the chief factor in the reputation for savagery which has ever since characterised the struggle. Hundreds of men were brought before the various tribunals established by the French and sentenced to death: between May 1809 and June 1812 Valladolid saw fifty-two death sentences for 'brigandage', whilst 1811 saw another twenty-two in Jaén alone. Such formal proceedings were but the tip of the iceberg, however, the memoirs of French soldiers being littered with accounts of wayside shootings and hangings, whilst there were plenty of

French commanders who executed prisoners and hostages without trial (to take just one example, General Kellermann became known as the 'hangman of Valladolid'). In October 1809, for example, there were at least eighteen such executions in Pamplona, two other mass shootings in July 1811, and December 1812 accounting for another seventy-eight. In Galvana in the province of Palencia thirty-two 'brigands' were hanged in April 1809, whilst in Olite July 1811 saw the execution of eight men whose sons were reputed to be with Espoz y Mina. And it was not just those taken in arms or their families who suffered: in January 1809 Chinchón witnessed the execution of a hundred people chosen at random in reprisal for the murder of two or three French soldiers. To all this, the guerrillas responded in kind. Tales of wholesale torture are probably exaggerated, though Elzéar Blaze complains that a friend 'was buried . . . in the ground, all but his head, which served the savages as a mark at bowls'.[13] But, even so, things were bad enough. As Bell wrote:

Great ferocity existed . . . amongst the guerrilla chiefs . . . The curate Merino . . . was revolting in cruelty: he took some hundred French prisoners on one occasion and hanged fifty or sixty of them . . . in order to avenge the death of three of his men.[14]

Moving on, one has the impression of the generation of a see-saw struggle that neither side could win. Typical enough, perhaps, are the experiences of Bigarré as temporary governor of Aranjuez in 1811:

The guerrilla leaders, Morales and El Abuelo, were constantly making incursions in the vicinity . . . One extremely hot day, the sentries stationed at the Ocaña gate were taken by surprise, and these two chieftains . . . galloped down the street that led to the main square . . . shouting, 'Long live Fernando VII!', followed by 500 of their men. Warned of what was going on by one of the sentries, I jumped on my horse, and . . . charged them with such impetuosity that they took flight, galloped out of the gate, and dispersed in the countryside . . . Seeing that [El Abuelo] was only a short distance ahead of us, I rode out to get him followed by my aides-de-camp and about twenty chasseurs . . . With my horse at top speed, I suddenly found myself faced by a canal eighteen feet wide. This I attempted to leap, but my horse was not good enough to make such a jump, and I was thrown right into the middle, along with my aides-de-camp and four of the light horsemen . . . I felt the effects of the fall for some months, but I was not going to let El Abuelo . . . get away with it . . . On 6 June I heard from one of [my spies] . . . that El Abuelo and his guerrillas were going to spend the . . . night of the seventh at Uclés . . . At a quarter to ten, 400 infantry . . . and twenty-five light horse . . . arrived outside the town . . . Charging into the town, they met no resistance . . . Having been shown the house where El Abuelo stayed whenever he spent the night at Uclés, I ordered it to be surrounded . . . Several shots were fired at us . . . but in the same instant the doors were forced by some *voltigeurs* . . . Rushing inside, they killed four guerrillas . . . but El Abuelo, who had been in bed with his wife, saved himself by scrambling out of an attic window . . . in his nightshirt, and jumping down into the garden. Although more than twenty shots were fired at him, he then managed to gain the safety of the open country.[15]

In fact, however, by dint of bitter fighting and much hard marching, it *was* possible to subdue the *partidas*. By early 1810, for example, Suchet had captured such guerrilla strongholds as Benasque, Nuestra Señora de la Aguila and Nuestra Señora del Tremedal, won a series of skirmishes, laid waste a number of districts particularly noted for their support of the guerrillas, sacked, amongst other places, Calatayud and Saliente, and carried out many executions. The troops endured heavy casualties and were worn out by the endless marching and counter-marching, whilst final success remained dependent both on protecting the conquered territories with adequate garrisons and clearing Navarre, La Mancha or Catalonia as well. Yet the achievement is still worthy of note: for the next two years Aragón remained quieter than many other provinces.

Given sufficient time and sufficient troops, then, the French could restore order in the occupied territories. All the more is this the case because there was a gradual change in the nature of *la guerrilla*. Throughout Spain, in the early days of occupation the *partidas* for the most part consisted of small groups of men who dispersed to their own homes after each operation and were bound together only by the most informal links. This was never wholly the case: we find, for example, that the Aragonese band of Felipe Perena, active from January 1809, was in fact a unit of infantry raised in May 1808 entitled the Segundo Regimiento de Voluntarios de Huesca that had been serving as the garrison of Huesca, and, further, that Perena himself was a regular officer who had spent the period since 1795 hunting down bandits in the region and had been appointed governor of the city by José Palafox.* But even such bands as fitted the stereotype could not long maintain it. Both Martín Javier Mina and El Empecinado, for example, are supposed to have started with twelve men. Backed by followings of this sort, they could indeed live and fight amongst the populace. Once the twelve men had become several hundred, though, this clearly became impossible, the guerrilla bands tending to assume a semi-permanent status and live *off* the populace.

---

* Also worth noting here is the fate of Perena's men. Active throughout 1809 and into 1810, the band disappeared following the capture of its chief base of Lérida in May of the latter year.

According to the traditional view, this ought to have posed no problems, but in fact the people as a whole were for the most part not interested in fighting, as witness, for example, the picture presented by the Condado de Niebla at the moment of its occupation early in 1810:

All energy and patriotism was gone. The egoism of many landowners . . . the fear and ignorance of the mass of the people, and the sagacity of the enemy, who had been both buying the hearts of the rich and . . . terrifying the spirits of the poor, ensured that many *pueblos* submitted to the yoke of *el rey intruso*. As for those places that remained free, they suffered from the same egoism, their justices acting in an arbitrary manner that did not recognise . . . any other law than that of their caprice . . . From this it followed that in every *pueblo* many stragglers and deserters were hidden without either the justices or, much less, their parents . . . making any attempt to get them to return to their regiments.[16]

For an authentic view from the *populacho*, meanwhile, we can do no better than turn to the memoirs of Gregorio González Arranz, a peasant from Roa, who had just turned twenty when the war began and had been managing the family farm following the death of his father the previous year. Thus:

In the course of 1811 the guerrillas . . . of General Jerónimo Merino and . . . El Empecinado caused my mother many worries by continually trying to force me to take up arms and fight against the usurpation. I was having to bear the full weight of our small holding, as my mother was not accustomed to go out of the house except . . . to go to church, whilst her other children, my sisters, were only little girls. Although we repeatedly made great financial sacrifices to secure my exemption, the pressure did not cease, and so my mother advised me to get married. On 6 February 1811 I therefore wed María Berdón Altable.[17]

To get information, supplies and reinforcements, then, the guerrillas had increasingly to resort to violence, whilst the tendency was increased still further, as we shall see, by the dubious nature of many of their leaders, not to mention their general wastefulness and lack of system.

So general is the picture of the brutality and oppression associated with the guerrillas that it is impossible to deny it. From all sides the story is the same. To quote Heinrich von Brandt, for example:

The guerrillas cared even less about their compatriots than we did and certain chiefs held sway over the countryside by terror alone. When they intercepted requisitioned cattle, it was in order to confiscate them for their own profit. When they themselves requisitioned something it was usually upon pain of death.[18]

If Brandt is deemed suspect as a representative of the imperial forces, then let us take Augustus von Schaumann, a fellow German serving as a commissary in Wellington's army. Thus, speaking of the forces of Julián Sánchez – of whom the British officer, William Bragge, wrote that he had never seen 'a more verminous looking set of fellows'[19] – he remarked:

They were very much feared. No Spanish municipal authority would have dared to refuse them anything. Even the inhabitants of small towns submitted to their orders without complaining. Let me give just one example of this. One of my muleteers had a young and extraordinarily pretty girl with him . . . One afternoon . . . a guerrilla dashing past, suddenly halted and . . . peremptorily commanded her to jump up behind him on the horse's back and galloped away with her. The parted couple did not dare to protest against this treatment by even one syllable of complaint![20]

Turning to Spanish sources, we find complaint after complaint. Let us quote, for example, the Marqués de la Romana on the subject of Juan Díaz Porlier, whom a British liaison officer described as 'a vain boy not above eighteen . . . who is at best but chief of a band of robbers who can by no means be said to be under his command or . . . ever be induced to make an attack on any force capable of resistance'.[21]

The complaints against Don Juan Porlier with regard to the misuse of the powers that he claims to have been conceded him have been so repeated that I consider it of absolute necessity that Your Excellency . . . make him understand how reprehensible his conduct is, and that . . . true patriots should only occupy themselves in offending the enemy.[22]

Lower down the ranks, we have Luis de Villaba, an artillery officer who served in the siege of Zaragoza. Thus:

The guerrillas who go by the name of Patriots should be exterminated: they are gangs of thieves with *carte blanche* to rob on the roads and in the villages. If some of them have brought benefits, the damage that others have wrought is one thousand times greater . . . Those who believe these bands . . . to be very useful are many, but if they meditate on the desertion from the enemy that has not occurred for fear of being murdered . . . the burnings and other disasters suffered by the villages . . . the many highwaymen and bandits who carry out their crimes under this pretext, and finally the manner in which their disorder and independence has caused all kinds of evil, they will understand how far the disadvantages outweigh the benefits.[23]

As regular officers, La Romana and Villalba might be expected to disapprove of irregular forces. However, their opinions were also shared by the civil authorities. In the words of the Junta of Najera, for example, 'All [the guerrillas] wish to be independent commanders, and to dispose of the effects of the nation, and, still worse, the municipalities and the citizenry, as sovereigns, whilst they frequently make use of the infamous word "traitor" to satisfy their greed.'[24] Still more explicit is the report of Manuel Loynaz, a government commissioner sent to Navarre by the Junta Central in June 1809:

Who would believe that, in addition to the continual vexations that they experience at the hands of the French, these loyal . . . vassals of Your Majesty are experiencing others just as bad at the hands of Spaniards in the form of the so-called guerrilla bands that have been infesting this unfortunate kingdom, along with the neighbouring districts of Castile? The disorder which these men commit is such that it is impossible to portray it without feeling a sense of horror. The least they do is to demand exhorbitant rations . . . They all ride about on the horses which they have stolen from unfortunate peasants who need them for their labours. As I myself have experienced, no respectable citizen can ride from one *pueblo* to another without being robbed . . . Almost all the leaders . . . are men long known for their misconduct . . . and the consequence is that they wage war on the richest pockets.[25]

The result of all this was a vicious circle of alienation that played straight into the hands of the French. To quote Suchet:

The Aragonese . . . felt a growing affection for the . . . troops . . . 'Los nuestros' they always said when speaking of us . . . They considered our steady and regular occupation as a means of escaping the frequent inroads of Mina and Villacampa, which, from the very circumstances of their being transitory, were attended with disorder and only left evil consequences behind them without being productive of any salutary result.[26]

This, doubtless, is over-congratulatory, but, even so, by the winter of 1809 Villacampa was complaining that he was 'unable to supply the troops . . . because the inhabitants abandon their homes the moment they have news of our arrival'.[27]

What is beyond doubt, meanwhile, is that the guerrillas' best efforts were not enough to halt the march of French occupation. The latter was slowed down, certainly – so busy did the Aragonese and Navarrese guerrillas keep Suchet in the summer and autumn of 1809 that the march on Valencia which was supposed to follow the fall of Zaragoza had to be postponed until the following year, and even then was undertaken with so few troops that it had to be abandoned. Yet, for all that, no territory could be claimed to have been liberated by partisans alone: lacking artillery, the *partidas* could not batter down the walls or gates of the fortresses improvised from old castles or monasteries into which French garrisons withdrew when they were in trouble (when, that is, they did not enjoy the protection of city walls or Vauban-style bastions), and were rarely granted the time necessary to reduce a target through starvation. And, at the same time, the French still made significant gains, defeating the Spanish field armies, taking Gerona and occupying the whole of Andalucía.

Such was the obvious truth of this point that, despite much propagandist cant, a clear realisation emerged that it was futile to trust to the guerrillas for Spain's salvation. Let us take as an example a pamphlet that was published in Cadíz in 1810:

As a method of waging war, popular insurrection is almost always . . . far more costly than the use of regular forces. When protected by a regular army, at the right moment the former can reinforce the latter, but otherwise the only result is momentary success avenged later with great sacrifice . . . Is it still doubted that the kingdom is lost if we do not raise large armies? Let us suppose that Spain becomes the tomb of twenty thousand French soldiers every year . . . Napoleon has necessarily to subjugate Spain or lose his reputation . . . and, now that the north [i.e. Austria] is quiet . . . it is not difficult for him to send . . . 100,000.[28]

Nor was this an end to the argument:

It is held . . . that our arms cannot match those of the enemy when both sides are fighting in large forces. From here stems the foolish idea that instead of increasing our armies, we should rely solely on the use of *partidas* and the defence of towns [by the inhabitants] when the war that we are waging on the contrary demands large armies that are capable of imposing themselves on the enemy . . . It is true that Madrid was defended heroically by its own people, that La Mancha has devoured many Frenchmen without the aid of any troops, and that the enemy was expelled from Galicia by the peasantry alone. Nevertheless, Madrid is occupied by the enemy and La Mancha in reality controlled by them, whilst Galicia would also fall into their hands if there was not a large army to protect it. Little by little the French extend their dominions whilst we celebrate a riot in some village or an attack by some guerrilla band.[29]

In view of the fact that he was the commander of the much vaunted forces of the Serranía de Ronda, the ideas of José Serrano Valdenebro in this respect are still more interesting. Thus:

Although war is being waged in these mountains in the style of Viriato,* flattering results cannot be expected ... A band of patriots situated in mountains that are almost inaccessible will hold off the bravest soldiers. However, should the latter fall back to more accessible terrain, the picture changes ... The peasant wages a petty war ... How can this man fight in a terrain where infantry can press upon him or cavalry ride him down? Furthermore, the peasants are ... little more than unmanageable. There is neither union nor regularity ... in their movements. This is not surprising: amongst troops who have not been fashioned by the strictest discipline, they cannot be achieved ... Valiant in skirmishing, they do not understand that shock action is the chief weapon on the battlefield ... Whilst troops do not realise that battles are won by the sword and bayonet, all is lost. Fire is only a chimera ... Advancing on the enemy with union and bravery ... is what brings victory.[30]

Such doubts were also shared by many British observers. To quote Sir Thomas Graham:

There are points where it is of infinite consequence ... that there should be armies, for, useful and important as ... the guerrillas are, that is not enough, let them be ever so much spread over the face of the country. They can never stop the march of a considerable body of the enemy.[31]

The guerrillas, then, were neither invulnerable to defeat nor in themselves sufficient to save Spain. Still worse, however, in a number of ways they sapped the ability of unoccupied Spain to defend itself. Eager to expand their forces, guerrilla leaders kidnapped parties of regular troops, seized horses that might otherwise have mounted much-needed cavalry units, and hijacked men who had been raised for the army by the *quinta*. Meanwhile, aided and abetted by press and propaganda alike, they much exaggerated their exploits – in Wellington's army 'to lie like a guerrilla' was a common-place remark – with the result that the increasingly desperate position of the Spanish armies was to some extent hidden from view, thereby providing unwilling local authorities with a splendid pretext for failing to enforce conscription. But, above all, the mere existence of the guerrillas encouraged desertion. Strongly influenced by traditional fears of military service and forced into the ranks by ballots characterised by corruption and injustice, the soldiery soon found that life in the army confirmed their worst sus-picions. Not only were food, clothing and pay all in short supply, but disease was rampant and casualties heavy. By contrast, the guerrillas, whose praise

---

* A reference to the leader of the guerrilla war waged by the Iberians against the Roman empire.

the Patriot press was singing ever more loudly, offered multiple advantages, including freer discipline, a better chance of survival, greater rewards and, perhaps above all, the chance to remain in the *patria chica*. With desertion easy – many Spanish soldiers had to wear at least some items of civilian clothing, whilst both march and camp discipline were notoriously lax – we therefore continually come across such figures as Josep Bosoms, a Catalan infantryman turned bandit who escaped from jail to become a guerrilla, and José Fombella, an Asturian cavalryman who established himself at the head of a group of fellow deserters in the Cantabrian mountains. Nor were such cases isolated, every defeat seeing hundreds of men scattering into the hills to join existing bands or form new ones of their own. Amongst the leaders we have mentioned alone, indeed, Amor, Príncipe and Espoz y Mina were all deserters. As the British diplomat, Thomas Sydenham, put it, the *partidas* therefore 'prevented the recruiting of the regular armies, for every Spanish peasant would naturally prefer rioting and plunder and living in free quarters with the guerrillas to being drilled and starved in the regular army'.[32]

It will, of course, be objected by admirers of the guerrillas that true examples of the *genre* did not engage in 'rioting and plunder'. Such arguments are not helpful, however. Thus, even leaders who seem to have been genuinely altruistic in their motives attracted followers of baser intent. Equally, to pretend that *partidas*, commanded by men who quickly revealed themselves to be bent on nothing more than plunder and personal aggrandisement, were not guerrillas when they regularly attacked the French and their collaborators is completely unsatisfactory. French-style accusations that none of the guerrillas were anything more than brigands go too far, but even so the association of *partidas* and plunder was strong enough to become proverbial, '¡Viva Fernando y vamos robando!' ('Long live Fernando and let's go robbing!') becoming something of a catch-phrase. The question is one to which we must return, but for the time being let us simply note the ambiguity inherent in the figure of a *cabecilla* named Vitoriano Díez encountered by Elzéar Blaze. Nicknamed 'Chagarito', he cut a sinister figure:

This chief ... after making war upon the French, turned his arms against the Spaniards in his leisure moments in order to keep his hand in. He had struck such terror into Castile that the Spaniards had joined the French to endeavour to take him. Betrayed by one of his men, he was seized in a *venta* ... A few days afterwards he suffered the most horrible of deaths ... but this example did not deter other brigands from pursuing the same course.[33]

To argue, then, that the guerrillas were at the very least a mixed blessing is therefore sensible enough even if it is going too far to maintain that they inflicted more damage on the Allies than they did on the French (the very circumspect opinion of Thomas Sydenham was that 'the guerrillas did as much mischief to the country as they did to the French, but, in as much as they certainly did considerable damage to the enemy, they were on the whole useful to the common cause'[34]). From the very beginning, indeed, both juntas and generals did everything that they could to encourage the formation of partisan bands. In June 1808, for example, no less a figure than the highly conservative Gregorio García de la Cuesta sent an officer named Manuel García del Barrío to raise the upper Pisuerga valley in revolt; in July José Palafox sent two agents to do the same in Navarre; and in December the Marqués de la Romana attempted to stir up resistance amongst the inhabitants of Galicia and León, one of his staff officers even producing a manual of guerrilla warfare, notable though this was more for its enthusiasm than its practicality (one of its suggestions was for a wheeled *cheval de frise* that could be propelled into action by galloping horses in the style of an equine bulldozer!). Not to be undone was the Junta Central, which, as we have seen, issued commissions to large numbers of petitioners who wanted to raise guerrilla bands and encouraged enlistment in their ranks by means of the decree of the *corso terrestre*.

From this it follows that the guerrillas as a whole always had much closer connections with the military and civil authorities than has generally been suggested. Who, however, were the guerrillas, and why did they spring to arms? Though some chieftains have come down to us as mere names, of others we know a great deal. Francisco Espoz y Mina, Juan Martín Díez ('El Empecinado'), Julián Sánchez ('El Charro'), and Francisco Aznar Moreno were peasants; Francisco Abad Moreno ('Chaleco') and Antonio Jaureguí ('El Pastor') shepherds; Ignacio Gómez a retired sergeant; Toribio Bustamente ('Caracol'), a postal courier; Francisco Longa a blacksmith; Antonio Pedrazuela an unemployed actor; and Antonio Piloti a gunsmith. Jerónimo Merino, Lucas Rafael, Antonio Marañón ('El Trapense'), Ramón Argote, Antonio Jiménez, Policarpo Romeo, Antonio Temprano – a rogue figure chiefly interested in pillage – José Pinilla, Juan de Tapía, Jácobo Alvarez, Francisco Salazar, Juan Délica, Juan Mendieta ('El Capuchino'), and Agustín Nebot ('El Fraile') were all priests or ecclesiastics. José Serrano Valdenebro was an ageing naval officer known for his writings on the art of war caught by the French conquest of Andalucía on his estates at Cortes de la Frontera, whilst other men of property who became *cabecillas* include the *labradores*, Cámilo Gómez and Miguel Sarasa, and the Aragonese textile manufacturer, Fidel Mallén, in which connection we should also mention such representatives of the professional classes as Isidoro Mir, José Martínez de San Martín and Alfonso Marzo y Torres. Martín Javier Mina ('El Mozo') and Juan Palarea ('El Médico') were both students. Amor, Príncipe and Fombella were deserters of dubious intent. Pedro Juanez, Mariano de Renovales, Saturnino Abuín ('El Manco'), Anselmo Alegre ('El Cantarero'), Ignacio Alonso ('Cuevillas'), Díez, Bosoms, Saornil, and the future Valencian leader, Jaime Alfonso ('El Barbudo'), were all bandits or smugglers (though Renovales had succeeded in obtaining the rank of brigadier from Palafox and began his career as a partisan after escaping from a convoy of prisoners being sent to France). Finally, Manuel Jiménez Guazo and Juan Manuel de Soria were officials, and Pedro Villacampa, Felipe Perena, Juan Díaz Porlier ('El Marquesito'), José Joaquín Durán, Pedro Lamota, Juan López Campillo, and Antonio Cuesta, all serving or retired army, navy or *resguardo* officers.

This wide variety of social background encompassed a wide range of motives. Setting aside a handful of mavericks who were eager to escape the cloister or influenced by liberal views, the dozens of ecclesiastics who headed guerrilla bands may be assumed to have seen the war in terms of the defence of the Church and the traditional order (it is notable, for example, that Merino ended his days as a Carlist, although, with a brother who was a bandit, it is clear that he also had links with the world of crime). For many of the representatives of the propertied classes, too, the issue may be assumed to have been at root an ideological one, although one in this instance dominated more by concern for the privileges of the nobility. Much the same applies to many of the army officers, although here other pressures – desire for promotion or the orders of superiors – could also have been involved. Beyond the established oligarchy, however, the situation is less clear. There are many stories of rape or murder leading to a desire for revenge (as is, in fact, the case with such figures as Jerónimo Merino, Lucas Rafael and Cámilo Gómez as well), whilst traditional accounts have always made much of patriotism and love of Fernando VII. The existence of such factors is impossible to prove or disprove, but in view of the widespread disaffection which we have already noted the influence of *dios, rey y patria* must at the very least be doubted. Leadership of a guerrilla band could bring enormous gains – in 1808 a younger son of an extended peasant household with few prospects, by the end of the war Espoz y Mina was a *mariscal de campo* with hopes of gaining the viceroyalty of Navarre* – and it is therefore

---

* Espoz y Mina's rank has been the subject of much confusion among anglophone historians. The literal translation of *mariscal de campo* is 'marshal of the field', but this did not equate to 'field marshal'. In the Spanish service the equivalent of field marshal was *capitán general*. *Mariscal de campo* ranking two steps below this, the correct translation is therefore major-general.

impossible not to suspect, say, the two Minas of being nothing more than adventurers. In the cases of Pedrazuela and Piloti, meanwhile, the evidence is even clearer: the former was eventually executed by the Spanish military after engaging in a reign of terror in the Montes de Toledo which cost the lives of at least sixty innocent civilians, and the latter revealed as a fraud. As for the plethora of bandits and deserters, to believe in stories of their patriotism stretches credulity to the extreme. In the circumstances of 1808 violence and extortion could very easily be garbed in a cloak of patriotism, and thus it was that many bandits simply continued in their old ways in the guise of freedom-fighters. In one or two cases, indeed, the uprising came as a godsend: in Málaga, for example, one enterprising chieftain whose band had just been imprisoned by the authorities hatched a daring plot to rescue his followers by petitioning the Junta Central for permission to recruit a guerrilla band from imprisoned bandits and smugglers as the men most accustomed to irregular warfare. Entirely happy to prey on the French (so long, of course, as the targets were suitably 'soft'), they in practice had no allegiance to either side, and were in fact frequently recruited by the invaders as spies or counter-guerrillas, a good example here being Saturnino Abuín, a bandit who for some time served under El Empecinado before falling out with him and going over to the French. En route from Ronda to Málaga, indeed, Joseph personally secured the services of a noted local smuggler named López.

So much for the leadership, but what of the rank and file? A substantial force – according to a press report that circulated very widely at the end of 1812, at that point the 20 most important *partidas* numbered no fewer than 38,500 men – the bulk of those involved came from humbler elements of the rural populace. Of one group of nineteen captured *vallesoletano* guerrillas, for example, seven were peasants, three shepherds, two barbers, one a shoemaker, one a butcher and one a tailor. Equally, of fifteen volunteers from the valley of Echauri, fourteen were peasants. As for the remainder, aside from a smattering of students, clerks, shopkeepers and taverners, most seem to have been ecclesiastics, there even being a few bands known as *cruzadas* whose ranks were entirely composed of monks and friars.

Why, though, did these men fight? The traditional view, of course, is that they rushed to take up arms in defence of *dios, rey y patria* – in short, that they were engaged in an ideological struggle – but, setting aside the ecclesiastics, only in such exceptional cases as the district of northern Navarre known as La Montaña is there any evidence that this was the case. In this area, the rural populace was relatively prosperous with the vast majority of households not only owning their own land but possessing holdings of a size that was sufficient for their own needs. Even those who rented land were for a variety of reasons assured of dues that were as low as they were stable. Thanks to the mild climate, steady rainfall and use of appropriate techniques that were well within the capacities of even the humblest households, productivity was high as well, whilst both the cost of living and taxation were much lower than elsewhere. Social tensions were also low – differences in wealth between neighbours were rarely noticeable and municipal government organised on an extremely democratic basis – and *señorialismo* hardly an issue at all: very few villages in the Montaña had to pay feudal dues and *mayorazgos* were hardly to be found, whilst in some districts as much as eighty per cent of the population could claim noble status. Last but not least, relations with the Church were excellent: almost no land was in ecclesiastical hands, there were few monasteries or convents, the district was free of the clerks in minor orders and the like who were such a parasitical presence elsewhere, and parish priests lived in close proximity to their flock, came from the same stock and existed in sufficient numbers to minister to their congregations on a regular and effective basis. In such areas, defence of the traditional order made perfect sense, whilst agriculture was organised in such a way that production could continue even if the bulk of the men were away, the terrain of the district perfect for irregular warfare, and the people accustomed to the idea of fighting invaders as irregular *miqueletes*. Given the rapacity and violence of the French forces, the anti-clericalism of the *josefino* régime, the economic disruption caused by the transfer of Spain's customs frontier to the Pyrenees – thousands of the inhabitants of the Montaña either marketed produce in France or were engaged in the wholesale smuggling of French imports to the rest of Spain – it is therefore hardly surprising that participation in the guerrillas was widespread.

Elsewhere, however, it is a rather different story. Even in Navarre there were strong regional differences. The south of the province lies in the Ebro valley – the Ribera – and is in many respects a complete contrast to the Montaña. Rather than dispersed as in farmsteads of the north, the populace were concentrated in large 'agro-towns' such as Corella and Tudela, of which most were *señorios* of either the Church or the upper nobility. Peasant proprietorship was unknown and even tenant farming scarce and more precarious, the bulk of the inhabitants being dependent on day labour. Municipal government was in the hands of closed oligarchies drawn from the propertied classes, whilst the towns were filled with numerous clerks in minor orders and other ecclesiastics who seemed to do little to earn their privileged position, and dominated by numerous religious houses that owned much land. Parishes, too, were much bigger than those of the Montaña with the result that the Church was far less able to reach out to the populace through the medium of pastoral care. With patterns of labour much less compatible with periods of absence – in the Montaña much cultivation was carried out jointly by the extended family or even the entire community, whilst women were able to take over much of the work – it is therefore hardly surprising that the Ribera produced far fewer recruits for *la guerrilla* than did the regions further north.

Whatever their state, the populace often had good reason to hate the French. For a classic instance of the supposed result, we have only to turn to the memoirs of Joseph Sherer:

In a village about three leagues from Pamplona . . . I met with a very fine man, a native of Aragón and a guerrilla . . . I asked him where he lived and under whom he served. 'Señor,' said he, 'I have no home, no relations, nothing save my country and my sword. My father was led out and shot in the market place of my native village; our cottage was burned; my mother died of grief; and my wife, who had been violated by the enemy, fled to me, then a volunteer with Palafox, and died in my arms in a hospital in Zaragoza. I serve under no particular chief: I am too miserable, I feel too revengeful to support the restraint of discipline and the delay of manoeuvre . . . But I have sworn never to dress a vine or plough a field till the enemy is driven out of Spain.'[35]

Yet despite such evidence, it is clear that only in relatively small parts of northern Spain can the guerrilla struggle be said to fit the normal stereotype. On the other hand, hatred of the French and devotion to *dios, rey y patria* were by no means the only reason to join the *partidas*. For example, Próspero Marco, who enlisted in Merino's band, wanted to avenge himself on a local landowner who had tried to eliminate him as a rival for the hand of a particular girl by having him arrested by the French, and El Empecinado's sometime lieutenant, Abuín, was a murderer on the run from justice. Equally, of the group of nineteen guerrillas from the Valladolid area mentioned above, no fewer than ten were deserters, whilst at Horcajo de los Montes an agent of the Junta Central named José Crivell formed a band of sharpshooters by the simple means of threatening to march any man who refused to enlist off to the nearest headquarters (at nearby Navahermosa, however, Crivell was less fortunate, the population rising in revolt rather than submit to his demands). Rather less ambiguous, perhaps, was the action of the many prisoners of war who gave their guards the slip and found refuge with the nearest *partida*, but even so there is no firm evidence that such fugitives were motivated by anything other than opportunism.

Finally, also in flight, except in the opposite direction, were the assorted Italian, German and Polish deserters who ended up with such bands as that of Espoz y Mina.

If service with the guerrillas was frequently purely a means of escaping worse alternatives, it was also very often the fruit of economic necessity. Not only was the burden of French requisitioning and taxation extremely heavy, but the populace were already for the most part poverty-stricken, and the propertied classes only too eager to save themselves at the expense of the poor (French levies were, for example, frequently funded by imposing extra taxes on basic foodstuffs). As a further means of raising money, meanwhile, many municipalities sold off considerable amounts of common land, thereby depriving many of the humbler elements of the community of firewood, pasturage, food and raw materials (chestnuts and wild asparagus came from the commons as did the esparto grass used in such activities as basket-weaving). As most municipalities had also rented out parts of the common land in small parcels at reasonable rents, there also disappeared many vital tenancies. In such places as the Montaña where the land involved was sold off in small parcels, this policy was softened in its effects, but all too often it went in large units, the result being that the oligarchy consolidated their control of the local economy still further. A good example is Guipúzcoa where a study of 9 *pueblos* has shown that 14 per cent of the 1,458 purchasers got 71 per cent of the land (and, still worse, that a mere 12 purchasers took almost one-fifth of the property involved). Thanks to the requisition of so many draught animals and carts by the contending armies, in many areas agricultural activity seems virtually to have come to a standstill, whilst nature was no more kind to Spain in the period 1808–1814 than she had been in the years before the war. Thus, the harvest of 1811 was particularly disastrous, the result being that wheat prices shot up dramatically (in Burgos, for example, wheat rose from 80 reales the *fanega* in June 1811 to 244 by the close of the year). Yet the populace were in no condition to respond to the crisis. With the French imposing strict limits on movement and clamping down on many traditional aspects of street life, opportunities to find alternative sources of income were limited, and all the more so as industry was at a standstill and many *señores* unable to pay their existing retainers and domestic servants, let alone take on fresh hands. In short, hunger and despair reigned on all sides.

Let us quote, for example, Carnicero's account of life in Madrid:

There were so many unfortunates in the streets . . . that it was impossible to move along them without the stoniest heart being wrung and saddened . . . Some people could be heard complaining that it was three o'clock in the afternoon and they had still not broken their fast; others had death clearly written in their faces; others were fainting from want; and still others had just breathed their last . . . At one spot there was a group . . . of children abandoned by their parents crying and begging for bread; at another there was a number of tearful widows surrounded by their little ones; a little further some young girls assuring passersby that they were begging so as not to prostitute themselves; on this corner a few priests humbly asking for alms, and on the next persons of the highest character . . . doing exactly the same. So many were the poor . . . that however much they wandered the streets . . . they could not get enough to see them through the day . . . Going back to their homes . . . they therefore quietly . . . lay down to die.[36]

Faced by such a situation, for many young men the guerrillas offered an attractive alternative, and all the more so given the decree of the *corso terrestre* of 25 February 1809. Thus, Matías Calvo – a deserter who had fled the second siege of Zaragoza – joined the forces of Espoz y Mina when the death of his father pushed his family over the edge, whilst one of Merino's earliest collaborators was Julián Pablos, an erstwhile member of Godoy's bodyguard who had been living in poverty in his home town of Lerma ever since the dissolution of his regiment at Aranjuez. With the guerrillas also engaging in forced requisitioning, banditry – always an escape for the poor – had now been legitimised, whilst the war against the *afrancesados* meant that plenty of pretexts could be found to settle scores with the *pudientes*; hence the scenes witnessed when Ronda was briefly occupied by the *serranos* in March 1810:

The very day . . . we left Ronda, the mountaineers entered it . . . shouting with joy and discharging their pieces exultingly in the streets. The inhabitants of each village arrived together, marching without order, and . . . loaded their asses with whatever they found . . . till the poor beasts were ready to sink under the weight of the booty . . . The prisons were forced, and the . . . criminals they contained ran instantly to take revenge on their judges and accusers. Debtors obtained receipts from their creditors by forcible means, and all the public papers were burned in order to annul the mortgages that the inhabitants of the town had upon the . . . mountaineers.[37]

The evidence that the leitmotiv of the rank and file of the guerrilla movement was plunder rather than patriotism is overwhelming. British soldiers, for example, often found themselves under attack, O'Neil complaining that the guerrillas 'often fell upon and murdered our men if they strayed from the ranks', and even going so far as to say that 'they were almost as great a terror to us as to our foes'.[38] Even if such events as the fight O'Neil describes between himself and a guerrilla sporting a musket and a pack that had once belonged to a British rifleman are put down to attempts on the part of civilians to defend their property, in Navarre Espoz y Mina suppressed a number of bands who had been oppressing the populace, whilst he famously complained to a friend that he was terrified of his men and feared that they were capable of stabbing him to death at any moment. In view of the sack of Ronda, also interesting is Francisco Ballesteros' account of what he found when he took over command in Algeciras in 1812:

The commander of the *cruzada*, his guerrilla band, and all the others that infested the region were one of the objects that called for my consideration. They had lent many services, but the *pueblos* . . . were loudly complaining of their excesses and vexations. I examined the truth of their expositions with my own eyes. The commander of the *cruzada* might have been a man noteworthy for his patriotism, but his disposition did not appear to me to be one suitable for a guerrilla. As for the *partidas* . . . I became convinced that they were . . . prejudicial to the nation, and did not hesitate a moment in ordering their disbandment.[39]

Just as interesting is the response of many guerrillas to the attempts at militarisation that we shall discuss below, the response of rank and file often being desertion, mutiny or other forms of resistance.

To all this there can be opposed many qualifications. For example, it is clear enough that the many bands that were operating with the sanction of the appropriate civil or military authorities ought to be distinguished from the many gangs of freebooters that roved the countryside entirely on their own account. Operating without any check at all, indeed, it was doubtless the latter who should be held accountable for many crimes. Still worse, perhaps, were the large gangs of deserters that preyed on all sides indiscriminately. Travelling to Madrid with his family, for example, a leading *josefino* official from Palencia was held up and robbed by a gang of twenty French deserters, whilst in 1809 the village of Pajares de Adaja witnessed a group of Irish soldiers, who had fled Wellington's army, rob several houses and then murder the mayor and the parish priest. Yet, for all that we are a long way from the legend, and even the hope of plunder was not sufficient to bring in the recruits required, with many of the *partidas* in practice relying on compulsion. For example, on 30 August 1811 Longa visited Orduña with a force of cavalry and forced all the young men of the district to come away with him, whilst according to the founder of the Bank of Spain, Ramón Santillán, on 13 June 1809 Merino descended on Lerma and 'threatened to treat as traitors any young men who refused to join him immediately'.[40] Santillán was taken, but his neighbour, González Arranz, was more lucky:

Married though I now was, there was no escape. A party under the command of a brother of El Empecinado named Don Damaso Martín . . . carried me off with a number of other young men, both married and unmarried, to the town of Riaza, which was where El Empecinado was at that point. Such was the distress of my mother at my absence . . . that, leaving our house, she set off in pursuit, dragging my father-in-law along with her. Arriving at Riaza, she managed to secure my definitive exemption by means of a combination of pleading and bribery. My companions were less fortunate, for they were taken away . . . very few of them ever returning to their homes.[41]

González Arranz, it transpires, was doubly fortunate, the Aragonese *cabecilla*, Sarasa, supposedly executing twenty men of Ainsa who tried to prevent him from taking their sons. With many of the local juntas established in the occupied regions also doing their best to enforce the *quinta*, towns such as Ciudad Rodrigo therefore saw the arrival of streams of fugitives. Many of the *partidas* were in any case actually flying columns of regular troops such as those commanded by Pedro Villacampa, and there were even generals who became directly involved in *la guerrilla*, as witness, for example, La Romana's surprise attack on Villafranca del Vierzo in March 1809.

If, as is obvious, a large number of modifications have to be made to the traditional picture of the guerrillas, how should this affect our perception of their value to the Allied war effort? As we have seen, the *partidas* were incapable of preventing the French armies from occupying ever greater tracts of Spanish territory, let alone ejecting them from any that they had conquered, whilst their presence may well have accelerated the disintegration of regular resistance. This said, it can be argued that such was the state of the Spanish armies that Spain would have been certain to have been overrun anyway, the guerrillas at the very least serving to slow down the French advance, disrupt the consolidation of the *josefino* state, force the French to abandon their cloak of benevolence, keep alive the spirit of resistance, persuade the British that Spain was still worth fighting for, force Napoleon to pay a heavy price for intervention in the Peninsula, and save Wellington from being thrown into the sea. Such arguments cannot be entirely set aside, for the complexity of *la guerrilla* did not prevent it from causing the invaders immense difficulties. Subject to constant harassment, the imperial troops lost thousands of unnecessary casualties and found it hard to engage in both reconnaissance and foraging. Isolated garrisons were constantly being blockaded with the result that much time had to be wasted in rushing to their relief. Communication between different forces became extremely difficult to maintain, the isolated courier and his escort being an ideal target for the *partidas*. Convoys were forever being held up and ambushed, with the result, as with dispatches, that they had to travel under the protection of many hundreds of troops. Every square inch of conquered territory had to be physically garrisoned and still more men deployed in mobile columns to scour the hills and mountains for the guerrillas and destroy their bases. More and more replacements and reinforcements were required from France with the result that public confidence in the emperor was undermined, and yet the armies actually facing Wellington and the Spanish armies remained starved of men: organised in temporary 'march battalions', many of the new conscripts were sucked into the struggle to keep open the roads that led to the frontier, in which task they invariably suffered much heavier losses than would have been the case had it been possible to dispatch them directly to their units. The constant threat of retribution helped restrict collaboration with the *josefino* régime (in many areas *afrancesado* officials were regularly kidnapped and put to death). And, finally, the discipline and morale of the occupying forces were seriously damaged: in Jaca, for example, half the garrison appears to have deserted in a single month in 1809, whilst more than one observer spotted the graffito, 'This war in Spain means death for the men, ruin for the officers, and a fortune for the generals.'[42] At times, indeed, one comes across a sense of genuine despair. July 1810 saw one officer complain, 'I really cannot do this any more . . . Every wood, every mountain hides a band of insurgents, and in every town that has not been abandoned we have as many enemies as there remain inhabitants.'[43] But most graphic of all is a dispatch sent to Marshal Berthier by the French officer entrusted with Asturias after its reoccupation in 1810:

My situation calls for Your Highness' attention. The forces of the enemy are growing whilst their organization is gaining in consistency . . . Pablo has united Barcena and Porlier under his command . . . and is maintaining himself . . . on the Pigüeña. A number of small parties are operating in the area of Teverga and Quirós. The road from Oviedo to León is frequently attacked by Castañón. Escandón.is raiding my posts along the coast . . . The destruction of various bridges has made it very hard for the little help that I can send to arrive as promptly as it should, whilst matters are being made worse by the fact that all the little combats that are taking place are causing me dead and wounded. The action that has just taken place at Fresno cost me 160 combatants. Meanwhile, the number of sick is being augmented by the bad weather and the state of nakedness in which the soldiery finds itself . . . A spirit of discontent is growing and desertion has begun to make itself felt . . . The spirit of insurrection impedes all supply, for the inhabitants flee before our troops . . . I need at least 2,000 men, replacement officers and NCOs, and a shipment of powder, and for the rest will do the impossible.[44]

If more specific justification is required for the role played by the guerrillas in the first years of the war, it is only necessary to look at some of the events of the campaign. It was the irregular resistance springing up in the Sierra Morena that persuaded Dupont to halt his march before the battle of Bailén. It was a letter intercepted by Spanish guerrillas at Valdestillas that allowed Sir John Moore to launch the offensive of December 1808 in reasonable safety. It was the guerrillas of Old Castile who hid Soult's travails in Portugal from the eyes of Ney, Victor and Joseph, forced the French commanders to engage in full-scale military operations just to decide what they should do next, and persuaded them to evacuate Asturias almost as soon as they had conquered it. It was the guerrillas of Aragón who saved Valencia from invasion in 1809. And finally it was the capture of a secret message from Joseph to Soult by some guerrillas near Avila that saved Wellington from disaster in the aftermath of Talavera.

Clearly, then, the guerrillas played a major role in the campaigns that have been examined thus far. That said, though, it is difficult not to feel that the guerrilla movement's many peculiar characteristics were an obstacle in its operations. Love of booty, for example, could reduce attacks on the French to a farce: when the bands of Mina the younger and a noted smuggler named Ignacio Alonso joined forces for an attack on Tudela on 28 November 1809, the two groups ended up pillaging the town and then fighting one another over the spoils. Rivalry between different commanders meant that even this level of co-operation was not always forthcoming, whilst there were also endless disputes over the control of territory. So serious were they that the more unscrupulous *cabecillas* were not above murdering their rivals: one of the first steps that Espoz y Mina took in Navarre, for example, was to arrest and execute the head of another band named Pascual Echevarría. All too often the result was chaos. Nowhere was this problem worse than in the area south of the River Ebro centred on the modern-day provinces of Soria and Logroño where two royal commissioners, numerous local juntas and a multiplicity of guerrilla bands were all jockeying for position with one another by the autumn of 1809. As a memorial from Logroño complained:

The various juntas that control the province all regarding themselves as being equal, they all act as they see fit without agreeing any plan or system and in consequence frequently fall foul of each other. The result is mutual jealousy . . . and endless quarrelling . . . This evil has spread to the guerrillas, and it is unfortunately . . . the case that the important services which they have been rendering . . . have been marred by disputes . . . which have often ended up with the weaker band being disarmed.[45]

Meanwhile, the more irregular *partidas* could never be relied upon to harass the enemy on a consistent basis, just as many *cabecillas* found it impossible to prevent their men from coming and going more or less at will. As for doing any fighting, they could be all but useless. Thus:

I went on my way without incident as far as . . . Briviesca, but between that place and Burgos we saw twenty mounted Spaniards appear suddenly around a low hill. They fired several shots at us without effect; then my escort [of six *gendarmes*], my servant and I drew our swords, and went forward without deigning to reply to the enemy, who, judging from our resolute attitude that we were the kind of people to defend ourselves vigorously, went off in another direction . . . Between Palencia and Dueñas I fell in with an officer and twenty-five men of the Young Guard escorting a chest of money for the garrison at Valladolid. The . . . *guerrilleros* of the neighbour-hood were just attacking the detachment. On seeing my escort galloping up . . . they stopped short . . . But one of them . . . called out that no French troops were in sight, whereupon the brigands advanced boldly towards the tempting treasure wagon. I naturally took command and bade the officer of the guard not to fire until I gave the word. Most of the enemy had dismounted . . . and . . . many had only pistols. I had placed my infantry behind the wagon, and as soon as the Spaniards were within twenty paces I made them come out and gave the order to fire. This was obeyed with terrible precision: the leader . . . and a dozen of his men dropped. The rest bolted at full speed towards their horses.[46]

Nor is this surprising, the fact being that many so-called guerrillas really were nothing but brigands. Typical enough were the so-called *muchachos de Santibáñez*, a gang of bandits hailing from the district of Plasencia headed by Miguel Caletrión, Miguel Dosado and Antonio Serrano. Throughout their career, they pretended to be partisans, but in fact the majority of their victims, whom they regularly treated with the utmost cruelty, were shepherds, migrant labourers, muleteers and peasants.

The Patriot authorities were not unaware of these deficiencies, nor, still less, of the pillage on which many of the bands subsisted. From as early as December 1808, then, the Junta Central was issuing orders whose purpose was to impose a structure on the guerrillas whilst at the same time ensuring that every band was subordinated to the appropriate military authorities. Very soon, indeed, those wishing to organise a *partida* had to obtain the sanction of the Junta Central itself, one of the *comisarios regios* that it sent out to act as its representatives in the occupied provinces, a provincial junta, or the commander of the army based in the district in which the person concerned wished to operate. Muddled though the chain of command often remained, the result was that at least in theory a gap began to open up between those who were genuinely fighting the French and those who were simply bandits.

Though far from perfect – many *partidas* that regularised their positions continued to lead a distinctly chequered existence – this development was reinforced by the efforts that were made to form the guerrillas into regular units subject to military discipline. The advantages of this course of action were many: as regular soldiers dressed in uniform, the guerrillas would find it harder to abscond; as regular soldiers trained to fight in a formal fashion, they would be more effective than a mob of individuals; as regular soldiers subject to discipline, their excesses could be contained more easily; and as regular soldiers organised in units, they could supply themselves from the countryside in a far more efficient and less wasteful manner than could mere *partidas*. From as early as 1809, then, the civil and military authorities alike embarked on a policy of, quite literally, regimentation. Many of the irregulars' rank and file were bitterly opposed to this process, fearing that it would make them soldiers by the back door. Yet the guerrillas did not present a united front on this issue. On the contrary, their chiefs were frequently eager allies of the authorities. By forming their followers into regular commands, they could assure themselves of receiving the support of the government in arms, uniforms and supplies. Not only did this increase their military capabilities, but it also reinforced their prestige, a vital consideration given the *ad hoc* nature of their authority. At the same time, the introduction of military discipline provided them with a greater chance of quelling discontent amongst their followers, whilst, with disciplined troops at their command, they were more able to overawe rival leaders and to portray them as mere bandits. Possession of regular commissions could also offer an escape from the tutelage of local juntas – El Empecinado, for example, had a hard struggle to shake off the pretensions of the Junta of Guadalajara – whilst, at least until the reforms enacted by the *cortes* of Cádiz, it also brought entitlement to the numerous judicial and fiscal advantages conferred by membership of the officer corps. Finally, there was also the question of the inferiority complex evidently suffered by many guerrilla commanders of civilian origins *vis-à-vis* the often disdainful and supercilious officers of the regular army, in which respect the adoption of military norms also became a form of self-defence.

By the end of 1811 all the most famous bands had undergone the process of militarisation. However, the adoption of military forms brought with it unexpected drawbacks. As bands became more complex in their structure, so they presented the French with an easier target. To quote Heinrich von Brandt:

Rendered incapable by their great numbers to conceal themselves from a vigilant enemy and suddenly to disappear from him without giving battle as they had formally done, they were now frequently overtaken, surprised, defeated and dispersed.[47]

Nor was this an end to it. Militarised though they may have been, the guerrillas could not be trusted to put up a good fight. As Porlier complained:

We will continue to . . . find it hard to obtain any result from the troops for a long time unless they are organised as they ought to be . . . I say this on account of what happened in the last action: I would have lost half my men had not the cavalry saved everyone. It was impossible to contain the infantry's disorder or . . . remedy their confusion and fear.[48]

Increasingly dependent on the structures of the Patriot state for orders, arms and ammunition, the more or less regularised *partidas* of such figures as Espoz y Mina, El Empecinado, Sánchez, Durán, Villacampa, Longa, Merino and Porlier were in effect tied to the fortunes of the regular armies. That left, of course, the cloud of bands that remained wholly irregular in nature, but, for all their considerable nuisance value, Chagarito and the rest were little threat, and could not hope to withstand the might of the imperial state. Meanwhile, the fortunes of both regular and irregular bands were linked to those of the regular armies in yet another sense: in Aragón, for example, *la guerrilla* had flourished in the course of Blake's offensive in the summer of 1809, only to be placed under increasing pressure following the disaster at Belchite. Capture such cities as Tarragona, Valencia, Badajoz, then, and the French would be well on their way to the defeat of the *partidas*.

Where, then, is one to leave the question? All too clearly, the guerrillas were not the heroic defenders of the fatherland of legend. A complex phenomenon that in many respects defies definition, they embraced a variety of forms and motivations, but it is evident that the rank and file, and even some of the leaders, were little interested in questions of ideology or patriotism. Yet, even at its most primitive, *la guerrilla* was always a considerable nuisance to the French. By 1812, moreover, it had evolved considerably. As brigades and even divisions of regular troops, such bands as those of Espoz y Mina undoubtedly packed a heavier punch, whilst they had also begun to establish liberated zones from which they were increasingly difficult to expel. In this way the seeds were laid for the very important role that they played in the eventual liberation of Spain. The costs, however, had been enormous. The resistance of the regular armies had been sapped, large parts of Spain had been overrun, and relations with the populace had generally gone from bad to worse: guerrilla requisitioning was hated, the *partidas* blamed for every French reprisal, and the invaders provided with considerable mileage for their propaganda. French rule remained unpopular, certainly, but there was less and less inclination to resist. In short, the political advantages that supposedly accrued to the Patriot cause through the actions of the guerrillas had ceased to apply, if, that is, they had ever applied in the first place. As for the military advantages associated with them, even though they had helped to keep the war alive this hardly served as a substitute for the disciplined regular armies which Spain so desperately needed.

Spain, then, most certainly was not saved by the guerrillas, the fact being that it is quite clear that until 1812 the French had the potential to overrun the entire Peninsula. Pour more men across the Pyrenees, indeed, and Napoleon would eventually win. Yet, if only because the military record was so dismal in other respects, many Spanish politicians and publicists took exaggerated comfort from the activities of the guerrillas and elevated them to the role of national heroes, whilst the issue was also exploited by the important faction determined to argue that the struggle against Napoleon was a veritable 'people's war'. In doing so, however, they obscured the equally valuable contribution of the unlucky but ever-persevering regular army. Humiliated and jealous, considerable elements of the officer corps were thereby impelled towards the political interventionism that plagued Spanish history for the next century and a half. The military impact of the guerrillas may therefore still be open to question, but the bitterness of their legacy is undisguised.

11

Cádiz

THE MAKING OF THE SPANISH REVOLUTION, 1810–1812

The hastily converted theatre was stuffy in the late summer heat. Crowded around a central dais were the ninety-nine deputies who had arrived in time to attend the first session of the new assembly whilst the public galleries were thronged with army and militia officers, churchmen, place-seekers, journalists, the representatives of polite society and a variety of British and Portuguese guests. After hours of debate the moment had arrived for the first vote. On the table was a decree introduced by the Extremaduran deputies, Diego Múñoz Torrero and Manuel Luján. It was a dramatic moment. The renunciations of Bayonne, it was proclaimed, were null and void on the grounds that the monarch did not have the right to dispose of the throne without consulting the Spanish people. As for the cortes, *it was, the two deputies argued, a legitimate assembly that embodied the sovereignty of the nation. As such, it had the right to embark on a fundamental reform of the governance of Spain, which, for good measure, would take as a basic principle the separation of powers between the executive, the legislative and the judiciary. At stake were the very principles of absolutism. Yet, to immense applause, the measure was carried by a large majority. Spain, it seemed, had formally embraced the course of revolution.*

Implicit in the decree passed on the evening of 24 September 1810 were the seeds of deep division, but for the time being all was jubilation and excitement: politically naive as they were, many of the delegates had not realised what they had done, whilst the decree was in any case susceptible of interpretations that constituted no threat to the old order whatsoever. When one of the regents – the aged Bishop of Orense, Pedro Quevedo y Quintana – refused to swear the oath of loyalty to the *cortes* which was immediately required of every authority in Spain, he therefore received no support. Meanwhile, the general mood of harmony and optimism was reinforced by a certain sense of security. Although the French had in theory been besieging the new capital for the past seven months, in practice it was impregnable. Cádiz was built at the end of a sand spit nearly five miles long jutting out from a triangular piece of land known as the Isla de León. To reach the island, meanwhile, an attacker would have to fight his way across a wide strip of creeks and salt marshes known as the Río Sancti Petri which could only be traversed by means of a narrow causeway-cum-bridge known as the Puente de Suazo. As for bombardment, the only possible site for a siege battery – a peninsula that half closed the mouth of the great harbour protected by the Isla – was held by troops ensconced at its seaward end in the fort of Matagorda. Batteries and redoubts commanded the entire length of the Sancti Petri; the Puente de Suazo had been blown up; the isthmus was studded with defences; and Cádiz itself protected by massive walls. Every boat for miles around, meanwhile, had been scuttled, burned or taken over to the Isla de León, whilst the harbour was full of British and Spanish warships, the Spaniards having also fitted out a large number of gunboats and launches that could patrol the whole length of the Sancti Petri. Troops, meanwhile, existed by the thousand, Alburquerque's army and the Voluntarios Distinguidos having been reinforced by 3,000 soldiers who had fled Seville and reached the sea at Ayamonte and a strong Anglo-Portuguese brigade commanded by General William Stewart (shaken by their experiences, the Spaniards had abandoned their earlier scruples about a British garrison). Finally, in September the local authorities decreed the mobilisation of the entire male populace between the ages of sixteen and fifty-five, laying down that, depending on their resources, they should join either the privileged Voluntarios Distinguidos or the ordinary *milicias urbanas* (those who were unfit to serve were to pay a redemption fee proportionate to their income).

In the face of these resources, the French had had to confess themselves thwarted. Once a forlorn effort to persuade the garrison to surrender had been rejected, all that could be done was for the French troops that had reached the shoreline (the corps commanded by Marshal Victor) to make camp and embark on an attempt to bombard the city into surrender (in addition, Joseph wrote to Napoleon appealing for naval assistance, but this was never forthcoming, the emperor knowing better than to risk a second Trafalgar). Large numbers of troops and guns were therefore pushed forward to attack Matagorda and this was eventually subjected to so much punishment that the garrison was evacuated on 22 April. For a graphic description of the fighting, we have only to turn to the memoirs of Joseph Donaldson, a young Scottish soldier of the Ninety-Fourth Foot, who had been ordered to help man one of the fort's cannons. Thus:

At last when everything was prepared, they commenced their operations . . . Five or six batteries, mounting in all about twenty guns and eight or ten mortars, opened their tremendous mouths, vomiting forth death and destruction ... Death now began to stalk about in the most dreadful form. The large shot were certain messengers where they struck. The first man killed was a sailor ... The whole of his face was carried away ... The French soon acquired a fatal precision with their shot ... killing and wounding men with every volley. I was on the left of the gun at the front wheel. We were running her up after loading. I had stooped to take a fresh purchase [when] a cannon ball ... carried the forage cap off my head and struck the man behind me on the breast, and he fell to rise no more ... The carnage now became dreadful: the ramparts were strewed with the dead and wounded, and blood, brains and mangled limbs lay scattered in every direction ... The action was kept up the whole of that day during which we lost the best and bravest of our men ... By this time three of our guns were rendered unfit for service, and they had made a great impression on our parapet, with a breach in the end of the bomb-proof [sic] ... It being found that we could not keep the place, boats were sent to convey us to Cádiz.[1]

With Matagorda in their hands, the French could harass the harbour and isthmus and even shell Cádiz itself. Special mortars of an enormous size were eventually constructed for this purpose at Seville, and the city was thereafter periodically bombarded. The gunners' efforts, however, proved completely ineffectual and the only result was to swell the confidence of the *gaditanos* and persuade them that they were heroes. As Alcalá Galiano wrote:

From December 1810 bombs ... fired by the enemy batteries had started to fall inside Cádiz. However, these shots ... came very infrequently, and then only a few at a time. At the same time, in order to carry so far, the projectiles had had to be increased in weight, and were consequently mostly made up of lead without much space for powder. As a result, they caused little damage ... and in the end little notice was taken of them other than to make them the subject of humour. In theatre and streets, then, a popular couplet was sung ... 'From the bombs fired by the popinjays, the girls of Cádiz make hair curlers.'[2]

With food abundant and even falling in price, there was in fact no hope of success, and that despite both hurricane and epidemic – a great storm destroyed many ships in the spring of 1810, whilst the city was for much of the time ravaged by yellow fever.

For the time being, then, all eyes could focus on the political situation. In essence, this was dominated by three factors: the instructions that had been left by the Junta Central concerning the convocation of the *cortes*; the installation of a new council of regency; and the emergence of Cádiz itself as a major player in the political process. In so far as the first is concerned, on 28 October 1809 the Junta Central had, as we have seen, announced that, after a three-month electoral process beginning on the first day of the New Year, the *cortes* would open on 1 March. On 1 January 1810, meanwhile, instructions had appeared that the suffrage was to be extended to all male house-holders over the age of twenty-five. Voting was to be public, whilst the electors were to choose not deputies but parish representatives whose job it was to attend district-level assemblies. These would then choose deputies to send to the provincial meetings that would be the bodies from which the members of the *cortes* would finally emerge, the number involved being determined by a ratio of one deputy to every fifty thousand inhabitants. Also allowed to elect deputies (one in each case) were the provincial juntas and all those towns and cities that had been represented in the *cortes* of the *antiguo régimen*. All that was left unclear was the crucial question of whether or not the new assembly should have a single chamber, or, to put it another way, whether the clergy and nobility should have their own organs of representation.*

From 1 February 1810 – the date when it first met – the implementation of these various decrees had been in the hands of the new council of regency selected in its death throes by the Junta Central. Composed of General Castaños; the erstwhile minister and president of the Junta of Seville, Francisco de Saavedra; Admiral Antonio Escaño; an official of the Ministry of State named Miguel de Lardizábal who had represented his native Mexico in the Junta Central; and the Bishop of Orense (who was then still in Galicia and did not appear in Cádiz until 29 May), this was a highly conservative body which in theory enjoyed absolute power. As the leading reformer, Argüelles, complained:

Its authority was as absolute and arbitrary as that of the governments of the past. There was no remedy against the use of power. The freedoms of speech and of publication . . . were as chained up as they were before the insurrection.[3]

Nor was this surprising, for the new body was in large part a creation of the amalgam of all the old councils of the Bourbon state set up by the Junta

---

* Conservative historians have always maintained that on the very last day of its existence the Junta Central issued orders for the election of a second chamber, only for liberal elements in the administration to take advantage of the general confusion to suppress the document. However, the fact that the assembly was unicameral did not make it democratic. At best, the vote went only to heads of families, but the decree of 1 January 1810 was so vague that in many areas everyone was excluded except *vecinos* (roughly, 'citizens'; broadly speaking, owner-occupiers who paid a certain level of taxation). Add to this the many opportunities that existed for pressure of one sort or another, and it will be agreed that the *cortes*' democratic credentials are open to serious question.

Central known as the Consejo Reunido, the members of this body being deeply opposed to all forms of political progress. However, its leading figure, Castaños, was much given to dissemblance and compromise, and forswore a second chamber in favour of restoring the various councils brought together in the Consejo Reunido in the hope that such a move would clip the wings of the new assembly in a fashion that, whilst more subtle, was no less effective. With this matter out of the way, the Regency reserved its energies for matters more directly related to the war effort. Over the course of the next few months, a series of decrees appeared that limited the power of the provincial juntas still further, established a permanent general staff, formed a new artillery academy in place of an earlier one that had been destroyed when the French captured Seville, and gave the Spanish infantry a new table of organisation that would have got rid of many surplus regiments. At the same time, too, such aid as was possible was funnelled to the struggling Spanish armies, whilst a conscious attempt was made to improve relations with the British, whose interests in Patriot Spain were now represented, after a brief interregnum in which the embassy had been occupied by Frere's brother, Bartholomew, by Wellington's youngest brother, Henry Wellesley.

Despite these efforts, in practice little changed. The individual members of the Regency attracted much scorn, the only joy that one British officer could find being that Wellesley now had 'only five blockheads to transact business with instead of thirty-four'.[4] Though few statesmen would have been equal to the task, it therefore proved incapable of satisfying the army's wants, checking political intrigue, or completing the fortifications of their capital. Meanwhile, intrigue was rife and the Minister of War, General Eguía, an inveterate nepotist. As for the administration, such was the muddle that in May 1810 an obscure Treasury official in the pay of Cuban agents was able to cause chaos by getting a fake decree granting free trade to all Spain's colonies promulgated by slipping it in with a pile of papers that had been sent to the Minister of Finance for signature.

Not surprisingly, Britain's new ambassador, Henry Wellesley, was in despair:

It is impossible not to perceive that they have many of the same defects which so strongly characterised the proceedings of the Supreme Junta . . . The same want of energy and firmness, the same system of procrastination . . . prevails, I am sorry to say, in the proceedings of the Council of Regency . . . Although six weeks have elapsed since the Spanish army arrived at the Isla de León . . . no attempt has been made to render them more efficient . . . They continue to be ill-clothed, . . . ill-fed, and their discipline totally neglected. The pay of some of the . . . corps is eight, and of others (I believe) fourteen months in arrears.[5]

In fairness to the Regency, however, it was operating under difficult conditions. Not the least of its problems was the behaviour of the Junta of Cádiz. A new body that had ousted its predecessor in a *de facto coup d'état* in the chaos of January 1810, it was dominated by a clique of merchants headed by one Tomás Istúriz, and later described as being perhaps 'the one which has aspired to most power among all the juntas of Spain'.[6] Intent at the beginning on seizing the very governance of Spain, it was only persuaded to recognise the Regency with the greatest difficulty and thereafter devoted itself to the alternative policy of seizing control of as large a share of the revenue as possible so as to force the radical political agenda which it espoused upon the new régime. Knowing that he was an 'out' who had fallen foul of the Junta Central, the junta had invited Alburquerque to become its first president, but the latter very soon got wise to its designs and denounced it to the Regency, accusing its members of overweening ambition and financial peculation. Much too afraid of the junta, which had behind it the weight of the entire merchant community, to respond to this warning, the Regency chose rather to pack Alburquerque off to London as its ambassador. Already undermined by the fact that it could be represented as a creature of the despised Junta Central, the result was that it found itself saddled with a situation in which it had no option but to accede to the junta's demands for control of the whole of Cádiz's customs revenues. As Blanco White noted, indeed:

A government established as if by a favour or condescension must needs be the slave . . . of a junta that had in its favour . . . the fact that it was composed of respectable inhabitants of the city to which it could be said that . . . Spain had been reduced. The opinion of Cádiz was inevitably in favour of its junta and against the last fruit of the *central*.[7]

Although the loss of so much territory meant that the duties paid in Cádiz now represented a disproportionately large part of the government's domestic income, matters might not have been so bad but for two other issues. In the first place, the junta was not particularly efficient: as one British observer wrote, 'The members are too numerous for an executive government, and . . . have so ill arranged the distribution of the different branches of the government that in the few days they have acted, they have already been found to clash.'[8] Far more important, however, were developments in central and South America. From the days of Carlos III the *criollo* community had come increasingly to resent Spanish rule, such feelings having been much sharpened by the extension of Godoy's *desamortización* to America, the evil reputation of the Spanish court, and the manner in which the intermittent war against Britain from 1796 to 1808 had both given the inhabitants a taste of the benefits of free trade and convinced them that they now had much less need of Spanish protection. Inspired by loathing of the French and fear that their influence might stir up the same sort of bloody racial revolts as those that had rocked the Caribbean in the 1790s, the *criollos* had initially joined the *peninsulares* in rallying to Fernando VII. Patriotic donations poured in, whilst Santo Domingo – today the Dominican Republic – which had been ceded to France in 1795 in the Treaty of Basle, was reconquered by local militias dispatched from Puerto Rico who defeated the French garrison at Palo Hincado. Yet the colonies remained restive: other than suspending a much resented decree of 1804 that had effectively forced all those who had borrowed from Church funds – the chief source of credit in America – to pay back what they owed to the state, the Junta Central had failed to address *criollo* grievances. For example, the local authorities continued to be dominated by *peninsulares*, whilst an offer of political representation was marred by the fact that the colonies were only allocated ten deputies as opposed to twenty-six for metropolitan Spain. In just the same way, whilst the latter was allotted one *cortes* deputy for every fifty thousand inhabitants, the American territories got one for every hundred thousand with the added stipulation that the headcount would only include pure-blood Europeans. Add to all this the fact that the Junta had proved completely inept in its handling of the rather confused situation that had developed in the Viceroyalty of the Río de la Plata in the wake of the British invasion of 1806–7, and it will be appreciated that an explosion was inevitable.

As early as the summer of 1809 revolts therefore broke out in La Paz and Quito. These were suppressed, but the arrival a year later of news of the fall of Andalucía changed matters completely. One interpretation is that, as Spain seemed to be falling, the *criollos* had no option but to look to themselves. Another is that the groups that were bent on independence saw a golden opportunity and seized it with both hands. At all events, between April and October 1810 parts of the territories now called Venezuela, Argentina, Colombia, Ecuador, Chile, Mexico, Bolivia, Paraguay and Uruguay all rose in revolt, the only areas of Spanish rule to remain loyal – Peru, Cuba, Puerto Rico, Santo Domingo and central America – being those where racial fears were particularly intense. This was but the beginning of a long story: in Mexico and Venezuela social unrest led to the wholesale defection of the *criollos* and the restoration of the *status quo*; in Bolivia, Ecuador and Chile Peruvian expeditionary forces were able to crush the rebels; and in Colombia serious splits in the insurgent camp enabled loyalism to maintain a foothold. However, Argentina, Paraguay and – with certain limitations – Uruguay all remained independent, whilst such was the disruption caused by the fighting that financial support for Spain fell dramatically. Thus, whilst 225,500,000 reales were received from across the Atlantic in 1810, the figure for 1809 had been 860,000,000. As total domestic receipts in 1810 were only 182,200,000 reales, the Regency was presented with a serious problem. As Sir Thomas Graham noted in April 1811, indeed, 'The government is quite bankrupt.'[9]

It might be objected here that British aid was so generous that the Spaniards ought to have had little to fear. However, whilst the Spaniards were provided with immense quantities of weapons, uniforms, ammunition and other military necessities, money was a different matter. No regular treaty of subsidy was signed, whilst the Spaniards had to compete for money with Britain's other allies – most notably, the Portuguese and the Austrians. With the Continental Blockade's effects still almost at their very worst, the consequence was that, not counting whatever was left over from a sum of £650,000 that Frere had been given when he first went to Spain as ambassador in the autumn of 1808, in 1809 the financial support received from this source had amounted to only £214,000 (*c.* 2,000,000 reales). An attempt had also been made by the Junta Central to negotiate an enormous loan on the London market that would be guaranteed by the British government, but such were the sums involved – the minimum figure mentioned was £10,000,000 – that Canning had laughed the idea to scorn. Doubtless the Spaniards did not make things easy for themselves, but the fact was that, so long as the British were maintaining a large army in Portugal, money for other purposes was desperately short. Thanks in part to Henry Wellesley, who, to the intense disapproval of Spencer Perceval, advanced large sums of money to the Regency on the promise of payment from future consignments of specie, a further £445,000 – *c.* 40,000,000 reales – was received in 1810, but attempts to reintroduce the idea of a privately financed £10,000,000 loan were thrown out, and it was all too apparent that bankruptcy was just around the corner.

With power in the hands of *gaditano* commerce, things could only get worse. Having profited immensely from the colonial trade – in 1802, for example, Cádiz is claimed to have imported goods from Spanish America of a value equivalent to the whole of Britain's total exports for that year – the merchants who dominated the junta were unlikely to look kindly on a rabble of rebellious *criollos*, pardos and *mestizos*. As well as having to fight the French, successive Regencies therefore found themselves committed to a highly expensive second front, which by 1814 had absorbed some 20,000 troops. The reverse side of the coin, meanwhile, was that the government was not allowed to make any significant concessions, as witness, for example, the furious reaction occasioned by the fake decree of free trade, not to mention the constant refusal to admit that there was any serious cause for rebellion (at best the insurgents were regarded as self-seeking degenerates – there was a common perception that the American climate had encouraged sexual profligacy and sapped the moral and intellectual fibre of the *criollos* – who had gulled the savage and uncivilised masses into following their lead).

Whilst worsening the Regency's financial difficulties, the American revolutions also affected relations with the British. As had been made clear after Talavera, Wellington's forces could not be expected to intervene in the hinterland of Spain until relations between the Allies had been placed on a very different basis. From the beginning Canning had sought to link aid to Spain with greater access to the trade and bullion of her colonies on the grounds that the Continental Blockade would otherwise render further assistance impossible. Reasonably enough given the immense quantities of British goods being smuggled into the American territories – £1,000,000 worth was shipped to them in 1808 from Jamaica alone – the Spaniards saw things very differently. Only a few years before, British troops had attacked Buenos Aires and Montevideo and allowed them to be swamped with cheap goods, whilst the British in any case had a long record of preying on the American trade and had in recent years given succour to such fugitives as the Venezuelan revolutionary, Miranda. Fearing that relinquishing the mother country's commercial monopoly would jeopardise the Patriot cause's most important source of income, the Junta Central had therefore refused to make any concessions except in exchange for a guaranteed subsidy. Yet obduracy on the part of Spain provoked intransigence on the part of Britain, and thus it was that the American colonies came to be a major bone of contention.

With the revolts of 1810, matters became more complicated still. On the one hand, the Perceval administration could not openly support a revolt against its most important ally, but, on the other, it feared that the rebels might be driven into the arms of the French, wished to forge good relations with them, and had a strong interest in seeing them attain their independence. The result was a most unhappy compromise. Whilst British representatives in the Caribbean and elsewhere were forbidden to give direct assistance to the rebels, insurgent emissaries were received in London.

Furthermore, rather than agreeing to Spanish demands that it should help put down the rebels by force, the British government offered to mediate between the belligerents in the hope of securing terms – amongst them, needless to say, a liberalisation of trade – that would restore the Americans to their allegiance.

To the Spaniards, of course, all this was totally unacceptable, for inherent in the very concept of mediation was the idea that they should make substantial concessions. As a result, the Regency would only agree if the British promised to assist in repression should the negotiations fail. As for the British, they were regarded with more hostility than ever. Writing from La Coruña, Sir Howard Douglas noted a worrying tendency 'to attribute all our measures to selfish policy', whilst Henry Wellesley went so far as to claim that the American revolts 'have been the principal cause of all the trouble and vexation I have met with in my different communications with the government'.[10] Only to be expected, this obduracy aroused much anger in London, and all the more so when it began to be coupled with the dispatch of troops to America, the consequence being that a British campaign in Spain was rendered less likely than ever.

In the early months of its existence, then, the Regency was in serious trouble. The war continued, certainly, but such was the battering to which the Spaniards had been subjected that there seemed to be little in the way of the occupation of most of what remained of Patriot Spain. Asturias and Galicia had been stripped of most of their troops for the campaign of Tamames and Alba de Tormes, and plunged into confusion by La Romana, who, not content with overthrowing the junta in Oviedo, had also outraged the Galician notables by trying to substitute military for civilian government. The 10,000 soldiers who remained were deserting in droves and terrorising the populace, whilst in Galicia in particular the *alarmas* were running amok, the effect of popular mobilisation having been to form 'gangs of smugglers and bandits who are better dressed and armed than our own troops'.[11] Not that this was difficult: one British officer described the Galician forces as 'a wretched rabble ... attended by a numerous corps of officers equally ignorant of military duty as the men, who ... were all raw recruits not exercised above eight days and the greater part not even knowing how to load and fire'.[12]

Galicia, indeed, provided the Patriot authorities with the problems with which they would everywhere have to contend in the wake of liberation. Arms, uniforms and equipment were all wanting. Costs were enormous: La Coruña was swarming with supernumerary officers, whilst the province had to sustain two different headquarters as the territorial command was in the hands of the Captain General, Noroña, and its field counterpart in those of General Mahy. Thanks to an increase in smuggling, a general breakdown in law and order, the collapse of trade and industry, and the death or flight of many local magistrates, income was in decline (46,000,000 reales were received as income in 1808 as opposed to only 38,500,000 in 1810): by the end of 1811, indeed, there was a monthly deficit of some 5,300,000 reales. How this situation was to be resolved was not clear, however. For example, an extraordinary contribution of 60,000,000 reales levied in April 1811 produced only 7,250,000 reales in the first six months, the re-established Junta of Galicia complaining bitterly of 'the league that we note among the well-to-do classes to avoid contributing to the public necessities, a monstrous league that is sustained by every kind of crime'.[13] Nor were the military authorities much help, Mahy having fallen out with the new junta and being described as a man whom 'nothing appears capable of moving ... to exertion'.[14] But, above all, the whole province was swarming with bandits. Always a problem in poverty-stricken and over-populated Galicia, their numbers had been swollen by draft evasion, desertion, despair, the sale by fleeing soldiers of their arms and ammunition, and the fact that many jails had been thrown open by the insurgents of 1808. A series of draconian proclamations and police regulations did no good whatsoever. The number of bandits seems to have roughly doubled, gangs in operation in 1810 including those of Antonio Ferro, Tomás Mínguez, Bernardo Montans, Antonio Vázquez and Francisco Rodríguez. Noted for their cruelty – the usual tactic amongst such groups was to descend on isolated farmhouses and carry off all that they could find, having first employed the most horrific tortures to reveal the presence of any hidden valuables – such men instilled a common sense of insecurity and lack of confidence that augmented the general unrest and made it still harder for the authorities to impose their writ.

Help, then, could not be expected from Galicia and Asturias, but what of the Kingdom of León? Setting aside Astorga, which was garrisoned by the Galicians, the chief bastion of resistance here was the fortress of Ciudad Rodrigo which was reasonably well-garrisoned, but gripped by social ferment. Thus:

We find ourselves in something approaching a state of anarchy here, and are exposed to the risk of tragedy, for the junta is consumed with fear of the people and dares not bring either delinquents or deserters to justice ... In eight months of horrible events, we have not seen a single punishment.[15]

Composed largely of rebellious part-time local militia – the Voluntarios de Ciudad Rodrigo – the garrison was in any case unable to undertake much more than the cavalry raids of Julián Sánchez (now the commander of a regiment known as the Lanceros de Castilla). As for the Army of the Left, terribly mauled at Alba de Tormes, this had spent the winter cantoned in the barren mountains between León and Extremadura and had lost over half its strength to desertion and disease. As the Junta of Ciudad Rodrigo reported:

The army is at present occupying the Sierra de Gata . . . If the station of the troops is judged solely in terms of fighting battles, it can with all security be said that it is as advantageous as could possibly be desired. But as it is also necessary . . . to think in terms of the means that the countryside can provide, it must be confessed that they could not be more fatal . . . Rich in wine and oil, the area does not produce grain . . . and this has produced a complete want of discipline amongst the soldiery, who are going out to steal on the public roads in the guise of foraging.[16]

Very soon, moreover, the area was weakened still further. Confirmed as commander of the Army of the Left by the new régime – it will be remembered that he had been reappointed to the position by the insurgents who had briefly seized power in Seville in January 1810 – La Romana had led most of the troops that remained southwards to establish a fresh base at Badajoz. However, though not without its problems, La Romana quickly falling out with the Junta of Extremadura, this did at least create a solid nucleus of resistance on King Joseph's western flank. Indeed, reinforced by such troops as Albuquerque had left in the Extremaduran fortress and provided with fresh supplies of food and clothing, the Army of the Left was to cause considerable mischief in the months that followed. As the British intelligence officer, Cocks, wrote, 'The Marquis of Romana's corps now forms part of our army . . . The men are very good: I saw part of them engaged the day before yesterday and they behaved most bravely.'[17]

Badajoz, then, represented a solid bulwark, but, across the whole of the south of Spain from the Portuguese border to Alicante, there was nothing other than the even more imposing focus of resistance represented by Cádiz. Thus, most of the remnants of the old Army of the Centre had reached safety in Murcia and been taken over by General Blake, who had just resigned the Catalan command after a bitter dispute with the Junta of Catalonia over the fall of Gerona, but the state of these forces was desperate in the extreme and it was to be the winter before they were even remotely ready for action. Another force had reached the Condado de Niebla, but its state was much the same: all the units were infected by 'the seed of dispersion', whilst the cavalry 'lacked carbines and pistols, and in some instances had no swords . . . or saddles'.[18] And even the garrison of Cádiz was not to be trusted.

According to Roche, for example, 'They ... are, if possible, of a worse description than I have seen in the armies ... badly fed, paid and almost without clothing'.[19] As for Sir Thomas Graham, he was even more scathing:

The Spanish cavalry is an encumbrance and worse than none, and their means in field artillery very trifling ... It is undoubtedly trusting to a broken reed to confide in the steadiness and discipline [of] such troops in the open field.[20]

Finally we come to the Levante and Catalonia. Taking Valencia first of all, its forces numbered only 12,000 men, most of whom were untried, whilst its political situation was extremely unstable. Thus, from May 1808 to March 1809 the original Captain General, Conquista, had come under unremitting attack from La Romana's brother, José Caro – in 1808 an obscure naval captain whose dreams of grandeur fitted in very well with the demands of family loyalty – and the revolutionary faction headed by the Bertrán de Lis clan. Thanks very largely to the support given to the anti-Conquista camp by the Barón de Sabasona, who had been sent to Valencia by the Junta Central as its commissioner, this struggle was eventually ended by Conquista being forced to resign. However, the results were not those foreseen by the progressive elements who had dominated the campaign against the old Captain General. Thus, appointed to the Captain Generalcy in Conquista's place, Caro arrested all the *bertrandelistas*, drove out Sabasona, and mobilised the mob to ensure that the government allowed him a free hand, thereafter running Valencia very much as a personal satrapy whose rule, as one observer put it, was characterised by 'neither courage, nor strength, nor talent'.[21]

Next, then, is Catalonia. Though large parts of the south and west were still free, including the fortified cities of Lérida, Tarragona and Tortosa, its forces were even less able to undertake anything of any consequence than those of Valencia. Whilst a new commander had been found in place of Blake in the person of the young Enrique O'Donnell, who had made a name for courage and daring in the operations round Gerona, no more than 7,000 men were available for field operations, whilst attempts to introduce conscription merely stirred up popular hostility and undermined the new Captain General. In truth, however, O'Donnell was hardly an inspiring leader, Lord Holland very fairly describing him as 'unsteady, intemperate ... unreasonable and regardless of truth and character'.[22] As for the *somaténes*, they were now so wedded to banditry and pillage that they were all but useless. *La guerrilla* continued, true – on 18 December 1809, for example, the commander of the French forces in the region, Marshal Augereau, was himself ambushed near Figueras in the course of his return from a short vist to Perpignan – but for a long time most of the fighting had been the work of detachments of regular troops and the volunteer *tercios de miqueletes* formed by the Junta of Catalonia at the start of the war.

Wherever one looks, then, the picture is the same. Popular disaffection, lack of resources and political intrigue together ensured that the Patriot armies could henceforth seek to do little more than hang on to such territory as they still occupied whilst at the same time joining with the guerrillas of the interior in harassing the invaders. Worse, the situation was still deteriorating. Hastily organised expeditions against Astorga, Ciudad Rodrigo, Tarragona, Valencia and Badajoz may all have failed to obtain the surrenders expected in the wake of the fall of Seville, but Asturias and central Extremadura were reoccupied and the city of Murcia raided and stripped of its valuables, whilst in Catalonia Augereau inflicted terrible punishment on the *somaténes* of the north, revictualled Barcelona, and, despite a gallant and prolonged defence, eliminated the strategically placed fortress of Hostalrich. In Aragón, meanwhile, having captured the younger Mina and inflicted several other blows on the guerrillas, who had seized the opportunity constituted by the abortive march on Valencia to make all sorts of trouble, Suchet resolved to attack Lérida. An important objective whose capture would open the way for co-operation between the garrisons of Aragón and Catalonia, this city was well-fortified and full of troops, whilst its governor, García Conde, put up a fierce fight, but on the night of 13–14 May the walls were successfully stormed. Built on a towering hill above the town, the citadel might have held out for some time more, but Suchet dealt with the threat in ruthless fashion by first driving the unfortunate civilian population inside its walls at bayonet point and then subjecting its packed courtyards to heavy artillery fire. The effects were appalling – at least 500 people died, including many women and children – and within twenty-four hours García Conde had duly surrendered. With Lérida secured, Suchet then turned on Mequínenza and besieged that place as well, securing its surrender on 12 June. And, finally, and in some ways most importantly, on 21 March Junot's corps attacked Astorga, which was protected only by its old city wall, and proceeded to subjugate it in a month-long siege, in which the Spaniards distinguished themselves by fighting an attempt to storm the defences to a standstill and only surrendering when they ran out of ammunition.

It should not be thought that the Spaniards had been idle in the course of these campaigns. On the frontiers of Galicia an attempt was made by Mahy to check the siege of Astorga. Equally, in Catalonia Enrique O'Donnell launched attack after attack on Augereau's forces and came very close to winning a considerable victory at Vich, though a risky dash at Lérida took his army out of the shelter of the mountains and led to a severe reverse at Margalef. From Badajoz, meanwhile, two divisions of La Romana's army – those of Ballesteros and Contreras – were dispatched to the remote Condado de Niebla from where they repeatedly sallied out and attacked isolated French garrisons, at one point advancing to within twenty miles of Seville. At the same time, assured of the help of the British fleet, possessed of numerous safe harbours and well provided with schooners, launches, gunboats and other small craft, the Patriots were also able to make much use of seapower. From the late spring, then, La Coruña and Cádiz saw the departure of a series of expeditions in which small forces of regular troops either landed in remote towns and villages and established bases from where they could harass the French or launched surprise commando-style attacks on such vulnerable enemy garrisons as that of Santoña.

In the interior, too, the struggle continued. As an example, one might cite the case of El Empecinado. Now the head of a band of volunteers that numbered at least 500 men, on 9 March, for example, the Castilian commander attacked a French column near Sigüenza, evaded an attempt to take his men in the rear by a second force that was lying in wait for just this purpose, and finally fought off the combined forces of his assailants. For some time chiefly engaged in hunting down bandits and recruiting his forces, on 30 June he reappeared and forced the garrison of Brihuega to take refuge in the castle that dominated the town. Further raids followed: on 7 July the target was Sigüenza, on 16 July Brihuega, and on 26 July Torrelaguna. Despite being immersed in a series of intrigues, meanwhile, Porlier was just as active. No sooner had Bonet got his troops into Oviedo, for example, than the guerrilla leader descended on Infiesto and captured many prisoners and supplies, his efforts leading to Oviedo being given up twice over before the invaders finally settled down within its walls.

Spanish heroism notwithstanding, the French were clearly in the ascendant. With Patriot Spain gradually being ground down, indeed, defeat could only be avoided if the British consented to take a greater role in the struggle. Yet Britain's ability to save Spain promised to be distinctly limited. Content though Napoleon was to see what remained of the Patriot cause conquered and overthrown, his attention was fixed on Portugal. Exasperated with the inability of his generals to finish the job, he had throughout the autumn been talking of leading an army on Lisbon and throwing Wellington into the sea. Engrossed in his divorce of Josephine and search for a new bride, in the end he did not come, but the project of an attack on Portugal was not forgotten, and on 17 April the corps of Soult (now commanded by General

Reynier), Ney and Junot and a variety of others units – most importantly, a temporary corps of reinforcement battalions that was still in France – were designated the Army of Portugal, and Marshal André Masséna appointed to be their commander. Avaricious, lecherous, and in poor health, Masséna still rated among the very best of Napoleon's commanders, and, after a series of discussions in which it was decided that he should march on Lisbon via Ciudad Rodrigo and Almeida, on 26 April he set out for Spain.

Awaiting the marshal were some 65,000 men. However, all was not well with this army. The ponderous siege train that would be needed to breach the walls of the two fortresses that blocked the way was still on the road from France. Junot and Ney were notoriously obstinate and self-willed characters who were jealous both of each other and of Masséna. ('The emperor does not believe that Ney and I are capable of commanding our troops', Junot told his wife. 'We have been put in a state of tutelage.'[23]) With feelings already running high, Masséna did not help matters by, first, turning up with his latest mistress dressed in dragoon uniform and sporting the coveted cross of the Legion of Honour, and, second, offending Ney by interfering with his staff. At the same time, several of the divisional generals were nursing grievances of various sorts; many of the troops were inexperienced conscripts; morale was low; and sickness was widespread. In consequence, the campaign opened in an atmosphere of acrimony. There were also serious supply difficulties, whilst the guerrillas caused the French enormous problems. The troops, wrote Masséna's chief-of-staff, Pelet, 'never had wine or brandy and often no more than a half or even a quarter ration of bread . . . and . . . lacked cartridges even at the beginning'; meanwhile, 'Several Germans, Swiss and Italians have deserted from the French . . . who all speak with horror of prolonging the war in Spain as they dare not individually leave their camp. The Spanish guerrillas lie in wait to destroy them, and have become so impudent of late that they have even attacked a mass of considerable force.'[24]

In consequence, it was not until mid-June that operations began with Ney's corps laying siege to Ciudad Rodrigo. A fairly small place, Ciudad Rodrigo was imperfectly fortified, but its garrison was more than adequate and possessed of plentiful supplies of food and ammunition, whilst its governor, Andrés Pérez de Herrasti, was a good soldier whose resolve was strengthened by the belief that he could count upon the support of Wellington's army, whose advanced elements were only a few miles to the west. Guarantees, indeed, had been received that Wellington would do everything that he considered possible to relieve the city, but careful reading of the British commander's letters should have shown Herrasti that in practice relief was unlikely. Given the fact that 12,000 of his troops had had to be detached to the Guadiana valley to keep watch on Reynier, who had until this point been occupying the area around Mérida, Wellington had only 33,000 men on the Ciudad Rodrigo front. Sufficient to drive away the besieging forces though these were, any such action must inevitably have produced the immediate concentration of enemy troops numbering some 50,000 men. Even if the Anglo-Portuguese army escaped disaster, it would still have had to retreat post-haste and leave Ciudad Rodrigo to its fate, so why, Wellington reasoned, incur the risk in the first place?

With the outposts of the famous Light Division literally in sight of their lines, the French were therefore left to proceed with the siege in peace. Hindered by heavy rain and a series of sorties, progress was slow, but on 25 June all was finally ready for the bombardment. The scene is described by Pelet:

At dawn every battery opened fire at the same time with their forty-six guns . . . Soon guns were firing vigorously from both sides and the noise was terrible. Those who had never before seen a siege believed that everything would be destroyed.[25]

In the face of this barrage, Pérez de Herrasti put up a good fight, whilst he was ably supported by Julián Sánchez, who had led his cavalry out of the town and 'did good service by making frequent attacks on our trenches'.[26] French casualties were heavy – Masséna himself was badly bruised when a bursting shell pelted him with stones and earth – whilst food and ammunition were soon running short. Ney's troops were growing more and more frustrated – there was talk, indeed, of killing the entire garrison – but at length a combination of mining and bombardment produced a major breach in the southern perimeter. As for the situation in the city, it was impossible:

Bombs were falling . . . with great rapidity . . . On every side arose thick clouds of dust and smoke, pierced by the flames of the fires. The wreckage . . . was tumbling down with great noise, and . . . small magazines exploded periodically with tremendous detonations . . . Everything adjoining [the breach] had been crushed, pounded and destroyed. The . . . devastation extended to the middle of the city.[27]

Exhausted and deprived of all hope, on 9 July the governor surrendered, though even then he delayed until the last minute: the column organised for the assault was actually rushing in when the white flag was finally raised.

Militarily correct though the decision not to help Ciudad Rodrigo was, in political terms it was unfortunate. Many officers of the Anglo-Portuguese army questioned the failure to advance, thereby initiating a mood of doubt and disillusion that was to dog Wellington for much of the coming campaign.

As for the Spaniards, they were furious. Pérez de Herrasti openly accused Wellington of betrayal, whilst the local population complained bitterly that the British were simply trying to prolong the war for their own selfish ends. Collaboration with the French was thereby stimulated – some members of the garrison were so angry that they changed sides – and further doubts sown with regard to British good faith. As even Wellington was forced to admit, indeed, 'However unreasonable it may appear . . . the people of Spain are by no means satisfied that His Majesty's troops have taken so active a share . . . in the war as might have been expected from them.'[28]

With the fall of Ciudad Rodrigo the road was open for the invasion of Portugal, but this must be left to a later chapter in favour of the political situation in Cádiz. Amidst a military situation that was deteriorating by the day – the one bright spot was that in Valencia Caro's arrogance and incompetence had led to his being overthrown by his own officers – preparations had been going ahead for the opening of the *cortes*. In those areas that were unoccupied by the enemy, the elections had been held in regulation fashion, whilst they also went ahead even in a few of the provinces that were dominated by the French. Few details have survived as to the sort of debates and discussions that accompanied the electoral process, let alone whether there was any of the manipulation, falsification and official pressure that was later to be so characteristic of the Spanish political system. All that can be said is that, the indirect voting system favouring property and education, two-thirds of the 725 *electores de partido* were drawn from the clergy, and the remainder from administration, local government and the liberal professions (or, to put it another way, the landed classes, and, in particular, those who had profited from *desamortización*).

In cases where there was no possibility at all of holding elections, or where, as in the cases of the colonies, they would inevitably be much delayed, a different procedure was followed. Such provinces were initially represented by substitute deputies chosen by such of their residents who happened to be present in Cádiz and the Isla de León. A census was organised to discover who was eligible to vote in these contests, and the electorate was found to total 1,334. Small though the resultant provincial electoral colleges undoubtedly were, they do not appear to have been much smaller than those that met in other parts of Spain, whilst their assemblies were certainly not hole-in-the-corner affairs, but formal meetings presided over by senior officials. Setting aside the thirty American deputies, moreover, only twenty-one representatives of Spanish constituencies were ever elected in this fashion, whereas the total number of seats in the *cortes* came to over 300. Also significant is the social composition of the deputies. Of the 185 deputies elected for metropolitan provinces (as opposed to the provincial juntas and the cities represented in the assemblies of the *antiguo régimen*), 42 were officials; 61 ecclesiastics; 16 army officers; 23 members of the liberal professions; 10 noblemen or landowners (though see the qualification made above); and the remaining 33 unknown. Taking all categories of deputy together, around two-thirds of the total were members of the clergy. By contrast, merchants and manufacturers were notable for their scarcity, and the *populacho* wholly absent.

If considerable attention has been paid to these issues, it is because of the controversy that has always attached to the elections of 1810 and, still more so, the events that followed. When the *cortes* opened, it was, as we have already seen, quickly captured by a radical agenda. For those hostile to the work of the *cortes*, this was the result of force, fraud and circumstance: heavily influenced by the Enlightenment, Cádiz was the only city in Spain where it was possible to stir up a mob in favour of radical reform; the mercantile community controlled the government; the principle of representation by estates had been overthrown; and the interior, supposedly conservative, was under-represented, with such deputies as it had being *suplentes* elected by undemocratic means and drawn from elements that were likely to sympathise with revolutionary politics. For liberal and Marxist historians, by contrast, the picture is very different: far from being an unrepresentative minority who had gained power by foul means, the political movement that became known as the liberals were rather a group who were backed by the full weight of public opinion and, more particularly, a Spanish bourgeois revolution.*

In reality, however, neither explanation is wholly tenable. Implicit in such arguments is the concept of a head-on clash between revolution and counter-revolution, but in 1810 only a tiny minority would have had such a perception of the situation. Thus, if we take the question of whether the *cortes* should have one chamber or two, men of clearly progressive tendencies – the most obvious example is José Blanco y Crespo, a liberal of such heterodox views that he fell out with the clique who came to dominate *gaditano* politics and had to go into exile in England where he adopted the name Blanco White – could be found supporting the bicameral thesis and men of traditionalist ones the unicameral alternative. In just the same way,

---

* Like 'guerrilla', 'liberal' (in its political sense) is a term that entered the English language during the Peninsular War, *los liberales* being the nickname applied to the most progressive group in the *cortes* on account of their frequent use of the words 'free' and 'freedom' (*liberar; libertad*).

the principle of popular sovereignty received the backing that it did because many traditionalists believed that the renunciations of Bayonne had broken fundamental laws which laid down that any change in the succession had to be laid before a *cortes*.

Nor are arguments of a social or geographical nature much help. One of the few manufacturers to be found amongst the deputies – the Catalan, Salvador Vinyals – was to prove an arch-traditionalist, and one of the few titled aristocrats – the Conde de Toreno – a leading liberal. As for the ecclesiastics, the fact that many of them were both Jansenists – a group within the Catholic Church that wished to see the power of the Pope reduced in favour of that of the bishops – and members of the secular clergy ensured a considerable degree of clerical support for the radical programme. Finally, there is little hard evidence that men duly elected in the Castiles or Navarre would have voted any differently in 1810–1812 from the *suplentes* that took their place in Cádiz. In any event this latter group were in no way a united force: if they included the liberal leaders, Agustín Argüelles, Manuel García Herreros and Evaristo Pérez de Castro, they also threw up the reactionary Peruvian, Blas Ostolaza, and Francisco Eguía, a singularly old-fashioned Bourbon general who was to play a major role in the restoration of absolutism in 1814. Moreover, even if the emphasis given to the question of the *suplentes* is not as misplaced as this suggests, they were balanced by the fact that the two provinces with the most deputies – Galicia (twenty-three deputies) and Catalonia (twenty) – both produced delegations that were strongly traditionalist.

The answer to this question, in fact, lies in nothing more complicated than muddle. Three different programmes were on offer at Cádiz, but this was in large part simply not appreciated. Of the three positions found in the *cortes*, the most coherently expressed and argued was that of the liberals. Underpinning this was a classic combination of political perception and economic interest. Influenced by Rousseau and Smith, a growing minority had come to argue the need for a thorough renovation of society, the starting point of their theory being that in the Middle Ages Spain had enjoyed an age of liberty – and hence felicity – which had then been eclipsed by centuries of despotism. To restore this 'golden age' it was necessary to take account of the basic rules that in their eyes governed human conduct – first, that all men were employed in the pursuit of happiness; second, that the only possible measure of happiness was material wealth; and, third, that all men were created equal. From this it followed that the role of government was to create a society in which prosperity could be pursued by all men on an equal basis, this in turn requiring that all men should enjoy equality before the law and have the absolute right freely to acquire, own and dispose of property as they saw fit. Given the war, however, all this was doubly important, for the liberals argued that the people had risen against the French not to sustain the rights of despotism, but to recover their own lost liberty. Viewed in this fashion, indeed, the *cortes* became 'the reward for the constancy and heroism of the Spanish nation, which, having bought its liberty at the cost of such generous sacrifices, earned the right to come together . . . to break the chains of external and domestic tyranny alike'.[29]

According to liberal rhetoric, Spain owed such success as she had won in the war to the people, from which it followed, first, that the privileged estates had lost their right to pre-eminence, and, secondly, that reform was the key to victory, every defeat being blamed on failure to keep up its momentum, and thus to keep popular devotion at white heat. To quote Argüelles:

Reform was an essential part of the mission of the congress. Circumstances insepar-able from a popular insurrection . . . stamped it with the . . . aspect that it displayed from its very origins [and] conserved throughout its work . . . But even if this had not been the case, reform was a weapon that could not but be employed against a conqueror as crafty as he was daring who was himself using it to subjugate the nation.[30]

But reform was necessary not just for the present, but for the future, because only thus could Spain's independence be safeguarded once and for all. As one liberal newspaper later proclaimed:

The Spaniards are fighting to be independent, to be free. But will shedding their blood, facing death and exterminating the French be enough to achieve these two great objects? Let us suppose that the latter are ejected from our territory. If virtue, love of the fatherland and the conviction of what we ought to be do not put us in the respectable position that is the child of enlightenment (without which there can be no nations, but only hordes of savages); if we do not establish a system of government founded on just, wise and beneficent laws; if we do not banish from amongst us the multitude of errors of every sort that has kept us brutalised . . . will we truly be able to acclaim our victory? Will we really be safe from fresh attempts on the part of the usurper, or any other power that wishes to enslave us?[31]

In *ancien-régime* Spain, however, liberty was an impossibility, for freedom of property was blocked by the extensive lands held in perpetuity by the Church and the nobility, and freedom of occupation by such obstacles as the influence of the guilds and the nobility's monopoly of direct entry to the officer corps. Meanwhile, too, there was no semblance of equality before the law, with the Church, the nobility, the army, the military orders, the guilds and the Basque provinces all enjoying their own *fueros*, the Mesta – or sheep-owners' confederation – possessing the right to let their flocks traverse the length and breadth of the land without let or hindrance, and large areas still being governed by seigneurial jurisdiction. What was required was therefore the destruction of all forms of privilege, the creation of a free market in land with all its attendant property rights, the sale of the lands of the Church, the abolition of all restrictions on economic activity, and the establishment of a unitary state. Also vital was a written constitution that would guarantee basic freedoms, impose limits on the power of the monarchy, and provide for the representation of the people on the basis of proportionality rather than of privilege (the old estates would therefore be swept away in favour of a unicameral assembly). Finally, the Church must be reformed so as to reduce the power of the papacy and purge it of the Inquisition and the religious orders, thereby making it both more 'national' and less burdensome.

Thus far Spanish liberalism appears a model of patriotic altruism, but in fact it dovetailed neatly with the interests of substantial elements of the propertied classes. Despite all their praise for the people, few even of the most radical could conceive of their direct participation in politics. Products of a cultured élite, the liberals were terrified of the unruly mobs who had overthrown the old order and determined to defend private property, their arguments being a reflection of powerful economic interests. Thus, by 1808 Spain was witnessing the emergence of a prosperous oligarchy of notables that, whilst often noble in origin, in practice owed its status to commercial investment. Reinforced by the influx of wealth brought by the commercial boom of the late eighteenth century, these *nouveaux riches* had sought to capitalise upon their prosperity through the acquisition of status, land and office, and benefited greatly from *desamortización*, whilst also acquiring substantial interests as government creditors (it was in large part their money that had financed the extensive issues of paper currency on which Godoy had increasingly relied). Clearly, then, the creation of a free market in land acquired a new significance, for it implied the entrance into the market of enormous holdings that had never been available before. Spain, in short, was to be reordered for the benefit of a new élite, the much-lauded Spanish people actually having little stake in the future for which they were supposedly fighting.

Between this programme and that of the second position revealed in the debates of 1808–10 there was a surprising amount of common ground despite the fact that the latter may essentially be described as legitimist. Prior to the uprising Spain had, as we have seen, been a bastion of enlightened absolutism. In the course of the uprising of 1808 many of the ministers and officials who had been active in this tradition had given their allegiance to Joseph Bonaparte, but some had chosen the Patriot cause, the most notable being Jovellanos and Floridablanca. With the death of the latter in December 1808, the chief proponent of this position became Jovellanos, and it was largely his influence as one of the representatives for Asturias that has allowed some observers to stigmatise the Junta Central as being conservative and even counter-revolutionary. Yet, in fact, Jovellanos shared many of the liberals' perceptions. Heavily influenced by Adam Smith, he had always condemned such phenomena as entails, the prohibition of enclosure in favour of the rights of pastoralists, and the survival of communal property. A Jansenist, he had also favoured the hispanisation of the Church and the abolition of the Inquisition (or at least the transfer of its powers to the episcopate). Like the liberals, too, he opposed provincial privilege, and, above all, was deeply committed to progress in science and education, calling for freedom of the press, a reduction of illiteracy, and greater study of agronomy and economics. Where Jovellanos differed from the liberals, however, was in his political analysis. Terrified by the French and Spanish revolutions alike and unable to conceive of a society that could function without the guidance of the nobility and the Church, he never argued for the abolition of entail *per se* but merely suggested its limitation. At the same time, still less did he desire a new concentration of the land in the hands of wealthy oligarchs, looking rather to the creation of a settled and prosperous peasantry. Faced by the events of 1808 he had concurred in the resumption of sovereignty by the nation, but wanted to balance this by maintaining the bicameral principle and opposing the radical programme of political and institutional reform proposed by the liberals. For Jovellanos, in fact, Spain already had a constitution in the form of the fundamental laws that she had inherited from the medieval era, and all that was necessary to abolish despotism to restate them.

Cautious though this programme was, it formed a marked contrast to that of the traditionalist party who had emerged as the third main element in Patriot politics. With all their dreams of a puppet monarchy swept away by Napoleon's overthrow of the Bourbons, the outbreak of a general uprising they were unable to control, the elimination of José Palafox, and finally the formation of the Regency, they yet remained a powerful force that embraced substantial elements of the clergy and nobility. Insisting that the rising was a crusade for Church and King so as to undermine arguments in favour of radical change, their tactic was on the one hand to demand that the *cortes* concentrate on the war effort, whilst on the other interpreting reform as a return to Spanish tradition. An exemplar of this programme's many advocates was Juan Pérez Villamil, the senior official who had helped pen the famous *bando de los alcaldes de Móstoles* in the wake of the Dos de Mayo (cf. p. 46). Though as much enamoured of popular heroism as any liberal, for Pérez Villamil the past was still valid, liberty – and, indeed, a constitution – lying in the existence of the fundamental laws inherited from the past. Far from being overthrown by the introduction of dangerous foreign innovations – it was a constant theme of traditionalists that the ideas of the liberals were drawn from the French Revolution – these should rather be reinforced. We thus return to the position adopted by Jovellanos, but, for all that, it would be a mistake to believe that Pérez Villamil was in agreement with him. On the contrary, for Pérez Villamil and his fellows, the royal reformism that the erstwhile minister represented was just as much a cancer as the ideas of the liberals, the solution being to turn back the clock: in 1810, for example, we find the future traditionalist deputy, Francisco Borrull, not only defending the rights of the nobility but also demanding the restitution of the Valencian *fueros* overthrown by Felipe V in 1707.

The trouble was that these three positions not only had a great deal in common with one another – after all, all of them coincided in upholding the sovereignty of the people, denouncing 'ministerial despotism', and calling for a return to a mythical medieval 'golden age' – but also employed a common discourse, it being *de rigueur* for all parties to lard their speeches and pamphlets with endless references to a mass of medieval precedents. For political neophytes of the sort that filled Cádiz and the Isla de León in the autumn of 1810, it was therefore all too easy to fall into the trap of co-option and manipulation, and all the more so as there was a general desire for reform: the *informes sobre cortes* solicited by the Junta Central had almost all called for a *cortes* and expressed particular interest in changes in the military estate, there being widespread agreement on the need for the subordination of the military to the civil power, the exclusion of the army from the administration, the opening of the officer corps to all classes of society, and the suppression of the army's numerous privileges. Beyond that, it is true, there was little agreement, but the deputies could easily be persuaded to vote for those who had the most radical answers to what, after all, were radical problems. All that was required was clever oratory and a measure of political organisation, and these the liberals possessed in abundance. Thus, the best speakers in the assembly, most notably the Asturian deputy, Agustín Argüelles, were all liberals, whilst they had in many cases known one another for years. Argüelles, Toreno and the most capable of their many allies in the press, Alvaro Flórez Estrada, whose paper, *El Tribuno del Pueblo Español*, was to become the most outspoken mouthpiece of the liberal cause, had all studied at the University of Oviedo, for example, as had the slightly more moderate Angel de la Vega Infanzón, and the senior Treasury official, José Canga Argüelles. A tight, united group who met regularly outside the chamber, possessed a clear agenda, planned their tactics in advance and trusted one another implicitly, these men were quickly able to forge alliances with such like-minded deputies as the progressive ecclesiastics, Juan Nicasio Gallego, Diego Múñoz Torrero and Joaquín Lorenzo Villanueva. Through long-standing links with the mercantile community – many of them had, after all, been resident in Cádiz since the start of the siege – they were also able to conjure up a mob. Thus, as traditionalist critics have always argued, the public galleries were frequently packed with crowds that had been primed to applaud liberal orators and decry their opponents, one or two of whom were on occasion all but lynched, even some liberals becoming alarmed at 'the disorderly manner in which the crowd that filled the public galleries took part in debates and coerced the deliberations of the *cortes*'.[32]

What counted, then, was discipline, organisation and financial support. Backed by these advantages, the small group of very talented ideologues that was all that Spanish liberalism could count upon was able to impose its will upon a confused and divided *cortes* and time and again win the support of the mass of deputies who were committed to the principle of reform, but had no clear idea as to what reform should entail. Thus it was that the *cortes* embarked upon the course encapsulated by the Constitution of 1812. Great stress was placed on the idea that this document was a reflection of tradition, but this was a mere fiction: for all the liberals' claims, its roots lay firmly in the Enlightenment, establishing, as it did, all the basic civil liberties except that of religion, and in general dealing a heavy blow to corporate privilege. Thus, the *cortes* itself, being unicameral, made no recognition of the estates, whilst there was to be equality before the law, freedom of economic opportunity and employment, and equal liability to taxation and military service. Meanwhile, the principle of the separation of powers was declared, the nation proclaimed to be sovereign and the most severe restrictions placed upon the power of the king. Real power therefore belonged to the *cortes*, which was to meet each year and to enjoy complete control of taxation as well as a dominant role in legislation. Last but not least, no changes in the Constitution would be permitted for at least eight years, Fernando being expected to swear an oath of loyalty to the entire document as soon as he returned from exile.

Though it was hostile to the throne, in many respects the Constitution followed the goals of enlightened absolutism. Thus, provincial privilege was removed and Spain declared a unitary state, her governance being completely remodelled. The king was to be aided by a council of state whose composition was laid down by law, and the network of councils that had stood at the apex of administration and justice was replaced by seven new ministries. As taxation was to be assessed in an equal and proportionate fashion, it followed that the nobility and the Church, and, indeed, such favoured provinces as the Basque territories, would now lose their fiscal exemptions and have to contribute their full share of revenue. And, in contrast to the confusion that had characterised the *antiguo régimen*, uniformity would also characterise local government and the administration of justice. Thus, Spain would henceforth be divided into provinces of equal size administered by civil governors known as *jefes políticos*, who would be assisted by elected councils. Also elected, meanwhile, would be the councils that would rule each locality, the system being completed by a unitary system of law courts which envisaged a supreme court in Madrid, a district court in each province and a stipendiary magistrate in every district.

In forcing this programme through, the liberals did not, of course, have things all their own way. The number of hardline traditionalists in the assembly might have been relatively few, but they were not devoid of courage, whilst they had also been encouraged by the relatively lenient treatment accorded the Bishop of Orense, who had simply been allowed to retire to his diocese. As one liberal muttered darkly, indeed:

It appeared that the Bishop of Orense counted for more than the whole of the nation . . . there emerging a party that supported his opposition. In that moment, perhaps, was born the discord that eventually degenerated into civil war. What was the obstinate refusal of that prelate to swear free and full obedience to the *cortes* if not the seeds of civil war?[33]

Nor did the liberals' enemies lack talent. Rather than simply opposing reform *tout court*, for example, traditionalist clerics such as Francisco Javier Borrull, Pedro de Inguanzo and Jaime Creus made use of the arguments of Montesquieu in favour of mixed monarchy to defend the privileges of the nobility and press for a second chamber, and they often cut an impressive figure in debate. Traditionalist pamphleteers, meanwhile, began to publish newpapers that openly opposed the liberals, whilst producing a series of biting critiques of Spain's military performance that rubbished notions of 'people's war' and pressed the idea that the *cortes* should not waste time on political reform but rather dedicate itself to the war effort. Still other figures, meanwhile, chose the path of open confrontation: the deposed regent,

Lardizábal, for example, caused a storm of controversy, by publishing a bitter denunciation of the *cortes* in which he denied its legitimacy, opposed the principle of the sovereignty of the people and claimed that it was dominated by a faction of unrepresentative *suplentes*, whilst the Marqués del Palacio resigned his command rather than swear the oath of allegiance required by the decree of 24 September 1810.

As the traditionalists (or, as they gradually became known, *serviles* – literally, 'the slavish ones') soon learned, however, they were powerless. Hardly surprisingly, they therefore turned to intrigue. No sooner had the *cortes* opened than the Castaños regency had resigned, the liberals securing its replacement by an anodyne body composed of General Blake and two obscure admirals named Ciscar and Agar. To redress the political balance, it was obvious that the *serviles*' best hope was to engineer a change, and they soon discovered that they found ready allies in agents of the wife of the Prince Regent of Portugal, the *infanta* María Carlota. The sister of Fernando VII, *la Carlota* or the Princess of Brazil, as she became known, was a tough and determined woman who saw herself as duty bound to conserve all the rights and prerogatives of the Spanish throne, whilst at the same time harbouring dreams of an Iberian monarchy that would unite Portugal, Spain and the whole of Latin America. From 1808 onwards, she had therefore been scheming both to establish a regency in Spain and to place herself at its head. With the formation of a regency, these efforts were redoubled, and the *serviles* not surprisingly welcomed them with open arms, whilst at the same time seeking to win the support of the British, who were known to be most dissatisfied with the failure of the *cortes* to address Spain's military needs. As Wellington complained:

The *cortes* appear to me to suffer under the national disease to as great a degree as the other authorities; that is, boasting of the strength and power of the Spanish nation till they are seriously convinced they are in no danger, and then sitting down quietly and indulging in their national indolence.[34]

Underpinning Wellington's dissatisfaction was a measure of ideological alarm. As he wrote to Henry Wellesley, indeed, 'I am apprehensive that the *cortes* are becoming a national assembly.'[35] Yet even so there is no doubt that the liberals had a real case to answer. Setting aside the fact that the Constitution of 1812 proved shot through with flaws that made it very difficult to operate, as even the highly progressive Blanco White admitted:

The debates of the *cortes* are full of knowledge and excellent ideas, but they more resemble conversations than debates . . . In the same day a multitude of matters are dealt with, at times in accordance with what occurs to each [deputy], and it is not seen . . . that speaking other than to the motion is not allowed, that one speaker cannot be interrupted by another, and that an individual cannot speak more than once upon a subject.[36]

Still worse was the fact that the military situation continued to deteriorate. For the liberals, the Constitution was 'the most formidable army that the French have had to face, for it has transformed . . . a horde of savages into a nation of free men'.[37] Yet in practice the reforms supposed to revive Spain's fortunes made no difference whatsoever. In consequence, *servil* pamphleteers were provided with the most obvious arguments for undermining the whole liberal project. To quote *El Ciudadano Imparcial*:

If the time that many learned men have until now employed on matters concerning friars and the Inquisition . . . had been spent on alerting the nation, discussing the means of subsistence . . . the organisation of the armies and the . . . supply of clothing, food and arms . . . there would undoubtedly be more enthusiasm among the troops, a greater willingness to serve . . . fewer desertions, better discipline, and less indulgence towards criminals who are at present generally seen . . . as miserable victims of nakedness and hunger.[38]

Once again such views were echoed by Blanco White, who was rapidly earning the hatred of his erstwhile friends. Thus, condemning the *cortes*' 'absolute lack of attention to the improvement of the Spanish army', he complained:

This truly clamours to the sky. The human mind can hardly conceive the idea of putting under discussion and controversy how and with whom Fernando VII should be married when there is within sight of the *cortes* a disorganised army, incapable of doing anything in favour of the cause . . . which is the mockery of its enemies for its want of discipline . . . What have the *cortes* done in this most important matter, the only one, it could be said, which clamours for their attention?[39]

What made matters still worse was that fear of reaction in the eyes of many critics had very quickly led the liberals to force through a *reglamento* that reduced the power of the Regency to a cypher. To quote Blanco White again:

They have done very well in overthrowing the Regency which wanted to impede their congregation so badly, but they have done very ill in forming a most weak executive power as a result. They wished to conserve the sovereign power, but have lost it for themselves and the executive power, their creation.[40]

For the supporters of the Princess of Brazil, this, of course, was a godsend, for traditionalist pamphleteers could argue that the root of Spain's ills was weak government, from which it followed that what was needed was a strong regency headed by a member of the royal family. Thus:

Bad as our former system of government was, we should not have changed it at so critical a time . . . but, supposing that we had to do so, we should have preferred that constitution which, although perhaps not the most free . . . was by its nature the most energetic . . . Yet what we have done is precisely the opposite . . . We say that the entire nation should not breathe anything but war, but we wish to wage this war without subjecting ourselves to the severe discipline of a military government and idle under the rule of a democracy that comes very close to anarchy and is incapable of preserving tranquillity and good order.[41]

In the end, as we shall see, these arguments were to destroy the liberals, but such was the dexterity of their leaders that in the short term they were more than a match for them. Exploiting the fact that the princess was a notorious opponent of the British, they hinted that Wellington might be offered the command of the Spanish armies – a constant goal of Marquess Wellesley, who had now become Foreign Secretary. Meanwhile, when criticism of Spain's deteriorating military situation finally became too intense to ignore, in an extremely clever move they launched a pre-emptive strike by replacing Blake and his colleagues with a new five-man body headed by the Duque de Infantado (a noted *servil*, Infantado could hardly be objected to by traditionalists, and yet he was at the same time no danger, being notoriously indolent and simple-minded).

In political terms, then, the liberals were able to maintain control of the situation. Nor, indeed, were they quite so negligent as their opponents implied. Hardly had the *cortes* met, for example, than it decreed a new levy of 80,000 conscripts whilst in March 1811 it firmly threw itself behind the principle that military service should be universal. Various efforts, too, were made to improve the quality of the troops, most notably through the establishment of a central training depot on the Isla de León, whilst, in a major change, the armies were stripped of their old territorial denominations.* Meanwhile, a variety of reforms were enacted that aimed to restore order in the colonies, whilst liberal deputies and pamphleteers never ceased to preach the need for all-out war against the French and to attempt

---

* The forces of Catalonia became the First Army, those of Valencia the Second, those of Murcia the Third, those of Cadiz the Fourth, those of Extremadura the Fifth, and those of Galicia the Sixth.

to whip up popular enthusiasm for the struggle. Last but not least, the *desamortización* that was at the heart of their social and economic policy had become the one means by which the war could be financed, for it was only through the expropriation and sale of the lands of the Church and the municipalities that the state could obtain the revenue that it needed.

Yet in the last resort all this is by the by. The new Regency was, if anything, worse than its predecessor. As García de León y Pizarro complained, indeed:

The office of the Regency was a sorry picture ... Ever frivolous, Infantado disrupted every discussion with irrelevancies, and spent most of his time fiddling with sword or braid, or looking at a miniature or something else of the sort ... Except when some matter relating to the navy came up, when he would regularly come out and force through the most unwise decision. Villavicencio, who was a man but little committed to justice, spent all his time pacing up and down and smoking cigars in a lavatory next to the office. Abisbal had more spark, but no judgement to go with it, whilst Wellesley had only to offer him 200 pairs of shoes for the troops for him to forget honour, the decorum of the fatherland and the public interest alike ... Mosquera was punctual, hardworking and honourable, which is more than can be said for the others, but his knowledge was limited to a few old laws ... As for Rivas, I shall not even speak of him, for, though ill-intentioned, he was insignificant.[42]

By the time that the new Regency had been installed in January 1812, Patriot Spain's situation had deteriorated still further. Having seized power in Cádiz, the liberals could not escape responsibility for this situation, whilst the divisiveness of the various measures that we shall see them introduce in the period that followed the promulgation of the Constitution on 19 March 1812 ensured that they became still more enmired. In the end Spain was to be saved from disaster but not so the liberals. Committed to the fiction that the struggle against Napoleon was a people's war, they had sought to justify their revolution in military terms. Offering the people nothing, however, they were unable to kindle the sort of enthusiasm of which they dreamed. For the moment the revolution might continue, but in reality the liberals were doomed.

12

Torres Vedras

THE DEFENCE OF PORTUGAL,
JULY 1810 – MARCH 1811

The stench hung heavy in the air. In the rubbish-strewn streets nothing moved except a few emaciated dogs who snarled at one another over the corpses lying everywhere. As the British troops moved into the village, they looked at one another in horror. Hardened veterans though they were, nothing they had seen had prepared them for this. The entire population, it seemed, had been massacred. Most of the houses had been reduced to blackened shells whilst the few that had not contained still more bodies, many of which showed signs of torture or rape. In the churches what could not be burned had been smashed, whilst the very tombs had been flung open, and their contents strewn about or propped up in a variety of mocking attitudes. As for food or items of value, there were none, the French having stripped the place bare. All around, meanwhile, the smoke rose from other ruined villages, whilst to add to the horror there began to appear haggard skeletons desperate for food and shelter.

If these sights were shocking, however, they were also the mark of Allied victory. Implicit in the savagery visited on the unfortunate inhabitants of such towns as Venda Nova, Pombal and Leiria in March 1811 was a winter of suffering that had broken Marshal André Masséna's Army of Portugal, and put an end to a campaign that had seemed to offer the hope of victory. To understand Wellington's triumph, we must return to 1809. As the British commander realised, Austria's defeat at Wagram would almost certainly mean the invasion of Portugal. But for Wellington such a prospect held no fear, for he was convinced that, unless the French came in absolutely overwhelming force, such an invasion could be thrown back. (His political masters, by contrast, were less sanguine, but, as they could not simply abandon Portugal, they left Wellington to act very much as he wished.) In essence, his plan started with the integration of the Portuguese troops and his own forces to allow him to do battle with the invaders and throw them back at an early date, to which end a number of obvious defensive positions along the roads from the frontier were strengthened with redoubts and other fortifications. Should the French prove unstoppable, however, then the defenders would fall back on Lisbon, which he planned to cover with an impregnable system of defence works – the famous Lines of Torres Vedras – whilst at the same time stripping the countryside of its resources and mobilising a guerrilla war. With the French brought to a standstill and restricted in their foraging, victory was assured. Though convoys of food and reinforcements might with some difficulty be got to them from the border, it was unlikely that enough men could ever be brought up to allow the French to break through. Even if they did, the entire field army would be available to fling them back as Wellington planned to garrison his forts solely with militiamen. Provision, it is true, was made for evacuation from the port of São Julio south-west of Lisbon, but the further line of fortifications built to protect this bolt hole did not seem likely to be needed. With the Lines impossible to outflank, the Tagus impossible to cross, and the Allies able to bring in unlimited food by sea, sooner or later the French must retreat.

Though not without its problems, this plan was one of the most perfect schemes of defence that has ever been devised. Thus, making use of the facts, first, that the French could only conquer Portugal by conquering Lisbon, and, second, that they could in practice only reach Lisbon from the north, it exploited both the Portuguese capital's geographical situation and the poverty of the Portuguese countryside to the full, whilst at the same time bringing into play traditional responses to invasion in the form of the *ordenança* and the devastation of the countryside in a scorched-earth policy (a similar tactic had actually been employed against the Spaniards as recently as 1762). In consequence, despite serious worries about his army, Wellington was quietly confident. As he wrote to Lord Liverpool on 14 November 1809:

From all I have learned of the state of the enemy's force at present in the Peninsula, I am of opinion that unless the Spanish armies should meet with some great misfortune, the enemy could not make an attack upon Portugal; and [that] if events in Spain should enable the enemy to make such an attack, the force at present in Portugal is able to defend that country. If in consequence of the peace in Germany the enemy's army in the Peninsula should be largely reinforced, it is obvious that the enemy will acquire the means of attacking Portugal . . . Even in this case, however, I conceive that till Spain shall have been conquered . . . the enemy will find it difficult, if not impossible, to obtain possession of Portugal.[1]

Yet implementing his plan would not be easy. Whilst Wellington would obviously need the co-operation of the Portuguese Regency (see Chapter 4,

p. 104), this was distinctly uncertain. Thus, the Convention of Sintra (see Chapter 4) and Beresford's ruthless remodelling of the army had already given rise to many fears of British intentions, whilst matters were not helped by British opposition to their allies' pursuit of the restoration of Olivenza – a small frontier district seized by the Spaniards following the 'War of the Oranges' of 1801. With other quarrels developing over slavery, free trade and the payment of the subsidy (fixed in December 1809 as the cost of maintaining 30,000 men), it was hardly to be expected that Wellington would have everything his own way.

Though some elements of the Portuguese administration might snipe at the British general, in the long run they could not prevail. Sometimes bamboozled by the intrigues of his wife, the Prince Regent nevertheless remained loyal to the Alliance, it being thanks to him, indeed, that Beresford had been appointed to command the army. Determined to restore order to the Alliance, in August 1810 João therefore took advantage of the resignation of one of its members to remodel the Regency along lines that he hoped would make for smoother relations. Thus, both the British ambassador, Charles Stuart, and a member of the powerful Sousa Coutinho family were offered a place in its ranks. Sousa Coutinhos already holding the posts of Secretary of State, ambassador to London and ambassador to Cádiz, it was clearly hoped that the clan would feel that its interests were so bound up with the British Alliance that it would have no option but to sustain it for good.

Until these changes occurred, however, the Portuguese administration was free to resist British influence more or less as it wished, Beresford's position being rendered tolerable only by the firm support of the Minister of War, Miguel de Pereira Forjaz. In so far as the condition of the army was concerned, then, much less was achieved than Wellington would have liked, but even so enough was done to allow it to take the field alongside the British. Thus, when Beresford arrived in Portugal, its troops were in a ruinous condition. Arms, clothing and footwear were all in short supply – as late as December Beresford was complaining, 'Few regiments of militia . . . are complete in arms, and we have not even enough for the regulars when completed'[2] – whilst the men were described as 'very obedient, willing and patient, but also naturally dirty and careless of their persons, dreadfully sickly and [possessed of] a natural . . . want of fortitude which makes them yield immediately to . . . fatigue'.[3] Recruitment having been slow, the regiments, as we have seen, had still been scattered around the country in their depots, whilst desertion was rampant, fifty men fleeing a unit stationed at Peniche in a single night. To quote Wellington:

The Portuguese army is recruited by conscription constitutionally, very much in the same manner with the French army, but . . . it must be recollected that for the past fifty years . . . the troops have never left their province, and scarcely ever their native town; and their discipline, and the labours and exertion required from them, were nothing. Things are much altered lately, and, notwithstanding that the pay has been increased, I fear that the animal is not of the description to bear up against what is required of him, and he deserts most readily.[4]

Yet this was not the worst of the trouble. Very poorly paid, the officers consisted of a mixture of men who had grown old in the service without hope of obtaining promotion and inexperienced boys who had joined up since 1808. Such men being incapable of instilling their units with fighting spirit – many of them, indeed, were perpetually absent – the rank and file lacked any pride in their appearance and made little effort to master their calling. No sooner had he arrived, than Beresford plunged into a sustained campaign to restore the army's morale. The officer corps was purged – in 4 months no fewer than 215 officers were cashiered and at least a further 107 ordered to retire – whilst a series of regulations both stressed the need for discipline, cleanliness and attention to duty and laid down severe penalties for those who broke them. Degrading punishments and the casual use of violence were forbidden; an intensive programme of training instituted; and the men given proper medical treatment. Pay was raised for all ranks, whilst considerable efforts were made to ensure the men's comfort, whether it was through the replacement of the cauldrons traditionally used for cooking with smaller and more manageable camp kettles, or the issue of orders directing that blankets were not to be used to keep out the rain on the march, but rather kept dry and only got out at night. And, last but not least, the campaigns of 1809 were made use of to give the troops some experience of life in the field, the result being that by the end of the year there had been a considerable improvement. To quote Charles Boutflower:

On the twenty-eighth [of December] we . . . marched to Thomar. Marshal Beresford is at present there. We had an opportunity of seeing one of the regiments at parade . . . They were well clothed and made an excellent appearance. The soldier-like manner in which they went through their evolutions astonished the English officers. I should really expect much from them if opposed to an enemy.[5]

Despite doubts that 'their . . . officers, though very much improved and mostly young men, have scarce experience and firmness enough to control them as we could wish', such opinions were shared by William Warre. At least the officers now had the means 'of living like gentlemen and with respectability', whilst, as he continued:

I am anxious that the campaign should begin, and to be able to judge of what our Portuguese will in reality do. I confess I have very great hopes of them. Their discipline is most wonderfully improved, perhaps fully as good as necessary for active service, and only wants confirming . . . Our cavalry is also getting into a very respectable state, and [is] now very tolerably mounted.[6]

In all this, meanwhile, Beresford, who had been given the rank of field marshal, was assisted by large numbers of British officers and sergeants (indeed, Beresford contended that their presence was not just a help but an absolute necessity, his argument being that the Portuguese were so lazy by nature that only British officers could be trusted to get anything done). Initially drawn from volunteers procured amongst the forces of Sir John Cradock, they were later supplemented by men recruited from units that were still at home, enthusiasm for such transfers being stimulated by the fact that they were accompanied by a guaranteed step in rank (so that a captain in the British service became a major in that of Portugal). Initially distributed amongst the Portuguese at a rate of about three per battalion, the 350 men who were eventually involved undoubtedly engendered much jealousy. In some ways, however, this was all to the good, while Beresford was careful not to let the British dominate the army altogether: plenty of Portuguese officers were allowed to command battalions, regiments and brigades, whilst all units or sub-units placed under the command of British officers had Portuguese seconds. To save face still further, Portuguese generals were given territorial commands or appointed as governors of fortresses such as Elvas, and the army allowed to form brigades of its own rather than being split up amongst British units.

The British officers sent to Portugal were not all paragons of virtue: indeed, Wellington, who had opposed the promotion automatically given them in the Portuguese service, considered their selection to have been 'unlucky'.[7] But at least their presence served to homogenise the Allied armies. Thus, Portuguese line infantrymen carried 'Brown Bess' muskets and learned the British system of drill and manoeuvres, whilst the existing force of light infantry was expanded by fifty per cent and in some cases equipped with the Baker rifle. Other issues, however, proved harder to deal with. Because of a lack of horses, for example, only a relatively small force of cavalry could be built up. Far worse, however, was the attitude of the populace to the war. The picture that we have of Portugal, indeed, is rather similar to that which we have of Spain. Amongst the propertied classes there was much froth – the merchants of Lisbon, for example, rallied enthusiastically to the special militias that they raised and enjoyed putting on fine uniforms and playing at soldiers in the safety and comfort of the capital – but the people were a different matter. Banditry was rife – even wounded British soldiers were not safe from robbery – and the *ordenanças* behaved in a notoriously disorderly manner during the campaign of 1809, a number of regular troops having to be left in Oporto on account of 'the possibility of the people being unquiet'.[8] A new system of conscription was introduced, but military service was, as before, thoroughly detested. Despite intensive efforts to evoke a patriotic response amongst the populace, indeed, resistance remained the norm. Many of them being criminals, troublemakers, village idiots or men suffering from serious physical handicaps, conscripts often had to be locked up and manacled. The men, wrote Aitchison, 'are pressed like seamen in England and bound together', whilst in Douglas' words, 'You must not expect to hear of a sergeant conducting a party of men voluntarily enlisted as soldiers, but fancy for a moment a . . . mounted policeman with a rope fastened to the saddle . . . of the horse, and at a distance of two yards . . . twenty or thirty on the string.'[9] Not surprisingly, then, between May 1809 and October 1810, no fewer than 10,224 of the 23,885 men inducted into the army ran away. Savage penalties were decreed for the punishment of deserters and those who harboured them, but, with deaths from disease also very high, the army grew very slowly and never attained full strength (assessed at a nominal strength of 56,000 men, in September 1808 it possessed 18,000 men; in September 1809 42,000; and in August 1810 perhaps 47,000).

The reasons for this situation were simple. In the first place, the mass of the inhabitants were essentially apolitical. In the words of the commissary, Augustus Schaumann:

One hears no more patriotic sentiments from [the populace] than joy over the liberation of their precious selves from French molestation . . . National freedom on a grand scale . . . and the desire for a national constitution . . . are matters in which they are not interested.[10]

Thus they would only fight the French if their homes and families were directly threatened, whilst the existence of the *ordenanças* seemed to suggest that the regular army was redundant. At the same time, there was also a problem of authority, the local magistrates knowing all too well that they had few means of either imposing conscription or staving off the anger of the inhabitants. As Wellington noted:

The military forces stationed in the provinces enabled the civil government to carry into execution the conscription, but, under present circumstances, [it] is . . . removed to a distance. The civil government . . . can hardly be said to exist, and . . . the people . . . are all armed, and . . . defy the . . . government.[11]

Matters might have been somewhat easier had Beresford been able to reform the army's supply system as he wished, but in this respect he got nowhere. If it was to operate successfully the army needed a permanent corps of transport as well as the ability to pay for its provisions on the spot. However, beyond transferring supply from the Ministry of Finance to the Ministry of War, Beresford was unable to make much progress. Lacking funds, the army had to muddle through on the basis of wagons, pack mules and draught animals hired on a short-term basis from the local populace. As for its debts, it had to rely on bills of credit presented to the central Junta da Viveres and generally only settled months in arrears. Because the populace in consequence preferred to sell to the British commissariat, the troops tended to go hungry and fall sick or deserted at an even faster rate than would otherwise have been the case. For an angry denunciation of the chaos, let us turn to Beresford's chief-of-staff, Sir Benjamin d'Urban:

The Marshal is arranging with Lord Wellington some certain means of subsisting the Portuguese troops when their own supplies fail . . . This is absolutely requisite or the troops will often starve, for such is the poverty, imbecility and total want of arrangement of the Portuguese government that any regular system of supply is not to be expected . . . The whole civil branch of the army is in such a state of confusion that I hold it utterly impracticable to carry on operations with it for more than a week or two together, if even so long.[12]

Knowing that military service was liable to mean semi-starvation, the townspeople and villagers of Portugal were nudged still further in the direction of resistance. And, as if this was not enough, there was also the question of what might happen to their families in their absence. As British writers have always stressed, Wellington from the beginning took the utmost pains to prevent his soldiers from plundering the populace. Yet all his hanging and flogging made no difference. On the contrary, complaints abounded. For example: 'The commander of the forces is . . . obliged again to complain of the conduct of the troops; not only have outrages been committed by entire corps, but there is no description of property, of which the unfortunate inhabitants of Portugal have not been plundered by the British soldiers whom they have received into their own homes.'[13] And again: 'I am concerned to tell you that . . . the conduct of the soldiers is infamous. They behave generally well with their regiments . . . but, when detached and coming up from hospitals, although invariably under the command of an officer, and always well fed and taken care of . . . they commit every description of outrage.'[14] Though still ruinous enough to the peasantry, some of this plundering was committed in a spirit of light-heartedness, as witness, for example, Schaumann's account of robbing beehives (an affair which ended in his being badly stung and soaked from head to foot in honey). But on other occasions scenes took place that were as least as bad as anything perpetrated by the French. Thus:

The night before last a most horrid murder was committed a short distance from this place. There is too much reason to suppose that the perpetrators were British. I was directed by the general . . . to go down there . . . Three bodies, viz. a man, a woman and their daughter, a child of about eight years of age, lay on the floor, weltering in blood . . . A hatchet lay beside them with which the deed had evidently been completed . . . the heads of the deceased were literally beat to a jelly.[15]

This, perhaps, was an exception, but for many soldiers it is all too clear that pillage was a way of life. As for the civilian population, they were habitually treated with the utmost callousness. Taking Sergeant William Lawrence as an example, we find him by his own confession stealing a pig, a hen, a cock, the entire contents of the oven of a bake house, and a large sum of money that the owner of the house he was billeted in had concealed in the cellar. As he himself admitted, indeed, the British 'often committed depredations on the inhabitants almost as bad as the enemy'.[16]

Desertion, then, remained a serious problem. Yet the Portuguese army was still much better than before. What, though, of Wellington's plans for the construction of field fortifications? Here matters proceeded relatively smoothly. Two of the chief routes from the frontier of León across the highlands of Beira were blocked by chains of redoubts at places suitable to make a stand, whilst a third was wrecked by demolitions. That left just one more. Seemingly neglected as an unlikely route for Masséna to take, it was along this one that the latter came, but such were the defensive positions that it offered that the oversight hardly mattered. All the more was this the case as the Lines of Torres Vedras were well advanced. Commenced towards the end of 1809, these consisted of two lines of heavily armed forts that stretched from the Atlantic to the Tagus. Constructed along the crest of a series of rocky hills by gangs of peasants and militiamen, these were pro-tected by a broad belt of *abattis*, pits, inundations, palisades, *chevaux de frise* and man-made escarpments. Meanwhile, everything that might provide the French with cover was torn down, special roads constructed to allow the defenders to rush troops from one sector to another, and a semaphore telegraph set up that could relay messages the whole length of the line in less than ten minutes.

As Masséna was the first to recognise when he finally encountered them – and it should be noted that almost no news of their construction reached his ears – these works were simply not amenable to being stormed by an army of the size that he possessed, and all the more so as Wellington's entire field army was available for counter-attacks, the Lines themselves being largely manned by militiamen and *ordenanças* (in this case formed into regular units on the lines of the Voluntarios Distinguidos de Cádiz – the merchant units referred to above (see p. 316) – Sherer describing the men involved as being 'most handsomely clothed and appointed'[17]). As Wellington had always planned, these forces were also to play an important role outside the lines. Badly trained, unreliable and ill-armed as they were, the 45,000 militia under arms in 1810 (out of a theoretical total of some 70,000) helped to man Almeida, Elvas, Abrantes and other places and made up the bulk of the weak covering forces that Wellington had left to watch the frontiers of Galicia, Extremadura and Andalucía, whilst also being charged with the task of harassing the enemy's flanks and rear and preventing the French from sending out forage parties. In short, they were to act as guerrillas, in which task it was, as we have seen, expected that they would be joined by the *ordenanças*. With the latter ready to be called out at a moment's notice and the authorities carefully primed with regard to what was expected of them when it came to the implementation of a scorched-earth policy and the evacuation of the civilian population, the invaders were in for a most unpleasant surprise.

Before we go on to discuss what actually happened in the third invasion of Portugal, we must say a little more about the Allied field army. Thus, in addition to the 26,000 Portuguese regulars who were available for service in the summer of 1810 and such oddments as the survivors of the Loyal Lusitanian Legion, Wellington had perhaps 31,000 British troops. His army now assumed the basic shape that it was to retain for the rest of the war, consisting, as it did, of five British line infantry divisions, the 'light' division, and four cavalry brigades. Each infantry division consisted of between two and five infantry brigades, of which at least one was usually Portuguese, and a battery of artillery, and each brigade consisted of three or four infantry battalions and an extra company of riflemen (the remaining Portuguese troops were formed into an independent infantry division, three independent infantry brigades and a cavalry brigade). Special mention ought to be made of the Light Division, whose two brigades each only mustered two and a half battalions and were the only ones in the army to contain both British and Portuguese battalions. Highly trained and possessed both of many riflemen and of a high opinion of themselves, they were an élite force. As for the generals who commanded the divisions and brigades, whilst they numbered several products of seniority whose competence and courage alike have been called into question – as Wellington complained, 'Really when I reflect upon the characters and attainments of some of the general officers of this army ... I tremble'[18] – their ranks also included some of Britain's very best commanders. Thus, in command of the Second Division was the genial Sir Rowland 'Daddy' Hill, a bluff, solid and reliable figure much liked by all who came into contact with him, whilst the Third Division was led by the tough and indomitable Sir Thomas Picton, and the Light by Robert Craufurd, a highly efficient soldier who had proved his worth over the past few months commanding the army's front-line pickets. As for the troops, although sickness was a problem amongst those units that had been sent to Spain following involvement in the abortive Walcheren campaign,* they were fresh, rested and raring for a fight. To quote the guards officer, Aitchison, '[The troops] are in high health and excellent spirits, and should it be our lot to engage the French on 27 or 28 July we shall celebrate the anniversary of Talavera in a victory as brilliant and more complete.'[19]

This opinion, to be sure, was not shared by every officer in the army – on the contrary, throughout 1810 Wellington had been plagued by 'croakers' who had been writing home prophesying disaster – but the British commander was supremely confident. 'I am positively in no scrape,' he wrote to William Wellesley-Pole, 'and, if the country can be saved, we shall save it.'[20] As for the chances of the French actually taking Lisbon, he thought it highly unlikely, informing Henry Wellesley that 'three times [20,000 men] will not obtain possession of Portugal, or possibly four times'.[21] And even then all would not be lost:

All the preparations for embarking ... the army ... are already made ... If the enemy should invade this country with a force less than that which I should think so superior to ours as to create the necessity for embarking, I shall fight a battle to save the country ... and if the result should not be successful ... I shall still be able to retire.[22]

Whether or not this optimism was justified, the invasion of Portugal was certain to prove extremely difficult, and all the more so as Masséna initially had only 68,000 men (even that figure, indeed, could only be obtained by

---

* This was a disastrous attempt at an amphibious invasion of the Low Countries.

calling in the corps of Reynier which until then had been occupying the Tagus valley and keeping open communications with Marshal Soult). Despite a desperately difficult supply situation, however, on 21 July the French crossed the frontier and headed for Almeida, which, in spite of strong suggestions from Wellington that it should retreat, was still being covered by the Light Division. Retreat would certainly have been advisable, for Almeida lies some two miles east of the River Côa, which flows in a deep gorge and in 1810 was only crossed by a single narrow bridge. Craufurd, though, was a reckless, quarrelsome and touchy figure, bitter at what he felt to have been a blighted career. Rendered overconfident by several months of skirmishes in which the French had never once bested his men, he therefore decided to stand and fight. Yet in doing so he was taking a great risk, and that for no good reason, for he could hardly hope to stave off the coming siege for more than a day or two. All that can be said in Craufurd's favour, indeed, was that he had managed to find a reasonably good defensive position for his men; that he kept a sharp watch; that his handling of the battle that followed was reasonably skilful; and, finally, that he had brought the Light Division to such a pitch of readiness that it proved equal to almost any crisis.

Yet at all events disaster was averted. Fighting began at dawn on 24 July with a general advance on the part of Ney's corps that was fiercely contested by Craufurd's men:

The whole plain in our front was covered with horse and foot advancing towards us. The enemy's infantry formed line and, with an innumerable multitude of skirmishers, attacked us fiercely; we repulsed them; they came on again, yelling, with drums beating, frequently the drummers leading ... French officers like mountebanks running forward and placing their hats upon their swords and capering about like madmen, saying as they turned to their men, 'Come on, children of our country. The first that advances, Napoleon will recompense him!'[23]

Quickly turned out of their initial position, the troops were soon scrambling for the bridge, and for a moment catastrophe threatened. The bridge became blocked by Craufurd's guns and transport, whilst French cavalry charged in amongst the retreating infantry and began to cut them down. The Forty-Third regiment, indeed, were soon in real trouble:

Our line was ... contracted, and brought under the edge of the ravine. In an instant 4,000 hostile cavalry swept the plain, and our regiment was unaccountably placed within an enclosure of solid masonry at least ten feet high ... with but one narrow outlet ... A few moments later and we should have been surrounded, but ... we contrived to loosen some large stones, when by a powerful exertion we burst the enclosure . . . There was no room to array the line, no time for anything but battle; every captain carried off his company as an independent body, the whole presenting a mass of skirmishers, acting in small parties and under no regular command . . . Having the advantage of ground and number, the enemy broke over the edge of the ravine . . . and their hussars . . . poured down the road, sabring everything in their way.[24]

However, launching his British infantry on a knoll above the crossing, Craufurd managed to hold out long enough for the cavalry, *caçadores*, artillery and wagons to get across and then to disengage his rearguard as well. It was, though, a desperate affair. 'In ascending the hill, a musket-shot grazed the left side of my head, and buried itself in the earth close by', Leach remembered. 'Both my subalterns, who were brothers, were severely wounded, and . . . we were . . . the whole time exposed to such a fire . . . as might have satisfied the most determined fire-eater in existence.'[25] Amongst those who fell was George Simmons:

The enemy . . . kept up a terrible fire . . . Lieutenant Harry Smith, Lieutenant Thomas Smith and Lieutenant Pratt were wounded, and I was shot through the thigh . . . Captain Napier took off his neckerchief and gave it to a sergeant, who put it round my thigh and twisted it tight with a ramrod, to stop the bleeding. The firing was so severe that the sergeant . . . fell with a shot in the head. Captain Napier was also about the same time wounded in the side.[26]

Foolishly, Ney then ordered several battalions to assault the bridge, but in three separate assaults they were shot to pieces, the battle eventually being ended by a heavy thunderstorm.

Claimed by both sides as a victory, the combat of the Côa, as it became known, was essentially a draw. Though driven back, the Light Division had fought well and suffered far fewer losses than the French. Still, Masséna's troops were much encouraged, whilst their morale was now to be raised still further. A much better fortress than Ciudad Rodrigo, Almeida, which was strongly garrisoned, well-provisioned and built on rocky ground that made the task of digging trenches very difficult, might have held out for a considerable time. Such were the problems that the French had in getting up their siege guns and supply trains that it was not even formally besieged until 15 August. Still more time was then lost in scraping out the first parallel and its accompanying batteries, and it was therefore not until the early morning of 26 August that the French guns opened fire. Some thirteen hours later they were still firing when suddenly the fortress disappeared in an almighty explosion. As Pelet wrote:

Suddenly I felt the earth tremble strongly under my feet. I heard a vast and deep noise . . . My first thought was for our powder, but . . . an officer arrived from the trenches and announced that he had seen an awful explosion in the middle of the fortress followed by a violent fire, and that a rain of huge stones and debris together with a small piece of artillery had fallen on our approaches.[27]

Caused by a freak shot that touched off its main powder magazine, the blast reduced every building in the place to ruins, atomised the castle in which the powder had been housed, and killed 500 of the garrison (an all-Portuguese force composed of the Twenty-Fourth Line Infantry, and the militia regiments of Arganil, Trancoso and Viseu). The walls still stood, it is true, but the surviving troops were dazed with shock, many guns had been smashed, and all the stores had been destroyed. The governor, a British officer named William Cox, tried hard to prolong the defence for a further couple of days in the hope that Wellington might come to his rescue, but, led by one or two officers who had quarrelled with Beresford, his men mutinied, and the following night the fortress surrendered.

Coming, as it did, in the wake of the Côa, this was a serious blow to the Allies, for Masséna had been spared a long siege. Yet supply problems – notably, the devastation of the countryside around Almeida, and the destruction of several convoys by Spanish guerrillas on the road from Salamanca – kept the French from pushing forward immediately, and it was only by a huge effort that the two weeks' food supplies were amassed that Masséna regarded as the minimum for any further advance. Even then, transport was so short that a third of the artillery's horses had to be handed over to the supply columns, each infantry division in consequence only being accompanied by eight cannon and howitzers instead of the usual sixteen. Good maps, too, were lacking, the efficient and conscientious Pelet having to produce a whole new set for the army's use. And, to cap it all, the simmering discontent in the high command erupted afresh when Masséna's 'dragoon' suddenly appeared at the army's advanced headquarters on the frontier, an increasingly concerned marshal having in the meantime come to the conclusion that he had been betrayed by the emperor. As Pelet writes, 'The great difficulties of the war and the inadequacy of our resources were so well known that it was thought Masséna's expedition had been sacrificed to Napoleon's jealousy of him.'[28]

This was ridiculous – much more to the point is Thiébault's suspicion that Napoleon 'expected Masséna to work miracles'[29] – but even so it was 15 September before the French got under way again. When they did so, however, rather than following Wellington's army along the main Almeida–Coimbra–Lisbon road, or striking southwards along the rougher and more circuitous route that eventually joined the former near Santarem, Masséna turned off on a particularly bad side-road that led him many miles to the north. This is sometimes put down to poor maps, the misleading information given him by the score of *afrancesado* Portuguese officers who had been attached to his army and his inability to carry out proper reconnaissance in the face of *ordenanças*. In fact, the decision rather rested, first, on the discovery that every other route was blocked by entrenchments, and, second, on the hope that the districts further north might not have been 'scorched', for, as Marbot remarks, 'Lord Wellington, being allowed a perfectly free hand by the government, used it to compel all the people to leave their houses, destroy all provisions and mills, and retire with their cattle to Lisbon'.[30] As Warre wrote, 'It was most distressing to see them abandoning their habitations and flying away ... loaded with what little they could carry ... crying and lamenting [and] followed by their helpless children.'[31] Yet the new route did not prove much better: progress was extremely slow; the troops were exhausted; and the artillery and wagons fell behind, at one point the whole siege train almost being captured by a brigade of Portuguese militia commanded by a redoubtable British officer named Nicholas Trant. Nor did the march even gain the French anything in the way of a tactical advantage, for Wellington merely shifted his army to a new position lying along a great north–south ridge known as the Serra do Buçaco that the French would have to cross if they were ever to reach Coimbra.

Although he knew that the Serra lay ahead, Masséna apparently did not expect that it would be defended, and it was therefore with some surprise that news reached him on the evening of 25 September that a substantial force – 52,000 men with 60 guns – was concentrated in his front. For a variety of reasons the battle that followed two days later has become shrouded in controversy. Attempts, for example, have been made to claim that Wellington merely wanted to blood the Portuguese army, gain more time for his measures of devastation, calm the population of Lisbon, still growing criticism of his tactics in the Portuguese Regency, reassure the Perceval administration in London, or even engineer a pretext for the highly expensive Lines of Torres Vedras. For all of these arguments some shred of justification may be found: Lisbon, for example, was on the verge of panic; a faction in the Regency headed by José Antonio Sousa Coutinho and the Bishop of Oporto was claiming that the British were out to wreck Portugal as a commercial rival; Wellington was suspicious of the Cabinet's commitment to the struggle, and aware that some of his officers were writing private letters that were bitterly critical of their commander; and there are oddities in his dispositions which could possibly be explained by a positive desire to see the French advance continue. In the last resort, however, all this falls down. Battle may have become a good idea in political terms, but the British commander had always intended to turn and fight, his calculation being that this was an almost risk-free option that might turn back the French without incurring the horrors that would certainly accompany a retreat to Torres Vedras.

Whatever the origins of the decision to give battle, the Serra do Buçaco was certainly a good place to fight. An undulating granite ridge some nine miles long dotted with outcrops of rock, it was extremely steep and rose high above the French positions, the ground about its foot also being cut up with woods and gullies. Troops on the summit could not be bombarded by artillery, whilst men sent against it would be certain to reach its crest in a state of considerable disorder. Yet rather than immediately looking for a way round, the French chose to attack head on: lacking personal experience of the British, Masséna had little regard for them, whilst he was, for obvious reasons, anxious for a victory. On the morning of 27 September, then – it had taken two days to get enough troops up to launch an assault – Ney and Reynier threw their infantry against the Allied centre-left. Despite a thick mist that cloaked their advance, Reynier's men were attacked on all sides at the summit and after some sharp fighting forced to retreat in disorder. For a good account we may turn to William Grattan:

Wallace and his regiment, standing alone without orders, had to act for themselves . . . The colonel sent his captain of grenadiers (Dunne) to the right where the rocks were highest to ascertain how matters stood . . . In a few moments Dunne returned almost breathless; he said the rocks were filling fast with Frenchmen, [and] that a heavy column was coming up the hill beyond . . . Wallace, with a steady but cheerful countenance turned to his men, and . . . said, 'Now Connaught Rangers . . . when I bring you face to face with those French rascals . . . don't give the false touch, but push home to the muzzle! I have nothing more to say, and if I had it would be of no use, for in a minute there'll be such an infernal noise . . . you won't be able to hear yourselves.' This address went home to the hearts of us all, but there was no cheering: a steady and determined calm had taken the place of any lighter feeling . . . Wallace then threw the battalion from line into column . . . and moved on . . . at a quick pace. On reaching the rocks, he . . . threw himself from his horse and . . . ran forward . . . into the midst of the terrible flame in his front. All was now confusion and uproar, smoke, fire and bullets; officers and soldiers . . . knocked down in every direction; British, French and Portuguese mixed together; while in the midst of all was to be seen Wallace fighting . . . at the head of his devoted followers and calling out to his soldiers to press forward.[32]

To the right, meanwhile, things went even worse for the French. Ney's men moved forward in fine style, but they were much harassed by skirmishers from the Light Division, which happened to be holding the sector which they were attacking. Waiting in hiding for them, meanwhile, were the rest of Craufurd's men, together with the Portuguese brigade of Pack, and they therefore marched straight into an ambush:

No sooner did [the enemy] crown the height, then he found us drawn up to receive him, and his column became exposed to a most destructive fire, both of musketry and artillery. This . . . was but of short duration, yet . . . the leading regiments of the assailants were almost totally annihilated. A charge of bayonets followed: the whole column was routed and driven down the hill with prodigious slaughter.[33]

Junot's corps was still intact, but to carry on was clearly pointless, and so the battle ended.

The French had suffered a severe reverse. For the loss of only 1,252 Allied troops – a total, incidentally, split exactly between British and Portuguese – they themselves had lost almost 4,500 men. On top of this, confident predictions that the Portuguese would disintegrate at the first shot had proved to be sadly wrong, whilst Wellington had proved once again that he was outstanding as a defensive commander and had won back much of the respect that he had lost on the frontier. Commenting on his 'extraordinary circumspection, calm, coolness and presence of mind', for example, Schaumann remarked:

His orders were communicated in a loud voice, and were short and precise. In him there is nothing of the bombastic pomp of the commander-in-chief surrounded by his glittering staff. He wears no befeathered hat, no gold lace, no stars, no orders – simply a low plain hat, a white collar, a grey overcoat and a light sword.[34]

Masséna was now totally cut off from Spain by the militia and the *ordenança*, tied to one of the worst roads in the entire Peninsula, surrounded by towns and villages from which everyone had fled, and running short of food. A lesser – or wiser – man might well have given up the whole campaign at this point (indeed, Ney and Junot pressed for just such a course), but the marshal was a determined individual possessed of an outstanding reputation as a commander, and pride alone was therefore enough to keep him going. At all events, large cavalry patrols were soon riding out to examine the countryside, and within a matter of hours an unguarded track had been discovered that led northwards around the Allied line.* Many miles from Buçaco, it was well out of reach of any sudden counterstroke. By the evening of 28 September, then, the Army of Portugal was pulling out from the positions that it had occupied before the Serra de Buçaco and heading north-west, leaving Wellington with no choice but to retire on Coimbra and Lisbon.

The retreat that followed saw morale in the Allied army plummet. Masséna had been badly beaten, and officers of less skill and foresight than Wellington believed that the French army might have been destroyed altogether. This view was unfair, but the grumbling continued none the less, much swelled by the pathetic columns of refugees that now clogged the roads. With the autumn rain falling in torrents, it was a miserable scene:

My pen altogether fails me: I feel that no powers of description can convey . . . the cheerless desolation we daily witnessed on our march from the Mondego to the Lines. Wherever we moved, the mandate which enjoined the wretched inhabitants . . . to forsake their homes had gone before us. The villages were deserted; the churches . . . were empty; the mountain cottages stood open and untenanted . . . The flanks of our line of march were literally covered with the flying population of the country. In Portugal there are at no time many facilities for travelling, and these few the exigencies of the army had very greatly diminished. Rich indeed were those . . . who still retained . . . any mode of transporting their families and property . . . for respectable men and delicate women . . . might on every side be seen walking slowly and painfully on foot, encumbered by heavy burdens of clothes, bedding and food.[35]

The plight of the refugees was harrowing. Douglas admits that he and his comrades regularly plundered them – as on the road to La Coruña straggling and drunkenness were rife – whilst, as Schaumann wrote:

The nearer the procession came to Lisbon, the greater was the number of animals . . . that fell dead either from fatigue or hunger, and very soon ladies were to be seen wading in torn silk shoes . . . through the mud. It was a heart-rending sight.[36]

As for the troops, they were little better off:

___

* The failure adequately to block this road is puzzling. Trant's militia had been sent to hold it, but Wellington's correspondence makes it clear that the British commander did not believe that they could do so. The best answer would have been to blow it up, but no one had expected Masséna to come via Buçaco. A strong force of regular troops might also have done the job, but such a move would have left Buçaco badly undermanned. In short, by doing the unexpected, Masséna had wrong-footed Wellington, and frustrated his plan to turn back the invasion before it reached Lisbon.

We ... encamped in a beautiful field of grapes, but in the course of the night it commenced to rain with a gale of wind, and we were awakened in the morning ... [by] the water running over us in the trench as we lay between the bushes. To attempt a description of our misery would be a task too hard for my old pen ... All the resource we had was to stand upright and let the water run off as well as possible.[37]

With the French burning village after village, engaging in wholesale pillage, killing large numbers of the inhabitants, and executing any *ordenanças* who fell into their hands, Sousa and his allies continued their struggle to halt the retreat, but nothing would induce the British commander to turn and fight, and by 10 October the whole of the Anglo-Portuguese army had fallen back within the Lines of Torres Vedras. In short, all seemed well, but in many cases, the evacuation of the population had not taken place until the last minute, whilst some of the inhabitants had refused to leave their homes or had hidden food rather than carry it away. Rather than being forced to withdraw within a few days, as Wellington had hoped, the French therefore gained access to sufficient supplies to blockade the Lines in the hope that something – revolt in Lisbon, for example – might turn up. Gallant as this effort was, however, in his heart Masséna knew that he was in desperate straits. Depleted by battle casualties, sickness, desertion and the need to garrison Almeida, by early November the army was down to no more than 40,000 effectives. Food was limited, rain was falling steadily, the troops lacked adequate shelter, the Allied lines held firm, and there was no news from Spain. All around Masséna's positions lurked bands of militia and *ordenanças*, and Coimbra, which had been left in the hands of the tiniest of garrisons, was known to have been retaken by Trant with the loss of 4,000 sick or wounded soldiers who had been left there in hospital. Even ammunition was running low, whilst many of the men were sullen and disaffected. Yet, heartened by the fact that Wellington would not move, still the French held on, the only developments being the dispatch of a column of troops headed by a trusted staff officer named Foy to Spain in the hope of obtaining help, a retreat on the part of Masséna to a safer position at Santarem, and the arrival of 9,000 French reinforcements under General Drouet, who had been assigned a corps improvised from twenty fresh battalions belonging to regiments that were already serving in the Peninsula.

For the civilian population, the consequences of the long stand-off that was the fruit of Wellington's failure to move were terrible. For the people of Lisbon itself, life was not too bad, but for the refugees it was a different matter:

Thousands of the unfortunate inhabitants of the provinces through which our army had recently retreated . . . were endeavouring to exist between Lisbon and the Lines. There was, therefore, an immense population hemmed up in a small space of country, hundreds of them without a house to cover them or food to eat . . . In the course of the winter the number of Portuguese who actually died of want was quite dreadful. It was not unusual to see hordes of these poor wretches, old and young, male and female in rags, the very picture of death, round a miserable fire, on which was placed an earthen vessel, full of such herbs as could be gathered in the fields and hedges. Thousands contrived to drag on a miserable existence on this vile sustenance. Their . . . emaciated faces were sufficient to have touched the heart of the most callous and unfeeling.[38]

For these unfortunates, little or no official provision was ever made. Some assistance was forthcoming from the Church, private charity, and the British army, but famine and exposure nevertheless took the life of many thousands, whilst there were still plenty of soldiers who remained all too willing to terrorise the populace. As a result Sousa and his allies continued to cause trouble, whilst a few Portuguese officers became so angry that they even deserted to the French. Despite the growing criticism, however, Wellington chose this moment to renew his quarrels with the British government, which he again accused of starving him of money. At the best of times his complaints would have been unfair: faced by a genuine shortage of specie, possessed of only a slim majority in the House of Commons and beset by an Opposition that lost no opportunity to argue that the war in Portugal had become a question of pouring good money after bad, the government had in fact done its utmost to support Wellington. In January 1811, however, the charges were downright maladroit: not only had growing economic difficulties produced much agitation in favour of peace, or, at the very least, an end to the shipping restrictions that had been Britain's answer to the Continental Blockade, but King George III had just been smitten by a terrible attack of porphyria that left him permanently disabled. With the Prince of Wales – hitherto notorious for his friendship with the Whigs – now Prince Regent, the Cabinet could not be certain of survival. As it happened, the danger faded away – for a variety of reasons 'Prinny' had fallen out with the Whigs – but not until February 1811 did the future George IV announce that he would keep the government in office. Until then it seemed that the slightest slip might lead to disaster, and it is therefore hard not to conclude that Wellington would have been better employed attacking Masséna, and all the more so as his inactivity was straining the patience of the beleaguered Spaniards.

For week after week, however, the stalemate continued, for a combination of energy, enterprise and sheer terror had netted Masséna's troops far more food than Wellington had hoped. By the middle of February, however, the peasants' hoards had been all but exhausted, whilst the army was on the brink of collapse: a large band of deserters, for example, had clubbed together in the hills near Santarem and were living as bandits under the command of an elected 'general'. However, what could Masséna do? An attack on the Lines was still out of the question, but, after Drouet's arrival, the only help from Spain was a small column of drafts and convalescents brought in by Foy, who had eventually reached the frontier by means of forced march through the desolate Tagus valley. A pontoon bridge had been made ready in an attempt to gain access to the south bank of the Tagus, but, even if the army could have crossed the river, there was no chance that it could have entered Lisbon. Some more food could have been collected, perhaps, but in the end things would have remained much the same. In short, there was nothing for it but retreat, and all the more so as Wellington obviously could not be depended on to remain inactive for ever.

On 5 March 1811, then, the marshal pulled out. Delayed by supply problems, the Anglo-Portuguese forces did not come up with his men for several days, and even then were kept at bay by a series of rearguard actions that cost both sides many casualties. To hasten their retreat still further, the French abandoned most of their baggage and by 22 March the exhausted survivors were once more in contact with Spain. Once again, the horrors of war were all too evident. Appalling atrocities were committed by the French as they fell back. At Porto de Mos, for example, 200 of the inhabitants were burned to death in the parish church, Donaldson describing how he went in and found 'the half-consumed skeletons of human beings on every side; some lying, others kneeling and more of them standing upright against the walls'.[39] Similarly, of Carapeta, Simmons, who complained bitterly that it 'is beyond everything horrid the way these European savages have treated the unfortunate Portuguese', wrote, 'I saw a woman laid in the street near her own door, murdered. The ruffians had placed upon her bosom a huge piece of granite taken from the market cross, so heavy that it took me and six men to remove it. The blood was running from her ears and mouth.'[40] Often macabre humour added to the horror:

Never during the whole of the war did I again see such a horrible sight . . . Murdered peasants lay in all directions. At one place I halted at a door to beg water of a man who was sitting on the threshold . . . He proved to be dead, and had . . . been placed there ... for a joke. The inside of the house was ghastly to behold. All its inmates had been murdered in their beds ... The corpse of another ... peasant had been placed in a ludicrous position in a hole in a garden wall ... to make fun of us when we came along.[41]

All this was visited on a population ravaged by starvation, for in many villages there was literally nothing left. As Wheeler remarked, 'Thousands must have died ... and thousands more must perish, for there is no help at hand: rich and poor are all reduced to the same state.'[42] Time and again, the British came across the most distressing scenes. For example:

A large house ... was discovered near the line of our route. Prompted by curiosity, several men turned aside to inspect the interior, where they found a number of famished wretches crowded together ... Thirty women and children had perished for want of food, and lay dead upon the floor, while about half that number of survivors sat watching the remains of those who had fallen. The soldiers offered some refreshment to these unfortunate persons, but one man only had sufficient strength to eat.[43]

And again:

On the top of a hill ... we found three children lying, two already dead but the other ... still breathing. There were pieces of biscuit lying beside them, which our soldiers had brought, but it was too late ... One of them had expired with [a] bit in his mouth.[44]

The French, however, did not escape scot-free. Indeed, with discipline and comradeship in a state of collapse, they were by now at the last extremity:

When men became so fatigued with marching and want of food that they could not go further, they were left to perish on the roadside. Disease raged freely in their ranks, but the men ... would not even lift their comrades to the side of a wall to die in peace, but allowed them to ... be trodden to death under the feet of the baggage mules ... Those French soldiers who were lying on the roads in a still sensible state soon suffered retribution at the hands of the Portuguese peasantry. Wherever they were found ... the first step was to strip the victims of all clothing and leave them in a state of nudity. Those still living were summarily dispatched by having their brains ... dashed out ... or [being] stabbed, and when all else failed suffered the death of stoning ... The very bodies of the dead were kicked about as if they had been footballs, and every indignity that could be heaped upon the inanimate frame was resorted to.[45]

By now, then, the French were little more than a horde of fugitives. Wellington's pursuit having soon been outstripped, logic dictated a retreat to Ciudad Rodrigo. The travails of the Army of Portugal were not yet over, however. To the astonishment and consternation of his subordinates, on 22 March Masséna suddenly issued orders for a march on the Tagus valley in the hope of getting into contact with the French forces in Andalucía and again threatening Lisbon. In the circumstances no plan could have been worse. Masséna's desire to salvage some crumb of justification from the campaign is understandable enough, but the district into which he was proposing to march was one of the most barren in the entire Peninsula, whilst, deeply demoralised, the troops had little food, ammunition, clothes, footwear or transport. Absolutely horrified, Ney therefore refused to obey and tried to continue the march on Almeida and Ciudad Rodrigo, only to be removed from his command and sent to Spain in disgrace. With 'the bravest of the brave' gone, all resistance collapsed and the miserable columns therefore dragged themselves into the wild mountains of the Serra da Estrella. For a few days the attempt to reach the Tagus was sustained, but very soon the plan collapsed. Food could not be found, most of the roads were impassable to wheeled transport, and the troops were in many cases in a state of complete disbandment. At this even Masséna had to give up, and on 29 March he finally ordered the Army of Portugal to head for the frontier. This was all very well, but the Anglo-Portuguese were now closing in again. Extraordinarily, Masséna, who now had less than 40,000 men, still did not make all speed for the shelter of Ciudad Rodrigo, but rather lingered in a defensive position strung out along the River Côa in the faint hope that he might somehow avenge Buçaco. In this too he was to be disappointed. Attacked in a thick fog and pouring rain on the morning of 3 April 1811 by three Anglo-Portuguese divisions at Sabugal, Reynier's corps fought astonishingly well, launching a series of heavy counter-attacks and inflicting some casualties on the Light Division, whose first brigade got lost and ended up fighting the French almost single-handed. It was a bitter struggle:

Two guns opened on us and fired several discharges of round and grape. The guns were repeatedly charged, but the enemy were so strong that we were obliged to retire a little. Three columns of the enemy moved forward with drums beating and the officers dancing like madmen with their hats frequently hoisted upon their swords. Our men kept up a terrible fire. They went back a little and we followed ... Lieutenant Arbuthnot was killed, Lieutenant Haggup wounded [and] Colonel Beckwith wounded and his horse shot.[46]

However, by midday the French were fleeing north-eastwards in considerable disorder, leaving behind them over 600 casualties.

Sabugal being only a few miles from the Spanish frontier, the third invasion of Portugal was finally over, the only Frenchmen left in arms in the country being the garrison of Almeida. Badly battered though it was, the Army of Portugal was still a fighting force, but even so the blow to French arms had been significant enough. At least 25,000 men were missing from the ranks, whilst the troops involved had lost almost all their baggage and many of their guns. Particularly serious, given the difficulties that were always found in replacing such losses, was the death of almost half the Army of Portugal's horses. On the other side, meanwhile, military casualties had been insignificant by comparison (indeed, Wellington's strength had been all but doubled by the knowledge that he could now trust the Portuguese army in major field operations). Yet victory cannot just be reckoned in terms of so many soldiers killed or wounded. At least 80,000 Portuguese civilians had perished, and whole areas had been completely devastated. From this blow the Portuguese war effort never really recovered, but still worse was the fact that Masséna's courage had tilted the balance of forces heavily against the Allied position.

At first sight, this seems a strange claim, and all the more so if we look at *la guerrilla*. In Navarre, for example, the ruthless figure of Espoz y Mina had now emerged as the commander of a semi-regular force of three battalions of infantry and a squadron of cavalry, at the head of which he tied down thousands of French troops, fought off a number of enemy attempts to destroy him, won several small victories, and was even able to charge customs duties on goods and animals crossing the frontier. A little further south the chaotic situation that had characterised the area of Soria and Logroño the year before had been much improved by the concentration of most of its guerrillas into a single force under the command of the regular army officer, José Joaquín Durán y Barazábal, who, like Mina, had won a series of minor actions after turning his men into regular troops. Further south again, the genuinely heroic El Empecinado had done much the same in the area of Guadalajara and Molina de Aragón and had even been known to appear on the very outskirts of Madrid (on one occasion, indeed, he almost captured King Joseph himself). In and out of touch with El Empecinado to the east, meanwhile, was the flying column of regular units commanded by Pedro Villacampa which in the autumn of 1810 caused Suchet many problems in the area of Teruel.

If the broad band of territory running from Navarre to the northern parts of La Mancha was one zone in which guerrilla resistance was a major problem, another was to be found in the area stretching from the Basque provinces along the Cantabrian mountains and then southwards into León. Beginning with Alava and Vizcaya, yet another semi-regular division was being formed in this area under the command of Francisco Longa. In the mountains of Santander and Asturias the naval officer, Juan Díaz Porlier, headed another such force and was harassing the garrison of Oviedo and at times coming down to the coast and taking part in the maritime operations of which we shall read below. And finally in León, Julián Sánchez headed a band of irregular horsemen that eventually provided the basis for two regiments of cavalry.

Setting aside the multitude of other bands both fair and foul that swirled around these relatively well-organised and disciplined forces, Mina and his fellows were by the end of 1810 causing the French serious problems. Thus, in León, for example, cavalry sweeps dispatched to hunt down Sánchez found themselves lunging into empty air. 'We rode for nine days without encountering any guerrillas', complained one officer. 'It was not that there were none in the region, but the local population warned them of our arrival, and . . . they did not allow us to catch up with them.'[47] As Thiébault wrote, 'The difficulty was to get at [Sánchez], and do something more against him than execute . . . movements . . . which generally ended only in seasoning [the guerrillas] while tiring the troops.'[48] Through various subterfuges, he eventually succeeded in inflicting a serious reverse on the guerrilla leader that cost him many casualties, but 'El Charro' was undaunted, inflicting heavy losses on 400 troops who had been sent to escort a courier to Ciudad Rodrigo, and capturing a substantial supply convoy at Tamames.

Far more important as a factor in la guerrilla even than such raiders, however, were the forces of Allied regulars that continued to be scattered around the periphery of Spain. In western Andalucía, for example, the much-travelled division of General Ballesteros spent most of 1810 fighting Soult in the Condado de Niebla, whilst Extremadura had seen several attempts on the part of the Marqués de la Romana to march on Seville. Similarly, in Asturias Patriot forces were clinging on to a small area in the western part of the province from where they from time to time sallied out to attack the French around Oviedo. And, last but not least, all round the coasts of Spain considerable efforts were being made to make use of the benefits of seapower. Thus, in September 1810 Enrique O'Donnell wiped out an entire brigade of German troops at La Bisbal in a clever operation that combined a hazardous march through the mountains of central Catalonia, with a surprise amphibious descent on the coast. Meanwhile, a month later the erstwhile leader of the insurrection in the Roncal, Mariano de

Renovales, sailed eastwards with a number of battalions of the Army of Galicia and a force of British marines and stormed the port of Gijón. At about the same time, too, a small Anglo-Spanish force was dispatched to attack the coast of Málaga, but in this instance it was routed with some loss at Fuengirola.

Greatest of all these raids, however, was the operation that was launched at Cádiz in February 1811. The besieging forces having been for various reasons so reduced that they were actually outnumbered by the garrison, the Regency duly proposed a major attack on the French rear. This, indeed, was to be rather more than a mere raid: the object was to raise the siege of the city, defeat the invaders in a full-scale field battle and destroy the French lines. At first all went well enough, the troops involved – Sir Thomas Graham's Anglo-Portuguese division, two Spanish infantry divisions and a Spanish cavalry brigade – disembarking safely at Algeciras and Tarifa. Unfortunately for the Allies, however, affairs thereafter were mishandled. Command of the landing force was in the hands of the Spanish general, Manuel La Peña, a man whom even Spanish sources are agreed was a man of neither courage, nor energy, nor ability. Far from striking inland – a course which offered great success – La Peña chose rather to take a road that led directly back to Cádiz and then proceeded to fall straight into a clever trap led by Marshal Victor. Thus, whilst one infantry division checked the Allied column just short of the Isla de León, two others fell on its flank and rear. Known variously as the battle of Chiclana or Barrosa, the battle that followed on 5 March generated immense controversy. The chief weight of the French assault fell on Graham, whose badly outnumbered men put up a heroic resistance, as, for example, when a composite battalion of flank companies found itself taking on an entire division single-handedly:

All being now ready, Colonel Browne rode to the front of the battalion, and said in a voice to be heard by all, 'Gentlemen . . . General Graham has done you the honour of being the first to attack those fellows. Now follow me, you rascals!' He pointed to the enemy, and [gave] the order to advance . . . As soon as we crossed the ravine close to the base of the hill . . . a most tremendous roar of cannon and musketry was all at once opened . . . Nearly 200 of our men and more than half the officers went down by this first volley . . . In closing on the centre and endeavouring to form a second line, upwards of fifty more men were levelled with the earth; and . . . the remainder of the battalion now scattered. The men commenced firing from behind trees, mounds or any cover which presented, and could not be got together.[49]

A variety of factors eventually sent the French scurrying from the field, but the Allied victory was not exploited. A cowardly figure – even the Spaniards knew him as Doña Manolita – La Peña had failed to send any troops to help Graham although he had plenty to spare and knew that he himself was in no danger. Still worse, despite the fact that Victor was in complete disorder – his losses totalled two thousand men and five guns – the Spanish general ordered his entire force to cross over on to the Isla de León by means of a pontoon bridge that had been constructed across the Sancti Petri. Bewildered and not a little relieved, Victor was therefore enabled to resume the blockade. Back in Cádiz, meanwhile, Graham and La Peña were almost literally at daggers drawn. Graham having lost a quarter of his men, his anger was understandable enough, whilst La Peña inflamed matters still further by a mendacious attempt to pretend that the decision to fall back on the Isla had been precipitated by the British commander. Rightly superseded by the Regency, he continued to wax righteous – 'I have just gained a victory, and not only am I prevented from taking advantage of it, but I am deprived of the command which gained it'[50] – but the British stood firm and hinted openly at treachery. Thus:

Nothing but the extraordinary coolness ... and quickness of arrangement which General Graham showed on that day could have extricated us out of the scrape which our allies had drawn us into ... Although we occupied the whole force of the enemy ... the Spanish general not only did not show a single battalion to save us, but he did not profit by the moment and get possession of the French lines, which were then deserted. He either wanted curiosity or nerves to come himself to see how the affair was going on with us [and] he did not send any of his staff to enquire. I think myself that, if the commander-in-chief did not act in concert with the French, the *chef d'état major*, General Lacy ... certainly knew of and favoured their plan, which was to cut us off from the Spaniards and then either to capture or annihilate us.[51]

With Anglo-Spanish relations already strained by events in Latin America and Portugal, the whole affair was most unfortunate, and all the more so as *gaditano* opinion sided wholeheartedly with La Peña.

To return to the war as a whole, *la guerrilla* could not disguise the fact that the French had continued to make steady progress. Setting aside the capture of the strategic Catalan town of Tortosa on 2 January 1811 after a siege of a mere eighteen days, this was at its most spectacular in Extremadura where Soult had launched an offensive in the hope of forcing Wellington to detach troops from Lisbon. By cutting his garrisons to the bone – hence the shortfall in Victor's forces at Barrosa – Soult managed to put together 20,000 men, and on 31 December he duly set out from Seville. After only a few days, however, things went wrong. Setting aside drenching winter rain,

Ballesteros suddenly appeared on the invasion force's left flank with the result that half Soult's infantry had to be dropped off to chase him away. Though the Spaniard was eventually beaten at Villanueva de los Castillejos and forced to take refuge in Portugal, this took some time, whilst Soult also had to capture the minor fortress of Olivenza into which the Spaniards had foolishly thrust a large garrison. Badajoz, then, was not invested until the end of January, whilst even then Soult did not have sufficient troops to surround the city altogether (Badajoz lying on the southern bank of the broad River Guadiana, to have done so would have been to risk disaster, for the attackers would necessarily have been split in two). For a moment the campaign hung in the balance, for on 5 February Mendizábal suddenly appeared on the north bank of the Guadiana at the head of the erstwhile Army of the Left, which had until then been encamped at Alburquerque.* Yet, rather than falling on the overstretched and undermanned French siege lines with his 15,000 men, he simply set up camp across the Guadiana. The result was catastrophe. Throwing a pontoon bridge across the river, on the night of 18 February Soult sent 7,000 troops against the new arrivals. Failing to detect the noise of the crossing, the Spaniards were taken completely by surprise, and ridden down by a large body of French cavalry that had circled their position until it had reached a point where it could ride in upon Mendizábal's open left flank. The troops posted in this sector broke and fled immediately, but to their right Mendizábal was able to form a number of regiments into a gigantic square. It was, however, to no avail. As one Spanish infantryman remembered, the enemy's horse being unable to break its ranks, 'their artillery played upon it in a most horrible fashion until it became first an oval and then an unformed mass that the cavalry were able to penetrate and take prisoner'.[52] Some 4,000 men either got across the river into Badajoz or managed to escape to the west, but Spanish casualties numbered 8,000 men, whilst gone, too, were all the army's guns and baggage. As for the French, they had barely lost 400 men. After this there is little to tell. The defenders for some time continued to show much vigour, but on 4 March their courageous commander, Rafael de Menacho, was killed, and his successor surrendered the city a week later.

The surrender of Badajoz was a strange affair. The city had plenty of provisions, whilst its garrison was still in good shape. At the time of the

---

* For the whole of 1810 the Army of the Left had been headed by the Marqués de la Romana, but the latter had been suffering from syphilis and on 23 January 1811 he died suddenly of heart failure. Meanwhile, in accordance with the decree of 31 December 1810, his forces had been redesignated as the Fifth Army.

surrender, meanwhile, the breach was not practicable, whilst Menacho's successor, one José Imaz, knew not only that Wellington had dispatched three divisions to his relief under Beresford, but that the troops involved were only a few marches away. Treachery has been suggested, but the truth seems rather that Imaz's nerves simply gave way in the face of the pressure of events. At all events, for the French, Badajoz was a stunning victory. Though the city was to absorb large numbers of French troops and prove costly to defend, its possession made an Anglo-Portuguese offensive south of the Tagus far more difficult than before, whilst some 20,000 Spanish troops had been put out of action. Even more irreplaceable, meanwhile, were the immense quantities of armaments, munitions and foodstuffs that were lost with them, together with the men and money of southern Extremadura. Wellington, indeed, was dismayed. As he wrote to Liverpool:

Although experience has taught me to place no reliance upon . . . Spanish troops . . . this recent disaster has disappointed and grieved me much. The loss of this army and its . . . consequence, the fall of Badajoz, have materially altered the situation of the Allies . . . and it will not be an easy task to place them in the situation in which they were, much less in that in which they would have been if this misfortune had not occurred.[53]

To the physical damage done by the disaster, then, was added a further blow to Anglo-Spanish relations, Wellington complaining that the defeat 'would certainly have been avoided had the Spaniards been anything but Spaniards'.[54]

To conclude, then, despite Wellington's triumph in Portugal, the efforts of the guerrillas, and much use of seapower, Masséna's dogged persistence had eroded the foundations of Spanish resistance still further. Thus, every lost fortress and every shattered army brought the day closer when the *partidas* could be hunted down and exterminated (as had just happened to the last of the insurgents in Calabria, where a savage guerrilla struggle had been raging since 1806). Wellington, indeed, was deeply concerned, as witness the consternation and anger with which he greeted the news of the defeat of Mendizábal. According to the traditional view, each fresh advance on the part of the French only rendered them more vulnerable to defeat, but, as the next chapter will show, so long as the French remained willing to send adequate reinforcements and replacements across the Pyrenees, there was nothing inevitable about this process. And, though British morale had been boosted, and, with it, the willingness of the Perceval administration to pour still more resources into the fight, terrible strain had been placed on the Anglo-Spanish Alliance. Thus, the Spaniards blamed the British for their misfortunes, whilst the British had been presented with further examples of Spanish incompetence and were furious at what they perceived as a failure to use the respite supposedly provided by the attack on Lisbon to rebuild their forces. In March 1811, in short, it was still entirely reasonable to think in terms of a French victory.

13

Albuera

STALEMATE ON THE PORTUGUESE
FRONTIER, MARCH–DECEMBER 1811

A motley collection of blue and white and brown, the Spanish line was trading volley for volley with its opponents. Dead and wounded littered the ground, musketry and canister were flaying their ranks, the shallow valley beneath them was hidden by a veritable forest of Frenchmen, and the troops were soaking wet, the sunny weather with which the day had begun having suddenly been banished by a torrential downpour. Yet, encouraged by their officers, the Spaniards were holding their ground, and they did not flinch even when a mass of enemy cavalry, many of them armed with the long lances dreaded by all infantrymen, suddenly thundered along their rear ranks, slashing and stabbing at anyone who got in their way, cutting down the red-coated fugitives who were fleeing before them and enveloping a group of generals and staff officers who had come up to observe the fighting at close quarters. Despite the fact that many of his comrades were being struck down by bullets aimed at the cavalry from the rear, one unknown infantryman even snatched a guidon from its bearer, whilst the Spaniards were still unbroken when they were ordered to retire perhaps half an hour later. It was truly the Spanish army's finest hour.

The terrible engagement fought out around the Extremaduran village of La Albuera on 16 May 1811 may be regarded as a metaphor for the campaigns of 1811. A bloody stalemate, indeed, was not the sort of battle that had been expected to follow Masséna's expulsion from Portugal. His confidence and moral authority having been much boosted by Torres Vedras, the spring of 1811 found Wellington intending to move over to the offensive, for which policy he had received *de facto* authorisation from his political masters in London, where talk of major reductions in the size of the army employed in Portugal had been replaced by promises of major reinforcements. Supply difficulties, sickness amongst the troops and want of siege artillery ensured that in the short term no great strokes of strategy could be envisaged, but it was hoped that Almeida, Ciudad Rodrigo and Badajoz might all be recaptured, thereby opening the way for lightning strikes on such targets as Salamanca or Seville. In the event, however, success was limited, the story of the rest of 1811 essentially being one of failure and frustration.

In March 1811, however, such a prospect would have been hard to envisage. In Cádiz, true, there had been fresh trouble in that, beguiled by *serviles* eager to engineer British discontent with the Regency, Henry Wellesley had been tricked into putting forward a plan much favoured by both himself and his eldest brother, the marquess, whereby Wellington would be given the command of the Spanish army and British officers posts in its ranks, in exchange for which Britain would grant the enormous loan which the Spaniards had for some time since seen as the only way out of their penury. In political and financial terms alike, this was utterly impractical – *gaditano* opinion was hostile, whilst Lord Wellesley's enthusiasm failed to win over his Cabinet colleagues. Only slightly less maladroit, meanwhile, was a follow-up suggestion that the provinces bordering on Portugal should be placed under British authority, this idea, too, being rejected out of hand. However, with the French still ensconced in Almeida, Ciudad Rodrigo and Badajoz, the problems which the measures were designed to combat – essentially, a repetition of the troubles of the Talavera campaign – remained wholly academic.

With no political considerations to get in the way, operations began immediately, the first blow being struck in Extremadura, where we left Beresford marching to the relief of Badajoz with 18,000 men. A French force that had captured the minor strongpoints of Alburquerque and Campo Mayor having been chased off, the field marshal crossed the swollen River Guadiana at Juromenha some twenty miles downstream. Badajoz could not be attacked immediately for want of a siege train, but Olivenza was retaken and the French field forces that had remained in the region forced to withdraw across the Sierra Morena. Eventually, however, all was ready. Very considerable numbers of Spanish forces having come up to join Beresford, there were plenty of troops, whilst the want of siege guns had been remedied by sending up twenty-three heavy cannon from Elvas.*

There was much optimism in the Allied camp: 'We looked forward with eager hope', wrote Sherer, 'to ... a triumphant march over the Sierra Morena ... The towers of fair Seville ... seemed to ride before us, and in

---

* The Spanish troops concerned were what was left of the Fifth Army, which was now commanded by Castaños, and three divisions of the Fourth, including that of Ballesteros, and two more from Cádiz, which had sailed to Ayamonte under Blake and then marched up the Portuguese frontier.

imagination we were already wandering . . . on the banks of the far-famed Guadalquivir.'[1] But very soon things were going wrong. When the heavy cannon finally arrived, most were found to be very old (four, indeed, dated from the first half of the seventeenth century). Varying enormously in calibre, they had also proved difficult to supply with proper ammunition, and, this, together with their casting defects and lack of modern sights and elevating gear, suggested that their fire would be distinctly inaccurate. Meanwhile, the walls of Badajoz had been thoroughly repaired, matters being made still worse by the fact that Beresford and Wellington settled on a faulty plan of operations. Whereas the best chance of success was to concentrate on the southern walls – the section of the defences which had been breached by Soult – it was decided to mount no more than a secondary assault in this sector, most of the attackers' resources rather being deployed against the detached fort of San Cristóbal. Perched on its lofty bluff across the river, this fort was crucial, for such was its command of the town that the latter could not be held without it. On the other hand, however, it was also immensely strong and built on stony ground that was hard to work.

When operations began on 8 May, progress was very slow: the attackers were hampered by heavy rain; the French guns outmatched those of the besiegers at every point; two-thirds of Beresford's limited number of engineer officers were killed or wounded in the trenches; and the governor, Armand Philippon, was a most determined opponent. Nor, it seems, did Beresford help. According to Edward Pakenham, 'Indecision has been his bane, and want of strength in command his misfortune. He has the cards to play that ought to have made him a peer of the realm, but still continues Sir William . . . and I fear . . . posterity will have no . . . ground to defend him on.'[2] The result was much dithering. To quote one of the British commander's engineers, 'The investment having been completed on the morning of the eighth . . . Marshal Beresford was pressed to allow us to begin . . . our principal attack on the next night . . . but it was not until the . . . twelfth that [he] finally consented to our beginning.'[3] As a result morale plummeted in the Allied camp: 'Little has been done . . . and we are all in a state of complete despondency at having witnessed so much bloodshed in vain; the blame rests somewhere, and our brigade have . . . been the victims of some shameful mismanagement.'[4] Time, meanwhile, was exactly what the attackers did not have, for Soult had long since resolved to march to the relief of Badajoz. At the head of 25,000 troops on 12 May he crossed the Sierra Morena, whereupon the largely Spanish covering forces that had been watching the passes hastily fell back to the rendezvous point that had previously been agreed at the village of La Albuera. Knowing that he could count on the Spaniards, whose behaviour throughout had been impeccable, Beresford resolved to fight and by 15 May some 35,000 Allied troops were blocking Soult's way.

Outnumbering Soult by almost three to two, Beresford's army was drawn up in a strong position along the crest of a line of low hills. In the centre of the Allied position – of which the Anglo-Portuguese occupied the left and centre and the Spaniards the right – the closely packed houses of La Albuera provided a natural defensive redoubt, whilst the ridge provided plenty of shelter for the defenders. Soult, however, was no mean general, and, reconnoitring his own position, which was thickly covered with olive and ilex trees, he perceived that he was well placed to outflank the Allied right without Beresford realising what was happening. Accordingly, a little while after what appeared to be a strong French thrust opened against Albuera itself, a massive column debouched from the woods facing the troops of Blake and Castaños. Swinging beyond the Spaniards' flank, these forces – the infantry divisions of Girard and Gazan and a brigade of cavalry – crossed the stream and began to ascend the heights on the near side with the obvious intention of rolling up Spaniards and Anglo-Portuguese alike.

In the face of this brilliant piece of grand tactics, Beresford and Blake proved slow to react (Castaños had surrendered the command of the two brigades that were all that he had contributed to the Allied array to the latter*). Thus, both seem to have remained convinced that a huge French force was still hidden in the woods to their front, and that Soult's outflanking move was little more than a dramatic feint. Beyond sending over a cavalry brigade, Beresford therefore initially left his Spanish allies to deal with the threat, and even sent troops to reinforce Albuera. As for Blake, meanwhile, he wheeled back only a single infantry brigade, supported though this was by the 1,000-strong brigade of Spanish cavalry that he posted to guard the end of his line.

If disaster was averted, it was therefore no fault of the Allied commanders. What saved them was, first, the fact that the French strike force had to deploy from column of march into a formation more suited for field action, and necessarily took much time in doing so. No frontal attack of the sort

---

* According to General Long, Castaños appeared 'a perfect old woman, whose sole occupation is powdering his hair and patrolling about . . . with a suite of servants and soldiers from fifty to sixty in number, at which the common people gaze with admiration and cry out, "¡Viva!" '.[5] But documents discovered as this book was going to press suggest a different picture, the reality being that, but for Castaño's efforts to get him to stand and fight, Beresford would have retreated behind the Guadiana.

that Beresford and Blake feared being forthcoming – on the contrary, some of the troops who had initially threatened the Allied centre could now be seen marching to their left – it finally dawned on them that they had been outwitted. Desperate to remedy matters, the British commander immediately ordered the Second Division of William Stewart and the Fourth Division of Lowry Cole to follow the cavalry he had already sent to support Blake, leaving his centre and left to be held by no more than an independent King's-German-Legion brigade that had been placed in Albuera itself, the Portuguese division of General Hamilton, and a brigade that had been improvised from a few Portuguese regulars that had remained in the Alentejo during the blockade of Lisbon. Galloping over to the right flank, meanwhile, Beresford found Blake frantically trying to get more of his men into line, but by then it was too late: commanded by José de Zayas, four Spanish infantry battalions and a single battery were facing the onslaught of two entire divisions.

Coming on one behind the other, with the first in *ordre mixte* – a formation in which column was mixed with line in an attempt to combine impetus with firepower – and the second in a dense mass of battalion columns, and supported by three batteries of artillery, the French ought in theory to have made short work of the Spaniards. However, we now come to the second factor that saved the Allies from disaster. Thus, Blake's troops (those of Castaños were at this point still in reserve) were the best in the entire Spanish army. The two divisions brought up from Cádiz – in origin the troops of Alburquerque – had remained intact since the middle of 1809 and had, with the exception of the brief Barrosa campaign, spent the whole of the past year in training on the Isla de León. As for Ballesteros' men, they had been intact for even longer, whilst a year of marching and counter-marching in western Andalucía had turned them into hardened veterans. At all events, positioned on a small rise, the four Spanish battalions stood firm and opened fire on the French, who responded not by rushing in with the bayonet – a tactic that might well have succeeded – but by slowing their advance and firing back.

Even as the bloody duel that resulted began, help was starting to arrive. On either side of and behind the defenders, many more Spanish battalions were filing into position, whilst some way to the right rear the first brigade of Stewart's division had made its appearance. On the right, meanwhile, the Spanish cavalry of Loy had been joined by two regiments of British heavy dragoons. Beresford had been planning a great counter-attack involving both Stewart's division and the increasing numbers of cavalry that were reaching the right flank (not far behind the British heavy dragoons was the brigade of cavalry belonging to the Fifth Army commanded by Penne Villemur). However, hot-headed and ineffectual, Stewart ruined this scheme by going straight in without waiting for the rest of his men. Speed was of the essence, true – what would have happened had Zayas' men collapsed before the counter-attack was ready? – but what Stewart cannot be excused for is the order in which he made his attack. Despite the fact that Girard and Gazan's flank was protected by cavalry, the troops were sent in in line. Stewart may have expected the Allied cavalry to protect his advance, but even so this was an extremely dangerous manoeuvre. Wheeling to their left so as to advance against the French infantry, the brigade concerned, which belonged to John Colborne, necessarily had completely to expose its right flank, whilst matters were further complicated by the onset of a sudden thunderstorm. With their own cavalry apparently blinded by the deluge, Colborne's men therefore suddenly found themselves attacked by a brigade of enemy horsemen. Caught in the open, three-quarters of them were killed, wounded or taken prisoner, whilst two squadrons of British heavy dragoons that attempted to effect a rescue were themselves charged in the flank by a unit that had been kept in reserve for just such a purpose and they were driven off in disorder. As for the cavalry, they were merciless:

Part of the victorious French cavalry were Polish lancers. From the conduct of this regiment . . . I believe many of them to have been intoxicated, as they rode over the wounded, barbarously darting their lances into them . . . I was an instance of their inhumanity: after having been most severely wounded in the head, and plundered of everything that I had about me, I was being led as a prisoner between two French . . . soldiers when one of these lancers rode up, and deliberately cut me down. Not satisfied with this brutality, the wretch tried by every means in his power to make his horse trample on me.[6]

With exultant cavalrymen and desperate fugitives streaming past their rear ranks and many men felled by a volley fired at the enemy horsemen by the newly arrived brigade of General Hoghton, the Spaniards still did not break, whilst their fire had done so much damage to their French assailants that the latter broke off their assault and tried to bring forward their second division (that of Gazan). This, however, led to chaos: with the two divisions much too close together to allow them freedom of movement, they merged into a single confused mass. With all forward movement impossible, Soult should either have disengaged, or flung in the two infantry brigades that he had in reserve, along with his powerful cavalry, in a last-ditch attempt to tip the balance. Such a stratagem might yet have succeeded, but, whilst Soult was in his element when it came to formulating battle plans, he was less effective when it came actually to implementing them, let alone to reacting to changing conditions on the battlefield. Taken completely by surprise, he therefore failed to issue the fresh orders that were needed, condemning his men to a most ill-deserved defeat.

For the Allies, meanwhile, things were beginning to look much better. Stewart's remaining two brigades – those of Hoghton and Abercrombie – had now been formed in line behind Blake's troops, and the latter now filed to the rear, Sherer remembering how 'a very noble-looking young Spanish officer rode up to me and begged me . . . to explain to the English that his countrymen were ordered to retire [and] were not flying'.[7] With Hoghton's men facing the mass of Frenchmen on the ridge and Abercrombie's prolonging the line downhill to the left, what remained of Stewart's division now advanced. Disordered though they might have been, the French infantry were not cowards, whilst they could scarcely have run even had they wanted to, and there therefore followed a terrible firefight which earned one of the regiments involved – the Fifty-Seventh Foot – its long-standing nickname of 'The Die-Hards'. Fighting in Abercrombie's brigade, Sherer was an eyewitness:

This murderous contest of musketry lasted long. We were the whole time progressively advancing upon the enemy . . . The slaughter was now . . . dreadful: every shot told . . . To describe . . . this wild scene with fidelity would be impossible. At intervals a shriek or a groan told that men were falling around me, but it was not always that the tumult . . . suffered me to catch these sounds. A constant feeling [i.e.: closing in] to the centre . . . more truly bespoke the havoc of death.[8]

Faced only by French skirmishers, Abercrombie's three battalions might have attacked the French in flank, but for reasons which are not entirely clear they did not do so. Orders are supposed to have been sent to them to this effect, but it is possible that they never arrived, whilst their commander may also have been worried at the possibility of an attack on his rear by the French troops around La Albuera. Once having ordered them up, meanwhile, Beresford seems simply to have forgotten them. Much shaken by the charge of the French cavalry (in which he and his staff had actually been caught up, the British general supposedly having dispatched one of the enemy horsemen with his bare hands) and all too well aware of the large numbers of horsemen further along the ridge and in the shallow valley on its northern side, he was now engaged in the fruitless task of bringing up the infantry brigade of Carlos de España belonging to the Fifth Army to guard Hoghton's right (fruitless because the three battalions of which it was composed had all been at the battle of the Gebora, and in consequence refused to move). Also to hand was Cole's Fourth Division and three brigades of cavalry, all of which were currently echeloned to the right, but these troops Beresford left alone for fear of incurring another disaster along the lines of that which had befallen Colborne, instead fixing on the astonishing plan of calling up more troops from his left and centre.

With men falling thick and fast, this can only be described as quite crazy, for the troops concerned could not have arrived for some time. Luckily for Beresford, however, an exasperated staff officer rode over to Cole and urged him to take the offensive. Having first obtained a promise of cavalry support and arrayed itself in a formation in which it would be safe from enemy horsemen, the Fourth Division therefore advanced across the valley. Flayed by French artillery fire, it was immediately charged by four regiments of dragoons, only for the Portuguese brigade facing them to perform the extraordinary feat of repulsing them without forming square. On the ridge, meanwhile, Soult had ordered forward the strong brigade of General Werlé to protect the left flank of Girard and Gazan, and, as Cole's troops mounted the slope, this opened fire with considerable effect. Twice as strong as their assailants though they were, however, Werlé's men had come forward in three closed columns of three battalions each, and they were therefore unable either to bring many muskets to bear or to deploy with any ease, and, after a fierce fight, they broke and fled. At about the same time, Abercrombie had finally led his troops up on to the summit of the ridge from the other side. Unable to take any more, Girard and Gazan's divisions disintegrated in their turn, and within minutes the whole of the French left wing was in retreat. Fighting went on for a little while longer around La Albuera itself, but, with the Allies too exhausted to pursue, to all intents and purposes the battle was over.

Thus ended a terrible day. Not counting several hundreds of prisoners, the Allied armies had lost 5,380 men dead or wounded. As for Soult's losses, they were still worse, the marshal having lost at least a quarter and possibly a third of his 24,000 men. As Long wrote, 'I never . . . saw such a scene of carnage . . . The field of battle was a slaughter house.'[9] Despite the heroism of many of his soldiers, Beresford had little cause to glory in his victory. Completely misjudging the situation at the start of the battle, he had then lost confidence in himself to such an extent that he became incapable of fighting it in an effective fashion. Badly served by some of his subordinates though he may have been, the fact is that he was simply not suited to the role of a battlefield commander, having been given the command of the southern front only because the solid and reliable Rowland Hill – Wellington's usual choice when it came to appointing an independent commander for part of his army – had fallen sick. Surrounded by scenes of the utmost horror, meanwhile, Beresford seems to have experienced some sort of nervous collapse: letters written by him after the battle suggest a man gripped by panic and shock, whilst his official dispatch had to be substantially 'written up' by Wellington before he could send it on to London.

Yet whatever criticisms may be made of Beresford, the fact is that Albuera had ended any immediate hopes Badajoz may have had of relief, for Soult had to withdraw. What is more he did so amidst scenes of demoralisation and horror. French prisoners, for example, 'called Soult bloodthirsty and avaricious, saying that he cared not how he sacrificed his men, and that he was wholly bent on the pursuit of dignities and wealth'.[10] As for the wounded, their sufferings were appalling:

About two o'clock in the morning the main convoy of wounded, amounting to near 4,000 in all, was put in motion. Dreadful were the cries of these poor . . . wretches! Had my heart been made of adamant I must have felt for the pitiable condition to which the ravages of war had brought them . . . Two or three hundred . . . died on the seventeenth, and between 600 and 700 more expired on the road to Seville.[11]

At the same time, the battle had at least shown that co-operation between the British and the Spaniards was possible, and, further, that Spanish troops could put up a good fight when they had to. Nor was any military harm done by the heavy Allied losses: for reasons which shall become clear shortly, Wellington was quickly able to make good the damage and resume the siege of Badajoz. Nevertheless, the battle did little for Anglo-Spanish relations. Wellington put the bulk of the blame for what had occurred on Blake, and was at best grudging in his praise of the Spanish infantry. Thus:

The Spanish troops, I understand, behaved admirably. They stood like stocks, both parties at times firing upon them, but they were quite immovable, and this is the great cause of all our losses. After they had lost their position, the natural thing to do would have been to attack it with the nearest Spanish troops, but they could not be moved. The British troops . . . were brought up, and must always in these cases be brought up, and they suffered accordingly.[12]

Although much of this was unfair, there was a kernel of truth here: most Spanish troops were, quite literally, incapable of manoeuvre. Needless to say, a very different story was soon being put about: Leith-Hay, for example, states categorically that Beresford's difficulties were 'occasioned in the first place by the Spanish troops giving way'.[13] As for William Lawrence, a sergeant who fought in Cole's charge, he was even more damning:

The Spaniards . . . soon gave way in great disorder, leaving the brunt of the battle to the British . . . It was always a bother to get them to stir forward during a battle, but retreating was what they were best at, and then it was always in confusion.[14]

Irritation, meanwhile, was turned into fury when the dispatch that was read out in the *cortes* made it impossible to believe that the British had played anything but a minor role in the fighting. Some fair accounts of the battle did appear in the Spanish press, but, as Graham complained:

The news of the victory in Extremadura has filled the minds of the people . . . with the most determined belief of the superiority of the Spanish army, which now in the public opinion neither admits of nor requires improvement, being already perfect. Without being a witness to this unfortunate national egoism . . . it is not to be believed, nor would anyone imagine it possible that people of all ranks should be so ready to deceive themselves and others. Instead of a grateful and generous feeling of sympathy for the loss of the British troops at Albuera, the people here universally believe that it is purposely exaggerated . . . and that at all events the safety of the British and Portuguese was entirely owing to the intrepidity of the Spanish soldiers, and the activity and judgement of their leaders.[15]

What rendered the Spaniards' grumbling still more irritating was the fact that Wellington had just obtained an important victory on the northern front. Following Sabugal, the British commander had invested Almeida, which he believed he could starve into surrender long before Masséna's army could come up to the front (thoroughly exhausted, it had retreated deep into Spain and was now refitting around Salamanca and Toro). Ciudad Rodrigo, too, it was hoped might be forced to surrender, for its reserves of food were known to have been stripped to feed Masséna's men, but the troops concerned – the Light Division, which had for some time been in the hands of the singularly incompetent Sir William Erskine, and the guerrillas of Julián Sánchez – failed to keep an adequate watch and thereby let a large supply convoy slip through. Realising that a long blockade would have risked a repeat of the Côa, Wellington therefore pulled the Light Division back and concentrated on Almeida alone.

In the event, this proved just as well. Nothing if not resourceful, Masséna succeeded in rebuilding his army far more quickly than had been expected, and by the end of April reports were coming in that the French were on the move. Though his men lacked horses and had not been properly reclothed, Masséna was determined to make one last effort. Reinforced by a small cavalry division brought up by the commander of the Army of the North, Marshal Bessières, on 26 April 'the darling child of victory' moved forward to the attack.* Ostensibly this move was aimed at allowing Almeida to be revictualled, but the French did not have the transport to bring up more than a moderate amount of food, and could not possibly maintain themselves in the vicinity of their target for any length of time. The real object, then, was Wellington's destruction. Would a battle have brought such a result, however? Wellington could only field 37,000 men to Masséna's 48,000; his newly formed Seventh Division was largely composed of raw recruits and foreign deserters; and the open nature of the border country made his marked shortage of cavalry particularly worrying. Yet all this only begged the question of whether Wellington would fight. As Masséna knew all too well, the British commander could simply withdraw beyond the Côa and wait for hunger to force the French to retreat, whilst if he fought at all it would be on ground that was immensely strong. Nor was the Army of Portugal in the happiest frame of mind. Thirsting for revenge for the horrors of the last eight months, the men were willing enough: 'Everyone', says Parquin, 'was eager to come to terms with the English.'[16] Amongst the generals, however, the atmosphere was even more poisonous than it had been in 1810. Constant buccaneering had led to incessant squabbling that almost led Generals Poinsot and Fournier to fight a duel. Unwilling to fight any more under Masséna, Drouet had just tried to take advantage of fresh orders he had received from Paris to depart for Andalucía with most of his men. And finally, Bessières had welched on promises to bring up at least a full infantry division, and was adding insult to injury by claiming that he had 'come, like a French cavalier, at the head of a handful of heroes'.[17]† As Masséna remarked, 'He would have done better to have sent me a few more thousand men . . . than to come examining and criticising what I am going to do.'[18] Well might Marbot write, 'The many annoyances which [Marshal Masséna] had all around him did a good deal to embitter his naturally vindictive temper'.[19]

As it happened, Wellington decided to fight it out, but from the French point of view the whole affair seems singularly pointless. With the high command in such disarray, victory was never likely, whilst the position chosen by Wellington for this fresh battle was readily defensible. The Allied army was stationed along a line of low hills between a ruined fort and the village of Fuentes de Oñoro, whilst its centre and left were screened by a

---

* Only formed in January 1811, the Army of the North was a new force composed of the garrisons of Old Castile, Navarre and the Basque provinces.
† Bessières, doubtless, was influenced by jealousy, but he could only have brought up more men by allowing large parts of northern Spain to slip out of French control, whilst the extra troops would have made little difference.

deep ravine through which ran a stream called the Dos Casas. Encountering this position on the morning of 3 May, Masséna quickly decided that the best means of making progress was to seize the village, which, strongly garrisoned, was thrown forward on the slopes that led down to the Dos Casas. Early in the afternoon, then, his leading infantry division charged across the river and into its warren of alleys and courtyards. For several hours there followed a bitter fight, which cost the two sides over 900 casualties. Something of the chaos is captured by one of the defenders:

The overwhelming force which the French now pushed forward on the village could not be withstood by the small number of troops which defended it [and] they were obliged to give way ... While retreating through the town, one of our sergeants ... being pushed hard by the enemy, ran into one of the houses. They were hard on his heels and he just had time to tumble himself into a large chest ... when they entered and commenced plundering the house ... and they were in the act of opening the lid of his hiding place, when the noise of our men cheering as they charged the enemy ... forced them to take flight.[20]

At length the attackers were thrown out and forced to retire by a ferocious charge of the Seventy-First Foot, though the French cause was not helped by the fact that one of their units was the red-coated Légion Hanovérienne:

The result was a cruel blunder. The [French] Sixty-Sixth Regiment, having been sent to support the Hanoverians, who were in the fighting line, mistook them in the smoke for an English battalion, and fired into them ... Another regiment, which was entering the village at that moment, seeing the red coats on their flank, supposed that the position had been turned ... and the enemy cleverly took advantage of the resulting confusion to recapture Fuentes de Oñoro.[21]

Thus baulked, Masséna spent the whole of the next day reconnoitring the Allied position, and at length concluded that the best means of defeating Wellington would be to march around his left flank and leave him the choice of retreating or facing a pincer attack in which 20,000 men would move north against the southern end of his ridge whilst 14,000 more stormed Fuentes. Realising that something of the sort was afoot, Wellington sent out his new Seventh Division to occupy the area of the village of Pozo Bello two miles south of the end of his line, but, like Beresford at Albuera, he had badly misjudged the situation, for, very weak in terms of both numbers and quality, this force was unlikely to be able to stop a serious attack. Also available, true, was the whole of the Allied cavalry – four regiments of regulars and Sánchez's guerrillas – but even so the Seventh Division could well have been annihilated.

In the end, however, disaster was avoided. No sooner had dawn broken on 5 May than thousands of French troops began to envelop Pozo Bello. Fighting bravely, the Allied cavalry tried to slow them down, but their best efforts were to no avail. As William Tomkinson remembered:

Our men rode up and began sabring, but were so outnumbered that they could do nothing and were obliged to retire . . . the enemy having brought up more troops at that point. Captain Belli was wounded . . . and taken; Sergeant Taylor . . . and six men . . . were killed . . . in attempting to rescue him.[22]

With the French in overwhelming strength, the village's garrison was quickly overwhelmed, and the main body of the Seventh Division, which had been drawn up in line of battle under its commander, General Houston, a little to the west, was forced to retreat in search of safer ground:

We retired through the broken ground in our rear . . . and were pretty safe from their cavalry, but they had brought up their guns . . . and were serving out the shot with a liberal hand. We continued retiring and soon came to a . . . rapid stream. This we waded up to our armpits, and from the steepness of the opposite bank we found much difficulty in getting out. This caused some delay [but] the regiment waited until all had crossed, then formed line and continued [its] retreat in quick time. Thanks to Colonel M. we came off safe . . . He dismounted . . . faced us and frequently called the time . . . He would now and then call out, 'That fellow . . . cannot march; mark him for drill, Sergeant Major. I tell you they cannot hurt us if you are steady; if you get out of time, you will be knocked down.' He was leading his horse and a shot passed under the horse's belly, which made him rear up. 'You are a coward', he said, 'I will stop your corn for three days.'[23]

Stiffened by such gallantry, Houston's men were able to reach a good defensive position some way further back. Here the retreat stopped, for, after several charges had been cleverly repulsed, the French horsemen found that they could make no further progress, whilst the infantry that had followed them had swung northwards and were now heading for Wellington's main position.

Here, however, the crisis had already passed. Now fully aware of the danger, Wellington had ordered two of his best infantry divisions and a further brigade of Portuguese troops to form a new line angling back across the ridge from Fuentes de Oñoro towards another little river – the Turón – that ran along the rear of his original position. This was likely to prove a hard nut to crack – aside from anything else, the ground fell away sharply in front of the new line – and Wellington could therefore feel perfectly at ease. All that troubled him, indeed, was the situation of the Seventh Division, which was still dangerously isolated. To avoid the possibility of Masséna securing even the partial success that would have been achieved by its destruction, the British commander therefore sent orders for it to fall back still further whilst at the same time dispatching the Light Division (now once more led by Craufurd, who had fortuitously resumed its command only the night before) to cover its retreat.

There followed the most famous episode of the battle. Marching out along the slopes that led to Houston's position, Craufurd's men briefly drew up in line. No sooner was the Seventh Division on the move, however, than they began to file back again. The French cavalry having now re-formed, they immediately tried to ride them down, but the same cavalry units that had already fought so well to protect Houston now again came to the rescue. What could have been a situation of extreme danger was therefore avoided, the battalion squares into which Craufurd had formed the bulk of his men being able to retire in good order. However, even then the retreat was not without its moments of crisis: a section of the horse artillery battery attached to the Light Division only saved itself by charging at full gallop some French cavalry that had cut it off, whilst the French also got in amongst the skirmishers covering the main line and caused one hundred or so casualties. Yet even this minor success was dearly bought:

General Fournier . . . Captain Lasalle [and] Lieutenants Labassée and Hymonet, as well as several chasseurs, were unhorsed by the enemy artillery and infantry fire, and a bullet fired at point-blank range smashed into my face and knocked out six of my teeth.[24]

At this point it should have been clear to Masséna that the battle was lost, for the British position was once again too strong to force. Knowing that defeat meant sure disgrace, however, the marshal could not afford to back down. Thus, as soon as his outflanking move was seen to be making progress, the French had once again charged across into the village. Since then, a desperate fight had been taking place that saw first one side gain the advantage and then the other, as well as forcing both the contending commanders to feed more and more troops into the struggle. On at least two occasions French troops made it to the very last buildings of the village, but each time they were hurled back. After the battle the dead offered mute testimony to the ferocity of the fighting:

Among the dead that covered the streets . . . it was quite a common thing to see an English and a French soldier with their bayonets still in each other's bodies, and their fists convulsively grasping the butt ends of their muskets, lying on top of each other. At one spot I saw seven, and at another five, French officers killed by bayonet wounds.[25]

Unlike on 3 May the French were not expelled from Fuentes altogether – on the contrary much of the lower part of the village was still in their hands – but for Masséna this was not enough. Realising that no attack on Wellington's main position could succeed until the village had fallen, he seized upon Bessières' refusal to release the division of cavalry he had brought for a final charge on Wellington's line as a useful pretext, and called off the action. Casualties were 1,452 for the Allies and 2,192 for the French, or, taking both days of the fighting together, 1,711 and 2,844.

All in all, then, Fuentes de Oñoro had not been a good bargain for Masséna. Large quantities of supplies had been consumed for no purpose, and it had not been possible either to reach Almeida or to inflict serious damage on Wellington. There yet remained a consolation prize for the French, however. Although Masséna had no option but to withdraw, he first managed to smuggle a message to the garrison of Almeida ordering it to slight its defences and try to escape. Thanks to a series of lapses on the part of the forces watching the place, this ploy proved remarkably successful: having fired the fuses of a number of mines that a few minutes later blew great holes in the walls, on the night of 10 May the entire garrison dashed out of one of the gates. Assailed from all sides, they were almost caught at the bridge that crossed the River Azava at the village of Barba del Puerco, but their commander's courage and resource kept them going, and for the most part they eventually reached safety.

Unwelcome though this may have been, Wellington could on the whole feel well satisfied. His army had succeeded in winning a clear victory, and the way was now open to him to concentrate on capturing Badajoz, which he rightly judged to be the most valuable of the two possible objectives facing his forces (indeed, no sooner had Masséna departed, than Wellington set out for Extremadura with two infantry divisions). Moreover, although he was not to know it, if Fuentes de Oñoro had shown that adventures in the plains of León and Old Castile were still a dubious proposition, it proved a turning point in the war, for a delighted Cabinet suddenly switched from suggesting cuts in the size of Wellington's army – under existing circumstances always a possibility once the safety of Portugal had been assured – to promising 8,000 fresh troops and sending out a proper siege train. On top of this munificence came fresh instructions. No longer confined to the defence of Portugal, Wellington was henceforward to have full discretion in what he did. At no point was it specifically said that he should advance, but the implications were clear: sooner or later, the Anglo-Portuguese army would be taking the offensive with a view to driving the French from Spain.

To return to Extremadura, meanwhile, Wellington found that matters were on a tolerable footing. Thus, Soult could be expected to be out of the fight for some time whilst Badajoz had been hastily reinvested by Allied troops returning from La Albuera (though not before Philippon had demolished all the Allies' siege works). Fully recovered from his illness, General Hill had also turned up, Wellington immediately placing him in charge of the covering force – the remains of the Second and Fourth Divisions plus some other troops – that was watching Soult. No sooner had siege operations been recommenced, however, than it became obvious that Wellington still did not have the resources that he needed to take a major fortress. Matters were not helped by various geographical accidents, the gallantry and resourcefulness of Philippon, and faulty planning that dissipated the Allies' scanty resources and once again pitted them against the immensely strong San Cristóbal, but the key factor was the dubious Allied siege artillery. Still composed almost entirely of museum pieces, this proved incapable of either suppressing the fire of the defenders or blowing adequate breaches in the walls. For the troops in the trenches the siege was in consequence a miserable affair, Donaldson remembering how they 'suffered severely from the enemy's shot and shell, with which they . . . plied us hotly', and Wheeler how they were, 'almost suffocated for . . . want of air and nearly baked by the sun', and were 'kept in constant motion by swarms of flies'.[26] Though some damage was eventually done, the courage and fortitude of the defenders ensured that two assaults on 6 and 9 June were beaten off with heavy losses. A participant in both attacks, Wheeler gives a graphic description of the scene:

We advanced up the glacis . . . Not a head was to be seen above the walls, and we began to think the enemy had retired . . . when sudden as a flash of lightning the whole place was in a blaze. It will be impossible for me to describe to you what followed. You can better conceive it by figuring . . . a deep trench or ditch filled with men who are endeavouring to mount the wall by means of ladders. The top of this wall crowded with men hurling down shells and hand grenades on the heads of them below, and when all these are expended they each have six or seven loaded firelocks which they discharge . . . as quick as possible. Add to this some half a dozen cannon scouring the trench with grape . . . heaps of brave fellows killed and wounded, [and] ladders shot to pieces, and falling together with the men down upon the living and the dead . . . But in the midst of all these difficulties . . . we should have taken the fort, but for an unforeseen accident that could not be remedied . . . The ladders were too short . . . As soon as this was discovered, all hopes of gaining possession was abandoned, and the order was given to retire.[27]

Had the Anglo-Portuguese only been able to hang on, starvation alone might have been enough to defeat Philippon, but by now large forces were marching to Badajoz's relief. Such was the strategic importance of the fortress that Wellington had always expected that besieging it would attract the attentions of more of the enemy than even he could handle. And so it transpired. Even before Albuera had been fought, Soult had written to the Army of Portugal warning it that Badajoz was in danger and that he might have to call on it for help. Arriving on 14 May, this letter found not the notoriously mean and selfish Masséna, but a new commander in the person of Marshal Marmont. Younger and more personable than his predecessor, who had just received the inevitable news that Napoleon had decided to dismiss him from his post, Marmont immediately agreed to move south. Given his character, this was, perhaps, a little surprising, for the Army of Portugal's new commander was just as vain and self-centred as Masséna, but he was a good strategist, whilst, as the only French general with no great expanse of territory to defend, he had nothing to lose in marching to Soult's aid. On the contrary, indeed, doing so would win plaudits in Paris and might even secure him the credit for a remarkable success.

For the moment there was much to do, for the Army of Portugal was in desperate need of re-equipment and fresh troops, whilst the forces of Soult and Marmont alike had been ordered to rid themselves of their old corps structure. Possessed of great energy and enthusiasm, however, Masséna's replacement proved more than up to the job. In a short time, the surviving soldiers had been concentrated in a smaller number of battalions and squadrons, cadres of every infantry and cavalry regiment sent back to France to absorb fresh conscripts, and part of Drouet's Ninth Corps dispatched to reinforce Soult.* At the same time, large stocks of clothing and shoes had been issued, and the morale of officers and men greatly revived. Now possessed of an establishment of only 36,000 men, the army was much smaller than it had been under Masséna, whilst for the time being it could only put about half its cavalry and artillery into the field for want of horses (of which large numbers were being dispatched from France). However, with most of its old senior officers got rid of, the increasingly vitriolic

---

* Composed of twenty new battalions raised for infantry regiments already serving in the Peninsula, the Ninth Corps had only ever been conceived of as a temporary formation. Caught up in Masséna's travails, it had survived longer than intended, but now that opportunity offered its units were sent to join their parent formations, Soult's share amounting to eleven battalions.

atmosphere of the last few months was at an end, and the Army of Portugal a more cohesive and battle-worthy force than it had been for some time. As Marmont wrote, 'A month before seemingly so disorganised, so discouraged, so incapable of taking the field, the army . . . had recovered its vigour, its élan and its confidence.'[28]

Despite Albuera, Soult's position was therefore by no means as desperate as it might have been. Forewarned of his plight, Marmont had begun to edge his command southwards even before he had heard the result of the bloody combat of 16 May, and in consequence was on the march as early as 1 June. Hearing of the move, Bessières was furious, arguing – totally speciously – that his domains would now be exposed to attack from the west, that Soult (whom he hated) could shift for himself, and that Marmont would be better employed resting his army, but Marmont ignored him. Feinting at Almeida to bluff the substantial forces left in the north by Wellington into quiescence, by 11 June he had got the first of his troops to the Tagus at the Puente de Almáraz, the British commander in consequence deciding that he had no option but to raise the siege of Badajoz. With Hill's covering forces in full retreat as well, Soult moved north and on 18 June the two marshals met at Mérida.

According to a somewhat smug Marmont, Soult was 'little accustomed to such comradely conduct' and was in consequence 'overwhelmed with joy and gratitude'.[29] As for Badajoz, it was safe again, but what should the French now do? Once they had joined forces, Soult and Marmont had 60,000 men, but Wellington had fallen back across the frontier and taken up a strong defensive position behind the River Caya between the fortresses of Elvas and Campo Mayor, where he was soon joined by all the forces that he had left to cover Almeida. Reconnoitring this position, the French commanders decided that pushing on any further would be madness, for the Anglo-Portuguese army was clearly of a strength not far short of their own. There followed an uncomfortable stand-off. 'Our foreign troops, German and French, have been deserting in numbers lately', complained the Guards officer, John Mills. 'Fifty of the Chasseurs Britanniques went over . . . a few nights ago and a night or two afterwards the same number of Germans . . . played the same trick.'[30]* And the entire army suffered terribly from heat and thirst:

---

* Wellington's army had many foreign regiments, including not just the Chasseurs Britanniques (supposedly a unit of royalist *émigrés*) but also those of the King's German Legion, a force originally recruited from the exiled Hanoverian army. By 1811 composed almost entirely of deserters and prisoners of war, they generally fought well, but were prone to desertion.

Our life in this camp was by no means pleasant . . . All day long we were infested with snakes, blowflies and other vermin . . . At night we were plagued by scorpions, mosquitoes and a piercingly cold wind . . . All kinds of typhus and ague began to break out . . . The heat was so oppressive that Captain von Müller, who was president of the officers' mess, was obliged to find out the precise spot which at five in the afternoon happened to be shaded by two old cork trees, so that we could at least enjoy a meal . . . protected from the sun.[31]

Yet, the army was safe, for no attack came. And if the French could not attack, they could not keep 60,000 men in Portugal for very long either, for, setting aside the problem of supplies, it was clear that in both León and Andalucía the Spaniards were capable of considerable mischief (indeed, the French did not know it, but Wellington had already got Blake to march southwards in the hope that he might threaten Seville). Within a matter of days, then, Soult was heading back to Andalucía and Marmont to León. Assisted by the arrival of the troops brought by Drouet, the former was able to leave 15,000 men to hold down Extremadura, but once again the initiative was in the hands of the Allies.

What, meanwhile, had been happening in the rest of Spain? In brief, the Allies' position in the Peninsula had been continuing to deteriorate. This is not, of course, to say that Spanish resistance was in any way diminishing. Thus, in Navarre, Aragon, the Basque provinces, León, the two Castiles, Andalucía and Catalonia, the guerrillas continued to wreak havoc. In the Serranía de Ronda, for example, José Serrano Valdenebro's mountaineers were now organised into three infantry battalions, a squadron of cavalry, and a home guard called out in the event of emergency. Much strengthened as a result, these forces engaged in frequent combats, severely harassing a French column sent to levy contributions from the district of San Roque, defeating an attempt to capture their headquarters of Gaucín and repeatedly attacking Ronda. As elsewhere, meanwhile, the irregulars were seconded by regular forces: in June 1811 a column of Polish troops sent to reinforce Ronda was defeated at Dehesa de Gaena by a division of the Fourth Army landed from Cádiz under General Antonio Begines de los Ríos, and eastern Andalucía invaded by General Freyre's Third Army. Far away in the north, meanwhile, another force on the move was the Sixth Army, which had been asked by Wellington to mount an offensive in León so as to neutralise Bessières.*

---

* Castaños was at this time nominally commander of both the Fifth and the Sixth Army, as well as Captain General of the regions in which they were based. In practice, the Captain Generalcy of Galicia was filled by Castaños' deputy, Mahy, who in turn delegated field operations to a General Santocildes.

Able to put some 15,000 men into the field, the Galicians moved forward on 12 June, regained Astorga, which had been hastily evacuated, and won a minor victory at Cogorderos on 23 June. After some weeks of marching and counter-marching, the Sixth Army fell back, but by then the French had been forced to give up not only Astorga but also Asturias, whilst the concentration of much of the Army of the North against its forces had effectively given free rein to the guerrillas of Old Castile. On 14 August, for example, Porlier stormed Santander, whilst more irregular bands blockaded Palencia and Valladolid. Indeed, all that rescued the French was the arrival from France of several divisions of reinforcements (for at this time Napoleon was still pouring fresh troops into the Peninsula).

The greatest coup of all pulled off by the Spaniards at this time, however, was the work of the Catalans. Thus, aided by three young clerks who were employed by the garrison, on the night of 9–10 April the erstwhile cleric, Francisco Rovira, was able literally to let himself into the very strong fortress of Figueras at the head of 2,000 men. Because it commanded the main road from Barcelona to the frontier, its loss was not to be tolerated, and, after confused fighting in which Rovira and his men received some rather ineffectual support from troops of the First Army brought up by its latest commander, the Conde de Campoverde, the fortress was besieged (or, to be more precise, blockaded: reckoning that relief was unlikely, the commander of the French Army of Catalonia, who was now Marshal Macdonald, eschewed formal siege operations in favour of simply starving the defenders into surrender). Defended largely by irregulars though it was, the fortress hung on for much longer than expected, but on 17 August, with every scrap of food gone, it was finally forced to capitulate after a desperate attempt at a break-out was foiled. As Macdonald wrote:

The unevenness of the ground caused the head of the columns to waver and made their weapons jingle, and this attracted the attention of our advanced outposts . . . We awaited their approach, and as soon as they opened the attack we threw some hand grenades amongst them . . . The Spaniards lost a large number of killed, wounded and . . . prisoners; on our side no one had a scratch. Next day the enemy ran up the white flag . . . I accorded them the honours of war. The garrison laid down their arms and remained prisoners; out of respect for their bravery the officers retained their swords.[32]

Counting losses due to sickness, some 4,000 Frenchmen died in the operations round Figueras, whilst for several months the Army of Catalonia, its ranks swelled by a fresh division sent across the border by Napoleon, was rendered incapable of carrying out the task it had been set of conquering the Catalan interior. Yet, for all that, the gallantry of neither Catalans, nor Navarrese, nor Galicians, nor Andalusians made any difference, for the machine of French conquest continued to grind on unchecked. In all the areas where imperial control had been shaken by the campaigns of the spring and summer of 1811, the situation was soon returned to the position in which it had stood at the beginning of the year (the Third Army, for example, was forced to retreat after one of its divisions was defeated by Soult on 9 August at Zujar). Still worse, having made serious inroads on Spain's limited resources – the Sixth Army was left in a very weak condition by the campaign in León, Walker reporting that the troops were in a 'wretched state . . . in want of almost everything, one third part at least without shoes, and dependent for subsistence on the precarious collection of the day'[33] – the fighting had not even prevented the French from seizing still more ground. Next to feel the weight of the emperor's armies was the vital city of Tarragona. The chief reason why the Spaniards had for so long been able to maintain a regular army of however small a size in southern and central Catalonia, Tarragona was at one and the same time a great port, a major fortress, and the key to the Levante – the last region whose resources remained intact as far as the Patriot cause was concerned, and a very wealthy one at that. Not surprisingly, then, the emperor had deemed that it should be taken. Told off for this task was the Army of Aragón under its commander, General Suchet, the latter being given a third of the Army of Catalonia so as to ensure that his operations could not be marred by friction with Macdonald. In consequence, Suchet now had some 43,000 men, but so many had to be left behind to provide for the defence of Aragón that he was only left with 20,000 men for his offensive. Nothing daunted, however, the French commander was soon on the march. Much aided by the fact that Campoverde and most of his army had gone north to take part in the operations round Figueras – a curious example of guerrillas distracting Allied rather than French troops from the chief object of the moment – on 3 May he appeared before its walls.

The siege that followed was long and bitter. Reinforced by troops brought back from northern Catalonia by sea and the fire of British warships in the harbour, the garrison launched many sorties and put up a desperate defence of Suchet's first target, an important outwork known as Fort Olivo. At first the defence was headed by Campoverde, but after nearly a month of fighting that officer left the city to try to organise an army of relief from such troops of the First Army as had remained outside the city together with some reinforcements which he had begged from Valencia. Great difficulty was experienced in getting together a force of reasonable size, however, whilst Campoverde showed little enthusiasm for a battle, contenting himself instead with sending false promises of help that ended up doing more harm than good. Inside the city, meanwhile, all was far from well: with the French trenches edging ever closer and the walls crumbling under the constant bombardment, the garrison was increasingly disheartened, whilst matters were not helped when Fort Olivo was stormed in a gallant action fought on 29 May:

Between eight and nine in the evening . . . the signal was given for the assault . . . By a fortuitous coincidence . . . a column of 1,200 men coming from the town to relieve the garrison of the fort began to enter it just at the moment when our columns of assault were debouching from the trench . . . The first was commanded by *chef-de-bataillon* Miocque, and proceeded directly towards the breach. The second under *commandant* Revel . . . turned to the right of the fort to attack the gorge. Captain Papigny of the engineers . . . reached the gate at the moment of its being shut: the . . . 1,200 Spaniards had just entered precipitately, followed by a detachment of the First Light [Infantry], which . . . had rushed in pell-mell with [them]. The sappers endeavoured to break down the gate with their axes, but . . . though there was some confusion within, a terrible fire was opened and several of the sappers fell . . . While the column was crowding up to the gate, *commandant* Revel ordered some of the sappers and grenadiers to apply long ladders to that part of the scarp which was without ditch: our brave fellows on reaching the top rushed . . . the gate, opened it and admitted their colleagues . . . At the same instant . . . Miocque . . . arrived with his column facing the point battered by our artillery, and, as the breach was neither sufficiently wide nor very practicable, he caused the ladders to be applied to get upon the scarp . . . It was twenty feet in height and the ladders were only fifteen. Serjeant Meunier . . . placed himself on top of the longest and made the *voltigeurs* clamber up on to his shoulders . . . but this method was too slow . . . Fortunately . . . the Spaniards had imprudently preserved . . . the aqueduct . . . at the extremity of the ditch on our left . . . The grenadiers . . . rushed forward into this narrow and dangerous passage . . . They penetrated into the interior of the fort, and, proceeding along the rampart, overthrew, killed or put to flight such of the enemy as were engaged in . . . opposing the escalade.[34]

Discouraged by Suchet's success, the defenders did not put up much of a fight when the French stormed the city's first line of defences on 21 June. All that was now left to the garrison was the old town which was situated on a high bluff overlooking the harbour. A belated attempt at relief by Campoverde failing through want of will on his part, morale slumped still further when a British expeditionary force that had appeared in the harbour left without firing a shot (sent up by Graham from Cádiz, it was under orders not to disembark unless it could guarantee its escape).

The end came on 28 June: bombarded by twenty-two guns brought up to the closest possible range, the wall of the old city was breached, and late in the afternoon the French advanced to the assault. For a little while the defenders fought bravely, but most of their guns had been put out of action and the attackers soon broke through. As Suchet remembered:

At five in the afternoon . . . our brave men . . . issued from the trenches . . . and dashed onto the breach . . . The Spaniards then hurried up, lining the breach with the most valiant of their officers and men . . . A shower of case-shot poured upon the head of the column. For a moment fortune seemed to waver . . . [but] the columns rallied [and] the mass formed anew, dashed on, reached the summit, and, like an irresistible torrent . . . inundated the ramparts.[35]

A resourceful and courageous soldier, however, the governor, Juan Senan de Contreras, had barricaded the streets, and fighting continued in the interior of the city for some hours. Contreras himself was captured leading a counter-attack; many groups of soldiers found themselves trapped and fought to the death, including 300 men who were caught in the cathedral; and a considerable number of survivors were got together by a General Courten and tried to break out of the city so as to join Campoverde, only to be ridden down by French cavalry. Inside the city, meanwhile, there were scenes of horror, the victorious French thoroughly sacking the old town and killing at least 2,000 civilians. As Suchet admitted of his men:

Their excitement had reached the highest pitch: it was not possible . . . amid such a scene to moderate them by words. They were inebriated . . . by the noise, smoke and blood, by the recollection of danger, by the desire of victory, by the thirst for revenge. Their uncurbed fury would listen to nothing; nay, they were almost deaf to the voice of their officers.[36]

At length the slaughter came to an end, but nothing could hide the magnitude of the disaster which had beset the Patriot cause. As the Junta of Catalonia lamented:

Catalonia has . . . lost the only port which remained to her . . . The most . . . fertile part of the principality is in possession of the enemy . . . and the mountainous parts alone must support the burden of the war . . . From the loss of the park of artillery and the very great want of ammunition in that part of the country which remains free, the army finds itself incapable of undertaking military operations, and the enemy, beholding our constrained inactivity, will no doubt advance without the least delay, and thus very soon become master of the whole province.[37]

Setting aside the enormous quantities of stores and munitions that had been consumed in the siege, fully two-thirds of the First Army had been put out of action – there were 9,000 prisoners alone – and the remainder reduced to a demoralised mob with no confidence in its commanders, for no one could understand why Campoverde had not made a greater effort to raise the siege. Over the next few weeks there was therefore a considerable increase in desertion, whilst the *somaténes*, too, went to ground. Abandoning several hospitals full of wounded men, who had been evacuated from the city by boat, as well as the stores that it had amassed to throw into its magazines, the army fell back to Cervera where Campoverde and his subordinates engaged in bitter recriminations which eventually led to the departure of the Valencians (through a rapid descent on the coast, the infantry were got away by sea, but, in what is possibly the most extraordinary feat of the entire Peninsular War, the 900 cavalry elected to try to ride home, and eventually made it all the way to Murcia after a 600-mile odyssey through Aragón, Navarre and La Mancha).

At this point, with the remains of the First Army having fallen back deep into its mountain fastnesses in the interior, Campoverde was replaced by Luis Lacy, but, if the latter was a better general, there was little that he could do to improve matters. Inheriting no more than 3,000 men, he tried hard to increase his strength, but the populace were now even less disposed to serve as regular soldiers than before – an attempt to impose a *quinta* of 6,000 men in September 1812 produced less than one sixth of that number – whilst he himself appears to have been an unpopular character blessed with little in the way of personal charisma. As a result there was nothing he could do to stop Suchet from following up his success by relieving Barcelona, which had once again been blockaded by the *miqueletes*, and driving the latter from the great massif of Monserrat, which they had made into an important base. With Figueras also gone, had Suchet been willing to pursue operations in Catalonia any further, it is clear that he might have crushed the Catalans once and for all, but the French commander had other plans and Lacy was therefore afforded a breathing space.

Of this Lacy made good use, launching a series of attacks on the French that re-established a variety of somewhat precarious links with the sea, but in the grand scale of things this made little difference, Tarragona remaining a blow from which the Catalans never recovered. Indeed, the whole affair is an excellent case study with regard to the impact of French offensives on *la guerrilla.* In particular, the spirit of the populace had been completely broken:

Let us undeceive ourselves: the fruit one expects to reap sweetens the labour . . . The soldier who is destitute of everything . . . [sees] the enemy's well clothed and fed, and [is] . . . offered security and [the hope of being] restored to his family, . . . deserts, [and] the army is therefore continually decreasing.[38]

If the towns and villages of occupied Catalonia teemed with men on the run from the armies – in March 1813 the Ampurdán alone was estimated at hosting at least 12,000 – the *somaténes* also proved little help. Lacy tried to give them new life, but the results were disappointing, the Spanish commander running into precisely the same problems that had dogged his predecessors:

[The general] . . . authorised several men who enjoyed the confidence of the people to collect a certain number of soldiers and form companies called *patriótas.** These parties killed a great number of Frenchmen, but, on account of a general pardon having been granted to all deserters, and a great many of them having joined those parties in preference to the regular corps, introduced great disorder . . . in the different places they were stationed. To remedy that in future, they were ordered to dress uniformly, got a regular commandant put over them, and, [having] begun to assume some regularity . . . were by force incorporated in the regiments of the line. This disgusted the greatest part of them [and they] immediately deserted and filled the province with robbers instead of augmenting the army.[39]

Pushed back into the interior, meanwhile, the First Army suffered terribly. The mountainous districts around Vich and Seo de Urgel, which now constituted its only base, could supply it with neither sufficient money, nor sufficient men, nor sufficient provisions, and it was in consequence reduced to penury. A British report of 1813 described the troops as being tough and well-armed, but suffering from 'much deficiency of accoutrements . . . very bad clothing . . . and . . . a complete want of shoes'.[40] The result was paralysis:

In the state in which Catalonia and her army find themselves, every type of assistance is needed if the offensive is to be taken and the enemy reduced to the walls of their fortresses. With an army that scarcely amounts to 7,000 men . . . we have with difficulty been able to stop the French from raiding the most inaccessible parts of the

---

* This is unlikely to be clear to modern readers. The units referred to were entitled *companías patriótas* (i.e. companies of patriots).

region, but we have had to abandon the richest and most productive areas of the province to their mercy ... As a result we have been denied their resources and manpower alike, the French having shut them in behind a line of fortified posts protected by a field force far superior to anything that we can oppose to it.[41]

In sum, then, as a British liaison officer reported, 'Without an additional force of 6,000 or 8,000 men, nothing offensive can be undertaken.'[42]

As if all this was not bad enough, the Anglo-Portuguese forces' record in the second half of 1811 was distinctly disappointing. Following the non-battle on the River Caya in the last week of June, Wellington had been left free to do more or less as he wanted, for the French had adopted an essentially defensive posture: the much-tried Army of the North holding open communications with Ciudad Rodrigo with no more than one division; Soult leaving only a relatively small force of troops in Extremadura; and Marmont occupying the Tagus valley, this being a position from which he could strike either north or south as required (of great importance in this respect was the bridge of Almáraz, which, as the only good crossing of the central Tagus, the French had protected with a ring of imposing forts). Ciudad Rodrigo being a weaker fortress than Badajoz, Wellington therefore marched north once more, leaving Hill in the Alentejo with the Second Division and some Portuguese units.

Yet the autumn of 1811 saw no siege of Ciudad Rodrigo. Although a blockade was imposed as early as 11 August and the siege train sent from Britain was ordered up from Lisbon, no sooner had the French gathered together the necessary supply convoy, than they struck again. Thus, on 22 September Marmont and Dorsenne (who had replaced Bessières as commander of the Army of the North, and had access to far more troops) swept forward with some 58,000 men. With only 46,000 men Wellington realised that he could not stop so powerful a force, but, in the apparent belief that the French commanders intended only to revictual Ciudad Rodrigo, he neither pulled back the troops that had been watching it as far as he might have done nor bothered to concentrate his army properly. Marmont and Dorsenne, however, had more fighting spirit than the British general had allowed for. Thus, far from quietly bivouacking around Ciudad Rodrigo, which was relieved on 23 September, two days later all the cavalry that the French could muster suddenly moved forward, and fell on Picton's Third Division at El Bodón. Though badly outnumbered, the troops concerned fought bravely. Thus:

The French cavalry charged ... The Fifth Regiment were lying down ... The commanding officer would not allow them to get up until the enemy was close to them. At the distance of a few yards this little regiment poured a volley into the enemy, and, dashing on through the smoke with the bayonet, charged the . . . cavalry [and] drove them back.[43]

It was, however, an unpleasant affair:

We kept our post gallantly, surrounded by about 2,000 cavalry, until at last, the French infantry being brought up, we were ordered to retreat in squares . . . The French cavalry, seeing us prepared for retreat, rushed furiously on, and the various squares were now successively charged by powerful masses of their cavalry . . . but they halted and repulsed them with the utmost steadiness and gallantry. The French . . . suffered severely, having a tremendous fire poured in on them each time . . . We were much annoyed by shot and shell from the heights where the French artillery were posted, some of which falling in the squares did great mischief, killing and wounding several of our men, and blowing up our ammunition. We had about six miles to retreat in this manner before we reached the body of the army, with the French cavalry hanging on our flanks and rear.[44]

In the end all the men involved got away, but even so Wellington was in serious trouble, for initially he could get together only a mere 15,000 men. Further retreat at first being impossible for fear that the French might defeat the army in detail, the British commander had no option but to try to bluff things out by adopting a strong defensive position at Fuenteguinaldo.

Fortunately for the Allies, the gamble came off, for Marmont refused to move. Attacking Wellington whilst his forces were spread out over miles of countryside was one thing, but taking him on in a position of his own choosing was quite another, the very fact that he was willing to stand and fight suggesting that he must have more troops than at first met the eye:

At length, Marmont and Dorsenne appeared at the head of their gorgeous staffs . . . Hardly, however, had these gentlemen come up than they dismounted and began to examine the English camp . . . 'Yes', said the marshal, making efforts to see what was not there through a telescope supported on my aide-de-camp's shoulder. 'Yes, my information is correct; the right of the English line rests upon an impracticable escarpment.' Thereupon I again took up my own glass . . . and could discover no indication of such an escarpment. General Dorsenne was equally unable to see it, and told the marshal so. He made no answer but continued, 'That camp is covered by revetted works.' After exchanging one or two . . . looks with me, General Dorsenne further observed that it was all he could do to see a few places where the ground had been thrown up. At length, the marshal finished his examination, adding, as though no-one else had spoken, 'And . . . those revetted works are armed with heavy guns . . . so there is nothing to be done.'[45]

In consequence, the opportunity was lost. At nightfall on 26 September Wellington quietly retreated to Alfayates, where he picked up the rest of his forces before occupying another natural fastness at Aldeia Velha. This the French reconnoitred, but, if they had been unwilling to attack at Fuenteguinaldo, they were even less willing to do so now, and the campaign therefore petered out, Marmont and Dorsenne retreating to Ciudad Rodrigo.

If he had in the end escaped with no serious losses, the period from March to September 1811 had therefore seen Wellington receive two bloody noses on the Portuguese frontier. Twice his forces had advanced to attack the fortresses which blocked the roads into Spain and twice they had been forced to retreat by superior concentrations of French troops. His siege train had now come up and was ready for action – stationed at Almeida, indeed, it could be got into action against Ciudad Rodrigo in a mere two days – and yet, so long as things remained unchanged in terms of the disposition and strength of the French armies, it was clear that nothing more could be attempted. And, if Wellington was powerless to effect any change in the situation, for all the petty victories that their forces won, how much more was this true of the Spaniards' skeletal armies and empty pay chests? For the French, however, matters were very different. Their forces in Spain having reached a strength of over 350,000 men in the summer of 1811, they had demonstrated all too clearly that they possessed sufficient troops to contain the Anglo-Portuguese, keep the guerrillas under control, and launch fresh offensives against the remnant of Patriot territory that was the key to victory in Spain, and, by extension, Portugal.

One should not, of course, exaggerate here. If Wellington was being contained on the Portuguese frontier, it was only at the cost of immense trouble and difficulty. The logistical problems involved in the concentration of large armies in the devastated and largely infertile regions that marked the frontier of Spain and Portugal were extremely difficult to resolve, whilst more worrying still was the fact that the Caya and Fuenteguinaldo had shown that even the French generals had lost all confidence in their ability to defeat the Anglo-Portuguese army in open battle. In consequence, the thousands of dead who littered the fields of Albuera and Fuentes de Oñoro therefore represented something more than just another 'butcher's bill', Wellington having established a clear moral superiority over his opponents, and firmly wrested the initiative from them. Gone for ever, too, was the chance that lack of confidence in London would place Wellington in a strait-jacket, let alone produce an evacuation of the Peninsula, whilst the successes of the first part of the year had also increased the chances of Napoleon getting into difficulties with Austria, Russia and Prussia (indeed, an increasingly unhappy Alexander I had even briefly considered going to war).

None of this is to say that the French were not still winning the war, but the gains of 1811 had for all that given rise to serious problems for their commanders. All too clearly, they faced a dangerous opponent in Wellington. Thanks to their determination to eradicate Spanish resistance, meanwhile, their troops had become more and more spread out. As we shall see, indeed, with French troops marching on Valencia (see below), extension was rapidly becoming over-extension. As yet, the situation was still under control – more than that, the French could still go on to victory – but one false move would be enough completely to destabilise the whole edifice of Napoleonic rule. As 1811 drew to a close, then, much hung in the balance.

14

Badajoz

THE ANGLO-PORTUGUESE
OFFENSIVE OF 1812

Tumbled untidily on the steep slope, the dead and wounded were in places four deep. Some, the luckier ones, had just been shot, but others had been drowned, trampled to death, torn apart, burned alive, or impaled. Silhouetted against the sky, a single macabre figure hung from the great cheval de frise *that crowned the slope. Scattered about among the bodies lay the inevitable detritus of war – discarded cartridge boxes, broken muskets, ripped haversacks, trampled shakos, officers' swords, torn letters, blood-soaked testaments. In the air the stench of powder, burned flesh, urine and excrement assailed the nostrils whilst the city hidden behind the walls resounded to shots, screams and the crackle of flames. Sitting on his horse on the lip of the ditch, Wellington was silent, and then, visibly overcome, he turned away: there was suddenly a war not just to fight but to win.*

Badajoz, then, had fallen. With Ciudad Rodrigo – the prize of a similar action some seven weeks previously – also in Allied hands, the way was clear to end the frustrating stalemate of 1811, march into Spain and reap the fruits of victory. Yet in itself the bloody triumph gained at Badajoz was not a turning point, but rather the consequence of developments far away in which the Peninsular War played no part. In the early autumn of 1811 the French had still been in a position to take the initiative in Spain, given that they had sufficient resources simultaneously to contain the Anglo-Portuguese, hold their own in *la guerrilla*, and embark on the conquest of still more Patriot territory. This, of course, depended on the arrival of more and more troops from France. There having been no major challenge to Napoleon since 1809, for some considerable time this had been no problem, the troops already in Spain having been kept up to strength, and many fresh units sent to join them. Implicit in this situation was the absence of any other employment that would require an overwhelming effort on the part of the emperor's soldiers, but in the autumn of 1811 just such a demand suddenly emerged. Ever since 1808 relations between Napoleon and Alexander I had been growing frostier by the month, and matters had now reached such a point that the former had decided to go to war. Very soon, then, orders were going out for the *grande armée* to concentrate in Poland. For *josefino* Spain the implications were very serious. Thus, by January 1812 all troops of the Imperial Guard and units of Polish origin serving across the Pyrenees were called back to France. These troops amounting to well over 25,000 men, a great hole was torn in the armies defending Joseph Bonaparte. Worst hit was Dorsenne who lost two full infantry divisions and the best part of his cavalry, whilst Suchet and Soult each lost some 6,000 infantry.

Grievous blow as this was, it was made still more dreadful by the fact that the Peninsula had altered dramatically in the course of 1811. Wellington was stronger than ever before, possessed of a powerful siege train, and all but unbeatable on grounds of his choosing. The *partidas* had been reinforced by Spanish regulars and in many cases given a degree of military organisation. And, above all, the French armies were overstretched by occupying huge expanses of territory that had still been in the hands of their opponents in January 1811. But even this is not an end to the matter, for Napoleon compounded his errors by insisting on an offensive policy. Annoyed at the evacuation of Asturias, he directed that it should be reoccupied immediately by the Army of the North, and, whilst Oviedo and Gijón were taken with ease, the result was that the unfortunate Dorsenne had to hold down yet more territory. Asturias, however, was a mere mouthful. Thus, for Napoleon, 'The great affair of the moment is the capture of Valencia'.[1] No sooner, then, had Figueras fallen, than Suchet was ordered to march on the Levante post-haste:

Everything . . . induces the belief that terror reigns within the walls of Valencia, and that, after . . . a defeat of the enemy in the open plain, the city will surrender to our arms . . . Happen what may, your headquarters will be within the territory of Valencia, and as near as possible to the gates of that city, on or about the fifteenth of September next.[2]

Any worries Suchet had, meanwhile, were swamped by a flood of reassurances. 'Send an officer to Marshal Suchet', the emperor told Berthier. 'Inform him . . . that the very day that he thought Mina had joined El Empecinado to assist Blake, the same Mina was in the vicinity of Mondragón, being vigorously pursued by General Bourke. Tell him that . . . General Decaen has left to relieve Barcelona . . . Advise him that the British have 18,000 sick . . . and are in no state to undertake anything . . . and that he should therefore launch a powerful attack on Valencia.'[3] Yet, as even Napoleon recognised, such orders had certain corollaries. In the current circumstances, each fresh advance created the necessity for a fresh garrison, whilst it had fallen to Suchet's lot to have to deal with some of the most determined guerrilla forces in the entire Peninsula in the form of Espoz y Mina, Durán, El Empecinado and Villacampa. So many troops were needed to face these adversaries, to say nothing of the Catalans, that Suchet could demonstrate to his imperial master that, unless he received external support, Valencia could only be gained by losing Aragón.

The logical conclusion here, of course, was that the French armies in Spain should maintain a defensive posture until such time as the Russians had been dealt with. For Napoleon, however, such a confession of weakness was intolerable, and, as implied above, he therefore responded to Suchet's pleas by forcing Dorsenne both to loan him men from Navarre and to release a division intended for the Army of Aragón which had been detained in anti-guerrilla operations along the way. Yet if Aragón was stronger, the Basque country and Navarre were now much weaker. What, then, was going on in the imperial mind? In brief, the answer is that Napoleon was simply becoming detached from reality. Contemptuous of the Spaniards and, more especially the guerrillas (a force whom he regarded as mere brigands), Napoleon saw no problem in either reducing the garrison of northern Spain or landing Suchet with the problem of holding Valencia.

Even with the aid sent him by Napoleon, Suchet could only muster 26,000 troops for the march on Valencia, but these were, without exception, experienced veterans of the highest calibre. Facing them was a distinctly mixed array consisting of the ill-trained and generally rather demoralised Second Army (or, rather, its regular divisions: in theory, the forces of El Empecinado, Durán and Villacampa were also part of the Valencian command) and the much better divisions of Zayas and Lardizábal, which had been sent round by sea from Cádiz. Cantoned at various places in Murcia, but available for service so long as Soult did not make a move from the direction of Andalucía, was the Third Army, although this, too, was a force with a long record of defeat. Though at least 40,000 men were available to defend Valencia, and the whole assemblage handed over to Blake, who had also been made Captain General of both Valencia and Murcia, British observers painted a grim picture:

Palacio* has given himself up to . . . the most extreme superstition . . . He attends all processions and puts his baton in the hands of the Virgin. There is no use, it appears, in change: we go from bad to worse. Nothing short of a miracle can save

---

* The Marqués del Palacio, titular commander of the Second Army.

Valencia . . . The number of souls in the town . . . is 150,000 at present, and, if the enemy approaches, the population would be doubled. Suchet need only blockade them for a few days, and they must starve or surrender.[4]

On 15 September 1811 the campaign began. French columns coming from southern Aragón and Tortosa poured across the northern frontiers of Valencia and advanced along the coast meeting little resistance, Blake having decided to abandon the border region without a fight in favour of concentrating his forces for the defence of Valencia itself. Here the enemy could be brought to a halt before a strong line of entrenchments that had been constructed along the River Guadalaviar, on whose southern bank the city stood, by which time Blake hoped that far away in Aragón and Navarre, Espoz y Mina and the other guerrillas (to whom he had sent messages asking for their co-operation) would have wrought such damage that Suchet would have no option but to turn for home. However, to win time, he also deployed a garrison in the ruins of Roman Saguntum, these occupying the top of a steep and rocky hill high above the town of Sagunto. Patched up and adapted for artillery, on 23 September this fort was invested by the French. Eager to waste as little time as possible, Suchet resolved on an attempt simply to rush its walls, and on the night of 27–28 September columns duly approached two points in the *enceinte* that were particularly weak. However, the element of surprise was lost, and the attackers found themselves under heavy fire. To quote their commander:

They placed the ladders against the walls, and . . . an officer of sappers and a few grenadiers . . . reached the summit, but they were . . . either killed or driven back, whilst shot and grenades filled with glass were poured in torrents upon the body of the assailants who were hurrying to the foot of the rampart.[5]

With casualties mounting, the French eventually had to fall back, there now being no option but to wait for the army's siege train. The heavy guns not coming up till 16 October, there followed a prolonged lull in operations which was to have a dramatic effect on the entire war.

Thus, far away in Paris, Napoleon, from news of the check before Saguntum, jumped to the entirely erroneous conclusion that Suchet did not have enough troops to capture Valencia. Afraid of another Torres Vedras, he decided that the Levante ought to be threatened from the west as well as the north, and therefore told Joseph to send part of his Army of the Centre towards Valencia, and Marmont to send part of the Army of Portugal to take over the districts evacuated by Joseph. In short, the forces facing Wellington were to be significantly weakened, thereby compounding the errors already committed with the Army of the North. Once again, though, there was no danger so far as Napoleon was concerned. Thus, despite everything, the emperor was convinced that Wellington was not a threat, the stated grounds for this argument being that, in Berthier's words, 'the English have 20,000 sick, and can only put 20,000 men into the field'.[6] Also operative, however, was a serious underestimation of Wellington as an opponent: the campaigns of 1809, 1810 and 1811 having painted a picture of a cautious general unlikely to take dangerous risks, the idea that he might suddenly erupt across the border was laughed to scorn.

In fact, it was Napoleon who was taking the risks, whilst, to make matters infinitely worse, he was not even doing so on the basis of up-to-date information. The orders issued to Marmont and Joseph went out on 18 October, but on 12 October Suchet had received his guns. With these in action, within four days the walls of Saguntum were breached, and, although another assault was beaten off, it was clear that the garrison's days were numbered. Sitting behind his fortifications twenty miles to the south, Blake was thereby placed in an impossible dilemma. All too obviously, relying on the guerrillas was proving a failure. Thus, the garrisons of Calatayud and Ayerbe were forced to surrender by the *partidas*, that of Molina de Aragón blockaded in the castle that served as its citadel, and that of Ejea de los Caballeros forced to make a dramatic break-out, whilst 800 Italian auxiliaries were captured at Plasencia de Gállego.* Despite these successes, however, Suchet showed no signs of retreating. All that was left, then, was to march to relieve Saguntum, and yet that would involve fighting the very battle in the open that Blake had been striving to avoid.

In reality, however, Blake had little choice in the matter as he knew that failure to move would lead to accusations of treason or cowardice, and possibly even his removal from the Regency (of which he was still the president). Waiting only for the arrival of some troops he had been promised from the Third Army and the return of a division he had sent to conduct a reconnaisance in force on the frontiers of La Mancha, on 24 October he crossed the Guadalaviar and headed for Saguntum. Battle was joined next day a few miles south of the fortress on either side of the Valencia–Tarragona highway. Blake's plan – in brief, to pivot on his right wing so as to allow his much stronger left and centre to roll Suchet up and drive him into the

---

* As we have already seen, Napoleon employed large numbers of German, Polish and Italian forces in the Peninsular. It was the contention of some observers that reliance on such troops was one of the factors in the French downfall, but in practice the foreign auxiliaries seem to have performed no worse than their French counterparts.

sea – was a good one, but his misgivings proved all too well-founded. To carry out their brief the Spanish centre and left had to cross a range of hills that jutted out into the coastal plain, and the commander of the French forces opposed to them waited only for them to lose their dressing on the steep slopes before hurling his 4,300 men upon them. The result was total chaos, the leading Spanish troops fleeing for their lives and sweeping away the troops who were coming up in their rear. Only a few men were killed, but several hundred were taken prisoner and the rest reduced to a horde of fugitives. On the right, meanwhile, the high quality of the divisions of Zayas and Lardizábal had brought some progress (the Spanish cavalry shone for once, indeed). As Suchet later admitted:

We perceived . . . the Spanish columns advancing upon the high road . . . with a regularity and determination which they had not yet displayed on any occasion . . . Our hussars were charged and driven back. Our artillery was attacked by the enemy sword in hand, and a few pieces . . . fell into their hands.[7]

Despite this display of courage, Suchet had sufficient reserves to tip the balance and Blake's whole army was soon fleeing the field in great disorder. Left behind were over 5,000 casualties, most of them prisoners.

Given that Suchet had only 14,000 men to Blake's 27,000, this was one of the more extraordinary battles of the Peninsular War, whilst it also sealed the fate of Saguntum, whose bitterly disappointed garrison surrendered the next day. After this affair, too, it was clear that Valencia would be unlikely to resist for very long either. As Wellington wrote, indeed, 'The Spaniards will owe the loss of another kingdom . . . to the insatiable desire of fighting pitched battles with undisciplined troops led by inexperienced officers.'[8] Yet news of the victory did not make Napoleon any happier, for on 21 November he sent a fresh order to Marmont instructing him to get together a force of 12,000 men to assist Suchet.

According to Napoleon, of course, such a move was perfectly safe, the emperor being immovable in his belief that Wellington would not attack. Yet at the very time that Marmont was being given his orders, news was coming to light that suggested a picture that was far less rosy. Thus, the two French divisions left to hold Extremadura under Drouet (who had replaced Mortier) were having to cover the whole front from the Sierra Morena to the River Tagus, the Army of Portugal having withdrawn the division which it had for a little while kept around Trujillo. Seeing his opportunity, Hill, who was still covering Elvas with the Second Division and a variety of Portuguese troops, secured the support of those elements of the Fifth Army which were in the vicinity, and marched to attack the northernmost of

Drouet's two divisions. 'The rainy season had commenced', remembered George Bell, 'and the weather was dreadful.'⁹ On 28 October the French were taken by surprise at the isolated village of Arroyomolinos de Montánchez, and, after a confused fight, badly beaten. Amongst the participants was Robert Blakeney:

About dawn . . . favoured by a dense fog, the troops were formed . . . within half a mile of the enemy, who, strange to say, did not present even a single vedette . . . All being prepared, all suddenly moved forward . . . and the dense fog clearing away, our left column were absolutely entering the town before the enemy were aware of our vicinity . . . The Seventy-First and Ninety-Second Regiments cheered and charged through the town, taking a few prisoners . . . The enemy . . . formed in two columns on the plain outside . . . The fire from the Seventy-First . . . disturbed their close formation, and in the meantime the Ninety-Second . . . formed line on the enemy's flank [and they] commenced a rapid retreat . . . The British cavalry having at length come up . . . [a] brisk charge put the French cavalry to flight. Their infantry still pushed forward with uncommon rapidity, yet . . . as they approached the eastern horn of . . . the Sierra [de] Montánchez, they were met directly in front by our right column . . . The enemy perceived it impossible to pass by us, and as our left column was moving up in their rear . . . they made a rush at the [mountain].¹⁰

By scrambling up the rocky hillside, a number of French troops managed to escape along with their commander, General Girard, but even so over 1,000 men laid down their arms.

This little campaign should have shaken Napoleon out of his misapprehensions but it did not. In this respect it may not have helped that Arroyomolinos had witnessed the début of a somewhat farcical attempt to instil the Spanish armies with the spirit of the 'golden age' of the sixteenth century. This was the brainchild of a hispanophile adventurer named John Downie, who had originally been a commissary in Wellington's army. Securing the backing of La Romana and Castaños, he had himself appointed as the commander of a new 'legion' of cavalry and infantry, of which the chief basis was a number of depleted units drawn from the Fifth Army. Some material support was also got from London, but Wellington himself disapproved (indeed, he is reputed to have observed that Downie was Spanish down to his shirt). Sadly, his doubts were well-founded, for Downie proceeded to dress his men in sixteenth-century costume. 'Anything so whimsical and ridiculous as the dress of this corps,' complained Sherer, 'I never beheld . . . The turned up hat, slashed doublet and short mantle might have figured very well in the play of Pizarro . . . but in the rude . . . bivouac they appeared absurd and ill-chosen.'¹¹ And at all events Downie's fancies served no purpose whatsoever. 'Clothed like harlequins', wrote Blakeney, 'this fantastic and unruly squadron . . . displayed neither order nor discipline. Intractable as swine, obstinate as mules and unmanageable as bullocks, they were cut up like rations or dispersed in all directions like a flock of scared sheep.'[12]

Marmont, meanwhile, was just as complacent. For reasons that are not entirely clear he too believed that Wellington would remain inert. As one of his aides-de-camp told a worried Thiébault, for example, 'The preparations of which you speak . . . have no other object but to lead us into making false movements. The English army is not ready for any important operation and will undertake none before spring.'[13] As a result, headed by General Montbrun, three infantry divisions and a brigade of cavalry were soon moving south-eastwards, only to find that by the time they reached the frontiers of the Levante their services were no longer required (of rather more use was the small contingent contributed by King Joseph, for, by occupying Cuenca, this did at least succeed in tying down a few troops that had been marching to help Blake). Nor was this an end to the calls on the Army of Portugal. Eager to help Suchet, who had proved slow to follow up his victory at Saguntum, Napoleon had authorised him to draw still more troops from Aragón, these being replaced by others from the Army of the North. But with Dorsenne's forces already badly over-stretched by the recall of so many of his troops for the campaign in Russia, Napoleon decided that he could not leave matters there. Hitherto responsible for the whole sweep of territory from the French frontier to Ciudad Rodrigo, the Army of the North was now charged only with Santander, Burgos, Navarre and the Basque provinces. The Army of Portugal was to be in charge of León and Asturias, and so it suddenly acquired territorial responsibilities that far outstripped the relatively minor task of holding down the lower Tagus valley that was all that had fallen to it in 1811. Two of the divisions that had been manning the areas concerned remained where they were and therefore joined the Army of Portugal, but Dorsenne was allowed to withdraw a third, together with some other troops, to his much reduced bailiwick further east. Very soon, then, Marmont was sending large parts of his army north-eastwards to take over from the troops withdrawn by Dorsenne, all that was left to contain Wellington being a mere two divisions.

What, though, of Valencia? After the battle before Saguntum, Blake had fallen back to the Guadalaviar, but for a long time Suchet made little move to pursue him, realising that any further advance was impossible unless he could draw in more troops from Aragón. Blake, then, was given the chance to strengthen his earthworks, fill up his battered regiments with fresh conscripts, and send off a few regular troops to encourage guerrillas to fresh efforts. However, his appeals had little effect – the various commanders were unwilling to collaborate with one another, and resentful of Blake's interference – and by Christmas the French were ready. On the night of 25 December Suchet's army marched out to attack the Spanish positions along the Guadalaviar. Defended by some 23,000 men, these were heavily fortified, but far too extensive for Blake's mediocre troops, whilst both flanks of the position had been neglected in favour of the centre (constituted by the city of Valencia itself). Hardly surprisingly, then, Suchet sent the bulk of his troops to strike each end of Blake's line with the aim of swinging inwards and encircling army and city alike. In this situation, there could be little contest. Some of the defenders fought bravely enough, but Blake failed to act with the energy that was the only thing that might have saved something from the situation and the bulk of his forces were therefore forced to withdraw inside the city. Perhaps 5,000 troops got away to join such forces of the Third Army as had not succeeded in reaching Valencia in time for the assault, but there were too few men to launch a counter-attack and no source of reinforcements nearer than Cádiz. In short, the city was doomed, for, though well fortified, it had less than three weeks' food in its magazines. An attempt at a mass break-out on 29 December was foiled by bungling and irresolution, whilst on 5 January Suchet opened fire on the city. Three days later it was all over. With the population on the point of revolt, Blake capitulated, leaving Suchet to march in and avenge the massacre of 1808: several hundred people were executed, all the city's monks and friars deported to France, and the authorities forced to pay a fine of 200,000,000 reales.

Even by Spanish standards Valencia was a disaster. Well over 20,000 troops had been lost in the campaign, including the best two divisions in the Spanish army, whilst Suchet had captured immense stocks of war material and perhaps 500 guns. Politically and strategically, too, the affair was a source of real worry. As Wellington wrote:

The greater number of grandees of Spain have estates in Valencia upon the revenues of which they have subsisted since they have lost everything elsewhere. It may be expected, therefore, that the loss of the kingdom will induce many to . . . submit to the French yoke . . . There is also another view in which the loss of Valencia is a shattering misfortune, and that is that this conquest, unlike the others which the enemy have made in Spain, will promote the concentration of their forces. Even if Suchet should not be able to press on further to the southward . . . [he] will be able to communicate with a shorter route than he had with the Army of the Centre and the Army of Portugal [and] he will be on the back of the Empecinado, Mina and [the] others, and will cut off the supplies which they received through Valencia. If the people of Valencia should submit as soon as the military force of the kingdom will be subdued, which, from what I hear of them, I think probable, Suchet's force will then be disposable on the left of Soult or to support the [armies] more immediately opposed to us.[14]

Wellington was not the only commander to feel alarmed. In another example of the way in which French conventional successes favoured the defeat of the guerrillas, Espoz y Mina later professed that he was horrified at the news:

As well as causing me much sorrow, the loss of Valencia did me a great deal of damage. In this respect, the worst problem was the manner in which it deprived me of a point to which I could turn for munitions, and in fact these immediately began to run short. At the same time I feared that some of the enemy troops that had taken part in the conquest of the city would ... fall on the area in which I had been operating.[15]

Yet Valencia was the high tide of French conquest. As we have seen, irregular resistance continued under such leaders as the friar, Agustín Nebot. In consequence, Suchet's troops were too overstretched to be able to advance very much further, whilst such help as was available from outside was insufficient to allow the French to occupy the rump of Spanish territory in the Levante. Montbrun, true, advanced all the way to Alicante, only to be forced to turn tail when the garrison refused to surrender, whilst Soult, who had also received orders to go to Suchet's assistance, could in the end do no more than raid the city of Murcia, the Army of the South's small field force having spent the autumn and winter attempting to take the minor coastal fortress of Tarifa, and fighting Ballesteros, who had been transferred to the vicinity of Gibraltar. Stretched to their very limits, the French had finally shot their bolt.

At this moment nemesis struck. Far from being incapable of taking the field, Wellington had all along been ready to march on Ciudad Rodrigo at a moment's notice. The British had many men sick, certainly, but in the course of 1811 they had been so heavily reinforced that they still had 45,000 men ready for duty. Eighteen months, meanwhile, of continual fighting against the French had honed the tactical skills of the infantry beyond measure, whilst there were now twice as many cavalry as at the start of the year as well as a reasonable complement of field and horse artillery and a fine siege train. Supporting them were some 33,000 Portuguese regulars, many of whom had now earned an excellent reputation. Financial problems abounded, true – even with the British subsidy, Portugal's income amounted to only half what the Council of Regency needed, whilst Wellington was short of specie – but in the last resort these were never more than an irritant and certainly not enough to frustrate the hammer blow that Wellington was about to deliver.

Thus, no sooner had the British commander received word that the Army of Portugal was sending troops northwards and eastwards – or, to put it another way, that Napoleon had destabilised the position of the whole of the French forces in Spain – than his troops were set in motion. Despite severe winter weather, Ciudad Rodrigo was invested on 8 January 1812 – the day that Valencia capitulated – and thereafter matters were pushed at great speed, Wellington being well aware that sooner or later the French would concentrate their forces against him (in this, of course, he was perfectly correct, but it appears that he was unaware of just how severe the problems faced by his opponents were in this respect). The French were quickly driven from their chief outwork and in a mere six days sufficient spade work had been completed for twenty-seven guns to be brought up and set to work to smash a breach in the walls. Two holes having been torn in the defences, on 19 January Wellington ordered an assault. In an ideal world, there is no doubt that it would have been better to wait a little while longer before throwing the army at the breaches. Thus, assault trenches might have been dug closer to the walls or the ditch blown in so that the troops did not have to negotiate a sheer drop before gaining access to the breaches, but such was the pressure on Wellington that he would brook no further delay. In the early evening of 19 January, then, the assault began, the troops having first been provided with sacks of hay to break their fall when they jumped down into the ditch. At the lesser breach, the assailants came from the Light Division. Amongst them was George Simmons:

The forlorn hope and storming parties moved on at about seven o'clock, and the head of the column followed close behind. A tremendous fire was opened upon us, and, as our column was entering the ditch, an expense magazine on the ramparts blew up . . . The night was brilliantly illuminated for some moments, and everything was made visible. Then as suddenly came utter darkness, except for the flashes from cannon and muskets, which threw a momentary glare around.[16]

Facing the other breach, meanwhile, was Joseph Donaldson:

Some time after it was dark, we . . . advanced rank entire under a heavy fire . . . to the brink of . . . the ditch. After descending, we moved along towards the breach.

Our orders were to remain there and protect the right brigade, but, our colonel finding no obstacles in the way, pushed up the breach . . . In mounting the breach, we found great difficulty in ascending from the loose earth slipping under our feet at every step . . . the enemy at the same time pouring their shot amongst us from above.[17]

Despite gallant resistance on the part of the French, who had placed cannon to sweep the breaches and booby-trapped the rubble, the walls were carried, albeit not without the loss of Robert Craufurd, who was mortally wounded by a round of canister. Not for the last time, there followed scenes of great disorder. A town taken by storm was by tradition regarded as the legitimate prize of the men concerned, and, whilst the events that took place were by no means as terrible as those that were to follow elsewhere, they were still distressing enough. As Swabey wrote:

Our troops, as soon as the breach was gained, more eager for plunder than their duty, broke and ran in defiance of their officers . . . and committed shameful excesses disgraceful to the whole army. [There was] not a soul that was not rifled, and the dead were scarcely cold when they were inhumanly stripped . . . No intentional murders were committed, though some men were so drunk that they fired promiscuously in the streets and killed many of their comrades.[18]

Even more dramatic is the version given by Grattan of the Eighty-Eighth:

Scenes of the greatest outrage now took place, and it was pitiable to see groups of the inhabitants half-naked in the streets . . . while their houses were undergoing the strictest scrutiny. Some of the soldiers turned to the wine and spirit houses, where, having drunk sufficiently, they again sallied out in quest of more plunder; others got so intoxicated that they lay in a helpless state in different parts of the town, and lost what they had previously gained.[19]

All that can be said in mitigation of the disorder is that the soldiers were not the only culprits, being joined in their ravages by some of the poorer elements of the inhabitants. Nor was the sack prolonged: through the most determined efforts, a semblance of order was soon restored. And, at all events, Ciudad Rodrigo was in Wellington's hands, along with 1,300 prisoners and the whole of the Army of Portugal's siege train.

What, though, of the French? So effective were the cavalry of Julián Sánchez in isolating Ciudad Rodrigo from inquisitive French patrols that Marmont did not hear that the fortress was under attack until 14 January. By then, of course, nothing could be done, but Marmont was not to know this, and made desperate efforts to remedy the situation by calling in troops from all sides. Hearing of the surrender two days after the fortress had fallen, he contemplated an immediate counter-attack, but heavy rain, the absence of faraway Montbrun, and the arrival of news that the Army of the North had its hands full with Espoz y Mina, who had just defeated the governor of Navarre in a major action at Rocaforte, all ruled this out. All that Marmont could do, then, was to put up a brave front and pray that Wellington's next target was not Salamanca, whilst fuming at the governor of Ciudad Rodrigo, General Barrié, whom he later described as 'a detestable officer, without either resolution or foresight'.[20] At root, however, the fault was not Barrié's, nor even Marmont's, but rather Napoleon's: '[The emperor] withdrew all the Young Guard . . . as well as five regiments of Poles. In this manner he weakened the number of troops in the Peninsula by 15,000 men with the result that the remainder were simply insufficient to defend the immense amount of territory that had been occupied.'[21]

To return to Wellington, a march on Salamanca seemed pointless, for Marmont had only to fall back on Dorsenne to be safe, whilst the French might ultimately have concentrated so many troops against him that he might have been turned out of Ciudad Rodrigo (which required some weeks' work before it could face an attack). Far better, then, to move against Badajoz, and all the more so as the Army of Portugal would now find it far harder to help Soult. Undeterred by a political crisis in London which removed Lord Wellesley from the government and could have reduced its commitment to Iberia, as early as 25 January Wellington issued the first orders for an attack on Badajoz.* By late February, then, his forces were heading south, leaving Ciudad Rodrigo to be held by the Spaniards of Carlos de España. Realising what was afoot, Marmont began to make preparations for another march across the Tagus. In this, however, he was frustrated by Napoleon who insisted that the best way of succouring Badajoz was to keep the Army of Portugal in León and Old Castile whence it could march on Ciudad Rodrigo, Almeida and Lisbon should Wellington head south (for good measure, Marmont was also castigated for calling back the garrison of Asturias – the division of General Bonet – in the course of his attempt to save Ciudad Rodrigo, and ordered to hand over yet more troops to Dorsenne). Frantic to get Napoleon to understand the increasingly dangerous

---

* As Foreign Secretary, the marquess had been a firm – even over-enthusiastic – supporter of the Peninsular War, and as such had played a key role in getting the extra support that had enabled Wellington to carry the war across the frontier. But, if Wellington had any fears at all about this crisis, whose most notable result was the replacement of Wellesley by Castlereagh, he need not have worried: the Cabinet was strengthened in the Commons and proved positively fawning in its efforts to retain his goodwill and assure him of its support.

nature of the situation, the marshal dispatched a senior aide to Paris in the hope of changing his mind, only to find that the French ruler was utterly inflexible:

It was something truly inexplicable. The emperor completely ignored the real state of the question . . . The mission of Colonel Jardet was fruitless. Many long conversations with the emperor had the air of convincing him, but they did not bring any change in the . . . orders that had been given.[22]

Stripped of their wilder aspects – supply problems alone, for example, rendered a march on Lisbon out of the question – Napoleon's ideas were not so crazy as has sometimes been suggested, for Ciudad Rodrigo might just possibly have been recaptured, the fortress being ill-supplied and garrisoned by troops of the poorest quality. That said, however, the plan was a highly risky one, depending, as it did, on the assumption that Wellington would value keeping Ciudad Rodrigo more than taking Badajoz, whilst at the same time surrendering any chance of saving the latter by more direct means. Soult, Napoleon claimed, could look after his own, but, as the events of the previous year showed, he simply did not have the strength to relieve Badajoz without outside aid. Still worse, 'King Nicholas' did not even know that he was on his own until much too late, Marmont having written to him in all good faith that he would march to his assistance the moment that he was certain Wellington had moved south.

Curiously enough, at the very time that Napoleon was wreaking such havoc in the affairs of the Army of Portugal, he had taken a step that might have done much good, for, as we have seen, on 16 March 1812 he appointed Joseph to the post of commander-in-chief of the French armies in Spain. In many ways this was no bad thing, for the King and his chief-of-staff, Marshal Jourdan, possessed a clearer understanding of the situation in Spain than anyone except Marmont. Recognising that the chief priority at the present moment was supporting Soult, they in consequence ordered Dorsenne, Suchet and Marmont to concentrate a relief force in the Tagus valley. Yet for Badajoz the appointment could make no difference: even if the various commanders had been disposed to accept Joseph's authority – which none of them were – the *masse de manoeuvre* he was trying to create could not possibly have been got together in time. Nor was it any use that at the last minute Marmont was granted permission to head south, for the dispatch concerned did not reach the marshal's headquarters until 27 March, by which time he was irrevocably committed to a thrust into Portugal.

In fairness to Marmont, it has to be said that, good soldier as he was, he did his best. Ciudad Rodrigo was blockaded, and Almeida investigated with a view to a possible escalade, but the latter was judged impracticable, Marmont then marching south-westwards into the depths of Beira in the faint hope that Wellington might at least detach some forces to defend his flank and rear. Without supply trains, however, Marmont could not possibly sustain such a movement, for, as he wrote, 'Without means of transport, and with very little food, how could the army have successfully completed a march through a barren countryside that had been abandoned by its inhabitants?'[23] Castelo Branco was occupied, a brigade of Portuguese militia routed at Guarda, and some minor supply dumps overrun, but on 15 April news reached the marshal that Badajoz had fallen, the result being that he retired in some haste, all his efforts having therefore gone for nothing.

Once again, in fact, Napoleon had got it wrong, though Wellington still did not have it easy. Arriving before Badajoz on 16 March, the Anglo-Portuguese army found a fortress rendered even stronger than it had been in 1811. An officer of great courage and determination who later distinguished himself by making a daring escape from captivity in England, Philippon had done all that he possibly could to prepare for another attack. The breaches had all been repaired; various sections of the *enceinte* had been reinforced; mines had been driven outwards under parts of the glacis to blow up any approach trenches dug across them; the fort of San Cristóbal had been given a new outwork; the Pardaleras fort that protected the city on its southern side had been connected to the walls by a covered way; and a stream that ran along the eastern side of the defences had been dammed so as to produce an impassable inundation, some of the water also having been used to fill a broad trench dug in the bottom of the main ditch. Given the extent of the perimeter, men were not over-abundant, true, but food, cannon and munitions were all plentiful, whilst the defenders were all seasoned veterans.

Taking Badajoz, then, was always likely to be a costly business, but at least Wellington now had the benefit of past experience. In consequence, the mistakes of 1811 were firmly avoided, the attack this time falling not on San Cristóbal, but rather the south-eastern corner of the defences. On this side of the city, the ground was much easier to work, whilst constant rain shielded the men involved from the enemy even if it also flooded the trenches and constantly washed away parapets and revetments: 'We were working,' complained Donaldson, 'up to our knees in mud.'[24] Meanwhile, the work was pushed with the utmost speed. On 25 March the Picurina redoubt, which had to be taken before the attackers could implement their plans, was stormed with some loss, and five days later the bombardment of the walls began. The French fired back with great courage, and there were many losses among the troops in the trenches. Thus:

On the twenty-ninth poor Major Thomson was killed by my side in the eight-gun breaching battery. We had been walking together in the trenches and went down to see how far the battery was advanced . . . We were standing up with Major McLean of the First Caçadores when [the enemy] fired at us and hit poor Thomson through the head . . . I fortunately jumped down in time and escaped, as they hit instead the sand-bag I was leaning against which did quite as well.[25]

To this fire, however, the British had an answer in the form of the crack shots of the Ninety-Fifth Rifles: 'Three or four heavy cannon that the enemy were working were doing frightful execution amongst our artillerymen . . . I selected several good shots and fired into the embrasures. In half an hour I found the guns did not go off so frequently as before.'[26] But in fact the British guns needed little support: so heavy was the weight of fire that the new siege train could bring to bear that the defenders were quickly overwhelmed, and no fewer than three separate breaches blown in the defences.

By 6 April, it was decided that all was ready for an assault. This, in fact, was questionable – as at Ciudad Rodrigo the glacis and ditches had not been blown in – but Soult was on the march, whilst it was still unknown whether or not Marmont would join him. At the same time a series of embarrassing contretemps was giving reason to suggest that Sir Thomas Graham, who had come from Cádiz to take charge of some of the troops watching Soult, was not wholly to be trusted. Waiting two or three more days would doubtless have made more sense, but in the circumstances the best thing seemed to be to go in straight away: better that, perhaps, than to risk another Albuera. Though it has been often recounted, what followed was a terrible affair. The breaches had been booby-trapped with mines and combustible material, encumbered with a wide range of unpleasant devices designed to injure anyone trying to climb them, and crowned with *chevaux de frise*, and the men defending them provided with hand grenades, incendiary bombs and extra muskets. Unknown to the British, meanwhile, they were also protected by the deep canal that had been cut in the bottom of the ditch. Set to attack these grim defences at ten o'clock in the evening, the men of the Fourth and Light Divisions set to with a will, but they became hopelessly entangled with one another and quickly suffered appalling casualties. Many men were drowned in the wet ditch, for example, and another 500 blown up when the French exploded their mines. In the lead was William Lawrence:

I was one of the ladder party . . . On our arriving at . . . the wall . . . a shower of shot, canister and grape, together with fireballs, was hurled . . . amongst us. Poor

Pig [Harding] received his death wound immediately . . . while I myself received two small . . . shots in my left knee, and a musket shot in my side . . . Still, I stuck to my ladder and got into the [ditch]. Numbers had by this time fallen, but . . . we hastened to the breach. There, to our great . . . discouragement, we found a *cheval de frise* had been fixed . . . Vain attempts were made to remove this fearful obstacle, during which my left hand was fearfully cut by one of the blades, but, finding no success in that quarter, we were forced to retire for a time . . . My wounds were still bleeding, and I began to feel very weak. My comrades persuaded me to go to the rear, but this proved a task of great difficulty, for on arriving at the ladders, I found them filled with the dead and wounded, hanging . . . just as they had fallen . . . so I crawled on my hands and knees till I got out of the reach of the enemy's musketry.[27]

Joining Lawrence at the ladders, there came a wounded sergeant of the Forty-Third who describes how, having stumbled down the breach with the help of his musket and dragged himself through the flooded ditch, he 'scrambled up with extreme difficulty', to the accompaniment of 'bullets whistling through the rounds of the ladder'.[28] Also to the fore, meanwhile, was Sergeant Anthony Hamilton:

On reaching the glacis we were discovered by the garrison, and instantly a tremendous fire opened. Though the carnage in our ranks was very great, we continued our advance . . . Owing to the darkness of the night . . . we came unexpectedly upon the counter-scarp, and nearly half our party, myself among the number, were precipitated into the ditch below. Much bruised by the fall I lay a few minutes insensible, till on the arrival of the main body, the ladders were fixed . . . and the descent into the ditch quickly effected. Though the formation of the troops was necessarily broken in these operations, they immediately advanced against the breaches . . . but such were the obstacles prepared by the enemy that it was found impossible to surmount them . . . To overcome these obstacles many gallant . . . attempts were made by our troops, but . . . we were at length compelled to retire . . . Twenty-one officers of the regiment were either killed or wounded, and of the ten men of our company who volunteered for the forlorn hope only myself and a man by the name of Cummings came back alive, both wounded.[29]

Fighting alongside Hamilton in the Light Division was George Simmons:

Our columns moved on under a most dreadful fire . . . that mowed down our men like grass . . . Eight or ten officers and men innumerable fell to rise no more. Ladders were resting against the counter-scarp . . . Down these we hurried and . . . rushed forward to the breaches, where a most frightful scene of carnage was going on. Fifty times they were stormed, and as often without effect, the French cannon sweeping the breaches with a most destructive fire. Lights were thrown amongst us . . . that burned most brilliantly, and made us easier to be shot at . . . I had seen some fighting, but nothing like this.[30]

For two hours the fighting continued, but around midnight Wellington decided that he could not ask any more of his men and ordered them to fall back.

The troops involved having suffered some 2,000 casualties, it looked as though the assault had failed. However, at the last minute Wellington had agreed to the idea of secondary assaults on the castle and the bastion of San Vicente, both of which were points far removed from the breaches. At the castle the assailants suffered heavy casualties. As Donaldson recalled:

At last the order was given, and with palpitating hearts we commenced our march . . . Being apprised of our intentions, they threw out fire balls in every direction . . . By this means they were enabled to see . . . our columns, and they opened a fire of round and grape shot which raked through them, killing and wounding whole sections . . . We still advanced as before . . . and got down into the ditch. The ladders were not yet brought up, and the men were huddled on one another in such a manner that we could not move . . . When we first entered the [ditch] we considered ourselves comparatively safe, thinking that we were out of range of their shot, but . . . they opened several guns . . . and poured in grape shot upon us from each side . . . Our situation at this time was truly appalling . . . When the ladders were placed, each eager to mount, [the soldiers] crowded them in such a way that many of them broke, and the poor fellows who had nearly reached the top were precipitated a height of thirty to forty feet and impaled on the bayonets of their comrades below. Other ladders were pushed aside by the enemy on the walls, and fell with a crash on those in the ditch, while [men] who got to the top without accident were shot on reaching the parapet, and, tumbling headlong, brought down those beneath them. This continued for some time, until at length, a few having made a landing . . . [they] enabled others to follow.[31]

By these means, the castle was taken, but even then the town might not have fallen but for the fact that there were too few men to guard the bastion of San Vicente. With the troops who had been sent to attack that sector soon over the wall, the breaches were taken in the rear and the garrison forced to lay down its arms. Badajoz, then, belonged to Wellington's army. Let us quote, for example, Robert Blakeney:

There was no safety for women even in the churches, and any who interfered or offered resistance were sure to get shot. Every house presented a scene of plunder, debauchery and bloodshed committed with wanton cruelty . . . by our soldiery, and in many instances I saw the savages tear the rings from the ears of beautiful women

... When the savages came to a door which had been locked or barricaded, they applied ... the muzzles of a dozen firelocks ... against that part of the door where the lock was fastened, and ... fired [them] off together into the house and rooms, regardless of those inside ... Men, women and children were shot ... for no other ... reason than pastime; every species of outrage was publicly committed ... and in a manner so brutal that a faithful recital would be ... shocking to humanity. Not the slightest shadow of discipline was maintained ... The infuriated soldiery resembled rather a pack of hell-hounds vomited up from the infernal regions for the extirpation of mankind than ... a well-organised, brave, disciplined and obedient British army.[32]

Much the same scenes are recorded by the surgeon, Henry:

I beheld a scene of the most dreadful drunkenness, violence and confusion. Parties of intoxicated men, loosed from all discipline and restraint and impelled by their own evil passions, were roaming and reeling about, firing into the windows, bursting open the doors ... plundering, shooting any person who opposed them, violating and committing every horrid excess and sometimes destroying each other.[33]

One could continue almost *ad infinitum*. Grattan writes of 'a scene of plunder and cruelty that it would be difficult to find a parallel for'; Bell of 'scenes that were shocking ... not fit to be recorded'; Gomm of 'a plundering scene which was a jumble of all that was horrible'; and Donaldson of 'scenes which ... are too dreadful and disgusting to relate'.[34] Many officers did their best to save Spanish civilians – one or two, indeed, were murdered in the attempt – but the men were open in their contempt for authority, insisting that plunder was their right, and it was not until gallows were erected and many soldiers flogged that the army was restored to order.

In the meantime, the war went on. Gathering together his battered army – in all, Badajoz had cost him 4,670 casualties of whom 3,713 had fallen in the storm – Wellington initially hoped to smash Soult's isolated command in southern Extremadura. However, 'King Nicholas' retired in great haste, having discovered not only that Ballesteros had gone on the offensive again, but also that the small force of troops belonging to the Fifth Army had, at Wellington's request, moved down the Portuguese frontier and launched a sudden thrust at Seville. Meanwhile, the British commander had in any case become increasingly anxious about Ciudad Rodrigo, of whose blockade he had just learned. Losing this so soon after it had been gained would hardly be politic, and Wellington therefore left Hill to protect Badajoz with the same troops that normally made up his command, and once more set off for Ciudad Rodrigo, which he relieved in the very nick of time on 22 April.

For the next month Wellington remained quiet on the frontiers of León, supervising the repair of Ciudad Rodrigo, resting his weary troops, and considering his next move. Setting aside the central issue of whether the British should strike in the north or the south, one point that had become obvious was that the Puente de Almáraz possessed immense strategic importance. Carrying the only decent road across the Tagus between Madrid and the Portuguese frontier, it was the quickest way for Marmont to move south or Soult to move north. Such French forces as had been left in Extremadura having retired to the frontiers of Andalucía, Wellington decided that Hill should attack it with his independent corps. Taking with him the bulk of the Second Division, at six o'clock on the morning of 18 May, Hill therefore hurled himself upon the fort that guarded its southern end. Known as Fort Napoleon, this was overwhelmed in a matter of minutes, whereupon the garrison of the forts across the river abandoned their positions and made off, leaving Hill to burn the bridge (the original masonry one having been blown by the Spaniards in 1809, it was a wooden pontoon affair) and demolish its fortifications.

Having thus wrought incalculable damage on the French cause – with no means of repairing the bridge, the invaders could henceforth only communicate between north and south by means of a long detour via Madrid – Hill headed back to Mérida. However, at this point the political situation in England once again took centre stage. On 11 May Perceval was mortally wounded in the Palace of Westminster by a merchant named Bellingham who had recently gone bankrupt and blamed the government for his travails. This event came at a moment of great tension: the harvest had been very bad; parts of the north had been gripped by the movement of machine-smashing, riot and intimidation known as Luddism; agitation against the trade restrictions imposed in response to the Continental Blockade was reaching a climax (they were, in fact, shortly to be repealed); and there was a growing peace movement. Yet, much acclaimed though the assassination was in those parts of the country which had been hit hard by the war, Bellingham's action did not, as was briefly feared, presage revolution. Panic-stricken rumours of secret rebel armies notwithstanding, the government was at no point distracted from the war in the Peninsula (the claim, for example, that more troops were deployed against the Luddites than Wellington had under his command in Spain is disingenuous nonsense). As for Bellingham, he had acted entirely alone and was absolutely lacking in political motivation. The shooting did, however, plunge politics into crisis. Chosen to take over as Prime Minister, Lord Liverpool tried to make up for losing Perceval by recalling Canning and Wellesley, but neither of them was willing to co-operate. Without them, the Commons felt that the old administration could not carry on and therefore demanded a replacement. In so far as the war in Spain was concerned, this move was truly frightening, for it implied bringing in either Wellesley and Canning or the Whigs. Yet Wellesley and Canning were seriously lacking in political judgement, and, in the case of the former, notoriously lazy, whilst the Whigs, though no longer opposed to the war against Napoleon *per se*, were deeply pessimistic about the Peninsula, inclined to a defensive strategy and eager to cut expenditure. In the end, however, all was well. Ever more enamoured of the military glory his sometime friends were so keen on scorning, the Prince-Regent would not back the Whigs of his own accord, whilst the latter could not muster the support they needed in the Commons to force him to do so. As for Wellesley and Canning, neither of them proved capable of forming a government. All the alternatives having been tried and failed, there was no choice but to bring back Liverpool and his colleagues, and on 17 June a distinctly humbled Commons confirmed them in office by a majority of 100 votes.

Given the close understanding that by now existed between Wellington and the ministers that had made up the old Perceval administration, no result could have been more welcome, whilst the latter's commitment to the strategy of fighting the French in the Peninsula was soon to receive still further confirmation. Wellington's problem was that for reasons that were quite beyond the control of the British government, he continued to be short of specie. The flow of bullion from Latin America having collapsed, rising demand had driven prices ever upwards, whilst efforts to find alternative sources of supply had delivered very little. By the time that Badajoz fell, Wellington was in genuine distress for want to funds, and this situation the new Liverpool administration now made great efforts to resolve. Various schemes for the purchase of specie on the open market having been rejected on the grounds, first, that Britain's revenue was insufficient to bear the cost, and, second, that buying more gold would ineluctably lead to fresh price increases, less orthodox measures had to be tried. In consequence, a near-forgotten law that allowed the government to export guineas (which was normally prohibited) if the object was to pay British troops engaged in service abroad was used to force a reluctant Bank of England to disgorge huge sums of money, Wellington then being secretly instructed to spend the extra money as he saw fit rather than simply on the pay of his soldiers. This was illegal, whilst the release of so much gold could easily have led to a major financial crisis. Yet in reality there was little else to be done, and in the end the collapse of the Continental Blockade made all secure once more.

Yet, illegal or not, it would be winter before the extra money began to appear in Wellington's coffers. As so often before, however, there was an element of 'crying wolf' in the British commander's dealings with the government. Money was short, yes, and there were a number of ways in which the Anglo-Portuguese army was seriously inconvenienced, but Wellington was nevertheless planning fresh victories. Having resolved that it would be better to strike Marmont rather than Soult (on the grounds that the liberation of northern and central Spain would infallibly bring with it the evacuation of Andalucía, whereas the liberation of Andalucía would in itself make no difference in the north), towards the end of May he had begun to concentrate all his troops save those of Hill in the vicinity of Ciudad Rodrigo. Given the continued dispersion of the Army of Portugal from Asturias to the Tagus valley, initial success of some sort was certain, but Wellington knew that with every step that he advanced the French were more able to fall upon him in overwhelming force. Since every step that he advanced also took him further from the safety of Portugal, as many of the enemy as possible had to be neutralised.

For this purpose, a variety of devices lay readily to hand. Though he had no official authority over the Spanish forces, Wellington now had considerable prestige in Patriot Spain, the liberation of Badajoz and Ciudad Rodrigo having done much to wipe out the unhappy memories of 1808, 1809 and 1810. Fulsome displays of pro-British feeling therefore began to appear in the press; there were ecstatic demonstrations when the British commander returned to Ciudad Rodrigo on 26 April; and a handful of British officers had even been allowed to embark on the reform of the army through the establishment of training depots and model divisions.* In consequence, Wellington had only to suggest a plan for the Regency – since 21 January a new body headed by the emollient Infantado – to agree. By this means, then, Ballesteros was directed to strike at Seville; the Sixth Army to besiege Astorga; Porlier, Longa and Espoz y Mina – now grouped together as the Seventh Army under Gabriel Mendizábal – to tie down the Army of the North, in whose command Dorsenne had just been replaced by Caffarelli; and the Second and Third Armies to tie down Suchet. The great diversion was not just to be left to the Spaniards, however. Thus, Hill was instructed to head south should Soult press Ballesteros; the British squadron on the

---

* The most prominent examples were Charles Doyle, who had been permitted to establish a training depot on the Isla de León; Phillip Roche, who was allowed to take over a division of the Third Army; and Samuel Whittingham, who was given an independent division that had been organised in Mallorca. As the troops of Roche and Whittingham were paid and supplied by the British, they generally proved fairly reliable.

north coast of Spain to raid the French garrisons dotted along the coast; and finally the governor of Sicily, Lord William Bentinck, to send a division to the coast of Catalonia.

Some minor hiccups aside, this scheme functioned extremely well. In Andalucía the end of May saw Ballesteros strike inland and attack a French division at Bornos. Though he was beaten and forced to retreat, this did not matter, for Hill immediately came forward in Extremadura, with the result that Soult had to send many troops to reinforce Drouet. Whilst Hill then entangled the latter in a complex war of manoeuvre, Ballesteros sallied out again, briefly occupied Málaga, and then led as many as 10,000 French troops a merry dance through the wilds of Granada before finally heading back to the coast. In the north, the British squadron, which was commanded by the adventurous Sir Home Popham, sailed up and down the coast, landing naval guns and parties of marines to attack such garrisons as Lequeitio, Guetaria, Castro Urdiales and Santander in company with the guerrillas of Longa and Porlier. Not all these operations succeeded – indeed, Popham and Mendizábal suffered a number of minor defeats – but the Army of the North was run ragged trying to keep the situation under control, Bilbao occupied for a fortnight, and the major port of Santander left in Allied hands for good. With Mina, too, extremely active, Caffarelli was therefore, like Soult, out of the fight. In the east, by contrast, matters did not go quite so smoothly. Thanks to a combination of foolishness on the part of Bentinck and growing political tension in Sicily, far fewer troops were sent over than had originally been expected, whilst those that did come arrived much later than planned and eventually did nothing but collect Whittingham from Majorca and disembark at Alicante. As for the Third Army, commanded by José O'Donnell, it eventually struck north, only to be heavily defeated at Castalla in what was more a gigantic ambush than a battle. Yet, again, the fact that the Sicilian expedition proved a damp squib and O'Donnell particularly maladroit mattered not a jot. Ringed by enemies, and unable to borrow any troops from Catalonia, where Lacy was continuing to do his best to cause trouble (his actions at this time included a surprise attack on Lérida timed to coincide with an explosion in the city's main powder magazine set off by Patriot sympathisers), Suchet had no chance of sending troops to central Spain and that was all that mattered.

This complicated web of diversion helped Wellington but it was in reality hardly necessary. To have any serious chance of blocking Wellington, the French would have had to give up part of their dominions, but Napoleon was so obsessed by questions of prestige that he could not tolerate a repeat of the evacuation of Galicia in 1809, and had, in fact, forbidden any such move. Nor was this an end to the matter. Of the various French commanders, other than Joseph and Jourdan, only Marmont – the very general most in need of help – ever thought in wider terms than those of his own satrapy, the rest being inclined to give their fellows only minimal assistance, if indeed they gave them any at all. In this there was selfishness and egotism in plenty, but in the circumstances of 1812 it was also entirely understandable, for the French were so hard-pressed that reducing one garrison in favour of another was almost certain to lead to disaster. The struggle being just as much about prestige as it was about anything else, politically the French could not afford to take such risks, whilst Figueras alone showed how inconvenient they could be in military terms. In the last resort, then, the real issue was not the personal failings of Soult and the rest, but rather want of troops, and, beyond that, Napoleon's belief that he could have his cake and eat it.

Of this, however, he was soon to be disabused. Thus, on 13 June, Wellington advanced into León with his 48,000-strong main army, the Sixth Army in the meantime sallying forth from Galicia to blockade Astorga whilst a force of Portuguese militia tackled Zamora. No sooner had the Allies taken the field than Marmont set about concentrating all the men he could, requested help from Caffarelli and Joseph and, in flat defiance of Napoleon, called back Bonet from Asturias. However, whilst he intended to fight, it would be some time before he got enough troops together and in consequence he fell back behind the Duero, leaving Salamanca to be defended by a small force ensconced in three fortified convents that had been converted into an improvised citadel. Much stronger than the British at first realised, these held out bravely. As Mills wrote, for example:

Our people are beginning to find out that these . . . forts are stronger than they at first gave them credit for . . . The fire . . . is incessant, but their men are so well covered it is almost impossible to hit them. We have already lost fifty or sixty men.[35]

Beating off an attempt at a storm, the garrison only gave up on 27 June after their position was set on fire by red-hot shot.

Amidst the firing, there was much popular excitement. According to Simmons, the inhabitants 'expressed their joy in a most frantic fashion and praised their deliverers, as they called the English, and expressed their abhorrence of the French', whilst, to quote Wheeler, 'Every afternoon the people pour out of the city by thousands to enjoy themselves with song and dance, so that our camp every evening presents one of the liveliest scenes imaginable'.[36] Yet amongst the British there was also much cynicism, many of them realising that delight at liberation did not necessarily amount to enthusiasm for the cause. Thus:

The people, alternately in the power of friends and foes, show indifference to both. They cannot take a part without danger to themselves; they prefer consequently personal security to a display of unseasonable loyalty or patriotism. In their hearts I believe they hate the French, but they have at the same time no great love for us.[37]

Much the same point was made by Aitchison. As he remarked, 'I cannot say whether the people are happy at our entrance . . . It is all the same to the poor man whether the enemy take by force or the British lay all the provisions under contribution for payment.'[38] As the army advanced into León, indeed, many instances were uncovered of the local authorities attempting to insure themselves against a return of the enemy. And, as ever, the behaviour of the soldiers did not help. In the words of a general order of 10 June 1812:

The commander of the forces is sorry to observe that the outrages so frequently committed by the soldiers when absent from their regiments, and the disgraceful scenes which occurred upon the storming of Badajoz, have had the effect of rendering the people of the country the enemies instead of being the friends of the army.[39]

To believe, then, that liberation would produce anything other than cheers and flowers was optimistic. At the same time, although Wellington was now the master of León, the campaign had not gone entirely as he had wanted it to, for he had hoped that Marmont might have been tempted into launching a head-on attack at Salamanca. As the marshal had refused to take the bait, however, there was no option but to advance to the Duero where Wellington proceeded to sit down to wait for the Sixth Army to appear in the rear of the enemy (the latter's orders had been not just to besiege Astorga but to keep pace with Wellington's army as it moved eastwards, thereby both trapping Bonet in Asturias and threatening Marmont's flank). Had all gone to plan, the marshal would have had to send a division or two to hold off the Spaniards, so weakening the line of the Duero that Wellington could have tried an attack. Yet the Sixth Army failed to appear, its troops having for the most part advanced no further than Astorga, whose garrison was still holding out most stubbornly.

In many ways, the stand-off on the Duero was to prove extremely beneficial to Wellington, for it appears to have convinced Marmont, who was, after all, possessed of the smaller army, that Wellington was on no account an attacking general and, in consequence, an opponent with whom he could take every risk. At the time, however, the non-appearance of the Spaniards was extremely frustrating for it allowed Marmont to regain the initiative. Thus, having at last been joined by Bonet, on 15 July the marshal suddenly sent his troops back across the river. For this he has been bitterly criticised on the grounds that, had he only waited, troops would have reached him from both Burgos and Madrid. Thus, Caffarelli, having earlier told him that he could spare him no assistance, was sending him a cavalry brigade, whilst a deeply alarmed Joseph had decided to march to join him with virtually every soldier he could muster (deducting a minimal garrison for Madrid, some 14,000 men). In fairness to Marmont, however, it must be said that he not only did not know that these moves were under way, but had no reason to believe that they would ever come to pass, whilst, at 44,000 men, his forces were not very much smaller than those of Wellington.

At first, certainly, all went well enough. Completely deceiving Wellington by some clever feinting, the marshal managed to get across the Duero unchallenged, and over the next few days forced him to retreat on Salamanca by a series of elaborate outflanking manoeuvres designed to threaten his communications with Portugal. By 22 July the Allied army was drawn up just to the south-east of Salamanca along a line of low hills whose southern end was marked by a pronounced butte known as the Arapil Chico. Marmont, however, had no intention of trying a frontal assault, and on the morning of 22 July, having first seized the much larger butte known as the Arapil Grande that stood a few hundred yards due south of the Arapil Chico, he therefore began to march his entire army round its southern flank. Seeing what was going on, meanwhile, the British commander swung division after division back from their original positions to form a new line running west from the Arapil Chico along a convenient spur that extended for about a mile to the west. Last but not least, having until now been covering the eastern approaches to the city of Salamanca itself, the Third Division and some Portuguese cavalry were brought across the rear of the army to an altogether hidden position beyond the right flank of Wellington's new line near the village of Aldea Tejada.

By early afternoon, then, the bulk of the Allied army was facing south (the Light Division and a few other troops had been left in their original positions just in case Marmont was trying another feint), whilst the French were circling westwards around the two Arapiles. At this point, however, Marmont made a terrible mistake. Having mounted the Arapil Grande, he could see much of what was going on in the Allied position, but such was his conviction that Wellington was a cautious general who much preferred the defence to the attack that he drew quite the wrong conclusion from what he saw. Thus, in his eyes, the movements were explained by preparations for a retreat to a fresh position a few miles to the west behind the River Zurgaín, and he in consequence determined to push his vanguard even further westwards in the hope of outflanking this new position as well. Thus far, the

French had not advanced beyond his viewpoint, but some time after midday Marmont ordered four of the five infantry divisions that he had to hand to advance along a long ridge that ran westwards towards the Zurgaín, together with a division of light cavalry under Curto.

In acting in this fashion, Marmont was taking an awful risk, one of the most basic rules of 'horse and musket' warfare being never to march across the front of an opponent. Convinced that Wellington would not attack, Marmont was blind to the danger, but in reality his men were marching straight into a trap. Not only did the move further west lead to the French becoming more and more strung out, but Wellington had for the past few hours actually been contemplating an attack. Surveying the French through his telescope in between bites at a leg of chicken, the British commander saw his moment. Exclaiming, 'By God, that will do!', he tossed the half-finished chicken leg over his shoulder, leaped on his horse, and set off at high speed for Pakenham's Third Division with its attendant Portuguese cavalry.

The events of the next hour or so were to prove a bitter awakening for the French. Alerted by Wellington, Pakenham led his men to the westernmost end of the ridge along which the French were advancing and then faced left and burst over the crest to envelop the leading French division (that of Thomières). There followed a sharp clash:

We were going up an ascent on whose crest masses of the enemy were stationed. Their fire seemed capable of sweeping all before it . . . Truth compels me to say . . . that we retired before this overwhelming fire, but . . . General Pakenham approached and very good naturedly said, 'Reform', and in . . . a moment, 'Advance . . . There they are my lads; just let them feel the temper of your bayonets.' We advanced, everyone making up his mind for mischief. At last . . . the bugles along the line sounded the charge. Forward we rushed . . . and awful was the retribution we exacted for our former repulse.[40]

A long way from its nearest fellow and supported only by Curto's light cavalry, Thomières' division was overwhelmed with the loss of almost half its strength, Pakenham then pursuing its remnants eastwards until he came upon the next French division – that of Maucune – which had halted to cover the march westwards of the rest of the French infantry. Maucune, too, was in trouble, however, for, after setting Pakenham in motion, Wellington had ridden back to his main position and ordered the troops there to attack in echelon from the right. First off were the Fifth Division of General Leith, and the cavalry brigade of General Le Marchant. Seeing the British cavalry, Maucune ordered his men to form in squares, only for the first troops to hit home to turn out to be Leith's infantry. Caught in the act of changing formation, the French were therefore soon vanquished:

The spirit of our people rose . . . and when they reached the enemy's solid columns, which opened a fire like a volcano upon them, there was . . . a general shout of exultation . . . The enemy wavered . . . till at length it was impossible to withstand the ardour of our soldiers . . . and complete rout ensued.[41]

Thrown into confusion, the unfortunate French soldiers were then struck by Le Marchant and utterly broken, once again with heavy casualties. As Bragge recalled, 'We quickly came up with the French columns and charged their rear. Hundreds threw down their arms.'[42] Caught up in the rout, meanwhile, was Taupin's division, which had been marching across Maucune's rear to fill the gap between him and Thomières at the moment of the British attack.

In only an hour of fighting, then, Wellington had broken the entire French left – three full divisions – and taken 2,500 prisoners, 12 guns and 2 eagles. Thomières was dead and Marmont, who had been caught by a chance shell, badly wounded. However, although the afternoon was far advanced, the battle was not yet over. Thus, shortly after Leith had advanced against Maucune, part of Fourth Division and Pack's independent Portuguese brigade had advanced on the divisions of Clausel and Bonet, which had held the eastern end of the ridge, and the Arapil Grande. Both forces, however, were repulsed – the French 'did pepper them most dreadfully', remembered Dyneley[43] – whilst Clausel and Bonet tried to follow up their success by charging across the valley that separated them from the British ridge and trying to break the Allied centre. Brave move though this was, it was doomed to failure, for Wellington had plenty of reserves and simply moved the fresh Sixth Division to plug the gap, the initial French onrush having been first checked by the Portuguese brigade of the Fifth Division which had attacked Clausel in flank. Urging them on, however, Beresford was shot in the chest and forced to quit the field.

Very soon, then, the French centre had joined the left in falling back in complete disorder, abandoning the Arapil Grande in the process. Three infantry divisions which had formed the French reserve – those of Ferey, Sarrut and Foy – were available to cover the retreat, and they fought back bravely as the whole Allied army pressed forwards to finish the job: ordering up the hitherto unengaged Light Division, indeed, Wellington himself had a lucky escape when a bullet struck his saddle holster and bruised his thigh. In most sectors they do not seem to have been pressed too hard, however: most of the Allied troops, after all, were exhausted after hours of marching and fighting in blazing heat. Only Ferey, indeed, found he had a real job on his hands, being forced to face a full-scale assault by the whole of the Sixth Division. Anglo-Portuguese casualties were heavy, but in the end Ferey too gave way, the Army of Portugal only being saved from complete destruction by the onset of darkness. Thus ended the battle of Salamanca, or, as the Spaniards called it, Los Arapiles. Known, and for good reason, as 'Wellington's masterpiece', it had cost the Army of Portugal 12,000 casualties, 2 eagles and 12 guns (Anglo-Portuguese casualties, by contrast, numbered some 5,000). These losses might have been still higher had the pursuit been pressed with any vigour, but in the darkness and confusion, Wellington's forces appear to have quite lost their cohesion (claims that the entire French army would have been destroyed had the Spaniards only kept a garrison in Alba de Tormes are highly disingenuous: the garrison was withdrawn, it is true, but its presence would have made little difference). Only the next day did the pursuit get under way properly, although there still proved time to inflict yet more damage on the French at the village of García Hernández where the King's-German-Legion heavy dragoons distinguished themselves by achieving the near impossible feat of breaking a battalion of infantry in square.

After García Hernández, however, the Army of Portugal was allowed to fall back on Valladolid and Burgos unmolested. Wellington would doubtless have liked to have done still more damage to Clausel (on whom command of the Army of Portugal had eventually devolved), but further pursuit would simply have driven him into the arms of Caffarelli whilst yet leaving his forces intact, for the French commander would never have risked a battle. Still worse, it would have put the Anglo-Portuguese army at great risk, for logic dictated that Soult and Suchet would send large forces to Madrid and join with Joseph in an offensive across the Sierra de Guadarrama that might easily have cut it off from Portugal. Considering that the Army of Portugal was shattered, it made better sense to march on Madrid, whose liberation would for obvious reasons constitute a terrible humiliation for the enemy. The French might well still join up against Wellington, but if they did he could always retreat, whilst there was also a chance that they would not march against him in sufficient strength to force him back at all. As a result, leaving a single division at Valladolid, together with two divisions of Spaniards who had come up from Astorga, on 6 August the Anglo-Portuguese army set off for Madrid.

As the capital's occupation was the result of a series of events in the French camp that need to be discussed at some length, we shall deal with it in the next chapter. In any event, what mattered was the fact that the stalemate on the Portuguese frontier had been broken. What, though, had brought about the Allied cause's change of fortune? In answer we should turn neither to Wellington's prowess as a general, nor to the mistakes of his opponents, nor to the quality of his army, nor even to the resistance of the Spaniards. All these played their part, but in the end Napoleon had no one to blame but himself. Had he only left the forces in the Peninsula in the state in which they had been in the early autumn of 1811, there is little doubt that they could have held back Wellington and the Spanish armies, whilst setting about the guerrillas in the methodical fashion known to produce success. Adopting a defensive posture was not to Napoleon's taste, however, and, whilst stripping his generals of vital troops, he refused to recognise reality – an early instance of a trait that was to become all too typical – and instead demanded fresh offensives. The result was disaster, Soult and Marmont finding themselves unable to counter Wellington in an effective fashion. Whether the latter could consolidate his gains was another matter, of course, but for the time being he was fighting a very different war.

15

Burgos

THE AUTUMN CAMPAIGN OF 1812

Beneath a cloudless sky regiment after regiment tramped across the bridge and entered the canyon-like street leading into the heart of the city. Faded jackets, battered shakos, shapeless forage caps, and trousers of assorted shades of grey, blue and brown proclaimed that this was no ordinary parade, but rather the arrival of an army straight from the field. Amongst the troops there rode the modestly attired but unmistakeable figure of Wellington, several brightly uniformed Spanish generals and half-a-dozen swaggering guerrilla commanders, one of whom attracted especial attention by sporting a captured French shako whose imperial eagle had been turned upside down. In the narrow streets progress was near impossible, however. Beneath high buildings whose every balcony was hung with drapes and tapestries, a huge crowd surged forward to greet their liberators, shouting, 'Long live Wellington! Long live El Empecinado and the six-farthing loaf! Long live Fernando and the return of abundance!' Reduced over the past year to a state of semi-starvation, they fell upon the troops, flung branches, cloaks and shawls in their path, plied them with wine and tobacco, and showered them with kisses, whilst Wellington and his fellow horsemen were almost pulled from their mounts. Lost in the throng disgusted privates angrily fended off men who were attempting to embrace them, but otherwise it was truly an exhilarating moment – indeed, perhaps the most exhilarating moment of the entire war.

Accompanying the Allied liberation of Madrid on 12 August 1812, these scenes were the culmination of a series of triumphs that had completely turned the tide of the war in Spain. Whereas the beginning of 1812 had seen the French armies winning fresh conquests, within eight months they had been ejected from as much as half the territory that they had managed to occupy since 1808. As for the future, all seemed set for further victories and a continued thaw in Anglo-Spanish relations. Yet, as so often before, appearances were deceptive, the next three months bringing failure and humiliation to British and Spaniards alike. In one sense, this was only to be expected: with every step that Wellington advanced, the French had less territory to garrison, whilst they still had some 210,000 troops with the colours compared to the British commander's 60,000. Yet in theory the Spaniards could put at least 100,000 more men into the field, whilst the liberated territories offered them the prospect of fresh resources. It being the inability of the Allies to capitalise on this additional contribution that tipped the balance, it is Spanish affairs that must take precedence in our consideration of the autumn of 1812.

Before looking at the issues concerned, however, we must examine the aftermath of Salamanca. As we have seen, the occupation of the Spanish capital was the result of Wellington's decision that his troops would be more gainfully – and less dangerously – employed moving on central Spain than attempting to destroy the remnants of the Army of Portugal. On 6 August, then, the victors of Salamanca set off for Madrid from Valladolid. Facing them were Joseph and Jourdan, but, with only 22,000 troops, many of them *juramentados* of little reliability, they were in no position to defend the capital. In this a large part of the responsibility must be borne by Marshal Soult, who, determined to hang on to his viceroyalty, had for the past two months been ignoring demands that he send a substantial force of troops to the Tagus. Covered by a screen of cavalry which succeeded in inflicting a sharp reverse on some Portuguese dragoons at Majadahonda, on 10 August a great convoy consisting of Joseph's troops, the royal household, 2,000 wagons and perhaps 15,000 civilian refugees set off along the highway that led through Aranjuez and Albacete and thence to Valencia. Progress was slow; the heat terrible; the dust choking; water almost unobtainable; and the troops mutinous and undisciplined, many of those that did not desert pillaging the unfortunate civilians they were supposed to be protecting. As for Madrid, the only French presence was now a small garrison left in the great earthwork citadel that had been built on the high ground occupied by the present-day Retiro park.

In Andalucía, meanwhile, so bad had communications become between his Viceroyalty and central Spain that Soult did not get certain news of Salamanca until 12 August. Left with no hope but to retreat, within two or three days the Army of the South had also started to evacuate its positions. On 25 August the siege of Cádiz was abandoned, and on 27 August Seville (with the exception of a small rearguard that was ejected the next day by a hastily improvised Anglo-Spanish division which had been sent up from Cádiz). Falling back eastwards in the company of the same masses of refugees that encumbered Joseph in La Mancha, Soult was joined at Córdoba by the troops of Drouet from Extremadura, and then headed for Granada,

The Duke of Wellington. Painted by Lawrence at the end of the Peninsular War, this famous portrait captures the aloof dignity that was the hallmark of his public persona.

(*top left*) André Masséna. Notoriously avaricious, 'the darling child of victory' was a spent force when he arrived in Spain in 1810, but he still pushed Wellington harder than any other of his opponents.

(*top right*) Claude-Victor Perrin. Always known as Victor, the 'shining sun' gained significant successes at Uclés and Medellín, but was badly beaten by Wellington at Talavera.

(*left*) A successful administrator of the territories seized by France in present-day Slovenia and Croatia, Marmont was an excellent choice for the Spanish theatre, but his Peninsular career was cut short by defeat and the loss of an arm at Salamanca in July 1812.

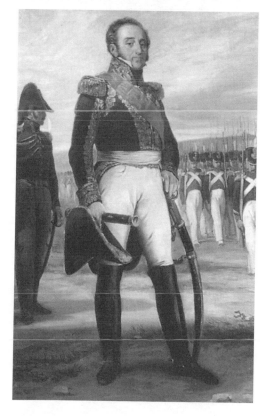

(*top left*) A hot-tempered adventurer, Michel Ney not only failed to distinguish himself in the Peninsula but also quarrelled with almost every general with whom he served.

(*top right*) Joseph Bonaparte's most trusted military confidant, Marshal Jourdan showed genuine vision in the two periods in which he served as his chief-of-staff, but he was unable to impose his authority on his fellow commanders and was completely outwitted at Vitoria.

(*right*) Conqueror of Tarragona and Valencia, Louis Gabriel Suchet was the only French commander to win a marshal's baton in the Peninsular.

Pictured with his wife, Laure – a vivacious woman who became Metternich's mistress during his embassy to Paris and was described by Napoleon as his 'little pest' – Jean-Andoche Junot commanded the French forces defeated at Vimeiro in 1808.

Sir John Moore. Brave, popular and a noted military reformer, Moore died a hero but was nevertheless a complicated figure whose quarrels with his political superiors almost led to disaster in 1808.

Notoriously brutal and foul-mouthed, Sir Thomas Picton was an extremely good soldier whose resolution and energy made him one of the best of Wellington's divisional commanders.

Marshal Soult surveys the horror of the broken bridge as Oporto falls to the French on 29 March 1809. As proof that not all French soldiers were brutes, in the foreground a grenadier rescues an orphaned baby.

Spanish infantry, cavalry and artillery help repulse the advance of the division of General Leval at the battle of Talavera on 28 July 1809.

A contemporary engraving of the assault on Ciudad Rodrigo on 19 January 1812. Headed by the editor of Wellington's dispatches, Lieutenant Gurwood, the forlorn hope of the Light Division rushes the lesser breach, whilst, to their right, a French booby-trap explodes in the rubble of the main breach.

Inside the Castle of Burgos, the embattled garrison of General Dubreton hold on amidst a storm of shot and shell in the siege of October 1812.

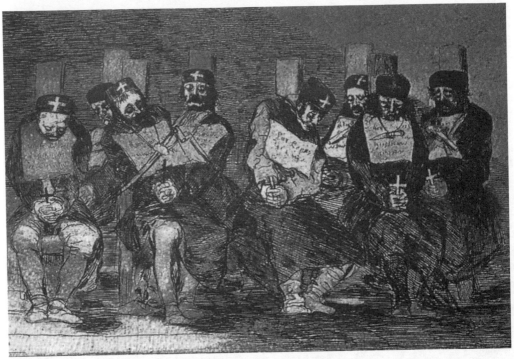

'It is impossible to find out the reason.' Goya's response to the sight of these victims of the garotte sums up the ambiguity of the guerrilla struggle against the French.

British cavalry riding down confused and exhausted French infantry are counter-charged by enemy lancers in the closing stages of the battle of Vitoria on 21 June 1813.

where he picked up the garrison of the eastern part of his territories and engaged in some last-minute requisitioning before finally marching for Valencia on 16 September.

In Cádiz, of course, all this was accompanied by great jubilation. The news of Salamanca caused a great stir. As Henry Wellesley wrote to Wellington:

I heartily wish you joy of your glorious victory, and I wish you could have witnessed the effect it produced here . . . A deputation of the *cortes* came to congratulate me upon the victory, and the people assembled under my windows, hailing you as the saviour of Spain.[1]

But the greatest moment, as Alcalá Galiano recalled, was the departure of the French from the shores of the bay:

At this time the siege of Cádiz was raised. The day this happened was one of unequalled joy. The people rushed to embark in boats to visit the abandoned French encampment . . . There was a great desire to walk on the earth of the continent, to breath in fresh air . . . I went with the officials of the Ministry [of State] . . . Accompanied by a numerous crowd we went round . . . the batteries which had contained the mortars whose effects we had been experiencing for such a long time. On the way back . . . all the boats carried a bunch of grass at their mastheads as a way of showing that they had completed a return trip that had been denied to the inhabitants . . . for more than thirty consecutive months.[2]

In the space of less than two months, then, New Castile, Extremadura and Andalucía had all been cleared of the enemy with scarcely a shot being fired. As Wellington advanced on Madrid, meanwhile, it appeared to have rekindled popular enthusiasm. At Segovia, for example, the inhabitants 'waylaid him at the entrance to the town with a cracked trumpet, an old kettle-drum and two miserable wretches dressed in scarlet robes, [and] conveyed him nearly half a mile to the market place, where he was obliged to stand with his hat off until they had done "viva-ing" him'.[3] It was at Madrid, however, that excitement and optimism were at their height. To quote Cocks:

The earl made his way into this place on the twelfth . . . Our arrival produced a joy far beyond description . . . I was never kissed by so many pretty girls in a day in all my life, or ever expect to be again. If we moved on horseback, the animals were embraced and pulled one way, and we were hauled and caressed the other. On foot it was impossible to make your way . . . Unless the emperor gets through the Russian war with perfect *éclat*, the French must no longer think of acting south of the Ebro.[4]

For a Spanish view, we may again turn to Carnicero:

When the bells began to announce the entrance of our troops at about ten o'clock, it was wonderful to see the people rushing to ... the Portillo de San Vicente, which was the one through which they were said to be coming. A new town council was formed, and this immediately set forth to greet ... the immortal Wellington ... To the accompaniment of a crescendo of bells, the people massed in ever greater numbers round the Plaza de la Villa. When a portrait of our Don Fernando [i.e. Fernando VII] was placed in the window of the town hall, they simply went mad. The cheering was incessant; hats and caps were thrown in the air; on all sides people were giving thanks to God; and everyone was filled with the greatest joy and happiness. Another of the incidents that made the day shine out was the behaviour of the women and children of the poorer quarters. Joseph ... had made a new avenue from the palace to the Casa de Campo [i.e. the royal hunting park] ... This had been lined with fruit trees ... but the crowd ... fell upon them ... and ripped them up ... When Lord Wellington arrived, many of the people who greeted him were therefore carrying branches and sprigs of greenery which they waved in time with their cheers and happy shouts of greeting. In this manner he was accompanied to the town hall. When he got there the cheering redoubled, and all the more so when ... he came out onto one of the balconies accompanied by El Empecinado. Amidst thunderous applause, everyone flung their arms around one another, and gave themselves over to congratulating their neighbours in the most unreserved fashion.[5]

Very quickly, however, it became apparent that victory was not, as the British had hoped, to be followed by the formation of large Spanish armies that could assist them in the expulsion of the French from the Peninsula. Thus, in Madrid, for example, the days following the departure of the French had gone by in a whirl of celebrations. The Constitution of 1812 was proclaimed and sworn allegiance to in a series of ceremonies across the city; illuminations and open-air dances were held every night; and there were a series of free bullfights (fox-hunting men though they were, Wellington's officers were on the whole revolted by the spectacle). Meanwhile, the troops mingled with the crowds, who continued to swarm around them happily, the general atmosphere of goodwill being reinforced by the food which was shared with the starving (two colonels are even supposed to have fed 200 of the city's poor for several days out of their own pocket). Yet, although weapons, uniforms, artillery and ammunition existed in abundance in the citadel, which had been forced to surrender after a brief fight, there was no sign of general mobilisation. On the contrary, there seemed to be a general feeling that all and sundry could rest on their laurels. 'Nothing has disgusted me for a long time,' complained Sydenham, 'so much as the juvenile exultations and absurd fanfarronade with which all the late Cádiz papers are filled. The editors seem to think that the war is at an end, and that nothing more is to be done but to cut their jokes upon the flying and discomforted French. They talk in passing of the *ilustre* Wellington, the *valiente* Beresford, and the *sabio* [i.e. wise] Silveira (what names to associate!), but they evidently attribute all the great events of the campaign to the invincible spirit and miraculous exertions of the Spaniards.'[6]

The British, then, were filled with gloom. As Wellington wrote, 'Everything in which the Spaniards are concerned is going as badly as possible, and I really believe there is not a man in the country who is capable of comprehending, much less of conducting, any great concern.'[7] Nor were his subordinates any happier. 'It is impossible at this moment to say what efforts will be made by the Spanish authorities in consequence of our arrival, but there appears to be no form of direction ... Nothing could be so hopeless', complained James Willoughby Gordon, whilst in the words of Wellington's favourite aide-de-camp, the Spaniards, 'expect us to do everything, and have not the least idea of their being able themselves to assist us'.[8] Such views could only be reinforced by what little was to be seen of the Spanish army. Thus, Thomas Browne noted that the Spanish troops he saw were 'badly clothed and equipped and ... had the appearance of not being more than half fed', George Hennell that, although he had heard that 'great numbers' of fresh troops were to be raised, he had seen 'nothing like it', and William Bragge that their boasting 'put one in mind of the foppish midshipman who marked his only two shirts fifty-nine and sixty'.[9]

To many British observers, of course, all this was yet another instance of Spanish laziness and incompetence, whilst the more informed amongst them were also furious at the manner in which the authorities had been 'hurried by a spirit of revenge into the most absurd and impolitic measures against the persons who have from necessity been compelled to accept office under the government of Joseph Bonaparte'.[10]* However, rather than seeking explanations in some supposed national character, they would have done better to look at the general state of Patriot Spain. Taking the Infantado Regency as an example, it may have been a collection of mediocrities headed by a simpleton, but the fact was that its powers were very limited. Since the moment that the *cortes* had first assembled, ever tighter controls had been placed upon the executive power's operations by the liberals who regarded

---

* Sanctioned by a series of vengeful decrees, the witch-hunt that followed the Allied advance was grim indeed: in Madrid alone arrests numbered at least 150, whilst there were many executions. However, according to the British, many of those concerned had been secretly helping Wellington as spies.

all governments as a threat to liberty. In consequence, the Regency had been left no function beyond implementing the will of the *cortes*. As before, however, the assembly was uninterested in the real problems that dogged the war effort: in the autumn of 1812 the chief subject under discussion was the abolition of the Inquisition, the provision that no deputy could hold government office depriving the Regency of any chance of giving the deputies a lead. Denied the chance to defend itself, it also became the subject of a chorus of criticism that had the effect of both discrediting the Regency and inhibiting its actions still further. With the administration in chaos and corruption and nepotism widespread, the work of government was all but paralysed.

With a modicum of popular goodwill, there was nothing here that need have got in the way of the formation of a new army. But confidence in the régime was lacking: 'If the authority of the government has not hitherto been respected in the country', wrote Henry Wellesley, 'it is solely to be ascribed to the neglect of all the measures necessary to assist the exertions of the people, and to the want of public confidence in the regular armies and the officers selected to command them.'[11] In Madrid, Salamanca and Badajoz alike, meanwhile, there could be no certainty that the Anglo-Portuguese forces would be able to hold their ground against the French. Yet the heart of the matter was simply that even after years of occupation military service was still anathematised. The crowds that had welcomed the Anglo-Portuguese army in Salamanca, Valladolid and Madrid had cheered, certainly, but they had been more interested in cheap bread than marching off to war. At the same time, with the harvest of 1811 a disaster, all normal economic activity at a standstill, the populace frequently taxed by both sides simultaneously, and the countryside stripped bare of all it contained by army after army, popular suffering had become intense (many areas, indeed, were in the grip of outright famine). As Hennell wrote of Madrid, for example:

The poor are very numerous here, and many are most wretched objects. In the great streets you are stopped every five or six yards, and frequently by six or seven at once . . . I have seen children five or six years of age lying on the pavement with scarcely one ounce of flesh on their arms and making a piteous moaning. After dark they lie down against a door doubled almost together . . . some sleeping, others crying.[12]

Yet the return of Spanish authority brought no help. Police regulations that differed hardly at all from those of the French were imposed on a populace that in many cases could only survive by resorting to crime, or, at least, economic activities of a sort that the authorities were inclined to frown upon, such as peddling and prostitution. No more in 1812 than in 1808, meanwhile, were there any serious moves in the direction of greater social justice. Thus, whilst the *cortes* in principle abolished feudalism, nothing was done to prevent the *señores* from continuing to levy their old feudal dues on the grounds that they were owed to them as rent. Nor, still less, were their tenants given the land. Equally, as in 1808, power stayed as firmly in the hands of the same local oligarchies as ever. In areas which had always remained in Patriot hands and those which were newly liberated from the French alike, there therefore arose a widespread movement of agrarian protest that the authorities were powerless to control. Dues went unpaid, the symbols of feudal rule were torn down, and *pueblo* after *pueblo* protested at the actions of their *señores* or challenged their rights. As for the *quinta*, meanwhile, it was ignored: hungry and desperate, a few individuals may here and there have answered the increasingly pathetic appeals of the Regency, but to expect anything more was out of the question.

If any further evidence is needed of the true state of popular feeling about the war effort, one has only to look at the *partidas* of the liberated areas, for their behaviour in no way matched the degree of commitment to the struggle that might have been expected had they been the patriots of legend. Indeed, the more the French receded from occupied Spain, the more *la guerrilla* appeared in its true colours. In northern Spain irregular resistance reached fresh heights – having defeated one substantial French force outside Vitoria, on 19 August Mina routed another at Tiebas midway between Tafalla and Pamplona – but in the liberated territories there emerged a sorry picture. Thus, deprived of the cloak of patriotism, many of the guerrillas were revealed as the brigands which they had always been, whilst there were few signs of a willingness either to pursue the French to fresh hunting grounds or to enlist in the regular army. From all sides, indeed, came complaints of pillage and highway robbery, whilst, as in the years 1808–1810, the problem was again swelled by young men taking to their heels to avoid military service. Still worse, meanwhile, even relatively well-disciplined forces such as those of El Empecinado generally spent their time, in Wellington's words, 'getting quietly into the large towns and amusing themselves or collecting plunder of a better or more valuable description'.[13] As for the few units that took the field with the regular armies, such as Sánchez's Lanceros de Castilla, they were soon shedding deserters by the dozen, whilst they proved little use in regular military operations: 'They are worse than useless ... for they only consume the produce of the country ... None of the guerrillas can act in line with regular troops.'[14] From this there followed but one conclusion: 'In proportion as we advance ... the guerrillas must be reduced into regular troops, or driven from the provinces as a pest and useless burden to the country.'[15]

Large parts of the country, then, had been to all intents and purposes reduced to anarchy. Rarely, however, could an administration have been in less of a position to assert its authority. *Jefes políticos*, Intendents and 'constitutional' town councils were appointed in the liberated territories, certainly, but all too many of the officials concerned were mere placemen who had found favour with the new authorities, relations between which were in any case often very confused. As for the *ayuntamientos*, in town after town life was disrupted by constant skirmishing as various local factions jockeyed for position and hurled accusations of treason at one another.

None of this made for efficient administration. Also extremely damaging was the manner in which cities such as Cádiz, La Coruña, Ciudad Rodrigo and Alicante had all become crammed with supernumeraries with perfectly legitimate claims to pay and employment. As Mahy complained of this last city, 'The immense gathering of . . . officers of every class that has come together in [Alicante] is absorbing all the resources [of] the territory that has not yet been occupied by the enemy . . . In consequence, Your Highness must decide what should be done with all those who are not legitimately employed with the army.'[16] Nor were matters helped by the exceptionally wasteful structure that was given to the Spanish army in the course of 1812. Thus, to accommodate the swollen officer corps that had emerged from the war, the Captain Generalcies were kept separate from the field commands, and each regiment given only a single battalion, each brigade only four regiments, and each division only two brigades (in the French army, by contrast, regiments had four battalions, brigades eight, and divisions sixteen).

Economy was essential, however. Thanks to the advance of the French armies and the continued chaos in America, revenue had been falling steadily – from 407,700,000 reales in 1810 to 201,600,000 in 1811 and only 138,000,000 in 1812. Falls in the amounts dispatched from the colonies had been particularly sharp – as much as ninety-three per cent in the period 1811–12 – and, even though a measure of order had now been restored in Mexico, a variety of factors ensured that shipments of bullion would never regain their previous levels. Notwithstanding the fact that it was the key to Spain's situation, however, consideration of the American problem had been relegated to a secondary level by the *cortes*. Repeated efforts were made by the American deputies, many of whom were anything but eager for a total rupture with metropolitan Spain, to introduce genuine measures of reform, but these either foundered for lack of interest, or were brought down by the determination of merchants to protect their commercial interests, liberals to safeguard the principle of a unitary state, and traditionalists to defend the patrimony of Fernando VII. Even the political equality offered by the *cortes* on 14 October 1810 was hedged about with qualifications that effectively rendered it null and void, whilst many of its general reforms actually exacerbated American grievances. As *gaditano* opinion had also continued to block the commercial concessions being pressed for by the British, the Spanish revolution had therefore offered the colonies almost nothing.

Yet without stability in America, Spain was bankrupt: indeed, had the British government not agreed to supply the Regency with a subsidy of £600,000 in 1812, it is hard to see how the struggle could have been continued at all. Even in the moment of victory, then, Cocks was writing, 'All will depend on the power with which we shall be entrusted [to make] the Spaniards what they are capable of being made . . . Drilled by us and led by us and mingled with us, no soldiers will be more formidable. Left to themselves, they will afford more proofs that . . . discipline is far superior to courage.'[17] In these circumstances, it is natural to assume that conciliating London would have been the foremost item on Spain's political agenda in the summer of 1812, and it is in consequence highly tempting to see the offer of the command-in-chief of the Spanish army that was suddenly made Wellington by the *cortes* on 22 September 1812 in this light. As a delighted Henry Wellesley wrote:

After the experience of four years there is no-one in Spain who believes that this country will be saved by the measures of this or any other government composed of Spaniards, and it is to the prevalence of this sentiment in the *cortes*, as much as the increasing confidence of the nation in the British army and in its commander that we are indebted for the sacrifice of those prejudices which existed to placing a foreigner at the head of the Spanish armies.[18]

Nothing could have been further from the truth, however. As we have already seen, ever since 1810 a traditionalist minority known as the *serviles* had been struggling to resist the *liberales*, but, until the ratification of the Constitution in March 1812, the use of ambiguous language and medieval precedent had generally given the latter the support of enough deputies to render a successful challenge unlikely. In the autumn of 1811, indeed, merely voicing support for the Princess of Brazil – the great hope of the *serviles* – had led to the arrest of the erstwhile regent, Lardizábal, and the suspension of the entire Council of State. With the Constitution out of the way, however, the *cortes* could not avoid confronting major issues on which there was no possibility of compromise or obfuscation, the most notable of these being the position of the Church. At the same time, as a constituent body only, the *cortes* should in theory have dissolved itself in favour of an 'ordinary' assembly, but the liberal leaders insisted on keeping it in being, on the grounds that the new political system had not been fully elaborated. In consequence, passions in chamber and press became more inflamed by the day, matters finally being plunged into crisis by the disastrous Spanish defeat at Castalla on 21 July 1812, which for a variety of reasons raised the possibility that the Regency might have to be re-modelled.* Fearing at the very least the formation of a regency of a less docile cast, if not one headed by the Princess of Brazil, the liberals decided to launch a pre-emptive strike. For this, however, British support was essential, and to this end the Asturian deputy, Andrés Angel de la Vega, a moderate who had been one of the emissaries dispatched to Britain in 1808, paid a call on Henry Wellesley. Informed that Vega and his friends were anxious for his opinion, the ambassador replied that he would not back any government that did not immediately appoint a commander-in-chief and give him the power necessary to turn the Spanish army into an effective fighting force.

Well aware what was being hinted at, Vega returned the very next day with the news that a motion would shortly be introduced in the *cortes* appointing Wellington to the command of the Spanish armies, the liberals duly forcing this through in secret session in the face of only minimal opposition (the few objections came chiefly from Catalan deputies anxious at the threat British influence might pose to Catalonia's cotton industry). Yet there was more to this than meets the eye. Obsessed with the threat of military despotism suggested by the arrogance and ostentation favoured by many generals, the liberals hedged the appointment round with a series of qualifications that prohibited Wellington from altering the structure of the army or exercising any control over the civilian authorities. Also present in the monstrously tortured language of the actual decree passed by the *cortes*, meanwhile, was the strong implication that Wellington should operate at the orders of the Regency rather than acting as a free agent: no more would the British be able – from the Spanish point of view – to take flight whenever it suited them, added weight being lent to this point by claims that the loss of Andalucía had been the result of Wellington's refusal to lend the Junta Central military support in the autumn of 1809.

The idea of Spanish control being one that filled Wellington with horror – the thing he was most determined to guard against, he wrote, was 'the

---

* In brief, the beaten commander was the brother of Enrique O'Donnell, who had been rewarded for his exploits in Catalonia with the title Conde del Abisbal and a place in the Infantado regency. Believed to be a supporter of their cause, his presence had reassured the liberals, but press criticism of the battle led him to resign in outrage. Meanwhile, Villavicencio was also on the verge of quitting and Infantado thoroughly discredited.

pretension which the Spanish government might form to direct the operations of the war in consequence of this appointment'[19] – this was a recipe
for disaster, and all the more so as the decree failed to give him the powers
that both he and Henry Wellesley were convinced were necessary if the
command was to be of any value.* A clash, in short, was inevitable, the
only reason that it was postponed being that Vega was blithely promising
that the *cortes* would readily pass any amendments that Wellington might
think necessary. From politics, however, we must now return to the battlefield, particularly as events at the front were materially to affect the chances
of Wellington getting what he wanted.

With Wellington in occupation of Salamanca, Valladolid and Madrid,
and the French falling back on Burgos and Valencia, a serious problem
threatened to develop. The more that the French were driven back, the
more they were able to concentrate their forces, and the more that they
concentrated their forces the more they were able to outmatch those of the
Anglo-Portuguese. Meanwhile, it was clear that little could be expected
from the Spanish regular armies beyond the rather limited assistance that
Wellington was receiving from them as things stood, and, further, that the
guerrillas could not be counted on to halt a French counter-offensive. The
Anglo-Portuguese forces in the south could now be brought up to Madrid,
true, but even so Wellington would be able to field no more than 60,000
men. This figure might perhaps be increased to 70,000 through the incorpor-
ation of such Spanish troops who were ready to take the field in central
Spain, but the Armies of the Centre, Portugal and the South – all of which
had now been freed from garrison duty – alone amounted to over 100,000
men, whilst there was no guarantee that further forces might not be obtained
from Suchet and Caffarelli. Splendid though Wellington's forces were, these
were not odds of a sort to be faced in the depths of central Spain, and all
the more so as the French were in a position to launch a concentric attack.
Yet the British commander could hardly abandon Madrid in favour, say, of
his old position at Salamanca. This dilemma was only resolved by Clausel
suddenly moving west to re-occupy Valladolid with a view to rescuing the
beleaguered garrisons of Astorga, Toro and Zamora. Presented with a

---

* As Wellington had written earlier in the year, 'I consider troops that are neither fed, nor
paid, nor disciplined (and they cannot be disciplined . . . unless they are paid and fed) to be
dangerous only to themselves when collected in large bodies . . . I never will voluntarily
command troops who cannot and will not obey, and therefore I am not desirous of having
anything to say to the command of the Spanish troops till I shall see the means provided for
their food and pay, and till I shall be certain that the regular issue of these has been the effect
of introducing among them a regular system of subordination and discipline.'[20]

wonderful opportunity to lessen the odds against him before Joseph and Soult could arrange a counter-offensive in New Castile, on 31 August Wellington therefore moved north.

With the British commander were just 21,000 men, the rest of his forces being left to hold Madrid where they were eventually joined by Hill's corps, and the division which had been stationed at Cádiz, both of which were still coming up from the south. Necessary for political reasons, this left Wellington dangerously short-handed, but it was hoped that the want might be made up by the Sixth Army, which had just forced Astorga to surrender, and was therefore in a position to fall on Clausel from the north-west. In dividing his forces in this fashion, however, Wellington was taking a serious risk, and, what is more, one that he well knew might not come off. As he had written to Bathurst on 18 August:

I do not expect much from the exertions of the Spaniards . . . They cry 'viva' and are very fond of us . . . but they are in general the most incapable of all the nations that I have known, the most vain, and at the same time the most ignorant . . . I am afraid that the utmost we can hope for is to teach them how to avoid being beat.[21]

As for the siege of Astorga, the fact that the French had been overcome could not disguise the fact that it had been a considerable embarrassment: for want of sufficient artillery, the Sixth Army had been forced to rely on mining, but operations had gone so badly that, faced by the prospect that he might run out of food before the garrison did, a desperate Castaños had eventually written to the governor offering him any terms he cared to propose in exchange for his surrender. In retrospect, it would therefore probably have been better to risk the censure of Cádiz and strike north with a much larger force, for it was, after all, fairly clear that Soult and Joseph would be unlikely to be able to march on Madrid for at least a month. As it was, indeed, the scheme miscarried, for the Sixth Army was slow to appear and even then came forward with less than half its disposable strength. In consequence, having first rescued his two surviving garrisons, Clausel was allowed to evacuate Valladolid and fall back on the Ebro without a fight. Hardly surprisingly, British fury knew no bounds. As Sydenham wrote:

Lord Wellington declares that he has not yet met with any Spanish officer who can be made to comprehend the nature of a military operation. If the Spanish officers had knowledge and vanity like the French, or ignorance without vanity as our allies in India, something might be done with them. But they unite the greatest ignorance with the most insolent and intractible vanity. They can therefore be neither persuaded, nor instructed, nor forced to do their duty.[22]

To add insult to injury, meanwhile, the Spanish forces consisted of 'about 10,000 men badly clothed and equipped and still worse in discipline'.[23]

In the circumstances, it would be wrong to be too hard on the Spaniards, for Wellington had known all along that he could not rely on them and in fact had had no need to do so And they certainly cannot be blamed for what followed. The offensive having failed, Wellington's best move would have been to return to Madrid in the hope that one or other of the two 'army groups' facing him might prove incautious and afford him the opportunity of a crushing blow. Instead, however, he continued his advance until he came to Burgos, which was currently being pillaged unmercifully by swarms of irregulars who had rushed into the city in the wake of the retreating French. Clausel having left a garrison in the castle overlooking the famous cathedral, Wellington then sat down to besiege the place as the only means of salvaging something from what would otherwise have been a completely wasted march.

Taking the castle, however, proved beyond the capacities of Wellington's forces. The troops selected for the offensive in Old Castile were not the cream of the Anglo-Portuguese army; the Allies had very few heavy guns, no trained sappers and only a small number of engineer officers; the governor of the castle, a General Dubreton, was another Philippon; the garrison was both very strong and composed entirely of veteran troops; and the castle, which was amply supplied with food and munitions, occupied a dominant position on a steep hill and had been reinforced by a variety of earthworks. Put all this together, and the result was entirely predictable. Wellington's troops quickly stormed the fortress' main outwork, albeit at very heavy cost. As Mills remembered:

The redoubt was ordered to be stormed. The Forty-Second, as the strongest regiment in the division, was selected for the purpose, supported by the light companies of the Highland brigade and General Pack's Portuguese brigade. At eight o'clock they advanced . . . but the Portuguese, who thought to raise their spirits by it, began to shout . . . and thereby drew the enemy's fire upon them. The Forty-Second advanced gallantly and planted their ladders which proved to be too short, and after persisting for some time they were beat back. They returned again, and with Major Cocks and his light . . . companies got in . . . scrambling over without ladders.[24]

However, an attempt to escalade the main line of defences was beaten back. To quote the same observer again:

Our men got the ladders up with some difficulty under a heavy fire . . . but were unable to get to the top. Hall of the Third Regiment [of Foot Guards] who mounted first was knocked down. Fraser tried and was shot in the knee. During the whole of this time [the French] kept up a constant fire from the top of the wall and threw down bags of gunpowder and large stones. At last, having been twenty-five minutes in the ditch and not seeing anything of the other parties, [our men] retired, having lost half their numbers in killed and wounded . . . Thus ended the attack, which was almost madness to attempt.[25]

Thanks to the inadequacy of their siege artillery – just three eighteen pounders, which, after one had a trunnion knocked off, were nicknamed Thunder, Lightning and Nelson – the Allies were then forced to try the extremely time-consuming expedient of mining. However, the first mine was not pushed far enough under the defences with the result that its detonation caused only limited damage, the troops sent in to seize the walls in its wake making no headway. A second mine was more successful and nightfall on 4 October therefore found British infantry ensconced in a large breach in the outer wall. After that, however, progress was minimal. Heavy rain, mounting casualties and growing demoralisation among the troops made digging the fresh trenches that were required inside the *enceinte* very slow, whilst two of the only three Allied heavy guns that were of any use were badly damaged. Nor did it help that the French launched repeated sorties that resulted in desperate fighting, particularly on 7 October. Thus:

Aided by the most tremendous fire which I ever saw of cannon, they succeeded in driving us out . . . but a small party of about thirty of our men maintained themselves behind a breastwork, the enemy being on the near-side and stabbing at [them] with bayonets, and from their spirited conduct the work was regained . . . An officer on our side was wounded . . . and our whole loss . . . about 120.[26]

Only on 18 October, then, was an assault deemed feasible. Once again there was fierce fighting:

Our party was to escalade the wall in front. Burgess ran forward with thirty men, [and] Walpole and myself followed with fifty each . . . A most tremendous fire opened upon us from every part which took us in front and rear. They poured down fresh men, and ours kept falling down into the ditch, dragging and knocking down others. We were so close that they fairly put their muskets into our faces, and we pulled one of their men through an embrasure. Burgess was killed and Walpole severely wounded. We had hardly any men left on the top, and at last we gave way. How we got over the palisades I know not . . . the fire was tremendous: shot, shell, grape, musketry, large stones, hand grenades and every missile weapon were used against us.[27]

The retreat was due to too few men being employed in the attack. Such mismanagement, indeed, had been a feature throughout. As Aitchison complained, for example, 'It appears to me that to ensure success men should have confidence in themselves, which in all desperate cases is to be acquired by numerical superiority', whilst, as D'Urban noted, the problem was compounded by the habit of employing small parties of men from different regiments: 'Corps [i.e. complete units] and not detachments . . . should always be used for services . . . of more than ordinary danger. In the former there is a common feeling of honour and shame. The officers know the men, the men the officers. In the latter the very contrary of all this is the case, and the effects correspond with the causes.'[28]

Frustrating though the failure of this assault was, for three more days siege operations continued. Had Wellington but known it, however, he was in deadly danger, for Caffarelli had temporarily vanquished the guerrillas of the Basque provinces and brought up a considerable field force with which to aid Clausel. In all, indeed, supported only by 11,000 men of the Sixth Army, the 24,000 Anglo-Portuguese troops at Burgos were threatened by some 50,000 Frenchmen. What finally tipped the balance, however, was the arrival on 21 October of news from Madrid to the effect that Joseph and Soult were advancing into La Mancha in overwhelming force. The game was up, and there was clearly nothing for it but to retreat. It was, however, a distinctly sullen army that took the road. Officers and men alike were exhausted, whilst casualties in the siege had amounted to over 2,000. Not surprisingly, therefore, there was much grumbling. 'I have not been in the habit much of questioning the conduct of our chief', wrote Aitchison, 'even when it differed from what I expected, but . . . it appears in this instance to be extremely impolitic, not to say most wantonly reprehensible.'[29]

For a variety of reasons, the news of the French advance in the south undoubtedly came as a great surprise to Wellington, who had assumed, first, that the autumn rains would block the roads in La Mancha, and, second, that the expeditionary force at Alicante and the Spanish Second, Third and Fourth Armies would between them ensure that the French could only send a moderate force against Madrid. In all this he was disappointed. Though Burgos was deluged, in central and eastern Spain the rains had been paltry by comparison. In the Levante the Allied forces were simply not strong enough to do more than ensure that Suchet did not add any forces to those of Soult and Joseph. And in the south the Fourth Army, which had been, at Wellington's request, ordered to cross the Sierra Morena and take up a position that would threaten the flank of any force moving from Valencia on Madrid, had failed to put in an appearance. Between them possessed of some 60,000 men, the Armies of the Centre and the South were therefore soon heading for the capital.

In British accounts, chief blame for this situation is usually laid at the door of the Fourth Army, but this is unfair. The force involved could bring up at best 16,000 men, and was simply too weak to do more than win the defenders of the capital a little time. That said, however, the behaviour of its commander, General Ballesteros, is hardly worthy of praise. Recently elevated to the command of the Fourth Army from that of his old division, the Spanish general had over the past three years gained a reputation as a fighter, certainly, but also as an officer who was bombastic, bullying and much inclined to fall out with the civilian authorities. A skilful self-publicist, he had quickly won the adulation of the liberal press, the latter having been delighted that a man forged in the revolution should have gained such renown (in 1808 a retired infantry officer employed in the state tobacco monopoly, Ballesteros had been promoted straight to the rank of brigadier by the Junta of Asturias). So successful was Ballesteros, indeed, that by the summer of 1812 he had become the centre of something of a personality cult. Mobbed by cheering crowds whenever he passed through Cádiz, he was presented with a large sum raised by public subscription for the support of his army, whilst the press outdid itself in singing his praises. For example:

> Ballesteros, honour of Spain,
> Warlike bolt of lightning that terrifies the Frenchman,
> The glory of victory and the crown of green laurel follows you . . .
> In the annals of the history of Spain
> Your great name should be immortal,
> For you liberated Andalucía
> From the lash of the infidel French.[30]

This extravagant praise was scarcely merited, for, as one British officer who was for a while attached to his forces noted:

Of all the unworthies produced by Spain during this war (and God knows there were plenty of them), this man was the greatest impostor and charlatan . . . He certainly kept a body of men together, but they proved only a curse to the inhabitants . . . [and] appeared to be composed of the débris of defeated and dispersed armies, men who would not fight, yet reassembled to obtain food because they were too idle or too dissipated to work. Whenever the French retired, the Spaniards followed, composing and reciting songs of victory, but at too respectable a distance to disquiet the enemy. If the French halted or attempted to pursue them, they soon found how vain was the undertaking . . . Ballesteros fought some actions, but they were all forced upon him ... and he was invariably beaten. His army never undertook the initiative in any operation that might entail contact with his adversaries.[31]

Even if this condemnation was a little exaggerated, it is clear, first, that the calls that were beginning to be heard for Ballesteros to be appointed commander-in-chief or even dictator were ridiculous, and, second, that the confidential circular informing the commanders of the various Spanish armies of Wellington's appointment came as a most unwelcome surprise to the Asturian general, who had been sitting on his laurels at Granada. With predictable violence, indeed, on 24 October he dispatched an open letter to the Minister of War, Carvajal, in which he made a great show of his patriotic services, claimed that Spain did not need foreign aid, denounced Wellington's appointment as a national humiliation, accused Britain of attempting to subvert Spain's independence, and threatened to resign unless the offending decree was immediately rescinded. Distributed throughout Patriot Spain, this document was little less than a call to arms, but in thus 'pronouncing' against the government Ballesteros had seriously miscalculated. His fellow commanders regarding him with a mixture of jealousy and scorn, they had no desire to follow his lead, and still less so in a cause which made such little sense. No support, then, came from the rest of the army, whilst the Asturian commander was even deserted by his own subordinates, the result being that the Regency had no difficulty in procuring his arrest.

In theory, the rebel general should then have been packed off to the penal colony of Ceuta, but he succeeded in delaying his departure for some weeks on the grounds of illness whilst in the process stirring up an immense press controversy. This, however, will be examined in its proper place (cf. p. 422), Ballesteros' revolt having exactly coincided with military nemesis. Split into two as they were, the Anglo-Portuguese forces had no chance of stopping either the 50,000 men of Clausel and Caffarelli in Old Castile or the 60,000 men of Soult and Joseph in La Mancha. United in and around Madrid, Wellington's men might just have been able to smash one of the two foes before rushing north or south to deal with the other, but as things were the only option was flight. During the night of 21 October, then, the siege of Burgos was abandoned, the troops involved proceeding to fall back in the direction of Valladolid amidst a series of sharp rearguard actions at such places as Venta del Pozo and Villadrigo. Initially, the plan was to make a stand on the line of the River Carrión forty miles to the north-east of Valladolid in the hope of giving Hill's corps time to get up from Madrid, but on 25 October the French defeated the Spanish forces holding Palencia and secured its bridge before it could be blown up, and within a few days

Wellington had in consequence lost Valladolid and been forced to retire behind the Duero. Even more might have been achieved by the French, but further difficulties were averted by elements of Mendizábal's Seventh Army which, in the absence of so many troops from the Army of the North, succeeded in re-capturing Bilbao. With his hold on the western parts of the Basque provinces reduced to the isolated garrisons of Santoña and Guetaria, Caffarelli was left with no option but to turn back, whereupon Clausel called a halt.

Thanks to the storm of Bilbao, Wellington had been saved from immediate disaster, but the advance of Joseph and Soult meant that the Allies remained in some danger. To the south-east, Hill had been preparing to fight the French from behind the line of the Jarama and Henares. On the very eve of battle, however, he received an order from Wellington telling him that he must retreat immediately. As a result 30 October saw his troops heading north-westwards for the Sierra de Guadarrama. A sharp rearguard action just north of Aranjuez notwithstanding, Madrid had to be left to its fate. It was a dismal scene. Amid general panic and despair, the Allies blew up the fortifications and magazines of the Retiro, whilst the *populacho* engaged in an orgy of looting. As for the British, already harassed by biting cold, they fell into despondency. As the artillery officer, Webber, remembered, 'I never recollect on any occasion . . . being more melancholy and depressed than in passing by the Puente de Toledo, and giving up Madrid to the plunder and wanton cruelty of the enemy. I would willingly have lost a limb in battle to have saved it, and I know every man felt the same sentiments.'[32]

Sullen, frustrated and much inclined to blame the Spaniards for their ills, the men took out their anger on the populace, one early casualty being the town of Valdemoro. 'Here a scene of the most disgraceful character ensued,' wrote Swabey. 'It was at the time of year when the new wine was in open vats and there were many at this place. Numbers of men fell out of the ranks and surrounded them, and I saw with my own eyes many actually drowned in the vats. They were bailing out the liquor with their caps to their comrades till overcome as much by the fumes of the wine as what they drank, they sank down and expired in their glory.'[33] Drunkenness was not the only crime committed by the soldiers, however. To quote Bell, 'Many peasants lay dead by the roadside, murdered . . . The old trade was going on, killing and slaying, and capturing our daily bread.'[34] As Long admitted, 'All this . . . has made our line of retreat as vandalic as any Frenchified Spaniards could wish, and it has distressed me not a little to witness it. The poor peasants have indeed abundant reason to be heartily sick of both friends and foes.'[35]

Fortunately for the British, perhaps, no attempt was made to press Hill's retreat and by 6 November his troops had pulled back so far to the west that there was no longer any danger of them being cut off from Wellington. With Hill safe, the latter was able to resume his retreat in turn, and the entire Anglo-Portuguese army was therefore soon converging on Salamanca, where it eventually took up a strong defensive position covering the city against any attack from the east and south-east. Wellington was now safe enough, but even so the campaign was far from over. Thus, Soult and Joseph had joined up with Clausel in their turn, and on 14 November 1812 their combined forces struck across the River Tormes well to the south of Salamanca in a repeat of Marmont's disastrous advance of 22 July. This time, however, there was no chance of fighting, with the result that the Allies were soon falling back in the direction of Ciudad Rodrigo. There followed a few days that many British soldiers remembered as being amongst the most miserable in the entire war: 'The Corunna [sic] retreat,' wrote Wood, 'from what I experienced of it . . . will bear no comparison.'[36]

Amidst torrential rain, the Allies had to retreat along roads that were, in Kincaid's words, 'nearly knee-deep in a stiff mud into which no man could thrust his foot with the certainty of having a shoe at the end of it when he pulled it out again'.[37] Still worse, an administrative mistake led to most of the troops losing contact with their supply trains, whilst, thanks to a lack of dry wood, there was no means of cooking the slaughtered livestock that was the only food to be had. The unfortunate men involved, then, had to scavenge for acorns, but even where better rations could be issued, things were little better. Typical enough were the experiences of the Connaught Rangers on 17 November:

Each man received his portion of the quivering flesh, but, before any fires could be relighted, the order for march arrived, and the . . . soldiers were obliged either to throw away the meat or put it with their biscuit into their haversacks . . . In a short time the wet meat completely destroyed the bread, which became perfect paste, and the blood which oozed from the undressed beef . . . gave so bad a taste to the bread that many could not eat it. Those who did were in general attacked with violent pains in their bowels, and the want of salt brought on dysentery.[38]

To the horrors of the retreat, then, was added sickness, and this, together with want of forage for the horses, produced sights that easily rivalled those found on the road to La Coruña. 'I never saw so many dead animals in so short a distance,' wrote Aitchison. 'Independent of these, however, our route was sufficiently marked by the bodies of men who had died from wounds or sickness, and others left to become prisoners . . . from want of means to bring them off.'[39]

Under these pressures, many units went to pieces, though it ought to be stressed that the Portuguese and Spanish soldiers were no better behaved than their British counterparts. To quote Wheeler, 'It is impossible for any army to have given themselves up to more dissipation and everything that is bad as did our army. The conduct of some men would have disgraced savages, drunkenness had prevailed to such a frightful extent that I have often wondered how it was that a great part of our army were not cut off.'[40] The answer to Wheeler's question is that, conducted only by the forces of Marshal Soult, the French pursuit was none too vigorous: Wellington, indeed, had only to make a show of resistance for his opponents to draw rein. Yet even so over 6,000 men were killed, wounded or missing. Amongst the prisoners was Sir Edward Paget, who had just come out to act as Wellington's second-in-command and was seized by some French horsemen in a minor skirmish on 17 November, whilst almost one third of Wellington's British troops were sick. It was an unhappy end to an unhappy campaign.

Except in Catalonia (where the First Army was still doing what it could to harass the occupying forces), the return of the Allied army to Ciudad Rodrigo brought field operations to an end for 1812. Most importantly, however, Espoz y Mina and other guerrilla leaders continued to harass the French. Fresh from helping to cover the retreat to Ciudad Rodrigo, for example, on 28 December Julián Sánchez defeated a column that had been sent out to requisition supplies at Vitigudino, whilst on 29 January El Empecinado routed a squadron of *juramentado* cavalry at Valdetorres de Jarama. However, by far the fiercest fighting took place in Navarre and northern Aragón. From the month of August onwards Espoz y Mina had been drawing the noose tighter and tighter around the beleaguered French garrison of Pamplona, and the absence of so much of the Army of the North in Old Castile had allowed him to devote more and more men to repelling the sorties of its increasingly desperate governor, whilst at the same time extending his operations into Guipúzcoa on the one hand and Aragón on the other. Thus, on 23 November troops led by Espoz y Mina himself ambushed a French convoy near Ayerbe, the same forces going on to attack Huesca four days later. Also active in Aragón, albeit further south, were the forces of Durán and Gayán, the latter forcing the evacuation of Calatayud and Almunia, capturing the garrison of Borja, and defeating a small enemy column at Herrera.

Coming back from the Duero, Caffarelli therefore found much of his command in chaos, and it was only through hard fighting that he was able to relieve his battered strongholds, clear away the guerrillas from the Basque coast and the main road to France, and reprovision Santoña. Even this much was not achieved in Aragón, however, the French hold in this area being reduced to a series of isolated garrisons dotted along the roads which linked Zaragoza with the French frontier, Navarre and Valencia. Indeed, throughout the Basque provinces, Navarre and Aragón the situation was bleak in the extreme. Increasingly numerous, well organised and well disciplined, the guerrillas were now strong enough to defeat the ever weaker flying columns that were all the desperately overstretched French could send against them (Espoz y Mina alone could now field nine battalions of infantry and two regiments of cavalry) and pen the invaders into their strongpoints. At the same time, the latter could often now be taken, for Espoz y Mina, Durán and other commanders had received a number of pieces of mountain artillery brought in by sea. Morale in the burgeoning guerrilla forces was therefore high. Assured by a grip on the countryside that on the French frontier was so tight they could even impose customs duties, their pay and supply were in good shape. Faced by precisely the opposite situation, the invaders, by contrast, were in despair, their garrisons therefore being reduced not just by casualties but by desertion. As Napoleon himself wrote, 'There is not a moment to lose . . . Tell [the king] that . . . things will turn out badly unless he puts greater activity and movement into the direction of affairs.'[41]

Crucial as all this was, for the time being, however, we must return to the aftermath of the retreat from Burgos. Both sides now went into winter quarters. For the Anglo-Portuguese army, this meant settling down in a series of towns and villages in eastern Beira. As for the French, meanwhile, the Army of Portugal occupied eastern León and western Old Castile, the Army of the Centre the district around Madrid, and the Army of the South northern La Mancha. Despite Wellington's retreat, 1812 therefore remained a good year as far as the Allies were concerned: after all, Andalucía, Extremadura and Asturias all remained in their hands. This, however, did not prevent the winter from witnessing the outbreak of fresh disputes between Wellington and the Spaniards. Thus, according to the British commander, the failure of his operations in the autumn of 1812 had been entirely the fault of the Spaniards. Their armies had proved of little worth; their commanders had proved either careless and dilatory, or, still worse, obstructive and rebellious; their administration had failed to deliver either fresh soldiers or adequate supplies; and their politicians had remained obsessed by questions that seemingly had little bearing on the conduct of the war. As for the guerrillas, meanwhile, close acquaintance had suggested that in many cases they were little more than a rabble of bandits and adventurers that were militarily useless and interested in nothing but pillage. Everything had in consequence been left to the Anglo-Portuguese army, which had ended up fighting the French all but alone. Thus:

My plan was to bring Ballesteros upon the left flank and rear of Soult's march . . . If this game had been well played, it would have answered my purpose . . . Had I any reason to expect that it would have been well-played? Certainly not. I have never known the Spaniards do anything, much less do anything well. Ballesteros has sometimes drawn the attention of a division or two for a moment, but that is all. Everything else you see and read is false and rotten. A few rascals called guerrillas attack one quarter of their numbers and sometimes succeed and sometimes not, but, as for any regular operation, I have not known of such a thing and successful in the whole course of the war.[42]

This critique was vociferously echoed by many British observers. To quote Swabey, for example:

The fundamental cause of our giving up Madrid I attribute . . . to the total abandonment by everyone of the slightest hope that the Spaniards will ever do anything to help themselves. The trial was fairly made during our possession of Madrid. The imbecility of their government, but more than all their national vanity, blinded them to the necessity of active and efficient measures and rendered the opportunity useless. The moment of action whilst the country was in possession of their government was lost. They were then too short-sighted to fancy anything further necessary, they failed in their engagements to Lord Wellington, and lost their independence for ever . . . In stating an opinion of the regular Spanish troops already in the field, it may be said that the same causes render them collectively useless. They will not face the enemy, and, excepting at Zaragoza and Gerona, they never have done so. They are deficient in officers, and the leading feature in those they have is presumption. So great is this national fault that it extends to all ranks . . . For want of co-operation with the civil authorities, a large army of Spaniards cannot be supplied without plundering . . . the inhabitants: this is carried on without regard to humanity, and starvation is not the only evil accruing from it.[43]

Much of this criticism, of course, was unfair. Whatever Wellington may have seen in the liberated territories, Espoz y Mina and his fellows had elsewhere contained many troops that would otherwise have been available for operations against his forces, whilst, for all the mediocrity of Castaños, the folly of José O'Donnell, and the rebelliousness of Ballesteros, even the Spanish regulars had played a far greater role in affairs than he was inclined to admit. Considering, too, that Wellington himself had repeatedly stated that he did not believe that the Spanish armies could save him, it is simply absurd to blame them for the retreat from Burgos. Spanish failings had not helped, certainly, but the Anglo-Portuguese forces simply did not possess the strength to fight the sort of armies that the French could field once they had evacuated Extremadura and Andalucía. Still worse, the one chance of success in the autumn of 1812 was thrown away by Wellington when he got bogged down in a pointless siege for which he lacked the necessary resources. To say that Wellington should not have attacked Burgos is to miss the point, however. Quite clearly, the Spanish regular army had somehow to be rendered fit for large-scale regular operations, for otherwise the Allies could not hope to expel the French from the Peninsula. As Wellington himself admitted, 'It is obvious that we cannot expect to save the Peninsula by military efforts unless we can bring forward the Spaniards in some shape or other.'[44]

No sooner, then, had Wellington returned to the Portuguese frontier than he was informing Liverpool that he intended to travel to Cádiz to see what use could be made of his newfound command of the Spanish armies. According to Henry Wellesley, the powers that he required would be granted him without difficulty, but such a view was extremely over-optimistic, Spanish confidence in the British having been shaken to its very foundations. Once again, the redcoats had marched into Spain and once again they had fled before the enemy, and this time without even the saving grace of a Talavera, an Albuera or a Fuentes de Oñoro. Once again, the soldiers had behaved in an abominable fashion. And, once again, it was the Spaniards who were abandoned and blamed for everything. Insult was added to injury, meanwhile, by the British being seemingly bent on ruining the Spanish economy. Dark mutterings, for example, had been heard at the fact that amongst the installations blown up by the British in Madrid was its noted but hopelessly uneconomic royal porcelain factory (the fact that it had been reduced to a mere shell and pressed into service as a powder magazine deterred no one). At the same time, the American question had also flared up again. For reasons which have already been explained, ever since the outbreak of the *criollo* revolutions Britain's policy had been to reconcile the contending parties, to which end she had eventually proposed that a joint commission should mediate between the two sides. Thanks to Spanish recalcitrance, negotiations had dragged on interminably, but by September 1812 the British government felt that it could wait no longer. Only four days after Wellington's appointment, Henry Wellesley had therefore written to the Spanish Secretary of State, Ignacio de la Pezuela, claiming that the failure to make any progress was not only threatening the Allied cause with bankruptcy but throwing up the danger that the rebels might seek support from France. The key obstacle having been the refusal of the Spanish authorities to grant the colonies full commercial freedom and allow the mediation to be extended to the whole of the empire, Wellesley made a number of concessions on these issues, but, as the Spaniards saw full well, they were still one way or the other being expected to allow their colonies to trade freely with the British. Whether this was likely to produce peace in America was debatable, but what was certain was that Britain's commercial interests would be advanced and those of Spain severely damaged, the fact being that Wellesley was laying himself open to charges of blackmail and duplicity.

With matters in this state, the Ballesteros controversy – the first news, incidentally, that public opinion had of Wellington's appointment* – did not help in the slightest. In manifesto after manifesto, the Asturian general claimed that he was defending the liberty of Spain against foreign domination, protested his innocence and demanded a fair hearing, whilst he was joined in his protests by a variety of pamphleteers who lauded his patriotism, accused the British of being motivated solely by their own national interests, questioned Wellington's integrity, denounced the decree of 22 September as damaging to the morale of army and populace alike, and even denied the need for British aid. Even more insidious was the pamphlet entitled *Vallesteros* (contemporaries spelt the name as frequently with a 'V' as they did with a 'B'):

Whilst noting that the value of what we would have to give them could well be doubled were the British to have control of our armies, let us set aside for a moment . . . the compensation which they are certain to demand for the greatest sacrifices of every sort which they have made for us . . . The British would be very foolish if they did not take advantage of the fact that, whilst still obtaining the same results, they could reduce the amount of blood they had to shed by drawing on ours. Putting it another way, we would be the first when it came to danger and the last when it came to glory.[45]

Even though these claims were received with a storm of ridicule by other writers, the seeds of doubt had been sown: there were, for example, shouts of 'Viva Ballesteros!' at a parade in Córdoba, whilst the governor of Ceuta treated him as an honoured guest.

---

* Offered the command on 22 September 1812, Wellington had insisted on referring the matter to London for approval. Until an answer was received on 21 November, the matter therefore had to be kept secret.

Muttering was soon to become mutiny: indeed, had Ballesteros acted a few weeks later, the outcome of the crisis could have been very different. Even before Wellington had arrived in Cádiz, it was made clear that what he wanted was not just to exercise the command of the various Spanish forces scattered around the Peninsula, but also to have the power to intervene in the structure and organisation of the army itself, and, above all, ensure that the troops were paid, supplied and kept up to strength. What all this boiled down to was on the one hand making him a generalissimo in the style of Godoy and on the other subordinating the civil authority to its military counterpart. Utterly scornful of the Spaniards' ability to manage their own affairs, only thus, he felt, could a force of troops be enabled to take the field that was of a strength sufficient to prevent any repetition of the setbacks of the autumn of 1812. As he wrote:

We must not conceal from ourselves that there is but little authority of any description whatever in the provinces which have been occupied by the enemy, and even that little depends on the exercise of military power. It is vain to expect a gentleman called an Intendent will exercise the power to realise the resources of the country . . . without the assistance of a military force, which military force in the existing state of the army will destroy more than its effects would produce . . . I am aware that it is wrong in principle to invest military men with civil powers, but when the country is in danger that must be adopted which will tend most directly to save it . . . whatever may be the constitutional principles invaded by those measures.[46]

First outlined in a letter to the Minister of War, José María de Carvajal, on 4 December 1812, Wellington's demands were therefore dramatic. Setting aside the obvious provision that only his headquarters should have the right to communicate with the Spanish field armies, he asked, first, that he should have control of all promotions and appointments; second, that he should have the power to purge the officer corps; third, that he should have control of the military budget; fourth, that the number of field armies should be greatly reduced in the interests of economy; and, fifth, that provincial and local government alike should be subordinated to the army's Captains General. In military terms, all this was fair enough. The uncontrolled expansion of the army in 1808 had produced an officer corps that was much too big for the number of troops that Patriot Spain was actually able to field. As for the civil authorities, the autumn of 1812 had shown that in the current circumstances they were all but helpless when it came to enforcing conscription and taxation. Yet what to Wellington was a matter of common sense to the Spaniards was something else altogether. The supporters of the appointment were still thinking in terms of Wellington being given no more than command of the Spanish field armies whilst in effect being subjected to the authority of the Spanish government. Already under constant threat, the Regency now found that it was to be stripped of the control of much of its revenue, deprived of much patronage and prevented from having any say in the conduct of military operations. When the British commander arrived in Cádiz on 24 December 1812, he was therefore confronted by determined opposition, shrouded though this was in much obsequious language. In this, moreover, the Regency received the support of not just the rag-bag of dissidents who had rallied to Ballesteros, but even a number of leading liberals.

At first sight, this is a little surprising: the liberals, after all, had taken the leading role in Wellington's appointment. Yet in fact many of them were hostile to any extension of British influence. Closely connected with the mercantile community in Cádiz, they had no desire to see any concessions to the American rebels. Nor did it help that Wellington showed a marked propensity to associate with figures whom the liberals had some reason to distrust: his chief Spanish confidant in the Burgos campaign, for example, was Miguel de Alava, an aristocratic officer who had originally proffered his allegiance to Joseph Bonaparte. One particular enemy was the radical newspaper editor, Alvaro Flórez Estrada. A leading light in the rising in Asturias in 1808, Flórez Estrada had been forced to flee his native province by La Romana's coup, only to find that Wellington and his brothers were backing the marquess against all-comers in the furore that followed. Suspicious of both military despotism and British support for *servilismo*, he was therefore horrified to discover the sorts of thing that Wellington was demanding. Very soon, then, Flórez Estrada's *Tribuno del Pueblo Español* was waxing furious at 'the monstrous and despotic union of political, civil and military authorities' that Wellington was proposing. Thus:

Is it credible that Lord Wellington, who was born . . . in a free country where such a union of authorities is entirely unknown . . . could have made such a proposal? How could a general destined to have the glory of bringing liberty to a nation which esteems it so much . . . have made so absurd a mistake? How could this illustrious soldier have persuaded himself that a plan so degrading to a nation that has sacrificed itself for its liberty . . . could have been . . . heard by the heroic Spanish people without the author of so impertinent . . . an idea having aroused their anger? Let us not deceive ourselves. The Spaniards have not only shed their blood so as not to suffer the yoke of Napoleon; they have shed it so as not to suffer any yoke at all.[47]

The British commander having given much offence by the arrogance of his behaviour – the natural acerbity of his temper had not been improved by a painful attack of lumbago and the long and difficult ride to Cádiz from his headquarters at Freneda – the Regency was encouraged by this show of defiance to dig in its heels, only to be informed that failure to comply would lead to Wellington's immediate resignation. At this, resistance collapsed. According to a decree of the *cortes* of 6 January 1813, the Regency was henceforward to be permitted to unite the Captain Generalcies with the command of the relevant field armies; the civil authorities to be subject to their military counterparts in all matters relating to the conduct of the war; every army to have an Intendent General to which the provincial Intendents – the Treasury officials responsible for the pay and supply of the army – would be answerable; and a fixed proportion of the revenue of each province devoted to the war effort. In addition to all this, meanwhile, the Regency agreed that all appointments were to be made at Wellington's recommendation; that the new commander-in-chief was to have the power to send away – though not to cashier – undesirable officers and determine the employment of the military budget; that all communication with the Spanish forces would henceforth be through his headquarters; that the Chief of the General Staff and the Inspectors-General of infantry and cavalry should all be attached to his person; that ninety per cent of revenue should henceforth be spent on the army; and that the Spanish armies should be reorganised more or less as Wellington wanted.*

Despite these concessions, Wellington remained unhappy, his chief complaint being that the civil authorities were still not totally under the control of the military. However, though convinced that the Spaniards could have gone further – as he pointed out, in Cádiz fears for the sanctity of the Constitution had not prevented the post of *jefe político* from being given to the military governor – he reluctantly decided that enough had been achieved to allow him to accept the command. The experiment had to be tried, certainly, but it is quite clear that Wellington was far from certain that there was much to be gained from it. Setting aside the enormous problems facing the army, the protests of Flórez Estrada had soon been resumed with even greater ferocity than before. According to the Asturian journalist, indeed, the powers were not only unconstitutional, but anti-constitutional: Spain had been placed under the tutelage of a foreign power and exposed to precisely the same sort of attack as she had suffered in 1808 and all for the sake of provisions that had no foundation in necessity, Flórez Estrada

---

* The First Army was left unchanged, the Second and Third Armies amalgamated as the Second Army, the Fourth Army renamed the Third Army, and the Fifth, Sixth and Seventh Armies united as the Fourth Army.

arguing that Spain's existing laws and procedures had only to be properly enforced for all to be well. These fulminations striking a general chord, it was not long before the entire alliance was coming under hostile scrutiny. For the *Diario Redactor de Sevilla*, for example, 'the most heroic people in the world' had not fought the French for four years to be made 'the slaves of Albion', the effect of Wellington's appointment having been 'to subordinate Spain to the will and caprice of a foreign general and government'.[48] Still more acerbic was the noted radical, Juan Romero Alpuente. As he wrote:

Offering Wellington so great a dignity . . . overlooks the . . . Nation's sons and gives preference in their despite to a foreigner, whilst extinguishing all enthusiasm, and with it the hope of victory . . . Opposed to justice and liberty, it also . . . risks us . . . becoming the slaves of the enemy who is defending us . . . It is true that British blood has been shed in Spain, but . . . for every drop . . . that has been shed, a sea of Spanish blood has been poured out . . . Let us open our eyes . . . and take France, our greatest enemy . . . as our point of comparison. Pretending to be friends, the French took over the greatest fortresses that defended our land frontiers . . . Pretending to be friends, the British have taken over the greatest fortresses that defend our coasts . . . The French . . . have stripped us of all the treasure that we did not manage to hide, and . . . the British have stripped us of all the rest. The French have not furthered either their agriculture, their industry, or their commerce at our expense, but the British have furthered each one . . . at the cost of our ruin. The French have not augmented their navy with our own, and yet our ships have either been reduced to rotting hulks or all but absorbed into the British fleet . . . The French have murdered thousands of our brothers . . . but in the midst of our shipwreck the British have cut off the very hands by which we were clinging to the land.[49]

So angry was the Minister of the Interior, García de León y Pizarro, meanwhile, that he resigned. ' "The war! The war!" everyone cried,' he wrote, 'and as a result the nation's honour was sacrificed in order to increase Britain's influence and glory at the cost of our own.'[50]

Wellington, then, was in for a rough ride, whilst his powers remained extremely circumscribed: the wholesale cull that had to be undertaken in the officer corps was quite beyond his means, for example. Nor did it help that in the course of his visit to Cádiz, news had arrived of Napoleon's defeat in Russia, for this seemed likely only to stiffen Spanish resistance: without Spain's example, many Spanish newspapers affirmed, Alexander I would never have stood firm. When he left Cádiz, then, Wellington did so with a sense of deep dissatisfaction. Yet there was no option but for him to make the best of what he had been offered, for the French armies continued to dwarf his own. Mina and the rest might do something to redress the balance, but, for all the havoc that they were wreaking in northern Spain, they could hardly be relied upon. In short, the French would be driven across the Pyrenees with the help of a revived Spanish army, or they would not be driven across the Pyrenees at all.

16

Vitoria

THE DEFEAT OF KING JOSEPH,
JANUARY–JUNE 1813

Yelling and cheering the men fell on the van. Smashing open its doors with their musket butts, they dropped back in astonishment, for the interior was packed to the brim with church plate, bags of coin, caskets and treasure chests. Forcing their way through the throng, two mounted officers initiated the scramble, one of them grabbing a large chalice and the other a likely looking casket. Around them, meanwhile, in the midst of a chaotic jumble of wagons, tents and animals of every sort, the wildest scenes were taking place. One man was standing on a wagon full of shoes and throwing them out to the crowd; another covered from head to foot in flour; another standing knee-deep in a pile of pillage and drunkenly inviting all and sundry to come and take their pick; another slaughtering a sheep with his bayonet; another running around with a shako full of Spanish dollars and offering anyone who would listen to him the whole lot for a handful of British guineas. To complete the scene there were crowds of drunken women dressing themselves in fine court dresses; girls in mock military attire begging for protection; and groups of soldiers fighting over the spoils, drinking themselves senseless, conducting impromptu auctions, or methodically stripping wagon after wagon. It was 21 June 1813.

Witnessed at the end of the battle of Vitoria, these scenes marked the end of the Bonaparte kingdom of Spain. Almost captured in the rout himself, Joseph was forced to flee his domains and the military power of the French in the Peninsula was decisively broken. It was arguably Wellington's greatest victory, and yet in many respects Vitoria was lost by the French as much as it was won by the Allies. Certainly, the invaders had been riding for a fall. By the end of 1812 the *grande armée* that had invaded Russia had ceased to exist. Unable to resist the oncoming Russians, the French also had to evacuate East Prussia and the Grand Duchy of Warsaw. With both Austria and Prussia likely to join his opponents, Napoleon responded by withdrawing more troops from Spain. In brief, every battalion of infantry, regiment of cavalry and battery of artillery was ordered to dispatch a certain number of picked men for the Imperial Guard, whilst in some cases these were accompanied by the cadres needed for the formation of duplicate units in France. Also taken were a few more foreign units, together with the three battalions of sailors who had been sent to assist with the siege of Cádiz. At some 20,000 men, the numbers were not overwhelming, but even so the occupying forces were left in a very difficult position. In much of the area that was supposedly under their control – the Basque provinces, Navarre, Aragón, Old Castile, La Mancha, the Levante and parts of Catalonia and León – their only presence was a few scattered garrisons, and even then their forces were very thinly spread. Trying to hold a front line that stretched in a great arc from Bilbao to Valencia, they were clearly almost as vulnerable to an assault as they had been in 1812, and, with hopes of victory abandoned, the best policy would therefore have been to have fallen back to the Ebro. But such a course of action was more than Napoleon could have stomached. If imperial prestige had always made retrenchment very difficult, in 1813 the political situation rendered it out of the question. With dozens of German princes nervously eyeing the oncoming Russian armies and wondering whether they ought to change sides, the last thing that was needed was a confession of weakness. In consequence, all that Napoleon would sanction was the evacuation of La Mancha and the transfer of the capital to Valladolid. This was better than nothing, especially as the defiant and unco-operative Soult was recalled to help the emperor in Germany, but even so the French remained badly overstretched. At the same time, of course, their prestige had suffered a great blow, for on 17 March *el rey intruso* duly left Madrid in the company of another vast caravan of refugees.

For Wellington, meanwhile, the chief feature of the early months of 1813 was his difficulties with the Portuguese and the Spaniards. Setting aside the frictions that were inevitably engendered by British control of the army and the continued misbehaviour of the rougher elements among the British troops, the chief problem with the former was financial. Thanks to the devastation of much of the country in 1810–11, Portugal was producing far less food than would normally have been the case, whilst the absence of so many men with the armed forces ensured that production was depressed still further. As Sir Augustus Frazer noted, for example:

It is true that these three days of our march have been holidays, but I have not yet observed one soul at work . . . I was assured today by the commandant that a whole estate of a countess of his acquaintance . . . [went] untilled last year for want of husbandmen, and that this want of men is severely felt all over the kingdom.[1]

In consequence, the Regency remained desperately short of money, not simply because tax revenue was low, but also because much revenue had to be spent on buying wheat from abroad. To cover the deficit, large quantities of paper money had been issued, but this had lost much of its value, whilst the promissory notes used by the army's commissaries to pay for their requisitioning were also all but worthless. In consequence, the Portuguese troops continued to suffer terribly from want of food, pay and clothing. As for the populace, they were becoming ever more alienated from the war effort, in which respect it did not help that the propertied classes remained unwilling to go to war, Frazer complaining that Coimbra was full of students who 'are said to learn nothing but how to be idle and to avoid joining the army'.[2] Heavily taxed – one estimate was that peasants were paying a third of their income – and largely destitute, the inhabitants also continued to be subject to the attacks of plundering British soldiers. The latter could sometimes be dealt with with grim efficiency: 'The Portuguese . . . considered it no greater crime to kill a British subject than one of their dogs. They generally carried a large knife concealed up the sleeve of their coat, and be assured they knew how to handle it.'[3] But even so the inhabitants had continued to flee from their homes with the result that the countryside was swarming with brigands. Of the district of Fronteiras, for instance, Schaumann remembered, 'Nobody dared to go about unarmed. Not a day passed without a murder or robbery being committed . . . The *juiz de fora*, for fear lest he should be shot in the street by one of the robbers in disguise, locked himself up in his own house, and would only take a walk if we went with him.'[4] So bad was the situation, indeed, that in some places the populace were in a state of near insurrection, as in the neighbourhood of São João da Pesqueira where Wellington informed Beresford that he had been forced to order General Cole 'to employ armed parties to protect his foragers . . . and to call upon the magistrates of the district . . . to perform their duty . . . in repressing the disposition of the people in that part of the country to oppose the military'.[5]

Portugal, then, was in much the same state as Spain, but the Regency was no more capable of restoring order than was its Spanish counterpart. The worst problems of law and order could be dealt with by the dispatch of troops, but finance was another matter. Consideration had been given to the possibility of selling off the estates of the Crown and the Church, but, amidst loud claims of bankruptcy, the project had been abandoned in favour of simply asking Britain for more money. According to an increasingly irate Wellington, however, the underlying problem was not shortage of resources at all. On the contrary, he argued, money was plentiful, and particularly so amongst the mercantile community, which had supposedly gained enormously from speculation and war profiteering. What was required was therefore the eradication of corruption, economies in the machinery of government, and an end to the propertied classes' evasion of their responsibilities (a ten per cent levy, for example, had been imposed on all commercial profits, but this was honoured more in the breach than in any other manner). Determined to improve matters, the first half of 1813 therefore saw him put great pressure on the Portuguese authorities. Angered by his failure to obtain a satisfactory response from Lisbon, he even appealed directly to Prince João. Thus:

I request permission to call the attention of Your Royal Highness to the state of your troops . . . in consequence of the great arrear of pay which is due to them. According to the last statements which I have received, pay is due to the army of operations from the end of last September, to the troops of the line in garrison from the end of last June, and to the militia from February . . . The serious consequences which may result from the backwardness of these payments . . . and the uniform refusal of the governors of the kingdom to attend to any one of the measures which I have recommended either for temporary or permanent relief have at last obliged me . . . to express . . . in the most decided manner my very ardent wish that Your Royal Highness will be pleased to return to your kingdom to take charge of its government.[6]

Wellington's problems with the Portuguese were as nothing in comparison with his problems with the Spaniards, however. As we have seen, the key to his strategy for 1813 was the transformation of the Spanish regular army into a force capable of playing a full part in regular operations, to which end a stream of plans and suggestions was soon flowing from his headquarters at Freneda. Given the problems faced by the army, it is in fact doubtful whether anything would have made much difference. With desertion rife and conscription barely functioning, many units were badly under strength; large numbers of the 130,000 men theoretically serving with the colours were sick; there was insufficient cavalry and artillery, the little that there was also being dispersed amongst the different divisions in penny packets; the troops were at best ill-supplied and at worst on the brink of actual starvation; footwear and transport were lacking; indiscipline of all sorts was rife; and far too many officers still served no other role than to add a military air to the streets of Cádiz, La Coruña or Alicante. At the same time, many towns were gripped by feuding between rival factions of the oligarchy, whilst the countryside was still in uproar. In so far as the latter was concerned, matters were not helped by the efforts of liberal officials to undermine the Church and the nobility, but in fact the populace needed little in the way of egging on. In part, their discontent was expressed by revolt against the *señores*, as occurred at the Andalusian *pueblo* of El Coronil, but the most characteristic form of dissidence continued to be banditry. In La Mancha, for example, El Empecinado was spending more of his time chasing bandits than fighting the French, whilst even the liberals – hitherto the greatest admirers of the guerrillas – had started to call for their suppression, not to mention the formation of new gendarmeries and civic militias. Typical was an article that appeared in *El Conciso*:

Why do we hesitate in lifting the thick veil that hides the atrocities, outrages and insatiable rapacity of these gangs of bandits who so unjustly usurp the respectable name 'patriot'? Because they kill Frenchmen? Could they not do it at less cost? Woe on us if our salvation is to come from such men. Did Lord Wellington liberate Portugal with *partidas*? Did he defeat Marmont with them? And what have we achieved with them, but to complete our ruin, denude our provinces of resources, retard the growth of patriotism, disorganise our armies, fill with sorrow . . . hundreds of families whose only crime was to have money or daughters, and throw entire *pueblos* into the blackest desperation. Patriots of Cádiz . . . your opinion is horribly mistaken: the majority . . . of those you believe to be heroes are nothing more than infamous bandits who recognise neither law nor discipline nor compassion.[7]

So bad had the situation become that French successes were now applauded, as when a punitive column succeeded in surprising the *partida* of the notorious 'Borbón' at Fuentecen, the comment of one Granada newspaper being that 'as a result of their frequent bad behaviour in the *pueblos*, the death of these soldiers means almost as much as does that of the enemy'.[8] With the French gone from much of Spain, the link between irregular resistance and banditry at last became well understood. From all sides, indeed, complaints flowed in. 'The *partidas* of Príncipe and Marquínez have converted themselves into highwaymen', raged one correspondent. 'They respect no class of traveller and rob and violate everyone.'[9] Even the better units were not immune from the problem. Thus: 'The deserters from the band of Don Julián are causing the greatest damage. Exploiting the fact that they are Spaniards, they deceive and surprise not just individuals, but even entire *pueblos*, whilst their cruelty and inhumanity are such that they gouged out the eyes and cut off the buttocks of a group of soldiers whom they surprised.'[10] As for fighting the French, it was in many areas but a memory. As the British liaison officer, Leith-Hay, wrote of the district of Guadalupe, 'The Médico has remained in a state of inactivity, and made no exertion whatever to prevent the small parties which the enemy have . . .

sent into the mountains ... to forage, and which from the nature of the country might have been very severely molested.'[11]

However, the issue was not just the Augean nature of Wellington's task but also the impenetrable wall of obstruction and non-co-operation that he faced. Though he took care to pay lip-service to the Constitution, the arguments of Ballesteros, Flórez Estrada and Romero Alpuente had struck a chord with the liberals, who were clearly dismayed to find that their plans had backfired in so dramatic a fashion. As for the Regency and the *generalato*, they, too, could not but feel alienated and humiliated. The French defeat in Russia having inflamed feelings still further, there was therefore a strong disposition to resist Wellington's instructions.

Meanwhile, a series of issues continued to suggest that the British were not to be trusted. Chief amongst these was the situation in America. In the territory now known as Venezuela, for example, January 1813 saw the disembarkation of a rebel expedition that had assembled at Port of Spain in British-ruled Trinidad. Still worse, at the head of this band was a group of insurgents who had been rescued by a British ship from the coastal town of La Guaira at the time of its recapture by loyalist troops. Great offence, too, was caused by the British ambassador to Brazil, who succeeded in negotiating an armistice between the Argentinians and the Brazilian forces that had occupied Montevideo in support of Spanish rule. As Henry Wellesley complained:

I should not so often recur to the subject of America if affairs in that quarter ... did not influence the conduct of this government ... in all their transactions with Great Britain. Even those who have given unequivocal proofs of their attachment to Great Britain ... consider it to be our policy to establish a commercial intercourse with the Spanish colonies, and they think that in the pursuit of this object we have given a degree of countenance to the insurgents which by exciting jealousies here has considerably weakened our influence.[12]

Closer to home, meanwhile, chronic fears of foreign intervention were inflamed by talk of the possible arrival of a wholly imaginary Russian expeditionary force. With Henry Wellesley continuing to press for a free-trade agreement and Wellington refusing to resume operations until the spring, the result was to fuel accusations that the British were simply prolonging the war for their own benefit. Hence the publication of such diatribes as that which appeared in *El Español Libre*:

We, whose services with respect to Great Britain are much superior to those she has received from our other allies, have been placed in a worse situation than any of them . . . Let us look among ourselves for the commander we need, let us reanimate the enthusiasm of the people, and let us consolidate the throne of justice proclaimed by the wisdom of our constitution. Let us resolve to accomplish alone . . . the enterprise which we sustain alone, and afterwards enter into negotiations with our allies.[13]

Hardly surprisingly, then, Wellington's proposals for reform were ignored, whilst a variety of devices were employed to harass or impede the British. To take just one example, Alvaro Flórez Estrada was made Intendent of Seville, and his younger brother, Antonio, *jefe político* of the vital port of Santander. At the same time, in defiance of its agreement with Wellington, the Regency continued to send orders of its own to the Spanish forces. In this last respect, however, the desire to obstruct British control of the armed forces was married to other considerations. Once again we come to the ever-growing tension that was gripping Cádiz. In the course of the last few months debate in the *cortes* had been dominated by the religious question. The Constitution of 1812 had declared Spain to be Catholic in perpetuity and prohibited the practice of any other faith, but that did not mean that nothing would change. Many churchmen, including a number of those with seats in the *cortes*, were themselves bitterly critical of the Church as things stood, whilst the Inquisition, the religious orders, clerical jurisdiction, ecclesiastical taxation and the lands of the Church were all natural targets of liberal reform. As Argüelles wrote, change was essential 'if the nation was not . . . to be sacrificed to the ill-considered plan of upholding unchanged the temporalities of an ecclesiastical establishment that had been remade by the insurrection, and . . . could not resist for much longer . . . the noble and generous spirit that animated all the useful and active classes'.[14]

First of these issues to raise its head was the Inquisition. Effectively defunct since 1808, it had been unable to do anything to check the increasing tendency towards anti-clericalism that had surfaced in the *gaditano* press, papers such as *El Robespierre Español* losing no opportunity to satirise the Church and condemn its privileges. In response angry ecclesiastics and conservatives published counterblast after counterblast of their own, whether it was in newspapers such as *El Censor General* and the *Procurador General de la Nación y del Rey*, or in pamphlets such as those penned by the Dominican, Francisco de Alvarado. Meanwhile, moved by a particularly violent torrent of invective written by the librarian of the *cortes*, in April 1812 the *serviles* made a determined attempt to have the Inquisition formally re-established. Referred to the committee of the *cortes* that dealt with matters relating to the Constitution, the matter was effectively shelved for the next nine months, but, for all that, it remained a matter of intense public controversy, with many bishops, in particular, petitioning the deputies for its restoration. Returning to the assembly in January 1813 with the report of the Constitutional committee, the matter was finally decided in a series of debates that were marked by some of the most violent confrontations the *cortes* had yet seen. In line with the committee's recommendation, on 22 January the Inquisition was duly abolished by ninety votes to sixty, the liberals having in effect lost two-thirds of their majority.

The struggle, however, was far from over, the resistance of the traditionalists being reinforced by the fact that the past two years had seen a variety of measures that in one way or another tended to reduce the power of the Church. Financial exigencies, for example, had forced the State to seek an even greater share in ecclesiastical wealth and revenue than it had before 1808, the *cortes* having voted to appropriate all plate not actually required for the celebration of normal services, the income accruing to the Church from such sources as vacant benefices, and no less than thirty per cent of the tithes. Abolished altogether was the Voto de Santiago (on the grounds that it infringed the principle of equality of taxation), whilst the religious orders were in large part forbidden from re-establishing convents and monasteries shut by the French, the property of these foundations in effect being expropriated. Outlined, though not acted upon, meanwhile, had been moves towards wholesale *desamortización*, whilst the attack on feudalism threatened the Church's income on yet another front.

None of this represented an attempt to overthrow the Church *per se*. In common with the caroline reformers of the period 1759–1808, the liberals were determined to break its hold on the cultural and economic life of the country, and coveted its land both for the State and, one suspects, themselves. Yet, with the exception of a few extremists, the liberals were all loyal Catholics (some of their leading figures, indeed, were even priests). Thus, the decree abolishing the Inquisition retained the principle of ecclesiastical censorship, whilst there was much interest in aiding the poverty-stricken parish clergy. For traditionalists, however, much though they pretended otherwise, the safety of the Church was not the issue. Many ecclesiastics had welcomed the *cortes* because they believed that revolution would enable the Church to shake off the regalism of the eighteenth century. Yet state control had in effect been reinforced, their anger naturally throwing them together with the increasingly desperate *señores* (to whom they were in many cases already bound by ties of family: the prominent Carmelite traditionalist, Manuel Traggia, for example, was the brother of the Duque del Parque, a general who had repeatedly given evidence of his hostility to the liberal system). Still further allies, meanwhile, were to be found amongst the personnel of the administrative and judicial system ousted by the Constitution of 1812, not to mention the more fortunate elements of the Church's tenantry, a good example of the latter being the *foreros* of Galicia. Wealthy local notables enabled by various regional peculiarities to rent Church land at minimal cost and then sublet it to the peasantry at a huge profit, these men were for obvious reasons terrified of *desamortización* and had been using their considerable economic power to whip their tenants into a state of near revolt. With the Archbishop of Santiago and the Bishop of Orense both deeply opposed to the *cortes'* religious policy, the result was that Galicia became a hotbed of reaction.

Somewhat alarmed at the extent of the opposition, the liberals drew back a little. Thus, the previous year a *cortes* committee had been established to clarify the many ambiguities of the decree that had abolished feudalism, and, on the recommendation of this body, on 27 March 1813 it was agreed that individual dues would only be revoked if the communities subject to them could prove that they had been levied as fees rather than as rents. Yet this move proved counter-productive, for the net result was simply to stir up more trouble in the countryside. In any case, relations between the two sides had already reached crisis point. Published on 22 February 1813, the decree abolishing the Inquisition was supposed to be read out on three successive Sundays in every parish church in both Spain and her empire. Needless to say, this attempt to force the whole Church publicly to back the régime's religious policy met with massive resistance. Secretly encouraged by the papal nuncio, Pedro Gravina, many bishops sent letters of protest, whilst a few refused point-blank to comply, in one or two cases even going so far as to flee their dioceses or threaten their clergy with excommunication should they comply with the order. Equally mutinous, meanwhile, was the cathedral chapter in Cádiz, which not only refused to obey, but sent emissaries to Seville, Málaga, Jaén and Córdoba to encourage revolt there as well.

By the beginning of March 1813, then, Cádiz had been plunged into crisis. As Alcalá Galiano remembered:

It began to be whispered that the regents were trying to make head against the *cortes* ... that the Duque del Infantado could count upon the Reales Guardias Españolas regiment, of which he had once been colonel ... [that] the violent and firm-willed Villavicencio was attempting to stiffen the more timid duke. Conjecture was rife.[15]

For the liberals, however, the events precipitated by the abolition of the Inquisition came more as an opportunity than as a threat. It had been clear since the previous summer that the Infantado Regency was a lost cause, and all the more so as Abisbal had eventually been replaced by the ultra-conservative, Juan Pérez Villamil. In the course of the autumn of 1812, meanwhile, it had been discovered that the Regency had been secretly funding the extremely hostile *Procurador General de la Nación y del Rey*, whilst evidence was also coming to light that it had been seeking to allow some of the religious houses closed by the French to reopen.

For a long time, then, the liberals had been hoping to free themselves of Infantado and his fellows, the Regency's failure to smash the protests now providing them with all the ammunition that they needed. Fuel having been added to the flames by the sudden replacement of the governor of Cádiz – an admiral known to be friendly to the liberals named Cayetano Valdés – by a noted *servil*, on 8 March an emergency session of the *cortes* duly established a new regency consisting of the three most senior members of the Council of State, these being the Cardinal Archbishop of Toledo, Luis de Borbón, and Admirals Ciscar and Agar, both of whom had served in the old Blake Regency. With this fresh change of personnel, the Regency was neutralised, for Borbón was a regalist much opposed to the Inquisition and Ciscar the brother of a leading liberal deputy. Just to make certain, however, the *cortes* also took the opportunity to strip the Regency of the last remnants of its independent power, the government also being remodelled so as to include several noted liberals. In short, the *serviles* had been thoroughly trounced. Cádiz too remained in liberal hands. Not only was Valdés restored to his position, but Abisbal was appointed to the wholly new post of Captain General of Cádiz and commissioned to form a fresh force entitled the Army of Reserve of Andalucía.

This new army having been formed without the slightest reference to Wellington, the commander-in-chief was understandably furious. Privately contemptuous of the Constitution of 1812, whose failure to provide separate representation for the interests of property inclined him to see it as the harbinger of social revolution, he was already distressed by his experience of the workings of the Spanish administration. 'It is impossible to describe,' he wrote, 'the state of confusion in which affairs are at Cádiz. The *cortes* have formed a constitution very much on the principle that a painter paints a picture, viz. to be looked at, and I have not met . . . any person of any description . . . who considers the constitution as the embodying of a system by which Spain is, or can be, governed.'[16] As for the overthrow of the Infantado Regency, he saw it as inconsiderate and ungracious: 'I have never known a shoe-black dismissed in such a style!'[17] – and in consequence sought, unsuccessfully, to find Infantado a command. More to the point, however, setting aside the fact that little progress was visible in the state of the army, the agreements that had been made with him were now being flouted virtually by the day, with the result that the Spanish government was soon in receipt of a series of angry protests. As Wellington told his ally, Vega:

> I am fully alive to the importance which has been attached . . . to my having been entrusted with the command of the Spanish armies . . . But I have a character to lose, and, in proportion as expectations have been raised by my appointment, will be the extent of the disappointment . . . at finding that things are no better than they were before. I confess I do not feel inclined to become the object of those disagreeable sensations . . . and unless some measures can be adopted to prevail upon the government to force the Minister of War to perform the engagements of the government with me, I must . . . resign a situation . . . which I should not have accepted if these engagements had not been entered into.[18]

The more Wellington protested, however, the more he was identified with the cause of reaction and foreign domination, matters being made still worse by the fact that London had decided that the best way out would be to shift the capital from Cádiz to some other city. In consequence, obstruction intensified, the *cortes* in the meantime pressing on with a series of measures that could not but increase the chaos. One issue here was a plan to reduce the number of convents and monasteries and, above all, restrict membership of the orders of friars, who were, as we have seen, in many parts of Spain the chief agents of evangelisation and focus of popular religiosity. Far more important, however, was *desamortización*, this being inextricably linked with the desperate need to restore some measure of financial stability. Thus, whilst the immense *mayorazgos* of the nobility were left untouched, on 4 January 1813 the *cortes* had ordered the sale of half of the common lands possessed by every municipality (in a rare gesture of benevolence, the remainder were supposed to be distributed to deserving war veterans). Also put up for sale, meanwhile, were certain Crown lands, and the estates of all those declared to be traitors, the military orders – the four orders of knighthood that had emerged in the course of the *reconquista* – the Inquisition and those religious houses closed by the French.

Very much in line with general liberal economic policy, all these sales were intended to restore the régime's credit and check the growth of the soaring national debt (7,000,000,000 reales in 1808, this had risen to 12,000,000,000 reales by 1814), and yet their chief result was to pour fuel on the flames. The brunt of the cost of the war having been borne by the small tenant farmer or proprietor, there was no way that these groups could buy any of the land. In consequence, the populace found themselves excluded from all reward, whilst at the same time seeing the commons, much of which had hitherto been let out to the peasantry in small lots, dwindle away. With rents in the meantime generally going up as purchasers strove to gain some return on their investments, the situation of the poor therefore became grimmer than ever. It was a historic failure. Setting aside the fact that a land reform angled towards the populace might have done much to restore order in the countryside, the curtain had been raised on a series of errors that were eventually to bring Spanish liberalism to complete and total ruin.

What did all this mean for the war effort, however? With the new campaign season rapidly approaching, there was no sign of the Spanish armies attaining the strength and capacity with which Wellington had hoped to endow them. Men, money and transport all remained short, whilst obstruction, procrastination and political interference were also causing problems (large numbers of units, for example, had been transferred from the field armies to Abisbal's new command). As Whittingham complained:

Lord Wellington's memorable battle of Salamanca put the Spaniards in possession of the best part of their country, and gave them the means of forming great and powerful armies. Have they taken advantage of these circumstances? Have they done anything for their salvation? Their whole time has been occupied in the forming of a cursed constitution, and their army has been forgotten and neglected! We have not . . . increased our army [by] 20,000 men in the last year, nor is there in my opinion any hope of amendment. About four months ago General Freyre, with 3,500 cavalry, was sent to Seville . . . to clothe, arm, equip and instruct the corps. I saw a letter . . . in which he states that he had received nothing, and that he was not able to exercise his cavalry for want of money to pay for the horses' shoes.[19]

For all that, however, the British commander had no hesitation in planning a new offensive, the situation facing him having been transformed. Much here was owed to the guerrillas, or, at least, their more organised elements. Thus, the first months of 1813 had not witnessed the slightest improvement in the French position in the occupied territories. In the Levante the tough, violent and daring Agustín Nebot – El Fraile – had established a liberated area centred on the isolated mountain town of Vistabella del Maestrazgo complete with tax collectors, arms depots, magazines, hospitals, clothing workshops and town councils established according to the provisions of 1812. So many men had to be held back to watch his forces, indeed, that Suchet's army had ground to a halt, an attempt to march on Alicante having been defeated at Castalla for want of sufficient troops. In southern Aragón Villacampa had survived a French offensive and was threatening to cut communications between Zaragoza and Valencia. In northern Aragón, having captured the important Navarrese town of Tafalla, Espoz y Mina was attacking in the district known as the Cinco Villas, whilst *miquelete* units headed by Francisco Rovira and the Barón de Eroles were closing in on the garrisons that protected the line of the River Ebro. In La Mancha El Empecinado was successfully resisting all attempts to clear him away from the vicinity of French-held Guadalajara. In Navarre the garrison of Pamplona remained under close blockade. And in the Basque provinces not only had the border fort of Fuenterrabia been captured in a surprise raid, but Santoña and Bilbao had once again been sealed off from the outside world.

All this, of course, was the product of the garrisons of the occupied territories having been stretched to such an extent that they were no longer equal to the task facing them. Every so often, a few thousand men might be got together for an attack on one guerrilla stronghold or another, but their departure from their garrisons was usually the signal for the latter to be attacked, whilst they generally achieved no more success than to drive back the troops facing them for a few days. With more troops the French might yet have remedied matters, but no such forces were available. Napoleon was not blind to the serious situation that had developed in northern Spain: not only was the highway from the French frontier to Madrid impassable except to substantial bodies of troops, but it was by now obvious even to the emperor that the countryside was so out of control that Joseph's administration could not pay its way. His answer, however, was a repeat of the disastrous mistake that he had committed the previous year. Again deeming Wellington unlikely to take the offensive, Napoleon ordered Joseph to send the Army of Portugal to assist in the suppression of Espoz y Mina and his fellows.

The emperor's reasons for this decision are not hard to establish. Wellington's army had, so he thought, been badly damaged during the autumn campaign, whilst news had reached the emperor both of the dissension in the Allied camp and of suggestions that some of Wellington's troops, which he estimated at no more than 50,000 men, might be used to attack the French in Holland or Germany. Yet this reasoning was flawed from start to finish. Not counting such Spaniards as might come to his aid, Wellington had 80,000 men at his disposal rather than 50,000, the losses of the Burgos campaign having been made up by substantial reinforcements. British and Spaniards might have been at daggers drawn, but the Alliance was still intact. And, finally, the idea of an expedition to northern Europe had been firmly quashed, the Liverpool administration having decided that its forces were best employed in the Peninsula. More than that, the army had more cavalry and artillery than ever before, whilst it was also better financed and better commanded (many of Wellington's more unreliable subordinates had gone home, whilst one, the drunken and half-blind Sir William Erskine, had obligingly committed suicide). Wellington being Wellington, he still found many things to complain of – above all, London's insistence on withdrawing veteran units which had been reduced to mere skeletons and the continued indiscipline of the soldiers – but in his more generous moments he had in consequence been heard to express the view that his forces were ready for anything. As he wrote to Lord Bathurst, indeed, 'I never saw the British army so healthy or so strong . . . We have gained in strength 25,000 men since we went into cantonments . . . and infinitely more in efficiency.'[20]

Wellington's Peninsular army was never quite the equal of the legend that it has generated. That said, however, the spring of 1813 still found it at its apogee. Keenly aware of the sufferings of his troops the previous winter, the British commander had personally looked into the care of the wounded and taken steps greatly to improve the army's medical services (one consequence of this was that far fewer men were sick than Napoleon had anticipated). Aware, too, that his men had spent week after week sleeping in the open in drenching rain, and had frequently not had either the time or the facilities to cook their meat properly, he had also addressed the question of their equipment. As Larpent recorded:

Last year the mules per company allowed by government were employed in carrying the heavy iron camp-kettles, and our men had no tents: though they were allowed them, they could not be carried. This year Lord Wellington had light tin kettles made, one for every six men, for the mess, to be carried by one of the men . . . This plan sets the mules free, and thus three tents have been carried for every company, and . . . this now . . . contributes much to the health of the army.[21]

This improvement had the knock-on effect of lightening the load carried by each man, for it was deemed that they could now do without their heavy greatcoats. This, perhaps, was not the best of moves – in the rain-swept Pyrenees the soldiers again suffered dreadfully – but for the time being the men were happy enough. The bitter grumbling of the autumn had subsided, whilst faith in Wellington was general. New uniforms had been issued, and great efforts had also been made to improve training: 'We were very busy,' wrote Bell, 'with parades and drills and field days.'[22] Not surprisingly, then, morale was very high. As Simmons wrote, 'The army is in high health and spirits. In a few days we shall take the field . . . The campaign bids fair to be most brilliant', whilst, to quote Bell again, Wellington 'never came near us without a cheer from the men that made the woods ring'.[23]

If the Allies' prospects were good, it was largely the result of Napoleon's decision to make use of the Army of Portugal in the Basque provinces, Navarre and Aragón. Originally, Wellington's plans for an offensive had been postulated on the use of large numbers of Spanish soldiers. These were not forthcoming, but, as division after division of the Army of Portugal headed east, it became clear that the great offensive of which he had been thinking that would take him all the way to the Pyrenees was still a possibility. In brief, Espoz y Mina and his fellows could make up for the absence of the Spanish regulars Wellington had felt he needed in León and Old Castile. Meanwhile, as he had always intended, Suchet would be tied down by the Anglo-Sicilian expeditionary force that had been sent to Alicante, together with whatever troops the Spaniards could get into the field in the Levante. Left to face the Anglo-Portuguese hosts all but alone, the Armies of the Centre and the South could not hope to hold out, and, with an advance to the Ebro a near-certainty, Wellington therefore felt it safe to order the transfer of his forward base to Santander.

In this situation, all that could have saved the French was the rapid defeat of the northern insurrection. This, however, was impossible. A real discovery of the campaigns of 1812, the energetic, enterprising and extremely competent General Clausel was placed in command of the Army of the North, whilst the guerrillas were hit by as many as 40,000 men. But resistance was fierce. A detachment belonging to the Army of Portugal was destroyed at Lerín on 30 March, for example, whilst it took over a fortnight just to reduce the port of Castro Urdiales. Still worse, the *partidas* were no sooner threatened in one place than they simply melted away to reappear somewhere else. Bilbao, indeed, was almost lost again, whilst such successes as were secured by the French in practice meant very little. Many villages were burned and many guerrillas caught and killed, but in the last resort the insurrection survived, Clausel eventually being left with no option but to confess that he needed at least another 20,000 troops.

By now, however, it was May, and all was ready for Wellington's offensive. Operations began on 22 May. Whilst the Light Division and Hill's old corps headed for Salamanca, the bulk of the Anglo-Portuguese army marched northwards under the command of Sir Thomas Graham. Crossing the River Duero on a pontoon bridge that had been brought up from the sea, they then turned east, bridged the River Esla with the help of Wellington's pontoon train, and advanced on Valladolid. Carefully planned and brilliantly executed, these orders quickly brought success. With such troops as were left in the western parts of their dominions hopelessly outnumbered and scattered widely across the countryside, within two weeks Joseph and Jourdan had been forced to evacuate Valladolid and Madrid. Some thought was given to the idea of defending the line of the Pisuerga and Carrión rivers, but all Wellington's forces had now met up at Toro. Such a mass of troops being quite impossible for them to take on, the French were therefore soon falling back on Burgos.

For the Allies, all this came as revenge for the horrors of the previous autumn. As Wood remembered:

Our march for the first two or three hundred miles was like a party of pleasure in comparison to others we had encountered. We passed through a most delightful level country, abounding in all the verdant beauties of nature ... Everything and every countenance now wore the aspect of joy, the men singing and telling their jocose stories as they passed along hill and dale.[24]

Normally reserved and unemotional, even Wellington seems to have caught the general excitement, for, as he rode across the frontier near Ciudad Rodrigo, he is supposed to have waved his hat in the air and shouted, 'Farewell Portugal! I shall never see you again!'* Practically the only sour note in the whole affair concerned the civilian population, who showed nothing like the excitement of the previous year. At the curiously named Wamba, Webber recalled being 'welcomed by the ringing of bells and cries of "Viva" from all the people', whilst at Zamora there was every 'demonstration of joy'.[25] Underlying the cheers was an atmosphere of tension, however, Hennell, for example, suggesting that two-thirds of the population 'would as soon give you some curses'.[26] But there was good reason for cynicism. Setting aside the bitter memories of 1812, the army was soon up to its old tricks. To quote Kincaid:

We were welcomed into every town or village through which we passed by the peasant girls, who were in the habit of meeting us with garlands of flowers ... and it not infrequently happened that while they were so employed with one regiment, the preceding one was diligently engaged in pulling down some of the houses for firewood.[27]

The further that Joseph and Jourdan fell back, of course, the greater the chance that they would be joined by the troops missing from the Army of Portugal or even reinforcements sent by Clausel, but Wellington remained more than willing to seek a battle, having with him not only his own 80,000 men, but also 20,000 Spaniards of the Fourth Army, the latter being described as being in better fettle than any Spanish troops the Anglo-

* There is some reason to be wary of this story. Yet of Wellington's general optimism there is little doubt.

Portuguese army had yet observed. At the same time, meanwhile, he had long since ordered immense convoys of ammunition and other supplies, including a powerful siege train, to be assembled at La Coruña. Transferred to Santander, these stores afforded the Anglo-Portuguese a second base which spared them the necessity of having to maintain their line of communications with Lisbon, the army meanwhile marching in such a direction that it also acquired an alternative escape route should the campaign go wrong. Thus, far from plodding along in the wake of the French along the direct road to Burgos, the Allies turned northwards and plunged into the rugged hills that filled the region to the north of the French stronghold. Circling eastwards, they then threatened Joseph's army with encirclement, with the result that, preceded by a great convoy of refugees, plunder and baggage wagons, *el rey intruso* had to order the destruction of the castle of Burgos and retreat across the Ebro. Even here he was not safe, however, for Wellington's army, which was now in easy touch with Santander, moved north-eastwards again, thereby getting across the headwaters of the River Ebro between Polientes and Puente Arenas on 15 June. Wheeling right on a broad frontage through country that was still rougher than any which had been traversed before, the army, which had just been reinforced by 5,000 more Spanish troops drawn from the commands of Longa and Porlier, finally swung southwards in an attempt to cut the French line of communication with the frontier.

The march of the Allied army from the Portuguese frontier to the Cantabrian mountains is an example of strategic brilliance that is without equal in the annals of the Peninsular War. In less than a month and with hardly any fighting, the French had been cleared from the whole of La Mancha, León and New Castile. Meanwhile, starting from positions over 120 miles apart, 100,000 troops had marched some 200 miles in four separate columns before finally being manoeuvred into a position from which they could fall on the enemy's flank and rear. Much of the march had taken place in mountainous terrain that was all but devoid of inhabitants, and yet the supply system had functioned with great efficiency, few of the troops ever going hungry (there were some exceptions: on 19 June Aitchison complained that bread was 'very, very scarce', whilst Wheeler maintained that by the morning of 21 June 'we had not seen a pound of bread these eleven days'[28]). And, last but not least, the army had been provided with a new base and saved from the necessity of having to drag up its cumbersome siege train all the way from Portugal.

Only one thing marred this extraordinary performance and that was that at the last minute the French realised the danger in which they stood and in consequence fell back from their cantonments on the Ebro to a somewhat safer position at Vitoria. Here, however, they turned at bay. Their reasons for this decision were obvious. Some of the stray units from the Army of Portugal having now been picked up, the forces available had risen to well over 60,000 men. Retreat any further, meanwhile, and Joseph looked likely to have no kingdom left, not to mention no opportunity to secure the help of the three infantry divisions of the Army of Portugal that were still missing but were currently supposed to be coming up from the east under Clausel. And, last but not least, Vitoria seemed to offer an excellent defensive position, in that the town could only be approached from the west – the direction from which it was presumed that Wellington would attack – by means of a long valley crossed by a series of defensive positions that seemed impossible to outflank (on the French right hand flowed the River Zadorra, whilst on their left hand stood a line of rugged heights that were largely inaccessible to formed troops).

Much of this thinking was perfectly reasonable, but it did presume that the army's will to fight had not been adversely affected by the long retreat. Indeed, the French commanders admitted this problem by electing to send off their baggage, which included vast quantities of loot, in the direction of the French frontier. Still worse, ignorant as ever of Wellington's movements, Joseph and Jourdan had missed the crucial fact that the Allied forces were not just approaching them from the west. Admittedly, the odds against the French had shortened: the Sixth Division having been left to cover the road to Santander, and most of the forces of the Sixth Army dispatched to threaten Bilbao in the hope of tying down the garrison of the Basque provinces, Wellington could only deploy some 75,000 men. However, even as the forces that had been concentrated at Vitoria made ready to resist the expected attack from the west, fully half the troops that had been brought up to fight them were swinging round their right flank and making for the Zadorra's many fords and bridges. Given the facts, first, that for the past month the whole of Wellington's strategy had centred on a series of out-flanking moves, and, second, that cavalry patrols had discovered that fewer troops lay to the west of them than might have been expected, it seems barely credible that Joseph and Jourdan failed to realise the same might happen again. What threw them seems to have been the idea that the roads which crossed the mountains that lay immediately to the north of the Zadorra were impassable to large bodies of men. If Wellington was shying away from a head-on attack, then, it followed that his troops were heading for Bilbao prior to making a fresh turning movement by way of the main road that ran south-eastwards from the city via Durango. This, however, would take many days to execute, whilst the troops that had been fighting Mina in Navarre were at worst only forty or fifty miles away. Were the Anglo-Portuguese forces really to be heading for Bilbao, in short, the French would soon have the strength to launch a counter-stroke on their communications.

The obvious flaw in this argument is that, having moved his main base to Santander, Wellington no longer had to worry about such a move, but this, again, Joseph and Jourdan did not know. Only at the last minute did they realise that all was not what it seemed, and send some forces from their reserve – the two infantry divisions of the Army of Portugal present on the field, Joseph's *juramentados* and royal guard, a handful of strays from the Army of the North and most of the cavalry – to guard the city of Vitoria and the road to France against an attack from the north. Consideration, too, was given to evacuating the western end of the valley and pulling back to a position whose left flank rested on the little village of Berostigueta, but Jourdan was feeling unwell and the necessary orders were never sent out to the troops concerned. Still worse, an entire infantry division was allowed to start out for the frontier in company with the first of the baggage, the result being that the French were left with just 57,000 men.

When battle was joined on 21 June Joseph and Jourdan therefore found themselves in a difficult predicament. Thus, the expected frontal assault failed to materialise, the first Allied troops to attack – Hill's old corps – instead clinging to the skirts of the heights that overlooked the French positions from the south whilst sending a few troops, most of them the Spaniards of Morillo's division of the Fourth Army, to seize the crest of the ridge. As L'Estrange remembered, 'A sharp firing on the right gave us notice that the ball had been opened in that quarter. It was Morillo's Spanish division that had come into contact with the most advanced part of the French army.'[29] Although they fought well – Morillo himself was badly wounded – the Spaniards made little progress, but they were soon reinforced by British and Portuguese troops. There followed some fierce fighting:

We were gaining ground along the side of the mountain, when we were met with a biting fire, and the battle here remained stationary for some time . . . Then, passing the Zadorra [on our left] we won the village of Subijana de Alava . . . and maintained our ground in spite of all opposition. There was a good deal of fighting in the churchyard, and some open graves were soon filled up with double numbers . . . As Colonel Brown said, 'If you don't kill them, boys, they'll kill you: fire away.'[30]

Much perturbed that Wellington might have out-guessed them and be marching on Vitoria from the south, Joseph and Jourdan responded by sending large numbers of troops to join the fight that was developing on the left flank, only to find that in doing so they had got themselves into worse difficulties than ever. Thus, not only did the First and Fifth Divisions and some additional Portuguese and Spanish troops suddenly appear out of the mountains to the north and threaten the troops – the single infantry division of Sarrut – that had been sent to hold the approaches to Vitoria from that direction, but the extreme right of the French front line found itself under attack from the Third and Light Divisions, of which the first had come through the mountains, and the second made use of woods and broken ground to creep across the French front from the western end of the valley.

Initially the Allied troops north of Vitoria did not prove much of a foe, for, though they had first appeared at nine o'clock, they did not actually attack the French positions in front of them for another four hours. To the west, however, matters were very different. Having crossed the river by an undefended bridge at Tres Puentes, part of the Light Division pressed forward, and, at some cost, distracted the attention of the French troops posted on the extreme right of Joseph's original front line. Present at this point was George Hennell:

Finding the fire heavy, we moved under a bank and lay down. At that moment a shell came hopping direct for me, but it was polite enough to halt . . . about six yards from us . . . and in about one minute it burst doing no harm. In another minute a ball struck the close column of the Seventeenth Portuguese . . . It killed the sergeant and took off the leg of each of the ensigns with the colours.[31]

From this predicament Hennell and his fellows were rescued by Sir Thomas Picton's Third Division. Having emerged from the mountains north of the Zadorra, Picton had been supposed to wait for the troops on his right – the Seventh Division of Lord Dalhousie – to attack before crossing the river himself. Dalhousie dithered, however, whereupon Picton, a fiery and impulsive man who deeply resented having to take second place to Dalhousie, took it upon himself to advance. Shouting 'Come on, ye rascals! Come on, ye fighting villains!', he therefore led his men across the river, whereupon the troops holding the French front line hastily retired to a second position above the village of Ariñez.

Well-supplied with artillery and reinforced by fresh troops brought up from the rear, the French now made a resolute stand. However, their right flank was being assailed not just by the Third and Light Divisions, but also the first troops of Lord Dalhousie. Supported by the Fourth Division, which had just entered the valley, the largest mass of artillery ever assembled by Wellington was at the same time pounding the unfortunate defenders. Fierce fighting continued on the extreme left, where the Seventy-First had an unpleasant experience when it was suddenly assailed in flank by a unit which it mistook for Spaniards. But at Ariñez there was no holding the Anglo-Portuguese attack. As Donaldson rather laconically notes, 'After crossing the river, our division advanced in two lines on the village where their artillery was posted under a tremendous fire, and succeeded, after an obstinate resistance in dislodging them.'[32] Also present was Wood of the Eighty-Second:

Our front was exposed to . . . a French regiment on the right of the battery, but, after politely receiving us with a few sharp volleys, which we as politely returned, they . . . retreated into a thicket. Towards this we advanced firing, and drove them furiously before us till they were completely routed.[33]

The French were still not quite finished, trying, with admirable determination, to form a new line based on the villages of La Hermandad and Gomecha. But, outnumbered, badly shaken, harassed by large numbers of skirmishers, and threatened from the south by Hill, who was now advancing along the crest of the heights, their men could take no more. In Long's words:

They behaved very ill. Their position was very strong and with common . . . spirit their defence might have been brilliant. But their infantry did not stand as I expected they would, their cavalry could be of no use from the nature of the ground, and when they saw themselves turned a panic seized the whole.[34]

Himself caught up in the rout, Joseph could only order a general retreat, but for many of his men there was no escape, for, as Simmons wrote, 'they had to pass over a fine plain, which enabled us from time to time to press them confoundedly'.[35]

In this predicament, one thing, and one thing only, saved the French from complete destruction. Had Sir Thomas Graham, who had been given command of the 20,000 troops sent to advance on Vitoria from the north, shown a modicum of initiative, Joseph would have found himself completely cut off, for Graham had only to seize the city – a relatively easy task given his numerical advantage – to trap almost the whole French army. However, mindful of orders that his prime objective was to cut the Madrid–Bayonne highway, which from Vitoria ran north-eastwards along the Zadorra, Graham struck east rather than south. Getting across the river at Durana, the Spanish division of Francisco Longa duly cut the road on the enemy's extreme right flank. In Gomm's words, 'His people behaved well and were of much service. He is a young man, and for one . . . so little used to control

I thought his behaviour admirable in falling so readily as he did into our plans.'[36] Of Graham, however, much less was to be said, the bulk of his troops becoming bogged down around the village of Gamarra Mayor. As Douglas remembered:

We reached the village, which we named Gomorrah as it was a scene of fire and brimstone. The enemy were driven . . . over the River Zadorra . . . The light company entered a house at the end of the bridge, from the windows of which a very destructive fire was kept up, while as many as could pushed across and formed as they arrived close to an old chapel. Here there appeared to be some want. Had the regiments which entered the village been pushed across the bridge . . . the wreck of the French would have been nearly as bad as Waterloo. [But] the enemy seemed to know the value of this spot and poured down a heavy fire on the few that got over and so obliged us to retrace our steps.[37]

Thanks to Graham, then, the French had an escape route, for a narrow road led eastwards from Vitoria in the direction of Pamplona by way of the pass of Salvatierra. Even so, things were bad enough, for the French rear was clogged up with Joseph's immense baggage train, every available track soon being jammed with fugitives. Fortunately for the defeated *rey intruso*, though, the victorious Allies' lust for plunder proved too much for them. Whooping with delight, many of the leading troops fell on the stranded wagons and gave themselves over to riot and debauchery. At the same time, the terrain to the east of the battlefield – a tangle of woods, vineyards, stone walls, and little villages – was scarcely conducive to rounding up large numbers of the enemy, whilst it must also be admitted that even such troops as remained in hand appear to have been poorly directed. Riding with Anson's brigade, indeed, William Hay even experienced a last-minute reverse:

In this order we . . . soon came in sight of the French cavalry. On seeing our advance, advantage was taken of some broken ground . . . to halt and form for our reception. As we approached this appeared madness, as their numbers did not exceed half ours. Our trumpet sounded the charge when . . . their flanks were thrown back, and there stood, formed in squares, about 3,000 infantry. These opened such a close and well-directed fire on our advance squadrons, that not only were we brought to a standstill, but the . . . leading squadrons went about, and order was not restored till a troop of horse artillery arrived on our flank and . . . opened such a fire of grape that . . . I saw men fall like a pack of cards.[38]

Still worse was the experience of the staff officer, Browne:

As I was accompanying a squadron of the Eighteenth Hussars in pursuit of the enemy, who were flying as fast as possible, we overtook a line of carriages and baggage, which offered so much temptation to many of the soldiers ... that they could not resist falling to the work of plunder, whilst others with their officers continued in pursuit. The squadron was thus considerably weakened in number, a circumstance which was observed by the French rearguard, near which we rapidly approached. They suddenly detached a body of cavalry from it, which, falling on the few of the Eighteenth who were in advance, killed some, wounded others, and took some prisoners. In this last lot I was myself included, my horse having been killed, and my head cut longitudinally with a sabre so as to knock me over.[39]

Thus protected, the bulk of the army's fighting men therefore got away to Pamplona (total French losses, including prisoners, were no more than 8,000 men). Their disarray was total, however. The apothecary, Blaze, for example, describes a scene of chaos:

I galloped along in the middle of a crowd of fugitives of whom the majority had flung away their arms so as to lighten their burden. None was better than the next – they had all run away rather than face the enemy – but all the same they still quarrelled with one another, calling one another cowards and poltroons, and even exchanging blows. On all sides one saw Spanish families who were abandoning their country rather than face the persecution which threatened them ... I saw a young girl running across the fields ... in satin shoes and a muslin dress; a woman bent by age supported by her daughter who was herself carrying a small child. Such distressing images appeared every instant, but they only inspired a sterile pity: everyone was fully occupied with his own person and could not aid others in their misfortune.[40]

Gone were all but one of Joseph's 152 guns; over 500 artillery caissons; huge quantities of supplies, clothing, footwear and equipment of all sorts; virtually all the transport that the French possessed; the personal baggage of the king, Marshal Jourdan (both of whom had come within an ace of being captured themselves) and many other senior officers; and the whole of Joseph's state papers and treasury, including 5,000,000 francs newly come from France. Stranded amidst the turmoil, too, aside from a swarm of camp-followers of all sorts, were many of the *afrancesado* officials who had been the very heart and soul of the Bonaparte administration. Thanks to the mistakes of Sir Thomas Graham, victory had not been total, but even so for the French there was no way back.

As so often before, however, the glory of victory was marred by the behaviour of Wellington's army. The captured French baggage train, as we have seen, presented an extraordinary sight. As commander of Wellington's artillery, Sir Augustus Frazer seems to have taken most note of the many books and papers strewn around:

The scene . . . baffles all description. I picked up a map large enough to cover the side of a small room . . . It proved to be a large map of the . . . palace and gardens at Aranjuez: I gave it to Sturgeon for the Quartermaster General. I gave him also . . . a beautifully bound copy of the regulations of the royal household . . . Joseph's . . . portable library was [also] in my possession, but I threw it away, having too much employment to attend to plunder.[41]

Of much more interest to most of the army, however, were other forms of spoil. As Bell remembered, 'Five million dollars [were] abandoned by the French and left upon the ground . . . There were little barrels of doubloons and *napoléons* . . . for the picking up, but rather heavy to put into one's haversack.'[42] Drink, too, was to be had by the barrel, but perhaps the most exciting feature of the scene was the women, the 500 or so prostitutes, officers' mistresses and other ladies of easy virtue who fell, quite literally, into the hands of the victors. What followed can be exaggerated: some men were too exhausted to be interested in much more than food and firewood, whilst others were kept firmly under control by their officers. Amidst the confusion there were also occasional acts of generosity, as in the case of the English cavalryman who picked up and cared for a lost child who turned out to be the daughter of the French general, Gazan, or the sergeant who took pity on a wounded officer and filled his pockets with money. Nor can blame be solely levelled at the soldiery, for muleteers, wagoners, camp-followers and other non-combatants were all well to the fore, whilst, according to Tomkinson, 'The inhabitants of Vitoria had not done plundering the day after, and many have amply repaid themselves for the sums taken from them in contributions.'[43] For a graphic description of the sort of thing that went on, we have only to turn to Wheeler:

I had not proceeded far when I met one of the Sixty-Eighth Regiment with a handkerchief full of dollars. He was followed by about a dozen Portuguese soldiers. One of these fellows . . . cut the handkerchief and down went the dollars. A general scramble followed. As the Portuguese were down on their hands and knees picking up the money, we paid them off in style with the sockets of our bayonets. After this fracas was over . . . I started off in the direction I heard most noise [and] soon came to the place where the money was. After much difficulty I secured a small box of dollars, and was fortunate enough to get back safe to camp.[44]

And, as ever, the troops did not just steal from the enemy. The complaints, indeed, of the citizens of Vitoria were very bitter:

It is impossible to give a clear idea of the abuses committed in this city ... The peaceful citizen is harassed; property is not respected; houses, shops and government offices are burgled; and the members of the town council ... are impeded in their efforts to supply the army. Nor is this the only problem. The inhabitants ... of the *pueblos* round about are hesitant about coming into town with the result that trade has fallen off [and] food run short.[45]

Wellington, needless to say, was furious. His victory, he said, had 'totally annihilated all order and discipline' and left the army 'incapable of marching in pursuit of the enemy, and ... totally knocked up'.[46] Yet, for all that, the fruits of victory remained enormous. Away from the main theatre of operations, the French had been holding their own. Much damage, for example, had been inflicted on the insurgents in the Basque country and Navarre, whilst the garrison of Valencia had checked the advance of the Second and Third Armies in an action at Alcira on 13 June. With more energy on the Allied side things might have been different, but the forces of El Empecinado, for example, had settled down to enjoy the fruits of victory in and around Madrid, whilst the Anglo-Sicilian expeditionary force had botched a descent on Tarragona. In the days following Vitoria, however, the Bonaparte kingdom of Spain collapsed like a house of cards. Immediately seeing that the game was up, Suchet ordered the evacuation of the Levante and Aragón, whilst, having hastily fallen back on Zaragoza, Clausel led the two divisions that he had got together back to France.* In the Basque provinces and Navarre, meanwhile, pursued by the Anglo-Portuguese, the French retreated to the frontier, leaving garrisons in San Sebastián, Pamplona and Santoña. All that was left, in short, was Catalonia, where Suchet still possessed sufficient men to hold his own, though even there part of the interior continued to be held by the First Army (not that the latter was strong enough to do more than mount the occasional raid).

With Wellington advancing to the Pyrenees and besieging San Sebastián and assorted Spanish forces settling down to blockade the isolated garrisons dotted from Pamplona to the Mediterranean, all was also up with Joseph Bonaparte, who on 11 July was directed to hand over the command of his forces to Marshal Soult and go into retirement. Yet for the time being there followed no invasion of France. Setting aside the fact that San Sebastián and Pamplona tied down large numbers of troops, the war in the rest of

---

* Despite the general retreat, there were a few exceptions. Thus, Saguntum, Peñíscola, Denia, Jaca and the castle of Zaragoza were retained in the hope that they might serve as *points d'appui* in the event of a possible counter-attack, whilst Morella, Mequínenza and Monzón either never received the order to pack up and leave or simply proved impossible to evacuate.

Europe was not going well, Napoleon having inflicted such heavy defeats on the Russians and Prussians that they had agreed to Austrian mediation and a temporary armistice. As it happened, nothing came of these developments, but Wellington rightly believed that there was a real chance of a compromise peace and in consequence decided to halt at the Pyrenees until such time as the situation was a little clearer, the need for caution being reinforced still further by the fact that fresh quarrels had just broken out with the Spaniards, with whom Wellington remained deeply dissatisfied. As he later told Lord Stanhope:

I had armies to co-operate with me upon whose operations I could not reckon owing to . . . their deficiencies of all kinds. I could not rely upon 10,000 of them doing what 500 ought to, or upon their doing anything, much less upon their doing what 10,000 ought to do.[47]

These quarrels we must leave for the next chapter. Suffice to say that for the time being the Allied cause was victorious. Despite his inability to make use of the Spanish army in the manner which he had intended, Wellington had still been able to launch the offensive he had hoped for. Thus, the guerrillas of Navarre and the Basque provinces had proved much more effective in their operations than the campaign of 1812 had led him to expect: better armed, better trained and more numerous than they had been in the past, they could no longer be contained by scattered garrisons and punitive columns, but required the attention of complete field armies. At the same time, Napoleon had compounded the difficulties faced by his commanders still further by withdrawing more troops from the Peninsula, refusing to send Joseph the reinforcements that were really needed, underestimating the British threat, and making use of forces badly needed at the front to hunt down Espoz y Mina and his fellows. So much did the situation play into Wellington's hands, indeed, that in the end he shrugged off chaos and harassment alike. Moreover, once the army was under way, the situation continued to favour Wellington, for Joseph and Jourdan were hampered at every step by the enormous trains that inevitably accompanied their forces, not to mention their own mediocrity as battlefield commanders. By 1813, meanwhile, the French were also suffering from a severe imbalance in the quality of the forces available to each side: whilst such Spanish troops as actually managed to take the field were infinitely superior to the levies of earlier years and the Anglo-Portuguese army self-confident, battle-hardened and almost impossible to defeat, Napoleon's soldiers were increasingly exhausted and demoralised.

That said, however, to explain Vitoria purely in terms of structural factors would be to do Wellington a disservice, for gone was the fumbling and hesitation of the autumn of 1812. Reacting quickly to changed circumstances, Wellington had realised that he could do without the Spaniards and gone ahead without them. Outwitting the French completely and pushing his forces through terrain so rough and deserted that parts of it had never yet been fought over, he repeatedly forced the French to retreat whilst eventually manoeuvring them into a position that could have seen the campaign culminate in a gigantic battle of encirclement. Meanwhile, in a classic example of the offensive use of seapower, the Anglo-Portuguese army had been freed from the constant worry of having to maintain its links with Lisbon by the establishment of a new base at Santander. In the event Vitoria had not entirely gone as planned, but the battle was still a fitting end to a great campaign, and, what is more, one that cost only 5,000 casualties.

The war, however, was not over. For all practical purposes, the Bonaparte kingdom of Spain was dead and buried, but most of France's troops had escaped intact, with the result that fresh armies were soon gathering beyond the Pyrenees. By themselves, of course, such forces were unlikely to secure more than one or two local victories, but, as Wellington saw all too well, the war in central and eastern Europe that had taken so many French troops could in no sense be taken for granted. Austria, Russia and Prussia might yet be beaten, whilst such were the divisions between the Allies that there was no guarantee that one power or another would not make a separate peace. By giving Britain somewhat more credibility on the Continent, Vitoria had helped a little (although it is certainly not true, as is sometimes claimed, that it was news of the battle that in August brought Vienna into the war), but the thought of Napoleon descending on the Pyrenees with the *grande armée* was still not one to be regarded with equanimity. Just as the period 1808–1812 had seen French success in the Peninsula rest on the defeat of Austria, Prussia and Russia, so the period 1813–1814 was to see Allied success in the Peninsula rest on their victory.

17

Pyrenees

THE INVASION OF FRANCE, JULY–NOVEMBER 1813

Crouching behind the dyke and still damp from the violent storm of the night before, the troops watched the sun come up and braced themselves to cross the estuary. Across the river all was silent, but even so the ordeal that faced them was a daunting prospect, for, low tide though it was, the further bank was more than a mile away, the fords the attackers were supposed to use largely unexplored, and the waters liable to turn with devastating speed. When the signal was given, however, unit after unit scrambled over the lip of the dyke and began to make their way across the sands. Very soon the leading troops were wading the narrow channel that was all that was left of the river, but, to their surprise, for a long while not a shot was fired. Only as the leading troops neared the shore, indeed, did the first enemy muskets sound, and even then it was soon apparent that the only opposition came from a few pickets. From further inland came sounds of tougher resistance, but here at least there was no doubt that the redcoats were triumphant.

It was a historic moment, for the river that the troops had crossed was the Bidassoa, and the ground that they occupied on the further bank was not Spain but France. Yet, curiously enough, it had been a distinctly reluctant Wellington who ordered his men across the river on 7 October 1813. Though heartened by the news that Austria had entered the war and, further, that the Allied armies had at least succeeded in avoiding decisive defeat in a major clash with Napoleon at Dresden the previous month, British head-quarters was filled with misgivings with regard to the eastern powers. As Wellington's brother-in-law, Edward Pakenham, wrote, 'I should think that much must depend upon proceedings in the north: I really begin to apprehend . . . that Boney may avail himself of the jealousy of the Allies to the material injury of the cause.'[1] But the defeat or defection of Austria, Russia and Prussia was not the only danger. It was equally by no means clear that Wellington could continue to count on Spanish support. Invasion seemed likely to be a rough ride even if Napoleon remained tied up in the east. To quote Wellington himself:

It is a very common error among those unacquainted with military affairs to believe that there are no limits to military success. After having driven the French from the frontiers of Portugal . . . to the frontiers of France, it is generally expected that we shall invade France, and some even here expect that we shall be at Paris in a month. None appear to have taken a correct view of our situation . . . An army which has . . . fought such battles as that under my command has is necessarily much deteriorated . . . The equipment of the army, their ammunition, the soldiers' shoes, etc., require renewal; the magazines for the new operations require to be collected . . . and many arrangements [have] to be made without which the army could not exist a day . . . Then observe that this new operation is the invasion of France, in which country everybody is a soldier, where the whole population is armed and organised under persons, not, as in other countries, inexperienced in arms, but men who . . . must, the majority of them at least, have served somewhere.[2]

Nor were things well with Wellington's army. Summer in the Basque provinces and Navarre is not the season of blazing heat to be found in the rest of the Peninsula, and in 1813 the weather appears to have been particularly bad. With the army drenched by incessant rain, the decision to strip the men of their greatcoats was looking singularly unwise. Sickness was widespread – at one point no fewer than one third of Wellington's British troops had been *hors de combat* – whilst there were also many fears as to the army's discipline and general reliability. Straggling had on 9 July been so general that Wellington reported that fully 12,500 men were absent without leave, whilst plundering had gone on without cease: 'We paint the conduct of the French in this country in very . . . harsh colours,' lamented Robinson, 'but be assured we injure the people much more than they do . . . Wherever we move devastation marks our steps.'[3] And, finally, with the army established on the borders of France, desertion had become a problem. Had the units affected only been those recruited from deserters and prisoners of war, this would have been bad enough: the nominally French Chasseurs Britanniques, for example, lost 150 men in a single night. But the problem was clearly much more general. Thus: 'The desertion is terrible, and is quite unaccountable, particularly among the British troops. I am not astonished that the foreigners should go . . . but, unless they entice away the British soldiers, there is no accounting for their going away in such numbers as they do.'[4]

As if this was not enough, there was also the question of the Spaniards. Thus, relations with the Spanish authorities had slipped to a lower ebb than that even of 1809, whilst matters were further complicated by the continued presence of substantial French forces in Catalonia, not to mention the fact that the onset of winter was wreaking havoc with Spain's ragged and ill-fed soldiers, commander after commander reporting that their men were starving and falling sick by the hundred. Also to be considered, meanwhile, were the linked questions of the conduct of the Allied armies and the danger of popular resistance likely to follow an invasion: if the behaviour of the redcoats was likely to be bad enough, the Spaniards and Portuguese for obvious reasons were likely to fall on the populace with the utmost savagery. As Edward Buckham noted, 'The Spaniards, elated with the prospect of entering the fine plains of France, boast that the time has come for the French to pay *la fiesta y el ajo* (the feast and the garlic too).'[5] If Wellington expressed the hope that he would not need the maps of France for which he asked the Horseguards and stressed that he was only asking for them because it was as well to have them as otherwise, in the last resort there was little choice. Britain had to offer further guarantees of her commitment to the struggle for fear that the emperor might otherwise once again divide and rule. And, if that were so, it was in Wellington's eyes best done on the Pyrenean front, there being no guarantee that the British government would not otherwise suddenly order the bulk of his forces to northern Germany or Holland in the belief that the Spanish frontier might safely be left to the Spaniards and Portuguese (in the wake of Vitoria, dispatches from London had repeatedly floated the utterly impracticable idea of fortifying the Pyrenees in the same style as the Lines of Torres Vedras). But enthusiasm was notably absent:

I see that, as usual, the newspapers on all sides are raising the public expectation and that the Allies are anxious that we should enter France, and that our government have promised that we should as soon as the enemy should be finally expelled from Spain . . . I think I . . . will bend a little to the views of the Allies, if it can be done with safety to the army, notwithstanding that I acknowledge I should prefer to turn my attention to Catalonia, as soon as I shall have secured this frontier.[6]

Only in one respect did the situation offer much comfort, and that was that Wellington was facing an enemy with a record of sustained defeat, for at the end of July and then again at the end of August the French had been severely beaten in a fresh series of battles whose object had been the relief of the major border fortresses of Pamplona and San Sebastián. Of these the former had been blockaded and the latter besieged: even with the increased resources now available to him, Wellington could only mount one formal siege at a time, whilst it was decided to plump for San Sebastián on the grounds that it was weaker, more accessible and open to resupply by sea. Yet San Sebastián was still a tough nut to crack. Situated on a narrow promontory that jutted out into the sea between the waters of the Bay of Biscay and the broad estuary of the River Urumea, the town was hard to get at and well fortified – it was 'the strongest fortification I ever saw, Gibraltar excepted', wrote William Dent[7] – whilst the governor, General Louis-Emmanuel Rey, was a coarse and foul-mouthed veteran of the Bourbon army who was very much out to make his name. Given a garrison of 3,000 seasoned infantry and gunners, Rey had accordingly been doing all that he could to make ready for a siege and had already inflicted several sharp reverses on the Spanish forces – erstwhile guerrillas from the Guipuzcoan hinterland now embodied as a division of the Fourth Army – who had closed in around the town on 29 June 1813.

To compound the problem, Wellington made a serious error. Two fronts of the town could be attacked: the bastioned *enceinte* that blocked the neck of the peninsula on which it stood, and the old medieval wall that rose above the Urumea on its eastern side. Of these, there was no doubt that the latter was easier to breach, and in consequence it was this that Wellington selected. If the garrison's morale collapsed (as the British commander appears to have expected), this was all very well, but if it stood firm, then trouble was certain. Thus, the river wall could only be approached at low tide and even then only by wading the Urumea or dashing northwards along its western shore under deadly flanking fire from the bastions that guarded the land approach to the city. Still worse, whichever route was adopted, the nearest trenches would necessarily be over half a mile away. And, finally, despite his behaviour at Vitoria, command of the siege was handed to the brave but otherwise singularly undistinguished Sir Thomas Graham, 'for which reason', wrote Aitchison, 'I am glad that we are to have nothing more to do with it than making gabions . . . for it at a distance'.[8]

The siege, then, proved a grim affair. From the beginning, indeed, the French put up a desperate resistance. Operations against the city began on 7 July, but the defenders had to be cleared from an outwork they had established in a convent outside the walls, whilst, forced to dig many of their batteries in sand dunes, the besiegers had their work cut out just to get their guns into position. 'We tumble and cry "Viva!" twenty times before we can get a twenty-four pounder to budge an inch', complained the artillery commander, Frazer.[9] Frazer thought the practice of the French guns to be not very good, but for the soldiers in the trenches, it was a different story:

We were completely deluged with shot from the half-moon battery. Lieutenant Armstrong commanded the working party, who did their utmost to dig a hole for shelter from this incessant fire but to no purpose as the earth was battered down as soon as raised, and scarcely a man left unhurt . . . Those who escaped . . . were assembled in the shelter of the walls [of the suburb of San Martín], yet here was no safety as the shot flew through the windows and doors, and, rebounding off the walls, hurt many, while stones and mortar falling in every direction bruised some and blinded others . . . We had scarcely got in shelter when a large shell dropped on the floor, rolling about, the fuse blazing. Armstrong stood looking at it, when I laid hold of him and dragged him to the rear of a broken wall at nearly the instant it exploded.[10]

In consequence, it was not possible to start bombarding the walls for twelve days, by which time the attackers had already suffered well over three hundred casualties. By 22 July, however, all seemed ready:

By midday yesterday the breach . . . was perfectly practicable, the wall being entirely levelled . . . The guns have each fired upwards of 300 rounds . . . daily between daybreak and sunset . . . Great part of the town is ruined by our fire. The crashing of houses and roaring of guns make a horrible din.[11]

Had an assault been launched immediately, the city might have fallen – most of its guns, for example, had been silenced – but for a variety of reasons Graham decided to delay the storm until 25 July. Needless to say, this allowed Rey to contrive a series of unpleasant surprises for the attackers, whilst the extra battering helped the attackers not at all, for the new breach that was its product was almost inaccessible to troops attacking along the river bank (the scheme settled on by Graham). Add to all this the most extraordinary mismanagement in the arrangements for the assault itself, and the results were predictable. Few men even reached the breaches, whilst those that did were for the most part quickly killed or wounded. As for the rest of the attackers, jammed together on the narrow strip of land between the defences and low-water mark, they, too, were decimated by heavy fire and eventually forced to fall back to their starting point. As Sergeant Douglas of the Royal Scots remembered:

Waiting for the tide to be sufficiently low to admit men to reach the breach, it was daylight ere we moved out of the trenches, and, having to keep close to the wall to be as clear of the sea as possible, beams of timber, shells, hand grenades and every missile that could annoy or destroy life were hurled from the ramparts on the heads of the men . . . Those who scrambled onto the breach found it was wide and sufficient enough at the bottom, but at the top . . . from thence to the street was at least twenty feet . . . Some little idea may be formed of the destructive fire of the enemy when [I say that] on the beach were left by the tide more [men] than would have loaded a wagon of fish, killed in the water by the shot of the garrison . . . And it not being sufficiently low at the time of the attack those who fell wounded and might have recovered were swept away by the current which runs here very rapid. Nor was it an easy matter for any man to keep his feet as the stones were so slippery.[12]

At Allied headquarters this costly repulse came as a serious blow: 'Lord Wellington was evidently much disappointed with the result of the attack, which I had an opportunity of ascertaining as I dined with him this day, and he scarcely spoke to anyone at table.'[13] All the more was this the case as news was coming in that thirty miles inland dense masses of French troops were pouring through the passes of Maya and Roncesvalles and heading straight for Pamplona. For the origins of this great counter-offensive we must look to events in the French camp following the fall of Joseph Bonaparte. Command of both the battered survivors of the Vitoria campaign and the large reserve forces stationed at Bayonne had been placed in the hands of Marshal Soult. In part, this was undoubtedly meant as one last snub for Joseph, who had, as we have seen, suffered much from Soult's presumption and insubordination, but there was, too, a measure of harsh reality: greedy and untrustworthy though he may have been, 'King Nicholas' was one of the very few subordinate commanders to whom Napoleon could give a command that numbered almost 85,000 fighting troops and, what is more, one on whom rested perhaps the only chance of persuading Austria, which was teetering on the brink of joining the Allies, to remain neutral. At all events, what was needed was an immediate counter-offensive. Displaying immense energy, Soult therefore threw himself into the task of getting his men ready for combat. Serious problems remained – the troops' morale and discipline were very brittle and transport in such short supply that the army in the end re-crossed the frontier with a mere four days' rations – but, by the time that operations at San Sebastián were reaching a climax, the French were on the march.

Creditable though the marshal's efforts were – by throwing his forces across the frontier at Maya and Roncesvalles, Soult wrong-footed Wellington, whose men were scattered across the whole district between Pamplona and the sea – it is hard to see what they were supposed to achieve, for, even if he managed to relieve Pamplona, Soult had no means of restocking its magazines and would have been hard put to maintain his forces in the countryside around it for any real length of time. Even had this not been the case, however, the offensive was soon in trouble. On the frontier itself, some success was obtained. Thus, despite having kept the French at bay for the entire day, the Allied commander at Roncesvalles, Sir Lowry Cole, lost his nerve and abandoned the pass during the night, whilst at Maya savage fighting also saw the French carry the summit. Amongst the casualties was Joseph Sherer of the Thirty-Fourth Foot:

In less than two hours my picket and the light companies were heavily engaged with the enemy's advance, which was composed entirely of *voltigeur* companies . . . These fellows fought with ardour, but we disputed our ground with them handsomely, and caused them severe loss . . . The enemy's numbers now, however, increased every moment: they covered the country immediately in front of and around us . . . The contest now . . . was very unequal. I saw two thirds of my picket . . . destroyed. Among other brave victims, our captain of grenadiers nobly fell, covered with wounds; our colonel [was] desperately wounded, and . . . [I] was myself made prisoner. I owe the preservation of a life, about which I felt . . . regardless, to the interference of a French officer who beat up the muskets of his leading section . . . with some speech about *un français sait respecter les braves*.[14]

Also present was Bell of the same regiment:

It was death to go on against such a host, but it was the order, and on we went to destruction. The colonel . . . was first knocked over, very badly wounded. The captain of grenadiers (Wyatt) . . . was shot through the head . . . My little messmate, Phillips, was also killed . . . Seven more of the officers were wounded . . . Different regiments scrambled up the hill to our relief as fast as they could. The old half-hundred [i.e. the Fiftieth Foot] and [the] Thirty-Ninth got a severe mauling . . . The Ninety-Second were in line, pitching into the French like blazes and tossing them over. They stood there like a stone wall, overmatched by twenty to one . . . When they retired their dead bodies lay as a barrier to the advancing foe.[15]

If the actions at Roncesvalles and Maya hardly constituted a great defeat, they were nevertheless something of an embarrassment. The troops concerned had on the whole fought well – undeterred by having run out of ammunition, the Eighty-Second, indeed, had even resorted to throwing stones at the enemy – but there had in the end been several instances of disorder: Keep, for example, says that he saw the Thirty-Fourth 'retreating most rapidly', and admits that his own Twenty-Eighth was 'forced instantly to flight'.[16] As for the retreat that followed, it quickly took on all the appearance of a rout. Thus:

On quitting this position, the most dismal sensations took possession of our breasts. Not a voice, not a sound was heard, save the slow step and casual murmur of the dejected soldiers, intermingled with the cries and groans of the wounded . . . In this state we kept moving . . . the whole of this sad and sorrowful night amidst the mountains, the woods and the rain, the way being so deluged with mire . . . that it was with difficulty we could wade through it . . . So entangled were we among carts, horses . . . mules, baggage and artillery broken down, together with artillery and other stores that lined the roads, that we could not extricate ourselves from these impediments.[17]

Wellington was much displeased, but his army was far from broken. Pushing on into Spain, the Roncesvalles wing of Soult's army, which was led by the marshal himself, had by 27 July got to within ten miles of Pamplona, only to find its way blocked by a substantial Allied force that had taken post on a high ridge in between the villages of Sorauren and Zabáldica. In command was Wellington himself, who had just reached the field from his headquarters at Lesaca (much to the delight of the troops, who, buoyed up by their faith in his leadership, greeted his sudden appearance in their midst with deafening cheers) whilst further south still more Allied forces, most of them Spanish, waited in reserve. Forced to attack head on on 28 July without the support of the three divisions that had forced the pass of Maya (commanded by the singularly lacklustre Drouet, these forces had been delayed in their march by a combination of bad weather and excessive caution), Soult tried hard to counter the usual Anglo-Portuguese advantage in such combats by making use of a very thick skirmish screen. For a good description of the scene we may turn to Browne, who was riding with Wellington's staff:

At daybreak the French columns were observed, formed in columns of attack and ready for battle. These columns were very deep and . . . moved steadily onwards in the most imposing masses I ever beheld . . . The enemy's grenadiers in their bear-skin caps with red feathers and blue frock coats appeared the most warlike body of troops possible. As they moved on they threw out their skirmishers, which were met by the British light troops, and thus the work of this bloody day began . . . I never remember to have witnessed so tremendous an onset.[18]

There followed ferocious fighting: Wellington, indeed, called it 'fair bludgeon work'.[19] Very much in the thick of things was Sergeant Lawrence of the Fortieth:

Orders had been issued by our officers not to fire till we could do good work, but this soon came to pass, for the French quickly sallied up, and fired first, and we returned it . . . I never saw a single volley do so much execution in all my campaigning days, almost every man of their first two ranks falling, and then we instantly charged and chased them down the mountain, doing still further and more fearful havoc. When we had done, we returned to our old summit again, where the captain cheered and praised us for our gallantry . . . Our likewise brave enemy tried again two hours later to shift us . . . but they were again . . . sent down the hill. We were again praised by our commander, who said, 'I think they . . . won't make a third attack in a hurry', but . . . fours hours had not passed before they were up again. Some of our men then seemed to despair . . . but we reloaded and were then ready to meet them . . . pouring another of our deadly volleys into their ranks and then going at them . . . with our bayonets like enraged bulldogs.[20]

Faced by resistance of this order, Soult could make no progress, practically his only success being the rout of two Spanish battalions that had been posted on an outlying knoll, and by the end of the day the French were back at their starting positions.

With food running out, perhaps 4,000 of Soult's men laid low and more Anglo-Portuguese troops coming up to join the action, the offensive was clearly in ruins. In consequence, the marshal would have been well advised to fall back immediately, but just at the crucial moment he heard that Drouet's men were at last coming up in his right rear, and this persuaded him to strike north-westwards through the foothills of the Pyrenees in an attempt to cut Wellington's army in two and reach San Sebastián. At best a risky proposition, set in motion on the night of 29–30 July, this plan led to disaster. The only possible chance of success rested on disengaging from the battlefield of Sorauren in secrecy, but, as was only to be expected, Wellington realised that the French forces facing him had started to edge away towards their right rear. No sooner had dawn broken on 30 July, then, than the victors of the battle of two days before were streaming down from their positions on the heights and attacking their unfortunate opponents. Caught at a hopeless disadvantage, short of food, demoralised by defeat and deprived of the leadership of their commander, who had ridden on ahead to join Drouet, the French were utterly routed. To quote William Wheeler:

Fifty buglers were sounding the charge, and the drums . . . were beating time to the music. A general rush was made by the whole brigade, accompanied by three British cheers. The concert was too powerful for the nerves of Monsieur . . . and off they danced, the devil take the hindmost, down the hill to our right, the only way they had to escape. We followed them close to their heels and soon got them on a small level, [where] they soon got huddled together like a flock of sheep. This place was well studded with thick bushes of underwood, and here and there a cork tree. As we were galling them with a sharp fire, they summed up resolution to turn on us and threatened us with a taste of steel . . . Now the tug of war began . . . As they could only get away a few at a time . . . many were the skulls fractured by the butts of firelocks . . . The enemy was soon thinned by some getting away and by their loss in killed and wounded, [and] the remainder we made prisoners.[21]

Here and there, fighting was fierce enough: a large force held out in Sorauren itself for two hours, for example, whilst the first battalion of the Eighty-Second Foot suffered very heavily, Wood remembering how 'in less than ten minutes one half my company were . . . knocked down and myself severely wounded by a musket ball'.[22] But by noon it was all over, the survivors of Soult's command either taking flight for the border or retreating along the Maya road to catch up with the marshal. Far to the north-west, Drouet's three divisions succeeded in winning a minor victory over Hill at Lizaso, but there were no troops left in a state fit to exploit this success, and it was in consequence clear that the only hope was flight. Cut off from their original line of communications by Allied troops that had pushed forward from Sorauren, the 35,000 men left with Soult and Drouet had no option but to retire by bad side roads to the valley of the Bidassoa. Aided though they were by a mixture of exhaustion and confusion in the Allied camp, the French were soon hard-pressed and there followed several days of fierce fighting as Soult and his men threaded their way through the mountains and forests that cloaked the entire region. French casualties were heavy and at one point it seemed as if the entire army might be encircled, but, despite much gallantry on the part of British, Spaniards and Portuguese alike, in the end the invaders got away and took up a strong defensive position on the frontier.

Thus ended the great French counter-offensive. Though Allied casualties had also been heavy, nearly 13,000 men had been killed, wounded or taken prisoner, whilst many of the survivors were scattered broadcast across the countryside and living by pillage. Discipline and morale alike had collapsed, and the very slightest pressure must have produced a rout that could have taken Wellington deep into south-western France. An invasion was briefly contemplated but the British commander soon abandoned the idea. It was a welcome relief, for Anglo-Spanish relations were again in the grip of serious controversy. Thanks to a combination of obstruction on the part of the Cádiz authorities, the collapse of local government, the devastation of the countryside, the depredations of many erstwhile guerrillas and, above all, want of revenue, far fewer Spanish troops had fought in the campaign of 1813 than Wellington had intended. However, Napoleon's mistakes had allowed success to be obtained anyway, whilst those Spaniards who had taken the field had all performed well enough, the consequence being that Wellington had set aside his irritation. With the French in eclipse, indeed, the way seemed clear for a general improvement in relations. Yet nothing of the sort transpired. On the contrary, the reduction of the French threat persuaded many Spaniards that they could do without Wellington. In the words of the *Diario de Gobierno de Sevilla*, indeed, it seemed that Spain was now the 'liberator of Europe'. Thus:

Spain has beyond doubt saved Europe, because without her Europe would have been irretrievably lost. Russia . . . has struck a mortal blow against the fantastical domination of France, but it was Spain who was holding the monster . . . for Russia to plunge in the dagger. Russia has defeated her armies and pursued them without let up, but it was Spain who with five years of war tore asunder the veil that had hitherto hidden the weakness of this power that claimed to be irresistible from the eyes of the nations . . . Russia has through her triumphs raised Europe anew against the tyrant, but Spain had first awoken Russia through her own. Russia has shown the peoples that they do not have to be slaves unless they chose to be so, but to prove the point it has had to hold up the example of the people of Spain. There is nothing, in short, that . . . has been done for the salvation of Europe in which Spain will not be found to have given the first impulse.[23]

Even before Vitoria had been fought, the leading liberals were therefore conspiring to engineer Wellington's resignation, in which task they had the willing support of the War Minister, General Juan O'Donoju. To get rid of Wellington, meanwhile, it was decided to make use of General Castaños, who, still the commander of the Fourth Army, was much distrusted on account of his links with Galicia, where anti-liberal feeling had been growing worse by the day. In consequence, on 15 June the victor of Bailén was without explanation ordered to relinquish his command and return to Cádiz to take up a place on the Council of State, several of his subordinates, including his nephew, Pedro Agustín Girón, also being transferred or dismissed. These actions (or, to be more precise, the designation of fresh commanders without consulting Wellington) constituted a clear breach of the conditions under which he had accepted the command-in-chief and Wellington was furious. As he wrote to Henry Wellesley:

I shall be very much obliged to you if you will call together Argüelles, Ciscar, Vega, Toreno and any other persons who may have been concerned in nominating me to the command of the Spanish army, and . . . tell them that if I have not some satisfaction for the insult offered me by these arrangements . . . it will be impossible for me to continue to hold the command . . . I judge from the measures adopted that it is intended to carry out the war against the bishops in Galicia,* for which I conclude that Castaños and Girón are not considered fit instruments. I wish that you

---

* It will be recalled that Galicia had for a variety of reasons (including, as Wellington implied, the attitude of the local bishops) become an important centre of anti-liberal feeling.

would take the same opportunity of pointing out to these gentlemen the danger and imprudence of such measures. It will now rest with the Archbishop of Santiago whether or not we have a civil war in our rear. If we have, we must take leave of all our communications and our supplies of all descriptions, and we shall soon feel the consequences. To be sure, it will be droll enough if, having commenced the war . . . with the clergy and the people in our favour . . . we should be compelled to withdraw by having the clergy and people against us.[24]

No movement was forthcoming, however, whilst the Regency chose to raise the stakes still further by completely disavowing the agreement made in Cádiz in January 1813 on the grounds that it could not consider itself bound by the word of 'its predecessor. But to take this line was to play with fire, for, hitherto neutral in the struggle between the liberals and the *serviles*, Wellington was already hinting not only that the *gaditano* régime should be overthrown, but also that Britain should withdraw from the Peninsula. As he wrote to Bathurst:

We . . . are interested in the success of the war in the Peninsula, but the creatures who govern at Cádiz . . . feel no such interest. All that they care about is the praise of their foolish constitution. There is not one of them who does not feel that it cannot be put into practice, but their vanity is interested in forcing it down people's throats. Their feelings regarding the Inquisition are of the same description . . . The bishops and clergy in Galicia have openly resisted this law, and . . . the people in that province are by no means favourably disposed to the new order of things. In Biscay the people positively refused . . . to accept of the constitution as being a breach of the privileges of their province . . . It appears to me that as long as Spain shall be governed by the *cortes* along republican principles, we cannot hope for any permanent amelioration. To threaten that you would withdraw your assistance without withdrawing if there was no amelioration would only make matters worse. You must be the best judge of whether you can . . . withdraw, but I acknowledge that I do not believe that Spain can be a useful ally . . . if the republican system is not put down.[25]

All through the summer, then, Wellington and Henry Wellesley did what they could to get Cádiz to back down. In this they were quite genuine, for, angry though they were, they at heart wanted to save the Alliance. As Wellington wrote, indeed, 'These fellows are sad vagabonds, but we must have patience with them, and the state of Europe, and of the world, and of Spain in particular, requires that I should not relinquish the command of the Spanish army if I should avoid it.'[26] Behind the scenes, meanwhile, Wellington, Castlereagh and Bathurst debated the pros and cons of intervening in the politics of Patriot Spain. On the whole, the politicians were delighted with the idea, but Wellington waxed hot and cold. Thus at one moment he was writing, 'Jealousy of the interference of foreigners in their internal concerns is the characteristic of all Spaniards, and any declaration of the British government against the liberals would give them more weight and power than they have already'; and, at another, 'It is quite impossible that such a system can last . . . I wish you would let me know whether, if I should find a fair opportunity of striking at the democracy, the government would approve of my doing it.'[27] In the end, however, the idea of a coup was rejected – aside from anything else, on 1 October the *cortes* was due to be replaced by its 'ordinary' and, so it was hoped, more friendly, successor – but that was not to say that all was well for the liberals. Sooner or later, Wellington believed, there would be a rebellion, and this, he continued, would 'enable us to declare openly likewise'.[28]

To save itself from this fate, Cádiz had only to climb down with regard to Castaños and Girón, but there was no sign of such a retreat. Meanwhile, matters were not helped by the behaviour of the Anglo-Portuguese army. Away on the frontier, the siege of San Sebastián had been resumed following the retreat of Soult's army. With the aid of extra siege guns brought in by sea, many fresh batteries were constructed, and on 26 August the bombardment was resumed. With the target once again the vulnerable river front, two great gaps had soon been torn in the defences, and low tide on 31 August therefore saw thousands of British and Portuguese troops hurl themselves upon the defenders. This time there was no mistake. So as to avoid congestion, whilst one column used the route along the foreshore, a second waded across the Urumea from trenches dug on its further bank. At the same time, the assault was distinguished by the daring use of artillery: when the French troops defending the breaches, which were by no means as practicable as they at first appeared, temporarily brought the assault troops to a halt, the siege batteries opened fire over the heads of their assailants and swept them away. 'The artillery in its fire on the curtain was beautifully directed', wrote Tomkinson. 'We looked at the point they were firing on, and . . . saw shot after shot strike in the right place.'[29] Within two hours the Anglo-Portuguese forces had therefore carried the walls, but for some little time more fighting continued to rage inside the town, Rey having barricaded many of the streets and houses. Too few French troops were still on their feet, however, and by late afternoon – the assault had been launched at eleven in the morning – the survivors of the garrison had fallen back into the castle that crowned the lofty northern end of the peninsula on which the town was built.

Thus far, San Sebastián had been a tale of ingenuity and heroism: Allied losses came to 2,376, whilst Douglas provides us with a graphic picture of the horrors experienced in the breach. Thus:

I was coming away making use of my firelock as a crutch, having received a grapeshot in the right leg . . . The scene before me was truly awful. Here you might observe . . . legs and arms sticking up, some their clothes in flames, [and] numbers not dead, but so jammed as not to be able to extricate themselves. I never expected to reach my trench with my life, for, not content with depriving me of my limb, the fire shot away my crutch also . . . Contrary to my expectations, I gained the trench which was a dreadful sight. It was literally filled . . . with the dead and dying. 'Twas lamentable to see the poor fellows here. One was making the best of his way minus an arm; another his face so disfigured . . . as to leave no trace of the features of a human being; others creeping along with the leg dangling to a piece of skin; and, worse than all, some endeavouring to keep in the bowels.[30]

Particularly noteworthy, meanwhile, was the courage displayed by the Portuguese troops who had waded the Urumea. 'It is impossible for troops to have behaved better', wrote Hennell, 'than the Portuguese did . . . They were up to the middle in water, grape . . . and musketry mowing down full half of the first regiment that advanced, and yet they did not hurry or spread, but marched regularly to the breach . . . to the admiration of all spectators.'[31]

But the picture now darkens tremendously. As we have seen, cities taken by storm were universally regarded by their conquerors as legitimate prizes, whilst in San Sebastián the task of controlling the troops was rendered still harder by the confused street fighting that had ended the action, not to mention the abnormally large number of officers that had fallen in consequence of the desperate efforts that had had to be made to get the faltering men to enter the breaches. Notwithstanding the presence of parties of provost marshals who roamed the streets dealing out summary floggings, the result was inevitable. As Gleig wrote:

As soon as the fighting began to wax faint, the horrors of plunder and rapine succeeded. Fortunately there were few females in the place, but of the fate of the few which were there I cannot even now think without a shudder. The houses were everywhere ransacked, the furniture wantonly broken, the churches profaned, the images dashed to pieces; wine and spirit cellars were broken open, and the troops, heated already with angry passions, became absolutely mad by intoxication. All good order and discipline were abandoned. The officers no longer had the slightest control over their men, who, on the contrary, controlled the officers, nor is it by any means certain that several of the latter did not fall by the hands of the former, when they vainly attempted to bring them back to a state of subordination.[32]

As with Ciudad Rodrigo and Badajoz, it would be easy to give page after page of such accounts. Suffice to say that Vivian remarked, 'Never did I see such an example made of a place'; Harley that 'I cannot give an adequate description of the horrible scenes that occurred'; and Schaumann that 'the horrors perpetrated in Magdeburg . . . during the Thirty Years' War were child's play compared with what occurred after the fall of San Sebastián'.[33] Schaumann, at least, was exaggerating – the civilian population was not put to the sword in its entirety as he suggests – but even so murder was common, and the sufferings of the populace severe in the extreme. 'The very few inhabitants I saw said nothing', wrote Frazer. 'They were fixed in stupid horror, and seemed to gaze with indifference at all around them.'[34] And to the horror of sack was added that of fire: thanks to a mixture of explosions and the carelessness of drunken soldiers, a major conflagration broke out which had soon consumed the bulk of the town.

In justification of the sack, it has often been alleged that the inhabitants of San Sebastián were pro-French, and, further, that they had collaborated with Rey in the construction of the barricades and retrenchments with which he sought to frustrate the assault. So common was this story that even Wellington repeated it, and, so far as can be ascertained, believed what he wrote. Thus:

In the course of the enquiry upon this subject, a fact has come out, which I acknowledge that I had not heard of before, and as little suspected . . . viz. that the inhabitants . . . co-operated with the enemy in the defence of the town, and actually fired upon the Allies.[35]

There is here, perhaps, a measure of truth, at least in so far as some of the leading inhabitants of the town are concerned. Thus, for many of the merchants and manufacturers of San Sebastián – the town had not only been an important port but the centre of an area of considerable industrial activity – the *antiguo régimen* had more than anything else signified economic discrimination, for the Basque provinces' privileged status had amongst other things carried with it exclusion from the Spanish customs frontier. In short, goods exported from Guipúzcoa (and, for that matter, Vizcaya, Alava and Navarre) to the rest of Spain had to pay a heavy duty, which had of late been steadily increasing as a means of putting pressure on the Basque notables. Still worse, perhaps, San Sebastián had also been specifically excluded from the decree that had opened the Spanish empire to trade with all Spain's ports. As if this was not enough, Guipúzcoa's industries – primarily iron and linen – had been in the grip of severe structural problems even before the outbreak of the French Wars, and had in consequence suffered even more from them than would otherwise have been the case. With the city the home of a strong French community that had remained undisturbed in 1808 and further alienated by the fact that the traditional provincial assembly was dominated by elements with a strong interest in the status quo, it was therefore hardly surprising that collaboration flourished within the walls, for what San Sebastián needed was either the abolition of Basque privilege (as offered by Joseph Bonaparte) or union with France (as offered by Napoleon).

Yet, in the last resort, all this is irrelevant. Unlike Badajoz, San Sebastián had never been occupied by the Anglo-Portuguese forces, and it was in consequence unknown to the troops. Nor, of course, can the horrors that were visited upon its population be excused by the pro-French attitude of its leading citizens. What took place was quite simply a disgrace – a war crime, indeed. And, in political terms, of course, it was a disaster. Thus, the *jefe político* of Guipúzcoa sent an angry protest to the Regency, accusing the Anglo-Portuguese of massacre, whilst, having grown considerably in the telling, the story was taken up by a number of liberal newspapers including one known to be edited by an employee of the Ministry of War. Amongst the claims that were floated was one to the effect that Wellington had ordered the destruction of the city in order to eliminate the threat that it posed to British trade. To quote *El Duende de los Cafées*:

Merely discussing these events is enough to plunge the imagination into a bottomless pit. At the same time, seeing that this did the British a lot of damage, we should not forget the commerce which San Sebastián was wont to carry on with France in time of peace. Also to be remembered is the fact that San Sebastián was a coastal fortress that under a wise government could have developed into a very respectable port.[36]

Much of this was simply ludicrous. Setting aside the fact that San Sebastián posed no commercial threat to Britain whatsoever, Wellington had specifically discouraged Graham from a general bombardment of the town and set his face against the use of rockets, when this was suggested to him, on the specific grounds that they were useless for anything other than setting fire to towns. Also noteworthy were the warnings that he had sent to Graham of the need to keep the men in hand after the storm. Yet, ludicrous or not, the charge stiffened resistance to Wellington, whilst the more the British protested, the more the Spaniards were inclined to stand upon their dignity. As one journalist wrote, on being taken to task for his criticism:

Enjoying freedom of speech as they do, Spaniards cannot place restrictions on this right without compromising the honour of the nation . . . In nothing do I believe myself to have been out of line, nor still less have I allowed myself to be carried away by foolish hatred of the British government . . . All I have done is to encourage my fellow Spaniards to meet every claim of British correspondents with another of their own, so that even with pen and ink no foreigner will ever defeat Spain.[37]

To expect the liberals and their creatures to give way over Castaños and Girón was therefore optimistic in the extreme. Indeed, the only bright spot was that the army was clearly loyal to Wellington. Thus, in Valencia and eastern Aragón, the garrisons left behind by Suchet had been blockaded by troops of the Second and Third Armies, whilst other troops from these forces had joined the Allied corps that had been sent to the Levante from Sicily the previous year in a renewed attack on Tarragona. A foolish mistake on the part of its new commander, Lord William Bentinck, saw him quite needlessly march the whole of the Third Army off to join Wellington, but this was in part made up for by the fact that the First Army sallied out of its mountain fastnesses and attacked a number of isolated French units (not that this prevented Suchet from evacuating the garrison of Tarragona and inflicting a sharp reverse on Bentinck at Ordal).

As might be expected, however, it was on the Pyrenean front that the Spaniards had their chief opportunity to make their mark. Having done what he could to restore the morale of his battered forces in the wake of Sorauren, Soult made one last attempt to save San Sebastián. On 31 August – the very day of the assault – one column of his troops marched directly across the River Bidassoa in the vicinity of Irun whilst another hooked inland and tried to penetrate the Allied line at Vera. There followed two distinct actions. Near the coast the French found themselves facing the foremost elements of the forces Wellington had left to cover the siege of San Sebastián. Composed of three divisions of the Fourth Army, these were posted on a dominant ridge overlooking the Bidassoa known as the heights of San Marcial. Undaunted by the oncoming French masses, they stood firm, and, waiting until the enemy infantry had reached the crest of the steep slope, drove them off by firing a single volley and then mounting a bayonet charge. Two attacks were beaten off in this fashion, but a third assault secured a lodgement on the heights. For a moment the exhausted Spaniards wavered, but in the end a fresh division threw back the equally weary French. If the victory was exclusively a Spanish one, however, the Spaniards owed this to Wellington:

At San Marcial . . . I had placed the Spanish troops in a position known all over the country for its strength . . . The same evening . . . as I was sitting on a rock watching what was going on, a fellow came up to me – one of their officers – and said he was desired . . . to tell me 'twas impossible they could hold out any longer, and requesting I would send my troops to assist them. I looked through my glass, and I observed that the French were already in movement to retreat . . . 'Well, then,' I said, 'had not you better keep your position a little longer and gain the honour of the day rather than give up the post to our troops?' They did so, and now I see . . . that they claimed this as one of their greatest victories.[38]

The other prong of the French offensive having been abandoned in the face of Allied demonstrations against its left flank, it might be thought that the victory at San Marcial would have done much to counter the effects of the storm of San Sebastián. Indeed, it is hard not to suspect that its all-Spanish nature was in part contrived to smooth ruffled feathers in Cádiz. Yet San Marcial had no impact at all in Spanish counsels – in fact it was rather overshadowed by claims that a group of grandees had offered Wellington the throne in exchange for a promise to convert to Catholicism – whilst harassment of the British on the part of the local authorities became more and more obtrusive. At the key staging point of Bilbao, for example, the *ayuntamiento* restored by-laws that prohibited the movement of wagons through the town, whilst in Vitoria and other towns the British were denied the use of buildings that they needed as billets, storehouses and hospitals. Meanwhile, at Santander British transports were searched for contraband, and the whole port – now Britain's most important base – eventually placed in quarantine on the pretext of a contagious fever that had supposedly broken out at a British military hospital.

The effect of all this, needless to say, was to enrage the British camp. Meanwhile, Wellington's irritation was further increased by the facts that such food as the Spanish armies in the north were receiving was coming from British magazines, that no supplies had been forthcoming from the liberated territories, and that the Spanish intendence and commissariat were costing more to maintain than they produced in the way of money and foodstuffs. Yet the misery which the Spanish armies continued to endure – in grave want of food, they were now also exposed to the sleet and rain of a Pyrenean winter – was not purely the result of *gaditano* machinations. Never likely to be able to cope with the demands of the tens of thousands of troops concentrated on their territory, Vizcaya, Alava, Navarre and Guipúzcoa had now been reached by the liberal revolution. This, however, was not a pleasant experience. For the notables who benefited most from the *fueros*, it represented a considerable blow to their vested interests, and for the mass of the population conscription and increased taxation (in most of the region neither the Church nor feudalism was much of an issue).

Meanwhile, insult was added to injury both by the depredations of the troops (Spanish, British and Portuguese alike) and the fact that the harvest of 1813 had been badly affected by a series of disastrous hailstorms. And, to cap it all, the powerful Espoz y Mina found that he could be 'king of Navarre' no more, the Cádiz government expecting him to surrender the *de facto* political authority that he had hitherto enjoyed into the hands of the new *jefe político*.

What all this meant was the frontier provinces became another stronghold of discontent. At Bilbao, for example, an attempt was made to resist the new political dispensation, whilst Espoz y Mina defied the new authorities and is reputed to have had a copy of the Constitution executed by firing squad. On a more popular level, meanwhile, at Vergara there was a serious tax riot, whilst at Olite and a number of other places British marauders were attacked and even murdered. However, if the troubles experienced by the district most directly affected by the war in the autumn of 1813 were particularly intense, the whole of Spain continued to be gripped by disorders of one sort or another. Thus, in the Levante the retreat of the French from Valencia saw the extension northwards of the anti-feudal disturbances already common in southern parts of the region for the past two years, whilst the old *señores* were also challenged, albeit more generally by legal means, in Castile and Aragón. Despite the spread of discontent, meanwhile, on 10 November 1813 the *cortes* ruled that, provided that they could present due title to their holdings, the nobility should be confirmed in their territorial rights (or, in short, that the populace could bid farewell to their dreams of land redistribution). Even more important as a cause of unrest than this, however, was the *cortes*' fiscal policy. Thus, already groaning beneath the weight of conscription, the populace also had to endure a much tighter system of taxation in the form of a new *contribución única* that took the form of a graduated income tax. In theory much fairer than the multitude of levies which it replaced, this was also harder to evade, whilst a series of oddities in the manner in which it was calculated produced great inequalities in its administration. Thus, Seville's fiscal contributions fell dramatically, whilst those of districts such as Segovia and Guadalajara quadrupled or even quintupled. To add insult to injury, meanwhile, one third of the money owed by each province for the year 1813/14 was ordered to be paid immediately. Hardly surprisingly, the result was pandemonium: so desperate was the situation of the populace that even the liberals' own supporters sometimes requested the suspension of the new system, whilst by March 1814 less than 25 per cent of the 161,000,000 reales demanded on account had come in.

Confirmed by much discussion of the need to form rural gendarmeries and a national guard recruited solely from the propertied classes, the decision of the *cortes* finally to come down on the side of the *pudientes* rather than the *pueblo* at the very least did nothing to reduce the level of banditry in the countryside, and that despite harsh justice of the sort meted out to a gang of marauders put on trial in Jaén in June 1813 (four of the ringleaders were sentenced to death, and the remainder to terms of between six and ten years' penal servitude). Against the robbers, indeed, even patriotism was no defence, Donaldson describing an encounter with a mysterious woman who had just been robbed who turned out to be none other than the almost sacred Agustina of Aragón.* Meanwhile, other problems that had sprung up in the course of the past year in various parts of the country also continued to make themselves felt. Even in the frontier regions, it was proving difficult to get many of the guerrillas to move against the French, whilst in the interior their bands were in many instances at best behaving as miniature armies of occupation. At the same time, though, even in regular units desertion and absenteeism remained very high. Yet most damaging of all were the determined attempts made by local representatives of the *serviles* to undermine the authority of all those tarred with the brush of liberalism. Thus, in Santander, for example, the *jefe político*, Antonio Flórez Estrada, was continually harassed by the cathedral chapter and defeated in his attempts to fill the province's seats in the ordinary *cortes* with loyal place-men. Equally, in Majorca elements of the local clergy stirred up serious riots against the rule of the constitutional *ayuntamiento*. Not for nothing, then, had the *cortes* in June issued an order banning members of the clergy from expressing any view, even in private, that could be held to denigrate, inspire opposition to, or undermine the authority of the régime. For the *serviles*, however, there was more than one way of securing their goals. Particularly useful was the charge of treason. Thus, many of them having come to Cádiz from provinces occupied by the French, the liberals were often open to charges of being enemy agents, as occurred in the case of the Intendent of Guadalajara and distinguished financial expert, José López Juana Pinilla.

To Wellington, however, all this was irrelevant. To him, indeed, all that mattered was that such Spanish troops as had reached the front were literally starving and in consequence had become more of a burden than a source of assistance. As if this was not enough, meanwhile, the forces whom he held responsible for the chaos seemingly remained bent on frustrating his efforts

* See p. 75

to restore order, whilst at the same time doing all that they could to postpone the evil day when they would, or so he assumed, be swept from power in the elections to the ordinary *cortes* (particularly noteworthy in this latter respect were the efforts of the liberal caucus to prohibit the election of priests to the new chamber, to permit members of the original *cortes* to retain their seats until such time as their replacements had arrived from the provinces, and to ensure that the new parliament met in Cádiz rather than Madrid).

Although the liberals were not always successful in these manoeuvres – the election of priests, for example, was never banned – Wellington was still thoroughly disgusted and on 5 October he finally tendered his resignation. A few days earlier, however, the constituent, or 'extraordinary', *cortes* that had assembled in 1810 had finally been replaced by its 'ordinary' successor. It had always been the hope of the British, and, for that matter, the *serviles*, that the new body would be less radical than its predecessor, whose liberal complexion was widely attributed to the excessive influence of Cádiz. There was a considerable degree of miscalculation here, the liberals having succeeded in maintaining a strong foothold in the new assembly. Nevertheless, even if the margin of victory was less than had been hoped, the change was still sufficient to overcome the forces opposed to Wellington. Thus, the Regency's behaviour having been condemned both by a special committee set up to look into the affair and by the Council of State, frantic liberal efforts to swing the final vote in their favour came to naught, and on the night of 28 November 1813 the British general was therefore confirmed in his command by a majority of fifty-nine votes to fifty-four.

By then, however, the affair of Castaños and Girón had in large part ceased to matter. As we have seen, in the autumn of 1813 the chaos that reigned in his rear and the impossibility of depending on Spanish support had been a major factor in dissuading Wellington from undertaking offensive operations in France. In the end, however, diplomatic considerations had outweighed these concerns and on 7 October thousands of British, Portuguese and Spanish troops crossed the frontier. Whilst the Fifth Division took the French by surprise by wading the estuary of the Bidassoa, the Light Division and powerful elements of the Fourth Army scaled the heights that overlooked the river further inland. In the coastal sector of the front, success was immediate, for there were few French troops in the vicinity. Amongst the troops who waded the river was Ensign Gronow of the Guards, for whom it was his baptism of fire:

We commenced the passage of the Bidassoa about five in the morning and in a short time infantry, cavalry and artillery found themselves upon French ground. The stream at the point we forded was nearly four feet deep, and had Soult been aware of what we were about, we should have found the passage of the river a very arduous undertaking. Three miles above we discovered the French army and ere long found ourselves under fire. The sensation of being made a target . . . is at first not particularly pleasant, but 'in a trice, the ear becomes . . . less nice' . . . The French army, not long after we began to return their fire, was in full retreat, and after a little . . . fighting, in which our division met with some loss, we took possession of the camp . . . of Soult's army. We found the soldiers' huts very comfortable: they were built of branches of trees and furze and formed . . . streets which had names placarded up, such as Rue de Paris, Rue de Versailles, etc.[39]

The mountains to the east having been fortified by a chain of redoubts, there was some sharp fighting before the defenders were put to flight. Drawn from the élite Light Division, however, the attackers were not to be checked. As Leach of the Ninety-Fifth wrote:

The business commenced by our third battalion climbing a small mountain on which the French had a small advanced post. After a sharp conflict the enemy was driven from it . . . and General Kempt's brigade was enabled, by a movement to its right and a flank fire on their engagement, to dislodge a strong force of French infantry, who must have been made prisoners if they had not bolted like smoked foxes from their earths. During these operations Colonel Colbourne's brigade had a much more arduous task to perform. His opponents could not be taken in flank and he was therefore obliged to advance straight against them, entrenched up to their chins . . . A succession of redoubts . . . were carried by the bayonet, and those who defended them were either shot, bayoneted or driven off the mountain.[40]

Only on their extreme left, where they were ensconced on the dominant peak known as La Grande Rhune, were the French able to hang on, and even here they abandoned their positions the next day on the grounds that they had become untenable. With only 1,600 casualties, half of them Spanish, the operation had been a great success, whilst there seemed nothing to stop Wellington from pushing deep into France, for Soult's troops were clearly both in poor heart and far too few in number.

Once again, however, the Allied army paused in its march, Soult being allowed to pull back to a new defensive position behind the River Nivelle. As before, the reasons were political. Although events were gradually moving Wellington's way in Cádiz, there was no guarantee that the battle would be won, nor, still less, that the Spanish forces that made up at least a quarter of his effective field strength could remain in action. Still worse, serious difficulties were also being experienced with the Portuguese. With the French now far removed from their borders, the authorities had little reason to continue their incessant struggle with the populace in the matter of conscription. At the same time the serious economic disruption consequent on the transfer of Britain's main supply port to Santander meant that the troops were now worse supplied than ever. Finally, there was great resentment of the British, and even some fear that Spain was bent on invasion. Through considerable effort, Beresford was able to avert a crisis, but for a time it looked as if the army's vital Portuguese contingent might literally dwindle away to nothing. Meanwhile, there still remained the campaign in Germany, which, for all Wellington knew, might still go either way, and Pamplona, whose blockade was tying down not just substantial Spanish forces, but also two of Wellington's Anglo-Portuguese divisions.

On 31 October, however, the starving garrison of Pamplona surrendered with the result that a fresh advance could be put off no longer. On the morning of 10 November, then, whilst several divisions contained the French right, 55,000 Allied troops moved forward against the rugged hills and mountains that marked the position of Soult's centre-left. The French had 60,000 men and had studded the line of the Nivelle with a complicated network of redoubts and other fortifications, but Soult's men were stretched very thin, as well as being hungry and demoralised. Within two hours the Light Division had stormed the outwork which the defenders had maintained on the commanding height known as the Petite Rhune: 'Some heavy cannon sounded the advance,' wrote Simmons, 'and in a moment everyone was in motion up the sides of this tremendous steep. Obstacles of an extraordinary nature were opposed to us, but nothing could impede the ardour of Britain's brave sons.'[41] Meanwhile, midday found the troops echeloned to the mountain's right deep inside the French positions. Here and there the fighting had been very sharp, and there had been plenty of casualties. Amongst the fallen was Robert Blakeney, who 'being struck by a shot which shattered both the bones of my leg . . . asked [Lieutenant Vincent] . . . to place me against a tree which stood close by . . . and then . . . cheered on the regiment'.[42] Also down was William Wheeler. The latter having left us a wonderful picture of the common soldier's view of a firefight, he is worth citing at some length:

On the top of the hill, they had a reserve: these came forward and gave us a crack . . . As I was in the act of pulling my trigger, I received a wound in both legs. The ball . . . scraped the skin just above the outside ankle of the left foot and passed through the gristle behind the ankle of the right, just missing the bone, [and] down I fell. I endeavoured to rise, but found I could not stand and that my shoe was full of blood. 'The devil's luck to you for a fool', said Ned Eagan. 'Now can't you be easy and lie quiet for a minute or so till we . . . send them in double quick over the hill?' At this moment, Hooker came to me and said, 'I hope . . . you are not much hurt. Take some of this rum' . . . Hooker was employed in emptying some of the rum into my canteen . . . when down [Eagan] came on top of us . . . shot through the body.[43]

Yet reserves of the sort encountered by Wheeler were few and far between, whilst many troops found that their flanks had been turned before they had had a chance to fire a shot. For a good impression of the fighting, one has only to turn to Donaldson of the Ninety-Fourth:

The enemy having been driven from the redoubts in front of Sarre, we advanced . . . to the attack of the enemy's main position on the heights behind it, on which a line of strong redoubts were formed with abattis in front . . . Colonel Lloyd, having pushed his horse forward before the regiment, advanced cheering with the most undaunted bravery, but before he reached the summit he received a mortal wound in the breast, and was only saved from falling off his horse by some of the men springing forward to his assistance. When this was perceived by the regiment . . . regardless of everything, they broke through all obstacles, and driving the enemy from their position, they . . . charged through their burning huts without mercy.[44]

In short, the French were heavily defeated, only the onset of night saving them from a major disaster. Even so, at 4,300 men their casualties much outmatched the approximately 3,000 suffered by the Allies, whilst they also lost 59 guns.

With the Nivelle breached, Soult had no option but to fall back once again, this time taking up a position that stretched south-eastwards from the fortress of Bayonne along the River Nive. However, for a variety of reasons there was no pursuit. No sooner had the battle of the Nivelle been fought than winter closed in, deluging the troops with rain and turning the roads into a quagmire. Despite Napoleon's decisive defeat at Leipzig, Wellington quite rightly remained suspicious that there were elements in the Allied camp who were still dreaming of a compromise peace that would have left Britain and her Iberian allies open to massive retribution. Despite encouraging signs that the people of south-western France were desperately war-weary and increasingly hostile to the imperial régime, there was no guarantee that full-scale invasion would not kindle a spirit of patriotism and defiance. Thanks to lack of naval support – the south-eastern reaches of the Bay of Biscay were a difficult station for British warships in the depths of winter – and the daring of French and American privateers operating out of Bayonne, there were delays in the arrival of food and coin from Britain. But, above all, there were once again problems with the Spaniards.

Thus, no sooner had Spanish forces crossed the frontier, than they had engaged in many acts of violence against French civilians. This, of course, was anathema to Wellington, and in consequence he decided to send almost all the Spanish troops with him back to Spain. As he wrote:

I despair of the Spaniards. They are in so miserable a state that it is really hardly fair to expect that they will refrain from plundering a beautiful country into which they enter as conquerors, particularly adverting to the miseries which their own country has suffered from its invaders. I cannot, therefore, venture to bring them into France ... Without pay and food, they must plunder, and if they plunder they will ruin us all.[45]

To add insult to injury, meanwhile, it was ordered that the soldiers concerned should be kept permanently under arms – in other words, formed up in their units – until they were well within the Spanish frontier. An act of some courage on the part of Wellington – he was effectively sacrificing his numerical superiority and at the same time sending back seasoned troops who had on the whole been fighting very well of late – this provoked fury among the Spanish generals, the latter feeling that they were being publicly humiliated and treated with the greatest injustice.

Whether these disputes would have any impact on the future of the Alliance remained to be seen – it should be noted that at this point the matter of Wellington's resignation still had to be decided on by the *cortes* – but, even if they did not, almost a quarter of the army that had crossed the Bidassoa was out of action. With the authorities in Cádiz in the meantime seemingly not making the slightest attempt to address the logistical situation and doing all that they could to subvert Wellington's control of the Spanish army (in particular, an attempt was made to remove the Inspectors-General of the cavalry and infantry – the officers responsible for the internal arrangements of these two arms of the service – from the British commander's headquarters), it also remained hard to discount the possibility of a complete rupture in relations. All the more was this the case as Wellington had resolved that the British subsidy should henceforth only be paid to troops who were actually present with his forces in France, the Regency having in the meantime gone so far as to release Ballesteros from captivity in the expectation that he would take over as supreme commander.

In the face of this hostility the British commander was deeply worried. As he wrote to Bathurst, 'Matters are becoming so serious with the Spaniards that I think it necessary to . . . request Your Lordship to consider what will be the consequence of this state of affairs, supposing that any reverse were to happen.'[46] Yet despite these troubles, Wellington could not remain where he was, for Soult's decision to hold the line of the Nive ensured that the Anglo-Portuguese army was trapped in an narrow salient running northwards along the coast from the Pyrenees. In these circumstances, staying put would be more dangerous than moving forward, and Wellington therefore decided to cross the Nive, advance to the River Adour, and close up on Bayonne. In itself there was nothing wrong with this plan, but it did mean that the Anglo-Portuguese army would necessarily be split in two by a major river that was now crossed only by a number of fords, the various bridges scattered along its length having all been destroyed by Soult's forces. Bayonne possessing no fewer than three bridges across the Nive, Soult therefore realised that the way was open to him to throw all his strength against one or other half of the opposing army in an attempt to defeat it in detail. And so it transpired. Somewhat to the surprise of Wellington's forces, on 9 December the Nive was crossed almost unopposed, the enemy troops on the far bank promptly melting away in the direction of Bayonne. Nor was any resistance experienced on the left bank of the river, where a strong force under the newly arrived Sir John Hope marched directly on the city from the south. By the evening, then, the Anglo-Portuguese army was drawn up in a great arc stretching from the southern bank of the Adour to the sea. Pontoon bridges had been laid to connect the two halves of the army whilst a bridge that had been destroyed by the French at Ustaritz some miles up river had been repaired and brought back into service.

All seemed well, then, but on the morning of 10 December Hope's forces were taken by surprise by a large force of French troops that suddenly emerged from the defences of Bayonne and crashed into their leading elements (so certain was Hope that Soult would remain on the defensive that at the close of the previous day he had actually ordered a third of his command to return to their starting point at the port of Saint-Jean-de-Luz some ten miles down the coast). Heavily outnumbered, the Allied troops in the path of this onslaught were driven back, and it was only with some difficulty that the French were finally brought to a halt at the Chateau of Barrouillet. Further to the right, however, the Light Division had had little difficulty defending the Church of Arcangues. According to Bell, indeed, 'The Light Infantry and Rifles liked the tombstones: they said they were . . . a steady rest for a pot shot and a good shield.'[47] Though indecisive fighting continued for the whole of the eleventh, and was resumed with greater force on the twelfth, when the French again almost captured the chateau, the attack had clearly lost impetus, and the evening of this third day of combat saw Soult's men fall back into the city.

The French, it seemed, had once again been defeated, but 'King Nicholas' was not yet finished. On the contrary, 13 December saw him switch his troops to the right bank of the Nive and launch them against the forces of Sir Rowland Hill. There followed a furious battle. For a while the Allies were in some danger: rain in the Pyrenees had sent a torrent of floodwater down the Nive and swept away their pontoon bridges, whilst the French made considerable progress. As Bell wrote:

Every point was attacked to weaken our force and keep us separate, their guns keeping up a terrific fire, knocking the dust out of Saint Pierre . . . ploughing up the side of the hill, thinning our ranks, and playing Old Harry, having no regard for life or limb . . . 'Dead or alive,' said our chief, 'we must hold our ground.'[48]

Yet the capable Hill had not won the reputation of being Wellington's most capable subordinate for nothing. Secure in the knowledge that reinforcements were on the way (for the bridges were hastily repaired and other troops sent up from the rear), he gathered his forces and launched a vigorous counter-attack that eventually succeeded in driving the French troops opposed to him back to the walls of Bayonne. So severe was the French rout, indeed, that a delighted Wellington observed, 'I have often seen the French licked, but I have never seen them get such a hell of a licking as Hill has given them.'[49]

Known collectively as the battle of the Nive, the fighting round Bayonne had been a bloody affair. In all, indeed, over 11,000 men had become casualties. The French losses, however, considerably outnumbered those of the Allies, whilst the gaps in Soult's ranks were increased by the desertion on the evening of 10 December of three battalions of German troops in response to a secret message from the Duke of Nassau – one of the many German rulers who had switched sides following Leipzig – ordering them to go over to the Allies. In addition to the 1,400 troops who went in this fashion, Soult and Suchet also lost the services of all the rest of their German units – another 3,000 men – as it was felt that they must in consequence be disbanded. Meanwhile, the Adour's defenders were not only much depleted, but all too clearly incapable of further offensive action. Twice, indeed, the whole of their disposable strength had fallen on a single wing of the army opposed to them, and twice it had been repelled. All Soult could now hope for, in short, was to defend the line of the Adour. As the battles of Orthez and Toulouse were yet to show, the *armée d'Espagne* was still not broken, but all chance of carrying the fight beyond the Pyrenees had gone.

By the end of 1813, then, although the French still held northern Catalonia and a series of outposts scattered from Santoña to Peñíscola, barring a stunning change of fortune in the rest of Europe, the Peninsular War had finally been decided in favour of the Allies. Soult was out of the fight and Suchet too weak to attempt anything, whilst the commands of both marshals were already being plundered for the cadres needed for the new armies that Napoleon was trying to form in place of the forces destroyed at Leipzig. Even had victory been achieved in the Pyrenees, it is hard to see how the French could have continued to maintain a foothold in Navarre and the Basque provinces, let alone reverse the verdict of Vitoria. By the autumn of 1813, indeed, their one hope on the Pyrenean front was that Britain, Spain and Portugal would fall out with one another. Herein, however, lay the rub. Inter-Allied relations were not good, and it is possible that in time the French might have won a great deal. Yet in the event, the Alliance was not found wanting: though the British, Spaniards and Portuguese hated one another, in the end they hated Napoleon still more.

18

Báscara

PEACE AND THEREAFTER

It was 24 March 1814. Near the village of Báscara the two armies faced one another across the bridge in the noon sunshine, Spaniards on the one hand and Frenchmen on the other. Yet not a musket sounded. Amongst the Spanish soldiers could be seen crowds of excited civilians, whilst the rival troops began to exchange cheers with one another. Alerted by a nine-gun salute, a group of Spanish officers arrayed in their brightest uniforms rode down to the bridge. Very shortly, there came a similar movement on the other bank, and soon a number of figures were being greeted on bended knee. From the hills all around, there immediately came a storm of cheering: King Fernando VII had returned.

Did the king enjoy his own again, however? Almost six years to the day since his tumultuous accession to the throne, Spain had changed immeasurably. In place of the absolute monarchy and strict censorship of 1808, she now possessed a Constitution and a flourishing press, whilst gone, too, were her feudal system, foral privileges, hereditary town councils, internal customs barriers, and archaic systems of conscription and taxation. All Spaniards were equal before the law, and, except in matters of religion, free, although even here there had been great change, the Church having experienced an enormous reduction in its power and wealth. Not all of this was necessarily anathema to Fernando, who secretly welcomed the manner in which certain goals that had eluded his father and grandfather for fifty years had suddenly been achieved, but at the same time it was clear that he was hardly being restored in the full plenitude of his power. With *el rey deseado* a rigid and unbending defender of the royal prerogative and the Constitution a document certain to give even the most moderate of princes much offence – even some liberals admitted that it treated the monarch as a dangerous wild beast – conflict between Fernando and the Patriot régime was inevitable. All that remained, indeed, was the question of whether or not the king would attempt to attack the new order head-on.

By comparison with the great political struggle that now unfolded, military affairs pale into insignificance. In France, after a considerable spell of inactivity in winter quarters, British, Portuguese and Spanish soldiers continued to battle the enemy, but the tale of how Wellington besieged Bayonne, liberated Bourdeaux, and finally defeated Soult's army at Toulouse is one that belongs not so much to the history of the Peninsular War as to that of the great invasion of France that produced Napoleon's abdication on 6 April 1814. Nor does much interest attach to such military events as took place in the Peninsula, for these boiled down to little more than a series of ineffectual blockades that are remarkable chiefly for the evidence they provide of the miserable condition of the Spanish army and the erstwhile guerrillas' lack of interest in prosecuting the war. The isolated French garrisons that remained had long since been besieged by a variety of Spanish forces. Mendizábal's division of the Fourth Army lay before Santoña and part of Mina's before Jaca, whilst the other strongholds absorbed all the forces of the Second Army except a single division – that of Sarsfield – that had been marched to Catalonia. To be precise, Peñíscola and Denia were guarded by the division of General Mijares; Sagunto by that of Roche; Tortosa by those of Villacampa and El Empecinado; and Lérida, Benasque, Mequínenza and Monzón by that of Durán.

As these dispositions reveal, the majority of the forces involved in these mopping-up operations consisted of troops who owed their origins to *la guerrilla*, whilst the proportion of erstwhile members of the *partidas* thus engaged was increased still further by Wellington's decision to confide the blockade of the minor French fortresses of Saint-Jean-Pied-du-Port and Navarrenx to troops from the divisions of Mina and Morillo (as Wellington had advanced deeper into France, so it had become more and more difficult to refrain from making use of Spanish troops, a large part of the Third and Fourth Armies eventually returning to French territory). Yet erstwhile guerrillas were not the troops best suited to protracted blockades and sieges. Never very happy about their subordination to military discipline in the first place, they lost what little interest they had ever possessed in the struggle, and all the more so as they were often almost as hard pressed for supplies as their opponents. Operations in consequence in most cases became very desultory and, even where they were pursued with greater vigour, the defenders were generally able to hold out without much difficulty. Thus, the only towns to fall were Denia and Morella, both of which were held by no more than a single company.

Only at the beginning of 1814 did the situation show some movement. In the first place Suchet, who, apart from a short-lived attempt to evacuate Tortosa and Lérida, had been keeping quiet on the Llobregat, was in January forced to retire to Gerona following the receipt of orders directing him to send off 10,000 men to assist in the defence of France, this leaving the Anglo-Sicilian expeditionary force (now commanded by Clinton), Sarsfield's division of the Second Army, and elements of the First Army free to close in on Barcelona. Still held by a substantial garrison, the city was to remain defiant until the fall of Napoleon and beyond – the last action of the war, indeed, was a sortie launched by its governor, General Habert, on 16 April 1814 – but in early March still further territory was given up by Suchet after fresh orders stripped him of nearly half his remaining 24,000 troops, the only ground that he still clung on to being the narrow district around Figueras.

Accompanied, as it was, by almost no fighting, the Spanish recovery of Catalonia was all but bloodless. Equally tame was the end of the few French garrisons that fell into their hands. Reduced to a state of complete starvation, Jaca gave up on 17 February, whilst Lérida, Mequínenza and Monzón were tricked into surrendering by a turncoat *juramentado* named Van Halen who succeeded in persuading their governors that Suchet had negotiated a convention for the evacuation of Catalonia. Troops of the Fourth Army fought well enough at the battle of Toulouse on 10 April 1814, but on the whole it was a singularly inglorious end to six years of hardship and sacrifice, the dissatisfaction of the Spanish generals being compounded by their troops' behaviour continuing to attract the most ferocious strictures from Wellington.

The humiliation and frustration experienced by the Spanish army in these last months of the war were to have a considerable impact on the fate of the liberal régime, but before looking at this issue we must first examine the dramatic developments that led to the release of Fernando VII at Báscara on 24 March 1814. Desired though he may have been, the young king was hardly deserving. Whilst Spain was devastated from coast to coast in his name, he had spent the war in comfortable imprisonment in Talleyrand's chateau at Valençay in the company of his uncle, Don Antonio, and his brother, Don Carlos, rebuffing attempts to organise his escape and penning numerous messages of congratulation to Napoleon and Joseph Bonaparte. Yet dubious as this conduct was, it persuaded Napoleon that Fernando was a fellow cynic, and thereby sowed the seeds of the final phase of his Iberian policy. Hitherto the interests of prestige had always precluded Napoleon from cutting his losses in the Peninsula, but there was no longer anything to lose, whilst Leipzig had dealt him such a blow that the damage that would be done by a climb down was now far outweighed by the cost of fighting on.

How, though, to slough off the Iberian entanglement? Herein, of course, lay the value of Fernando VII, for it seemed that there would be no difficulty in getting him to accept a deal that would place him back on the throne on Napoleon's terms. As to what these were, all Fernando had to do was to permit the evacuation of all the imperial forces from Spain, expel the British and Portuguese, sign a treaty of peace with France, accede to the Continental Blockade, and pardon all those who had collaborated with Joseph Bonaparte. To make these arrangements still more attractive, Fernando was promised the hand of the elder daughter of *el rey intruso*, whilst a picture of events in Spain was painted that was calculated to fill the monarch with fear and apprehension. Already concerned by what he had heard, Fernando was easy enough to win over, the monarch's only concern being that he avoid being damned as a mere tool of the emperor, to which end he insisted that he be allowed to consult with the Regency and *cortes*. Though a treaty was signed on 10 December, the Duque de San Carlos and José Palafox were therefore dispatched to Spain to secure its ratification, their private instructions suggesting that the king intended to stick by his agreement unless Regency and *cortes* proved willing to back the restoration of absolutism (or, in other words, that Fernando would happily ally himself with Napoleon to defeat the liberals).

Fernando, however, was out of touch with the realities of Patriot Spain. Difficult though relations with Britain may have been, neither liberals nor *serviles* could stomach the idea of an alliance with Napoleon. Despite British fears to the contrary, when San Carlos and Palafox arrived in Madrid – since the previous month once again capital of Spain – in January 1814, they therefore got nowhere. As soon as news arrived of Napoleon's offer, the current Spanish Foreign Minister, José Lujando, went to see Henry Wellesley and not only provided him with full details of the treaty, but declared that it was already a dead letter. As for the Regency, it wrote a polite note to Fernando informing him that the *cortes* had long since declared that any action taken by the king whilst he was still a prisoner would be considered null and void, whilst privately telling his emissaries that Fernando must look to the Allies for his salvation. At the same time, fearing that the king might be released from captivity anyway, on 2 February the *cortes* passed a decree imposing severe restrictions on Fernando should he cross the border, and issued a manifesto accusing Napoleon of trying to stir up civil war. And, at the front too, the Spaniards remained loyal. To quote Larpent:

I have just heard of another curious trick of the French here. They advanced towards Morillo's Spaniards [and] the latter fired at them. They sent in to say they were very much surprised, for they understood they were at peace with the Spaniards now as a treaty was signed. Morillo sent back for answer that he knew of no such peace, and [that], if the *cortes* . . . had signed such a peace, still he should continue to . . . fire at the French.[1]

For obvious reasons, all of this came as a pleasant surprise to the British. As even Wellington admitted, the Spaniards 'have conducted themselves remarkably well and with great candour and frankness upon this occasion'.[2] Indeed, conciliation seemed the order of the day. The hostile O'Donoju was dismissed as War Minister; attempts to charge customs duty on supplies and munitions imported for the use of the Anglo-Portuguese army were repudiated; free trade was hinted at; and Henry Wellesley was assured not only that Spain was opposed to a separate peace with Napoleon, but also that the *cortes* intended to prohibit any revival of the Treaty of Alliance that had bound Spain and France together prior to the French Revolution. All this, however, did not represent a sudden change of heart on the part of the liberals. Instead, it betokened a revival of the old strategy of turning to Britain for support in the face of domestic counter-revolution. Of this, there now seemed a real danger, but, despite their violent language, increased strength, and continued attempts to win over Wellington and Henry Wellesley, this did not come from the *serviles*. On the contrary, the first months of 1814 revealed the latter to be a paper tiger. Divided between traditionalists out to restrict royal authority and caroline bureaucrats eager to restore the situation of 1808, they completely failed to exploit the somewhat greater numbers which they enjoyed in the new *cortes*. Thus, clumsy tactics ensured the collapse of attempts to use the affair of Castaños and Girón to bring down the government, whilst plans to vote in a new Regency foundered over the question of its composition. With the liberals also much better at packing the public galleries with friendly crowds, their control of affairs therefore remained unshakeable. As a disgusted Henry Wellesley complained:

The jacobin party has . . . successfully resisted the feeble efforts of their opponents . . . Under the circumstances . . . it may be considered as fortunate that I am not in any way committed with a party which with a majority of two to one in the *cortes* has neither the courage, the activity nor the intelligence . . . to effect the object which they have in view.[3]

If the *serviles* were little threat, the British, too, had abandoned the fight. Unable to contemplate the loss of one of the chief props of their struggle to build a great coalition against Napoleon, the Liverpool administration had backed away from any confrontation with the *cortes*. As for Wellington, gloom over Spain's political situation was mixed with a recognition that relations with the Spaniards had indeed improved. 'The mob of Madrid,' he wrote, 'will be just as bad as the mob in Cádiz . . . Both are set in motion by the same machine, the press, in the hands, I believe, of the same people. The mercantile class will not have quite so much influence at Madrid, although they will not want partisans when they desire to carry a question by violence. The grandees had formerly a great deal of influence at Madrid, but they are too poor at present, and their situation is too degraded for them to be able to do much under existing circumstances.'[4] Yet that did not mean that he supported a change of régime:

Nothing can be more satisfactory than the . . . conduct of the Spanish government regarding the negotiations for peace, and I entertain serious doubts whether . . . the British government should be in any way party to a change under the existing circumstances. I am certain that no government would act better than they have in this most important of all concerns, and I doubt that any Regency under the existing constitution would have power to act better in other matters more peculiarly of internal concern.[5]

As for the idea of a British-led coup, this was in Wellington's eyes even worse, the British commander refusing point-blank to intervene on the grounds that it would be entirely counterproductive.

Yet danger there was, for the Spanish army – the one force that had the capacity to effect a change in the régime – was becoming more and more alienated. By January 1814, indeed, the Conde del Abisbal was suggesting to Wellington that troops should be sent to Madrid. To understand this situation, it is necessary to set aside preconceived ideas about armies as bastions of reaction, for there were many officers who owed a great deal to the revolution. For the third of the officer corps who had not been nobles in 1808, it had in many cases brought advancement, whilst many civilians had gained access to the military estate of a sort that would have been denied them under the Bourbons. This did not mean that the officer corps had been bourgeoisified: whilst the percentage of titled aristocrats in the *generalato* had declined from 23 per cent in 1808 to only 14 in 1814, of the 458 new generals appointed during the war, at least 173 had already been officers of the rank of *sargento mayor* (i.e. adjutant) or above at the beginning of the conflict, whereas only 9 are definitely known to have been civilians, and only 1 a member of the rank and file. Nevertheless, with the army an integral part of Bourbon reformism prior to 1808, even senior officers would not necessarily have sympathised with the *serviles*, all the more so given that many *serviles* supported the Church against the claims of the Spanish monarchy. With more thoughtful officers all too well aware that war on the scale of the struggle against the French empire demanded resources far beyond anything that the Bourbon régime could have mustered, the result was considerable support for liberalism (indeed, a number of liberal deputies and propagandists were actually army officers).

In short, self-interest and conviction coincided to produce a nucleus of liberal support within the officer corps, one of its greatest bastions being the general staff created in 1810. Nor was this support extinct in the last months of the war, as witness, for example, the flood of congratulatory resolutions of military origin-occasioned by the abolition of the Inquisition; the obstructive behaviour of Juan O'Donoju; and the angry response of the local military commanders to the attempts that were made to defend the Basque *fueros* from destruction at the hands of the Constitution of 1812. Indeed, with a number of the guerrilla commanders absorbed into the regular army in the last two years of the war being men who were for good reason overtly liberal, the cause may even be said to have received a certain degree of reinforcement.

The danger of a military coup, then, did not arise from some predisposition to reaction on the part of the officer corps. Much more to the point was the latter's experience of war and revolution. From the beginning the climate in Patriot Spain had been distinctly anti-militarist. Not only had many officers perished in the uprising of May 1808, but the authority of the army had been severely reduced and the autonomy of the military estate invaded in an unprecedented manner. Following the uprising, meanwhile, new officers and old had found themselves waging a desperate war against a powerful aggressor in the most unfavourable circumstances. Hostile to military discipline, the troops had been prone to riot and desertion, just as the populace had done all that it could to resist the draft. Meanwhile, unscrupulous and irresponsible propagandists had created false expectations of victory, whilst equally unscrupulous and irresponsible politicians had interfered in the conduct of military operations, failed to supply the army with the sinews of war, fomented alternative structures of military organisation that hindered the war effort as much as they assisted it, and made general after general scapegoats for disasters which were often none of their making. Typical, perhaps, was the deluge of complaints with which Castaños and other generals were bombarded after the disasters of November–December 1808. For example:

General Castaños is one of the most wicked men of our times. I say this because ever since he entered Madrid garlanded in laurels which he did not merit to the repeated cheers . . . of the inhabitants . . . he has spent all his time delaying the march of his troops, thinking up wrong-headed plans, changing his positions every other moment, discouraging his soldiers [and] opposing anyone who might frustrate his evil plans.[6]

Many of these denunciations were the fruit not so much of dissatisfaction with the officer corps *per se* as the scheming of such factions as the Palafox-ists. Needless to say, they were also frequently very unfair. As Castaños himself observed:

The word 'traitor' no longer signifies what we have understood until now: a traitor is a general who does not attack when a private feels like it, or when it is desired by those 200 leagues from the enemy; a 'traitor' is a general who retreats an army which is going to be enveloped and sacrificed without benefit or utility to the country.[7]

But the generals committed so many errors that they could not be exonerated from all blame. To quote a letter of the Junta of La Carolina written after the battle of Almonacid:

The caprice and arbitrary behaviour of the generals have led a defeated and demoral-ised enemy to victory . . . There can be no nation in history that has made war in the way in which we have been making it. Amongst our commanders co-ordination and intelligence are entirely unknown.[8]

From all this there stemmed a line of thought that was social and political dynamite. Denouncing all army officers as 'libertines', for example, one anonymous letter that was sent to the Junta Central argued that the only way to win was by 'making the veteran soldier a sergeant, the veteran corporal a captain, and the veteran sergeant a colonel'.[9] Even more explicit was the newspaper, *El Patriota*:

The shameful madness . . . of believing that the commanders of the old army . . . are the men most versed in the difficult art of war has caused us . . . the most bitter sorrow . . . In a new situation everything must be new, and so no general should be employed except those formed . . . in the revolution.[10]

All this was bad enough, but when the liberals came to power in 1810 the troubles of the officer corps were redoubled. At the heart of liberal ideology lay a conviction that regular armies were 'incompatible with the liberty of nations'.[11] Completely segregated from the rest of society, pro-fessional soldiers could have no interest in the liberty of their fellow citizens and were as likely to repress as they were to defend them. Little else could be expected, for their ordnances were 'truly despotic and suitable for slaves' and designed to make them 'the instrument of tyranny'.[12] Bound by rigid discipline and accustomed to violence and killing, soldiers automatically became 'the natural enemies of liberty' for they were incapable of recognising 'any other right than that of force, any other law than the demands of their officers'.[13] As proof of this argument, the liberals argued that, in ancient Rome, imperial Spain and revolutionary France alike, the substitution of a regular army for a citizen's militia had led to the emergence of despotism, whilst as time went on they could also point to the arrogance and Caesarism exhibited by many Spanish commanders. Convinced that a standing army was a threat to liberty, the liberals sought to prove that such a body was also a military liability. The essence of their claim was that the very existence of an army guaranteed the establishment of despotism, which in its turn led to national impotence. 'A slave people,' it was maintained, 'is incapable of any act of true valour because its sacrifices cannot bring it any reward.'[14] From this it followed that military strength was proportionate to freedom. Hence the decline of all the empires of the past and the prosperity enjoyed by Great Britain: whereas the former had all succumbed to despotism, the British had experienced a steady growth in their political freedom. Meanwhile, regular armies were no match for a free people. Regular soldiers would not fight bravely because they could not hope to improve their lot, whilst the brutal discipline to which they were habitually subjected meant that they could not be expected to show any fervour in the defence of freedom, the latter being a concept which was beyond them. In consequence, the liberal ideal was a citizens' militia. Not only would such a force pose no threat to liberty, but it would be fighting for home and freedom. As for the soldiers themselves, they would be better prepared for war by a healthy life in the fields than by the boredom, discomfort and disease of the barracks. A further barrage of historical precedent was laid down to support this conclusion, the Persian Wars, the Punic Wars, the *reconquista*, the Swiss revolt against the Habsburgs, and the American War of Independence all being cited as proof of the superiority of citizen armies. As if all this was not enough, further testimony to the superiority of the Nation-in-Arms was found in the prodigies ascribed to the Spanish guerrillas and the Voluntarios Distinguidos de Cádiz (though in fact the latter had never done anything more than perform guard duty). To reinforce their argument, meanwhile, the liberals drew a comparison between the French and Spanish revolutions. According to their version of events, at the start of the Revolutionary Wars France had possessed a powerful regular army, but she had nevertheless been consistently beaten until she had instigated the *levée en masse*. In Spain, the opposite had occurred, however, the armed people having everywhere defeated the French until they had been formed into regular armies. In the same way, defeat had allegedly been changed into victory in the Russian campaign of 1812 when 'the cabinet war waged by the Russians was converted into a national war by the people taking an interest in their own defence'.[15]

Reinforced by a distrust of the executive power that was almost paranoid in its intensity – it was held that the desire to find happiness and self-fulfilment ensured that rulers and governments could not but strive for absolute power – these views ensured that the liberals' priorities for the armed forces were far more political than they were military. Thus, their objectives were essentially two-fold: to ensure that the struggle against Napoleonic France should not be allowed to deteriorate into a mere cabinet war, and to neutralise the army as a factor in Spanish politics. In short, the liberals' chief interest lay in making sure that the struggle against Napoleon was a national war waged by the Spanish people, the obvious conclusion in the eyes of the more exalted being that the army should be got rid of in favour of a militia. Thus:

Who does not see that a militia composed of diligent and active men made strong by the constant labours of field and workshop, that is free of the corruption . . . of garrison life, [and] closely linked to the rest of the people . . . is more able to suffer the fatigues of war . . . and at least as capable of . . . learning the . . . mechanical science of a soldier? Nor can foreign invasion be avoided through the existence of a regular and permanent military . . . A daring . . . enemy will wait for an opportune moment, and then burst in like a torrent when he is least expected, but, if he is attacking a people whose soldiers have abandoned field and workshop to take up the sword, he will be somewhat less likely to succeed than if he were attacking multitudes of neatly lined-up mercenaries. Amongst such men, honour is . . . the only motive for their efforts, whereas . . . the militiaman is fighting for his liberty, for his laws, for the field that shortly before he was watering with the sweat of his brow, for the beloved who waits to see him return triumphant to reward him with her loving arms.[16]

In the end more practical views prevailed, but the military continued to be seen as a natural enemy. To rectify matters it was necessary to create a new army that 'has an incomparably greater interest in liberty than in slavery . . . [and] cannot be seduced by the false glory of a warrior king or a lucky general'.[17] In short, the first priority was to end the rigid distinction that had hitherto existed between soldier and civilian. Instead of being composed of men like criminals and foreigners who had no stake in society, the army would henceforth be recruited from free Spanish citizens serving in the greatest number and for the least time possible, it being in part for this reason that the *cortes* had declared all Spaniards to be 'soldiers of the Fatherland' in January 1811. Inducted into the army *en masse*, Spain's young men would in peacetime serve only for a few months of each year, whilst the opportunity would also be taken to indoctrinate them with the values of liberalism. Meanwhile, the institution in which they served would be purged of all features which reflected the *antiguo régimen*. Hence the restrictions that were imposed upon the *fuero militar*, the abolition of noble privilege in the officer corps, the creation of a more equitable system of decorations, and the numerous plans that were advanced for the reform or abolition of the royal guard. At the same time great importance was also placed on the reform of the army's *ordenanzas*. Gone, in particular, was the old emphasis on blind obedience: in future, the troops would be taught that there were limits to the authority of their officers, that they had a positive duty to disobey orders that jeopardised the public good, 'that the soldier is . . . a citizen before he is a soldier; that military law is inferior to natural law and civil law; [and] that the army has no other object than to defend the liberty of the citizen'.[18]

Considerable attention was also given to the question of the army's relation to the executive power. Initially there was much pressure for the army to be placed under the direct control of the *cortes*, but in the end the Constitution of 1812 compromised on the issue by giving command of the army and control of all military patronage to the monarch, whilst handing the deputies the right to determine the size of the army and the nature of its ordinances. Hence, too, the exclusion of all viceroys, captains general, military governors and other such figures from the exercise of civil authority and their subordination to the new *jefes políticos*. In case these provisions should still not be sufficient to prevent the army from being used against the Constitution, it was also decided that a new armed force should be created that would be wholly under the command of the civil authorities (though a further motive here was the protection of the interests of property in the face of the banditry and social unrest that gripped the countryside). Known as the national guard, this force was effectively to be a self-sufficient army in its own right, but its members were to be part-time militiamen who as such could be relied upon to retain their links with society and remain free of the corruption of military life.

In the event the national guard was not formally established till 15 April 1814, by which time it was far too late. As for the progress that was made with regard to the institutional liberalisation of the army, this was only slightly less chimerical. In June 1812 the *cortes* had admittedly established a special committee entitled the Comisión de Constitución Militar, but the officers who made up the bulk of its membership saw their brief in terms of restoring order, system and discipline to the army whereas the liberals saw it far more in terms of rendering the army compatible with the new political system. With the *serviles* and the more conservative members of the officer corps demanding that the committee should limit itself to military affairs and liberals such as Flórez Estrada accusing it of being incapable of carrying out its duties, debate on the issue became bogged down. Anxious to make progress, in October 1813 the liberal caucus in the new *cortes* succeeded in forcing the establishment of a second committee whose task it would be to elaborate a so-called 'military constitution' whilst the original body confined itself to anodyne questions of organisation and tactics, but in the end nothing was achieved.

Whether the liberals' much vaunted reform of the army's ordinances would have ended the danger of a military coup is a moot point, but what is certain is that their priorities were of little relevance to most military men. Even liberal officers protested that the new regulations would be useless unless the army was properly fed. Nor was the liberal programme any more satisfactory as an analysis of the Spanish war effort. Far from the successes of 1808 having been obtained by the armed populace, for example, they had rather mostly been owed to the despised regular army. As for the role-models constituted by the Voluntarios Distinguidos de Cádiz and the guerrillas, the former had sat out the war in safety, whilst the latter had, as we have seen, proved a double-edged sword. Indeed, popular fervour for the struggle had on the whole been sadly lacking, it having also to be admitted that the advent of the Constitution had not made the slightest difference in this respect.

Had the liberals' arguments been more plausible, there might have been some chance of retaining a real degree of support in the officer corps, but it was all too clear that what drove the army's antagonists was essentially the sectional interest of the groups from which most of them hailed. In their drive to create a nation-in-arms and ensure that the army could never again be used as a tool of despotism, they had also addressed many of the grievances which civilian notables had felt against the military estate prior to 1808. A satisfactory career in the officer corps was now open to all men of a reasonable degree of property and education; the military courts had been stripped of their right to try civilians; the army had been deprived of its role in local government and the administration of justice; and, perhaps above all, army officers could no longer expect to take instant precedence over their fellow citizens. Yet herein lay the rub. Whilst many army officers could agree with demands for the internal dynamics of the army to be placed on a more equal footing, few of them were willing to surrender their privileges, and particularly not if they had only just been able to gain access to them. Indeed, even liberal officers found it hard to abandon the notion that the army officer was not simply one more citizen, but rather a being set apart to whom society owed a special debt of gratitude (there is, in fact, good reason to believe that they were as much motivated by professional frustration as they were by ideological enthusiasm).

If sectional interest drove the liberals to become exponents of anti-militarism, so the same sectional interest converted more and more officers into bed-fellows of reaction. As a result *servilismo* had soon penetrated far beyond the elements that constituted its natural bastions within the officer corps (the pre-war *generalato*, the royal guard and the many pre-war officers who had found themselves passed over by the protégés of the juntas of 1808). By 1813, indeed, secret approaches were being made to Wellington to enlist his support for a coup, whilst a variety of officers were engaging in physical attacks on liberal journalists and publishing violent denunciations of the *cortes*' military reforms. First of all, it was argued, the army had been neglected by the *cortes*. To quote *La Milicia Desatendida en Tiempo de Guerra*:

If we examine with care the twenty-two volumes of the acts of the *cortes* . . . it will be seen that the army was not the issue that merited the primary attention of that congress. Despite having sat for three years, it closed without having elaborated the military constitution, without having established a complete and respectable army possessed of the reserves necessary to replace its continuous losses, and without having reformed the public finances so as to ensure the troops' subsistence and maintainance.[19]

More than that, however, with vainglory its besetting sin – Gleig remarks that, 'full of boasting', the officers he met in the Toulouse campaign 'gave themselves . . . as many absurd airs as if their valour had delivered Spain and dethroned Napoleon'[20] – the liberals were felt to have humiliated the officer corps by shaming it in the eyes of the British, and stripping its members of their chief sources of reward. On one level this was simply churlish – 'To have lavished our blood, and to have remained constant despite suffering infinite defeats: are these our crimes?'[21] – but on another the liberals had in effect left Spain defenceless:

Without an army . . . ruin and eternal slavery are inevitable . . . At the end of four years' cruel struggle . . . the military career has been despoiled of the few stimuli that made it attractive . . . What boy will take up so arduous a profession in the future?[22]

Much of this was so much cant – the real root of the trouble was, of course, the liberals' refusal to admit the officer corps' pretensions – but there is no doubt that the military had genuine grievances. In the eyes of many officers, for example, it really seemed that 'anybody now has the right to insult us', and that 'we are considered mercenaries, hired servants or paid assassins'.[23] As one liberal military man warned the *cortes*:

It is not enough that you sanction decrees in their benefit: it is necessary that you make their effects felt in the army with the speed of lightning . . . There is a large body of soldiers who . . . believe in good faith that you do nothing for this class . . . They do not read your decrees and discussions, and do not know them except by their consequences. As they do not have any effect . . . they are persuaded that they are null, and in consequence break out in imprecations which a lover of the Fatherland cannot hear without horror.[24]

Certainly, instances of provocation were numerous, as witness, for example, the constant denunciation of the forced requisitioning engaged in of necessity by many commanders; the arrogant and unhelpful manner affected by many civilian officials in their dealings with members of the officer corps; and the numerous attempts that were made to blame the sufferings of the army on wastefulness and ostentation. Nor were matters helped by British command of the army and, even more so, the failure of the Spanish army to achieve much in the way of glory in the campaigns of 1812 and 1813. If Wellington's appointment as commander-in-chief had been accepted with comparatively little in the way of overt resistance, this did not mean that it was popular. Arthur Wellesley was hardly the most emollient of leaders, whilst the campaigns of Vitoria and the Pyrenees showed that, at best, the Spanish armies could only expect a supporting role, still further damage being done by the quarrels that erupted in the wake of the invasion of France. These humiliations were blamed on the government's failure to meet the army's needs and it is entirely conceivable that, had Ballesteros launched his revolt in the autumn of 1813 rather than the autumn of 1812, he would have received much support.

As proof of this one has only to consider the case of Enrique O'Donnell. Ennobled for his services in Catalonia as Conde del Abisbal, O'Donnell was something of a favourite with the liberals – hence his appointment to the crucial Army of Reserve of Anadalucía. Yet by January 1814 the count was seething with resentment: not only had his forces played little part in the invasion of France, but Wellington had in the most acid tones rejected a pet scheme that envisaged giving O'Donnell command of all the Spanish forces on the frontier. Told by Wellington that independent Spanish armies had a habit of being beaten – a point whose wounding character was inflamed still further by a reference to the defeat of his brother, José O'Donnell, at the first battle of Castalla in 1812 – the count's answer was to get in touch with a number of leading *serviles* and make preparations for a march on the capital.

When San Carlos and Palafox arrived in Madrid in January 1814, they therefore found a situation that seemed to offer Fernando every hope of being able to overthrow the Constitution. Populace and army alike were deeply disaffected, whilst *servilismo* was growing in virulence by the day. Equally the atmosphere really did seem to presage the advent of a Jacobin republic, as witness the ferment in the countryside, and the brutal ejection from the chamber of a solitary *servil* deputy who had attempted to defend Fernando's right to negotiate with Napoleon. In consequence, though Palafox was more cautious, San Carlos returned to France as an enthusiastic proponent of a coup. On their arrival at Valençay, however, the two commissioners found that events had moved on. With nothing to lose, Napoleon had decided to release Fernando notwithstanding the refusal of the Patriot authorities to ratify his terms in the hope that the king's appearance in the Allied camp would lead to turmoil. Hence Fernando's appearance at Báscara on 24 March.

Fearing just such a move on the part of the emperor, the Madrid régime had taken a number of precautions, the decree of 2 February laying down not only that Fernando would not be recognised until such time as he had appeared before the *cortes* and sworn the prescribed oath of loyalty to the Constitution, but also that the Regency would stipulate the route by which he should travel to Madrid. No sooner had he crossed into the Spanish lines, indeed, than Fernando was presented with a copy of the *cortes*' decree together with an intinerary for his journey (he was to travel to Valencia via Tarragona, and then strike inland across La Mancha). Yet securing the compliance of the king was another matter. San Carlos was not alone amongst his followers in urging a coup – in the last weeks of his captivity, Fernando had been joined by a number of figures who were violently opposed to the Constitution – but at the time that he crossed the frontier the king was far from resolved on the course that he should adopt. Báscara, however, had provided him with much in the way of encouragement, for discreet enquiries had revealed that, whilst the commander of the First Army, General Copons, was loyal to the Constitution, many of his subordinates, including his second-in-command, the Barón de Eroles, were ready to overthrow it. Ever cautious, the king still would not commit himself either way, but, reinforced by the arrival of the master *frondeur*, Montijo, in a master-stroke of cunning the proponents of a coup succeeded in persuading him to defy the *cortes* and make a detour to visit Zaragoza. As they had expected, this trip filled Fernando's head with images of popular devotion to his person, whilst news was also beginning to come in of serious anti-liberal disturbances: as in 1808, the king remained the 'desired one' who would put all to rights, whilst agents of the *serviles* had been busying themselves circulating all sorts of alarmist rumours and hiring bands of thugs.

Ever cautious, however, Fernando wavered: the Englishman, Samuel Whittingham, indeed, claims that the king told him that he had found 'much that is good' in the Constitution, and, further, that 'if the refusal of my sanction is to cost one drop of Spanish blood, I will swear it tomorrow'.[25] Whether or not this anecdote is true, the die was not finally cast until his arrival in Valencia on 16 April. Deeply alarmed at the extent of the anti-feudal disturbances that had been rocking the province, the local nobility flocked to the royal standard, whilst the Marqués de Dos Aguas – a leading collaborator under the occupation régime – offered 2,000,000 reales to finance a revolt. Meanwhile, military authority in the city was in the hands of the Captain General and commander of the Second Army, Francisco Elío, who was an officer of a decidedly conservative stamp. Parading his troops before the newly arrived monarch, he therefore publicly swore to uphold him in the plenitude of his power. Having also by now been joined by many of those who had supported him in his struggle with Godoy as well as a variety of prominent representatives of the caroline bureaucracy, Fernando hesitated no longer, and all the more so as he had also been presented with a manifesto signed by sixty-nine *servil* deputies denouncing the *cortes* as both revolutionary and illegitimate.* Montijo, indeed, had already been sent to Madrid to sound out opinion, and, one suspects, organise the mob, whilst the beginning of May saw forces of the Second Army, together with the independent division commanded by Whittingham, take the road for New Castile.

In the capital all was confusion. The liberal press had reacted to the ambiguous letters which Fernando had sent to the Regency in the weeks since he had crossed the border with alarm and dismay, whilst further disquiet had been caused by the humiliating treatment meted out to Cardinal Borbón when he had travelled to meet the monarch in accordance with the decree of 2 February. Yet fighting the king was impossible: the few officers

---

* Known, from its opening words – an allusion to the Persian empire of antiquity – as the 'manifesto of the Persians', this document was written at the instigation of San Carlos, who wanted both to give Fernando the pretext for a coup and to hint at the concessions that the forces he represented would expect from an absolutist restoration.

willing to uphold the Constitution by force could not answer for the loyalty of their subordinates, whilst the much-vaunted National Guard existed only on paper. As for conciliation, a group of deputies sent to see the monarch was denied access to his person, stripped of its escort, and turned loose to make its way home as best it could. On the night of 10–11 May, then, the king's forces entered the capital without resistance. With many of the leading liberals under arrest and all the measures taken by the *cortes* proclaimed to be null and void, absolutism had been restored.

To these events there was no opposition. Delighted at the downfall of the liberals, whom they regarded as not just ingrates, but dangerous revolutionaries bent on attacking the whole of the social order, Wellington and Henry Wellesley made no move to assist their erstwhile tormentors. In the army faint stirrings of resistance in the garrison of Cádiz and the Third and Fourth Armies came to nothing. And, from one end of Spain to the other, *jefes políticos*, constitutional *ayuntamientos* and provincial *diputacíones* were ejected from power in scenes reminiscent of the rising of May 1808. Thus, in Astorga a copy of the Constitution was ceremonially burned in the presence of an ecstatic crowd in the main square; in Málaga a portrait of Fernando VII was paraded through the streets to the sound of artillery salvos; and in Oviedo and many other cities the tablet proclaiming the main square to be the 'Plaza de la Constitución' – a name imposed on every *plaza mayor* in Spain – was torn down and broken into fragments. Greeted though they were with immense popular jubilation, for the most part these events were carefully orchestrated – in Granada, for example, the popular revolt that swept away the city's authorities on 17 May was organised by a cabal that included representatives of the garrison, the local clergy and nobility – and, perhaps because of this, there were far fewer dead than in 1808. As for repression, this, too, was patchy, with the number of those arrested varying dramatically from region to region, many of those who had collaborated with the liberals in practice encountering little difficulty in finding a niche in the new order, and formal executions few and far between. But even so things were severe enough, Fernando earning a reputation for cruelty which was to dog him for the rest of his life and far beyond.

*   *   *

With the restoration of Fernando VII as absolute ruler of Spain, this chronicle of events must come to an end. What, though, was the significance of the Peninsular War? In this respect, one thing is clear: the conflict was of far greater significance in the history of Spain and Portugal than it was in the history of the Napoleonic Wars. According to the classic tradition, however, this was not so. On the contrary, to quote Napoleon himself, 'It was [the Spanish war] that overthrew me. All my disasters can be traced back to this fatal knot.'[26] Broadly speaking, the argument runs as follows. By intervening in Spain and Portugal, Napoleon involved himself in a struggle that would have been difficult to win at the best of times: so intense was the national spirit of these two countries, the French armies were confronted by a veritable people's war. As the emperor alleged, 'The system that I pursued in Spain . . . would have eventually been for the good of that country, yet it was contrary to the opinion of the people, and therefore I failed.'[27] With Iberian resistance reinforced by the deployment of a substantial force of redcoats in the Peninsula, the reorganisation of the Portuguese army and the construction of the Lines of Torres Vedras, victory receded still further. Yet retreat from the Peninsula would have been a catastrophic blow to the empire's prestige, and thus it was that for almost six years hundreds of thousands of French troops were tied down in a savage war that sapped their discipline and morale alike. The military consequences were dire: first, because the army that invaded Russia in 1812 would have been of infinitely higher quality had the place of its numerous foreign contingents been taken by the roughly equal number of veteran French soldiers who were fighting in Spain at that point; and, second, because Napoleon might have stemmed the Allied onslaught in 1813 and 1814 if he had not had to keep so many troops on his south-western front. But this was not the end of the story, the Peninsular War also proving both a political and a diplomatic disaster. Thus, inside France the dramatic increase in conscription of the period 1808–1812 – the direct effect of the struggle beyond the Pyrenees – caused growing disaffection amongst the populace. The Peninsular War was not the only problem here – also of importance were the serious economic difficulties that gripped the empire in 1810 and 1811 and the increasing lack of confidence felt in the emperor by the propertied classes – but, with Napoleon labelled as the 'man of blood', the titanic struggles of 1813 and 1814 received little support on the home front. Meanwhile, without the Peninsular War, there would probably have been no disasters of the sort that eventually occurred in Russia and Germany, and therefore no crisis of the sort that finally shattered France's acquiescence in Napoleon's rule. Thus, the war was instrumental in persuading Russia, Austria and Prussia to defy Napoleon in the first place, whether it was by convincing them of Britain's good faith, establishing the simple fact that the emperor was not invincible, or, in Germany in particular, encouraging the emergence of a new nationalist movement that was impossible to ignore. At the same time, the war offered the eastern powers proof that new forms of war effort that had hitherto been associated solely with the French Revolution could be employed in the service of the old order. Thus, just as in France in 1793, so in Spain and Portugal a 'people numerous and armed' had confronted foreign aggression and emerged triumphant. Understanding this, in Russia, Prussia, Austria and ultimately the turncoat states of the Confederation of the Rhine, the authorities had therefore sought to emulate the Iberian example. Whilst guerrillas harassed their rear, the imperial forces in consequence found themselves confronted by not the old professional armies of the *ancien régime*, but rather masses of hastily trained conscripts and militiamen, the result being, of course, that they were overwhelmed.

On the surface there is much evidence that can be cited in support of this analysis. Much more work is needed on the French home front, and all the more so as opposition to the draft actually declined between 1808 and 1812, but anecdotal evidence suggests that service in Spain and Portugal was deeply unpopular with the troops. As for the impact of the Peninsular War outside France, it is undeniable that many German nationalists were greatly enthused by the Iberian example, as were the leaders of the reform movement that revitalised Prussia in the wake of the humiliation of Jena and Auerstädt. Also true, of course, is the fact that Portugal in particular provided the British with a permanent foothold on the Continent of Europe – and, by extension, theatre of operations – that would for geographical and logistical reasons have been almost impossible to maintain anywhere else (much less convincing, by contrast, is the argument that the Peninsular War saved Britain from defeat at the hands of the Continental Blockade, for she would have been able to penetrate the vital South American market whether or not Spain and Portugal had broken with Napoleon).

Yet was the Peninsular War really so important a factor in the downfall of Napoleon? Let us take, for example, the question of the French army. The struggle in Spain, we are told, sapped morale, tied down hundreds of thousands of troops and cost immense numbers of casualties (imperial losses are hard to determine, but the total number of dead may have reached a quarter of a million). These remarks, however, beg a number of questions. In the Peninsula itself, it is clear that French commanders became less and less willing to throw their troops against Anglo-Portuguese forces arrayed on ground of their own choosing. Yet there is little firm evidence that, boosted as it was by a military machine gifted by an extraordinary capacity for enthusing the most unwilling conscript, the rank and file's fighting spirit witnessed the sort of decline that might have been expected. Meanwhile, even if some sort of case to this effect can be elaborated by reference to, say, Vitoria and Sorauren, the problem cannot be said to have spread very far, the troops who marched on Moscow, fought at Leipzig and defended France in 1814 performing prodigies of valour and endurance. What about the question of numbers though? By the end of 1813, certainly, the troops of Soult and Suchet would have been of inestimable service on the Rhine frontier, but they were not sufficient to have had much chance of turning the tide. At the same time, it is difficult to see how such victories as they might have helped obtain could have had any meaning unless Napoleon had settled for a compromise peace. The net effect of every victory the emperor succeeded in winning being to make him even more unyielding, maintaining that he was brought down simply by the need to defend the Pyrenees is highly disingenuous.

But would the situation in late 1813 and early 1814 ever have been so desperate but for the Peninsular War? With 260,000 extra troops – the number then deployed in Spain – the emperor might have triumphed in Russia, and thus short-circuited the formation of the great coalition that finally brought him down less than a year and a half after the débâcle of the retreat from Moscow. Yet none of this necessarily follows. The army that fought in Russia in 1812 was not short of numbers. Rather, what was lacking was the ability to make use of numbers, the communications, transport and supply arrangements of the *grande armée* all proving desperately inadequate for the needs even of the troops that Napoleon did take with him. Extra troops, in short, would not in themselves have allowed the emperor to pack a heavier punch. What, however, of the question of quality? Largely composed of Frenchmen, would not the troops in Spain have fought better than the Germans, Italians and others who made up so large a proportion of the invaders of Russia? Many problems are thrown up by this argument, but in fact the 'subject' troops who fought in Russia seem to have performed well enough. Even were this not the case, meanwhile, we find that as the years went by so more and more regiments of cavalry and infantry that were ostensibly French in origin had to find at least a percentage of their recruits from areas that were not part of France in any ethnic sense at all. Indeed, a few units had originally been parts of other armies altogether, the French having at one time or another simply press-ganged them into service.

It is not, then, especially daring to conclude that the war in the Peninsula had only a limited impact on the conflict in the rest of Europe, and all the more so as the chances of Napoleon staging another 1810 – when peace with Austria, Prussia and Russia had enabled the emperor to make much progress in Spain – could not be ruled out to the very end. By 1813 the chances of the French marching all the way to Lisbon or Cádiz were not very high, but the fact remained that the key to victory in the Peninsula was victory in Germany. British historians in particular would have this the other way about on the grounds that the Peninsular War stimulated resistance to Napoleon amongst the eastern powers. In practice, however, this argument does not stand up. In 1809, certainly, the Peninsular War contributed to Austria's decision to go to war against Napoleon and led some elements in the Habsburg court to back the organisation of a popular revolt in the recently lost Tyrol (it had been ceded to Bavaria in 1805). Yet it is abundantly clear that Vienna was moved not by heroic notions of national insurrection but the fear that the final eradication of the Bourbons as a ruling dynasty might be followed by that of the Habsburgs. Moreover, beaten at Wagram, the Austrians then allied themselves with Napoleon. Two years later, heartened by French difficulties in Spain, both Russia and Prussia considered going to war against Napoleon, whilst in the latter case leaders of the reform movement such as August von Gneisenau added to the pressure by painting pictures of people's war *a la español*. Yet in the end both Alexander I and Frederick William III rejected the idea of an attack, all that can truly be claimed being that the continuing war beyond the Pyrenees stiffened the tsar's determination to resist Napoleon should the latter actually attack him.

This, of course, Napoleon duly did, and within eighteen months he found himself facing a coalition of a magnitude that he had never had to deal with before. Was this, then, when the Peninsular War secured its moment in history? Again, however, the answer must be a doubtful one. In a general sense the Spanish ulcer constituted a guarantee of British good faith, but far more concrete was the reassurance provided by the immense subsidies that London lavished on any state that came out against France. Similarly, whilst every imperial soldier fighting in Spain was an imperial soldier who could not be fighting in Germany, confidence in Allied victory remained at best an uncertain quantity. If Russia decided to carry the war across the frontier into Germany and Poland; if Prussia and Sweden elected to throw in their lot with Russia; and if Austria finally abandoned her efforts to secure a general peace in favour of joining Napoleon's enemies, it was for reasons that had only the most indirect connections with the Peninsula. The hundreds of thousands of Allied troops who crushed Napoleon at Leipzig were the fruit not of events in Spain and Portugal, then, but rather of the emperor's refusal to accept reality and settle for a peace postulated upon the limitation of French influence. To put it another way, Napoleon fell not because the Peninsular War had any influence on Russian, Prussian or Austrian policy, but because it failed to have any influence on French policy.

This, perhaps, is to go too far. Clearly, French embarrassment in Spain did nothing to hinder Allied coalition building in 1813, whilst the complete elimination of Joseph Bonaparte at Vitoria relieved Britain of the need to get the Austrians, Russians and Prussians to recognise Fernando VII as king of Spain. But it is still difficult to accept the idea that events in the Peninsula had any major influence on the way in which the so-called 'War of Liberation' was actually conducted. In Prussia, certainly, the declaration of war on Napoleon was accompanied by a degree of popular mobilisation that was wholly unprecedented amongst the eastern powers, whilst the defection of most of the states of the Confederation of the Rhine to the Allied cause in the course of the autumn of 1813 was accompanied by measures of much the same sort. Thus, universal conscription and various forms of militias and home guards were very much the order of the day, whilst use was also made of guerrilla warfare and attempts to stir up popular insurrection. To say that the Peninsular War played no part in this would be foolish – many of the architects of the new Prussian army, in particular, had been deeply influenced by the Spanish model – but this is not the issue. Rather, what is striking is the obvious want of enthusiasm of the German rulers for such methods, which were in effect adopted *faute de mieux*, and, still more, the manner in which the rest of the Allied forces were completely untouched by the new developments. Add to this the general lack of popular enthusiasm for the struggle, and the influence of the Peninsula tends to look slight.

Once he had been beaten in Germany in 1813, Napoleon really had only one hope of survival short of accepting the compromise peace that at this point was still on offer, and that was to mobilise France herself for total war in a manner that had not been seen since the heroic days of 1793 in the hope that resistance might be prolonged long enough for the many fissures in the Allied camp to undermine its commitment to the common cause. In this, however, Napoleon was foiled by a combination of massive popular resistance to the enormous levies that the policy required and the wholesale withdrawal of the co-operation of the governing classes. Only here is it clear that the Peninsular War really did have a major influence on the situation. From 1808 until 1812 the struggle in Spain and Portugal had necessitated a very high level of conscription, but, although this was deeply resented, the régime had proved more than capable of imposing its will, maintaining a reasonable degree of order and, by extension, retaining the loyalty of the élites. After 1812, however, the situation changed. With the aid of the wider empire, it had proved possible both to maintain a substantial army in the Peninsula and to amass a large field force in eastern Europe without pushing the situation too far in France. Such were the demands that Napoleon made of his home base in 1813 and 1814, however, that the imperial system simply broke down, the emperor in the end being left all but alone. Yet even this does not make the Peninsular War a major factor in Napoleon's downfall. What broke the emperor in the end was his refusal to accept that there were limits to the capacities of his administration, his army, his subordinates and his own generalship. More simply still, victory in Spain and Portugal implied a restraint in the rest of Europe that Napoleon was incapable of delivering.

To regard the Peninsular War as a key factor in the defeat of the Napoleonic empire is therefore to miss the point. What cannot be denied, however, is the massive importance of the struggle in the modern history of Spain and Portugal. For both states the years from 1808 to 1814 constituted a truly horrible experience. Trade and industry had been ravaged, and, in the Spanish case, the vital link with America in large part broken. Towns and cities had been repeatedly sacked and in some cases literally reduced to ruin. Famine, epidemic and massacre had stalked the land. The countryside had been pillaged unmercifully, subjected to a process of destabilising social change and plunged into anarchy. And, to cap it all, such means as existed of palliating the situation in human terms – above all, the Church – had been stripped both of their resources and, in many cases, their very capacity to operate. For the population of the Peninsula, the consequences were well-nigh apocalyptic. Misery was general, whilst the number of those who died in Spain alone may well have numbered more than a million. In some areas the percentage of the population that was lost may well have been even higher than the ten per cent which this implies: round Tarragona, for example, the population of most towns and villages declined by between one quarter and one third, although at least a part of this loss may be attributed to flight rather than mortality.

If all this was not grim enough, in both Spain and Portugal the legacy of the conflict was almost certain to be civil war. Beginning with the former, the period 1808–14 is regarded as one of the defining moments of modern Spanish history. Not only did the conflict with the French provide a myth that was to become a central feature of political debate, but from it there are supposed to have emerged two Spains – the one clerical, absolutist and reactionary, and the other secular, constitutional and progressive – whose mutual incompatibility was to plunge the country into a prolonged era of confrontation and civil conflict. Such a picture is far too simplistic, however: closer examination shows the 'two Spains' to have been far less well-defined than this allows. Ideologically speaking, the liberals may have more or less conformed to the conventional stereotype, but their opponents were rather divided into different positions of which one stood for the perpetuation of eighteenth-century enlightened absolutism, and the other for a monarchy stripped of its Bourbon reformism that would only be absolute to the extent that it allowed the Church, aristocracy, and other corporations the untrammelled enjoyment of their privileges.

It is not enough, however, to talk even of three Spains. Caught between these forces was an increasingly radicalised *populacho* that identified with no goals more complicated than peace, bread and access to the land, and was as hostile to the 'freedom' of the liberals as it was to the 'chains' of the *antiguo régimen*. Loyal to none of the contending tendencies, the populace were open to manipulation by all three of them, whilst at the same time pursuing a dimly perceived agenda of their own, the popular disturbances and cheering crowds that greeted the return of Fernando VII being at one and the same time the product of bribery and coercion, a vague belief that somehow *el rey deseado* would put all to rights, and a swelling mood of protest that was but little connected with the cause of absolutism.

To make matters still more complicated, the Revolutionary and Napoleonic Wars had also given Spain an army that was deeply politicised: in 1808 the royal guard had overthrown Godoy; in 1809 the Marqués de la Romana had overthrown the Junta of Asturias; in 1812 Francisco Ballesteros had revolted in protest at Wellington's appointment as commander-in-chief; and in 1814 Elío had brought down the liberal system. At the same time, of course, the army had also been imbued with a strong sense of mission: interests that were essentially sectional having in each case been dressed up in the guise of patriotism, it came to believe that its goals – order, political unity, military primacy – were coterminous with those of the nation – indeed, that they were those of the nation. Certain sections of the press having meanwhile heaped praise on generals such as Palafox and Ballesteros, they were transformed into the veritable embodiment of patriotic heroism, and thus was born the concept of the military messiah.

Yet, as with the *populacho*, the army was in practice an operator that was separate from the liberals, the *serviles* and the enlightened absolutists. Thus, if sections of the army had risen in revolt in May 1814, they had done so in pursuit of essentially professional concerns whose satisfaction seemed most likely under the rule of an absolutist Fernando. Whether the new monarch would retain the army's support was doubtful, though: indeed, with much of the officer corps now a natural constituency of liberalism and Fernando's régime facing the task of cutting the swollen and inefficient army of the war against France down to size, it was hardly a likely prospect. Also operating on the government, meanwhile, was a series of financial constraints that were essentially related to the military situation that it inherited in 1814. The well-being of Bourbon Spain was absolutely dependent on the wealth of the American empire, but by 1814 four years of rebellion and civil war had ensured that the revenue derived from this source had slowed to a trickle (one could argue, indeed, that the impact of the Peninsular War was at its greatest not in Europe but beyond the Atlantic). To restore the *antiguo régimen*, then, what was required was the reconquest of Spanish America, and yet to reconquer Spanish America – indeed, to secure any measure of financial stability at all in a situation in which the national debt had doubled whilst revenue had fallen to less than half the average for the period 1798–1807 – it would clearly be necessary to adopt many of the practices of liberalism. Progress was only gradual – the process was not complete until the 1830s – but even the most tentative moves in this direction were sufficient to anger *señores* faced by wholesale refusal to pay the feudal dues owing to them, not to mention a Church whose fabric and finances had been badly shaken by years of war and occupation. Whilst trouble originally came from liberals and disaffected army officers – the years from 1814 to 1820 witnessed a series of plots and conspiracies that culminated in the revolution of 1820–23 – sooner or later a conflict with the *serviles* was inevitable. With liberalism gaining in support all the time amongst the bourgeoisie and the more realistic elements of the old order, the result was never in doubt, but no less than four civil wars had to be fought out before traditionalism would accept defeat.

The Peninsular War, then, gave birth to the violence and popular antagonism that, along with military intervention in politics, were to be nineteenth-century Spain's most pronounced characteristics. As for Portugal her position was only marginally more favourable. Revolt having failed to spread to Brazil, there was no colonial struggle to be waged, whilst there had been no attempt at political revolution. Yet even so the absolutist state faced precisely the same dilemmas as its Spanish counterpart, whilst in the devastated metropolis immense resentment was caused by the decision of the Regent, Prince João – from 1816 João VI – to remain in comfortable Rio de Janeiro in 1814. With matters far from helped by continued British domination in matters military and commercial, absolutism was overthrown in 1820 and João forced to return to Lisbon, but the price was the loss of Brazil in 1822, whilst it again cost a series of civil wars before the cause of traditionalism was destroyed.

A side-show in terms of the Napoleonic Wars, the Peninsular War was therefore a seminal event in the history of Spain and Portugal. Economically and financially devastating, it was the direct cause of the collapse of their American empires (at least, on the mainland, Spain holding on to Cuba and

Puerto Rico until 1898) whilst in Spain's case it shattered the last vestiges of her claim to be a great power on the European stage. Cruelly exposing the limitations of eighteenth-century enlightened absolutism, it also dealt a heavy blow to the pretensions of the Church and the nobility. Thus, the former had suffered appalling losses in terms of its personnel – as many as one third of the clergy may have died or been killed in the struggle – and been stripped of a considerable part of its physical presence in much of Spain, whilst *desamortización*, hostility to the tithes and the demands of French and Patriots alike for money had left it denuded of resources. As for the nobility, its hold on rural society had at the very least been severely shaken, whilst the return of absolutism failed to bring with it the full restoration of *señorialismo* that they had been expecting (in brief, Fernando refused to allow the return of the old manorial courts).

In the long run, all this ensured that the war ushered in an age of liberalism whose foundation was the Constitution of 1812. At the heart of the new dispensation was a serious mismatch between rhetoric and reality, however. Confronted by the resistance of bureaucratic absolutism on the one hand and reactionary traditionalism on the other, men such as Quintana and Flórez Estrada, who were the advocates of the new era, always argued that the people of Spain and Portugal had fought the French out of a desire not to preserve the chains of the past, but to reclaim the liberty which they had lost through centuries of despotism. From this it followed that the people might have been expected to secure some material benefit from their sacrifices, but this in fact was not so, the liberals offering the *populacho* nothing – even the abolition of *señorialismo* was framed in such terms that it was worth very little – and in practice regarding them with contempt. With much of the populace already exhibiting a yearning, however vague and inchoate, for social justice, thus were sown the seeds of still more conflicts, including, most obviously, the terrible disaster of the Spanish Civil War.

But did the people of Spain and Portugal fight in the manner in which their self-appointed champions alleged? On few areas of the conflict is further research more necessary, but it is all too clear that patterns of popular motivation and involvement in the struggle were, to say the least, much more complex than has generally been assumed. At certain times and in certain places, the French did find themselves facing a people's war of the sort that has so often been pictured, but the general picture that emerges is one of apathy and disaffection. Guerrilla warfare was a more acceptable alternative than enlistment in the regular armies, certainly, but for many of the *partidas* it is clear that what this meant was essentially pillage, extortion and highway robbery. This, of course, did not mean that the French and their supporters were never attacked, but what it does mean is that in the last resort they were often purely incidental targets – indeed, even secondary ones. Where guerrilla warfare was effective – and in much of northern Spain it was extremely effective – it therefore tended to be the work of either forces of the much derided regular army, or bands of irregulars that had been fully militarised.

Yet in the last resort, perhaps, the issue is irrelevant. Whether the forces that infested the countryside were gangs of bandits – as the French, in fact, always claimed – or guerrilla bands, they always had to be held down by enormous forces of regular troops. The problem was not in abstract terms an insuperable one – by 1808 the French had considerable experience of insurrectionary warfare whilst they proved capable of making progress even in the Peninsula – but so long as the invaders were also faced by substantial regular resistance, they could have no real hope of restoring order. In short, there is no reason to take exception with the generally accepted dictum that the French were defeated in the Peninsula by a combination of regular and irregular warfare, although much scope exists for greater recognition of the contribution of Spain's regular troops to this combination. What is less clear, however, is the issue of whether or not the invaders could have ever won. Setting aside the *sine qua non* of peace in the rest of Europe, even had they been reduced to Cádiz and Lisbon alone, it is unclear that the Spanish and Portuguese governments would ever have surrendered, for, as Graham wrote, 'We never can have such allies again, bad as their conduct has often been, and . . . much as we have daily reason to complain of it.'[28] Meanwhile, in Wellington the Allies possessed a field commander of almost unequalled calibre. Thanks to his prescience, the French faced a very difficult task, as well as the constant risk that any error that they made would be ruthlessly exploited. But even Wellington was not operating in a vacuum. As many as half his forces were drawn from the remodelled Portuguese army, whilst it is doubtful that even the Lines of Torres Vedras could have saved the Allied cause from the consequences of the collapse of Spanish resistance or the rupture in Anglo-Spanish relations that so often seemed a possibility. Under-lying everything, too, was the willingness of the politicians who made up the Portland, Perceval and Liverpool administrations to risk their reputations on a struggle that until quite late on seemed a dubious enterprise, not to mention the loyal support they gave a commander who consistently underestimated their problems, rarely let them into his plans and was always quick to find fault with their efforts. Victory in the Peninsula was therefore political and diplomatic as much as it was military. Hence the need for a history that has attempted to be something other than a mere list of battles.

Glossary

abatti	Obstacle constructed from felled trees.
afrancesado	Literally, 'frenchified one'; supporter of Joseph Bonaparte.
afrancesamiento	Literally 'frenchification'; sympathy with/attempt to implement French models, especially those of the Napoleonic empire.
alarma	Galician home guard.
alcálde mayor	local magistrate.
antiguo régimen	*Ancien régime*; old order.
audiencia	provincial high court and council of administration of lesser rank than a *chancillería*.
ayuntamiento	Town hall; town council; municipality.
bienes nacionales	Literally 'national properties'; property expropriated from the Church, the municipalities or, more rarely, political opponents.
cabecilla	Bandit or guerrilla chieftain.
caçador	Portuguese light infantryman.
cacique	Landowner or other local notable possessed of sufficient economic power to be able to exert political influence in his locality.
campesino	Literally 'countryman'; in practice, a generic term used to describe all those sectors of the rural lower classes engaged in agriculture.
carta de seguridad	Identity card.
cédula de crédito	Credit bond issued under Joseph Bonaparte.
chancillería	Provincial high court and council of administration.
chasseur	French light cavalryman (also soldier of a centre company of a French light infantry regiment).
cheval de frise	Beam embedded with sword blades used in the defence of breaches.
comisario regio	Royal commissioner.
consejo	Council (usually administrative).
contribución única	Literally 'the single contribution'; new system of taxation introduced by the *cortes* of Cádiz.

convento	Friary, convent, monastery.
corregidor	City governor-cum-chief magistrate appointed by monarch prior to 1808 (Portuguese: *corregedor-mór*).
corso terrestre	Literally 'land piracy', term used to describe irregular resistance to the French.
cortejo	Male lover-cum-companion of a married woman.
cortes	Parliament.
cortijo	Complex of barns, granaries and living accommodation that constituted the headquarters of a large landed estate.
costumbrismo	Nineteenth-century Spanish literary tendency associated with political conservatism.
criollo	American-born inhabitant of Spanish America, of European origins.
cruzada	Literally 'crusade'; generally a guerrilla band composed entirely of clerics, but occasionally a people's militia.
desamortización	Expropriation and/or sale of entailed land.
deseado, el	Literally 'the desired'; patriotic nickname for Fernando VII.
diputación	Provincial assembly or elected council.
doceañista	Literally 'man of 1812'; a veteran of the *cortes* of Cádiz.
electores de partido	District electors.
estado llano	Commonalty; third estate.
fanega	Unit of measurement equivalent to fifty-five litres.
fernandino	Supporter of Fernando VII.
fidalgo	Portuguese nobleman.
forero	Galician rentier.
forista	Galician landlord.
fuero militar	Privileges enjoyed by Bourbon officer corps prior to 1808.
fueros	Traditional rights/privileges/codes of justice (adjectival form: *foral*).
gaditano	Inhabitant of/pertaining to Cádiz.
garrochista	Andalusian lance-wielding cattle herder.
generalato	All army officers of the rank of brigadier and above.
generalísimo	Supreme commander; in contemporary Spanish usage the term implied control not just of the army's operations, but also of its organisation and discipline.
godoyista	Client of Godoy.
grandeza	Aristocracy.
guerrilla, la	Literally 'little war'; the guerrilla struggle against the French.
guerrillero	Guerrilla.
hijodalgo (hijosdalgo, plural)	Literally 'son of someone'; i.e. a member of the nobility.
huerta	Irrigated area devoted to fruit, market gardening, etc.
ilustrado	Literally 'enlightened one'; intellectual/man of letters.

infanta	Princess.
informes sobre cortes	Memorials and proposals requested by the Junta Central with regard to the establishment of a new *cortes*.
jacquerie	Agrarian rising.
jefe político	Literally 'political head'; provincial governor.
jornalero	Day labourer.
josefino	Supporter of Joseph Bonaparte; pertaining to Bonaparte Spain.
juiz de fora	Portuguese district magistrate.
junta	Committee of government or administration.
junta militar	Advisory council of generals established by the Junta Central.
juntero	Any member of a junta.
juramentado	Literally 'sworn one'; Spanish official or, more usually, soldier in the service of Joseph Bonaparte.
labrador	Landowner; prosperous tenant farmer.
leva	Forced levy of convicts, vagabonds, etc. to fill the ranks of the army.
madrileño	Inhabitant of/pertaining to Madrid.
maja	Feminine of *majo*.
majo	Literally 'fellow, lad, chap'; colloquial term used to describe the lower classes of Madrid.
malagueño	Inhabitant of/pertaining to Málaga.
malhechor	Literally 'evil doer'; criminal, bandit.
mariscal de campo	major-general (often mistranslated as field marshal).
mayorazgo	Estate held in perpetuity – i.e. in entail – by the Church or a noble house.
meseta	The high plateau of Central Spain.
Mesta	Powerful sheep-owners' corporation abolished by the liberals.
mestizo	Resident of South America of mixed race (Indian-European).
milicias honradas	Urban militia recruited solely from the propertied classes.
milicias urbanas	Urban militia; town guards.
miqueletes	Catalan militia.
motín	Riot.
ordenança	Portuguese home guard.
ordenanzas	Ordinances (generally military).
pardo	Resident of South America of mixed race (African-European).
partida	Guerrilla band.
patria chica	Literally 'little fatherland'; i.e. home district.
peninsulares	Literally 'men of the Peninsula'; Spanish-born residents of Spanish America.

petimetre	I.e. *petit maître*; ironic late-eighteenth-century nickname used to lampoon fashionable young men who had adopted French fashions and mannerisms.
plaza mayor	Literally 'Main Square', but in a few instances more accurately 'high street'; the hub of a city.
populacho, el	Literally 'the mob'; the lower classes.
pretendiente	Office-seeker.
procurador mayor	Senior prosecuting magistrate.
pudiente	Local notable; *cacique*.
pueblo	Town or village, but also the people.
quinta	Conscript; levy of conscripts.
real	Basic unit of Spanish currency prior to 1870.
regidor perpetuo	Hereditary town councillor for life.
reglamento	Regulation; ordinance.
renovación	Literally 'renovation'; reform, renewal.
renovador	Literally 'renovator'; most commonly, an opponent of the Constitution of 1812.
resguardo	Locally organised pre-1808 anti-bandit security forces.
rey deseado, el	Literally, 'the desired king'; i.e. Fernando VII.
rey intruso, el	Literally, 'the intrusive king'; i.e. Joseph Bonaparte.
reyes, los	The king and queen.
Rheinbund	Pertaining to the Confederation of the Rhine.
señor	Feudal lord.
señorialismo	Spanish feudal system.
señorio	Feudal fief; occasionally used in lieu of 'province'.
serranía	Mountainous district.
serranos	Literally 'mountain-dwellers' but especially used to refer to inhabitants of the Serrania de Ronda.
servil	Opponent of the Constitution of 1812.
sevillano	Inhabitant of/pertaining to Seville.
siempre, los de	Literally, 'the same ones as always'; i.e. the established local oligarchy.
somatén	Catalan home guard.
sorteo	Ballot for military service.
suplente	Substitute deputy in *cortes*.
tercio	Term used for the regiments of the Spanish army of the sixteenth century, and occasionally used to describe new infantry units raised in 1808.
tertulia	Group of friends; regular evening gathering.
tío pepe	Literally 'Uncle Joe'; common nickname of Joseph Bonaparte.
tirailleur	Skirmisher.
titulado	Titled member of the nobility.
valenciano	Inhabitant of/pertaining to Valencia.

vales reales	Credit bonds issued under Carlos IV to finance government expenditure.
vallesoletano	Inhabitant of/pertaining to Valladolid.
vecino	Literally 'neighbour'; propertied taxpayer.
venta	Inn.
voltigeur	Soldier of a light company in French line and light infantry regiments.
Voto de Santiago	Ecclesiastical tax payable by inhabitants of the Archdiocese of Santiago de Compostela.
zaragozano	Inhabitant of/pertaining to Zaragoza.
zarzuela, la	Traditional comic opera.

Notes

ABBREVIATIONS

AHN Est.   Archivo Histórico Nacional, Sección de Estado
BHS   Bulletin of Hispanic Studies
BL Add. Mss.   British Library Additional Manuscripts
BN CGI   Biblióteca Nacional, Colección Gómez Imaz
BS CGA   Biblióteca del Senado, Colección Gómez de Arteche
BUM   Boletín de la Univesidad de Madrid
CHJ   Cambridge Historical Journal
CIH   Cuadernos de Investigación Histórica
*CN   Correspondance de Napoléon I publiée par ordre de l'Empereur Napoléon
   III* (Paris, 1858–69)
CREP   Consortium on Revolutionary Europe Proceedings
EHQ   European History Quarterly
EHR   English Historical Review
EM   España Moderna
ESR   European Studies Review
HAHR   Hispanic American Historical Review
HJ   The Historical Journal
HMM   Hemeróteca Municipal de Madrid
HT   History Today
IHR   International History Review
JEH   Journal of Economic History
JLAS   Journal of Latin American Studies
JMH   Journal of Modern History
JSAHR   Journal of the Society for Army Historical Research
PRO FO   Public Record Office, Foreign Office Papers
PRO WO   Public Record Office, War Office Papers
QJE   Quarterly Journal of Economics
RAH   Real Academía de Historia
RHM   Revista de Historia Militar
RP   Review of Politics
SHM CDB   Servicio Histórico Militar, Colección Duque de Bailén

SHM CDF   Servicio Histórico Militar, Colección Documental del Fraile
SHM DG   Servicio Histórico Militar, Depósito de la Guerra
US WP   University of Southampton, Wellington Papers
WD   *The Dispatches of Field Marshal the Duke of Wellington . . . 1789 to 1815*, ed. J. Gurwood (London, 1852).
WSD   *Supplementary Dispatches, Correspondence and Memoranda of . . . Wellington*, ed. Second Duke of Wellington (London, 1858–72).

CHAPTER I

1. A. Alcalá Galiano (ed.), *Memorias de D. Antonio Alcalá Galiano* (Madrid, 1886), vol. I, pp. 127–8.
2. Earl of Ilchester (ed.), *The Spanish Journal of Elizabeth, Lady Holland* (London, 1910), p. 134; H. R. Holland, *Foreign Reminiscences*, ed. H. E. Holland (London, 1850), pp. 86, 107.
3. J. Blanco White, *Cartas de España*, ed. V. Llorens and A. Garnica (Madrid, 1972), pp. 262, 277.
4. Holland, *Foreign Reminiscences*, p. 136.
5. E. Gigas (ed.), 'Lettres d'un diplomate danois en Espagne', *Revue Hispanique*, vol. IX (1902), pp. 400–401.
6. M. de Godoy to María Luisa, 29 May 1801, Archivo Histórico Nacional, Sección de Estado (hereafter AHN Est.) 2821-1.
7. M. de Godoy to María Luisa, 8 June 1801, AHN Est. 2821-1.
8. A. Berazaluce (ed.), *Recuerdos de la Vida de Don Pedro Agustín Girón* (Pamplona, 1978), vol. I, p. 161; Gigas (ed.), 'Lettres d'un diplomate danois', p. 420.
9. Berazaluce, *Recuerdos de la Vida de Don Pedro Agustín Girón*, vol. I, p. 99.
10. J. García de León y Pizarro, *Memorias de la Vida del Excmo. Señor D. José García de León y Pizarro Escritas por el Mismo*, ed. A. Alonso Castrillo (Madrid, 1894), vol. I, pp. 105–6.
11. J. de Bourgoing, *A Modern State of Spain* (London, 1808), vol. III, pp. 359–60.
12. *Diario Político de Mallorca*, 18 June 1808, p. 13, Hemeróteca Municipal de Madrid (hereafter HMM) AH14-1 (2456); Earl of Stanhope, *Notes of Conversations with the Duke of Wellington, 1831–1851* (London, 1889), pp. 55–6.
13. *Cit.* Comte de las Cases, *Mémorial de Sainte Hélène*, ed. G. Walter (Paris, 1956), vol. I, p. 786.
14. Holland, *Foreign Reminiscences*, p. 110; Lady Jackson (ed.), *The Diaries and Letters of Sir George Jackson* (London, 1872), vol. II, p. 322; B. Alexander (ed.), *The Journal of William Beckford in Portugal and Spain, 1787–88* (London, 1954), p. 313; García de León y Pizarro, *Memorias*, vol. I, p. 229.
15. A. von Schepeler, *Histoire de la Révolution d'Espagne et de Portugal* (Liège, 1829–31), vol. I, p. 20; Berazaluce, *Recuerdos de la Vida de Don Pedro Agustín Girón*, vol. I, p. 140.
16. *Cit.* M. de Baudus, *Etudes sur Napoléon* (Paris, 1841), vol. I, p. 105.

17. M. Foy, *History of the War in the Peninsula under Napoleon* (London, 1827), vol. II, p. 34.

18. D. Thiébault, *The Memoirs of Baron Thiébault, late Lieutenant-General in the French Army*, ed. A. Butler (London, 1896), vol. II, p. 196.

19. Berazaluce, *Recuerdos de la Vida de Don Pedro Agustín Girón*, vol. I, pp. 190–91.

20. Thiébault, *Memoirs*, vol. II, p. 199.

21. Foy, *War in the Peninsula*, vol. II, p. 55.

22. *Ibid.*, vol. II, p. 87.

23. *Ibid.*, vol. II, p. 62.

24. J. Fouché, *Memoirs of Joseph Fouché, Duke of Otranto, Minister of the General Police of France* (London, 1892), p. 215.

25. Holland, *Foreign Reminiscences*, pp. 130–31.

26. *Cit.* Alcalá Galiano, *Memorias*, vol. I, p. 144.

27. Napoleon to Murat, 14 March 1808, *Correspondance de Napoléon I publiée par ordre de l'Empereur Napoléon III* (Paris, 1858–69; hereafter *CN*), vol. XVI, pp. 418–19.

28. L. Lejeune, *Memoirs of Baron Lejeune, Aide-de-Camp to Marshals Berthier, Davout and Oudinot*, ed. A. Bell (London, 1897), vol. I, p. 73.

29. Foy, *War in the Peninsula*, vol. II, p. 135.

30. *Cit.* A. Wilson (ed.), *A Diary of St. Helena (1816, 1817): the Journal of Lady Malcolm*, ed. A. Wilson (London, 1899), p. 141.

31. Foy, *War in the Peninsula*, vol. II, p. 20.

32. R. Brindle, 'A Brief Account of Travels, etc., in Spain' (MS), p. 10, Real Colegio de San Albano, Valladolid.

33. *Cit. Diario de Valencia*, 25 March 1808, p. 338, HMM RVP: T45.

34. Alcalá Galiano, *Memorias*, vol. I, p. 146.

35. Blanco White, *Cartas de España*, pp. 301–2.

36. J. Marcén (ed.), *El Manuscrito de Matías Calvo: Memorias de un Monegrino durante la Guerra de la Independencia* (Zaragoza, 2000), p. 177.

37. Alcalá Galiano, *Memorias*, vol. I, p. 160.

38. *Cit.* Las Cases, *Mémorial*, vol. I, pp. 780–81.

39. *Cit.* P. Roederer, *Mémoires sur la Révolution, le Consulat et l'Empire*, ed. O. Aubry (Paris, 1942), pp. 220–21.

CHAPTER 2

1. Lejeune, *Memoirs*, vol. I, p. 78.

2. Blanco White, *Cartas de España*, p. 305.

3. Alcalá Galiano, *Memorias*, vol. I, pp. 167–8.

4. Blanco White, *Cartas*, p. 309.

5. Foy, *History of the War in the Peninsula*, vol. II, p. 181.

6. W. Jacob, *Travels in the South of Spain* (London, 1811), p. 26; H. Swinburne, *Travels through Spain in the Years 1775 and 1776* (Dublin, 1779), p. 16.

7. J. Townsend, *A Journal through Portugal and Spain in the Years 1786 and 1787* (London, 1792), vol. I, p. 385.

8. Blanco White, *Cartas*, p. 71.

9. 'Plan sobre organización de dos batallones por regimiento y sobre sueldos', Real Academía de Historia (hereafter RAH), 2-MS135, No. 9.

10. Blanco White, *Cartas*, p. 321.

11. J. de Palafox, *Memorias*, ed. H. Lafoz (Zaragoza, 1994), p. 54.

12. J. Rico, *Memorias Históricas sobre la Revolución de Valencia que Comprehenden desde el 23 de Mayo de 1808 hasta Fines del Mismo Año, y sobre la Causa Criminal Formada Contra el P. F. Juan Rico, el Brigadier D. Vicente González Moreno, el Comisario de Guerra, D. Narciso Rubio, y Otros* (Cadiz, 1811), p. 16, Biblióteca Nacional, Colección Gómez Imaz (hereafter BN CGI) R61075.

13. Memorial of Fray Beda Peña, 5 July 1808, AHN Est. 74-A, No. 91.

14. R. Alvarez Valdés, *Memorias del Levantamiento de Asturias en 1808*, ed. M. Fuertes Acevedo (Oviedo, 1889), p. 27.

15. *Ibid.*, pp. 29–30.

16. Berazaluce, *Recuerdos de la Vida de Don Pedro Agustín Girón*, vol. I, p. 204.

17. Anon., *Manifiesto de las Ocurriencias mas Principales de la Plaza de Ciudad Rodrigo desde la Causa formada en el Real Sitio del Escorial al Serenísimo Señor Príncipe de Asturias, hoy Nuestro Amado Soberano, hasta la Evacuación de la Plaza de Almeida en el Reino de Portugal en el Dia de Primero de Octubre de 1808* (Salamanca, 1808), p. 23, AHN Est. 65-G, No. 264.

18. Brindle, 'Travels in Spain', pp. 11–12.

19. Memorial of Marqués de Usategui, 27 March 1809, AHN Est. 83-N, No. 395.

20. Berazaluce, *Recuerdos de la Vida de Don Pedro Agustín Girón*, vol. I, p. 217.

21. Conde de Noroña to Pedro de Rivero, n.d., AHN Est. 77-A, No. 106.

22. Anon., *Representación del Príncipe de Asturias, Don Fernando (ahora Nuestro Rey y Señor), a su Padre, Don Carlos IV, Hallada entre los Papeles de S.A.R., Escrita de su Mano, en Octubre de 1807* (Valencia, 1808), BN CGI R60124-1.

23. M. Andario, *Retrato Político del Emperador de los Franceses, su Conducta y la de sus Generales en España, y la Lealtad y Valor de los Españoles por su Soberano, Fernando VII* (Seville, 1808), p. 4, BN CGI R60124-10.

24. Anon., *Juicio Imparcial, Cristiano y Político sobre el Pérfido Cáracter del Emperador de los Franceses* (Seville, 1808), BN CGI R60124-11.

25. Berazaluce, *Recuerdos de la Vida de Don Pedro Agustín Girón*, vol. I, pp. 206–7.

26. Napoleon to Talleyrand, 9 June 1808, CN, vol. XVI, p. 284.

27. Napoleon to Bessières, 16 June 1808, *ibid.*, p. 314.

28. Napoleon to Berthier, 16 April 1808, *ibid.*, p. 8.

29. *Cit.* A. Bigarré, *Mémoires du Général Bigarré, Aide du Camp du Roi Joseph, 1775–1813* (Paris, 1903), p. 229.

CHAPTER 3

1. Napoleon to Murat, 5 May 1808, *CN*, vol. XVII, p. 63.
2. Napoleon to Bessières, 3 June 1808, *CN*, vol. XVII, pp. 266–7.
3. Foy, *History of the War in the Peninsula*, vol. II, pp. 123–5.
4. S. Blaze, *Mémoires d'un Apothécaire sur le Guerre d'Espagne Pendant les Années 1808 à 1814* (Paris, 1828), vol. I, p. 11.
5. Berazaluce, *Recuerdos de la Vida de Don Pedro Agustín Girón*, vol. I, pp. 208–9.
6. Baudus, *Etudes sur Napoléon*, vol. I. p. 111.
7. J. Moscoso, 'Memorias para las campañas de la Izquierda Militar de España' (MS), Servicio Histórico Militar, Colección Duque de Bailén (hereafter SHM CDB), 3/4/23, No. 1.
8. E. de Saint-Hilaire, *Souvenirs Intimes du Temps de l'Empire* (Paris, 1860), vol. II, pp. 232–3.
9. Foy, *History of the War in the Peninsula*, vol. II, p. 279.
10. Napoleon to Joseph, 17 July 1808, *CN*, vol. XVII, p. 403.
11. Blaze, *Mémoires d'un Apothécaire*, vol. I, p. 55.
12. *Ibid.*
13. A. Miot, *Mémoires du Comte Miot de Melito, Ancien Ministre, Ambassadeur, Conseilleur d'Etat et Membre de l'Institut* (Paris, 1858), vol. III, p. 15.
14. *Ibid.*, vol. III, pp. 6–7.
15. L. Gille, *Les Prisonniers de Cabrera: Mémoires d'un Conscrit de 1808* (Paris, 1893), pp. 78–9.
16. F. Guervos to his parents, n.d. RAH 11-5-7: 9003, No. 1.
17. Berazaluce, *Recuerdos de la Vida de Don Pedro Agustín Girón*, vol. I, p. 231.
18. *Cit.* Holland, *Foreign Reminiscences*, p. 156.
19. Napoleon to Clarke, 3 August 1808, *CN*, vol. XVII, p. 427.
20. *Cit.* Stanhope, *Conversations with the Duke of Wellington*, pp. 10, 22.

CHAPTER 4

1. *Cit.* R. Muir, *Britain and the Defeat of Napoleon, 1807–1815* (New Haven, Conn., 1996), p. 39.
2. E. Meteyard (ed.), *A Group of Englishmen, 1795 to 1815, being Records of the Younger Wedgewoods and their Friends* (London, 1871), p. 371.
3. A. Hayter (ed.), *The Backbone: Diaries of a Military Family in the Napoleonic Wars* (Bishop Auckland, 1993), p. 164.
4. *Ibid.*, p. 163.
5. L. Junot, *Mémoires du Madame la Duchesse d'Abrantes, ou Souvenirs Historiques sur Napoléon, la Révolution, le Directoire, le Consulat, l'Empire et la Restauration* (Paris, 1831–35), vol. XII, p. 64.
6. *Ibid.*, p. 71.

7. S. Morley, *Memoirs of a Sergeant of the Fifth Regiment of Foot, containing an Account of his Service in Hanover, South America and the Peninsula* (Ashford, 1842), pp. 45–6.

8. C. O'Neil, *The Military Adventures of Charles O'Neil, who was a Soldier in the Army of Lord Wellington during the Memorable Peninsular War and the Continental Campaigns from 1811 to 1815* (Worcester, Mass., 1851), p. 71.

9. A. Hamilton, *Hamilton's Campaign with Moore and Wellington during the Peninsular War* (Troy, New York, 1847), p. 11.

10. J. Leach, *Rough Sketches in the Life of an Old Soldier* (London, 1831), pp. 50–51.

11. C. Hibbert (ed.), *The Recollections of Rifleman Harris* (London, 1985), pp. 23–7.

12. *Cit.* Junot, *Mémoires*, vol. XII, p. 79.

13. G. Wood, *The Subaltern Officer: a Narrative* (London, 1825), p. 62.

14. R. Porter, *Letters from Portugal and Spain written during the March of the British Troops under Sir John Moore* (London, 1809), p. 2; E. Warre (ed.), *Letters from the Peninsula, 1808–1812 by Lieutenant General Sir William Warre, CB, KTS* (London, 1909), pp. 39–40.

15. Morley, *Memoirs*, p. 51.

16. Leach, *Rough Sketches*, pp. 55–6.

17. W. Wordsworth, *Concerning the Relations of Great Britain, Spain and Portugal to Each Other and to the Common Enemy at this Crisis, and Specifically as Affected by the Convention of Cintra* (London, 1809), p. 49.

18. Leach, *Rough Sketches*, pp. 56–7.

19. P. Roche to Castlereagh, 8 August 1808, Public Record Office, War Office Papers (hereafter PRO WO) 1/233, ff. 423–4; W. Parker Carroll to J. Leith, 8 September 1808, PRO WO 1/229, ff. 240–41.

20. W. Cox to Castlereagh, 3 August 1808, PRO WO 1/233, f. 320.

21. W. Cox to Castlereagh, 27 August 1808, PRO WO 1/231, f. 343.

22. J. Maurice (ed.), *The Diary of Sir John Moore* (London, 1904), vol. II, p. 261.

CHAPTER 5

1. Brindle, 'Travels in Spain', pp. 22–3.

2. Petition of M. Caval *et al.*, 28 June 1808, AHN Est. 74-A, No. 207.

3. Anon. to the Junta Suprema Central, n.d., AHN Est. 52-G, No. 403.

4. El Verdadero Español to the Junta Suprema Central, n.d., AHN Est. 52-E, No. 218.

5. Anon. to the Junta Suprema Central, n.d., AHN Est. 52-A, No. 27.

6. Anon. to the Junta Suprema Central, n.d., AHN Est. 52-G, No. 367.

7. El Sacerdote Celoso to the Junta Suprema Central, 29 January 1809, AHN Est. 52-E, No. 217.

8. Anon. to the Junta Suprema Central, n.d., AHN Est. 52-G, No. 312.

9. J. Kincaid, *Adventures in the Rifle Brigade* (London, 1909), p. 86.

10. Anon. to the Junta Suprema Central, n.d., AHN Est. 52-A, No. 82.

11. J. Patterson, *The Adventures of Captain John Patterson* (London, 1837), p. 216.

12. Junta of Santiago to Junta of Galicia, 16 December 1808, AHN Est. 74-B, No. 272.

13. Anon. to Junta Suprema Central, n.d., AHN Est. 52-G, No. 343.

14. S. Rodríguez to M. de Garay, 16 February 1809, AHN Est. 46-B, No. 56.

15. Junta of Mondoñedo to Junta of Galicia, 19 November 1808, AHN Est. 75-B, No. 222.

16. A. Ludovici (ed.), *On the Road with Wellington: the Diary of a War Commissary in the Peninsular Campaigns* (New York, 1925), pp. 79–80.

17. F. J. de Castaños to G. García de la Cuesta, 26 September 1808, PRO WO 1/227, ff. 395–9.

18. Holland, *Foreign Reminiscences*, p. 147.

19. W. Bentinck to Castlereagh, 14 November 1808, PRO WO 1/230, ff. 160–61.

20. W. Bentinck to Castlereagh, 19 October 1808, PRO WO 1/230, ff. 89–90.

21. Cit. Ilchester, *Spanish Journal of Elizabeth Lady Holland*, p. 412.

22. Alcalá Galiano (ed.), *Memorias*, pp. 201–2.

23. C. Doyle to C. Stewart, 12 August 1808, PRO WO 1/227, f. 134; S. Whittingham to W. Bentinck, 28 October 1808, PRO WO 1/230, ff. 140–41.

24. A. Pillado to M. de Garay, 6 December 1808, AHN Est. 17-1², f. 38.

25. M. Pró de Bayona to Barón de Sabasona, 26 January 1809, AHN Est. 17-1², p. 21.

26. F. J. de Cabanés, *Historia de la Operaciones del Ejército de Cataluña en la Primera Campaña de la Guerra de la Usurpación, o sea de la Independencia de España* (Tarragona, 1809), vol. II, p. 33, Biblíoteca del Senado, Colección Goméz de Arteche (thereafter BS CGA) 040126.

27. Jacob, *Travels in the South of Spain*, p. 17.

28. Anon., *El Duende de Nuestros Ejércitos Descubierto por un Buen Patriota* (Cádiz, 1810), p. 12, BN CGI R60087.

29. J. Green to E. Cooke, 1 September 1809, PRO WO 1/237, ff. 555–7.

30. Lady Jackson, *Diaries and Letters*, vol. II, p. 314.

31. F. Copons to F. Eguía, 21 April 1810, RAH 9-31-6: 6966.

32. A. de Rocca, *Memoirs of the War of the French in Spain*, ed. P. Haythornthwaite (London, 1990), pp. 43–4.

33. W. Broderick to Castlereagh, 10 September 1808, PRO WO 1/233, f. 16.

34. J. M. Sarasa, *Vida y Hechos Militares del Mariscal del Campo, Don Juan Manuel Sarasa, Narrados por el Mismo*, ed. J. del Burgo (Pamplona, 1952), pp. 10–11.

35. F. Whittingham (ed.), *A Memoir of the Services of Lieutenant General Sir Samuel Ford Whittingham* (London, 1868), p. 49.

36. Lady Jackson, *Diaries and Letters*, vol. II, pp. 298–9.

37. W. Parker Carroll to Castlereagh, 2 November 1808, PRO WO 1/229, ff. 468–72.

38. Sarasa, *Vida y Hechos*, p. 11.

39. J. Dellard, *Mémoires Militaires du Général Baron Dellard* (Paris, n.d.), pp. 266–7.

40. Sarasa, *Vida y Hechos*, p. 12.

41. *Cit.* 'Diario de operaciones del Ejército de la Izquierda al mando del Teniente General Don Joaquín Blake', SHM CDB 3/4/28.

42. J. North (ed.), *In the Legions of Napoleon: the Memoirs of a Polish Officer in Spain and Russia, 1808–1813* (London, 1999), p. 46.

43. García de León y Pizarro, *Memorias*, vol. I, pp. 251–2.

44. T. Morla to A. Cornel, 7 December 1808, SHM CDB 3/2/5.

45. J. Fortescue (ed.), *The Notebooks of Captain Coignet, Soldier of the Empire* (London, 1928), p. 167.

46. Duque del Infantado, *Manifiesto de las Operaciones del Ejército del Centro* (Seville, 1809), p. 16.

47. García de León y Pizarro, *Memorias*, vol. I, pp. 257–61.

48. Brindle, 'Travels in Spain', p. 24.

CHAPTER 6

1. J. Moore to J. W. Gordon, 4 October 1808, British Library, Additional Manuscripts (hereafter BL Add. Mss.) 49482, ff. 128–30.

2. J. Moore to Castlereagh, 24 November 1808, PRO WO 1/236, ff. 74–5.

3. Maurice, *Diary of Sir John Moore*, vol. II, p. 281.

4. J. Moore to J. W. Gordon, 29 November 1808, BL Add. Mss. 49482, ff. 156–8; Maurice, *Diary of Sir John Moore*, vol. II, pp. 347–8.

5. J. Moore to J. W. Gordon, 26 October 1808, BL Add. Mss. 49482, ff. 144–8.

6. A. Neale, *Letters from Portugal and Spain comprising an Account of the Operations of the Armies under Their Excellencies Sir Arthur Wellesley and Sir John Moore from the landing of their Troops in Mondego Bay to the Battle at Corunna* (London, 1809), p. 213; Patterson, *Adventures*, p. 70.

7. Porter, *Letters*, p. 101.

8. Ludovici, *On the Road with Wellington*, p. 70.

9. Maurice, *Diary of Sir John Moore*, vol. II, p. 284.

10. H. Wylly (ed.), *A Cavalry Officer in the Corunna Campaign, 1808–1809: the Journal of Captain Gordon of the Fifteenth Hussars* (London, 1913), pp. 102–3.

11. M. de Marbot, *The Memoirs of Baron de Marbot, late Lieutenant General in the French Army* (London, 1892), vol. I, p. 352.

12. Lejeune, *Memoirs*, vol. I, p. 107.

13. Fortescue, *Notebooks of Captain Coignet*, p. 168; T. Simmons (ed.), *Memoirs of a Polish Lancer: the Pamietniki of Dezydery Chlapowski* (Chicago, 1992), p. 47.

14. C. Hibbert (ed.), *A Soldier of the Seventy-First* (London, 1975), pp. 25–6.

15. Wylly, *Journal of Captain Gordon*, pp. 146–7.

16. C. Cadell, *Narrative of the Campaigns of the Twenty-Eighth Regiment since their Return from Egypt in 1802* (London, 1835), p. 45.

17. Wylly, *Journal of Captain Gordon*, p. 149.

18. Porter, *Letters*, p. 254.

19. J. Sturgis (ed.), *A Boy in the Peninsular War: the Services, Adventures and*

Experiences of Robert Blakeney, Subaltern of the Twenty-Eighth Regiment (London, 1899), pp. 49–50.

20. Morley, *Memoirs*, pp. 61–4.

21. La Romana to A. Cornel, 18 January 1809, AHN Est. 16-8, ff. 32–4.

22. J. A. Posse, *Historía Biográfica, o Historia de la Vida y Hechos de Don Juan Antonio Posse Escrita por El Mismo*, ed. R. Herr (Madrid, 1984; published as *Memorias del Cura Liberal Don Juan Antonio Posse con su Discurso sobre la Constitución de 1812*).

23. Ludovici, *On the Road with Wellington*, pp. 127–8.

24. L. Calvo de Rozas to M. de Garay (?), 6 January 1809, AHN Est. 17-1², f. 31.

25. Rocca, *Memoirs*, p. 68.

26. Berazaluce, *Recuerdos de la Vida de Don Pedro Agustín Girón*, vol. I, p. 271.

27. C. Doyle to W. Cooke, 30 November 1808, PRO WO 1/227, f. 567.

28. Berazaluce, *Recuerdos de la Vida de Don Pedro Agustín Girón*, vol. I, p. 242.

29. L. de Villaba, *Zaragoza en su Segundo Sitio* (Palma de Mallorca, 1811), pp. 20–32 *passim*, Servicio Histórico Militar, Depósito de la Guerra (hereafter SHM DG) 1811/6.

30. Marbot, *Memoirs*, vol. I, p. 360.

31. North, *In the Legions of Napoleon*, pp. 56–7.

32. Lejeune, *Memoirs*, vol. I, pp. 167–9.

CHAPTER 7

1. Junta Suprema Central to Junta of Murcia, 3 March 1809, AHN Est. 83-A, No. 1.

2. Anon. to Floridablanca, 12 November 1808, AHN Est. 52-A, No. 85.

3. *Semanario Político, Histórico y Literario de la Coruña*, No. 5, pp. 109–11 (NB facsimile edition, ed. M. Saurín de la Iglesia: La Coruña, 1996).

4. B. Hall, *Corcubión*, ed. J. Alberich (Exeter, 1975), p. 26.

5. Diary of Henri de Saint Simon (unpublished manuscript quoted here with the kind permission of M. Robin le Mallier).

6. F. Guervos to his parents, 18 November 1808, RAH 11-5-7: 9003, No. 4.

7. T. de Veri to M. de Garay, 17 March 1809, AHN Est. 17, 10-1, f. 35; C. Doyle to W. Cooke, 31 December 1808, PRO WO 1/227, ff. 651–2.

8. J. Blake to Junta of Catalonia, 15 September 1809, AHN Est. 38-E, No. 386⁸.

9. J. Queipo de Llano (Conde de Toreno), *Historia del Levantamiento, Guerra y Revolución de España* (ed. Biblióteca de Autores Españoles: Madrid, 1953), p. 190.

10. Anon. to Junta Central, n.d., AHN Est. 52-G, No. 303.

11. Anon. to Junta Central, n.d., *ibid.*, No. 306.

12. Junta de Vigilancia de Cádiz to Junta Central, 1 February 1809, AHN Est. 14-A:10¹, ff. 55–6.

13. Anon. to Junta Central, 20 June 1809, AHN Est. 52-E, No. 273.

14. Holland, *Foreign Reminiscences*, p. 146.

15. Jacob, *Travels in the South of Spain*, p. 33.

16. W. Thompson (ed.), *An Ensign in the Peninsular War: the Letters of John Aitchison* (London, 1981), p. 32.

17. *Cit.* Hayter, *The Backbone*, p. 211.

18. Bigarré, *Mémoires*, pp. 241–2.

19. Jackson, *Diaries and Letters*, p. 410.

20. I. Rousseau (ed.), *The Peninsular War Journal of Sir Benjamin D'Urban* (London, 1930), p. 48; Rocca, *Memoirs*, p. 78.

21. Rocca, *Memoirs*, pp. 79–80.

22. G. García de la Cuesta to A. Cornel, 7 April 1809, *cit.*, G. García de la Cuesta, *Manifiesto que Presenta a la Europa el Capitán General de los Reales Ejércitos, Don Gregorio García de las Cuesta sobre sus Operaciones Militares y Políticas desde el Mes de Junio de 1808 hasta el 12 de Agosto de 1809 en que Dejó el Mando del Ejército de Extremadura* (Valencia, 1811), pp. 41–45, BS CGA 040458.

23. Rocca, *Memoirs*, p. 80.

24. Rousseau, *Journal of Sir Benjamin D'Urban*, p. 48.

25. Hall, *Corcubión*, pp. 13–17 *passim*.

26. *Ibid.*, pp. 29–30.

27. Alvarez Valdés, *Memorias*, pp. 157–8.

28. *Ibid.*, p. 159.

29. C. Doyle to W. Cooke, 24 February 1809, PRO WO 1/241, f. 163.

30. L. Suchet, *Memoirs of the War in Spain from 1808 to 1814* (London, 1829), pp. 20–21.

31. North, *In the Legions of Napoleon*, p. 78.

32. C. Doyle to W. Cooke, 13 June 1809, PRO WO 1/241, f. 296.

33. *Gazeta Extraordinaria del Gobierno*, 3 July 1809, pp. 665–7, HMM AH17-2 (2925bis).

34. North, *In the Legions of Napoleon*, p. 80.

CHAPTER 8

1. Wood, *The Subaltern Officer*, p. 78.

2. *Ibid.*, p. 79.

3. Ludovici, *On the Road with Wellington*, pp. 155–6.

4. Wellington to Castlereagh, 31 May 1809, University of Southampton, Wellington Papers (hereafter US WP) 1/263.

5. J. Sherer, *Recollections of the Peninsula* (London, 1825), p. 130.

6. R. Buckley (ed.), *The Napoleonic War Journal of Captain Thomas Henry Browne* (London, 1987), p. 198.

7. G. Bell, *Rough Notes of an Old Soldier*, ed. B. Stuart (London, 1956), p. 43; S. Cassels (ed.), *Peninsular Portrait, 1811–1814: the Letters of Captain William Bragge, Third (King's Own) Dragoons* (London, 1963), p. 7.

8. Porter, *Letters*, pp. 7–8, 39–40.

9. W. Verner (ed.), *A British Rifleman: Journals and Correspondence [of George Simmons] during the Peninsular War and the Campaign of Waterloo* (London, 1899), pp. 49–50.

10. *Ibid.*, p. 94; J. Donaldson, *Recollections of the Eventful Life of a Soldier* (Edinburgh, 1852), p. 89.

11. Donaldson, *Recollections*, p. 58.

12. W. Grattan, *Adventures of the Connaught Rangers from 1808 to 1814* (London, 1847), vol. II, pp. 95–6.

13. Patterson, *Adventures*, p. 155.

14. W. Swabey, *Diary of the Campaigns in the Peninsula for the Years 1811, 12 and 13*, ed. F. Whinyates (London, 1895), p. 180.

15. Bell, *Rough Notes of an Old Soldier*, pp. 33–4.

16. W. Stothert, *A Narrative of the Principal Events of the Campaigns of 1809, 1810 and 1811 in Spain and Portugal* (London, 1812), p. 76; E. Costello, *The Adventures of a Soldier, or Memoirs of Edward Costello, K.S.F.* (London, 1841), p. 35.

17. A. Haley (ed.), *The Soldier who Walked Away: Autobiography of Andrew Pearson, a Peninsular-War Veteran* (Liverpool, n.d.), p. 65.

18. A. Wellesley to J. H. Frere, 24 July 1809, BL Add. Mss. 37286, ff. 118–21.

19. A. Wellesley to Castlereagh, 17 June 1809, US WP 1/266; A. Wellesley to J. H. Frere, 24 July 1809 (No. 2), BL Add. Mss. 37286, ff. 118–21.

20. A. Wellesley to Castlereagh, 24 July 1809, PRO WO 1/238, ff. 265–7.

21. Haley, *Autobiography of Andrew Pearson*, pp. 67–8.

22. *Ibid.*, p. 70.

23. *Ibid.*, p. 69.

24. Ludovici, *On the Road with Wellington*, p. 187.

25. J. Page (ed.), *Intelligence Officer in the Peninsula: Letters and Diaries of Major the Honourable Edward Charles Cocks, 1786–1812* (Tunbridge Wells, 1986), p. 39.

26. Ludovici, *On the Road with Wellington*, p. 189.

27. A. Wellesley to Richmond, 29 July 1809, US WP 1/270.

28. J. C. Carnicero, *Historia Razonada de los Principales Sucesos de la Gloriosa Revolución de España* (Madrid, 1814), vol. II, pp. 78–80.

29. *Ibid.*, pp. 93–4.

30. F. Venegas to M. de Garay, 7 August 1809, AHN Est. 15^1-8, f. 36.

31. Berazaluce, *Recuerdos de la Vida de Don Pedro Agustín Girón*, vol. I, p. 319.

32. Bigarré, *Mémoires*, p. 255.

33. Berazaluce, *Recuerdos de la Vida de Don Pedro Agustín Girón*, vol. I, pp. 320–21.

34. H. Mackinnon, *A Journal of the Campaign in Portugal and Spain containing Remarks on the Inhabitants, Customs, Trade and Cultivation of those Countries from the Year 1809 to 1812* (Bath, 1812), p. 39.

35. Verner, *A British Rifleman*, p. 23.

36. Wood, *Subaltern Officer*, pp. 87–8.

37. E. Shore (ed.), *An Engineer Officer under Wellington in the Peninsula: the Diary and Correspondence of Lieutenant Rice Jones, R.E., during 1808-9-10-11-12* (Cambridge, 1986), pp. 40–42.

38. A. Wellesley to Castlereagh, 21 August 1809, US WP 1/273.

39. A. Wellesley to R. Wellesley, 24 August 1809, US WP 1/273.

40. R. Wellesley to G. Canning, 15 September 1809, BL Add. Mss. 37289, ff. 41–70.

41. El Cura Andaluz, Amante de la Patria, to the Junta Suprema Central, 4 January 1810, AHN Est. 52-F, No. 282.

CHAPTER 9

1. Miot, *Memoires*, vol. III, p. 19.

2. Lejeune, *Memoirs*, vol. I, p. 83.

3. Rocca, *Memoirs*, p. 23.

4. Foy, *History of the War in the Peninsula*, vol. I, p. 200.

5. N. Edwards (ed.), *The Saint Helena Diary of General Baron Gourgaud* (London, 1932), p. 130.

6. P. Fleuriot de Langle (ed.), *Napoleon at Saint Helena: Memoirs of General Bertrand, Grand Marshal of the Palace, January to May 1821* (London, 1953), pp. 13–14.

7. Lejeune, *Memoirs*, vol. I, p. 95.

8. *Gazeta de Sevilla*, 7 January 1812, HMM RVP:T20.

9. Proclamation of the Conde de Montarco, 25 March 1812, BN CGI R60016-1[4].

10. Bigarré, *Mémoires*, p. 270.

11. North, *In the Legions of Napoleon*, p. 87.

12. *Ibid.*

13. B. Jones (ed.), *In the Service of Napoleon: the Military Memoirs of Charles Parquin* (London, 1987), pp. 113, 121.

14. T. Sydenham to H. Wellesley, 12 September 1812, US WP 1/361.

15. Miot, *Mémoires*, vol. III, p. 38.

16. Suchet, *Memoirs*, vol. I, p. 311.

17. Anon., *Gritos de Madrid Cautivo a los Pueblos de España* (Seville, 1809), p. 2, BN CGI R60124-8.

18. Proclamation of Marshal Berthier, 12 December 1808, AHN Est. 40-A, No. 23.

19. Miot, *Mémoires*, vol. III, p. 22.

20. Rocca, *Memoirs*, p. 33.

21. Thiébault, *Memoirs*, vol. II, p. 245.

22. S. Andrés de Embite to M. de Garay, 28 February 1809, AHN Est. 16-1, ff. 32–6.

23. M. de la Ceda to P. Rivero, n.d., AHN Est. 40-F, No. 228.

24. Miot, *Mémoires*, vol. III, p. 137.

25. *Ibid.*, vol. III, p. 138.

26. *Ibid.*, vol. III, p. 52.

27. Thiébault, *Memoirs*, vol. II, p. 274.

CHAPTER 10

1. Suchet, *Memoirs*, vol. I, pp. 52–3.

2. P. Haythornthwaite (ed.), *Life in Napoleon's Army: the Memoirs of Captain Elzéar Blaze* (London, 1995), p. 194.

3. Blaze, *Mémoires d'un Apothécaire*, vol. I, pp. 72–3.

4. Suchet, *Memoirs*, vol. I, pp. 47–51.

5. Bigarré, *Mémoires*, p. 277; Haythornthwaite, *Life in Napoleon's Army*, p. 102.

6. H. von Brandt, *The Two Minas and the Spanish Guerrillas* (London, 1825), p. 48.

7. *Ibid.*, p. 54; T. Sydenham to H. Wellesley, 10 October 1812, US WP 1/361; G. Larpent (ed.), *The Private Journal of Judge-Advocate F. S. Larpent, attached to Lord Wellington's Headquarters, 1812–14* (London, 1853), vol. I, p. 132.

8. Rocca, *Memoirs*, p. 21.

9. Miot, *Mémoires*, vol. III, pp. 56–8.

10. Brandt, *The Two Minas and the Spanish Guerrillas*, pp. 54–8.

11. Rocca, *Memoirs*, p. 89.

12. *Ibid.*, pp. 157–60.

13. Haythornthwaite, *Life in Napoleon's Army*, p. 58.

14. Bell, *Rough Notes of an Old Soldier*, p. 34.

15. Bigarré, *Mémoires*, pp. 284–7.

16. J. Ibañez, *Diario de Operaciones de la División del Condado de Niebla que Mandó el Mariscal de Campo, D. Francisco de Copons y Navía, desde el Dia 14 de Abril de 1810, que Tomó el Mando, hasta el 24 de Enero de 1811, que Pasó este General al Quinto Ejército* (Faro, 1811), pp. 3–4, Servicio Histórico Militar, Colección Documental del Fraile (hereafter SHM CDF), vol. CCCXLII.

17. E. Alonso (ed.), *Memorias del Alcalde de Roa, Don Gregorio González Arranz, 1788–1840* (Roa, 1995), pp. 23–4.

18. North, *In the Legions of Napoleon*, p. 89.

19. *Cit.* Cassels (ed.), *Peninsular Portrait, 1811–1814*, p. 57.

20. Ludovici, *On the Road with Wellington*, p. 325.

21. J. Walker to Liverpool, 1 November 1810, PRO WO 1/261, pp. 115–16.

22. La Romana to N. Mahy, 25 July 1809, SHM CDB 5/8/2, No. 5.

23. Villaba, *Zaragoza en su Segundo Sitio*, pp. 45–6.

24. Junta of Najera to Junta Central, 30 November 1809, AHN Est. 41-E, No. 124.

25. M. Loynaz to P. Rivero, 22 November 1809, AHN Est. 15-2⁴, ff. 70–74.

26. Suchet, *Memoirs*, vol. I, pp. 272–4.

27. P. Villacampa to J. M. de Carvajal, 27 February 1811, *cit. Gazeta de la Junta-Congreso del Reino de Valencia*, 5 March 1811, p. 293, HMM AH475.

28. Anon., *Medios de Salvar el Reino* (Cádiz, 1810), pp. 5–6, BS CGA 038158.

29. *Ibid.*, pp. 8–9.

30. J. Serrano Valdenebro to J. M. Carvajal, 4 April 1811, *cit. Diario de Algeciras*, 24 April 1811, pp. 357–61, HMM AH227.

31. T. Graham to H. Bunbury, 27 September 1810, PRO WO 1/247, f. 629.

32. T. Sydenham to H. Wellesley, 10 October 1812, US WP 1/361.

33. Haythornthwaite, *Life in Napoleon's Army*, p. 57.

34. T. Sydenham to H. Wellesley, 10 October 1812, US WP 1/361.

35. Sherer, *Recollections of the Peninsula*, p. 248.

36. Carnicero, *Historia Razonada*, vol. III, pp. 121–2.

37. Rocca, *Memoirs*, pp. 150–51.

38. O'Neil, *Military Adventures*, pp. 139, 145.

39. F. Ballesteros, *Repetuosos Descargos que el Teniente General D. Francisco Ballesteros Ofrece a la Generosa Nación Española* (Cádiz, 1813), pp. 21–2, SHM CDF CLIV.

40. R. Santillán, *Memorias de Don Ramón Santillán (1808–1856)*, ed. A. Berazaluce (Madrid, 1996), p. 50.

41. Alonso, *Memorias del Alcalde de Roa*, p. 24.

42. *Cit.* Jones, *Military Memoirs of Charles Parquin*, p. 126.

43. J. R. to Juillé, 19 July 1810, US WP 1/313.

44. J. Bonet to A. Berthier, 2 December 1810, *cit.* P. Rodríguez Fernández (ed.), *La Guerra de Independencia en Asturias: Correspondencia de General Bonet, 1809–1812* (Gijón, 1991), pp. 99–100.

45. P. del Canto and B. Bonifaz to Junta Central, 4 December 1809, AHN Est. 41-E, No. 127.

46. Marbot, *Memoirs*, vol. II, pp. 70–71.

47. Brandt, *The Two Minas and the Spanish Guerrillas*, pp. 65–6.

48. J. Porlier to N. Mahy, 25 March 1811, SHM CDB 25/36/24.

CHAPTER 11

1. Donaldson, *Recollections*, pp. 71–7.

2. Alcalá Galiano, *Memorias*, vol. I, p. 292.

3. A. Argüelles, *Examen Histórico de la Reforma Constitucional que Hicieron las Cortes Generales y Extraordinarias Desde que se Instalaron en la Isla de León el Dia 24 de Septiembre de 1810 Hasta que Cerraron en Cádiz sus Sesiones en 14 del Propio Mes de 1813*, ed. J. Longares (Madrid, 1970; published under the title *La Reforma Constitucional de Cádiz*), p. 90.

4. F. Roche to Wellington, 6 March 1810, PRO WO 1/243, ff. 490–94.

5. H. Wellesley to W. Wellesley, 12 March 1810, *cit.* F. Wellesley (ed.), *The Diary and Correspondence of Henry Wellesley, First Lord Cowley, 1790–1846* (London, 1930), pp. 54–5.

6. Duque de Alburquerque, *Manifiesto del Duque de Alburquerque Acerca de su Conducta con la Junta de Cádiz y Arribo del Ejército de su Mando a Aquella Plaza* (London, 1810), p. 75, SHM DG 1810/1.

7. *El Español*, 30 January 1811, p. 263, HMM AH4-2 (No. 711).

8. Jacob, *Travels in the South of Spain*, p. 366.

9. T. Graham to Liverpool, 23 April 1811, PRO WO 1/252, f. 291.

10. H. Douglas to Liverpool, 13 September 1811, PRO WO 1/261, f. 446; H. Wellesley to Wellington, 18 July 1811, US WP 12/2/2.

11. Conde de Noroña to Pedro de Rivero, n.d., AHN Est. 77-A, No. 106.

12. J. Walker to Liverpool, 1 November 1810, PRO WO 1/261, f. 114.

13. *Cit. El Redactor General*, 9 April 1812, p. 1177, HMM 6/3.

14. J. Walker to Liverpool, 4 October 1810, PRO WO 1/261, f. 87.

15. Bishop of Ciudad Rodrigo to G. de Jovellanos, 10 February 1809, AHN Est. 65-G, No. 267.

16. Junta of Ciudad Rodrigo to M. de Garay, 8 January 1810, AHN Est. 65-G, No. 343.

17. Page, *Intelligence Officer in the Peninsula*, p. 91.

18. Ibañez, *Diario de Operaciones de la División del Condado de Niebla*, p. 5.

19. P. Roche to Wellington, 6 March 1810, PRO WO 1/243, f. 490.

20. T. Graham to H. Bunbury, 28 March 1810, PRO WO 1/247, ff. 91–2.

21. Schepeler, *Histoire de la Révolution d'Espagne et de Portugal*, vol. II, p. 447.

22. Holland, *Foreign Reminiscences*, p. 158.

23. *Cit.* L. Junot, *Mémoires*, pp. 57–8.

24. D. Horward (ed.), *The French Campaign in Spain and Portugal: an Account by Jean Jacques Pelet* (Minneapolis, 1973), p. 51; Verner, *A British Rifleman*, p. 68.

25. Horward, *The French Campaign in Spain and Portugal*, p. 65.

26. Marbot, *Memoirs*, vol. II, p. 82.

27. Horward, *The French Campaign in Spain and Portugal*, pp. 78–80.

28. Wellington to Liverpool, 14 July 1810, PRO WO 1/245, ff. 92–3.

29. *Tribuno del Pueblo Español*, 6 July 1813, p. 253, HMM AH1-4 (No. 122).

30. Argüelles, *Examen Histórico*, p. 2.

31. *Diario Redactor de Sevilla*, 9 December 1812, SHM CDF, vol. CXXXII.

32. Alcalá Galiano, *Memorias*, vol. I, p. 282.

33. J. Villanueva, *Vida Literaria de Don Joaquín Lorenzo Villanueva*, ed. G. Ramírez Aledón (Alicante, 1996), p. 254.

34. Wellington to H. Wellesley, 2 December 1810, US WP 12/1/2.

35. Wellington to H. Wellesley, 21 October 1810, US WP 12/1/2.

36. *El Español*, 28 February 1811, p. 419, HMM AH4-2 (711).

37. *El Redactor General*, 1 March 1813, HMM 6/3.

38. *El Ciudadano Imparcial*, No. 2, p. 10, HMM AH5-1 (165).

39. *El Español*, 30 April 1811, p. 6, HMM AH4-2 (712).

40. *Ibid.*, 30 March 1811, p. 454, HMM AH4-2 (711).

41. Anon. *Indagación de las Causas de los Malos Sucesos de Nuestros Ejércitos y Medios de Removerlos* (Cádiz, 1811), pp. 7, 28, BS CGA 011166.

42. García de León y Pizarro, *Memorias*, vol. I, pp. 320–21.

CHAPTER 12

1. Wellington to Liverpool, 14 November 1809, *The Dispatches of Field Marshal the Duke of Wellington during his various Campaigns in India, Denmark, Portugal, Spain, the Low Countries and France from 1789 to 1815*, ed. J. Gurwood (London, 1852; hereafter *WD*), vol. III, p. 583.

2. W. Beresford to Wellington, 12 December 1809, *Supplementary Despatches, Correspondence and Memoranda of Field Marshal Arthur, Duke of Wellington*, ed. Second Duke of Wellington (London, 1858–72; hereafter *WSD*), vol. VI, p. 436.

3. Warre, *Letters from the Peninsula*, p. 78.

4. Wellington to Castlereagh, 25 August 1809, *WD*, vol. III, p. 453.

5. C. Boutflower, *The Journal of an Army Surgeon during the Peninsular War* (Manchester, 1912), p. 30.

6. Warre, *Letters from the Peninsula*, pp. 115–16.

7. Wellington to Castlereagh, 25 August 1809, *WD*, vol. III, p. 452.

8. Rousseau, *Peninsular War Journal of Sir Benjamin D'Urban*, p. 57.

9. Thompson, *Ensign in the Peninsular War*, p. 59; S. Monick (ed.), *Douglas's Tale of the Peninsula and Waterloo* (London, 1997), p. 19.

10. Ludovici, *On the Road with Wellington*, p. 162.

11. Wellington to Castlereagh, 25 August 1809, *WD*, vol. III, p. 453.

12. Rousseau, *Peninsular War Journal of Sir Benjamin D'Urban*, p. 103.

13. General Order, 29 May 1809, *WD*, vol. III, p. 258.

14. Wellington to Liverpool, 24 January 1810, *ibid.*, p. 700.

15. Boutflower, *Journal of an Army Surgeon*, p. 50.

16. G. Bankes (ed.), *The Autobiography of Sergeant William Lawrence, a Hero of the Peninsular and Waterloo Campaign* (London, 1886).

17. Sherer, *Recollections of the Peninsula*, p. 83.

18. Wellington to H. Torrens, 29 August 1810, *WSD*, vol. VI, p. 582.

19. Thompson, *Ensign in the Peninsular War*, p. 103.

20. Wellington to W. Wellesley-Pole, 5 September 1810, *WSD*, vol. VI, p. 589.

21. Wellington to H. Wellesley, 29 April 1810, *WD*, vol. IV, p. 38.

22. Wellington to Liverpool, *ibid.*, vol. III, p. 810.

23. Verner, *British Rifleman*, p. 77.

24. Anon., *Memoirs of a Sergeant Late in the Forty-Third Light Infantry Regiment, Previously to and during the Peninsular War* (London, 1835), p. 93.

25. Leach, *Rough Sketches*, p. 149.

26. Verner, *British Rifleman*, pp. 78–9.

27. Horward, *French Campaign in Spain and Portugal*, pp. 120–21.

28. *Ibid.*, p. 147.

29. Thiébault, *Memoirs*, vol. II, p. 288.

30. Marbot, *Memoirs*, vol. II, p. 108.

31. Warre, *Letters from the Peninsula*, p. 145.

32. Grattan, *Adventures of the Connaught Rangers*, vol. I, pp. 52–3.

33. Hamilton, *Hamilton's Campaign*, p. 89.

34. Ludovici, *On the Road with Wellington*, p. 249.

35. Sherer, *Recollections of the Peninsula*, pp. 115–17.

36. Ludovici, *On the Road with Wellington*, p. 261.

37. Monick, *Douglas's Tale*, pp. 21–2.

38. Leach, *Rough Sketches*, pp. 175–6.

39. Donaldson, *Recollections*, p. 104.

40. Verner, *British Rifleman*, pp. 152, 160.

41. Ludovici, *On the Road with Wellington*, pp. 290–91.

42. B. Liddell Hart (ed.), *The Letters of Private Wheeler, 1809–1828* (London, 1951), p. 52.

43. Anon., *Memoirs of a Sergeant*, p. 114.

44. Donaldson, *Recollections*, p. 104.

45. Haley, *Autobiography of Andrew Pearson*, pp. 78–9.

46. Verner, *British Rifleman*, p. 127.

47. Jones, *Military Memoirs of Charles Parquin*, p. 122.

48. Thiébault, *Memoirs*, vol. II, p. 304.

49. Sturgis, *Boy in the Peninsular War*, p. 190.

50. M. La Peña, *Representación hecha a las Cortes por el Capitán General de Andalucía y General en Jefe Interino del Cuarto Ejército* (Cádiz, 1811), p. 18, BL 9180.dd.1.

51. M. Spurrier (ed.), 'Letters of a Peninsular War commanding officer: the letters of Lieutenant Colonel, later General, Sir Andrew Barnard, G.C.B.', *JSAHR*, vol. XLVII, No. 191, pp. 135–6.

52. Sarasa, *Vida y Hechos*, p. 13.

53. Wellington to Liverpool, 23 February 1811, US WP 12/1/3.

54. Wellington to H. Wellesley, 23 February 1811, *ibid.*

CHAPTER 13

1. Sherer, *Recollections of the Peninsula*, p. 150.

2. T. Pakenham (ed.), *The Pakenham Letters, 1800 to 1815* (London, 1914), p. 89.

3. Shore (ed.), *Engineer Officer under Wellington*, p. 103.

4. Boutflower, *Journal of an Army Surgeon*, p. 91.

5. T. McGuffie (ed.), *Peninsular Cavalry General: the Correspondence of Lieutenant General Robert Ballard Long* (London, 1951), p. 96.

6. C. Oman (ed.), 'A Prisoner of Albuera: the Journal of Major William Brooke from 16 May to 28 September 1811', *Blackwood's Magazine*, vol. CLXXXIV, No. 1116 (October 1908), p. 428.

7. Sherer, *Recollections of the Peninsula*, p. 159.

8. *Ibid.*, pp. 160–61.

9. McGuffie, *Peninsular Cavalry General*, p. 106.

10. Sherer, *Recollections of the Peninsula*, p. 166.

11. Oman, 'A Prisoner of Albuera', p. 429.

12. Wellington to H. Wellesley, 22 May 1811, US WP 1/332.

13. A. Leith-Hay, *Memoirs of the Late Lieutenant General Sir James Leith, G.C.B., with a Précis of Some of the Most Remarkable Events of the Peninsular War* (London, 1818), p. 58.

14. Bankes, *Autobiography of Sergeant William Lawrence*, pp. 93–4.

15. T. Graham to Liverpool, 27 May 1811, PRO WO 1/252, ff. 331–2.

16. Jones, *Military Memoirs of Charles Parquin*, p. 134.

17. *Cit.* Thiébault, *Memoirs*, vol. II, p. 323.

18. *Cit.* Marbot, *Memoirs*, vol. II, p. 160.

19. *Ibid.*, pp. 158–9.

20. Donaldson, *Recollections*, pp. 123–4.

21. Marbot, *Memoirs*, vol. II, p. 162.

22. J. Tomkinson (ed.), *The Diary of a Cavalry Officer in the Peninsular and Waterloo Campaigns, 1809–1815* (London, 1894), p. 101.

23. Liddell Hart, *Letters of Private Wheeler*, pp. 55–6.

24. Jones, *Military Memoirs of Charles Parquin*, p. 134.

25. Ludovici, *On the Road with Wellington*, p. 303.

26. Donaldson, *Recollections*, p. 134; Liddell Hart, *Letters of Private Wheeler*, p. 59.

27. Liddell Hart, *Letters of Private Wheeler*, p. 61.

28. A. Viesse de Marmont, *Mémoires du Maréchal Marmont, Duc de Raguse, de 1792 à 1841* (Paris, 1857), vol. IV, p. 45.

29. *Ibid.*

30. I. Fletcher (ed.), *For King and Country: the Letters and Diaries of John Mills, Coldstream Guards, 1811–14* (Staplehurst, 1995), p. 47.

31. Ludovici, *On the Road with Wellington*, pp. 311–13.

32. E. Macdonald, *Recollections of Marshal Macdonald, Duke of Tarentum*, ed. C. Rousset (London, 1892), vol. II, p. 21.

33. J. Walker to Liverpool, 5 September 1811, PRO WO 1/261, f. 396.

34. Suchet, *Memoirs*, vol. II, pp. 52–7.

35. *Ibid.*, pp. 95–6.

36. *Ibid.*, pp. 99–100.

37. Junta of Catalonia to C. Cotton, 6 July 1811, US WP 1/343.

38. C. Zehnpfenning, 'Memorandum on the state of Catalonia', 1 January 1813, US WP 1/368.

39. C. Zehnpfenning to Wellington, 9 November 1812, US WP 1/353.

40. F. Adam to J. Murray, 24 March 1813, US WP 1/368.

41. Barón de Eroles to Wellington, 5 February 1813, US WP 1/366.

42. C. Zehnpfenning to Wellington, 17 March 1813, US WP 1/367.

43. Page, *Intelligence Officer in the Peninsula*, p. 144.

44. Donaldson, *Recollections*, pp. 142–3.

45. Thiébault, *Memoirs*, vol. II, pp. 344–5.

CHAPTER 14

1. Napoleon to A. Berthier, 19 November 1811, *CN*, vol. XXIII, p. 21.
2. A. Berthier to L. Suchet, 25 August 1811, *cit.* Suchet, *Memoirs*, vol. II, pp. 141–2.
3. Napoleon to A. Berthier, 19 November 1811, *CN*, vol. XXIII, p. 21.
4. E. Green to H. Wellesley, 30 July 1811, US WP 1/343.
5. Suchet, *Memoirs*, vol. II, pp. 160–61.
6. *Cit.* Marmont, *Mémoires*, vol. IV, p. 257.
7. Suchet, *Memoirs*, vol. II, pp. 183–6.
8. Wellington to Liverpool, 27 November 1811, *WD*, vol. V, p. 382.
9. Bell, *Rough Notes of an Old Soldier*, p. 10.
10. Sturgis, *Boy in the Peninsular War*, pp. 224–8.
11. Sherer, *Recollections of the Peninsula*, p. 168.
12. Sturgis, *Boy in the Peninsular War*, p. 226.
13. *Cit.* Thiébault, *Memoirs*, vol. II, p. 366.
14. Wellington to Liverpool, 4 December 1811, *WD*, vol. V, pp. 389–90.
15. F. Espoz y Mina, *Memorias del General Don Francisco Espoz y Mina, Escritas por el Mismo*, ed. J. M. de Vega (Madrid, 1851), vol. I, p. 237.
16. Verner, *A British Rifleman*, p. 221.
17. Donaldson, *Recollections*, pp. 150–51.
18. Swabey, *Diary*, pp. 70–71.
19. Grattan, *Adventures of the Connaught Rangers*, vol. I, pp. 207–8.
20. Marmont, *Mémoires*, vol. IV, pp. 184–5.
21. *Ibid.*, pp. 179–80.
22. *Ibid.*, p. 202.
23. *Ibid.*, pp. 206–7.
24. Donaldson, *Recollections*, p. 154.
25. Warre, *Letters from the Peninsula*, p. 237.
26. Verner, *A British Rifleman*, p. 221.
27. Bankes, *Autobiography of Sergeant William Lawrence*, pp. 112–13.
28. Anon., *Memoirs of a Sergeant*, p. 169.
29. Hamilton, *Hamilton's Campaign*, pp. 122–3.
30. Verner, *A British Rifleman*, p. 229.
31. Donaldson, *Recollections*, pp. 156–7.
32. Sturgis, *Boy in the Peninsular War*, pp. 273–4.
33. P. Hayward (ed.), *Surgeon Henry's Trifles: Events of a Military Life* (London, 1970), pp. 43–4.
34. Grattan, *Adventures of the Connaught Rangers*, vol. II, p. 3; Bell, *Rough Notes of an Old Soldier*, p. 28; F. Carr Gomm (ed.), *Letters and Journals of Field Marshal Sir William Maynard Gomm, G.C.B., Commander-in-Chief of India, Constable of the Tower of London, etc., etc., from 1799 to Waterloo, 1815* (London, 1881), p. 262; Donaldson, *Recollections*, p. 159.
35. Fletcher, *For King and Country*, p. 161.

36. Verner, *A British Rifleman*, p. 236; Liddell Hart, *Letters of Private Wheeler*, p. 81.

37. McGuffie, *Peninsular Cavalry General*, pp. 96–7.

38. Thompson, *Ensign in the Peninsular War*, p. 162.

39. General Order, 10 June 1812, *WSD*, vol. VII, p. 345.

40. Morley, *Memoirs*, pp. 114–15.

41. Carr Gomm, *Letters and Journals of Field Marshal Sir William Maynard Gomm*, p. 278.

42. Cassels, *Peninsular Portrait*, p. 64.

43. F. Whinyates (ed.), *Letters written by Lieutenant General Thomas Dyneley, C.B., R.A., while on Active Service between the years 1806 and 1815* (London, 1895), p. 33.

CHAPTER 15

1. H. Wellesley to Wellington, 6 August 1812, US WP 12/2/3.

2. Alcalá Galiano, *Memorias*, vol. I, pp. 316–17.

3. Whinyates, *Letters written by Lieutenant General Thomas Dyneley*, pp. 37–8.

4. Page, *Intelligence Officer in the Peninsula*, p. 191.

5. Carnicero, *Historia Razonada*, vol. III, pp. 153–6.

6. T. Sydenham to H. Wellesley, 12 September 1812, US WP 1/361.

7. Wellington to H. Wellesley, 12 September 1812, US WP 12/1/6.

8. J. W. Gordon to Duke of York, 13 August 1812, BL Add. Mss. 49473; A. Gordon to Lord Aberdeen, 7 September 1812, BL Add. Mss. 43,224 (I owe my knowledge of this latter document to my good friend and colleague, Rory Muir).

9. Buckley, *Napoleonic-War Journal of Captain Thomas Henry Browne*, pp. 185, 193; M. Glover (ed.), *A Gentleman Volunteer: the Letters of George Hennell from the Peninsular War, 1812–13* (London, 1979), p. 51; Cassels, *Peninsular Portrait*, p. 78.

10. H. Wellesley to Castlereagh, 19 November 1812, Public Record Office, Foreign Office papers (hereafter PRO FO) 72/132, ff. 278–83.

11. *Cit.* Wellesley, *Diary and Correspondence of Henry Wellesley*, p. 64.

12. Glover (ed.), *Letters of George Hennell*, p. 52.

13. Wellington to H. Wellesley, 23 August 1812, US WP 1/347.

14. T. Sydenham to H. Wellesley, 10 October 1812, US WP 1/361.

15. *Ibid.*

16. N. Mahy to Regency, 11 January 1812, SHM CDB 4/7/25.

17. Page, *Intelligence Officer in the Peninsula*, p. 191.

18. H. Wellesley to Castlereagh, 1 October 1812, PRO FO 72/132, ff. 105–7.

19. Wellington to Bathurst, 5 October 1812, US WP 1/351.

20. Wellington to H. Wellesley, 3 May 1812, US WP 1/347.

21. Wellington to Bathurst, 18 August 1812, US WP 1/347.

22. T. Sydenham to H. Wellesley, 12 September 1812, US WP 1/361.

23. Buckley, *Napoleonic-War Journal of Captain Thomas Henry Browne*, p. 185.

24. Fletcher, *For King and Country*, p. 226.

25. *Ibid.*, p. 229.

26. Thompson, *An Ensign in the Peninsular War*, p. 206.

27. Fletcher, *For King and Country*, p. 243.

28. Thompson, *An Ensign in the Peninsular War*, p. 208; Rousseau, *Peninsular War Journal of Sir Benjamin D'Urban*, p. 290.

29. Thompson, *An Ensign in the Peninsular War*, p. 210.

30. *Canción en Elogio del Exmo. Sr. D. Francisco Ballesteros, Capitán General de la Andalucías* (Jérez, 1812), SHM CDF, vol. CCLVI, pp. 101–2.

31. T. Bunbury, *Reminiscences of a Veteran, being Personal and Military Adventures in Portugal, Spain, France, Malta, Norfolk Island, New Zealand, Anderman Islands and India* (London, 1861), vol. I, pp. 111–12.

32. R. Wollocombe (ed.), *With the Guns in the Peninsula: the Peninsular War Journal of Captain William Webber, Royal Artillery* (London, 1991), p. 101.

33. Swabey, *Diary*, p. 151.

34. Bell, *Rough Notes of an Old Soldier*, p. 53.

35. McGuffie, *Peninsular Cavalry General*, p. 231.

36. Wood, *The Subaltern Officer*, p. 146.

37. Kincaid, *Adventures in the Rifle Brigade*, p. 92.

38. Grattan, *Adventures of the Connaught Rangers*, vol. II, pp. 134–5.

39. Thompson, *Ensign in the Peninsular War*, p. 219.

40. Liddell Hart, *Letters of Private Wheeler*, pp. 105–6.

41. Napoleon to Clarke, 9 February 1812, CN, vol. XXIV, p. 506.

42. Wellington to W. Cooke, 25 November 1812, US WP 1/351.

43. Swabey, *Diary*, pp. 157–8.

44. Wellington to Beresford, 10 December 1812, US WP 1/355.

45. *Vallesteros* (Cádiz, 1812), p. 3, BS CGA 431437.

46. Wellington to J. M. de Carvajal, 4 December 1812, US WP 1/355.

47. *Suplemento al Tribuno del Pueblo Español*, 1 January 1813, HMM AH1-4 (120).

48. *Diario Redactor de Sevilla*, 29 January 1813, SHM CDF, vol. CXLII.

49. J. Romero y Alpuente, *Wellington en España y Ballesteros en Ceuta* (Cádiz, 1813), pp. 21–40, BS CGA 032675.

50. García de León y Pizarro, *Memorias*, vol. I, p. 357.

CHAPTER 16

1. E. Sabine (ed.), *Letters of Colonel Sir Augustus Simon Frazer, K.C.B., Commanding the Royal Horse Artillery in the Army under the Duke of Wellington Written During the Peninsular and Waterloo Campaigns* (London, 1859), pp. 25–7.

2. *Ibid.*, p. 55.

3. Monick, *Douglas's Tale*, p. 68.

4. Ludovici, *On the Road with Wellington*, p. 361.

5. Wellington to Beresford, 2 February 1813, *WD*, vol. VI, p. 270.

6. Wellington to Prince João, 12 April 1813, *WD*, vol. VI, pp. 417–20.

7. *El Conciso*, 1 April 1813, pp. 3–5, HMM AH2-5 (351).

8. *Diario Crítico y Erúdito de Granada*, 10 April 1813, p. 38, HMM AH5-5 (1046).

9. A. Guillén to Wellington, 27 February 1813, US WP 1/382.

10. R. Escobeda to Wellington, 8 March 1813, US WP 1/367.

11. A. Leith-Hay to R. Hill, 24 January 1813, US WP 1/364.

12. H. Wellesley to Castlereagh, 25 May 1813, PRO FO 72/144, ff. 196–200.

13. *El Español Libre*, 4 May 1813, PRO FO 72/144, ff. 162–84.

14. Argüelles, *Examen Histórico*, p. 429.

15. Alcalá Galiano, *Memorias*, vol. I, p. 332.

16. Wellington to Bathurst, 27 January 1813, US WP 1/365.

17. Wellington to H. Wellesley, 15 March 1813, US WP 1/365.

18. Wellington to A. de la Vega Infanzón, 3 April 1813, US WP 1/370.

19. Whittingham, *Memoir of the Services of Lieutenant General Sir Samuel Ford Whittingham*, pp. 226–7.

20. Wellington to Bathurst, 5 May 1813, *WD*, vol. VI, p. 467.

21. Larpent, *Private Journal of Judge-Advocate F. S. Larpent*, vol. I, p. 226.

22. Bell, *Rough Notes of an Old Soldier*, p. 64.

23. Verner, *A British Rifleman*, pp. 277–8; Bell, *Rough Notes of an Old Soldier*, p. 63.

24. Wood, *The Subaltern Officer*, pp. 180–81.

25. Wollocombe, *With the Guns in the Peninsula*, p. 157; Buckley, *Napoleonic-War Journal of Captain Thomas Henry Browne*, p. 207.

26. Glover (ed.) *Letters of George Hennell*, p. 73.

27. Kincaid, *Adventures in the Rifle Brigade*, p. 103.

28. Thompson, *Ensign in the Peninsular War*, p. 241; Liddell Hart, *Letters of Private Wheeler*, p. 117.

29. G. L'Estrange, *Recollections of Sir George L'Estrange* (London, 1873), p. 29.

30. Bell, *Rough Notes of an Old Soldier*, p. 69.

31. Glover (ed.), *Letters of George Hennell*, p. 90.

32. Donaldson, *Recollections*, p. 203.

33. Wood, *The Subaltern Officer*, pp. 183–4.

34. McGuffie, *Peninsular Cavalry General*, p. 275.

35. Verner, *A British Rifleman*, p. 290.

36. Carr Gomm, *Letters and Journals of Field Marshal Sir William Maynard Gomm*, p. 307.

37. Monick, *Douglas's Tale*, p. 73.

38. W. Hay, *Reminiscences under Wellington, 1808–1815*, ed. S. Wood (London, 1901), p. 113.

39. Buckley, *Napoleonic-War Journal of Captain Thomas Henry Browne*, p. 214.

40. Blaze, *Mémoires d'un Apothécaire*, vol. II, pp. 364–5.

41. Sabine, *Letters of Colonel Sir Augustus Simon Frazer*, p. 165.

42. Bell, *Rough Notes of an Old Soldier*, p. 71.

43. Tomkinson, *Diary of a Cavalry Officer*, p. 253.

44. Liddell Hart, *Letters of Private Wheeler*, p. 118.

45. J. Gavieta to Wellington, 28 June 1813, US WP 1/371.

46. Wellington to Bathurst, 29 June 1813, US WP 1/370.

47. Stanhope, *Notes of Conversations with the Duke of Wellington*, p. 82.

CHAPTER 17

1. Pakenham, *Pakenham Letters*, p. 221.

2. Wellington to Bathurst, 8 August 1813, *WD*, vol. VI, pp. 663–4.

3. C. Atkinson (ed.), 'A Peninsular brigadier: letters of Major General Sir F. P. Robinson, K.C.B., dealing with the campaign of 1813', *JSAHR*, vol. XXXIV, No. 140, p. 165.

4. Wellington to Bathurst, 18 August 1813, *WD*, vol. VI, p. 690.

5. E. Buckham, *Personal Narrative of Adventures in the Peninsula during the War in 1812–1813 by an Officer late in the Staff-Corps Regiment of Cavalry* (London, 1827), p. 270.

6. Wellington to Bathurst, 19 September 1813, *WD*, vol. VII, p. 10.

7. L. Woodford (ed.), *A Young Surgeon in Wellington's Army: the Letters of William Dent* (Old Woking, 1976), p. 39.

8. Thompson, *Ensign in the Peninsular War*, p. 235.

9. Sabine, *Letters of Colonel Sir Augustus Simon Frazer*, p. 195.

10. Monick, *Douglas's Tale*, p. 77.

11. Sabine, *Letters of Colonel Sir Augustus Simon Frazer*, pp. 197–8.

12. Monick, *Douglas's Tale*, pp. 79–80.

13. Buckley, *Napoleonic-War Journal of Captain Thomas Henry Browne*, p. 226.

14. Sherer, *Recollections of the Peninsula*, pp. 258–9.

15. Bell, *Rough Notes of an Old Soldier*, p. 83.

16. I. Fletcher (ed.), *In the Service of the King: the Letters of William Thornton Keep* (Staplehurst, 1997), pp. 159, 161.

17. Wood, *The Subaltern Officer*, pp. 200–203.

18. Buckley, *Napoleonic-War Journal of Captain Thomas Henry Browne*, pp. 229–30.

19. Wellington to W. Bentinck, 5 August 1813, *WD*, vol. VI, p. 654.

20. Bankes, *Autobiography of Sergeant William Lawrence*, pp. 147–9.

21. Liddell Hart, *Letters of Private Wheeler*, p. 122.

22. Wood, *The Subaltern Officer*, p. 208.

23. *Diario de Gobierno de Sevilla*, 19 June 2001, p. 1121, SHM CDF, vol. CXLII.

24. Wellington to H. Wellesley, 2 July 1813, US WP 1/373.

25. Wellington to Bathurst, 29 June 1813, US WP 1/373.

26. Wellington to H. Wellesley, 9 August 1813, US WP 1/383.

27. Wellington to Bathurst, 12 July and 5 September 1813, US WP 1/373, 1/377.

28. Wellington to H. Wellesley, 26 October 1813, US WP 1/377.

29. Tomkinson, *Diary of a Cavalry Officer*, p. 271.

30. Monick, *Douglas's Tale*, pp. 82–3.

31. Glover (ed.), *Letters of George Hennell*, p. 127.

32. G. Gleig, *The Subaltern* (London, 1825), p. 56.

33. C. Vivian (ed.), *Richard Hussey Vivian, First Baron Vivian: a Memoir* (London, 1897), p. 141; J. Harley, *The Veteran, or Forty Years in the British Service, comprising Adventures in Egypt, Spain, Portugal, Belgium, Holland and Prussia* (London, 1838), pp. 83–4; Ludovici, *On the Road with Wellington*, p. 397.

34. Sabine, *Letters of Colonel Sir Augustus Simon Frazer*, p. 244.

35. Wellington to H. Wellesley, 23 October 1813, US WP 1/377.

36. *El Duende de los Cafées*, 27 September 1813, US WP 1/388.

37. *El Imparcial*, 13 November 1813, n.p., SHM CDF, vol. CCLV.

38. Stanhope, *Conversations with the Duke of Wellington*, pp. 106–7.

39. N. Bentley (ed.), *Selections from the Reminiscences of Captain Gronow* (London, 1977), p. 13.

40. Leach, *Rough Sketches*, pp. 341–2.

41. Verner, *A British Rifleman*, p. 321.

42. Sturgis, *Boy in the Peninsular War*, p. 319.

43. Liddell Hart, *Letters of Private Wheeler*, p. 137.

44. Donaldson, *Recollections*, pp. 214–15.

45. Wellington to Bathurst, 21 November 1813, BL Add. Mss. 38255, ff. 55–8.

46. Wellington to Bathurst, 27 November 1813, US WP 1/381.

47. Bell, *Rough Notes of an Old Soldier*, p. 108.

48. *Ibid.*, p. 111.

49. *Cit.* Glover (ed.), *Gentleman Volunteer*, p. 155.

CHAPTER 18

1. Larpent, *Private Journal of Judge-Advocate F. S. Larpent*, vol. II, p. 263.

2. Wellington to W. Clinton, 27 January 1814, US WP 1/396.

3. H. Wellesley to Castlereagh, 25 February 1814, PRO FO 72/159, ff. 133–6.

4. Wellington to H. Wellesley, 26 January 1814, US WP 1/396.

5. *Ibid.*

6. Anon. to Junta Central, 29 November 1808, AHN Est. 52-A, No. 40.

7. F. X. de Castaños, *Reales Ordenes de la Junta Central Suprema de Gobierno del Reino y Representaciones de la Sevilla y del General Castaños acerca de su Separación del Mando del Ejército de Operaciones del Centro* (Seville, 1809), p. 70, BL 9180.dd.1.

8. Junta de la Carolina to Junta Central, 15 August 1809, AHN Est. 17-11[1], ff. 4–5.

9. Anon. to Junta Central, 23 December 1808, AHN Est. 52-A, No. 43.

10. *El Patriota*, No. 1, p. 4, HMM AH 1-5 (158).

11. V. Sancho, *Ensayo de una Constitución Militar Deducida de la Constitución Política de la Monarquía Española* (Cádiz, 1813), p. 2, BS CGA 042094.

12. *Ibid.*, pp. 25, 33.

13. *Semanario Patriótico*, 27 October 1808, p. 153, HMM AH 1-6 (195).

14. *El Redactor General*, 11 April 1812, p. 1183, HMM 6/3.

15. *El Tribuno del Pueblo Español*, 9 March 1813, p. 183, HMM AH 1-4 (121).

16. *La Abeja Española*, 1 December 1812, HMM AH 6-5 (1250).

17. Sancho, *Ensayo de una Constitución Militar*, pp. 38–9.

18. *El Tribuno del Pueblo Español*, 30 March 1813, HMM AH 1-4 (121), p. 287.

19. Anon., *La Milicia Desatendida en Tiempo de Guerra* (Madrid, 1814), p. 38, BS CGA 039854.

20. Gleig, *The Subaltern*, p. 369.

21. T. Finestra, *Exposición que Hace un Oficial a sus Compañeros de Armas sobre la Decadencia de los Ejércitos Españoles* (Cádiz, 1813), p. 4, BS CGA 039854.

22. Anon., *El Ejército Español Destruido por las Leyes* (Alicante, 1813), pp. 7–8, BS CGA *carpeta* 304–1.

23. J. Liano, *Breve Discurso que Hace Don José Liano, Capitán de Husares de Granada Agregado a Cazadores de Sevilla, a los Generales sobre la Decadencia de los Ejércitos* (Isla de León, 1813), pp. 2–3, BS CGA 039854.

24. J. Alvarez Guerra, *Indicaciones Político-Militares del Estado de la Nación Española Dirigidas a la Oficialidad de los Ejércitos Nacionales y Dedicadas al Soberano Congreso de Cortes* (Madrid, 1814), pp. 50–51, SHM DG 1814/8.

25. Whittingham, *Memoir of the Services of Lieutenant General Sir Samuel Ford Whittingham*, p. 226.

26. Las Cases, *Mémorial de Sainte Hélène*, vol. I, p. 584.

27. Wilson, *Diary of St. Helena*, p. 104.

28. T. Graham to H. Bunbury, 12 July 1810, PRO WO 1/247, f. 452.

Further Reading

At first sight the literature of the Peninsular War seems overwhelming. Beginning with the strategic and diplomatic context, Schroeder [1994] is unsurpassed as an international history of the period, Esdaile [1995] and Gates [1996] detailed analyses of the Napoleonic Wars, and Esdaile [2001] a brief introduction. Meanwhile, the finest work on Napoleon Bonaparte remains Lefebvre [1969], the origins of the emperor's intervention in Spain and Portugal being discussed in full in Fugier [1930].

With regard to the Iberian background, Spain is well covered. For an introductory work that covers both the reign of Carlos IV and the War of Independence, see Hamnett [1985]. Lynch [1989], Anes [1972], Domínguez Ortiz [1976], and, despite its great age, Desdevises du Dézert [1897–1904], together provide an excellent introduction to government and society in the period before 1808, which may be supplemented by the essays contained in Molas [1991]. For the crucial issue of the army, see Esdaile [1988b] and Andújar [1991], whilst the Church may be studied in Callahan [1984]. Herr [1958] is very good on the impact of the Enlightenment and the conflict with Revolutionary France, and Hamilton [1944] and [1947] and Barbier and Klein [1981] useful guides to Spain's economic travails. On *desamortización* prior to 1808, see Herr [1989], whilst Fernández Albaladejo [1975] is a survey that examines social and economic change in the context of one particular province both before and after 1808. Seco [1978] is very helpful on Godoy, and Chastenet [1953] and González Santos [1985] his most recent biographers, whilst the politics of the court are covered by Hilt [1987] and Castro [1930–31]. On the overthrow of Godoy and Carlos IV, there is no substitute for Marti [1965] and [1972], but these should be supplemented by Izquierdo [1963] and the discussions of aristocratic discontent in Martínez Quinteiro [1977a] and Pérez de Guzmán [1909–10]. Of less use now, but still worthy of consideration, is Corona [1957]. Finally, the alienation of the populace and the nature of the uprising of May 1808 may be examined in Crowley [1981] and Herr [1965], and the political implications of the revolt in Moliner [1987] and [1997].

On Portugal, by contrast, the literature is much thinner. However, Labourdette [1985] and Bernardino [1986] together provide a solid introduction, and Ladner [1990] a brief view of her ruler, Prince João, whilst there is a mass of information in Medina [1994] and Veríssimo Serrao [1984]. Meanwhile, the occupation of 1807 can be studied in Brandao [1917] and MacKay [1992], whilst Southey [1823–32] contains a particularly detailed account of the uprising.

As might be expected from the general manner in which the historiography has developed, the war's military operations are the aspect of the subject that has received most coverage. For the actions of the Anglo-Portuguese army, in particular, Oman [1902–1930] and Fortescue [1899–1920] remain the obvious sources, but for the Spaniards they may be supplemented by Gómez de Arteche [1868–1903] and Priego López [1972–2000]. There are profiles of most of the leading French commanders in Chandler [1987], whilst, to pick just a few works from the overwhelming coverage of Wellington, James [1992] is a recent synthesis, and Bryant [1971], Glover [1968] and Griffith [1986] all studies that focus on his generalship and art of war. For some interesting examples of the anti-Wellingtonianism fashionable among some American writers, meanwhile, see Meyer [1989], [1990] and [1991]. Griffith [1999] will be found to contain much discussion of tactics and military organisation, whilst there have been a number of studies of Wellington's army, including Oman [1913], Rogers [1979] and Haythornthwaite [1994]. For the Spaniards, again, see Esdaile [1988b], and, whilst there is no comparable study of the French forces, Elting [1988] is a mine of information on the Napoleonic army in general. As for the Portuguese, they are best addressed by reference to Fuente [1983] and Horward [1989].

The guerrillas are a subject that is open to much debate, and, as such, they have spawned an extensive literature of their own. Classic 'Anglo-Saxon' views are to be found in essays in Alexander [1975] and [1985], Chandler [1994] and Uffindell [1998], as well as in Lovett [1975], whilst they are at first sight supported by Tone [1994] and [1996]. For a strong challenge, however, see Esdaile [1988a] and [1991], as well as the contributions by the same author to Berkeley [1991] and Fletcher [1998]. As yet the Spanish contribution to the debate, other than a flood of hagiography, has been limited, but Sánchez Fernández [1997] and [2000] provide encouraging evidence of the sort of work that might eventually be hoped for, whilst there is much of interest to be gleaned from Pascual [2000]. Finally, Vilar [1999] contains a thought-provoking French view.

A number of works address the Spanish experience of the War of Independence. Moreno [1997] paints a graphic picture based on a wealth of personal examples, whilst for many years the leading guide to the subject was the wide-ranging Lovett [1965]. For a more analytical approach stressing both Patriot Spain's military failure and the structural reasons for this problem, see Esdaile [1988c], [1989] and [2000]. Other than Lovett, the best guide to Patriot government and politics is Artola [1959], but this should now be supplemented by such works as Martínez de Velasco [1972], Fontana and Garabou [1986], Chavarri [1988], Hamnett [1977] and [1989], and Morán [1986] and [1994]. Also worthy of note here has been the major growth that has taken place in the study of local history in Spain. Pioneered by the Frenchman, Fugier, whose early efforts on Asturias have now been re-published in Spanish [Fugier, 1989], the result has been a series of monographs that provide many fresh insights into the Spanish struggle. Such works are too numerous for them all to be listed here, but particularly impressive examples include Ardit [1977], Carantoña

[1983], Moliner [1989], López Pérez and Lara [1993], Lafoz [1996], and Espinar [1994]. For military issues, see, in particular, Blanco [1988], Casado [1982] and Esdaile [1988b], whilst Canales [1988] is an example of the sort of work that is needed on popular responses to military service. As for the social unrest provoked by *desamortización* and the question of the *señorios*, this is addressed by Moxo [1965], Bernal [1974] and [1979], Lorente [1994], Hernández Montalbán [1999], and, albeit in microcosm, Morant [1984]. Finally, the coup of 1814 and restoration of absolutism are examined, not wholly convincingly, in Diz (1967) and Pintos [1958], the reassessment of *servilismo* on which the views of these authors are based receiving its fullest exposition in Suárez Verdeguer [1959] and [1965].

The Bonaparte kingdom of Spain, too, has attracted much attention. Pride of place here must go to Mercader [1971] and [1983] and Artola [1976], but there have again been a series of useful local studies, of which some of the more prominent are Cruz [1968], Bayod [1979a and b], Mercader [1978], Ollero [1983], Lorente [1990], Ramisa [1995], Moreno [1995] and Díaz Torrejón [2001]. For general studies of Joseph's experiences, meanwhile, see Abella [1997] and Glover [1971] as well as such biographies as Connelly [1968], Girod de l'Ain [1970] and Ross [1976]. Also worth examining is the imperial context, which can be examined in Connelly [1965], Ellis [1991] and Woolf [1991].

Turning now to the complicated subject of intra-Allied relations, these are covered by a variety of works. The Anglo-Spanish dimension is looked at by Villa Urrutia [1911–14], Azcarate [1961], Severn [1981], Rydjord [1941], Kaufmann [1967], Esdaile [1990] and [1992], Gil [1999], Sanudo and Stampa [1996], and Laspra [1992] and [1999], and the Anglo-Portuguese one by Fryman [1977] and Goldstein [1977]. Britain's strategy and foreign policy are examined in Hall [1992] and Muir [1996], and her domestic situation in Emsley [1979] and Harvey [1978] and [1992]. For foreign aid, see Sherwig [1969]. As for the question of Spanish America, Anna [1983] and Costeloe [1986] look at its impact in Patriot Spain, though Lynch [1973] is better as a guide to events.

Over the years, then, much work has been done, and there are aspects of the subject – most notably the campaigns of the Duke of Wellington – with regard to which it is impossible to imagine much else being added to the historical record. That said, however, many issues have yet to receive the attention which they deserve: there is, for example, much that we do not know about the uprisings of 1808, the formation of the new armies raised by Spain and Portugal, the response of the populace to conscription, and the nature of *la guerrilla*. Whether it is at a regional or a national level, then, there is still much to occupy historians of the Peninsular War, and, by extension, yet more further reading to look forward to.

Bibliography

A. ARCHIVAL SOURCES

Archivo Histórico Nacional, Madrid
Sección de Estado, Legajos 5, 14–17, 30–1, 33, 38–41, 46, 52, 60, 62, 65, 70, 75, 77, 80–3, 2821, 2959, 2995, 3010, 3566.

Biblióteca Nacional, Madrid
Colección Gómez Imaz, Volumes R60002, R60016, R60034, R60087, R60124, R60129, R61075, R60140, R62280, R63078

Biblióteca del Senado, Madrid
Colección Gómez de Arteche, Volumes 011166, 011634, 011867, 011961, 016544, 017057, 028477, 029083, 031030, 032589, 032605, 032675, 035255, 038158, 039054, 039809, 039854, 040126, 040270, 040325, 040458, 040733, 041437, 041478, 041970, 041996, 042062, 042070, 042092, 042094, 043523, 431437

British Library, London
Additional Manuscripts 37286–9, 37291–3, 37314, 38243–4, 38246–7, 38249–55, 49482, 64131.

Public Record Office, Kew
(a) War Office Papers, Series 1, Volumes 226–7, 229–52, 260–1.
(b) Foreign Office Papers, Series 72, Volumes 71, 73, 75, 108, 112, 121, 128, 131–3, 142–7, 150–5, 159–60.

Real Academía de Historia, Madrid
2-MS134; 2-MS135; 9-31-6: 6964–66; 9-31-7: 7021; 9-31-7; 7025; 11-2-2: 8154; 11-5-7: 9003; 14-9-6: 6925.

Real Colegio de San Albano, Valladolid
R. Brindle, 'A Brief Account of Travels, etc., in Spain' (MS)

Servicio Histórico Militar, Madrid

(a) Colección Documental del Fraile, Volumes XXVII, XXXII–XLI, CX, CXIV–CXVII, CXXXII–CLXIV, CXCI, CCLX, CCLIII–CCLXVIII, CCCXXXVI–CCCLI, CDLII–CDLXVII, DXL, DCXLVII–DCCLXIII, DCCLXXXIX, DCCXCI, DCCCLXIV, CMVIII, CMXXII.

(b) Colección Duque de Bailén, Carpetas 1/2/2, 1/2/8, 3/2/4–5, 3/4/23–4, 3/4/28, 3/4/32, 3/6/34, 4/2/10, 4/7/25, 5/8/1–10, 7/10/25–27, 18/22/71–79, 25/36/24, 32/49/21, 32/49/23, 34/52/53, 33/53/59, 36/54/1.

University of Nottingham

Portland Collection, Pwf. 8580–7, 9256–7; PwJc. 29–43, 47–60, 77–86, 131–42, 237–8, 188–93, 167–81.

University of Southampton

(a) Wellington Papers, Volumes 1/205, 1/207–14, 1/216, 1/263, 1/264–7, 1/269, 1/270, 1/273–7, 1/284, 1/290–5, 1/297–8, 1/311, 1/313, 1/315, 1/331–2, 1/341–56, 1/358–83, 1/387–420, 1/439–45, 1/447, 12/1/1–3, 12/1/5–6, 12/2/2–3.

(b) Carver Manuscripts, Nos. 8, 36, 53, 100.

B. PUBLISHED CONTEMPORARY SOURCES *

(a) Official Publications, Documentary Collections, etc.

Constitución Política de la Nación Española (Cádiz, 1812).

Correspondance de Napoléon I publiée par ordre de l'Empereur Napoléon III (Paris, 1858–69).

Correspondence, Despatches and other Papers of Viscount Castlereagh, Second Marquess of Londonderry, ed. Marquess of Londonderry (London, 1848–53).

The Croker Papers: the Correspondence and Diaries of the Right Honourable John Wilson Croker, LL.D, F.R.S., Secretary to the Admiralty from 1809 to 1830, ed. L. Jennings (London, 1884).

Diario de la Sesiones y Actas de las Cortes (Cádiz, 1810–13)

The Dispatches and Correspondence of the Marquess Wellesley during his Mission to Spain as Ambassador Extraordinary to the Supreme Junta in 1809, ed. M. Martin (London, 1838).

The Dispatches of Field Marshal the Duke of Wellington during his various Campaigns in India, Denmark, Portugal, Spain, the Low Countries and France from 1789 to 1815, ed. J. Gurwood (London, 1852).

---

* Considerations of space have made it impossible to list the numerous contemporary pamphlets, manifestos, treatises and apologias that have been used in the preparation of this work. Full details have been given in the notes to the chapters where these sources are quoted in the text, but the reader is otherwise referred to the catalogues of the collections in which they are housed (e.g. Colección Gómez Imaz, Colección Documental del Fraile and Colección Gómez de Arteche).

Estados de la Organización y Fuerza de los Ejércitos Españoles Beligerantes en la Península durante la Guerra de España contra Napoleón Bonaparte arreglados por la Sección de Historia Militar en 1821 (Barcelona, 1822).

Guerra de la Independencia: Proclamas, Bandos y Combatientes, ed. S. Delgado (Madrid, 1979).

Historical Manuscripts Commission Report on the Manuscripts of Earl Bathurst preserved at Cirencester Park, ed. F. Bickley (London, 1923).

Kalendario Manual y Guía de Forasteros en Madrid (Madrid, 1807, 1815)

Mémoires et Correspondance Politique et Militaire du Roi Joseph, ed. P. du Casse (Paris, 1853–54).

Ordenanzas de S.M. para el Régimen, Disciplina, Subordinación y Servicio de sus Ejércitos (Madrid, 1768).

Supplementary Despatches, Correspondence and Memoranda of Field Marshal Arthur, Duke of Wellington, ed. Second Duke of Wellington (London, 1858–72).

(b) Newspapers, Gazettes, etc.

Atalaya de la Mancha en Madrid (Madrid, 1813–14)
Correo de Murcia (Murcia, 1809)
Correo de Valencia (Valencia, 1811)
Diario Crítico y Erúdito de Granada (Granada, 1813)
Diario de Badajoz (Badajoz, 1808–9)
Diario de Gobierno de Sevilla (Seville, 1812–13)
Diario de Granada (Granada, 1808–9)
Diario de la Tarde (Cádiz, 1813)
Diario de Málaga (Málaga, 1808–9)
Diario Mercantil de Cádiz (Cádiz, 1813).
Diario Político de Mallorca (Mallorca, 1808)
Diario Redactor de Sevilla (Seville, 1812–13)
El Censor General (Cádiz, 1812)
El Ciudadano por la Constitución (La Coruña, 1813)
El Conciso (Cádiz, Madrid, 1812–14)
El Duende de los Cafées (Cádiz, 1813)
El Español (Cádiz, London, 1810–14)
El Español Libre (Cádiz, 1813)
El Fanal (Seville, 1812)
El Imparcial (Alicante, 1813)
El Patriota (Cádiz, 1812–13)
El Redactor General (Cádiz, 1811–14)
El Tío Tremendo o los Críticos del Malecón (Cádiz, 1813)
El Tribuno del Pueblo Español (Cádiz, 1812–13)
Gazeta de La Coruña (La Coruña, 1808)
Gazeta de la Junta Superior de la Mancha (Cuenca, 1811–12)
Gazeta de la Regencia de España e Indias (Cádiz, Madrid, 1810–14)
Gazeta del Gobierno (Madrid, Seville, 1808–1810)

La Abeja Española (Cádiz, 1812–13)
Los Amigos de Ballesteros (Isla de León, 1813)
Los Ingleses en España (Seville, 1813)
Memorial Militar y Patriótico del Ejército de la Izquierda (Badajoz, 1810)
Semanario Patriótico (Madrid, Seville, Cádiz, 1808–12)
Semanario Político, Histórico y Literario de La Coruña (La Coruña, 1809–1810)

(c) Memoirs, Diaries and Contemporary Accounts

A. Alcaide, *Historia de los Dos Sitios que Pusieron a Zaragoza en los Años de 1808 y 1809* (Madrid, 1830).

A. Alcalá Galiano (ed.), *Memorias de D. Antonio Alcalá Galiano* (Madrid, 1886).

A. Alcalá Galiano, *Recuerdos de un Anciano* (Madrid, 1907).

B. Alexander (ed.), *The Journal of William Beckford in Portugal and Spain, 1787–88* (London, 1954).

E. Alonso (ed.), *Memorias del Alcalde de Roa, Don Gregorio González Arranz, 1788–1840* (Roa, 1995).

A. Alvarez Valdés, *Memorias del Levantamiento de Asturias en 1808*, ed. M. Fuertes Acevedo (Oviedo, 1889).

Anon., *The Military Exploits of Don Juan Martín Díez, the Empecinado* (London, 1825).

Anon., *Memoirs of a Sergeant Late in the Forty-Third Light Infantry Regiment, Previously to and during the Peninsular War* (London, 1835).

A. Argüelles, *Examen Histórico de la Reforma Constitucional que Hicieron las Cortes Generales y Extraordinarias Desde que se Instalaron en la Isla de León el Dia 24 de Septiembre de 1810 Hasta que Cerraron en Cádiz sus Sesiones en 14 del Propio Mes de 1813*, ed. J. Longares (Madrid, 1970; published under the title *La Reforma Constitucional de Cádiz*).

C. Atkinson (ed.), 'A light dragoon in the Peninsular War: extracts from the letters of Captain Lovell Badcock, Fourteenth Light Dragoons, 1809–14', *JSAHR*, XXXIV, No. 138, pp. 70–79.

C. Atkinson (ed.), 'A Peninsular brigadier: letters of Major General Sir F. P. Robinson, K.C.B., dealing with the campaign of 1813', *JSAHR*, XXXIV, No. 140, pp. 153–70.

G. Bankes (ed.), *The Autobiography of Sergeant William Lawrence, a Hero of the Peninsular and Waterloo Campaign* (London, 1886).

R. Batty, *Campaign of the Left Wing of the Allied Army in the Western Pyrenees and the South of France in the Years 1813 and 1814 under Field Marshal the Marquess of Wellington* (London, 1825).

M. de Baudus, *Etudes sur Napoléon* (Paris, 1841).

G. Bell, *Rough Notes of an Old Soldier*, ed. B. Stuart (London, 1956).

N. Bentley (ed.), *Selections from the Reminiscences of Captain Gronow* (London, 1977).

A. Berazaluce (ed.), *Recuerdos de la Vida de Don Pedro Agustín Girón* (Pamplona, 1978).

A. Bigarré, *Mémoires du Général Bigarré, Aide de Camp du Roi Joseph, 1775–1813* (Paris, 1903).

J. Blanco White, *Cartas de España*, ed. V. Llorens and A. Garnica (Madrid, 1972).

S. Blaze, *Mémoires d'un Apothécaire sur le Guerre d'Espagne Pendant les Années 1808 à 1814* (Paris, 1828).

J. de Bourgoing, *A Modern State of Spain* (London, 1808).

C. Boutflower, *The Journal of an Army Surgeon during the Peninsular War* (Manchester, 1912).

H. von Brandt, *The Two Minas and the Spanish Guerrillas* (London, 1825).

E. Buckham, *Personal Narrative of Adventures in the Peninsula during the War in 1812–1813 by an Officer late in the Staff-Corps Regiment of Cavalry* (London, 1827).

R. Buckley (ed.), *The Napoleonic-War Journal of Captain Thomas Henry Browne* (London, 1987).

T. Bunbury, *Reminiscences of a Veteran, being Personal and Military Adventures in Portugal, Spain, France, Malta, Norfolk Island, New Zealand, Anderman Islands and India* (London, 1861).

C. Cadell, *Narrative of the Campaigns of the Twenty-Eighth Regiment since their Return from Egypt in 1802* (London, 1835).

J. Canga Argüelles, *Observaciones sobre la Historia de la Guerra de España que Escribieron los Señores Clarke, Southey, Londonderry y Napier* (Madrid, 1833–36).

J. C. Carnicero, *Historia Razonada de los Prinicipales Sucesos de la Gloriosa Revolución de España* (Madrid, 1814).

F. Carr Gomm (ed.), *Letters and Journals of Field Marshal Sir William Maynard Gomm, G.C.B., Commander-in-Chief of India, Constable of the Tower of London, etc., etc., from 1799 to Waterloo, 1815* (London, 1881).

Comte de las Cases, *Mémorial de Sainte Hélène*, ed. G. Walter (Paris, 1956).

S. Cassels (ed.), *Peninsular Portrait, 1811–1814: the Letters of Captain William Bragge, Third (King's Own) Dragoons* (London, 1963).

J. Cooper, *Rough Notes of Seven Campaigns in Portugal, Spain, France and America during the Years of 1809–10–11–12–13–14–15* (London, 1869).

E. Costello, *The Adventures of a Soldier, or Memoirs of Edward Costello, K.S.F.* (London, 1841).

H. Dalrymple, *Memoirs written by Sir Hew Dalrymple, Bart., of his Proceedings as connected with the Affairs of Spain and the Commencement of the Peninsular War* (London, 1830).

W. Dalrymple, *Travels through Spain and Portugal in 1774* (London, 1777).

J. Dellard, *Mémoires Militaires du Général Baron Dellard* (Paris, n.d.).

J. Donaldson, *Recollections of the Eventful Life of a Soldier* (Edinburgh, 1852).

R. Douglas (ed.), *From Valmy to Waterloo: Extracts from the Diary of Captain Charles François, a Solider of the Revolution and Empire* (London, 1906).

N. Edwards (ed.), *The Saint Helena Diary of General Baron Gourgaud* (London, 1932).

F. Espoz y Mina, *Memorias del General Don Francisco Espoz y Mina, Escritas por el Mismo*, ed. J. M. de Vega (Madrid, 1851).

W. Fernyhough, *Military Memoirs of Four Brothers (Natives of Staffordshire) engaged in the Service of their Country as well in the New World and Africa as on the Continent of Europe by the Survivor* (London, 1829).

C. Fischer, *A Picture of Madrid* (London, 1808).

C. Fischer, *Travels in Spain in 1797 and 1798* (London, 1802).

I. Fletcher, (ed.), *For King and Country: the Letters and Diaries of John Mills, Coldstream Guards, 1811–14* (Staplehurst, 1995).

I. Fletcher (ed.), *In the Service of the King: the Letters of William Thornton Keep* (Staplehurst, 1997).

P. Fleuriot de Langle (ed.), *Napoleon at Saint Helena: Memoirs of General Bertrand, Grand Marshal of the Palace, January to May 1821* (London, 1953).

J. Fortescue (ed.), *The Notebooks of Captain Coignet, Soldier of the Empire* (London, 1928).

J. Fouché, *Memoirs of Joseph Fouché, Duke of Otranto, Minister of the General Police of France* (London, 1892).

M. Foy, *History of the War in the Peninsula under Napoleon* (London, 1827).

J. García de León y Pizarro, *Memorias de la Vida del Excmo. Señor D. José García de León y Pizarro Escritas por el Mismo*, ed. A. Alonso Castrillo (Madrid, 1894).

E. Gigas (ed.), 'Lettres d'un diplomate danois en Espagne', *Revue Hispanique*, IX (1902), pp. 395–439.

L. Gille, *Les Prisonniers de Cabrera: Mémoires d'un Conscrit de 1808* (Paris, 1893).

G. Gleig, *The Subaltern* (London, 1825).

M. Glover (ed.), *A Gentleman Volunteer: the Letters of George Hennell from the Peninsular War, 1812–13* (London, 1979).

M. de Godoy, *Cuenta dada de su Vida Política por Don Manuel Godoy, Príncipe de la Paz, o sea Memorias Críticas y Apologéticas para la Historia del Reinado del Señor Carlos IV de Borbón* (Madrid, 1836–38).

W. Grattan, *Adventures of the Connaught Rangers from 1808 to 1814* (London, 1847).

J. Green, *The Vicissitudes of a Soldier's Life, or a Series of Occurrences from 1808 to 1815* (London, 1815).

J. Hale, *Journal of James Hale, late Sergeant in the Ninth Regiment of Foot* (London, 1826).

A. Haley (ed.), *The Soldier who Walked Away: Autobiography of Andrew Pearson, a Peninsular-War Veteran* (Liverpool, n.d.).

B. Hall, *Corcubión*, ed. J. Alberich (Exeter, 1975).

A. Hamilton, *Hamilton's Campaign with Moore and Wellington during the Peninsular War* (Troy, New York, 1847).

J. Harley, *The Veteran, or Forty Years in the British Service, comprising Adventures in Egypt, Spain, Portugal, Belgium, Holland and Prussia* (London, 1838).

P. Hawker, *Journal of a Regimental Officer during the Recent Campaigns in Portugal and Spain under Viscount Wellington* (London, 1810).

W. Hay, *Reminiscences under Wellington, 1808–1815*, ed. S. Wood (London, 1901).

A. Hayter (ed.), *The Backbone: Diaries of a Military Family in the Napoleonic Wars* (Bishop Auckland, 1993).

P. Haythornthwaite (ed.), *Life in Napoleon's Army: the Memoirs of Captain Elzéar Blaze* (London, 1995).

P. Hayward (ed.), *Surgeon Henry's Trifles: Events of a Military Life* (London, 1970).

C. Hibbert (ed.), *The Recollections of Rifleman Harris* (London, 1985).

C. Hibbert (ed.), *A Soldier of the Seventy-First* (London, 1975).

C. Hibbert (ed.), *The Wheatley Diary: a Journal and Sketchbook kept during the Peninsular War and the Waterloo Campaign* (London, 1964).

H. R. Holland, *Foreign Reminiscences*, ed. H. E. Holland (London, 1850).

D. Horward (ed.), *The French Campaign in Spain and Portugal: an Account by Jean Jacques Pelet* (Minneapolis, 1973).

Earl of Ilchester (ed.), *The Spanish Journal of Elizabeth, Lady Holland* (London, 1910).

Lady Jackson (ed.), *The Diaries and Letters of Sir George Jackson* (London, 1872).

W. Jacob, *Travels in the South of Spain* (London, 1811).

B. Jones (ed.), *In the Service of Napoleon: the Military Memoirs of Charles Parquin* (London, 1987).

L. Junot, *Mémoires du Madame la Duchesse d'Abrantes, ou Souvenirs Historiques sur Napoléon, la Révolution, le Directoire, le Consulat, l'Empire et la Restauration* (Paris, 1831–35).

J. Kincaid, *Adventures in the Rifle Brigade* (London, 1909).

L. Knowles (ed.), *The War in the Peninsula: Some Letters of Lieutenant Robert Knowles of the Seventh, or Royal, Fusiliers, a Lancashire Officer* (Bolton, 1913).

A. de Laborde, *A View of Spain* (London, 1809).

G. Larpent (ed.), *The Private Journal of Judge-Advocate F. S. Larpent, attached to Lord Wellington's Headquarters, 1812–14* (London, 1853).

J. Leach, *Rough Sketches in the Life of an Old Soldier* (London, 1831).

A. Leith-Hay, *Memoirs of the Late Lieutenant General Sir James Leith, G.C.B., with a Précis of Some of the Most Remarkable Events of the Peninsular War* (London, 1818).

L. Lejeune, *Memoirs of Baron Lejeune, Aide-de-Camp to Marshals Berthier, Davout and Oudinot*, ed. A. Bell (London, 1897).

G. L'Estrange, *Recollections of Sir George L'Estrange* (London, 1873).

H. Lewin, *The Life of a Soldier: a Narrative of Twenty-Seven Years' Service in Various Parts of the World* (London, 1834).

B. Liddell Hart (ed.), *The Letters of Private Wheeler, 1809–1828* (London, 1951).

J. Llorente, *Memorias para la Historia de la Revolución Española* (Paris, 1814).

A. Ludovici (ed.), *On the Road with Wellington: the Diary of a War Commissary in the Peninsular Campaigns* (New York, 1925).

E. Macdonald, *Recollections of Marshal Macdonald, Duke of Tarentum*, ed. C. Rousset (London, 1892).

T. McGuffie (ed.), *Peninsular Cavalry General: the Correspondence of Lieutenant General Robert Ballard Long* (London, 1951).

H. Mackinnon, *A Journal of the Campaign in Portugal and Spain containing Remarks on the Inhabitants, Customs, Trade and Cultivation of those Countries from the Year 1809 to 1812* (Bath, 1812).

M. de Marbot, *The Memoirs of Baron de Marbot, late Lieutenant General in the French Army* (London, 1892).

J. Marcén (ed.), *El Manuscrito de Matías Calvo: Memorias de un Monegrino durante la Guerra de la Independencia* (Zaragoza, 2000).

P. Marco, *El Cura Merino, 1808 a 1813: Memorias de un Contemporáneo* (Madrid, 1899).

A. Marmont, *see* A. Viesse de Marmont.

J. Maurice (ed.), *The Diary of Sir John Moore* (London, 1904).

M. de Mesonero, *Memorias de un Setentón* (Madrid, 1880).

A. Miot, *Mémoires du Comte Miot de Melito, Ancien Ministre, Ambassadeur, Conseilleur d'Etat et Membre de l'Institut* (Paris, 1858).

S. Monick (ed.), *Douglas's Tale of the Peninsula and Waterloo* (London, 1997).

J. C. Moore, *A Narrative of the Campaign of the British Army in Spain commanded by His Excellency Lieutenant General Sir John Moore, K.B.* (London, 1809).

S. Morley, *Memoirs of a Sergeant of the Fifth Regiment of Foot, containing an Account of his Service in Hanover, South America and the Peninsula* (Ashford, 1842).

A. Muriel, *Historia de Carlos IV*, ed. C. Seco (Madrid, 1959).

W. Napier, *History of the War in the Peninsula and in the South of France from the Year 1807 to the Year 1814* (London, 1828–40).

A. Neale, *Letters from Portugal and Spain comprising an Account of the Operations of the Armies under Their Excellencies Sir Arthur Wellesley and Sir John Moore from the landing of their Troops in Mondego Bay to the Battle at Corunna* (London, 1809).

J. North (ed.), *In the Legions of Napoleon: the Memoirs of a Polish Officer in Spain and Russia, 1808–1813* (London, 1999).

C. Oman (ed.), 'A Prisoner of Albuera: the Journal of Major William Brooke from 16 May to 28 September 1811', *Blackwood's Magazine*, CLXXXIV, No. 1116 (October 1908), pp. 425–48.

C. Ompteda, *In the King's German Legion: Memoirs of Baron Ompteda, Colonel in the King's German Legion during the Napoleonic Wars* (London, 1894).

C. O'Neill, *The Military Adventures of Charles O'Neill, who was a Soldier in the Army of Lord Wellington during the Memorable Peninsular War and the Continental Campaigns from 1811 to 1815* (Worcester, Mass., 1851).

J. Page (ed.), *Intelligence Officer in the Peninsula: Letters and Diaries of Major the Honourable Edward Charles Cocks, 1786–1812* (Tunbridge Wells, 1986).

T. Pakenham (ed.), *The Pakenham Letters, 1800 to 1815* (London, 1914).

J. de Palafox, *Memorias*, ed. H. Lafoz (Zaragoza, 1994).

J. Patterson, *The Adventures of Captain John Patterson* (London, 1837).

A. Paz (ed.), *Memorias de Don Juan de Escoíquiz* (Madrid, 1915).

V. Pina, *Paginas de 1808: Memorias de un Patríota* (Zaragoza, 1959).

R. Porter, *Letters from Portugal and Spain written during the March of the British Troops under Sir John Moore* (London, 1809).

J. A. Posse, *Historía Biográfica, o Historia de la Vida y Hechos de Don Juan Antonio Posse Escrita por El Mismo*, ed. R. Herr (Madrid, 1984; published as *Memorias del Cura Liberal Don Juan Antonio Posse con su Discurso sobre la Constitución de 1812*).

M. de Pradt, *Mémoires Historiques sur la Révolution d'Espagne* (Paris, 1816).

J. Queipo de Llano (Conde de Toreno), *Historia del Levantamiento, Guerra y Revolución de España* (ed. Bibliotéca de Autores Españoles: Madrid, 1853).

A. de Rocca, *Memoirs of the War of the French in Spain*, ed. P. Haythornthwaite (London, 1990).

P. Rodríguez Fernández (ed.), *La Guerra de Independencia en Asturias: Correspondencia de General Bonet, 1809–1812* (Gijón, 1991).

P. Roederer, *Mémoires sur la Révolution, le Consulat et l'Empire*, ed. O. Aubry (Paris, 1942).

I. Rousseau (ed.), *The Peninsular War Journal of Sir Benjamin D'Urban* (London, 1930).

R. Roy (ed.), 'The memoirs of Private James Gunn', *JSAHR*, XLIX, No. 198, pp. 90–120.

E. Sabine (ed.), *Letters of Colonel Sir Augustus Simon Frazer, K.C.B., Commanding the Royal Horse Artillery in the Army under the Duke of Wellington Written During the Peninsular and Waterloo Campaigns* (London, 1859).

L. Saint-Cyr, *Mémoires* (Paris, 1831).

E. de Saint-Hilaire, *Souvenirs Intimes du Temps de l'Empire* (Paris, 1860).

L. de Saint-Pierre (ed.), *Les Cahiers du Général Brun* (Paris, 1953).

R. Santillán, *Memorias de Don Ramón Santillán (1808–1856)*, ed. A. Berazaluce (Madrid, 1996).

J. M. Sarasa, *Vida y Hechos Militares del Mariscal de Campo, Don Juan Manuel Sarasa, Narrados por el Mismo*, ed. J. del Burgo (Pamplona, 1952).

J. Sarrazin, *History of the War in Spain and Portugal from 1807 to 1814* (London, 1815).

A. von Schepeler, *Histoire de la Révolution d'Espagne et de Portugal ainsi que de la Guerre qui en Résulta* (Liège, 1829–31).

J. Sherer, *Recollections of the Peninsula* (London, 1825).

E. Shore (ed.), *An Engineer Officer under Wellington in the Peninsula: the Diary and Correspondence of Lieutenant Rice Jones, R. E., during 1809-9-10-11-12* (Cambridge, 1986).

T. Simmons (ed.), *Memoirs of a Polish Lancer: the Pamietniki of Dezydery Chlapowski* (Chicago, 1992).

R. Southey, *History of the Peninsular War* (London, 1823–1832).

R. Southey, *Letters written during a Journey in Spain and a Short Residence in Portugal* (London, 1808).

M. Spurrier (ed.), 'Letters of a Peninsular War commanding officer: the letters of Lieutenant Colonel, later General, Sir Andrew Barnard, G.C.B.', *JSAHR*, XLVII, No. 191, pp. 131–48.

Earl of Stanhope, *Notes of Conversations with the Duke of Wellington, 1831–1851* (London, 1889).

C. Steevens, *Reminiscences of my Military Life from 1795 to 1818*, ed. N. Steevens (Winchester, 1878).

W. Stothert, *A Narrative of the Principal Events of the Campaigns of 1809, 1810 and 1811 in Spain and Portugal* (London, 1812).

J. Sturgis (ed.), *A Boy in the Peninsular War: the Services, Adventures and Experiences of Robert Blakeney, Subaltern of the Twenty-Eighth Regiment* (London, 1899).

L. Suchet, *Memoirs of the War in Spain from 1808 to 1814* (London, 1829).

W. Swabey, *Diary of the Campaigns in the Peninsula for the Years 1811, 12 and 13*, ed. F. Whinyates (London, 1984).

H. Swinburne, *Travels through Spain in the Years 1775 and 1776* (Dublin, 1779).

D. Thiébault, *The Memoirs of Baron Thiébault (late Lieutenant General in the French Army)* (London, 1896).

W. Thompson (ed.), *An Ensign in the Peninsular War: the Letters of John Aitchison* (London, 1981).

J. Tomkinson (ed.), *The Diary of a Cavalry Officer in the Peninsular and Waterloo Campaigns, 1809–1815* (London, 1894).

J. Townsend, *A Journal through Portugal and Spain in the Years 1786 and 1787* (London, 1792).

C. Vaughan, *Narrative of the Siege of Saragossa* (London, 1809).

C. Venault de Charmilly, *To the British Nation is Presented by Colonel Venault de Charmilly, Knight of the Royal and Military Order of St. Louis, the Narrative of his Transactions in Spain with the Right Honourable John Hookham Frere, His Britannic Majesty's Minister Plenipotentiary and Lieutenant General Sir John Moore, K.B., Commander of the British Forces* (London, 1810).

R. Verner (ed.), *Reminiscences of William Verner, 1782–1871* (London, 1965).

W. Verner (ed.), *A British Rifleman: Journals and Correspondence [of George Simmons] during the Peninsular War and the Campaign of Waterloo* (London, 1899).

A. Viesse de Marmont, *Mémoires du Maréchal Marmont, Duc de Raguse, de 1792 à 1841* (Paris, 1857).

J. Villanueva, *Mi Viage a las Cortes* (Madrid, 1860).

J. Villanueva, *Vida Literaria de Don Joaquín Lorenzo Villanueva*, ed. G. Ramírez Aledón (Alicante, 1996).

C. Vivian (ed.), *Richard Hussey Vivian, First Baron Vivian: a Memoir* (London, 1897).

E. Warre (ed.), *Letters from the Peninsula, 1808–1812 by Lieutenant General Sir William Warre, C.B., K.T.S.* (London, 1909).

F. Wellesley (ed.), *The Diary and Correspondence of Henry Wellesley, First Lord Cowley, 1790–1846* (London, 1930).

V. Wellesley (ed.), *The Conversations of the First Duke of Wellington with George William Chad* (Cambridge, 1956).

F. Whinyates (ed.), *Letters written by Lieutenant General Thomas Dyneley, C.B., R.A., while on Active Service between the Years 1806 and 1815* (London, 1895).

F. Whittingham, (ed.) *A Memoir of the Services of Lieutenant General Sir Samuel Ford Whittingham* (London, 1868).

A. Wilson (ed.), *A Diary of St. Helena (1816, 1817): the Journal of Lady Malcolm* (London, 1899).

R. Wollocombe (ed.), *With the Guns in the Peninsula: the Peninsular War Journal of Captain William Webber, Royal Artillery* (London, 1991).

G. Wood, *The Subaltern Officer: a Narrative* (London, 1825).

L. Woodford (ed.), *A Young Surgeon in Wellington's Army: the Letters of William Dent* (Old Woking, 1976).

H. Wylly (ed.), *A Cavalry Officer in the Corunna Campaign, 1808–1809: the Journal of Captain Gordon of the Fifteenth Hussars* (London, 1913).

(d) Secondary Sources

R. Abella, *La Vida y Epoca de José Bonaparte* (Barcelona, 1997).

R. Aldington, *Wellington* (London, 1946).

D. Alexander, 'The impact of guerrilla warfare in Spain on French combat strength', *CREP*, V (1975), pp. 91–8.

D. Alexander, *Rod of Iron: French Counter-Insurgency Policy in Aragón during the Peninsular War* (Wilmington, Delaware, 1985).

E. Alonso (ed.), *Memorias del Alcalde de Roa, Don Gregorio González Arranz, 1788–1840* (Roa, 1995).

M. Alonso, *El Ejército en la Sociedad Española* (Madrid, 1971).

F. Andújar, *Los Militares en la España del siglo XVIII* (Granada, 1991).

G. Anes, *Economía e Ilustración en la España del Siglo XVIII* (Barcelona, 1972).

T. Anna, *Spain and the Loss of America* (Lincoln, Nebraska, 1983).

Anon., *Historia de la Guerra de la Independencia Española: Años de 1808 a 1814* (Madrid, 1879).

M. Ardit, *Revolución Liberal y Revuelta Campesina: un Ensayo sobre la Desintegración del Régimen Feudal en el País Valenciano, 1793–1840* (Barcelona, 1977).

M. Arriazu (ed.), *Estudios sobre Cortes de Cádiz* (Pamplona, 1967).

M. Artola, *Los Afrancesados* (Madrid, 1976).

M. Artola, *La Burguesía Revolucionaria, 1808–1874* (Madrid, 1990).

M. Artola, *La España de Fernando VII* (Madrid, 1999).

M. Artola, *Los Orígenes de la España Contemporánea* (Madrid, 1959).

J. Aymes, *La Guerra de la Independencia en España, 1808–1814* (Madrid, 1975).

P. de Azcárate, *Wellington y España* (Madrid, 1961).

R. Barahona, 'Basque regionalism and centre-periphery relations, 1759–1833', *ESR*, XIII, No. 3 (July, 1983), pp. 271–96.

R. Barahona, 'The Napoleonic occupation and its political consequences in the Basque provinces, 1808–1813', *CREP*, XV (1985), pp. 101–16.

R. Barahona, *Vizcaya on the Eve of Carlism: Politics and Society, 1800–1833* (Reno, Nevada, 1989).

J. Barbier and H. Klein, 'Revolutionary wars and public finances: the Madrid treasury, 1784–1807', *JEH*, XLI, No. 2 (December, 1981), 315–39.

M. Barradas, *O General Gomes Freire de Andrade, 1788–1817* (Lisbon, 1892).

R. G. de Barthèlemy, *'El Marquesito': Juan Díaz Porlier, General que fue de los Ejércitos Nacionales, 1788–1815* (Santiago de Compostela, 1995).

C. Bartlett, *Castlereagh* (London, 1966).

R. Bayod, *El Reino de Aragón durante el Reino Intruso de los Napoleón* (Zaragoza, 1979a).

R. Bayod, *Suministros Exigidos al Pueblo Aragonés para el Ejército Napolénico-Francés* (Zaragoza, 1979b).

E. Becerra and F. Redondo, *Ciudad Rodrigo en la Guerra de la Independencia* (Ciudad Rodrigo, 1988).

N. Benavides and J. Yaque, *El Capitán General D. Joaquín Blake y Joyes, Regente del Reino y Fundador del Cuerpo de Estado Mayor* (Madrid, 1960).

A. Berkeley (ed.), *New Lights on the Peninsular War: International Congress on the Iberian Peninsula, 1780–1840* (Lisbon, 1991).

A. Bernal, *La Lucha por la Tierra en la Crisis del Antiguo Régimen* (Madrid, 1979).

A. Bernal, *La Propiedad de la Tierra y las Luchas Agrarias Andaluzas* (Barcelona, 1974).

T. Bernardino, *Sociedade e Atitudes Mentais em Portugal, 1777–1810* (Lisbon, 1986).

A. Blanch, *Historia de la Guerra de la Indepenencia en el Antiguo Principado* (Barcelona, 1861).

R. Blanco, *Rey, Cortes y Fuerza Armada en los Orígenes de la España Liberal, 1808–1823* (Madrid, 1988).

R. Brandão, *El-Rei Junot* (Lisbon, 1917).

M. Broers, *Europe under Napoleon, 1799–1815* (London, 1996).

A. Bryant, *The Age of Elegance, 1812–22* (London, 1950).

A. Bryant, *The Great Duke, or the Invincible General* (London, 1971).

A. Bryant, *The Years of Endurance, 1793–1802* (London, 1942).

A. Bryant, *Years of Victory, 1802–1812* (London, 1944).

C. Cáceres, *El Ejército de Andalucía en la Guerra de la Independencia* (Málaga, 1999).

A. Calama Rosellón, *La Guerra de la Independencia en Soria, La Rioja y Navarra: la Batalla de Tudela, 23-XI-1808* (Madrid, 1996).

W. Callahan, *Church, Politics and Society in Spain, 1750–1874* (Cambridge, Mass., 1984).

W. Callahan, 'The origins of the conservative Church in Spain, 1789–1823', *ESR*, X, No. 2 (April, 1980), pp. 199–223.

C. Cambronero, *El Rey Intruso: Apuntes Históricos Referentes á José Bonaparte y á su Gobierno en España* (Madrid, 1909).

E. Canales, 'La deserción en España durante la Guerra de la Independencia', *Bi-*

centenari de la Revolución Francesa (1789–1989): Le Jacobinisme (Barcelona, 1990), pp. 211–30.

E. Canales, *Patriotismo y Deserción durante la Guerra de la Independencia en Cataluña* (Coimbra, 1988).

F. Carantoña, *La Guerra de la Independencia en Asturias* (Oviedo, 1983).

F. Carantoña, *Revolución Liberal y Crisis de las Instituciones Tradicionales Asturianas* (Gijón, 1989).

P. Casado, *Las Fuerzas Armadas en el Inicio del Constucionalismo Español* (Madrid, 1982).

A. Cassinello, *Juan Martín, 'El Empecinado', o el Amor a la Libertad* (Madrid, 1995).

I. Castells and A. Moliner, *Crisis del Antiguo Régimen y Revolución Liberal en España, 1789–1845* (Barcelona, 2000).

C. de Castro, *La Revolución Liberal y los Municipios Españoles, 1812–1868* (Madrid, 1979).

H. Castro, 'Manejos de Fernando VII contra sus padres y contra Godoy', *BUM*, II (1930), pp. 397–408, 493–503; *ibid.*, III (1931), pp. 93–102.

J. Cepeda, *El Ejército en la Política Española, 1787–1843: Conspiraciones y Pronunciamientos en los Comienzos de la España Liberal* (Madrid, 1990).

M. Chamorro, *1808/1936: Dos Situaciones Históricas Concordantes* (Madrid, 1973).

D. Chandler, *The Campaigns of Napoleon* (London, 1966).

D. Chandler (ed.), *Napoleon's Marshals* (New York, 1987).

D. Chandler, *On the Napoleonic Wars: Collected Essays* (London, 1994).

J. Chastenet, *Godoy: Master of Spain, 1792–1808* (London, 1953).

P. Chavarri, *Las Elecciones a las Cortes Generales y Extraordinarias, 1810–1813* (Madrid, 1988).

E. Christiansen, *The Origins of Military Power in Spain, 1800–1854* (Oxford, 1967).

O. Connelly, *The Gentle Bonaparte: Biography of Joseph, Napoleon's Elder Brother* (New York, 1968).

O. Connelly, *Napoleon's Satellite Kingdoms* (New York, 1965).

C. Corona, *Revolución y Reacción en el Reinado de Carlos IV* (Madrid, 1957).

M. Costeloe, *Response to Revolution: Imperial Spain and the Spanish American Revolutions, 1810–1840* (Cambridge, 1986).

M. Costeloe, 'Spain and the Spanish-American Wars of Independence: the Comisión de Reemplazos, 1811–1820', *JLAS*, XIII, No. 2 (November, 1981), pp. 223–37.

C. Crawley, 'English and French influences in the *cortes* of Cádiz', *CHJ*, VI, No. 2 (1939), pp. 176–206.

C. Crowley, '*Luces* and *hispanidad*: nationalism and modernization in eighteenth-century Spain', in M. Palumbo and W. O. Shanahan, *Nationalism: Essays in Honour of Louis L. Snyder* (Westport, Connecticut, 1981), pp. 87–102.

J. Cruz, *Gentlemen, Bourgeois and Revolutionaries: Political Change and Cultural Persistence among the Spanish Dominant Groups, 1750–1850* (Cambridge, 1996).

N. Cruz, *Valencia Napoleónica* (Valencia, 1968).

J. Cuenca, *La Iglesia Española ante la Revolución Liberal* (Madrid, 1971).

D. Davies, *Sir John Moore's Peninsular Campaign, 1808–9* (The Hague, 1974).

H. Delavoye, *Life of Thomas Graham, Lord Lynedoch* (London, 1880).

J. Derry, *Castlereagh* (London, 1976).

G. Desdevises du Dézert, *L'Espagne de l'Ancien Régime* (Paris, 1897–1904).

F. L. Díaz Torrejón, *Osuna Napoleónica, 1810–1812* (Seville, 2001).

P. Dixon, *Canning, Politician and Statesman* (London, 1976).

M. Diz, *El Manifiesto de 1814* (Pamplona, 1967).

A. Domínguez Ortiz, *Sociedad y Estado en el Siglo XVIII Español* (Barcelona, 1976).

G. Dufour, *La Guerra de la Independencia* (Madrid, 1999).

G. Ellis, *The Napoleonic Empire* (London, 1991).

J. Elting, *Swords around a Throne: Napoleon and his Grande Armée* (New York, 1988).

C. Emsley, *British Society and the French Wars, 1793–1815* (London, 1979).

N. Epton, *The Spanish Mousetrap: Napoleon and the Spanish Court* (London, 1973).

C. Esdaile, *The Duke of Wellington and the Command of the Spanish Army, 1812–14* (London, 1990).

C. Esdaile, 'The Duke of Wellington and the Spanish Revolution, 1812–14', in C. Woolgar (ed.), *Wellington Studies, II* (Southampton, 1999), pp. 163–87.

C. Esdaile, *The French Wars* (London, 2001).

C. Esdaile, 'Heroes or villains? The Spanish guerrillas in the Peninsular War', *HT*, XXXVIII, No. 4 (April, 1988a), pp. 29–35.

C. Esdaile, 'Latin America and the Anglo-Spanish alliance against Napoleon, 1808–1814', *BHS*, LXIX, No. 3 (July, 1992), pp. 55–70.

C. Esdaile, 'The Marqués de la Romana and the Peninsular War: a case-study in Spanish civil-military relations, *CREP*, XXIII (1993), pp. 366–74.

C. Esdaile, 'Rebeldía, reticencia y resistencia: el caso gallego de 1808', *Trienio*, No. 35 (May, 2000), pp. 57–80.

C. Esdaile, *The Spanish Army in the Peninsular War* (Manchester, 1988b).

C. Esdaile, 'War and politics in Spain, 1808–1814', *HJ*, XXXI, No. 2 (1988c), pp. 295–317.

C. Esdaile, *The Wars of Napoleon* (London, 1995).

C. Esdaile, 'Wellington and the military eclipse of Spain, 1808–1814', *IHR*, XI, No. 1 (February, 1989), pp. 55–67.

C. Esdaile, 'Wellington and the Spanish army, 1812: the revolt of General Ballesteros', *CREP*, XVII (1987), pp. 93–108.

C. Esdaile, 'Wellington and the Spanish guerrillas: the campaign of 1813', *CREP*, XXI (1991), pp. 298–306.

A. Espinar, *Málaga durante la Primera Etapa Liberal, 1812–1814* (Málaga, 1994).

P. Fernández Albaladejo, *La Crisis del Antiguo Régimen en Guipúzcoa, 1766–1833; Cambio Económico e Historia* (Madrid, 1975).

F. Fernández Bastarreche, *El Ejército Español en el Siglo XIX* (Madrid, 1978).

V. Fernández Benítez, *Burguesia y Revolución Liberal: Santander, 1812–1840* (Santander, 1989).

V. Fernández Benítez, *Carlismo y Rebeldia Campesina: un Estudio sobre la Conflictividad Social en Cantabria durante la Crisis Final del Antiguo Régimen* (Madrid, 1988).

E. Fernández de Pinedo *et al.*, *Centralismo, Ilustración y Agonia del Antiguo Régimen, 1715–1833* (Barcelona, 1980).

A. Ferrao, *A Primeira Invasão de Junot vista atraves dos Documentos da Intendencia Geral da Policia, 1807–1808* (Coimbra, 1928).

J. Ferrer, 'Les Amis Réunis de Saint Joseph: la primera logía masónica de Vitoria', *CIH*, vol. III (1979), pp. 187–216.

J. Ferrer, *Masonería Española Contemporánea, 1800–1868* (Madrid, 1980).

M. Figueroa, *La Guerra de la Independencia en Galicia* (Vigo, 1992).

W. Fijalkowski, *La Intervención de Tropas Polacas en los Sitios de Zaragoza* (Zaragoza, 1997).

J. Fisher, 'Commerce and imperial decline: Spanish Trade with Spanish America, 1797–1820', *JLAS*, XXX, No. 3 (October, 1998), pp. 459–79.

I. Fletcher (ed.), *The Peninsular War: Aspects of the Struggle for the Iberian Peninsula* (Staplehurst, 1998).

F. Flores, *El Bandolerismo en Extremadura* (Badajoz, 1992).

J. Fontana, 'Catalonia, 1808–1814: how to name a war', *Review*, XII, No. 3 (Summer, 1989), pp. 397–403.

J. Fontana and R. Garrabou, *Guerra y Hacienda: la Hacienda del Gobierno Central en los Años de la Guerra de la Independencia, 1808–1814* (Alicante, 1986).

J. Fortescue, *A History of the British Army* (London, 1899–1920).

M. Fryman, 'Charles Stuart and the "common cause": Anglo-Portuguese diplomatic relations, 1810–1814', *CREP*, VII (1977), pp. 105–15.

F. de la Fuente, 'Portuguese resistance to Napoleon: Dom Miguel Forjaz and the mobilization of Portugal', *CREP*, XIII (1983), pp. 141–55.

A. Fugier, *La Junta Superior de Asturias y la Invasión Francesa* (Gijón, 1989).

A. Fugier, *Napoléon et l'Espagne, 1799–1808* (Paris, 1930).

P. García Gutiérrez, *La Ciudad de León en la Guerra de la Independencia* (León, 1991).

J. García Mercadel, *Palafox, Duque de Zaragoza, 1775–1847* (Madrid, 1948).

J. García Prado *et al.*, *Estudios de la Guerra de la Independencia* (Zaragoza, 1964–67).

M. García Ruipérez, *Revueltas Sociales en la Provincia de Toledo: la Crisis de 1802–1805* (Toledo, 1999).

N. Gash, *Lord Liverpool: the Life and Political Career of Robert Bankes Jenkinson, Second Earl of Liverpool, 1770–1828* (London, 1984).

N. Gash, *Wellington: Studies in the Military and Political Career of the First Duke of Wellington* (Manchester, 1990).

D. Gates, *The Napoleonic Wars* (London, 1996).

D. Gates, *The Spanish Ulcer: a History of the Peninsular War* (London, 1986).

A. Gil, 'Foreign military command and early nationalism in Spain during the Peninsular War', in C. Woolgar (ed.), *Wellington Studies, II* (Southampton, 1999), pp. 143–62.

G. Girod de l'Ain, *Joseph Bonaparte, le Roi Malgré Lui* (Paris, 1970).

M. Glover, *Britannia Sickens: Sir Arthur Wellesley and the Convention of Cintra* (London, 1970).

M. Glover, *Legacy of Glory: the Bonaparte Kingdom of Spain* (New York, 1971).

M. Glover, *The Peninsular War: a Concise Military History* (London, 1974).

M. Glover, *Wellington as Military Commander* (London, 1968).

M. Goldstein, 'The Stuart-Vaughan mission of 1808: the genesis of the Peninsular alliance', *CREP*, VII (1977), pp. 99–104.

J. Gómez de Arteche, *Guerra de la Independencia: Historia Militar de España de 1808 a 1814* (Madrid, 1868–1903).

M. Gómez Bajo, *La Guerra de la Independencia en Astorga, 1808–1814* (Astorga, 1986).

L. González Santos, *Godoy: Príncipe de la Paz, Siervo de la Guerra* (Madrid, 1985).

E. Goodman, 'Spanish nationalism in the struggle against Napoleon', *RP*, XX, No. 3 (July, 1958), pp. 330–46.

A. Grasset, *Málaga, Provincia Francesa, 1811–1812* (Málaga, 1996).

D. Gray, *Spencer Perceval, the Evangelical Prime Minister* (Manchester, 1963).

J. Grehan, *The Lines of Torres Vedras: the Cornerstone of Wellington's Strategy in the Peninsular War, 1809–1812* (Staplehurst, 2000).

P. Griffith (ed.), *A History of the Peninsular War, IX: Modern Studies of the War in Spain and Portugal, 1808–1814* (London, 1999).

P. Griffith (ed.), *Wellington – Commander: the Iron Duke's Generalship* (Chichester, 1986).

P. Guedalla, *The Duke* (London, 1931).

R. Guirao, *Guerrilleros y Patriotas en el Alto Aragón, 1808–1814* (Huesca, 2000).

R. Guirao and L. Sorando, *El Alto Aragón en la Guerra de la Independencia* (Zaragoza, 1995).

F. Guzman, *La España de Goya* (Madrid, 1981).

C. Hall, *British Strategy in the Napoleonic War, 1803–15* (Manchester, 1992)

E. Hamilton, 'War and inflation in Spain, 1780–1800', *QJE*, LIX, No. 1 (November, 1944), pp. 36–77.

E. Hamilton, *War and Prices in Spain, 1651–1800* (Cambridge, Mass., 1947).

B. Hamnett, 'The appropriation of Mexican Church wealth by the Spanish Bourbon government: the consolidation of the *vales reales*, 1805–1809', *JLAS*, I, No. 2 (November, 1969), pp. 85–113.

B. Hamnett, 'Constitutional theory and political reality: liberalism, tradition and the Spanish *cortes*, 1810–14', *JMH*, XL, No. 1 (March, 1977), on-demand supplement.

B. Hamnett, *La Política Española en una Epoca Revolucionaria* (Mexico City, 1985).

B. Hamnett, 'Spanish constitutionalism and the impact of the French Revolution, 1808–1814', in H. Mason and W. Doyle (eds.), *The Impact of the French Revolution on European Consciousness* (Gloucester, 1989), pp. 64–80.

J. Harbron, *Trafalgar and the Spanish Navy* (London, 1988).

A. Harvey, *Britain in the Early Nineteenth Century* (London, 1978).

A. Harvey, *Collision of Empires: Britain in Three World Wars* (London, 1992).

P. Hayman, *Soult: Napoleon's Maligned Marshal* (London, 1990).

P. Haythornthwaite, *The Armies of Wellington* (London, 1994).

F. Hernández Girbal, *Juan Martín, el Empecinado, Terror de los Franceses* (Madrid, 1985).

F. Hernández Montalbán, *La Abolición de los Señorios en España, 1811–1837* (Valencia, 1999).

R. Herr, *The Eighteenth-Century Revolution in Spain* (Princeton, 1958).

R. Herr, 'Good, evil and Spain's uprising against Napoleon', in R. Herr and H. Parker (eds.), *Ideas in History* (Durham, N.C., 1965), pp. 157–81.

R. Herr, *Rural Change and Royal Finances in Spain at the End of the Old Régime* (Berkeley, Calif., 1989).

C. Hibbert, *Wellington: a Personal History* (London, 1997).

A. de la Higuera and L. Molins Cabrera, *Historia de la Revolución Española: Tercera Guerra de la Independencia* (Madrid, 1940).

D. Hilt, *The Troubled Trinity: Godoy and the Spanish Monarchs* (Tuscaloosa, Alabama, 1987).

N. Horta Rodríguez, *D. Julián Sánchez, 'El Charro', Guerrillero y Brigadier* (Ciudad Rodrigo, 1987).

D. Horward, *Bussaco* (Gainesville, Fl., 1965).

D. Horward, *Napoleon and Iberia: the Twin Sieges of Ciudad Rodrigo and Almeida, 1810* (Tallahassee, 1984).

D. Horward, 'Wellington and the defence of Portugal', *IHR*, XI, No. 1 (February, 1989), pp. 39–54.

J. Iribarren, *Espoz y Mina, el Guerrillero* (Madrid, 1965).

M. Izquierdo, *Antecedentes y Comienzos del Reinado de Fernando VII* (Madrid, 1963).

L. James, *The Iron Duke: a Military Biography of Wellington* (London, 1992).

F. Jiménez de Gregorio, *Murcia en los Dos Primeros Años de la Guerra por la Independencia* (Murcia, 1947).

W. Kaufmann, *British Policy and the Independence of Latin America* (London, 1967).

J. Kinsbruner, *Independence in Latin America: Civil Wars, Revolutions and Underdevelopment* (Albuquerque, N. Mex., 1994).

G. Knight, 'Lord Liverpool and the Peninsular Struggle, 1809–1812', *CREP*, XX (1990), pp. 32–8.

J. Labourdette, *Le Portugal de 1780 à 1802* (Paris, 1985).

J. Ladner, 'John VI of Portugal: contemporary of Napoleon and Wellington', *CREP*, XX (1990), pp. 869–81.

H. Lafoz, *La Guerra de la Independencia en Aragón: del Motín de Aranjuez a la Capitulación de Zaragoza* (Zaragoza, 1996).

H. Lafoz, *José Palafox y su Tiempo* (Zaragoza, 1992).

A. Laspra, *Intervencionismo y Revolución: Asturias y Gran Bretaña durante la Guerra de la Independencia, 1808–1813* (Oviedo, 1992).

A. Laspra, *Las Relaciones entre la Junta General del Pruincipado de Asturias y el Reino Unido en la Guerra de la Independencia* (Oviedo, 1999).

G. Lefebvre, *Napoleon* (London, 1969).

J. Longares, *La Ideología Religiosa del Liberalismo Español, 1814–1843* (Córdoba, 1979).

E. Longford, *Wellington: the Years of the Sword* (London, 1969).

B. López Morán, *El Bandolerismo Gallego en la Primera Mitad del Siglo XIX* (La Coruña, 1995).

M. López Pérez and I. Lara, *Entre la Guerra y la Paz: Jaén, 1808–1814* (Granada, 1993).

L. Lorente, *Agitación Urbana y Crisis Económica durante la Guerra de la Independencia, 1808–1814* (Cuenca, 1993).

L. Lorente, 'Coyuntura económica y presión social en la España ocupada: el modelo tributario francés en Toledo, 1811–1813', in E. de Diego *et al.* (eds.), *Repercusiones de la Revolución Francesa en España* (Madrid, 1990), pp. 403–19.

L. Lorente, *Poder y Miseria: Oligarcas y Campesinos en la España Señorial, 1760–1868* (Madrid, 1994).

G. Lovett, 'The fall of the first Spanish liberal régime, 1813–1814', *CREP*, IV (1974), pp. 176–88.

G. Lovett, *Napoleon and the Birth of Modern Spain* (New York, 1965).

G. Lovett, 'The Spanish guerrillas and Napoleon', *CREP*, V (1975), pp. 80–90.

J. Lynch, *Bourbon Spain, 1700–1808* (Oxford, 1989).

J. Lynch, 'British policy and Spanish America, 1783–1808', *JLAS*, I, No. 1 (May, 1969), pp. 1–30.

J. Lynch, *The Spanish American Revolutions, 1808–1826* (London, 1973).

C. MacKay, 'Conflicting goals: Napoleon, Junot and the occupation of Portugal', *CREP*, XXII (1992), pp. 445–55.

H. Madol, *Godoy: the First Dictator of Modern Times* (London, 1934).

J. Marshall-Cornwall, *Massena* (Oxford, 1965).

F. Marti, *El Motín de Aranjuez* (Pamplona, 1972).

F. Marti, *El Proceso del Escorial* (Pamplona, 1965).

E. Martínez Quinteiro, 'Coyuntura económica y liberalismo, 1788–1810', *Hispania*, XLIII, No. 155 (September, 1983), pp. 581–98.

E. Martínez Quinteiro, 'Descontento y actitudes políticas de la alta nobleza en los origenes de la edad contemporánea', *Hispania*, XXXVII, No. 135 (January, 1977a), pp. 95–138.

E. Martínez Quinteiro, *Los Grupos Liberales antes de las Cortes de Cádiz* (Madrid, 1977b).

E. Martínez Ruiz (ed.), *II Seminario Internacional sobre la Guerra de la Independencia: Madrid, 24–26 de Octubre de 1994* (Madrid, 1995).

A. Martínez de Velasco, *La Formación de la Junta Central* (Pamplona, 1972).

J. Medina (ed.), *Historia de Portugal dos Tempos Pre-Historicos aos Nossos Dias, VIII: Portugal Liberal* (Lisbon, 1994).

J. Mercader, *Catalunya i l'Imperi Napoleònic* (Montserrat, 1978).

J. Mercader, 'La instauración primera del Ministerio del Interior en España bajo José Bonaparte en 1809', *Hispania*, XLII, No. 150 (January, 1982), pp. 183–206.

J. Mercader, *José Bonaparte, Rey de España, 1808–13: Estructura del Estado Español Bonapartista* (Madrid, 1983).

J. Mercader, *José Bonaparte, Rey de España, 1808–13: Historia Externa del Reinado* (Madrid, 1971).

J. Meyer, 'The battle of Busaco: victory or defeat?', *CREP*, XIX (1989), Vol. 1, pp. 514–29.

J. Meyer, 'The battle of Vitoria: a critical view', *CREP*, XX (1990), pp. 674–80.

J. Meyer, 'Wellington and the sack of Badajoz: "beastly mutiny" or deliberate policy?', *CREP*, XXI (1991), pp. 251–8.

F. Miranda, *La Guerra de la Independencia en Navarra: la Acción del Estado* (Pamplona, 1977).

P. Molas (ed.), *La España de Carlos IV* (Madrid, 1991).

A. Moliner, *La Catalunya Resistent a la Dominació Francesca, 1808–1812* (Barcelona, 1989).

A. Moliner, 'La Conflictividad social en la Guerra de la Independencia', *Trienio*, No. 35 (May, 2000), pp. 81–115.

A. Moliner, *La Guerra del Frances a Mallorca, 1808–1814* (Palma de Mallorca, 2000).

A. Moliner, 'Las juntas corregimentales de Cataluña en la *guerra del frances*', *Hispania*, No. 158 (September, 1984), pp. 549–82.

A. Moliner, 'La peculiaridad de la revolución española de 1808', *Hispania*, XLVII No. 166 (May, 1987), pp. 632–46.

A. Moliner, *Revolución Burguesa i Movimiento Juntero en España* (Lérida, 1997).

J. Montón, *La Revolución Armada del Dos de Mayo en Madrid* (Madrid, 1983).

G. Moore Smith, *The Life of John Colborne, Field Marshal Lord Seaton* (London, 1903).

M. Morán, *Poder y Gobierno en las Cortes de Cádiz* (Pamplona, 1986).

M. Morán, *Revolución y Reforma Religiosa en las Cortes de Cádiz* (Madrid, 1994).

C. Morange, *Siete Calas en la Crisis del Antiguo Régimen Español y un Panfleto Clandestino de 1800* (Alicante, 1990).

I. Morant, *El Declive del Señorio: los Dominios del Ducado de Gandía, 1705–1837* (Valencia, 1984).

M. Moreno, *Los Españoles durante la Ocupación Napoleónica: la Vida Cotidiana en la Voragine* (Málaga, 1997).

M. Moreno, *Sevilla Napoleónica* (Seville, 1995).

S. de Moxo, *La Disolución del Régimen Señorial en España* (Madrid, 1965).

F. Moya and C. Rey, *El Ejército y la Armada en las Cortes de Cádiz* (Cádiz, 1913).

R. Muir, *Britain and the Defeat of Napoleon, 1807–1815* (New Haven, Conn., 1996).

R. Muir, *Salamanca, 1812* (New Haven, Conn., 2001).

C. Mullet, 'British schemes against Spanish America in 1806', *HAHR*, XXVII, No. 2 (May, 1947), pp. 269–78.

J. Múñoz Maldonado, *Historia Política y Militar de la Guerra de la Independencia contra Napoleón Bonaparte desde 1808 a 1814* (Madrid, 1833).

B. Narbonne, *Joseph Bonaparte, le Roi Philosophe* (Paris, 1949).

A. Ollero, *Palencia durante la Ocupación Francesa, 1808–1814: Repercusiones Sociales y Económicas* (Valladolid, 1983).

C. Oman, *A History of the Peninsular War* (Oxford, 1902–1930).

C. Oman, *Wellington's Army, 1809–1814* (London, 1913).

A. Pacho, *Del Antiguo Régimen a la España Moderna: Manuel Traggia (de S. Tomás) OCD, Protagonista e Interprete del Tránsito* (Burgos, 1979).

J. Paget, *Wellington's Peninsular War: Battles and Battlefields* (London, 1990).

E. la Parra, *La Alianza de Godoy con los Revolucionarios* (Madrid, 1992).

P. Pascual, *Curas y Frailes Guerrilleros en la Guerra de la Independencia: las Partidas de Cruzada Reglamentadas por el Carmélita Zaragozana, P. Manuel Traggia* (Zaragoza, 2000).

S. Payne, *Politics and the Military in Modern Spain* (Stanford, California, 1967).

P. Pegenaute, 'La Abeja Madrileña de 1814: datos para su estudio', *Hispania*, XLIII, No. 155 (September, 1983), pp. 599–621.

J. Pérez Garzón, *Milicia Nacional y Revolución Burguesa: el Protótipo Madrileño, 1808–1874* (Madrid, 1978).

J. Pérez de Guzmán, 'El primer conato de rebelión precursor de la revolución de España', *EM*, CCL (1909), pp. 105–24; *ibid.*, CCLI (1910), pp. 48–68.

M. Pintos, *La Política de Fernando VII entre 1814 y 1820* (Pamplona, 1958).

J. Polt, *Gaspar Melchor de Jovellanos* (New York, 1971).

J. Priego López, *Como fue la Guerra de la Independencia* (Madrid, 1936).

J. Priego López, *Guerra de la Independencia, 1808–1814* (Madrid, 1972–2000).

P. Prieto, *El Grande de España, Capitán General Castaños, primer Duque de Bailén y primer Marqués de Portugalete* (Madrid, 1958).

M. Ramisa, *Els Catalans i el Domini Napoleonic* (Montserrat, 1995).

M. Ramisa (ed.), *Guerra Napoleònica a Catalunya, 1808–1814: Estudis i Documents* (Montserrat, 1996).

J. Read, *War in the Peninsula* (London, 1977).

I. Robertson, *Wellington at War in the Peninsula, 1808–1814: an Overview and Guide* (London, 2000).

W. Robertson, *France and Latin-American Independence* (Baltimore, 1939).

W. Robertson, 'The juntas of 1808 and the Spanish colonies', *EHR*, XXXI, No. 124 (October, 1916), pp. 573–85.

J. Rodríguez, *The Independence of Latin America* (Cambridge, 1998).

R. Rodríguez Garraza, *Tensiones de Navarra con la Administración Central, 1778–1808* (Pamplona, 1974).

C. Rodríguez López-Brea, *Frailes y Revolución Liberal* (Toledo, 1996).

E. Rodríguez Solis, *Los Guerrilleros de 1808: Historia Popular de la Guerra de la Independencia* (Madrid, 1887).

H. Rogers, *Wellington's Army* (London, 1979).

J. Rooney, 'The treaty of Valençay: an effort calculated to save an empire', *CREP*, XXI (1991), pp. 33–42.

M. Ross, *The Reluctant King: Joseph Bonaparte: King of the Two Sicilies and Spain* (London, 1976).

L. Roura, *La Crisi de l'Antic Règim a les Balears, 1780–1814* (Palma de Mallorca, 1999).

J. Rubio, *La Infanta Carlota Joaquina y la Política de España en América, 1808–1812* (Madrid, 1920).

R. Rudorff, *War to the Death: the Sieges of Saragossa, 1808–1809* (London, 1974).

J. Rydjord, 'British mediation between Spain and her colonies, 1811–1813', *HAHR*, XXI, No. 1 (February, 1941), pp. 29–50.

S. Saiz, 'Lerma en el levantamiento guerrillero de la Guerra de la Independencia', *RHM*, No. 63 (July, 1987), pp. 161–77.

J. Sánchez Fernández, 'El ejército contra las guerrillas: la jefatura militar frente al fenómeno guerrillero durante la Guerra de la Independencia', *RHM*, No. 87 (July, 1999), pp. 149–74.

J. Sánchez Fernández, *La Guerrilla Vallesoletana, 1808–1814* (Valladolid, 1997).

J. Sánchez Fernández, 'Las Juntas Criminales Extraordinarias en el reinado de José Bonaparte en España: el caso vallesoletano', *Aportes: Revista de Historia Contemporánea*, No. 40 (February, 1999), pp. 31–7.

J. Sánchez Fernández, *¡Nos Invaden! Guerrilla y Represión en Valladolid durante la Guerra de la Independencia Española, 1808–1814* (Valladolid, 2000).

J. Sanudo and L. Stampa, *La Crisis de una Alianza: la Campaña del Tajo en 1809* (Madrid, 1996).

J. Sarramon, *La Bataille de Vitoria: la Fin de l'Aventure Napoléonienne en Espagne* (Paris, 1985).

P. Schroeder, *The Transformation of European Politics, 1763–1848* (Oxford, 1994).

C. Seco, *Godoy: el Hombre y el Político* (Madrid, 1978).

J. Severn, *A Wellesley Affair: Richard, Marquess Wellesley, and the Conduct of Anglo-Spanish Diplomacy, 1809–1812* (Tallahassee, 1981).

J. Sherwig, *Guineas and Gunpowder: British Foreign Aid in the Wars with France, 1793–1815* (Cambridge, Mass., 1969).

A. Silbert, *Les Invasions Françaises et les Origines du libéralisme au Portugal* (Coimbra, 1990).

S. M. de Soto (Conde de Clonard), *Historia Orgánica de la Armas de Infantería y Caballería Españolas* (Madrid, 1851–62).

F. Suárez Verdeguer, *Conservadores, Innovadores y Renovadores en las Postrimerías del Antiguo Régimen* (Pamplona, 1965).

F. Suárez Verdeguer, *Las Tendencias Políticas en la Guerra de la Independencia* (Zaragoza, 1959).

G. Teffeteller, *The Surpriser: the Life of Sir Rowland Hill* (Brunswick, N.J., 1983).

G. Teffeteller, 'Wellington and Sir Rowland Hill', *IHR*, XI, No. 1 (February, 1989), pp. 68–75.

N. Thompson, 'Bathurst and Wellington: another 1812 overture', *CREP*, XIX (1989), Vol. 1, pp. 530–43.

J. Tone, *The Fatal Knot: the Guerrilla War in Navarre and the Defeat of Napoleon* (Chapel Hill, North Carolina, 1994).

J. Tone, 'Napoleon's uncongenial sea: guerrilla warfare in Navarre during the Peninsular War, 1808–14', *EHQ*, XXVI, No. 3 (July, 1996), pp. 355–81.

A. Uffindell (ed.), *On Wellington: the Duke and his Art of War by Jac Weller* (London, 1998).

M. Urban, *The Man who Broke Napoleon's Codes: the Story of George Scovell* (London, 2001).

J. Veríssimo Serrao, *História de Portugal, VII: a Instauracão do Liberalismo, 1807–1832* (Lisbon, 1984).

R. Vidal, *Historia de la Guerra de la Independencia en el Campo de Gibraltar* (Cadiz, 1975).

P. Vilar, *Hidalgos, Amotinados y Guerrilleros: Pueblo y Poderes en la Historia de España* (Barcelona, 1999).

Marqués de Villa Urrutia, *Relaciones entre España e Inglaterra durante la Guerra de la Independencia Española: Apuntes para la Historia Diplomática de España de 1808 a 1814* (Madrid, 1911–1914).

P. Vitorino, *As Invasoes Francesas* (Oporto, 1945).

S. Walpole, *The Life of the Right Honourable Spencer Perceval, including his Correspondence with many Distinguished Persons* (London, 1874).

S. Ward, *Wellington's Headquarters: a Study of the Administrative Problems in the Peninsula War* (Oxford, 1957).

J. Weller, *Wellington in the Peninsula, 1808–14* (London, 1962).

S. Woolf, *Napoleon's Integration of Europe* (London, 1991).

Index